D1559291

COGNITIVE PSYCHOLOGY AND INFORMATION PROCESSING:
An Introduction

COGNITIVE PSYCHOLOGY AND INFORMATION PROCESSING:
An Introduction

ROY LACHMAN
JANET L. LACHMAN
University of Houston

EARL C. BUTTERFIELD
University of Kansas
Medical Center

LAWRENCE ERLBAUM ASSOCIATES, PUBLISHERS
1979   Hillsdale, New Jersey

DISTRIBUTED BY THE HALSTED PRESS DIVISION OF
JOHN WILEY & SONS
New York   Toronto   London   Sydney

Lawrence Erlbaum Associates, Inc., Publishers
62 Maria Drive
Hillsdale, New Jersey 07642

Distributed solely by Halsted Press Division
John Wiley & Sons, Inc., New York

Library of Congress Catalog Card Number: 78-24744

Printed in the United States of America

Contents

Preface

PREMISE

Basic research, at its essence, is exploration of the unknown. When it is successful, isolated pieces of reality are deciphered and described. Most of the history of an empirical discipline consists of probes into this darkness—some bold, others careful and systematic. Most of these efforts are initially incorrect. At best, they are distant approximations to a reality that may not be correctly specified for centuries. How, then, can we describe the fragmented knowledge that characterizes a scientific discipline for most of its history?

The knowledge that a field claims at any point in its development cannot be unified, at that time, by a correct account of the phenomenon it studies; for that only becomes available much later. Throughout most of the history of a research science, reality does not unify its literature. What, then, does? It is our premise that the data, experiments, and theory of a developing field can only be fully understood by reference to the paradigmatic commitments of its practitioners. A dynamic field of science is held together by its *paradigm.*

Thomas Kuhn developed the concept of a scientific paradigm as part of a fundamental reformulation of views on the scientific enterprise. The paradigm, representing tacit commitments to a conception of reality that cannot be defended on rational or canonical grounds, stood in contrast to then-prevailing views of how science is done. Kuhn challenged the idea that scientific investigation is absolutely rational, thoroughly cumulative, and unequivocally objective. He highlighted the role of consensual judgments in determining what appears rational, objective, and worth cumulating. His most vociferous critics, philosophers of science by profession, have by now largely conceded his major points. Although some have relabeled the concepts and denied their source, the astute reader cannot fail to discern Kuhn's thesis lurking in such alternative formulations as research programs, scientific disciplines, and scientific domains.

As psychologists, we may ask whether these diverting echoes from philosophy of science have much to do with us. Does psychology have a paradigm? We suggest that, in fact, it has several; and a grasp of this reality and its significance is essential to an understanding of psychological research at either the graduate or undergraduate level. In the first chapter, we suggest a way to define and analyze psychological paradigms. The psychological research literature speaks effectively to the existence of something like paradigms in our discipline. In 1970, for example, Mostofsky edited a book on attention, containing 18 articles. One of these was authored by Donald Broadbent. It was entitled "Stimulus Set and Response Set: Two Kinds of Selective Attention," and it contained 34 citations. In the same book appeared another paper by Werner Honig, entitled "Attention and the Modulation of Stimulus Control," and it carried 38 citations. Of the 72 articles cited by Broadbent and Honig, *not one* appeared in both citation lists. Obviously, if two psychological researchers could write about attention without citing a single common paper, there must be two distinct psychological literatures on the subject. This is anomalous for a cumulative enterprise, but comprehensible in paradigmatic terms. Our example from the study of attention is not unique. Anyone who has considered the treatments of early childhood autism in the *Journal of Applied Behavioral Analysis* and childhood schizophrenia in the *Psychoanalytic Review* must conclude that the psychologists differ more than the children about whom they write.

How can a student approach this kind of discontinuity in the literature? One approach, sometimes tried by undergraduates, is to suppose that the apparently different views can be reconciled. This leads to tortured logic and bizarre reference lists in term papers, as well as unrelenting frustration for their writers and graders. One can only speculate on what these students think we are doing by the time they have completed the B.A. Another approach is more typical of graduate training. It involves mastering one of the literatures and rejecting several others. Unfortunately, the student may often be encouraged to believe that the chosen approach represents the only correct and defensible—even the only scientific—way to study the topic at hand. This is the purchase of coherence at a high price.

We do not claim, or even know, that a student can effectively bridge several paradigms in the course of graduate training; and mastery of one is essential to the practice of scientific research. What we do claim is that, if a scientist is to remain viable, he or she must be prepared in the course of a 40-year professional career to reject at least one paradigm in favor of another. This cannot be accomplished by one who equates the consensual judgments of his or her reference group with the rational methods of science. A paradigm change in mid-career is less dislocating for one whose graduate education has placed those consensual paradigmatic judgments in the broader epistemological context—in short, for one whose graduate training has included explicit accounts of paradigmatic commitments.

For the undergraduate student, the literature of a developing science often seems fractured and chaotic. Apparently important issues go completely unresearched; seemingly trivial issues fill chapters. Negative evidence is given heavy weight in one case and lightly dismissed elsewhere. These patterns are understandable if, and only if, one understands the pretheoretical commitments of the practitioners of the science—in short, their paradigm. Undergraduate readers have found this treatment of the literature highly congenial and comprehensible.

We think it is essential to adequate scientific education to teach paradigms, and we believe that there is an effective method. The method emphasizes the integral nature, rather than the objective correctness, of a given set of consensual commitments. Moreover, we believe that paradigmatic content can be effectively combined with the technical research literature commonly presented in scientific texts. This book represents the culmination of those beliefs. You, the reader, will make the final judgment of their validity.

CONTRIBUTIONS

A major problem we faced as authors is that the field of cognitive psychology has become exceedingly large. No one, today, can seriously claim expert knowledge of the entire range of cognitive literature. Indeed, it is increasingly difficult to keep up with the data accumulating in a subfield such as memory or perception. The field of cognitive psychology seems to have exploded in the middle 1960s and has not touched ground since.

Our strategy in dealing with this situation was twofold. To organize and interrelate the rather disjunctive literatures in the various subfields of cognition, we adopted the notion of consensual validation and an elaboration of the Kuhnian concept of a scientific paradigm. The idea and its development are the contribution of Roy Lachman, who conceived this book at a time when the field was much smaller than it is today. Second, we attempted to set up a division of labor so that significant aspects of the cognitive literature could be covered in a nonsuperficial way. We started with Roy Lachman, Janet L. Lachman, and D. James Dooling. As each of us completed a first draft, the other two criticized it for later revision. We soon added Earl Butterfield; his job was to evaluate the first drafts and their critiques, to resolve any inconsistencies between them, and, most important, to rewrite all material in a language that would be readable by nonspecialists. The objective was to ensure that the book did not assume professional expertise by our student readers, and to give the writing a coherence not always present in multi-authored texts. There were eventually some departures from this scheme, especially as the magnitude of the task became apparent. The final division of labor is represented in the following table:

Chapter	Short Title	Original Conception and First Draft	First Revision	Final Revision
1	Science and Paradigms	Roy Lachman Janet Lachman	Earl Butterfield	Roy Lachman Janet Lachman
2	Contributions from Psychology	Roy Lachman Janet Lachman	Earl Butterfield	Roy Lachman Janet Lachman
3	Contributions from Other Disciplines	Roy Lachman Janet Lachman	Earl Butterfield	Roy Lachman Janet Lachman
4	The Information-Processing Paradigm	Roy Lachman Janet Lachman	Roy Lachman Janet Lachman	Roy Lachman Janet Lachman
5	Reaction Time	D. J. Dooling	Earl Butterfield	Earl Butterfield
6	Consciousness and Attention	D. J. Dooling	Earl Butterfield	Earl Butterfield
7	Structure of Episodic Memory	D. J. Dooling	Earl Butterfield	Earl Butterfield
8	Episodic Memory Flexibility	Roy Lachman Janet Lachman	Earl Butterfield	Roy Lachman Janet Lachman
9	Semantic Memory	Roy Lachman Janet Lachman	Earl Butterfield	Roy Lachman Janet Lachman
10	Psycholinguistics	Janet Lachman	Earl Butterfield	Janet Lachman
11	Comprehension	Janet Lachman Roy Lachman	Earl Butterfield	Janet Lachman Roy Lachman
12	Global Models	Roy Lachman Janet Lachman	Earl Butterfield	Roy Lachman Janet Lachman
13	Pattern Recognition	Janes F. Juola	Earl Butterfield	James F. Juola
14	Epilogue	Roy Lachman	Janet Lachman	Roy Lachman Janet Lachman

ACKNOWLEDGMENTS

Drafts of the chapters were read and evaluated by countless devoted students, and we cannot begin to thank them all individually. However, special mention is due to those graduate students who gave us detailed written feedback on various chapters: Eric Block, Cameron Camp, Wendy Moore, Bettye Thompson, Don Taylor, Carroll Thronesbery, and Marilyn G. Boltz. Their commentary was always astute—sometimes profound. We also owe a debt of thanks to our many colleagues who have field tested the book for us by using parts of it in their classes, and to the many others who have given us their comments and suggestions. In this connection, we wish to extend special thanks to E. E. Smith, F. I. M. Craik, Irving Biederman, and one anonymous reviewer; all provided extensive feedback on many of the chapters. They are only to be credited with making the product better; if errors remain they are the responsibility of the authors.

The production of the book was especially facilitated by our graduate student Carroll Thronesbery, who worked with us on the innumerable last-minute details. We also could not have dispensed with those who helped with the typing and bibliography. Especial thanks for her competent and loyal assistance in typing go to our secretary Fern Tombaugh.

We are also very grateful to Mr. Larry Erlbaum for his support and continued faith throughout a very long process of completion.

ROY LACHMAN
JANET L. LACHMAN
EARL C. BUTTERFIELD

COGNITIVE PSYCHOLOGY AND INFORMATION PROCESSING:
An Introduction

1

Science and Paradigms:
The Premises of This Book

ABSTRACT

I. *Introduction*
   Technical competence in a science is possible without perspective, and perspective is possible without technical skill.
   A. *Perspective and Content are Both Important to Science Education.*
   B. *Beginning Definitions of Cognitive Psychology and Information Processing*
      A scientific field can be defined by its content, general approach, and specific approach. The content of cognitive psychology is the human higher mental processes, and the general method is the same as other sciences. The specific approach covered in this book is the information-processing paradigm.
   C. *Some Preliminary Examples of Cognitive Behavior* Automobile driving is the kind of activity that cognitive psychologists believe involves many important cognitive capabilities. We use this activity to introduce some of the emphases and assumptions of information-processing psychology.
   D. *The Significance of Information Processing and Cognitive Psychology* Paradigmatic views often find their way into the larger society, and we think the information-processing approach will have such an impact. Presently, it is most visible in cognitive science; but it is being extended. We advocate learning it along with other approaches.

II. *Cognitive Psychology as an Experimental Science*
   A. *Psychology Is a Research Science, Not a Mature System* This means that many psychological questions have not been clearly asked, let alone answered. The student should not approach an active research science seeking only established facts and agreed-upon theories. Learning about an unsettled research science involves learning the current questions, approaches, and controversies. These have their source in aspects of scientific practice that are often ignored in traditional descriptions of scientific method.

B. *A Fundamental Premise: The Rational and Conventional Rules of Science*   Every scientist operates within two sets of rules. One is the rational rule system of the scientific method, which has been widely described. The other is conventional and paradigmatic; it results from consensus among a group of scientists that a particular approach is worthy.
   1. *The Rational Rules*   While other human institutions make statements about mankind, scientific statements are unique. The rational rules of science are designed to obtain knowledge for its own sake. They are morally neutral and constructed to verify theoretical statements by observational methods.
   2. *The Conventional Rules*   The rational rules supply more guidance in how to make observations than in what to observe. Intelligent, well-trained, and honest scientists can disagree about what to observe and what a particular observation means. Groups of scientists tend to form, however, within which there is considerable consensus on what observations are worth making and how they should be interpreted. The tacit rules followed by these subgroups constitute the conventional component of their science, their paradigm.
C. *Normal and Revolutionary Science*   Thomas Kuhn (1962) suggested that advanced sciences cycle between "normal" and "revolutionary" science. During periods of normal science, there is a sense of progress within the context of a particular paradigm, and little questioning of its premises. However, as experiments are done, anomalies arise that cannot be handled within the existing paradigm. When there is sufficient weight of these anomalies, the discipline may go into crisis and alter some of its most fundamental paradigmatic commitments. Although Kuhn's contribution has been criticized, we think it is an excellent descriptive account of scientific activity and, with some modification, is highly appropriate to psychology.
D. *Paradigms in Psychology*   Psychology has always been, and still is, multiparadigmatic. However, at one time the dominant view was behavioristic. This has changed, partly due to the arrival of the information-processing approach. In cognitive psychology, the information-processing view was once revolutionary. It is now the dominant paradigm in cognition, and cognitive psychology now appears to be in a state of normal science.

III. *Characteristics of Paradigms*
   Paradigms are not the same as theories. We suggest six dimensions along which paradigms may be defined and differentiated.
   A. *Intellectual Antecedents*   These are the prior sources of the ideas and concepts that a scientist brings to his work.
   B. *Pretheoretical Ideas*   The working scientist draws on assumptions and tacit beliefs about the nature of the reality he is studying. These guide research and aid in the formulation of experimental questions.
   C. *Subject Matter*   The decision to study one facet of behavior and not another amounts to a judgment about which questions should be answered and which deferred.
   D. *Analogies*   When a scientist is studying a poorly understood system, it is useful to borrow concepts and ideas from better-understood systems. This borrowing is tantamount to analogizing the two systems and can be used to develop theories and formulate research questions.

E. *Concepts and Language* The terms in a paradigmatic language can be imported from the paradigm's intellectual antecedents, or from a discipline which is the source of an important analogy, or invented within the paradigm. The language used within a paradigm reflects the pretheoretical ideas of its users.

F. *Research Methods* Whereas the rational rules dictate observational methods, paradigms tend to develop preferences for particular kinds of observations, experimental designs, and variables.

IV. *Paradigms, Information Processing, Psychology, and Society*
It usually takes a long time for a paradigm to have an impact on the wider society outside the discipline in which it is used. We think that the information-processing view of human capacities will eventually permeate institutions outside cognitive psychology. Therefore, we have taken considerable trouble to present as explicitly as possible the pretheoretical ideas, intellectual antecedents, subject matter, concepts and language, analogies, and research methods of the information-processing paradigm.

The Lesson of the Copernican Revolution. In the Ptolemaic system, as in the cosmogony of the Bible, man was assigned a central position in the universe, from which position he was ousted by Copernicus. Ever since, writers eager to drive the lesson home have urged us, resolutely and repeatedly, to abandon all sentimental egoism, and to see ourselves objectively in the true perspective of time and space. What precisely does this mean? In a full "main feature" film, recapitulating faithfully the complete history of the universe, the rise of human beings from the first beginnings of man to the achievements of the twentieth century would flash by in a single second. Alternatively, if we decided to examine the universe objectively in the sense of paying equal attention to portions of equal mass, this would result in a lifelong preoccupation with interstellar dust, relieved only at brief intervals by a survey of incandescent masses of hydrogen—not in a thousand million lifetimes would the turn come to give man even a second's notice. It goes without saying that no one—scientists included—looks at the universe this way, whatever lip-service is given to "objectivity". Nor should this surprise us. For, as human beings, we must inevitably see the universe from a centre lying within ourselves and speak about it in terms of a human language shaped by the exigencies of human intercourse. Any attempt rigorously to eliminate our human perspective from our picture of the world must lead to absurdity.

—From the opening paragraph of
Personal Knowledge (Polanyi, 1962)

I.   INTRODUCTION

Science is an organized human activity having much in common with other human institutions. People can function effectively in a complex institution without necessarily understanding its history, social purpose, or properties. A businessman may know little of his nation's economy, yet earn great wealth. A general may not understand the causes of war, yet still win battles. A lawyer may know nothing of the history and social function of law, yet still win court cases. Beginning students sometimes do excellent technical work without necessarily knowing its importance. Scientists are human beings working within human institutions, just as are businesspeople, generals, and lawyers. Some of them can and do produce competent research without knowing its value, nor its place in the mosaic of knowledge, nor even the forces that directed them to the problems solved by their own findings. The point is that technical competence is not the same as perspective, in science or other human institutions. It is possible to have one without the other. The objective of this book is to provide both: a knowledge of the content of cognitive psychology, along with a perspective on that content.

Just as technical competence is possible without perspective, so perspective is possible without technical skill. People can grasp unifying views without practicing a specialty. They can understand war without fighting. They can understand law without trying cases. They can understand the economy without investing a dollar. Similarly, a student can gain a broad perspective on the sciences, or on a particular science, without earning a Ph.D. and setting to work in a laboratory.

A. Perspective and Content Are Both Important to Science Education

A few students intend to earn a Ph.D. in cognitive psychology and earn their living working in a laboratory; but the vast majority have no such intention. In this book, we hope to present the science of cognitive psychology so it can be grasped equally well by students who aspire to scientific specialization and those who do not. This requires that theories and data be analyzed relative to their place in the overall pattern of knowledge. Presenting technical facts, laws, and scientific theories is not enough, even though that is sometimes all one finds in science books and courses. We believe it is essential to bring broad perspectives to the teaching of science. Science and the student would benefit if more effort were spent on the pattern of knowledge to which theories and the data relate.

Science would benefit in two ways. Scientific research would be of better quality if all researchers understood where their work fit in the scheme of things, and the importance of science would be more widely understood and appreciated among the general public. Students would benefit by gaining greater enjoyment and understanding from a scientific education that imparted perspective. They would be excited by discovering adjoining pieces of the puzzle of knowledge, rather than bored by memorizing lists of experiments whose relations to one another sometimes seem obscure. Becoming educated should be intellectually exciting. It is science's big ideas and sense of discovery, not just its technical details, that carry its excitement. This is fortunate, because it is impossible in the 4 years of a diversified undergraduate education to master the details of even one scientific subdiscipline. On the other hand, it is quite possible to achieve a broad appreciation of a science on the way to a baccalaureate degree. But here is a dilemma: Most science courses are taught by specialists. A few of them may lack perspective on their own fields; for others, perspective has become so nearly second nature that they forget to teach it. Textbooks are also written by specialists. Only a rare textbook integrates a technical literature so that it is understandable and interesting to the general student and the aspiring scientist alike.

Our goal in this book is to present an overview and perspective that will bring coherence and significance to cognitive psychology and to the information-processing approach to cognition. In the process, we present many experiments and their results. As we describe these experiments, we explicitly address why they were done and how they reflect the basic commitments of the scientists who did them. Of course, we also cover what they seem to show about human beings—their properties and their nature. Together, the intellectual motivation for research and the interpretations of experiments render cognitive psychology coherent and exciting.

B. Beginning Definitions of Cognitive Psychology and Information Processing

Cognitive psychology is one branch of an extremely broad field. Many content areas fall within the field of psychology, such as brain physiology, social interaction, and intrapsychic dynamics. The topic area of cognition, then, is one way to distinguish cognitive psychology from other branches of the general discipline. Psychology also includes many different methods of study; there are literary psychologists, intuitive psychologists, humanistic psychologists, and scientific psychologists, among others. Different methods can be used to study what is apparently the same subject matter. For instance, social interaction is studied both by scientific psychologists in the experimental laboratory and by humanistic psychologists in the encounter group. In order to mark out an area of study such as "cognitive psychology," then, we must specify both the content and the general approach.

The subject matter of cognitive psychology could be broadly defined as "how the mind works," but as such it would be completely intractable. The cognitive psychologist, like any other student of nature, must limit the subject matter to keep it comprehensible and manageable. Therefore, those aspects that seem especially important to most cognitive psychologists are studied— the "higher mental processes," including memory, perception, learning, thinking, reasoning, language, and understanding. Most students of the higher mental processes, moreover, have made a commitment to the observational methods of science rather than to a literary, intuitive, or humanistic point of view. The typical cognitive psychologist is, therefore, a scientist motivated to understand a natural system consisting of the human higher mental processes.

The commitment to use the scientific method in studying the higher mental processes obviously sets limits on one's scholarly investigations. However, a multitude of further decisions must be made, implicitly or explicitly, before the first experiment is begun. What assumptions are reasonable? What ideas are relevant in creating hypotheses about the nature of mental processes? What hypotheses are plausible and worthy of study? What should be studied first, and what should be deferred until later? Scientific psychologists can legitimately differ in the way they resolve these questions. However, within scientific disciplines, there tend to form subgroups whose members adopt very similar resolutions. When a sufficiently large number of scientists in a field agree to a considerable extent on how such questions are to be resolved, they are said to share a *paradigm.* Information-processing psychology is one paradigm for studying cognitive psychology, and it happens that in recent years it has become the dominant paradigm in the study of adult cognitive processes.

As we shall use the term, *paradigm* refers to the common set of ideas a subgroup of scientists brings to their subject matter. We develop the concept of paradigm in considerable detail in the rest of this chapter, for it is a pivotal concept in our treatment of the literature on cognition. Although the same term has been used to refer to particular laboratory techniques, our usage is quite different. It is also different from "theory," but these differences are explored later.

Because of the enormous complexity of most natural and social systems, no scientist can study the totality of a major system. Research can begin only after manageable-sized subsystems have been defined. Significant research requires the knowledge, foresight, and luck to formulate the properties and states of a subsystem that corresponds reasonably well to the real world. The scientist's paradigm plays a central role in this very significant task. Cognitive psychologists within the information-processimg paradigm have a particular way of deciding which subsystems comprise the higher mental processes, some insights and intuitions about what they are like, and some commitments regarding how they should be studied. They have defined the area of study as the way man collects, stores, modifies, and interprets environmental information or information already stored internally. They are interested in knowing how he adds information to his permanent knowledge of the world, how he accesses it again, and how he uses his knowledge in every facet of human activity. Information-processing-oriented cognitive psychologists believe that such collection, storage, interpretation, understanding, and use of environmental or internal information *is* cognition. They believe understanding these processes is fundamental to understanding reading, speech production and comprehension, and creative thought. Indeed, many cognitive psychologists believe that this research will aid in understanding other human characteristics, such as emotion, personality, and social interaction. Some cognitive psychologists believe that the properties they study—speech, understanding, and thought—distinguish human beings from every other natural system on earth.

C. Some Preliminary Examples of Cognitive Behavior

So far, our discussion of information-processing psychology has been both brief and abstract. It is greatly extended in the next two chapters. Before that, however, it might be useful to concretize our brief description through a familiar activity, analyzed from the information-processing psychologist's point of view.

Most readers of this book probably know how to drive an automobile. Driving is the kind of activity that information-processing psychologists consider representative of tasks requiring many important cognitive processes. Although you are probably unaware of most of them, you perform countless internal acts as you drive your car. This is one characteristic of information-processing approaches to cognition: Many of the cognitive processes that interest information-processing psychologists occur without conscious awareness on the part of the individual who is performing them.

Consider your typical drive to your college or university. As you drive, you make various turns, each one signalled by some familiar landmark. These landmarks are so well known that you probably are not aware of "seeing" them each time. However, the information-processing psychologist is convinced that you must perceive each familiar landmark anew each time. You must recognize it as the same landmark that you have seen and used on previous occasions. How do you do this? From the information-processing viewpoint, you must have represented the landmark's appearance in your memory. When you see it again, you match up your current perception of the landmark to its stored representation; this is the process of *recognition*.

Recognition also makes available to you other stored information about the significance of the landmark. Thus, when you have recognized it you can know whether you should turn right or left, proceed straight ahead, get ready to turn, and so on. Information-processing psychology is fundamentally committed to the concept of representation: Everything you know is considered to be represented in your memory. How these representations are put to use is one of the central questions in many areas of cognitive psychology.

We have mentioned two kinds of information about the landmark: perceptual knowledge about its appearance and conceptual knowledge of its significance. Both kinds of information are presumably represented, and they are called into play whenever a driver correctly executes the actions necessary to get to his or her destination. Another question that intrigues information-processing psychologists is the *manner* in which different kinds of information are represented. The area of cognition is also characterized by an assumption that represented information is somehow *coded* for storage in the human nervous system. This means that external events are converted into an internal form according to some specifiable sets of rules. Perhaps there is a different code for perceptual and conceptual information; or perhaps there is a single code that can be reached on the basis of visual or conceptual stimuli. Many areas of cognitive psychology are concerned with the various forms in which content may be coded.

As you drive, you take in vast amounts of environmental data. You "see" dozens of other cars, many buildings and trees, signs and signals. Some of this material is almost immediately forgotten; for example, another driver who is behaving normally is unlikely to be remembered later. However, if a driver behaves erratically, you may subsequently recall his actions. Subjectively it seems as if you see only the erratic drivers. But the information-processing psychologist considers that you could not distinguish the erratic drivers from the others if you did not process information about them all. However, much of this processing activity did not result in memory for what was processed. This possibility indicates that there must be different *ways* of processing information—some that result in memory and some that do not. Cognitive psychologists are interested in what the different processing modes might be and how the human cognitive system sets one or another mode into operation.

As you drive you also make numerous decisions. Some are deliberate and conscious—for example, you decide to pass up a distant parking space in hopes of finding a better one. However, many are made without your attention or awareness. If your car has a stick shift, you decide repeatedly when to shift gears. You decide when to speed up and slow down, when to change lanes, when to pass and when to wait. When a green light changes to yellow, you decide whether to stop or proceed—incorporating into your decision an estimate of how long the yellow light will last, whether there are cars approaching from the other direction, whether someone is behind you, and the speed of your own vehicle and its distance from the intersection. Quite a bit of data goes into this decision making, although for the most part you can do it without thinking about it. What is more, the decision may depend in part on whether you are late for class, whether you have a new or an old car, or whether your insurance is paid up. Information-processing psychologists consider that much cognition depends on internal decision making. Some is conscious, some unconscious, and some is completely outside the control of the individual. Nevertheless, such decision making is an important part of the information-processing approach to cognitive psychology.

The conviction that cognitive processes occur over time, and that some take longer than others, is another feature of information-processing psychology. Many information-processing experiments are designed expressly to find out how long different activities take. Many conclusions are drawn from what the researcher discovers about how much time a cognitive operation consumes. Temporal measures are used to estimate how complex a particular task is or how many suboperations, such as decisions, recodings, and mental searches, may possibly be involved. Now that we have called attention to some of the things we do without thinking about them, you may be able to describe some of the internal activities involved in your own driving. In fact, rational and intuitive analyses are respectable tools in the information-processing paradigm. Scientists who work within this paradigm believe that they can gain important insights by informal analysis of cognitive activities. But information-processing psychologists know that they cannot rely on rational and intuitive tools alone, precisely because so many cognitive processes go on outside of people's awareness. To know how people's minds work, information-processing psychologists must also use experimental tools, and they do so extensively. Some of these techniques are elegant and yield unexpected insights into how people work. Herein lies part of the fun of studying the information-processing paradigm.

Like all paradigms, the information-processing approach to human cognition has an intellectual history, a set of research tools, and a language that sets it off from other paradigms. Without understanding these, it is impossible to understand the paradigm and, concomitantly, the experiments and theories the paradigm has stimulated. There is much more discussion of these matters in the next chapter and throughout the book. We have used the information-processing paradigm as our organizing theme. It has guided our choice of chapters and of what to include in them. We know that this is not the only approach to cognitive psychology, nor will it last forever. In fact, in our final chapter we briefly describe recent and potentially important changes in the approach. We simply believe that the scientific data on the higher mental processes are *currently* organized more comprehensibly by the information-processing paradigm than by any other view.

D. The Significance of Information Processing and Cognitive Psychology

For those who plan to obtain advanced degrees and become professional psychologists, the significance of cognitive psychology and the information-processing orientation lies in the fact that these are important parts of contemporary psychology. A professional education is incomplete without some mastery of them. But this book is also for psychology majors who plan to stop with a bachelor's degree and, indeed, for those who are not psychology majors. It is intended to give an appreciation and comprehension of mankind's finest faculties, his mental ones. In the process, it accounts for some of the most intriguing features of science: its paradigmatic conventions and its revolutions. The information-processing approach has been in the forefront of a scientific revolution; it has provided psychologists with a fundamentally new way of thinking about people. Past ways of characterizing the most central characteristics of humankind have been quite different. For example, Freudian psychology focused on the clash between rational and irrational forces in shaping the human personality. Conflict between the demands of civilized society and innate, instinctive forces, which occurred primarily during infancy and early childhood, was considered a fundamental determinant of later behaviors. More recently, psychologists have viewed the human being as a conditioned responder, waiting passively for stimuli to impinge on him before emitting the response he has been conditioned to make. Both these views have been invoked to explain emotional behavior and psychopathology. Information-processing psychology differs from both Freudian and conditioning psychology. Our paradigm focuses on normal and rational behavior, and views the human being as an active seeker and user of information.

No approach explains all behavior; certain approaches seem to work best for certain kinds of human activities. This will long be the case in a developing science such as psychology. At the moment, the information-processing view seems congenial mostly to scholars of intelligent human behavior—it seems to work best in accounting for people's ability to accomplish familiar, well-learned mental operations. For the time being, it has little to say about emotional behavior, mental illness, or individual differences. However, the number of scholars who share the information-processing view is increasing. Some have applied the paradigm to social psychology (Carroll & Payne, 1976; Hendrick, 1977), developmental psychology (Klahr & Wallace,

1976), and neuropsychology (Pribram, in press). Attempts have also been made to apply it to clinical psychology (Mahoney, 1974).

Freudian and behavioristic conceptions of man have been adopted by large segments of society. We anticipate that the information-processing conception will also work its way into social institutions outside of science. Information-processing conceptions are being used increasingly wherever survival depends on rapid and accurate dealings with changing and complex environments—for example, space travel and undersea exploration. The approach is also useful and will become increasingly important in school teaching, rehabilitation of perceptual and intellectual abnormalities, and in the communications fields.

Virtually every human activity is guided by a model of human nature. An implicit model of what people are like is responsible for the actions of police officers, salespersons, doctors, military officers, parents—in fact, everyone who interacts with other people. The use of some conception of man is universal and inescapable—whether the conception is valid or not. Insofar as the approach conveyed by this book is a valid picture of human capabilities, propensities, and behavior, learning it should improve one's effectiveness in many kinds of interactions with others.

We believe that an important piece of the truth is contained in the information-processing approach. It does not explain everything that humans do, but some human skills are explained more adequately in information-processing terms than in any other way. We advocate that a student learn this approach, and others as well. We believe that a complete education warrants learning a variety of approaches, such as dynamic, humanistic, and operant psychology, as well as information processing. A person who has mastered and understood several paradigms is in an excellent position to accomplish two important ends. First, he or she will be able to see the strengths and weaknesses of each approach as it applies to the aspects of human behavior that the person finds most interesting. The strengths of the information-processing view are most apparent to one who has tried to understand human intellectual capacities from behavioristic, psychoanalytic, and other viewpoints. Second, the person will be better able to deal with differences of approach, thus increasing receptivity to newer and more powerful conceptions as they are developed. Even the comprehension of established views will be facilitated. Each psychology course that is offered from a new vantage can increase a sense of disorder and chaos for the student who expects all of the facts collected by psychologists to fit into a coherent view. But for the student who has considered the similarities and differences between psychological paradigms, each new approach will fit a pattern and be easier to understand. Just as someone who knows two languages finds it easier to learn a third, so the student who understands scientific revolutions and how they evolve will not be dislocated each time he encounters another paradigm. Scientific perspective consists in large measure of understanding how paradigmatic conceptions change. Cognitive psychology provides an excellent opportunity to understand such change, because it has so recently undergone one.

II.   COGNITIVE PSYCHOLOGY AS AN EXPERIMENTAL SCIENCE

A. Psychology Is a Research Science, Not a Mature System

When they hear the word "science," many people think of mature systems, such as planetary mechanics, thermodynamics, electromagnetism, or optics. They do not recognize the differences between these relatively advanced systems (Hanson, 1958) and very active research sciences, such as molecular biology, microphysics, and most areas of psychology. Mature systems were once wide-open research sciences; many experiments were done to answer questions about their subject matters. But today, many questions have been answered. The natural systems associated with these fields are now well understood, although they are sometimes subject to reinterpretation. Today, experiments are rarely conducted on fundamental issues. In fields like psychology, however, scientists are actively engaged in the most fundamental kinds of research. The answers to most of their questions are not known. No field of contemporary psychology has achieved the status of a mature science. Psychology is dynamic, changing, and unsettled, and it ranks among the most exciting of research sciences. This is one reason that psychology courses often do not seem to hang together—changes are first taught in the area that originated them, and other areas may not reflect the change for some time.

Learning a dynamic research science is different from learning an advanced system. An immature research science has a multitude of unanswered questions, and the student will find that many of them have not even been clearly asked. There is often substantial disagreement between scientists over how to frame the questions and about what evidence would answer them. You will be frustrated indeed if you approach an active research science like psychology as if it were made up primarily of finished systems of established facts and agreed-upon theories. Learning psychology consists as much in learning the current questions, controversies, and research approaches as it does in learning established facts. There is no single theoretical scheme to organize the facts and questions of a dynamic research science, as there is for more established fields. Moreover, the questions, controversies, and approaches within an immature and dynamic research science have hardly ever been selected by applying textbook rules of scientific procedure. The choice of research questions, the character of current controversies, and the kinds of research approaches in use are comprehensible and interesting only in view of their social-intellectual roots. Throughout this book, we have provided the relevant contemporary antecedents and recent history to help make cognitive psychology orderly.

The controversies between scientists in an active research field can be particularly disorganizing for students. The student's problem is to distinguish the controversies that are central to the field, or at its frontiers, from those that are peripheral. Methodological issues can and often do fascinate research scientists; there are occasional researchers who make whole careers pursuing them. George Miller, a leading cognitive psychologist, has argued that methodological issues are bread and butter to the working scientist but can be spinach to everyone else. We have tried to avoid this source of difficulty by not presenting issues whose resolution will have limited effects on cognitive psychology. We have not presented data about issues which we judge peripheral, even if there are numerous experiments on them in the technical literature of our field.

It is also true of a research science that seemingly well-established facts are sometimes called into question by single pieces of conflicting data or by novel interpretations of old results. The facts and theories of a research science are variously qualified, depending on which other facts and interpretations one acknowledges. When writing about research sciences, textbook writers often try to present all possible qualifications to every fact or interpretation they discuss. This thoroughness can ensure that they will not offend the scientists who have discovered the qualifications, but it can also obscure the major generalizations that a student strives to grasp. The main outlines and important features of a research science can sometimes be seen more easily by simply ignoring data that are endlessly qualified and requalified. In this book, we have omitted qualifications that seem to confuse rather than clarify fundamental issues. We have tried, in short, to strike a balance between oversimplification and overcomplication.

Science is a human institution, and as such it suffers from human frailties and shortcomings. It is important to distinguish the actual from the ideal conduct of science as a preliminary to understanding the activities within a particular scientific field, such as cognitive psychology. Much of the chaos that so often seems to characterize an active research discipline results from an incongruence between the way the discipline is said to be studied and the way it is actually carried out. One reason research sciences often seem incomprehensible to the beginner is that the published research report often does not correspond in a one-to-one fashion to the actual conduct of inquiry. Scientific research is sometimes portrayed as if it were a completely rational, progressive business that moves steadily forward. New questions are supposedly generated only by gaps in knowledge or by unexplained facts. Experiments are presumably conducted only to test deductions from scientific theory. Theories are wisely discarded if the experiments give results that do not conform to the deductions from them; and the best theory is adopted, though only tentatively, of course. Few working scientists actually accept this as an accurate account of how science is done. A careful examination of the theoretical and experimental activities of scientists suggests that scientific inquiry is considerably more complicated and much more interesting than this false stereotype (Kessel, 1969).

This stereotyped view of science might be the only way to teach a high school course or the most elementary college course, but it causes great grief to the serious student. It provides no way of understanding why obviously important issues go completely unresearched, while experiments on some minor topics fill whole journals and books and then disappear. Why do so many experiments sometimes produce so little progress in theory? How can well-established theories be completely discarded and replaced by new ones? The stereotyped view leaves questions like these completely unanswered, and science ends up seeming incomprehensible. It is not. Questions like these can be answered. The answer begins here: There is more than one set of rules by which science is done.

B. A Fundamental Premise:
The Rational and Conventional Rules of Science

Every scientist has made a commitment to certain procedures that qualify his or her work as "science" rather than as something else. These rules are well known and publicized; they constitute the *scientific method*. The rational rules of science are quite similar from one discipline to another. They are shared by physicists, biologists, and social scientists. However, if you have ever tried to use your understanding of a physical science to understand psychological research, you have probably found that there were as many differences as commonalities. Understanding the rational rules is essential, but it is not enough to render the actual experiments and theories of a science obvious and comprehensible. The reason is that every scientist uses a second set of rules in addition to those of the scientific method. The second set of rules is *conventional*, in the sense that several or many scientists agree that they are appropriate. However, while every science has conventional rules, they are not the same from one scientific discipline to another. Even scholars within a single discipline may subscribe to different conventional rules. When a group of scientists share essentially the same conventional guidelines for formulating research questions and structuring experiments to answer them, they are members of the same scientific paradigm.

The *fundamental premise of this book* is that an active research science cannot be intelligently understood by reference to the rational rules of science alone. It is equally necessary to understanding the paradigm that guides the scientists who do the experiments. Without understanding the paradigm, a student may find the experiments unrelated to each other; or the answers the experiments are supposed to provide may seem incomprehensible. The questions the scientists have chosen to ask may seem trivial or exotic, and their controversies may resemble tempests in teapots. However, to the student who grasps the paradigm guiding the research, the relationship between theory and experiment will become clearer. The way in which experiments relate to each other will become more evident. The questions scholars in the field have chosen to ask will not seem so arbitrary, and their approach to answering the questions will look more reasonable. The field as a whole will have coherence and relevance to the student who understands the intellectual motives of the scientists who comprise it—include their rational rule system and their conventional, paradigmatic one.

1. The Rational Rules

Let us first consider the rational aspects of science, for it is these that distinguish science from other human institutions that make claims about human nature. Religion, art, poetry, political organizations, legal scholars, the military arts, encounter groups, and meditators are all sources of claims about people—their motives, essence, and actions. There are at least two fundamental differences between scientific methods for the study of mankind and nonscientific methods, such as religion and political ideology. The first concerns their objectives. Science may be unique, in that it is the only institution whose ultimate objective is obtaining knowledge for its own sake. The rational rules prescribe no prior commitment to what the truth is; the institution is designed to discover the truth and, when it is found, either to stop there or to transmit the findings to technology. Other institutions, such as religion and politico-legal systems, also make and defend claims about the way people actually are; but these claims are primarily in support of the institution's role in defining correct and incorrect action. The truth claims are not an end unto themselves, but are offered as foundations for prescribing moral rights and wrongs. The formal institutional rules of scientific method include no way to translate scientific discovery into prescriptions of the right thing to do; in fact, they preclude it. Science's rational component, for example, may be used to determine the number of deaths attributable to abortion or how to reduce this number, but it cannot render a judgment whether abortion is right or wrong. The rational rules can provide estimates of the incidence of premarital sex, but they cannot be invoked to judge the moral appropriateness of sex before marriage. It is true that scientists sometimes go on record for or against some moral principle, and this is legitimate if they are speaking as persons with moral views. However, the community of scientists does not accord universal adulation to a colleague who represents his moral conclusions as scientific discovery, however much they themselves may agree with the conclusions.

The second major difference between the rational rules for scientific conclusions and alternative methods resides in the scientific ideal for verification. The rational component of science demands that scientific beliefs at some point be tested against observable evidence. Science, in principle, has no axioms that are sacred and invulnerable to observational test. As we shall see, there are paradigmatic assumptions that may in fact never be tested, and that serve as a starting point for theory construction; but ideally even these assumptions are candidates for abandonment in the face of contrary observational evidence. As we shall also see, there is considerable latitude in the way observations relate to theoretical claims; but in the rational rules of scientific procedure, observational data provide the final criterion for determining the truth or falsity of such claims. Other sources of knowledge claims do no institutionalize observational data to this extent. In religion, for example, new claims are considered in light of their consistency with the axioms of the faith. Claims that are derived from the axioms are considered true; claims that are inconsistent with the axioms or their derivatives are false. The axioms are permanent, given, and unquestionable; their source is divine revelation. For example, Milne (1952) wondered whether Christian theology was threatened by the existence of countless planets in the universe, any one of which might contain intelligent beings. He noted that the Christian would either have to deny the existence of life on other planets or accept the possibility that the Incarnation of Christ was repeated countless times throughout the universe. A theologian (Mascall, 1956) considered this possibility from a theological point of view, and argued that Milne had a poor understanding of the fundamental Christian position on the Incarnation. Nothing in that position precluded the possibility that man might be one of a family of intelligent beings redeemed by Christ, or that man might be the only species that had fallen and needed redemption, or several other possibilities. The point here is that Mascall considered the findings of cosmology as they related to the axioms of Christianity. His theological judgment rested on consistency with these axioms rather than on observational test. Acceptability of truth claims, thus, rests on a different basis in religion and in the formal rules of science.

The test of truth in political ideologies is also consistency with a set of axioms, although these axioms may have a different source from those of religion. They may consist of truths held to be self-evident, as in the American Declaration of Independence. Or they may be rooted in divine will, as is the doctrine of the divine right of kings. They may rest on a particularly influential analysis of historical forces, as does Marxism. Whatever the source, however, the axioms that form the basis of political ideology are not open to question. New situations are analyzed in terms of the existing axioms and are not taken as potential evidence that the axioms are wrong. Political and religious institutions contain no mechanism for changing the axioms; such change is not part of the institution's internal structure. This is one difference between such systems and science. Even well-established beliefs in science are in principle open to question, and their occasional abandonment is considered an acceptable part of the way science is supposed to function.

Thus, the rational rules of science differentiate scientific claims from those of other institutions that also make assertions about nature. Perhaps for this reason, scientists are somewhat self-conscious about how they prove their claims. Many, many textbooks describe the rational procedures for scientific verification of truth. All scientists know these rules well, and there is no question that they guide scientists in their daily work. But they are not the only guide scientists use. There are also the conventional parts of scientific decision making.

2. The Conventional Rules

It has been known for a long time that scientific inquiry takes much of its direction from certain intellectual commitments that scientists have *not* clearly stated (cf. Polanyi, 1962; Popper, 1959). Still, until recently, most textbook accounts of the rational component of science presented it as if it were an essentially complete account of how science is done. The problem is that the rules are *prescriptive* and define how science should be done. To understand an actual science, a student really needs *descriptive* information about how the science is actually done. Otherwise, the student's position is analogous to trying to understand congressional action by reference to the U.S. Constitution and Robert's Rules of Order. Certainly, these codified rules place constraints on what senators and representatives do. However, much of what occurs in congressional sessions must be explained by reference to particular personalities and the characteristics of their constituencies, special relationships between individual members of Congress, temporary alliances, and a host of other factors that could not be codified in the Constitution or parliamentary procedural rules. This does not mean just covert violations of the rules, such as influence peddling or bribery. Many deals are made off the floor, with members of Congress agreeing to vote for each other's bills. This is a perfectly legitimate activity; it is not precluded by the Constitution, but neither is it explained by the Constitution. The length of filibusters, the function of party whips, and even the positions taken by members of opposite political parties can be understood only by reference to pragmatic factors outside the scope of the Constitution and Robert's Rules. It is not that these documents are wrong; but in accounting for the activites and votes of real senators and representatives, they are incomplete. So it is with the rational rules of science.

The canonical (rule-governed) component of scientific method requires that hypothetical accounts of natural-system properties be verified by observation. Empirical corroboration in science is a complex and controversial subject. However, even though it is an oversimplification, it is reasonable to say that the rules provide some guidance in how to make observations that will confirm or disconfirm proposed accounts of nature. There are prescribed methods, for example, of structuring an experiment so as to isolate the causal effects of a particular variable. However one views the current state of development of canonical methodology, the rules are of little help in choosing which variable to study. The rational component of science provides much more guidance in *how* to observe than in selecting *what* to observe. In selecting what to observe, a researcher must rely on other sources of ideas— and the source that most researchers use is the "collective wisdom"of other· researchers in the field. Such collective wisdom results partly from previous observation and experimentation; but it is also the product of "working assumptions" that others have made and found useful in formulating previous research. The working assumptions may never have been directly validated by experiment. They may have been indirectly supported, in the sense that productive experimentation has resulted from making them; and many scientists in the field may be quite convinced of their validity. However, the fundamental status of such working assumptions is different from empirically validated fact. They are consensually validated by collective judgment, not confirmed by direct experimental test.

Interpretations that are made of experimental data are also influenced by "collective wisdom." The rational rules of science impose some constraints on how a researcher may interpret his observations; for example, he cannot ignore the requirements of logic. Nevertheless, logical requirements do not completely determine a researcher's interpretations. The behavior of a rat in a Skinner box has at various times been interpreted as verifying, or not verifying, claims about how animals learn; and "animals" has been taken to include people. But to invoke the data of rat experiments in theories of complex human learning, one must assume that human and rat learning is similar in essential respects. Is this assumption empirically justified? Are there experiments in the psychological literature that have directly tested it? The answer is no, although for many years the assumption was widely accepted among experimental psychologists. Today, very few cognitive psychologists are comfortable with the assumption that complex human learning can be understood by extrapolation from the behavior of rats. Psychologists of human learning once supported such an assumption by consensus; but now their collective judgment has changed. Is this because experiments have proved the assumption wrong? The answer, again, is no. No one can point to a single experimental outcome that changed nearly everybody's mind. The change resulted from informal judgments rather than the application of formal scientific methods. The judgments were made by intelligent and well-read people who know a great deal about the experimental data of psychology; but they were judgments nonetheless. If the assumption of essential comparability between human and rat learning had been directly rejected by experimental observation, every respectable behavioral scientist who knew his trade would by now have abandoned it. However, there are perfectly respectable scientific psychologists, whose sanity, honor, and intellect are not in question, who still feel that animal behavior can illustrate important aspects of complex human learning abilities. Among students of complex human learning they are a vanishing minority, but their very existence is evidence that the rules of scientific procedure leave considerable room for different strategic interpretations of data on the part of decent, intelligent scholars.

The *central premise* of this book is that the character of a science is shaped as much by paradigmatic judgments as by the canons of scientific method. Consequently, understanding the paradigm is as much a part of learning the field as studying the experiments themselves. Like all judgments, paradigmatic ones leave room for fundamental differences in approach. If the rational rules of science determined all aspects of scientific decision making, there would be no room for different approaches and no need to learn paradigms. When differences of opinion arose, we would simply do the necessary experiment, and everyone would draw the same conclusion from the outcome. *This ideal state of affairs does not obtain and never will.* Partisans of different paradigms do not agree on what the "necessary experiment" should look like. Typically, they do not usually communicate and therefore do not discuss the matter. If they did communicate, competent scholars would still disagree on what the outcome means if they did not share the same conventions for interpreting results. It is not the *data* about which they might disagree; it is the *meaning* of the data. While all competent observers might agree that an experimental rat turned left at a certain time under certain conditions, some may absolutely refuse to draw any conclusion about human activity from this fact. Does this mean that a set of consensually validated judgments is essential to make rationally derived scientific observations meaningful? We think precisely so.

Seeing that both conventional and rational systems guide what scientists do is particularly informative for psychology students. The key point is that one cannot completely make sense of a scientific literature containing only the rational component. One must also understand paradigmatic decision making in science. Psychology has had more than its share of paradigmatic shake-ups in its short history, and these are best explained by reference to the tacit, conventional component of scientific psychology. The shake-ups are completely incomprehensible to the student who believes that a good scientist follows the data wherever they lead and that only incompetent or dishonest scientists let their preconceptions determine the experiments they do and how they do them. Actually, all scientists regularly let their preconceptions dictate what they will do next. They fall back on their conventional wisdom whenever the rational rules fail them, which is often. The scientist makes many decisions by reference to an inexplicit ideology acquired through years of professional training. This ideology—the researcher's scientific paradigm—should not be viewed as an irrational character flaw that detracts from the rationality of science. Rather, it is an essential supplement to the rational aspects of scientific procedure. The paradigm forms the context in which the rationally derived procedures of science can be meaningful and interpretable. Learning the paradigm of a scientific discipline is a large part of becoming an expert in the field. It is just as important to absorb the conventions for motivating experiments and interpreting experimental data as it is to become familiar with the facts. As our opening quote from Polanyi (1962) illustrates, the facts really do not "speak for themselves."

Thomas Kuhn (1962) was the first to introduce a systematic treatment of paradigms in science; and he did so in the context of a distinction he wished to make between "normal" and "revolutionary" science. The impact of paradigms on the practitioners of science is quite different in periods of normal and revolutionary science, but it is present in both.

C. Normal and Revolutionary Science

Since Thomas Kuhn published his book on comprehensive scientific paradigms in 1962, there have been several important reactions. Kuhn's book has become the most widely read interpretation of the nature of science. His original viewpoint has been the subject of a variety of criticisms in the literature on the philosophy of science. In response to his critics, Kuhn has changed various details of his position (1962, 1970a, 1970b, 1970c, 1974). Before publication of the original treatise, an "accumulation model" of scientific knowledge was the dominant conception. According to this view, progress in science consisted of the cumulative growth of factual discoveries, improvements in methods, and theoretical generalizations. Kuhn challenged this pervasive view. He argued that, in advanced and mature sciences, progress is not linear but alternating. He suggested that theoretical sciences cycle between a state he called *normal science* and a state of extraordinary or *revolutionary science.* Normal science consists of coherent traditions of day-to-day research activities. These activities are theoretical, methodological, and experimental; and they are justified and unified by the paradigm from which they emerge. The paradigm includes the intellectual commitments and beliefs of a community of like-minded scientists; it provides model problems to the community and defines the domain of acceptable solutions. The paradigm is not necessarily identified with a particular scientific theory, law, or method. It is more global, taking in the full range of implicit and explicit communal assumptions. Normal science is guided and structured by the paradigm. It produces research that extends and elucidates those facts that the paradigm suggests are most revealing. The paradigm sanctions methods known to, and accepted by, the paradigmatic community. In the course of normal science, the methods may also be extended, modified, and refined. As normal science proceeds under the auspices of a given paradigm, Kuhn describes two things that happen in advanced, mature disciplines such as physics: A stable body of knowledge grows and develops, and a small number of unsolved—perhaps insoluble—problems accumulate. The unsolved problems are called *anomalies*. One kind of anomaly is the failure of well-established theories, sanctioned by the paradigm, to predict experimental outcomes. Another is the failure of experiments to replicate. Whenever experimentation persistently fails to produce results consistent with the way the science has integrated and interpreted broad areas of prevailing knowledge, an anomaly exists. When enough anomalies arise, or when a particularly striking anomaly is reported, the discipline may go into crisis and change in character from normal to extraordinary science. If an alternative paradigm is put forth that can resolve the anomalies and shortcomings of the dominant one, a scientific revolution takes place. Scientific revolutions, in Kuhn's view, are noncumulative episodes in which most practitioners reject a dominant paradigm and accept, in whole or in part, the new commitments of a new paradigm. The revolutionary change to a new paradigm may mean significant changes in the scientists' conception of what problems are important, what solutions are acceptable, and what theoretical language is appropriate to those solutions. This is a truly revolutionary state of affairs, much like an ideologically based political revolution. As a matter of fact, the term "revolution" in politics came from science. It originated in the title of Copernicus' book referring to the revolutions of heavenly bodies—a book that provoked the archetype of all revolutions, intellectual or political.

Kuhn's book accelerated the rejection of views about science that had been accepted for many generations. Not surprisingly, his thesis has been vociferously attacked, mainly by philosophers of science (Lakatos, 1970; Popper, 1970; Shapere, 1971; Scheffler, 1972). One major objection concerns the concept of "paradigm," and a second is Kuhn's alleged acceptance of "irrationality."

Kuhn uses the paradigm concept in two important ways. One usage is essentially sociological, and refers to a community of scientists who function rather like a culture or subculture. The other usage refers to the particular commitments of the scientific culture: the scientific beliefs and values of the paradigmatic community and the particular puzzles, problems, and solutions those values support. Because a paradigm develops conventionally, without explicit documentation of its rules, some philosophers of science have rejected the "paradigm" concept as too vague and intuitive. But of course many useful concepts, such as "culture" and "common law," are likewise vague and intuitive and require development; nevertheless, they refer to a coherent reality. As a matter of fact, even critics who reject Kuhn's conception of the paradigm concept concede the distinction between normal and revolutionary science (e.g., Popper, 1970; Shapere, 1971). Because the rational rules do not change during revolutions, the distinction implies the existence of some other source of the overriding commitments that do change when scientific revolutions occur.

Other critics charge that Kuhn essentially defends irrationality (Suppe, 1977). This charge stems from the way Kuhn developed the concept of paradigms. His thesis implies that choice among paradigms cannot be made on reasoned objective grounds. One paradigm can never be objectively proven to be better than another. The problem is less with Kuhn, in this case, than with the philosophical conception of "rationality." The concept is somewhat underdeveloped, and for some philosophers encompasses only those judgments and conclusions that can be supported by existing formal or mathematical reasoning. Human reason, including that of scientists, no doubt includes components that have not yet been formally characterized. Kuhn's thesis is not that scientific judgments are made irrationally. We understand him to mean only that many such judgments involve a kind of reasoning that philosophers have not yet formalized.

Kuhn's conceptions on the growth of scientific knowledge have helped replace a long-prevailing view of science. That view, which grew out of the earlier tenets of logical positivism, fostered an unnaturally static view of the methodology of science. All competent students of science agree on the dynamic, everchanging character of the scientific enterprise: Methods, assumptions, facts, and theories are all continually modified, updated, reinterpreted, and sometimes abandoned. The process of change is surely one of the universal features of the scientific enterprise. Kuhn's formulations will likewise be altered, refined, and reinterpreted to give a richer and more accurate picture of modern science. Other philosophers of science are attempting to formulate their own accounts of the underlying systems of working assumptions used by scientists. These accounts are not identical with Kuhn's, of course, and their authors use different terms to avoid conceptual confusion. For example, Lakatos (1970) uses the term "problem shifts" rather than "revolution," and "research programs" instead of "paradigm." Toulmin (1972) characterizes scientific "disciplines" and their "evolution," and

Shapere (1977) describes scientific "domains" and how they are affected by "radical new hypotheses." The particulars of these alternatives differ from each other and from Kuhn's work. But all are attempting to deal with the reality that there are systems of assumption in science larger than formal theories, and to document how the assumptions change over time. Our treatment of the information-processing paradigm and its properties does not require a choice among the formulations that presently exist or are currently under development.

Kuhn's original analysis was developed for advanced, mature sciences, primarily the physical sciences. It requires some adaptation and modification as applied to psychology. We have taken the concepts of paradigm, normal science, anomaly, and revolution and have reconceptualized them to provide a novel account of cognitive psychology (cf. Segal & Lachman, 1972; Weimer & Palermo, 1973). Let us now take some of these rather abstract considerations and illustrate them by recent psychological events, in particular the decline of behaviorism. You have doubtless encountered aspects of behaviorism in one or more of your psychology courses, and we later describe in detail its impact on contemporary views of cognition. At one time, behaviorism was the dominant paradigm in American experimental psychology. It is no longer so. Let us consider this transition, which parallels the concept of a scientific revolution that Kuhn developed for mature sciences.

For many years, the majority of psychologists conducted normal scientific research into learning. Their research was based on certain important paradigmatic assumptions. They believed that most behavior was the result of learning and that relatively little could be attributed to innate abilities. They assumed that many species learned in the same way. They regarded learning as the formation of conditioned associations between external stimulus events and responses. These beliefs were not based on data, they were the conventional component of the scientific psychology of the time. The beliefs seemed plausible, and they helped psychologists decide what experiments were likely to be important and which observations would validly test their theories. For years, the study of learning proceeded as normal psychological science: Several theories of learning were formulated and tested with many experiments, which were usually performed on animals, such as the white rat.

Psychology entered a revolutionary period when many scientists began to question the conventional commitments of the learning theorists. The possibility of innate abilities was seriously reconsidered. Many psychologists came to believe that different species have different ways of learning. They raised the possibility that the formation of associations between stimuli and responses was not the only kind of learning. They even suggested that humans often learn in other ways. These changes in what psychologists believed were sometimes based partly on data, and sometimes on no data at all; but many researchers found the new commitments more plausible and more useful as guides to important and successful experiments.

The new beliefs were a massive challenge to learning theorists, because they struck at the very reasons for their research. If there were important innate abilities, then the centrality of learning to human behavior had been overplayed, and the energy devoted to studying it had been altogether disproportionate. If different species have different learning mechanisms, then data and theory about how animals learn might say nothing important about humans. If learning was not primarily a matter of conditioning, then painstakingly constructed theories of how stimuli are associated with responses by conditioning would be a small and perhaps trivial part of the science of psychology, rather than its very core. Such changed conceptions were revolutionary; they challenged the foundations on which most psychological theories were built; they implied that learning theory explained little of central importance. According to the new conceptions, it made no difference whether a particular learning theory was right or wrong: They were all seen as irrelevant, and research done to test any of them was uninteresting. The data collected when learning theory dominated normal psychological science were either reinterpreted in light of newer paradigms or discarded as insignificant. Although these newer views are not universally accepted, they represent the judgment of a substantial number of cognitive psychologists.

Scientific progress is cumulative, but only during periods of normal science. During scientific revolutions the conventional part of a science is changed drastically, and some or all of the data and theory of the preceding normal-science paradigm may be thrown out, ignored, or reinterpreted. Why do new paradigms replace old ones in psychology? Because many psychologists find them more helpful in their daily decision making and in becoming a successful scientist. They help answer questions like these: What are the probable components of the system I am studying? What are the important scientific questions of today? What observations can I make to help answer those questions? What experiment should I do first? Which experiments should be done at all? What should I measure? What conclusions do my observations justify? Scientists must answer these questions, and they regularly do, without reference to the rational rules. They answer such questions by referring to their conventional, paradigmatic beliefs.

The concepts and idea systems that make up a scientist's paradigm are usually learned while he is a student. They are learned primarily in graduate school, where the beginning scientist picks up the tricks of his trade. Some examples of conventionally accepted psychological concepts are the stimulus–response association, secondary reinforcement, uncertainty, representation, and propositional meaning. You may not have encountered the last two in previous courses, but they occur frequently in this book. Individual researchers may differ in how they use such concepts; but during periods of normal science, certain concepts are familiar to many scientists and their status is seldom questioned.

If scientists acquire their paradigms as students, what maintains their conventional beliefs later? The opinions of their peers, largely. Research is not a private matter performed alone in a laboratory. Psychologists, like all scientists, must regularly interact with one another. Although the public character of science is universally acknowledged, the extent to which the opinion of colleagues dictates a scientist's career and determines success is less widely appreciated. Whether or not a researcher publishes his experimental findings depends on other scientists; they read the reports and decide whether the work merits publication. When promotion is due, other scientists evaluate their colleague's scholarship and decide whether he or she will advance academically. When the scientist seeks money to support ongoing work, his or her research proposals are rated by colleagues; and unless they approve, the researcher receives no funds. Other scientists decide whether one's students should be graduated. When those students seek jobs, other scientists decide whether to hire them. Scientists have a deep personal investment in publishing their findings, in being promoted, in having the money to conduct their research, in having their students pass their doctoral examinations and find good jobs. These are some of the reasons it is to the scientist's advantage to gain and keep the high regard of fellow colleagues. This is far easier if one conducts one's research and trains one's students in a generally accepted paradigm.

Revolutionary science is extremely hard on established researchers, and this, too, contributes to the maintenance of normal science. Paradigmatic shifts beckon the established scientist to change his conception of reality and his view of his field. If he is to keep up, he must abandon familiar, well-understood concepts and ways of thinking; he must become something of a student again. He must retrain himself in a paradigm in which others are more expert. He may have to learn new research techniques. He may even have to abandon costly laboratory equipment that was suited to the old paradigm's research, and buy new equipment suited to the methods of the new paradigm. A scientist who is eminent in the practice of an established paradigm may become an obscure practitioner of an ascending one.

All this may suggest that scientists are bludgeoned into submission. On the contrary, most operate very comfortably within their scientific paradigm. Scientists have usually been trained in their paradigm, and they have a comforting sense of its correctness. It frees them from pondering extremely complex questions, such as "Where is my field going and how can I contribute to changing it?" It allows them to get on with their work. The community of scientists who share a paradigm function much like a family: They support one another; they provide validation for one another's work; they understand in a way that others do not. And the paradigm provides convenient ways to discount the work of incompetents and maniacs. Remember, scientists are human too.

How, then, does a paradigm ever die or decline? What brings on a scientific revolution? Why doesn't normal psychological science run forever? Paradigms fall slowly, from the weight of repeated failure. Problems that all agree need to be solved go untouched by research within the paradigm. Or, a particular kind of experiment may consistently fail to come out according to paradigmatic expectations. The unexpected results may be impossible to interpret within the paradigm unless the scientist makes absurd assumptions. Such occurrences can produce great dissatisfaction with a prevailing paradigm. Frustration can also result from the failure of experimental results to hold across similar settings. Experimental changes that are trivial according to the paradigm may completely reverse the outcome of an experiment. There is nothing quite so frustrating in the everyday life of a research psychologist as losing his usual findings by virtue of seemingly insignificant procedural variations. Another contributor to the fall of a paradigm is a sense that theory is not developing. Facts about the same behavioral system seem to remain unrelated for long periods of time. Even though there are many social pressures to continue normal science as usual, circumstances like these lead scientists to seek new ways of viewing their field. For example, one factor leading to the information-processing revolution was the lack of progress in understanding how people learn to read. There was enormous dissatisfaction with progress—in fact, there was none. A book written in 1908 remained, in 1968, the best available work on human reading, and was reprinted that year (Huey, 1908/1968). For a psychology that had for years been deeply committed to understanding learning, this was intolerable. The importance of reading could not be denied, but research based on learning theory ran into repeated dead ends. Ultimately, psychologists sought new approaches, and the information-processing revolution began. It has turned out to be more congenial to the study of reading; but most important to its initial success was the fact that it was there and that it represented a viable alternative.

Most scientific revolutions affect only the scientists whose old paradigm is replaced. Occasionally, however, enough sources of dissatisfaction with prevailing views come together to produce a seismic change in the general orientation, ideology, and activities of many scientists. A rare and very special type of scientific revolution changes even society's conception of man and the universe he inhabits. During the Copernican revolution, people's conception of their universe changed so that the sun rather than the earth came to be regarded as the center of their planetary system. The Copernican revolution also changed our view of how theories are "proved"; it was *the* scientific revolution. By believing Copernicus, Western society first accepted the view that observation and logic, not religious authority, should validate accounts of reality. In biology, the rise of Darwinian theory during the last century and, more recently, the ascendence of molecular biology are other examples of encompassing scientific revolutions. Freud presided over one such revolution in psychology, as did John Watson over another. In all of these examples, revolutionary conceptions of man and his universe spread through society. They profoundly influenced institutions outside of science: the church, the law, the educational system, politics, child-rearing, and so on (Segal & Lachman, 1972).

D. Paradigms in Psychology

Thomas Kuhn's ideas about paradigms and different kinds of science is gradually developing an enormous impact on how scientists think about themselves and their institutional enterprise. His views have also been extended and clarified by others. Masterman (1970), for example, has argued compellingly that paradigms play somewhat different roles in different sciences. She implies that there is a kind of developmental sequence of scientific disciplines. In the early days of a discipline, there is nonparadigmatic science: All facts are equally relevant; there are no overriding commitments to a particular conception of subject matter, to a particular method of study, or to a particular set of concepts. As the discipline develops, it becomes multiparadigmatic. Many paradigms vie simultaneously for the attention of the scientific community. Sometimes the different paradigms interact and influence one another; sometimes they do not. But eventually, in Masterman's scenario, one paradigm comes to dominate the discipline. This sets the scene for a scientific revolution. A new paradigm comes to challenge the prevailing one, and "a rank outsider with rudimentary new techniques may succeed in easily solving the major problems of the old paradigm (Masterman, 1970)."

This account describes science in a general way, but the real world is a bit more complicated. Certain branches of science may remain permanently multiparadigmatic. Several relatively dominant paradigms may maintain large constituencies and control most of the journals and meetings of the science. All the while, a number of less influential paradigms will continue to exist. This is now the state of science in psychology, and it may always be this way. The very early history of psychology may have been nonparadigmatic, but there have been multiple psychological paradigms since at least the turn of the century (Weimer, 1974; Weimer & Palermo, 1973). In our field, some paradigms simply change their relative dominance. Until the rise of Watsonian behaviorism, several paradigms claimed the allegiance of different groups of psychologists. Behaviorism appealed to more and more researchers until, by 1940, a variant called neobehaviorism had become the most dominant and popular approach to psychology. The dominance of neobehaviorism lasted for roughly 30 years, but no single paradigm replaced it. Today, psychology encompasses many paradigms, each of which is popular with a large identifiable group of scientists. The information-processing approach to cognition is one of these, and its influence is substantial.

III.   CHARACTERISTICS OF PARADIGMS

By now it may have occurred to you to ask whether paradigms are theories. They are not, even though major paradigms are often associated with particular theories. The Newtonian paradigm and Newton's theory of celestial and terrestrial mechanics illustrate the difference. The theory described and predicted the motions of the planets in our solar system and described the interaction of bodies on earth. Its subject matter was thus only a part of what concerned physicists. The Newtonian paradigm suggested, for the whole field of physics, which problems were important, how they should be studied, and what concepts would most advance knowledge. Its basic concepts of absolute space, absolute time, and absolute motion were not replaced until the Einsteinian revolution. The Newtonian paradigm far outlasted Newton's theory. Newton's theory of the motions of physical bodies had been revised and updated many times—for example, by William Rowan Hamilton and Carl A. Jacobi in the nineteenth century and by Joseph Louis Lagrange in the eighteenth. But the Newtonian paradigm continued to influence all physical sciences for over 200 years. By 1900, physicists had materially changed their factual statements about planetary motion, but their paradigm was what it had been for nearly three centuries. Shortly thereafter, the paradigm of physics changed as well.

How can one psychological paradigm be distinguished from another? Paradigms can differ in several ways, although they sometimes differ in only one or two. A psychological paradigm can be identified by its intellectual antecedents, by its pretheoretical ideas, by its subject matter, by the concepts and language that its adherents use, by their preferred analogies, or by the methods and procedures that its scientists employ. Paradigms are also sociological phenomena. They arise around groups of scientists who communicate mostly with one another. When a group of scientists communicate frequently and are aware of and cite one another's research, they very likely share a paradigm. Let us now look more closely at the characteristics of psychological paradigms. We use these characteristics in the next three chapters when we describe the information-processing paradigm.

A. Intellectual Antecedents

We said earlier that the nature of a science at any point in time is comprehensible and interesting largely in view of its intellectual antecedents. A scientist's beliefs about his work are frequently dictated by his intellectual predecessors. Paradigms, then, can be distinguished by the intellectual antecedents of their adherents. These antecedents can be historic or contemporary. They are the sources of concepts and views that the scientist applies to his work. Scientists often borrow ideas from mathematics, philosophy, and other sciences, and the disciplines from which a paradigm has borrowed are its intellectual ancestors. Freudian psychology borrowed heavily from medicine. Behaviorism was strongly influenced by British associationism and the philosophy of logical positivism. Information processing has drawn extensively on concepts from engineering, computer science, and communication science.

B. Pretheoretical Ideas

Because sciences have intellectual antecedents, the scientist does not approach his subject matter naively, even if it is a new subject matter about which very little is known. In formulating questions that he might answer scientifically, the scientist draws on notions about the reality underlying his subject. His notions may come from earlier observations, from knowledge about other phenomena that he thinks are similar to his area of study, from well-established beliefs passed on to him from his teachers, or perhaps from his own idiosyncratic insight. Every scientist depends on a network of notions, which Holton has called *themata* (Holton, 1973, 1975). We prefer the term *pretheoretical ideas* because that term has been employed previously in the psychological literature. Pretheoretical ideas guide research, motivate scientists, and sometimes constrain their efforts. Themata, or pretheoretical ideas, are present in most concepts, methods, and propositions of science. They manifest themselves in each of the other dimensions of paradigms: their subject matter, concepts, analogies, and so on.

   The pretheoretical ideas of cognitive psychology make up much of the next two chapters. Perhaps the best way to provide a preliminary sense of what we mean by pretheoretical ideas is through an example. To make it easier to distinguish our sample idea from validated scientific theory (which many pretheoretical ideas ultimately become), we will use an idea that proved incorrect. The work of Johannes Kepler provides such an example. Kepler was an astronomer who lived when planetary mechanics was a new science. To the study of planetary movements, Kepler brought his concept of the way things really were:

> The perfection of the world consists in light, heat, movement, and the harmony of movements. These are analogous to the faculties of the soul: light, to the sensitive; heat to the vital and the natural; movement, to the animal; harmony, to the rational. And indeed the adornment of the world consists in light; its life and growth in heat; and, so to speak, its action, in movement; and its

contemplation. . . in harmonies. (From Johannes Kepler, *Epitome of Copernican Astronomy IV and V,* translated by Charles Glenn Wallis, Great Books of the Western World, Volume 16, 853–857)

This notion of a universe characterized by harmony served Kepler as a pretheoretical idea. It suggested to him that planets traveled in circles, since circles are more harmonious than ellipses. His data were Tycho Brahe's observations of planetary motion, which did not immediately support the idea of circular orbits. However, for 19 years Kepler sought combinations of circles that would give him an orbit for the planet Mars that could be reconciled with Brahe's actual observations. He worked for all those years without success, and eventually he gave up the pretheoretical idea of circularity. Ultimately, Kepler himself demonstrated that it was much simpler to suppose that the planets actually traveled in elliptical orbits.

Incorrect pretheoretical ideas are easier to identify as conventionally derived than correct ones. However, our illustration should not suggest that such ideas are always—or even usually—wrong. Even those that do not seem to fit the data may not be wrong. An example of an extremely influential pretheoretical idea was the unshakable commitment by R. A. Millikan to an atomistic conception of electricity. Millikan lived early in this century, and his belief that electrical phenomena were the result of the actions of discrete elements, which we now call electrons, predated any experimental verification and was maintained in the face of indifferent data (Holton, 1973). Ultimately, Millikan conducted confirming experiments that gave his pretheoretical ideas an enduring scientific acceptance, unlike Kepler's idea of circular orbits.

Pretheoretical ideas operate in all sciences, and each paradigm within a science can be identified by its pretheoretical ideas. In information-processing psychology, most researchers believe that new inputs and old knowledge are represented in some "format" within the system. This pretheoretical idea is reflected in many of our theories involving formulations about the nature of mental searches, recoding of input into different formats, and internal-comparison operations.

A scientist's pretheoretical ideas are his conception of the reality underlying his subject matter. These ideas guide his definition of his subject matter by suggesting what are, and what are not, instances of the phenomena he wishes to study. They suggest what questions should be answered: For information-processing psychology, proper questions concern how information is represented, the nature of its code, how searches proceed, how "matches" are determined, and so on. By suggesting the questions, pretheoretical ideas often also suggest an appropriate methodology for obtaining the answers. Pretheoretical ideas often derive from a preferred analogy—a notion that one's science involves a reality similar to some better understood phenomenon. This in turn often suggests that terminology borrowed from the better understood area will be appropriate to the borrowing science as well. As you can see, then, the elements of a paradigm are not independent of each other; they function together as an interrelated system of ideas and concepts that give a scientist a particular "slant" on his field of study. We separate these elements for analytical purposes, but keep in mind that they are component pieces of a picture, each of which involves the other.

C. Subject Matter

Choosing a subject matter amounts to deciding what questions should be answered—selecting those questions whose answers seem to promise the most complete account of the natural system under study. In psychology, the natural system is the behavior of living creatures, especially human beings. Some psychologists believe that the most important aspect of people is their personalities. These researchers are likely to study individual differences, or people whose personalities are deviant. Others believe that learning is the most fundamental characteristic of living organisms, and they are apt to study how people and other animals acquire new responses. These psychologists will tend to overlook individual differences, and are usually more interested in typical performance than in extraordinary circumstances. Still other psychologists are interested in how people use language. They also are less likely to study individual differences, and are usually more interested in normal performance than deviant linguistic behavior.

The same questions recur continually within a conventional or paradigmatic group. While its choice of subject matter does not always define a particular paradigm, different paradigms are often best suited to the study of different subjects and hence become closely associated with them. Cognitive psychology is coming to be identified with the information-processing paradigm, because it has proved more successful than others in advancing our understanding of the higher mental processes.

D. Analogies

When scientists turn to the study of things they know little about, they often borrow principles from better-understood areas to guide their new research. When physicists first began to study gases, they borrowed principles from mechanics, postulating that gases were composed of something that behaved much like billiard balls or planets. Consequently, long before we understood molecules, the molecular action of gases was characterized with the same principles that accounted for the motion of visible bodies. Physicists could have used an analogy to some other phenomenon, such as ocean waves, and it would have misled them.

Analogies are also used to develop psychological theories. In Freud's psychoanalytic theory, sexual energy is viewed as a hydraulic system. According to this view, a person is subject to internal pressures that require release; if one outlet is plugged, the pressure will find another. This analogy directly underlies the psychoanalytic view of symptom substitution: If a patient's symptom is removed, but his basic personality remains unchanged, another symptom will appear to take its place. Freud's use of such analogies probably resulted from his medical training, according to which bodily organs were considered analogous to mechanical devices, such as pumps and levers. A paradigm's preferred analogies influence its choice of research questions, suggest hypotheses for experimentation, and help in theory construction. Different paradigms typically rely on different analogies.

E. Concepts and Language

Adherents of a paradigm often borrow terms from other disciplines, but they also invent terms to handle the concepts and data peculiar to their paradigm. There is some overlap between the languages of different paradigmatic groups, but each usually has a set of terms unique to it. These terms include names for conceptual entities and processes. Some people argue that this difference in language is "just semantic." They believe that the language of one paradigm is interchangeable with the language of another. It has been argued that it makes no difference whether a scientist says *stimulus* or *input,* whether he says *response* or *output* when referring to the conditions under which people behave and what they do. According to this view, all of the terms are mere jargon. We disagree. It seems to us that the terms that scientists use reflect their beliefs about the basic properties of the system they are studying. A psychologist's terminology often reflects fundamental conceptions of people and their capacities. Referring to behaviors as outputs rather than as responses implies very different pretheoretical ideas about the mechanisms underlying behavior.

F. Research Methods

The adherents of different paradigms often use different research methods. The paradigmatic, conventional component of science often includes preferences for particular pieces of apparatus, for particular experimental designs, for particular independent and dependent variables. Information-processing psychologists show a preference for human subjects and temporal measures, often using tachistoscopes and reaction-time data. They vary such factors as stimulus complexity and task demands; they control such matters as grammatical complexity and stimulus probability. These preferences, and the reasons for them, are developed in the next two chapters. They are not the only methods one could use, but they reflect the influence of the information-processing paradigm. Such methodological preferences are not perfect clues; but they often distinguish one paradigmatic group from another.

IV. PARADIGMS, INFORMATION PROCESSING, PSYCHOLOGY, AND SOCIETY

A paradigm reflects the thinking of a community of scholars who talk largely to one another, cite one another's findings, and do similar work. Paradigms are basic intellectual commitments about how to do a science, about the importance of different problems, about what are "facts" and what are not, about language and concepts that are appropriate, and about the suitability of different kinds of theory to a subject matter. Many paradigms can exist simultaneously in a given science, and in psychology several do. There certainly are differences among psychologists adhering to a given paradigm, but the similarities of their commitments outweigh the differences among them. Differences among paradigms are sometimes cast as issues of which is more scientific, but paradigmatic variations are far more subtle and more complex than that. Consider the metaphor of driving from New York to California. Many routes will get you there; no single way is absolutely correct. Some ways are more efficient than others; some are more beautiful; some are safer. People impose order on their world in their efforts to understand it; and it is impossible to absolutely value any single ordering scheme above all others. Nature can be ordered in many ways.

We have written this book from the point of view of one particular paradigm—information processing. We do not argue that it is *the* right way to understand and explain human mental processes, but we believe that it is at the present time the most comprehensive and comprehensible way. The recent ascendancy of information processing is a significant change in the study of higher mental processes. The change was essentially paradigmatic; it concerned man's basic character as well as theories of how he thinks. The information-processing paradigm made new questions interesting; it applied a new language to man's mental processes; it suggested new analogies for research into cognition; and it used some basically new techniques. This paradigm has potential applications beyond cognitive psychology—in clinical, social, and educational psychology, for instance. We would not be surprised to see the information-processing paradigm influence all of psychology. If it extends to the larger society as well, many people's conception of human nature will be affected.

It usually takes years for a change within science to affect the larger society. By now, most people have heard of Freud, but his impact on specialized psychology came over 50 years ago. Popular novels, child-rearing guides, and other printed materials now incorporate Freudian ideas, as if they were highly regarded and very contemporary among today's scientists. They are not; not many people realize how few courses in Freudian psychology are offered in most psychology departments today. The principles of behaviorism have been taught much more extensively over the last 40 years, but the general public knows far less about them. Some well-educated people have a general understanding of conditioning, but most do not. Information processing, which has been academically significant for 15 or 20 years, is still virtually unknown even to educated lay people. Students may come to college with a layman's acquaintance of approaches that may be 50 years behind events in particular sciences. In studying the contemporary literature, they must often leap over many years of thought within the science to catch up with prevalent paradigms. It is important for students to do this, both for themselves and for society at large. If only practicing scientists understand them, the newest paradigmatic developments will have little influence on society in general.

Even if we are wrong, and information-processing views never affect nonscientific social institutions, cognitive psychology has been profoundly influenced by the information-processing approach. Cognitive psychology is now identified as strongly with information processing as it is with the study of higher mental processes. The best way to understand this book and the field it deals with is to grasp the essentials of the information-processing paradigm. That understanding will make it much clearer why many rsearchers chose to do the experiments they did, and why they chose to do them as they did instead of some other way.

This book is designed to provide a thorough introduction to information-processing psychology. Chapters 2, 3, and 4 present in detail the characteristics of the paradigm and how it attained these characteristics. Later chapters present theory and data. As with all research sciences, the data are fragmented. The experiments will not answer all of your questions, as they have not answered all of the questions of the scientists who did them. But the studies represent what the science knows, where it is going, and how it expects to get there. The reader is not left to grapple alone with the fragmentation. Each chapter answers several of these organizing questions: Why are the contents of the chapter important? What do they mean to cognitive psychologists? What do the contents of the chapter add to our picture of humankind? How has the information-processing paradigm influenced the experiments discussed? We are convinced that if you learn the concept of a paradigm and the properties of the information-processing paradigm, you will be better able to tie together research on man's higher mental processes. Many students have used these ideas to make sense out of their other science courses as well.

2

Psychology's Contribution to the Information-Processing Paradigm

ABSTRACT

I. *How Do Antecedents Shape a Paradigm?*

Some influences are positive, and certain aspects of old paradigms are retained by new paradigms. Other influences are negative; the new approach takes a form that is expressly different from its predecessor. Sources of continuity include general methodological preferences, the training of scientists who shift to the new approach, and at least some well-established facts, laws, and theories. Discontinuity may be evidenced in any of the six facets of a paradigm. The nature of the anomalies, omissions, and perceived stagnation that engender a paradigm shift may determine the kinds of change that appear promising. Hence, the deficiencies of one paradigm may shape the characteristics of its successor.

II. *The Contribution of Neobehaviorism*

Neobehaviorists were committed to nomothetic explanation, laboratory experimentation, and the logical positivist philosophy of science. They were firmly antimentalistic. They emphasized learning and de-emphasized innate capacities as sources of behavioral explanation. To them, learning meant conditioning. Neobehaviorists also believed that learning was fundamentally the same process in all species that learned. Consequently, they were at home with animal experimentation and had no hesitation about generalizing the outcomes to human learners. They also preferred the study of laboratory-induced, conditioned associations to pre-existing associations.

From neobehaviorism, information-processing cognitive psychology took: (1) nomothetic explanation as its goal; (2) empiricism as its method of proof; (3) laboratory experiments as its mode of operation; (4) operationism as a way of describing experimental operations; and (5) the rational canons of science. However, contemporary information-processing psychologists have rejected: (1) extrapolation from a small set of principles; (2) animal data as a source of basic principles; (3) learning as the central psychological problem; (4) conditioning as the central form of learning; (5) logical positivism; (6) radical environmentalism and exclusion of innate capacities; (7) lack of interest in pre-existing associations; and (8) antimentalism.

III. *The Contributions of Verbal Learning*
Verbal learning shared many pretheoretical ideas with neobehaviorism, but it had its own flavor. It was functionalist, producing few major theories. Its criterion for evaluating research was "fruitfulness," or the number of additional experiments a particular study suggested. The major concerns of verbal learning were the acquisition and retention of such verbal units as letters, numbers, words, and nonsense syllables. The main techniques were paired-associates and serial-learning experiments. Many verbal-learning psychologists made an easy transition to information-processing psychology. The current paradigm retains: (1) memory as a key research area; (2) part of the data base of verbal learning; (3) many of its laboratory procedures and measurement techniques. The field of verbal learning also gave information-processing psychology: (4) many productive scientists. Contemporary cognitive psychology has rejected: (1) everything verbal learning shared with behaviorism and neobehaviorism except the rational rules of science; (2) verbal learning as a central psychological problem; and (3) the criterion of "fruitfulness" for evaluating research.

IV. *The Contributions of Human Engineering*
The field of human engineering burgeoned during World War II to deal with wartime problems in the area of skilled performance. Behavioristic pretheory and theory contributed little to the solution of such problems. New views of the human beings who operated wartime equipment had to be developed. Military psychology contributed the concept of the man/machine system and the human as an information transmitter. Some concepts were borrowed from the physical scientists with whom wartime psychologists collaborated. New interest arose in the problem of attention, and new approaches to perception emerged. The theory of signal detectability was developed to separate perceptual ability from decision making, and new interest was shown in the human being's decision-making capabilities. Because of the wartime applications of this kind of psychological research, it was generously supported by the Federal government, and there was increased access to sophisticated instrumentation.

From human engineering, information-processing psychology took: (1) the view of man as an information transmitter and decision maker; (2) the idea that there are limits to how much information he can transmit; (3) the theory of signal detectability; (4) continuing access to the concepts of the physical sciences; (5) a reliance on sophisticated instrumentation; and (6) a taste for Federal funding.

I. HOW DO ANTECEDENTS SHAPE A PARADIGM?

In this chapter, we are concerned with the impact of predecessor paradigms within the discipline of psychology. Intellectual antecedents from other disciplines generally make a positive contribution; the new paradigm borrows from them and uses their concepts. But previous paradigms in the same discipline can shape a new paradigm in either a positive or negative way. That is, characteristics of the new approach may be carried forward from the old approach, or they may be determined by reaction to perceived deficiencies in the old approach.

Earlier approaches—even when abandoned—do make positive contributions to the approaches that replace them. Kuhn's (1962) analysis of scientific revolutions generally neglected this source of continuity. His preoccupation with discontinuity was understandable, because earlier philosophies of science had emphasized continuity almost exclusively and, for the most part, had ignored the upheavals that Kuhn identified as revolutionary. Moreover, Kuhn's interest was in the conventional, paradigmatic aspects of scientific activity, and these aspects are more likely to show discontinuous change than the rational component. But some important sources of continuity can be identified.

A major source of continuity is in general methodological preferences. Scientists who shift paradigms are still the same individuals with the same basic training they received in graduate school. Moreover, they are still members of the same discipline, and scientific disciplines have characteristic methodologies that persist through paradigm shifts. For example, experimental psychology has for many years favored the experimental method of making observations (Koch, 1959; Woodworth, 1938). Other disciplines use other methods—for example, sociology makes wide use of survey research, and cultural anthropologists rely heavily on field studies. Although there have been changes in what psychologists select to observe and in the variables they prefer, psychological observations are still made in primarily experimental designs.

A second major source of continuity is the scientists who shift paradigms. The scientists who move from one approach to another are likely to retain their interest in particular research areas. They may adopt new ways of looking at these areas and design very different experiments to research them; but fundamental interest in a particular topic may be carried into the new paradigm by converts from the old. In cognitive psychology, an excellent example of this kind of continuity is our interest in memory, which has been a favorite research area in psychology since before any of us were born. One reason for this extensive interest is the relatively large number of verbal-learning psychologists who adopted the information-processing approach, bringing with them a fundamental commitment to the study of human memory capacity. Although some problem areas may be completely abandoned and others de-emphasized, some may retain their centrality in a new paradigm if many people who research it find the new paradigm congenial.

Third, there is continuity in at least some of the facts, laws, and theories of a field. Some facts and laws are so well established that it would violate the rational rules of science to dispute them, and some theories so broadly supported that they survive paradigm shifts. However, the paradigm shift may result in re-interpretation of such facts, laws and theories. For example, psychologists have long known that the middle items in a memorized list are likelier to be forgotten than the first and last few (McGeoch, 1942). This "serial position effect" is so reliable that no one doubts its reality. However, when conditioning was the primary basis for theory, efforts to explain the serial position effect usually relied on stimulus–response associations (e.g., Gibson, 1940). Information-processing psychologists explain the effect quite differently. As we see in Chapter 7, this well-known phenomenon is now thought to occur because items are differently processed depending on their position in the list.

Of course, there are many examples of the discontinuities that Kuhn emphasized when a paradigm shift occurs. Paradigm shifts occur because of wide-spread dissatisfaction with the dominant approach. The dissatisfaction arises from anomalies, absurdities, omissions, and perceived stagnation in the field. Consequently, the new approaches that appear most attractive are those that resolve the anomalies and absurdities, that rectify the omissions, and that give the practitioners a sense of progress in their work. The strengths of the new paradigm, then, and the problems it solves the best, are likely to be derivative from the weaknesses of its predecessor.

As we see in Chapter 3, paradigm shifts often result from new sources of ideas outside one's own discipline. However, the nature of the predecessor paradigm in one's own discipline may determine where the practitioners look for ideas. If, as in the case of neobehaviorism, there seems to be a lack of progress in the area of language, disciplines that concern themselves with language and other symbolic phenomena may appear especially attractive as sources of ideas. Indeed, much of the pretheory of contemporary information processing derives from just such disciplines: linguistics, computer science, and communications engineering. Hence, the new paradigm is shaped reactively as well as positively by its predecessors in the same discipline.

The polarization produced by scientific revolutions tends to reinforce the relationship between characteristics of a new paradigm and the perceived deficiencies of the old one. A prerequisite for scientific revolutions is a core of "revolutionaries"—people who are convinced that the old approach is fundamentally misguided and cannot be patched up. To support their arguments for a fundamental break, they may marshal "in principle" arguments to show that the dominant paradigm cannot, in principle, account for significant aspects of the discipline's problem area (e.g., Bever, Fodor, & Garrett, 1968). In the case of information-processing psychology, many early adherents of the new paradigm were influenced by the discipline of linguistics. Because neobehaviorists also accepted the importance of language behavior, language became a forum for a number of "in principle" arguments. Linguistically oriented psychologists argued that language could not, in principle, be learned through conditioning and reinforcement; that the conceptual apparatus of stimulus–response psychology was in principle inadequate to explain the grammatical characteristics of language; and so on. To buttress their view that the old paradigm is fundamentally wrong, proponents of the new one may give special weight to the problems that the old approach cannot in principle handle. Hence the central concerns of the new paradigm may result from the notable inadequacies of the old.

Let us now consider three psychological antecedents of the information-processing paradigm, and see how each influenced the character of the contemporary field.

II. THE CONTRIBUTION OF NEOBEHAVIORISM

A full appreciation of the information-processing approach requires an understanding of neobehaviorism. Neobehaviorism, sometimes called S–R psychology, exerted a profound influence on contemporary cognitive psychology—indeed, on most other areas of psychology as well. The reason is that, for about 40 years, neobehaviorism (and its parent paradigm, behaviorism) enjoyed an unprecedented degree of allegiance among American experimental psychologists.

Of course, psychology has always been multiparadigmatic. There has never been universal agreement on a single paradigm. But by about 1950, there was probably more agreement than at any time before or since. This is not to say that there was no controversy—quite the opposite. There were hot disputes over theory, but there was a striking consensus about what should be disputed. The dominant paradigm was neobehaviorism; the number of experimental psychologists who accepted its commitments was far greater than the number who did not. Some of these commitments have been maintained in our current approach, while others have been actively rejected. Let us consider what those commitments were, and how they have determined the character of the information-processing approach to cognition.

Neobehaviorism was profoundly committed to the empiricist tradition of Western science, and to a version of it that emphasized controlled laboratory experimentation and nomothetic explanation—accounts of general behavioral facts rather than the unique behavior of individual persons. These commitments were passed on to cognitive psychology. Whenever possible, cognitive psychologists make their observations under controlled laboratory conditions. They rely on laboratory analogues of the real world. In their experiments, cognitive researchers introduce causal agents in a planned and systematic fashion. They believe that this allows the strongest possible conclusions about the causes of behavior, and that it exposes most completely the recurrent regularities or laws of the cognitive system. Their goal is *nomothetic* theories of generalized human behavior rather than *ideographic* explanation of the behavior of individuals. These commitments to empiricism, nomothetic explanation, and laboratory experimentation were accepted by behaviorists and are now accepted by information-processing psychologists.

However, cognitive psychologists have rejected the philosophy of science called *logical positivism,* which was highly regarded by our immediate predecessors. These predecessors were actually the neobehaviorists rather than the original behaviorists such as Watson (1930). Neobehaviorism was an orderly outgrowth of behaviorism and had much in common with it; however, neobehaviorism permitted the limited use of theoretical concepts that could not be directly observed. Neobehaviorists were able to do this while maintaining their commitment to objectivity by virtue of their commitment to logical positivism.

Logical positivism was a highly developed philosophy of science, which arose in the aftermath of the Einsteinian Relativity and the Quantum Theoretical revolutions in physics. As a consequence of relativity theory, many of the concepts of the prerelativity or classical Newtonian paradigm were thought to be empty, meaningless, and unscientific. Logical positivists were bound together by their desire to rid science of meaningless and unscientific concepts, which they termed metaphysical (Ayer, 1959). They argued that only two kinds of statements were meaningful: logical or mathematical statements that derived their validity from rules for their manipulation and factual propositions that could be verified by observation. This argument drew the distinction between formal (theoretical) and empirical (experimental) aspects of science, and it relegated all other kinds of statements to the dustbin of nonsense. Finally, logical positivists held that all scientific statements or propositions could be translated into a common language: the language of physical things. Neobehaviorists were strongly drawn to logical positivism for reasons of their own. They were the intellectual descendants of the behaviorists, who had revolted against an approach to psychology that stymied progress. Before the behaviorist revolution, psychology had been concerned with philosophical questions about the relationship of mind and body, and about the fundamental nature of sensation and thought processes (Boring, 1950). To answer such questions, psychologists used the method of introspection—the systematic reporting of internal mental states. Unfortunately, this method often yielded nothing but fruitless polemics. Behaviorists justifiably wanted to free themselves of such unproductive procedures, and they turned to methods that seemed impeccably "scientific." They worked to align themselves with the methods of well-established sciences such as physics and biology rather than with approaches similar to speculative philosophy. Their descendants, the neobehaviorists, inherited this orientation.

During the 1920s, logical positivism gained wide currency as an account of the methods of the physical sciences. It provided rules for deciding which questions could be answered empirically, and it held that such questions were the only scientifically meaningful ones. When neobehaviorists discovered logical positivism (Stevens, 1939), they attempted to mold their scientific activities to fit its prescriptions about how science ought to be done. "Mentalistic" questions, which included some of those that had given earlier psychologists such trouble, were defined as meaningless by neobehavioristic interpretation of the rules of logical positivism. Consequently, neobehaviorists could continue to ignore such questions despite occasional objections. "Mind" was regarded as irredeemably mentalistic, and use of the concept was considered in some academic circles as *prima facie* evidence that a psychologist was either poorly trained or becoming demented. Their intense preoccupation with the pitfalls of mentalism led many of the psychologists of the time to dismiss as "unscientific" any explanation involving unobservable phenomena. The precepts of logical positivism permitted limited use of concepts that were not directly observable, provided extreme caution was used. But even so, most neobehaviorists were unwilling to consider such concepts as mind, idea, consciousness, and thinking as scientifically respectable. They wanted to account for what people do without positing thoughts, images, ideas, or other such mentalisms. In the principles of logical positivism, neobehaviorists found powerful support for the antimentalistic views that they had inherited from the behaviorists—who in turn had developed these views as a way out of the philosophical tangles of their own predecessors.

Time has not been kind to logical positivism. Philosophers of science have shown that many of its principles have insurmountable logical difficulties, and information-processing psychologists reject most of the doctrine out of hand. Nevertheless, logical positivism provided ideological support for many years to the passionate antimentalism of neobehaviorism. The ultimate result was a strong reaction or counterrevolution in information-processing psychology. It is the "mentalistic" features of people—their thinking, understanding, and ideas; their imposition of order on the universe; and all of the internal processes that underlie their behavior—that interest many of us. So with the information-processing revolution, logical positivism and related doctrine was rejected. Mentalistic concepts were reintroduced into psychology, and the processes they signify again became legitimate objects of study.

Today's cognitive psychology also rejects the way that neobehaviorists viewed learning. They generally minimized innate ideas, capacities, and instincts as suitable accounts of behavior, preferring the *tabula rasa* notion that at birth the human is equipped only with a maturational schedule and a generalized ability to learn. By this view, experience immediately begins to write its record in the form of a learning history, which, if it could be known, would explain all of the interesting aspects of the individual's behavior. It followed that learning was the central phenomenon to be explained (Estes et al., 1954). Neobehaviorists generally believed that good science demanded that behavior be attributed to learning, unless there was an overwhelming body of evidence suggesting otherwise. This kind of preoccupation with learning is not a part of the information-processing paradigm. While we do believe that much is learned, we are more willing than neobehaviorists to consider that innate abilities underlie many important human capacities. We do not feel that it is disreputable to posit innate abilities, and we are less likely than neobehaviorists to be primarily interested in learning. We view learning as only one of many human capacities, and not necessarily the central one.

Neobehaviorists were committed to large-scale theory construction, as are some information-processing psychologists. However, most neobehaviorist theories were theories of learning, and in those days learning meant some form of conditioning. Conditioning was considered the simplest and most basic form of learning (Hull, 1943), and it was thought to underlie virtually all behavior. Complex behavior was believed to be built up from simpler, mediated, conditioned associations. There was also substantial agreement that the principles of conditioning were the same for all species that learn. Hence, data about animal learning were taken as important and relevant to human behavior. Psychological laboratories were commonly packed with mice, rats, and pigeons; even the learning of cockroaches and worms was studied with avid interest. Those investigators who did study humans did not question the importance of learning nor the relevance of the animal data to it. Verbal-learning theorists, for example, incorporated principles that had been developed in the animal laboratory into their theories of human learning. Reinforcement was considered essential for verbal learning, some theorists likened forgetting to the extinction of conditioned responses (Gibson, 1940), and words that human subjects recalled were conceptualized as having habit strength. Notions such as reinforcement, extinction, and habit strength came straight out of animal experimentation. Information-processing psychologists, in contrast, largely ignore the literature on animals; the only animal data cited in this book are some interesting recent studies of language-like behavior in primates. Whenever higher mental processes are involved, we heartily disagree that human and animal behavior are necessarily governed by the same principles. We regard the human as a specialized product of evolution, as an animal whose cognition is also specialized. This means that humans and animals *may* share some cognitive abilities, but it is not a foregone conclusion that they do. Professor E. E. Smith (personal communication) has aptly captured the standard information-processing position on animal experimentation: "If there are any reasons at all to expect differences between animal and human behavior, then study the latter."

Finally, we have a very different perspective on the nature of association than S-R psychologists did. Because this goes to the heart of the difference between the paradigms, we pursue it. If you were to sit down, close your eyes, and seriously consider what it is to know something, you would very likely rediscover the concept of an association. Knowing has to do with relationships among things, and the person who *knows* has related things in particular ways. This conclusion has been inescapable since Aristotle. But in the intervening 2000 years, the idea of association has changed in many ways. Some of the changes in scholarly views about associations have concerned the nature of the units that are associated. Neobehaviorists believed that the units were stimuli and responses, but other theorists at other times believed that the units were sensations, ideas, thoughts, images, concepts, relations, propositions, and so on almost indefinitely. Students of human thought have also changed their views of the process by which associations are formed. Units have been said to become associated by contiguity, by similarity, by contrast, by causality, and by reinforcement, among other ways. Some neobehaviorists thought that associations resulted whenever stimuli and responses were contiguous in time, while others thought reinforcement was also essential. To see why neobehaviorists held their particular views, we should consider the British Associationists.

Between about 1700 and 1900, some of the foremost thinkers of Western civilization worked on and wrote about the problem of association. These British Associationists included John Locke, George Berkeley, David Hume, and James Mill. All of these men were impressed by the fact that events or sensations that had occurred close together in time were often remembered together. Their formulations were intended to explain this similarity between the succession of ideas and the succession of events giving rise to them. The mental units of concern to the British Associationists were ideas. For example, to John Locke ideas were logical concepts that could be expressed in words, even though the concepts themselves were not words. The process of association was intended to account for how ideas became bound together such that when one came to mind it consistently evoked another. Thus, since 1700 the process of association has served as a theory of memory, just as it did for neobehaviorists. As a consequence of their theorizing, Locke, Berkeley, Hume, and Mill made the process of association the basic mechanism of the human mind and the foundation of human knowledge. They dictated our modern concern with memory.

The British Associationists worked without benefit of laboratory data: They were armchair psychologists. Neobehaviorists rejected their armchair methods and their view that ideas were the mind's units. Ivan Pavlov, a Russian, and Hermann Ebbinghaus, a German, laid the foundations for these rejections beginning in about 1900. They provided the bridge from the British Associationists' to the behaviorists' and neobehaviorists' views by providing laboratory methods with which to study associations.

Pavlov (1927) discovered the conditioned response. He had a pervasive effect on every branch of S–R psychology. During his long research career, he defined and elaborated the major concepts of classical conditioning. He did this by studying how physicalistic stimuli can be made to elicit observable responses of animals. Because his stimuli were physically describable environmental events, such as ringing bells, and his responses were quantifiable glandular secretions or muscular movements, he made it possible to characterize associations without reference to such ephemeral terms as *idea*, whose definition came to plague armchair psychologists. Pavlov's classical studies involved the salivation of dogs. Dogs salivate naturally to meat powder. Pavlov coupled the offering of meat powder to the ringing of a bell. At first, the bell did not elicit salivation unless the meat powder was given at the same time; but after a number of pairings of the bell and the powder, the dogs salivated to the bell alone. The association that had formed between the bell and the meat powder was externalized in the observable fact of the dogs' salivation.

Behaviorists, and after them neobehaviorists, seized on this feature of Pavlov's work. For them, laboratory-induced associations became the most important if not the only scientifically legitimate ones. Neobehaviorists came to define the formation of associations as conditioning. As a result of Pavlov's work, they turned almost exclusively to the study of laboratory-induced associations between stimuli and responses. They totally neglected the pre-existing associations of ideas in men's minds that led Aristotle to the concept in the first place.

Ebbinghaus (1885) was the father of verbal learning, about which we have more to say shortly. Like Pavlov, he worked with laboratory-induced associations. He studied memory by memorizing and then attempting to recall literally thousands of lists of verbal items. However, he designed his lists in such a way as to *minimize* the influence of pre-existing associations on his learning and memory. Instead of using familiar or meaningful material, he used nonsense syllables to make sure that pre-existing associations did not "contaminate" his performance. From the idea that pre-existing associations were a contaminant, we may infer that Ebbinghaus considered his object of study to be the "pure" memory for laboratory-induced material.

Ebbinghaus and Pavlov both induced associations in laboratory experiments, and they are responsible for the fact that for 60 years psychological research focused so heavily on laboratory-induced associations.

The basic logic that gave rise to the concept of the association is still sound, and the idea that concepts in the mind are somehow connected to each other is still prevalent in cognitive psychology. However, some of our view of these connections is so different from that of the neobehaviorists that the term "association" really should not be used. One major difference is the extent of our interest in pre-existing associations. In contemporary cognitive psychology, research interest in the knowledge people bring with them to the laboratory is as great as our interest in their ability to learn and recall laboratory materials. In fact, three of our chapters—Semantic Memory, Psycholinguistics, and Comprehension—directly concern the use people make of knowledge they had before they entered the laboratory experiment. Another major difference concerns the content of the associations. For much of S–R theory (e.g., Underwood & Schulz, 1960), associations were treated as relatively content-free, whereas the majority of cognitive theories assume that they have content and that the content may be central. To illustrate this point, consider the pair of words TREE and LEAF. Both S–R theorists and cognitive information-processing psychologists recognize that their theories must accommodate the fact that people consider these words to be related. A popular approach in S–R theory was the word-association test, in which a subject is asked to respond to a word like TREE with the first word that comes to mind. Clinical psychologists use such tests for their own purposes (Milgram, 1961), but verbal-learning researchers have made extensive use of them as well (Deese, 1965). If a subject responds LEAF, the S–R theorist infers that at some time in his life, the individual had formed an association between TREE and LEAF such that LEAF is a strong response to the stimulus TREE. The association is nothing more, just an association, even if it is expressed in elegant quantitative terms. Information-processing psychologists approach the problem very differently. They assume that the person knows that TREE and LEAF are related; moreover, he knows how they are related. Implicit in the retrieval of LEAF, given TREE, is some use of the concept "to have as parts," because the person knows that trees and leaves are related by virtue of the fact that trees have leaves as parts. For contemporary cognitive theorists, then, associations are *labeled* with content of their own. The term "association," which was used for so long by psychologists who did not imbue associations with content, has seemed inadequate to most information-processing theorists, and they have substitued such terms as "relations" or "links" for what the previous paradigm called "associations" (Collins & Quillian, 1972). The word-association method, also, does not give the responder much opportunity to demonstrate his knowledge of the content of his associations or relations. Although word associations are used by cognitive psychologists, the most common approaches are quite different in information-processing studies. We take up these approaches in detail in our chapter on semantic memory.

Finally, the origin of associations or links between elements is differently conceived in S–R and information-processing terms. For most S–R theorists, associations were formed by a process analogous to conditioning. Through contiguous exposure, one element came to be associated with another— possibly requiring reinforcement for the association to be formed. No such assumption is made by most information-processing psychologists. In general, our paradigm has devoted relatively less study to the way in which conceptual elements come to be related. This neglect may be a reaction to the previous paradigm's preoccupation with learning, or it may derive from the general interest of information-processing psychologists in the performance of previously acquired competencies.

We have already mentioned the verbal-learning tradition, which began with Ebbinghaus. Before we turn to a more detailed consideration of how verbal learning influenced the information-processing paradigm, let us *summarize* the influence of neobehaviorism. Our paradigm has retained neobehaviorism's nomothetic approach: We are devoted to explaining man in general. It has preserved empiricism: Information processing psychologists believe that scientific observation provides the best proof of a knowledge claim. We have kept the laboratory tradition: Most information-processing experiments are done in laboratories under highly controlled conditions. We are also committed to theory building. However, we have rejected logical positivism and antimentalism. We rejected behaviorism's overriding interest in learning: Thinking, memory, and perception interest us at least as much. Whereas behaviorists rejected innate abilities and genetic determinants of behavior, we are now more willing to accept them. Few information processing psychologists study animals. While we have not abandoned the notion of association, we do not view it as conditioning but as relevant to meaning, and we are as interested in pre-existing associations as in laboratory-induced ones.

It is probably fair to say that much of the early *esprit de corps* among many of the psychologists who eventually identified with the information-processing paradigm resulted from their common rejection of, and often downright hostility toward, neobehaviorism. Neobehaviorists, in turn, had great difficulty accepting the new commitments of information-processing psychology; many never have. However, several generations of psychologists have received their graduate education in the period following the neobehaviorists' loss of dominance. They are not particularly interested in the paradigm clash that preceded their own professional training, and consequently the clash between the two paradigms has muted as the balance has tipped toward the new cognitive psychology. It is not clear whether information processing will become as prevalent as neobehaviorism was in the 1950s, permeating other areas such as social psychology, industrial psychology, and child psychology. However, it is currently in a period of normal science, guiding the research activities of a large community of psychological scientists whose primary area is human cognition.

III. THE CONTRIBUTIONS OF VERBAL LEARNING

During the heyday of neobehaviorism, verbal learning was already a clearly defined psychological subdiscipline with many highly productive practitioners. Even though their subject matter was the learning of verbal materials by human subjects rather than animal learning, verbal-learning psychologists shared many commitments with neobehaviorism. However, the relationship between verbal learning and information processing developed quite differently from that between information processing and neobehaviorism. For reasons we give presently, many verbal-learning psychologists found it relatively easy to accept the new commitments of the information-processing approach. Today, most verbal-learning researchers consider themselves information-processing psychologists as well.

We have already mentioned the work of Hermann Ebbinghaus, the indisputable father of the study of verbal learning. This master scientist brought the best traditions of Newton and Galileo to the study of learning and memory. He not only learned many thousands of nonsense syllables and tested his own memory for them, but also devised new quantitative measures of memory and new ways of eliminating errors from memory experiments. He advocated the use of constant experimental conditions and rigorous statistical analyses of the resulting data, and he invented procedures to accomplish these objectives. Many of his methods are still in use today, which gives his writing a strikingly modern tone. His influence has been altogether profound.

Before verbal-learning psychology began to absorb the ideas of contemporary cognitive psychology, it had a distinct paradigmatic flavor of its own. For one thing, the field of verbal learning merged Ebbinghaus' concepts and methods with the commitments and beliefs of the American Functionalists (Angell, 1907; Carr, 1925). A hallmark of functionalism was its considerable modesty in theory building, and the psychology of verbal learning inherited this modesty. Verbal learning psychologists preferred descriptive statements to grand theories of learning, and they preferred to report what happened in an experiment rather than to offer explanations for why it happened. When they did theorize, it was about restricted sets of data from a few experimental situations. An interesting implication of this sort of science is its criterion for evaluating research. For neobehaviorists, good science consisted of experiments that contributed to the development of positivist theory. But verbal-learning research could not be evaluated by the adequacy of the theory it generated, for it generated so little theory. It was evaluated instead by the quantity of additional research it stimulated. One aspect of good experiments, for the Functionalist, was their ability to suggest even more experiments. This criterion is called "fruitfulness." Verbal-learning psychology's commitment to the fruitfulness criterion helps account for the great productivity of its practitioners, but it also explains in part why they shifted paradigms so readily. Unlike the neobehaviorists, they had no great reason to protect a particular view of theory.

While neobehaviorism was the dominant paradigm in American scientific psychology, verbal learning was its close ally. This is not surprising, for the two approaches had much in common. Both emerged from empiricist traditions, both studied learning, and both induced associations in the laboratory. When neobehaviorism was at its zenith, verbal-learning psychologists looked to it for many of their concepts and for their ideology. Hence, the conventional components of their sciences were similar. Scholars of verbal learning agreed that learning was the central psychological problem. The very name of their field reflected their belief that the most interesting thing about verbal materials is how they are learned. They generally agreed with the neobehaviorists that learning is the same throughout the phylogenetic scale: They did not doubt that the learning of college sophomores had much in common with that of rats, pigeons, and other laboratory animals. It is clear that the great majority of them held a concept of "association" identical with that of the neobehaviorist student of animal learning. In fact, some viewed verbal learning as a special case of conditioning. Verbal-learning psychologists eschewed reference to innate capacities and were generally sympathetic to the logical positivist leanings of neobehaviorism. However, because they were less inclined to build grand theories, such philosophies of science were less relevant to them. Thus, while they were generally antimentalistic, they were more likely than the animal psychologists to tolerate occasional minor lapses into mentalism, probably because they studied humans. An otherwise antimentalistic verbal-learning psychologist, Norman Spear (see D'Amato, 1970) could nevertheless remark that "motivation" in the verbal-learning situation is typically quite high because the college sophomore would "like to avoid appearing dull." Such a foray into introspection would have been inexcusable in the typical animal laboratory. It seems fair to conclude that the antimentalistic component of the neobehavioristic paradigm was never a defining feature of verbal learning. Like their lesser commitment to theory this too contributed to the ease with which so many neobehavioristically oriented verbal-learning psychologists turned into information-processing psychologists. They were not as seriously offended as animal neobehaviorists by information processing's focus on cognitive events.

The similarities between the conventional commitments of neobehaviorism and verbal learning during the 1940s, 50s, and 60s, were not the defining features of verbal learning. Its defining features were the problems it studied, the methods it used, and the variables it manipulated. Thus, it could be concisely and satisfactorily summed up in a sentence: "Verbal learning deals with the acquisition, retention, and transfer of associations of verbal units formed under controlled laboratory situations (Jung, 1968, p. 3)." Clearly, verbal-learning psychologists were interested in learning and memory. Clearly, they were interested in associations. And, clearly, they considered themselves laboratory scientists. The verbal units they studied also defined their field: These were mainly words, pseudowords, and nonsense syllables.

One prolific experimenter described the verbal learner's object of study with this astonishing description: "the fundamental units of the language—letters and, in some cases, numbers." Verbal learning was generally unconcerned with such other units of language as phonemes, morphemes, phrases, sentences, and paragraphs. Verbal-learning psychologists were not in the business of studying natural language or the learning of ideas, abstract concepts, facts, or world knowledge.

Most verbal-learning experiments used one of two highly standardized laboratory tasks—serial or paired-associate learning. The subject in a serial-learning task was shown a list of items, one at a time, and then asked to recall them in the order in which they were presented. Normally, the items were presented on a memory drum, an apparatus on which printed items could be displayed through a small window. After the first cycle through an entire list, the subject would attempt to recall the first item. After a fixed interval of time, it would appear in the window, either confirming or correcting the subject's response. The subject would then try to recall the second item; in time it, too, would appear, whereupon the subject would see whether his recall was correct and try to recall the third item, and so on. The paired-associate task required a somewhat more elaborate memory drum, in which the left half of the window was always open and the right half was open only part of the time. The items came in pairs—for example, DAG-BIF. One member of a pair, called the stimulus, appeared in the left, open half of the window, and the other member of the pair, called the response, appeared in the right, closable half. During the first cycle through the list of pairs, both halves of the window remained open, exposing both the stimulus and response items. In our example, DAG would appear on the left, BIF on the right. After the whole list had been shown once, it was begun again; but now only the left side of the window contained a visible stimulus; the right side was closed, covering the response. The subject could see DAG, but BIF was concealed. His task was to recall the appropriate response to the stimulus shown on the left. After a fixed interval, the right-hand window would open, revealing the correct response, which the subject could compare to his own. Then the window would close, the drum would advance, and the subject would see the stimulus member of the second pair. The subject would try to recall the proper response, and so on through the rest of the list.

These tasks had endless possibilities for variations, and hence were exceedingly fruitful for generating new research. There were studies varying the length of the lists, the length of time the subject had to recall an item, the length of time the correct answer was exposed before the drum advanced, the number of times the subject was permitted to go through the list, the amount of rest permitted between the lists, the length of time between initial presentation of the list and attempted recall. There were studies varying characteristics of the material, such as similarity, meaningfulness, or pronounceability of nonsense syllables or the frequency of words in everyday language. There were studies varying conditions of learning, such as requiring subjects to learn several or only a few lists in one experimental session. And, of course, there were combinations and recombinations of these and other variations, which proved sufficient to sustain a substantial number of highly productive researchers for over 30 years.

The paired-associate study was the most popular, which reflects the concept of association that was current among verbal-learning psychologists of the time. These psychologists commonly recommended the paired-associate task because it was the most analytic, in that it allowed precise specification of the stimulus and it separated learning into components: the learning of stimuli, the learning of responses, and the learning of an association between them (Underwood & Shulz, 1969). Nowadays, it is clear that this task is analytic to the study of learning only if one is quite convinced that learning consists of these three components. It does not appear so analytic if one believes, for example, that learning consists of modifying the contents of one's store of knowledge in accordance with new information. A much more analytic technique than the paired-associate task, in this view, would be one that permitted the experimenter to specify the prestored information, the new information, and the modification performed by the subject.

The major issues addressed by verbal-learning psychologists during the 1940s, 50s, and 60s, as well as their choice of tasks, reflected their strong S–R orientation. What was the stimulus in serial learning, they wondered—was it the previous item or was it the position of the item in the list? They believed that learning would not occur if something were not serving as a stimulus. Another issue concerned whether paired-associate learning was all-or-none or incremental. This controversy concerned how the associative bond was formed between verbal stimuli and responses. To resolve this question would appear extremely important to someone who considered the formation of associative bonds to be the very heart of the process of learning verbal materials. But to someone with a different, non–S–R approach, resolution of this controversy might appear to be of minor concern.

The way in which verbal-learning psychologists interpreted their observations also drew on S–R theory. They knew, for example, that subjects used strategies to help them learn. These strategies were sometimes interpreted as the formation of associations that the experimenter did not plan (Jung, 1968). Interpreted this way, it was worthwhile to devote research effort to the phenomenon, which was called "mediation" (Dallett, 1964). As scholars of verbal learning saw it, a subject who was supposed to learn the paired associate BAC-FOD and who did so by thinking of BACKWARD–FORWARD, had formed three associations rather than one: He had associated BAC with *backward, backward* with *forward*, and *forward* with

FOD. He thus mediated his association of BAC–FOD, but only by the formation of associations unintended by the experimenter. One association, *backward–forward*, was a pre-existing association rather than an induced one.

Two other issues that occupied many verbal-learning psychologists concerned the serial position curve (McCrary & Hunter, 1953) and the phenomenon of forgetting (Postman, 1961). Interestingly, these two areas accounted for much of the limited theorizing in which verbal-learning psychologists engaged, and both are still significant issues in the information-processing-oriented verbal learning of today. Of course, the theories offered are quite different; today they rely on the pretheoretical ideas of the information-processing paradigm, whereas previously most theories were expressed in the concepts and language of stimulus–response associations. We encounter these new theories in Chapters 7 and 8.

What happened? Why did many of these verbal-learning researchers turn to information-processing psychology instead of continuing to do what they had been doing? Since their research was so productive, what led verbal learning to change? First, the fruitfulness of the limited set of problems studied by verbal learning began to wane: There are only so many meaningful and exciting serial and paired-associate experiments to be done. Second, the generality of their findings was too limited to satisfy many psychologists. Eventually, concepts borrowed from information processing proved more fruitful, and the new concepts changed the perspective of verbal-learning researchers on their science. Let us consider these factors in more detail.

The Functionalist tradition that characterized verbal learning in its earlier days emphasized descriptive statements and minimized theoretical explanation. While this tradition proved satisfactory to many verbal-learning psychologists, some felt the need for an explanatory framework to organize their data. It was difficult not only to make sense of vast amounts of data without the organizing function of theory, but also to distinguish important data from unimportant data. Verbal-learning psychologists were as committed to significant science as anyone, and some were no doubt distressed by the fact that some studies in the tradition could only be described as trivial. Others may have wished that their research had more analogues in everyday life. Although paired-associate studies were often justified by drawing an analogy with the learning of foreign languages, verbal-learning researchers knew that mastering a foreign language involves more than memorizing vocabulary items; languages have different grammars, as well. Similarly, serial learning was justified by noting that some everyday tasks require memory for order information; but most of what we remember is not serially ordered. Moreover, pre-existing associations continued to be, as they had been for Ebbinghaus, rambunctious variables that intruded even into pristine paired-associate learning experiments. Ebbinghaus started the use of meaningless units in order to minimize the influence of pre-existing natural-language associations and to reduce the tendency to use those associations to employ learning strategies. But his techniques, which were used so widely, did not lend themselves to the clear study of the everyday kind of use that people make of their natural-language associations; furthermore, they did not really succeed in eliminating strategies. All in all, when the concepts of verbal learning were invoked outside the laboratory, they explained disappointingly little of what people actually do. In its effort to study tractable problems in a rigorous way, the field of verbal learning had become the study of esoterica, of people in unique situations.

Then in 1956 George Miller published an exceptionally influential paper, "The Magical Number Seven Plus or Minus Two." Miller had been exposed to information theory (the influence of which we describe in later chapters), and he was impressed with the fact that, in a wide variety of situations, people remember approximately seven items—unrelated words, letters, different tones, or whatever. He found, too, that combining items into chunks increased the number of items recalled. For example, it is almost impossible for most people to recall the number sequence 1776149219181941 after hearing it only once; but if they divide it into four significant dates—1776, 1492, 1918, and 1941—the task becomes easy. In Miller's account, we cannot remember 16 things in the raw—digits, in our example—but if we recombine them into four larger chunks—important dates—we can remember them. Miller believed that chunking was necessary because humans have a limited capacity to remember. He suggested that this limitation was about seven, and if we must remember more than about seven things, we must do so by recombining them into larger units. Interestingly, chunks themselves appeared to obey the range of the magic number: Only about 5 could be remembered.

The notion that people have a limited memory capacity was not entirely new to psychology, but Miller put a new slant on it. Miller's perspective came from information theory, for which a chief problem was how to overcome limitations on the capacity of telephone and telegraph lines and radio frequency channels. Taken together with other changes in outlook, the idea of *human* capacity limitations turned out to be revolutionary for information-processing psychology. It was a fruitful idea, indeed, giving rise to an entirely new area of research. Verbal-learning psychologists began to study how people reorganize material to overcome the limitations of their immediate memories (Tulving, 1962, 1968). The research diverged in subtle but important ways from the older approach to verbal learning. Learning strategies had previously been considered extraneous to verbal-learning research, as nuisances that, if not controlled, would introduce distortions into the data. However, learning strategies soon became the phenomenon of interest. This in turn required verbal learners to change their conception of their human subjects. Whereas before they had been considered passive, now the subject had to be considered active. If one imagines that people simply wait for stimuli and automatically produce whatever response has previously been associated with the stimuli that impinge, then one has a hard time accommodating to the fact that people invent learning strategies.

New methods were devised and new measures invented to examine people's strategies. A method that had been used before, but was never especially popular, came into wide use (e.g., Deese, 1957; Ekstrand & Underwood, 1963; Murdock, 1960; Tulving, 1964, 1968; Waugh, 1961). It was the method of free recall, in which the subject is given a list of items to learn, but is left free to recall them in any order he prefers. While determined freely by the subject, this order was not random; if the subject was given the list over and over again with the words in a different order each time, he tended to recall them in a similar order from one trial to the next. He was apparently grouping the words together, or chunking them, according to some organizational scheme that he invented. Psychologists devised a measure to quantify this constancy of recall order, and they called the measure an index of subjective organization (Tulving, 1962, 1964, 1968). Another measure that became popular was intended to quantify clustering. Clustering occurred when people were given a list with a built-in order—for instance, a 20-word list containing five names of birds, five types of fuel, five forms of transportation, and five occupations. Even when the different kinds of words were ordered randomly, people recalled them together as groups of birds, fuels, and so on (Bousfield, 1953; Cofer, 1965).

These developments had a profound effect on verbal learning. For one thing, the nonsense syllable was generally abandoned, because it was so much easier to study organization of meaningful units, such as words. For another, the paired-associate paradigm was essentially useless for the study of subjective organization and clustering. But most important, verbal-learning theorists found themselves back in the business of pre-existing associations, for these were the stuff of which organizational strategies were made. Their laboratory operations looked much the same; their subjects now learned lists of words instead of nonsense syllables, and they recalled them in whatever order they liked. But the focus was no longer on the impact of external variables. It was on the internal activities of human subjects alone. The contrast with animal research was stark. The animal laboratory provided no concepts for the study of organizational strategies. Furthermore, psychologists shifted their primary concern from learning to performance; the subjects in these studies did not "learn" the items in the list; they already knew them. Instead, the task was to work out a way to decide which items were in the list and which were not when it came time to recall. Subjects did this by using pre-existing information about the relationships among the items in the list. Thus, the field of verbal learning began to shift from an interest in learning to an interest in performance. Acquisition—previously a major part of verbal learning—was de-emphasized, and considerably greater emphasis was placed on retrieval. This is not to say that learning was totally ignored; information-processing theories of free recall still included a learning component (e.g., Anderson, 1972). But the learning was quite different in conception from earlier, S–R theories. Anderson, for example, assumed that a subject learns to distinguish list items from other words, and his theory is quite unlike the theories of verbal learning that preceded information processing.

As interest developed in organizational schemes for recall, the aversion to meaning that had been typical came to appear somewhat misguided. Because meaning was essential to the construction of organizational strategies, the use of nonsense syllables diminished and more experimenters began to use lists of words.

Another major force for the change of verbal learning was launched in the late 1950s with a remarkable study by Peterson and Peterson (1959). These investigators were interested in a controversy over the cause of forgetting. Some theorists believed that forgetting resulted from "trace decay"; that is, when a list is learned, a memory trace is formed for each item in the list. With time, the trace becomes fainter, much as a weathered road sign becomes less and less readable. Other theorists felt that forgetting is due to interference; when the subject does other things between the time he learns an item and the time he tries to recall it, these intervening activities interfere with his ability to recall. Peterson and Peterson designed their study to address this issue. They used a technique developed by Brown (1958). Instead of giving subjects whole lists and testing them a few minutes later, they gave college students a single trigram—for example, PRF, which they had to recall after an interval of anywhere between zero and 18 seconds. When they were not required to recall immediately, they had to count backwards by 3s until it was time to recall. The Petersons found that subjects who had to count backwards often completely forgot the trigram after only 18 seconds! This arresting outcome could hardly fail to attract the attention of the verbal-learning research community, because of their interest in forgetting. But it did not resolve the interference versus decay controversy on one side or the other; the Petersons' experiment suggested a very different way of looking at memory and forgetting that incorporated elements of both interference and decay. It was generally agreed that the reason subjects forgot so quickly was that counting backwards by 3s prevents the subjects from *rehearsing*—that is, from repeating the item over and over to themselves until requested to recall it. But as reasonable as this seemed on the one hand, it seemed strange on the other. After all, subjects had been learning lists for 20 years in verbal-learning laboratories, and they did not forget immediately even though they could not continually rehearse. It began to look as if rehearsal actually served two important purposes. First, it "kept the item alive"; second, it helped the subject to get the item into a state that allowed him to remember it even if he could not rehearse it continually. But this, in turn, led to the supposition that there must be two kinds of memory states. There must be one kind in which rehearsal is essential if the item is not to be forgotten. There must be another kind that is established by rehearsal but that, once established, can maintain items even if the subject stops rehearsing them. Researchers soon postulated more than one memory: an immediate or "primary" memory, where the item goes when it is first presented, and a "secondary" memory, where an item goes as a result of rehearsal. Continued rehearsal is essential if an item is to be recalled from primary memory, but recall from secondary memory is possible long after rehearsal has ceased.

This kind of theorizing clearly fell outside the functionalist tradition. It postulated activities of the human mind. It postulated mental steps that a person performed when solving memory problems. Once verbal-learning psychologists began to think in terms of primary and secondary memory and of mechanisms for transferring items from one to the other, they were on the way toward abandoning the atheoretical orientation of functionalism. What is more, they could no longer look to the animal laboratory for theoretical constructs, because animal psychology was still involved in S-R theories of learning. Verbal-learning psychologists working in this area had become more interested in memory than in learning; they had to build their own theories of memory, and the ones they built were mentalistic. They had rediscovered the importance of meaning. They had joined forces with cognitive psychologists of the information-processing type.

From verbal learning, then, the information-processing approach took its focus on memory. It inherited a laboratory tradition complete with experimental procedures and response measurement conventions. But the most important contribution of verbal learning was people. They were among the most productive scientists in experimental psychology. These people have helped make cognitive psychology one of the fastest-moving parts of contemporary behavioral science. They brought their vigorous productivity and their considerable methodological sophistication to the study of memory, and when they adopted information-processing concepts, they turned the study of memory into one of the liveliest parts of the information-processing paradigm. In the course of their conversion from verbal-learning functionalism, they picked up many of the information-processing psychologists' conventional commitments, including the rejection of neobehaviorism, an interest in meaning and internal processes, a taste for computer analogies, and a conception of the human being as an active participant in the learning process. They lost their functionalist tradition and began to theorize forcefully. Because they abandoned the neobehaviorist concept of association as an S-R connection, they substantially changed the nature of the questions they asked and the problems they worked on. In fact, much of the contemporary study of verbal learning is in some respects indistinguishable from the study of short- and long-term memory, which in turn is a major part of the information-processing paradigm.

Besides neobehaviorism and verbal learning, which were two of the largest scientific traditions in psychology, information-processing has been considerably influenced by human engineering.

IV. THE CONTRIBUTIONS OF HUMAN ENGINEERING

Before World War II, almost all psychological research was done in universities. Most of it was basic research, and, as we have seen, it heavily concerned animal learning and the learning of nonsense syllables by college students. In addition, there was basic research on perception and on the senses of smell, taste, vision, and hearing, on emotions and feelings, and on thinking and problem solving. Like the learning research of those days, many of the studies of perception, emotion, and thinking were guided by the concepts, language, and ideology of neobehaviorism. In these areas, there was relatively little applied research, though a few psychologists did study motor skills, the measurement of intelligence, and other problems dealing with the school curriculum. Still, many of the most prominent researchers felt it beneath their dignity to involve themselves with the applications of their research.

World War II changed that. Many psychologists who had previously done only basic research were drafted and put to work on the practical problems of making war. Many who were not drafted received government contracts to work on similar problems. Thus, many basic scientists found themselves trying to understand problems of perception, judgment, thinking, and decision making. Many of these problems arose because of the sophistication of the weaponry developed for the war. Highly technical systems such as aircraft and devices like radar and sonar made exceedingly heavy demands on their human operators. Furthermore, the failure to meet these demands had drastic consequences. Serious military problems arose from accidents and errors made by human warriors. Objects on radar screens were misidentified. Aircraft with many people aboard crashed. Weapons were sometimes directed at friendly forces. Where could psychologists turn for concepts and methods to help them solve such problems? Certainly not to the academic laboratories of the day. The behavior of animals in mazes shed little light on the performance of airplane pilots and sonar operators. The kind of learning studied with nonsense syllables contributed little to psychologists trying to teach people how to operate complex machines accurately. In fact, learning was not the central problem during the war. Most problems arose after the tasks had already been learned, when normally skillful performance broke down. The focus was on performance rather than learning; and this left academic psychologists poorly prepared, because their paradigmatic commitments had led them to concentrate so much of their attention on learning.

Faced with the problems of war, psychologists had to develop a new view of man, and they soon did. An important concept emerged—that of the "man/machine system." This concept emphasized the functioning of the human being and the machine as an operating unit. How a pilot and a plane functioned together depended not only on the characteristics of the pilot and those of the plane but also on the relationship between these characteristics. In this view, a well-designed plane is one that a person can operate efficiently. This attitude developed in part from wartime psychologists' study of the relationships between human error and the design of the machines with which they erred. Psychologists could sometimes improve performance and save lives by remedying design faults in military machines. For example, one type of plane often crashed while landing. It turned out that the lever that the pilot had to use for braking was near the lever that retracted the landing gear. During landing, the pilot could not take his eyes off the runway: He had to work by touch alone. Sometimes pilots retracted their landing gear instead of putting on their brakes; they touched the ground with the belly of the plane at top speed. The best way to keep them from crashing was not to exhort them to be careful; they were already highly motivated to avoid crashing and getting killed. Improving training procedures was also an inefficient approach; pilots with many safe landings behind them committed this error as well as rookie pilots. The most reasonable approach was to redesign the craft's controls so that completely different arm movements were required for braking and for retracting the landing gear. This example also illustrates the problem of divided attention, which received some research interest in engineering psychology. If the pilot paid attention to the levers, making a difficult choice between similarly located ones, he had to reduce the amount of attention he paid to the fast-approaching landing strip. People cannot pay close attention to many things simultaneously. By redesigning the levers, plane manufacturers made it possible for pilots to select the correct one without taking their attention off the runway. As we see in a later chapter, the study of attention is an important part of information-processing psychology.

Other man/machine problems were best solved by retraining the men, and psychologists worked on that solution too. Still other problems required determining the conditions under which human beings simply could no longer perform well. This was the case with the tedious duty of watching radar screens and listening to sonar. There are limits to how long people can do such tasks accurately. The solution was to shorten duty periods so that operators were relieved before their performance broke down.

Psychologists who worked on such problems had to develop new ideas and concepts. They came to view their subject as the man/machine interaction, as a systems problem. They borrowed the systems notion from the physical scientists with whom they collaborated during the war. In this view, changing either component of the system—the man or the machine—changes the whole system's performance.

An important feature of the man/machine system concept was that the human operator served as an information transmitter and processing device interposed between his machine's displays and their controls. Thus, pilots read their plane's instruments, they interpreted those readings, and decided from those interpretations which controls should be operated, and how. The notion of man as an information transmitter thus has roots in military psychology, which came to be called human engineering.

Another important emphasis that was stimulated in part by wartime problems is cognitive psychology's interest in decision making. Many of the problems researched in the war years highlighted the central importance of human decision making. For example, a radar operator is supposed to report whether he has seen a point of light appear on his screen. These points of light can be very faint. The classical point of view was that the problem was perceptual: Did the operator perceive the "blip" or didn't he? How intense did the blip have to be before it could be perceived? However, the theory of signal detectability reconceptualized the entire situation as a perception-plus-decision problem. The operator's problem is only partly perceptual; given that he has been exposed to a very faint blip, he must decide whether or not he actually perceived anything. These decisons are determined to some extent by actual events—very strong blips are readily detected and reported. But when the signal is so faint that it is barely discernible, the operator cannot be absolutely sure he saw it. Still, he must decide whether he is sure enough he saw something to report the possible approach of enemy craft. This decision is subject to nonperceptual factors, including the relative costs of certain types of error. Failure to report a blip that turns out to be enemy craft is costly: It can affect the survival of thousands of fellow human beings. On the other hand, a radar operator whose superior threatens him every time he reports a "false alarm" may fear for his own well-being. The intensity of blip necessary to get the operator to report that he has seen something depends on how he weighs the costs of false alarms and the costs of significant "misses." These relative weights determine the operator's decision criterion. A radar operator with a lenient criterion will report anything that might be a blip; he will turn in many false alarms but he will not miss any enemy craft. An operator with a strict criterion will report nothing unless he is sure; he will seldom turn in a false alarm, but enemy craft will be relatively close by the time he tells anyone about it. Signal detectability theory provides a mathematical way of describing separately the perceiver's sensitivity to the signal and his decision criterion; these analytic conventions have been subsequently used in information-processing psychology to study perception and memory.

So, from human engineering cognitive psychology took its view of man as an information transmitter and decision maker. It retained the concept of human processing limits. In the military, psychologists came to appreciate the strength of sophisticated instrumentation, which information-processing psychologists still rely on. The lavish research support that the government made available during the war years left cognitive psychologists with an appreciation of federal research funding. Moreover, the increased contact with other disciplines stimulated by wartime research pointed up what valuable contributions other fields can make to the study of human behavior. Human engineering has been a valuable conduit of new concepts into psychology ever since the war. The man/machine concept was exceedingly valuable. Signal detectability theory has made important advances possible in several research areas. Its precise quantification of the consequences of internal mental events helped to legitimize the investigation of cognitive processes. Other contributions of human engineering that appear in this book are such notions as input, output, capacity, storage, filtering, and the like. About the only aspect of human engineering that contemporary cognitive psychology seems to have rejected is its focus on applied problems. Cognitive psychologists pick their research questions more for theoretical than practical reasons.

We have now covered the contributions of three antecedent psychological traditions to contemporary information-processing psychology. Several other disciplines have also exerted considerable influence on our approach. In the next chapter, we consider the contributions of information theory, communication science, and linguistics.

3 Contributions of Other Disciplines to Information-Processing Psychology

ABSTRACT

I. *Introduction*

Borrowing from another discipline may occur under a variety of circumstances. Sometimes scholars from different fields are thrown together to work on the same problems, as happened during World War II. Sometimes practitioners unhappy with the way their own fields deal with important problems "go shopping" for ideas from other disciplines that seem to handle the problems better. Sometimes, outsiders thrust themselves into a field—publishing in its journals and competing for the allegiance of its members. Borrowing may involve another discipline's emphasis, concepts, theoretical formalisms, terms, and units of analysis. It seldom involves the replacement of a discipline's general methodological preferences. At first, it is typical for borrower sciences to cast too wide a net, but as scientific investigation proceeds, the limits of the borrowed concepts are established.

II. *The Contributions of Communications Engineering and Information Theory*

Communications engineers, concerned with artifacts such as telephone and telegraph systems, have developed general principles applicable to any communication system. These are applicable to human beings if they can be correctly characterized as "communication channels." Early cognitive psychologists used just this metaphor, importing into psychology such concepts as coding, channel capacity, serial and parallel processing, efficiency, uncertainty, and information. Although information theory stimulated some important research, and the studies it suggested provided important insights, there are theoretical and practical limits to its utility.

From communications engineering and information theory, information-processing psychology took: (1) the analogy of human processors and information channels; (2) the notion of limited channel capacity; (3) the idea of coding to overcome capacity limitations; (4) an interest in serial vs. parallel processing; (5) some of the formal aspects of information theory; (6) the concepts of information and uncertainty; (7) an inclination to mentalism; and (8) an inclination toward structural theorizing. Our field has rejected: (1) the mathematical axioms of information theory; and (2) information measures based on number of physical alternatives, adopting instead measures based on number of mentally inferred alternatives.

III. *The Contributions of Linguistics*

The area of language was an important battleground in the paradigm clash between behaviorism and the nascent information-processing approach. Behavioristic theorists were beginning to extend their principles to language when a revolution occurred in linguistics. Linguists began to publish in psychological journals, and psychologists who felt that language was inadequately treated in psychology began to read their work. Linguists maintained that behavioristic psychology underrated the novelty, productivity, and complexity of human language use, and that they completely ignored its structured nature. They emphasized the importance of competence—rules in the head—and de-emphasized actual speech behavior. They also argued that language capacity is innate, not learned by principles of conditioning. They therefore challenged almost every important pretheoretical idea of behaviorism. The review by Chomsky (1959) of Skinner's book *Verbal Behavior* (Skinner, 1957) was an important milestone in the paradigm clash.

Information-processing psycholinguists found the arguments against behaviorism compelling, and they focused on language as a rule-governed, abstract system. They considered it important to develop theories of competence and imported such concepts as competence, grammar, and generative grammar. They adopted the sentence as the unit of analysis and set out to test predictions from Chomsky's own theories of transformational grammar. The use of intuition to produce testable hypotheses was resurrected, and a 10-year honeymoon took place between linguistics and cognitive psychology. The honeymoon has recently cooled somewhat.

From linguistics, our field has taken: (1) reasons to reject neobehaviorism; (2) reasons to reject animal experimentation; (3) biological and evolutionary explanations; (4) a focus on language as a central human behavior; (5) an interest in creativity and ruliness; (6) the competence/performance distinction and a concern with competence; and (7) intuitively derived hypotheses. However, we have rejected: (1) intuitions as data; (2) the denigration of performance; (3) the central role given syntax in linguistics; and (4) formal properties of grammars.

I. INTRODUCTION

A pervasive feature of the development of specialized science is the borrowing of concepts, methods, and theoretical formalisms between autonomous disciplines. The information-processing approach to cognitive psychology has been crucially influenced by communications engineering, computer science, and linguistics. We examine those properties of each discipline that helped to determine the current character of cognitive psychology. It is essential to understand how each external discipline initiated coherent traditions of normal science or influenced those already in motion.

Linguistics, for example, helped produce a puzzle-solving tradition with theoretical controversies and numerous chains of empirical findings. These are described primarily in the chapter on psycholinguistics. Information theory, in contrast, influenced our thinking about symbolic systems, but the normal science tradition in perception and performance that it impacted has been truncated or greatly diminished. The influence of computer science is pervasive, but it did less in its production of normal science than in its radical alteration of our thinking about a variety of ongoing research traditions.

There are several ways in which the scientists of one discipline can be exposed to the ideas of another. Events may throw them together to work on pressing problems, problems that the paradigm of no single discipline handles well in isolation. This happened to military psychologists. Their neobehaviorist paradigm alone was not sufficient when they went to war; so they borrowed from the engineers and physical scientists whom they met there. The result was an amalgam of the ideas and methods of several previously separate disciplines. The amalgam came to be called human engineering. Alternatively, scientists may actively search for new ideas and new approaches to their subject matter. They might do this simply because their discipline has ignored a problem that they find important or intriguing. This happened to psychologists who became interested in language during the 1950s and 60s. Neobehaviorism had given little serious attention to language, so that psychologists who became interested in it had little choice but to look to other disciplines for ways to study it. Or, scientists may turn to other disciplines after they have tried methods and concepts from their own and still failed to advance their understanding of a problem. This happened with psychologists who became interested in language. As neobehaviorists became convinced that it was important to study language, some of them tried to explain it within the constraints of their paradigm. They generally failed; so some looked to other disciplines for helpful concepts and tools. What they found contributed importantly to the information-processing paradigm. Finally, scholars in a separate field may directly contribute to a related discipline, publishing in its journals and arguing for the rightness of the outsider's approach. And so it was with linguistics at the start of the cognitive revolution in psychology.

Intellectual borrowing across fields may include some part of the emphasis of a second discipline—its units of analysis, concepts, and theoretical formalisms. Later, we show how those psychologists who were attracted to Chomskian linguistics initially appropriated its emphasis on syntax, the sentence as a unit of analysis, and the concepts of surface and deep representation of the sentence. However, the methods used were those of traditional psychology. Much of the training of scientists is devoted to research methods, and these are seldom abandoned in favor of another discipline's. When the central concerns and conceptualizations of a second discipline are appropriated, they are typically investigated according to the methods of the borrower discipline. So it was that the concepts from linguistics were investigated by the methods of experimental psychology.

In contrast, a formal analogy was central to the borrowings of cognitive psychologists from computer science as we see in the next chapter. Borrowing concepts from another field is like saying, "What I study is, in important respects, like what they study. I wonder whether I will learn more about my system if I think about it the way they study theirs." Scientists often draw analogies; and sometimes these underlie those wonderful inspirations that wrench a discipline out of its doldrums and immortalize their creators. It is important to remember that analogies are only partial. Unfortunately, many people, students and laymen alike, forget that crucial qualifier—*in important respects*—which goes along with every analogy and with most imported ideas. This becomes important later when we use computational concepts in the data chapters. It must be remembered that although the system under investigation is biological, the analogy suggests that it may be subject in part to the same principles that govern automata. This does not mean that information-processing psychologists believe that people *are* machines, or that they are *merely* machines. After all, when he said "Juliet is like the sun," Romeo hardly meant that she was merely an indescribably hot ball of gas.

In the first blush of their enthusiasm for concepts from a sister science, borrowing scientists may apply them too widely. There are examples of this in psychologists' use of notions from communications engineering and from linguistics. Initial overapplication is natural, because it is only by doing research that scientists come to know the limits of both their original and borrowed concepts. As time passes and research accumulates, the inapplicabililty of a new concept will show itself, and the notion may be used in a more limited way or fall completely out of use. Even when this happens, the borrowed idea may have made an important contribution. It may lose its identity as a concept that came from a different science, but leave behind an important new conception of the borrowing science's subject matter, a new perspective on its central problems, or a framework within which to solve them. This was the case with some contributions from both linguistics and information theory to cognitive psychology, and may ultimately be so with major concepts taken from computer science.

Besides drawing analogies and borrowing concepts and units of analysis, cognitive psychology appropriated formal methods from its sister disciplines. A formalism can be described as a set of symbols and as a precise set of rules for combining and transforming them without any consideration either of the meaning or reference of the symbols. A formalism with which you are probably familiar is the syllogism: If all As are B, and C is an A, then C is a B. This formalism can be used in discussing politics: "If all incumbents have an advantage, and Carter is an incumbent, then Carter will have an advantage." Notice that our syllogism is used to say something about the future. A biological example is, "If all female mammals bear live young, and women are mammals, then women bear live young." Examples are possible from all fields. The syllogism is typical of all formalisms in that it provides rules for manipulating symbol systems. The user must supply the content of the symbols.

There are formalisms called *grammars* used by linguists, and *propositional logic* used by computer scientists and philosophers, and *algebra* and *calculus* used by all scientists. All formalisms are abstract in the sense that they do not, initially, refer to any tangible piece of reality. Instead, they are used to describe ideal systems. An ideal system is an abstract and generalized description that is supposed to represent all instances of some part of nature. For example, physicists have written of an ideal gas, which is supposed to typify the performance of anything that is a gas. Similarly, communication scientists have described an ideal communication system, and linguists have conceptualized an ideal speaker–listener. Normally an ideal system is described within a single discipline. However, it is not unusual for scientists in another discipline to transfer an ideal system to a new context, sometimes with remarkable consequences to scientific knowledge. Cognitive psychologists have borrowed a number of ideal systems from other fields of study. They have also frequently borrowed the formalisms used by the parent discipline to describe the ideal system.

The fields from which information-processing psychology borrowed in major ways all dealt with the abstract representation and manipulation of symbol systems. Our discussion now turns to a detailed consideration of what was borrowed, what was later discarded, and what currently remain as important parts of our conceptualization of mankind's cognitive capacities.

II. THE CONTRIBUTIONS OF COMMUNICATIONS ENGINEERING AND INFORMATION THEORY

Modern technology has produced a large variety of communication systems: radio, telephone, television, and computer readout devices, to name a few. The development of this technology has been possible, in large part, because much is known about the abstract nature of communication systems. Communication scientists have formulated and tested many general laws that describe the abstract properties and generalized modes of operation of all communication systems, ideal and real. Interdisciplinary transfer of these conceptions is less obviously appropriate than the primary achievements. So it is necessary to emphasize that the concepts and laws of communication systems were extended to "exchanges" that are not normally viewed as communication. The astronomer's use of the telescope, for example, can be so viewed. The telescope, in this metaphor, becomes a "communications channel," and light output from heavenly bodies becomes a "message." In fact, the ideas inherent in an ideal communication system provided the methodology that was used to enhance visual or electromagnetic "messages" coming from deep space.

Can human beings also be viewed as communication channels? That is exactly the metaphor used by early cognitive psychologists. People were conceived of as an information-handling channel with built-in states and limitations. Work was initiated to determine the channel's properties and capacities for different types of information. A secretary, for example, taking shorthand and later converting it into a typed letter, can be viewed as a communications system. The boss' original speech is the "source" of the "message," which undergoes two encoding conversions if the secretary is viewed as a communication channel. The first is the transcribed shorthand, the second is typing with the typed copy as the "output." Whoever reads the typed copy may be viewed as the "destination." In both conversions, it may be meaningful to talk of channel "capacity" as the upper rate limits or top speed that the secretary can perform errorless transcription and errorless typed output. The secretary's performance also might be described in terms of information transmission, and the research psychologist might investigate environmental or internal "state" factors that influence the average rate of transmission.

Extending this metaphor a little further, we can view humans as information-transmission devices any time they respond in predictable ways to the information they receive. An airplane pilot, for example, looks at his instruments and, based on the readings, makes corrections in the trajectory of his aircraft. An automobile driver sees a traffic light turn red, and applies his foot to the brake. The pilot's movements and the action of the driver's foot preserve the information they received. In such situations, human capacities are analogous to those of any information-transmission device, and formulations that are true of information-transmission devices in general may also be true of people.

Like people, information transmitters work better under some conditions than others. Communications scientists have long asked, Under what circumstances do devices like the telephone completely preserve the information sent over them? A mathematician named Claude Shannon (1948) set out to answer this question. He wondered what circumstances permitted perfect transmission over a communication channel. The problem with these devices is that sounds other than those that people intend them to convey sometimes creep into the transmission channel; so the receiver hears other sounds, called "noise," along with the intended signal. In Shannon's channel, the noise came from physical sources and was similar to the static you hear on a low-quality radio, or over a good radio during a lightning storm, or near high-voltage electrical lines. Like the concept of message, the concept of noise can also be generalized. In the case of a young child trying to read a book, errors may originate inside his head, resulting in imperfect information transmission—that is, in imperfect reading. The secretary may make mistakes in her typing, which originate not in the message but in the secretary's typing habits; these errors may be considered as noise from the standpoint of an objective observer of the behavior. The pilot may misread his instruments or correct more than the instrument reading warrants, thus introducing noise into his performance. And the driver, because of some distraction, may fail to perceive a red light and so not stop. Such extraneous factors result in his performance being an imperfect mirror of the color of the traffic light. In all these cases, we can say that noise has reduced the accuracy of information transmission, just as it did in the physical channels considered by Shannon.

Shannon solved his problem and described the circumstances under which perfect transmission would occur in the presence of noise. He presented his solution as a mathematical formalism, as a general theory of communication. Shannon's mathematical theory of information applied to any message, from any source, transmitted by any means to any receiver. Because his theory was abstract, it fit a variety of real-world situations. It was borrowed by many disciplines, including engineering, astronomy, biochemistry, genetics, and psychology. Many psychologists recognized that information theory provided rich insights into psychological questions, even though it was developed to explain man-made physical systems such as the telegraph, rather than a biological system like man himself.

Man-made devices and systems are called artifacts, and while it may seem unlikely, the study of artifacts has frequently revealed important insights into natural systems. For example, major advances in the science of thermodynamics—the study of heat—came only after man invented the steam engine and was able to study its properties. While heat is heat, and the same general principles apply however it is generated, it was easier to study the steam engine than geysers, the sun, or volcanoes. Similarly, the science of aerodynamics advanced with the invention of the airplane, which is easier to study than the flight of birds. Electricity is another example: Major advances occurred after invention of the storage battery and coils, but not from the study of lightning. Inventing a device does not require full understanding of the principles by which it works, or an appreciation of all its properties and potentials. Quite the contrary, a man-made device can be just as mysterious, complicated, and poorly understood as a naturally occurring system. However, it is less likely to remain mysterious, for it is much easier to study something we have manufactured and can control than something we cannot control. That is one reason scientists so often rely on laboratory techniques and the study of artifacts. While this can make their work seem unnatural, it can also accelerate their progress, even when they seek to understand biological systems like human beings.

Shannon's theory of communication had direct and unexpected effects on the study of human behavior. Like any scientist's work, his contained some old ideas and some new ones. The old ideas had been around for a long time, but psychologists first encountered them in Shannon's writings. They found his new ideas useful, too. Let us first examine the concepts that predated Shannon's theory and see how they have influenced theory and research in cognitive and information-processing psychology. Then we look at the concepts Shannon himself introduced.

If you have ever used Morse code, you have probably thought how convenient it is that frequent letters are short and easy to send, while the code's long and cumbersome letters are relatively infrequent. This is not an accident: Samuel F. B. Morse arranged the code that way when he devised it in 1838. He represented the letters of the alphabet with dots, dashes, and blank spaces. The dots were short electrical pulses, the dashes were longer pulses, and the spaces were the absence of electric current. It is fastest to send a single dot and slowest to send a series of dashes. Laying underground cables or stringing wires on poles is expensive; so Morse sought a code in which messages could be sent as fast as possible, thereby maximizing the number of messages that could be sent over each communication channel. It must have been intuitively obvious to him that it mattered how the dots and dashes were matched up with letters. Morse designed his code so that frequently used letters could be transmitted faster than infrequently used ones. Table 3.1 shows the three most frequently used English letters and the two least frequently used, as counted by modern digital computers. The letter "E" occurs, on the average, 131 times per thousand letters; "T" occurs 105 times, and "A" occurs 82 times. In contrast, the letter "X" occurs about once per thousand letters and "Z" only about eight times per 10,000 letters. The

TABLE 3.1
The Original Morse Code and
Contemporary Letter Probabilities

	Code	Probability
High-probability letters		
E	•	.131
T	–	.105
A	• –	.082
Low-probability letters		
X	• – • •	.0012
Z	• • • •	.0008

efficiency of Morse code can be seen from the fact that it takes only about one-fourth as long to encode and transmit an E or a T as it does to send an X or a Z. If the codes were reversed, then one in approximately every five letters (E or T) would take four units of time, while a letter taking only one unit of time would turn up only occasionally. Morse did not have a computer. He estimated the letter frequencies by counting the number of type blocks in each compartment of a printer's box. This rough-and-ready method served him well, for according to modern estimates, the efficiency of Morse code could be increased only 15% (Peirce, 1961). While all of this is intrinsically interesting, we are concerned with its significance for cognitive psychology. Communications engineers were aware long ago of two concepts that cognitive psychologists use extensively today: the concepts of code (and its variants: encode, decode, coding) and of channel capacity.

Coding is a very general concept. Its core meaning is "a set of specific rules or transformations where messages, codes, signals, or states of the world are converted from one representation to another, one medium of energy to another, or one physical state to another." Thus, we use code in the familiar sense of Morse code or cryptographic code; however we also use it in less familiar senses to refer to the coding of experience into linguistic form (when we tell another person about what we see), the coding of experience into whatever form the brain requires to maintain a memory of the experience, and the recoding of a long list of single items into a shorter list of multiple items, such as the conversion of 16 digits into four dates that we mentioned earlier. In all these uses, coding merely refers to the conversion of information from one form to another. It is a striking fact that the word *coding* does not appear in psychology textbooks or research papers before the publication of Shannon's theory, while since then there are entire books devoted to the topic (Melton & Martin, 1972). The concept has at least six different meanings in contemporary psychology (Bower, 1972), and we have much to say about its use in later chapters.

The interest of psychologists in the concept of *channel capacity* also came from communications science. Telecommunications engineers knew well that there is a limit to how many signals a channel can carry in a fixed period of time, no matter how efficient the code. The economic, social, and military potential of telegraphy (later radio and, more recently, television) was immediately evident, and it was clearly desirable to maximize the number of messages that could be sent. The number of messages sent could be increased by adding more channels, but this also increases the cost. Twice as many channels mean twice as many cables. By using this solution to the problem of limited channel capacity, we would almost double the fixed costs to send twice as many messages. So communication engineers turned their attention to increasing *efficiency,* increasing the number of messages that could be sent per unit cost. Underlying most of the interesting economic questions was a technical property of communication channels: They are devices of limited capacity. This is an important part of the analogy of the human being as an information-transmission system.

A moment's reflection will show that there are limitations on many things that humans do. A person can read only one book, or listen to only one conversation, at a time. If he must monitor two conversations, he may switch back and forth and keep up reasonably well—but he will not actually hear all of either conversation. To keep up, he will have to fill in for himself what must have been said in one conversation while he was listening to the other. If the conversations are rapidly paced, he will not be able to keep up with both, for he will miss too much of one conversation while he is attending to the other. We can draw an analogy between a communication channel and each of many human cognitive capabilities, such as immediate memory, identification, thinking, and problem solving. Following this analogy, and recognizing that communication channels have capacity limits, a psychologist would not be surprised to find upper limits on how much a person can remember at once, how many things he can identify in a brief glance, how many things he can think about simultaneously, and so on. Yet before Shannon's contribution, psychologists had not regarded the limitations on such human capabilities as particularly important, even though they knew of data showing such a limitation. Long before psychologists knew of Shannon's work, considerable research had been done on the "span of apprehension"—the number of objects one could identify in a single glance (Woodworth, 1938). They knew that six to eight was the average number, but this fact was never interpreted as representing a very general principle until the analogy to a communications channel came into use. Once psychologists recognized the significance of capacity limits, they also realized that human beings have a large repertoire of behaviors with which to overcome these limitations. The study of these capacity-increasing behaviors has become a fascinating facet of cognitive psychology, and this can be attributed largely to the influence of communication engineering and information theory. Thus, the analogy of man as an information-transmission channel and the concept of capacity limits were borrowed with good results.

Two other concepts related to the notion of channel capacity crop up frequently in the information-processing literature. They are the ideas of *serial* and *parallel* processing. These concepts are related to information-transmission efficiency, for they concern the possibility of literally doing several things at the same time. Reading aloud is a serial process: You are physically incapable of simultaneously reading two stories aloud. You must read the words serially, each before the next. As a consequence, you can "transmit" only one story at a time. Switching back and forth between simultaneous messages, called multiplexing, is another serial process. Did you ever try to watch two television programs on two sets simultaneously?

This problem is somewhat different from listening to two conversations at once because the receptors must continuously reorient. As you switch your eyes back and forth, you will lose a piece of each program while you are watching the other. This process is serial because you look at the two TV sets one after the other. Even though you interleave your looks so as to see some of each program, you are receiving signals from only one program at a time. Parallel processing involves true simultaneity without loss of information; if you could watch both programs at the same time without losing a word or a gesture from either, that would be true television-watching in parallel. While you cannot do this in the case of watching television, it turns out that certain components of biological and communication systems are capable of parallel processing. That is, two messages can be transmitted simultaneously over a single channel without loss of information and without multiplexing.

In the case of telecommunications, the economic value of parallel processing was recognized early in the history of telegraphy, and parallel transmission over a single line was implemented by Edison in 1874. How this is done is illustrated in Table 3.2. Transmission of a single message in the dots, dashes, and spaces of Morse code required a minimum of two values of electrical current: "off" and "on." The "on" value is produced by a switch closure at the sender's location. At the receiver's end, the "on" may produce a click or drive a galvanometer. Both signals "on" and "off" can be either short or long. Suppose we assign 1 to "on," 0 to "off"; then a short 1 (on) is a dot, a long 1 is a dash, a short 0 (off) is a "space" between dots or dashes, and a long 0 is a "space" between letters. This is illustrated by the two serial messages in Table 3.2.

We must change the systems to four current values to send both messages at the same time; let's call these +3, +1, −1, and −3. To each of these we assign 0s and 1s for each message, as shown in the table. The assignment is partly arbitrary. The only restriction is that all possible binary code combinations are represented 00, 01, 10, and 11. Now, using the assignment table at the bottom of Table 3.2, let's convert the parallel transmissions at the bottom of the table into the two messages above. The first signal is +3, and the conversion table tells us that this transmits a 1 for both messages. The second signal is −3, yielding a 1 for Message 1, and a 0 for Message 2 in the second interval. The signals for the third and fourth interval are both +1, and they respectively convert into 0s and 1s for Message 1 and 2. This decoding procedure continues for the rest of the message. The four current values provide the physical representation for a code that is truly parallel; at any instant in time, its state has meaning for two separate messages. The exact same physical signal has carried TA for Message 1 and X for Message 2. If you study the assignment section of Table 3.2 awhile, you should conclude that it would take eight current values to transmit three simultaneous messages. Parallel processing results in an enormous cost savings by increasing the capacity of communication devices. If some of the capacities of biological

TABLE 3.2
The Use of Serial- and Parallel-Processing Concepts in Early Telegraphy

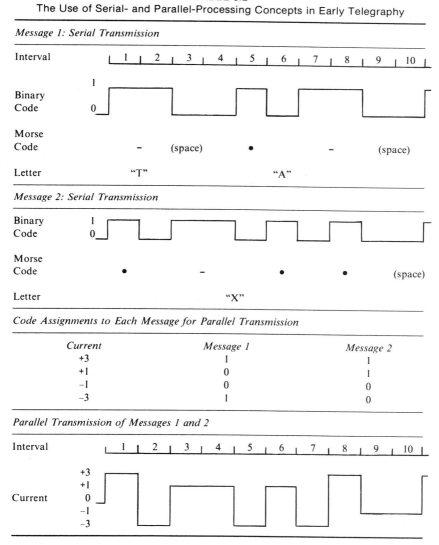

Message 1: Serial Transmission

| Interval | 1 | 2 | 3 | 4 | 5 | 6 | 7 | 8 | 9 | 10 |

Binary Code

Morse Code: – (space) • – (space)

Letter: "T" "A"

Message 2: Serial Transmission

Binary Code

Morse Code: • – • • (space)

Letter: "X"

Code Assignments to Each Message for Parallel Transmission

Current	Message 1	Message 2
+3	1	1
+1	0	1
−1	0	0
−3	1	0

Parallel Transmission of Messages 1 and 2

| Interval | 1 | 2 | 3 | 4 | 5 | 6 | 7 | 8 | 9 | 10 |

Current: +3 +1 0 −1 −3

systems could also capitalize on parallel processing, their efficiency would be similarly enhanced. It is therefore an interesting psychological question whether various cognitive processes can be performed in parallel, or whether they are restricted to serial execution. Such questions were never part of the idiom of behaviorism. They became sensible only when the human being was likened to an information channel. They were asked only after the advent of information-processing approaches to psychology.

The concepts of coding, limited channel capacity, increased efficiency, and serial and parallel processing had been in use in telecommunications engineering long before Shannon published his theory, but most psychologists had never heard of them. They had certainly never incorporated such concepts into their thinking about people. It was through psychologists' study of Shannon's theory of information that such ideas were introduced into the study of human cognition. It is interesting that they have had a longer-lasting impact on psychology than Shannon's own ideas, to which we turn now.

Shannon's central concepts were *information* and *uncertainty*. He developed these concepts—and a way to measure them—to clarify the properties of information channels. Given a message source, like English discourse, and a noisy transmission channel of known characteristics, Shannon's information theory showed how to encode a message into electrical signals so as to obtain the fastest possible transmission without error, despite the noisy channel. To develop his theory, Shannon had to be able to measure the transmitted commodity, so as to determine whether more or less of it is transmitted per unit time under various conditions. Shannon called the transmitted commodity *information,* which he measured in a metric called *bits,* which we illustrate in detail in Chapter 5. The information's transmission speed was measured in *bits per second.*

Shannon's mathematical theory applies to properties of a very general, abstract communication system like the one shown in Fig. 3.1. Shannon formulated mathematical axioms and proved theorems describing the properties of the class of abstract systems represented. The mathematical properties of the system represented in the figure have been successfully applied to the study and development of the telephone, radio, television, computer, and interplanetary communications. But the figure actually is concerned with any message encoded in any conceivable fashion and transmitted over any kind of channel. It is sufficiently general to apply to human information transmission, including the kind involved in a child reading, a secretary transcribing, and a driver hitting his brakes. The block diagram in Fig. 3.1 is an idealization represented in flowchart script. (Such flowcharts have proved very useful to cognitive psychologists trying to describe general, idealized, or hypothesized processing in the human mind. The use of flow diagrams came from communication engineering, and it has been carried to a high art by computer scientists. The use of flowcharts is also a pervasive feature of contemporary information-processing psychological theory.)

At first, Shannon's ideas were applied to many psychological problems, such as experiments described in our reaction time chapter, but the results of research gradually reduced the areas in which they were used. His theory requires that information be measured not only by the message or symbol that actually occurs, but also by the likelihood of occurrence of all the other possible messages or symbols that might have been sent instead. For

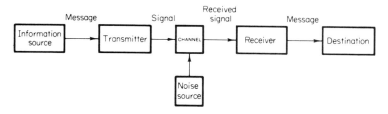

FIG. 3.1.   Shannon's general communications system.

information theory's formalisms to apply, information must be measured with reference to the entire set of available alternatives. The larger the set of available alternatives, the greater the *uncertainty* of the source and the more information in bits transmitted by that source.

It is difficult to give intuitive feelings for this important concept. However, consider the difference between a true–false examination and one consisting of multiple-choice questions with five alternatives each. Technically, more information is transmitted in the multiple-choice test. In a manner of speaking, you have to rule out only one alternative on a true–false test, but four on the multiple-choice test. In a sense, then, a "destination" given the correct answer among five likely choices finds out more, is given more information, than in a two-choice situation. Some of the early psychological studies using informational concepts confirmed the utility of this feature of Shannon's technical concept of information. It turned out that the effective stimulus in certain kinds of experiments was not solely the stimulus presented by the experimenter, but the entire set of symbols or stimuli from which that stimulus was selected. In other words, the cause of certain kinds of responses is not just the physically present stimulus, but the entire set of stimuli that *might* have been present. Think what this means for neobehavioristic metatheory. That paradigm's conventional wisdom demands that stimuli, the instigators of behavior, be defined in terms of physical operations executed in the here and now. How to do this with things that only might have happened must have been a puzzle. Later work heightened the puzzle by showing that behavior can be influenced not only by the other stimuli the experimenter might have presented, but also by stimuli the subject *thought* he might have presented (Garner & Clement, 1963). In these experiments, the effective causal stimuli are forever incapable of being defined in physicalistic terms.

Garner and Clement's (1963) experiment showed that presentation of a single stimulus produces an *inferred subset* of stimuli in the subject's mind, and the nature of this inferred subset produces his response. Suppose, for example, that the stimuli consisted of patterns of 0s and 1s. Then, subjects tend to infer that a pattern like 11111111 comes from a subset of two patterns: 11111111 and 00000000. In contrast, the pattern 10011100 is assumed to come from a much larger subset. Actually, in the idiom of probabilities, all stimuli came from the same set. The experimenter who is unaware of the subject's inferred stimulus set will predicate his theorizing on one definition of the stimulus, whereas the subject may be predicating his behavior on another. The novelty of Garner and Clement's outcome was its demonstration of situations in which the effective causal agent for an observed behavior was absent from the physically measurable outside world. The cause was in the subjective, internal, mental world of the experimental subject. Garner and Clement also showed that this mental world could be defined in the rigorous mathematical terms of Shannon's information theory. Such demonstrations were powerful reasons for psychologists to become mentalistic, and to be concerned with the structure of mental contents. The pioneers of behaviorism would have been astonished by such a turn of events were they alive to witness it, or if those who were alive bothered to read it. Remember that paradigms are social phenomena: Scientists tend not to read writings from other paradigms. Garner (1974) continues, at this time, to emphasize the psychological reality and importance of the inferred stimulus subset.

After a few years of research using information-theoretic concepts and measures, limitations on the applicability of some of the concepts began to show themselves. Precise measurement of the technical concept of information requires conditions that do not frequently obtain in the cognitive life of human beings. Though interesting, the number of experimental situations where information in bits can be measured is limited. The measurement of information in bits, and the use of the formalisms of information theory, are now restricted to a few areas of engineering psychology, and to certain aspects of perception, concept formation, and memory. The measurement of information requires that all the elements of the set of possible transmissions (messages or symbols) be known, or capable of estimation, along with their probabilities of occurrence. This is an easy business if we speak of letters of the alphabet, for we can estimate the probability of various letters by digital computer analysis of large samples of printed language. But probability estimates become difficult when we turn to words. The absolute probability of words may not be psychologically meaningful. The probabilities of words generally vary with context more than do the probabilities of letters. Even supposing we could identify the full set of words in a person's vocabulary, and the appropriate probabilities for each, when we turn to sentences the task becomes impossible even in principle. One of the central notions that cognitive psychologists have accepted from the field of linguistics is that the number of sentences a person is capable of understanding and uttering is infinite; thus we could never list that set of sentences and their probabilities, and the accurate measurement of information is impossible. Another more practical reason that information measures were abandoned is that they were of little use in the study of memory. This is a major point made by Miller (1956) in his paper on memory limitations described in the previous chapter.

So cognitive psychologists have mostly abandoned the formalisms of information theory. While few cognitive psychologists measure "information" in its technical sense nowadays, many still use the term. Whenever psychologists consider meaning or the meaning of messages, which was never part of information theory, they use the concept of information nearly as a synonym for knowledge. Contemporary research in the information-theoretic tradition is no longer concerned with quantity of information, but with the nature of psychological information and its structure (Garner, 1974). Garner's work on perception, in this tradition, is an important part of the cumulative knowledge of cognitive psychology (e.g., Garner, 1970, 1972, 1974; Garner & Felfoldy, 1970).

Let us summarize. Soon after psychologists encountered the ideas embodied in information theory, they likened various human capabilities to communication channels. They tried to measure the capacity of human information channels in bits. The outcomes of these efforts alerted them to the limited psychological applicability of the technical sense of "information." Still, these early efforts had surprising and important implications for cognitive psychology. They helped justify the rejection of antimentalism and a resurgence of thinking about mental structures that underlie behavior. And they led to a profoundly important conclusion: While human capacities are limited, their limitations are often not fixed like those of a passive communications channel. Humans can substantially increase their information-transmission capacities by recoding the material in accordance with information or knowledge stored in their permanent memories. It may even be that the most interesting aspects of human cognition—thinking, understanding, language, memory, knowledge, creativity—result from just such recoding operations in which the channel increases its own efficiency by altering, saving, reorganizing, and retrieving the information to which it is exposed. Psychology's search for ways of thinking about such constructive internal activity led it to turn to the burgeoning field of computer science. The way had been nurtured by information theory. It had prepared us to think about information and knowledge in terms of abstract symbol systems. Information theory also was a major impetus for a revolution in linguistics. The paradigm of transformational linguistics rejected most of the doctrine of information theory along with central aspects of the parent field. Major secondary shocks occurred as a result in psychology; we now examine the nature of what was once the "new" linguistics and its effect on psychology.

III.   THE CONTRIBUTIONS OF LINGUISTICS

The meeting of linguistics and psychology was different from the meetings of psychology and either communications engineering or computer science. In those fields, the systems studied were different from those studied in psychology. When our field borrowed concepts from them, their practitioners were pleased enough, but they had no real stake in how our discipline used the concepts. The cross-talk was predicated on analogies between their objects of study and ours.

Not so in linguistics. No analogy was involved; linguists and psychologists who studied language were concerned with the same phenomenon—human language. However, they held contradictory conventional commitments. The territory was not big enough for both, as it were; and the grounds were set for a paradigm clash of significant proportions. The resulting struggle was not exactly the sort of scientific revolution described in Chapter 1, for two different disciplines were involved. But when some psychologists picked up the linguists' colors and challenged their behavioristic colleagues, the battle of ideologies took on all the trappings of a classic Kuhnian revolution.

The first clash concerned whether language could ever be understood in behaviorist terms. Linguists were adamant it could not be. Again and again they emphasized the structure of language, its ruliness, its grammars. They relentlessly argued that the learning of rule systems could not be explained with the principles of stimulus and response learning. They won the argument—not with data, but with logic and compelling examples. The differences between the linguistic and the neobehavioristic approaches were so fundamental that it would have been impossible to marshal data to convert either group. They could never have agreed on what kind of data were convincing.

For one thing, they would have disagreed about what aspects of language were most important. The linguists who ultimately influenced psychology found novelty to be a highly compelling and central characteristic of language. They pointed out that a competent language user can understand and produce a potentially infinite number of linguistic utterances that he has never heard before. Behaviorists, in contrast, did not consider the novelty and productivity of language as central. They saw their task as explaining its recurring features, and it seemed reasonable to attribute these to learning and conditioning. The two approaches also differed widely on their perspective of the complexity of language. Neobehaviorists believed in explaining complex phenomena by reference to simple principles. This preference led them to emphasize those aspects of language that were most compatible with the simple principles they already had. In contrast, the linguists believed that complexity was a central characteristic of language. To them, the search for principles that explained only "simple" aspects of language was fundamentally misguided. They preferred to attack the complexity directly. The two approaches, as you might expect, differed widely in the samples of language they attempted to explain. Neobehaviorists dealt with such sentences as *Pass the salt* and *Tom is a thief,* which appeared simple. Linguists preferred to tackle sentences like *Visiting relatives can be bothersome* and *Several happy boys with masks on their faces frightened an old lady who had thought Halloween was over.*

Again and again, the linguists argued that language had structure. They believed that the use of language must be explained by reference to rules in the user's head that enable him to deal with that structure. Structure refers to the systematic relationships between parts of sentences, such as phrases, clauses, and so on. Mastering a language involved learning the system of rules governing those relationships. Structure is a concept that fit badly in neobehavioristic science. It was impossible to comfortably cast the learning of structure as the learning of physicalistic stimuli and responses. Rules in the head were considered irresponsibly mentalistic by behaviorists. Behaviorists resisted the notions of structure and rules for many years, though today some are working to condition "rule-learning behavior." This wrinkle on conditioning would have been unthinkable only a decade ago, before linguists influenced psychologists.

The importance of rules in the head was explicitly stated by the linguists in the "competence/performance" distinction. Competence is the knowledge of his language that a speaker carries around and uses to produce and understand utterances in his language. Performance is actual speaking and listening. In addition to drawing this distinction, linguists argued that nothing substantial could be learned about language by studying performance. They argued for devising explanations of competence. Even though the linguists relied on empirical facts about the language in deriving competence theories, the whole enterprise sat poorly with neobehaviorists. They defined psychology as the study of behavior, they regarded speculation about internal events as mentalistic and unscientific, and they certainly did not approve of building whole theories of such internal events.

Finally, the neobehaviorists' environmentalism left them loath to postulate innate capacities if other explanations would serve. Language seemed learnable to them, like table manners, roller skating, or karate. They assumed that language learning in children was accomplished by the automatic operation of conditioning principles. This assumption led them to overlook aspects of language acquisition that linguists found critically important. Although neobehaviorists made little of it, the linguists were struck by the fact that children all over the world, learning dramatically different native tongues, begin the acquisition process at about the same age. It takes them all about the same length of time to master the essentials of their language, and they go through strikingly similar steps in the process. What could account for this universality of the language-learning experience? To the linguists, it seemed reasonable that some aspects of language ability were innate. It made sense to view the child as a "language acquisition device"—preprogrammed by nature, as it were, to extract from his environment the information needed to acquire a linguistic system.

All of these paradigmatic differences converged on the question of whether conditioning could account for language. This was the battleground on which the paradigm clash was fought. Behaviorists proposed ways in which language could be handled with the concepts of conditioning, and linguists argued the inadequacy of the behaviorist proposals. Thus, B. F. Skinner (1957) attempted to turn a few simple principles of learning and reinforcement into a complete account of how people acquire and use language. His book *Verbal Behavior* was reviewed by a young linguist, Noam Chomsky. Chomsky's review constituted the opening shot in one of the great paradigm clashes of the century in psychology. The battle ended some 10 years later with the emergence of a new field called psycholinguistics, which now shares much with the information-processing approach to cognitive psychology.

Chomsky was well acquainted with behaviorism, for it had crept into linguistics. Leonard Bloomfield (1933) had successfully urged many of his linguist colleagues to purge themselves of mentalism and to adopt a more "objective" approach, as he believed psychologists had done. Chomsky was not convinced. He rejected the paradigm of behaviorism in toto. His review (Chomsky, 1959) of *Verbal Behavior* was an attack on all S–R accounts of language, not just on Skinner's. Skinner's thesis was that his explanation of language was more scientific than nonbehavioristic formulations, because it relied on terms whose meaning had been developed in the experimental learning laboratory. Skinner believed firmly in explanation by extrapolation of simple principles. The thrust of Chomsky's criticism was that Skinner had extrapolated the terms without their substance. In effect, he argued that while Skinner's words sounded scientific, his conceptualizations were more carelessly mentalistic than those of the traditional approach.

Here is an example to illustrate the critique. In the laboratory, a pigeon can be trained to peck a circle, by giving him food whenever he pecks it. It is further possible to get him to peck the circle when it is red, but not when it is green. This is done by feeding the pigeon only if the circle is red when he pecks it. His pecking gets no food when the circle is green. This common laboratory situation is a prototype of Skinner's explanations of language. The color of the circle is the *stimulus;* it elicits the *response* of pecking. In Skinner's terms, pecking is *under the control of* the stimulus, "red circle." The appearance of the food is a *reinforcer*. Because it comes right after the pigeon pecks, it causes the pecking response to persist, and even increases its frequency. The meaning of *stimulus, response, under the control of,* and *reinforcer* are thoroughly objective and precise in this situation. But this objectivity and precision of terms is directly predicated on two important facts about life in the laboratory. First, the experimenter has complete control over the environment and learning history of his animals, and second, the situation is exceedingly simple.

The experimenter can be reasonably sure that the red circle is responsible for the increased pecking because it is the only thing in the pigeon's environment that changes. It changes if and only if the experimenter wishes it to, and the experimenter knows that for all of his experimental life the pigeon has received food by pecking red circles but not green ones. Pecking is the only response the experimenter is interested in, and if the pigeon does other things the experimenter can safely ignore them. The pigeon is unlikely to surprise the experimenter very often because he does not do very many things. So it is possible to study the stimulus/response occurrence with great precision day after day. Reinforcement is also a precise term under the controlled circumstances of the laboratory. It is any event that increases the frequency of the just-preceding response. Thus, if food appears every time the pigeon pecks, and the pecking increases, the experimenter may be confident that this happens because of the reinforcing effect of the food. This is an excellent, uncircular definition in the laboratory because it is possible to determine experimentally which occurrences increase a response and which decrease it. For example, if the pigeon were given a mild shock every time he pecked, he would soon stop pecking. The decrease in pecking would identify the shock as aversive. If he is given food and the pecking increases, the increase is evidence for the reinforcing effect of the food. The experimenter need not introspect for the pigeon to know that he "likes" the food and "dislikes" the shock: Their aversive or reinforcing properties may be ascertained by the physical operations of experiments.

What happens, then, when we transport these laboratory terms into the arena of natural language, where precise control over the environmental circumstances is impossible and a vast range of complicated human responses is possible? According to Chomsky, what happens is "play-acting at science." When a person is shown a painting and responds "It's Dutch," Skinner claims that the response is under control of extremely subtle properties of the painting, which constitute the *stimulus* for it. But this is not the laboratory. The person might have said "It's hideous," "It's hanging too low," "I thought you liked abstract work," and so on. In any of these events, Skinner could only say the beholder must be under the control of some other subtle stimulus properties, and in none of these cases can he specify what those stimulus properties are. As a metaphor to the laboratory, there is nothing wrong with Skinner's claim that some stimulus prompts each language response, but as an explanation of language it offers nothing. Similarly, the term *reinforcement* loses all precision outside the laboratory. Skinner asserts that verbal behavior persists because it is reinforced, but there is often no observable reinforcing event for speech. For example, the babbling of babies, the conversations small children have with themselves, the poetry written by unknown poets, the reading of novels and newspapers, all seem to go unrewarded by specifiable events. To explain cases like these, Skinner made a heavy appeal to "automatic self-reinforcement"—the poet writes what he is reinforced by reading, the child alone in the nursery automatically reinforces his own babbling, and so on. Chomsky pointed out that this amounts to arguing that people say what they like, think what they like, and read what they like. He correctly argued that invocation of the laboratory term *reinforcement* serves a "purely ritual function" and does nothing to advance science.

Chomsky posed a dilemma: Either Skinner's system is a mere metaphor for laboratory experiments and not an explanation of language, or it is ridiculous. If the terms are taken literally, the consequence is scientifically absurd. If they are not taken literally, Skinner's system is a mere paraphrase of old-fashioned mentalistic accounts with scientific-sounding terms. For example, Skinner asserts that people respond properly to threats because of their reinforcement histories. If you say, *Give me the salt or I will hit you,* I give you the salt because to do so results in the cessation of the threat. But it can be reinforcing to get rid of this threat only if in the past it has been followed by the pain of being hit. Chomsky remarks: "It would appear to follow that a speaker will not respond properly to . . . *Your money or your life* unless he has a past history of being killed." But if the reinforcement history need not be explicit, only imaginary, then what difference is there between Skinner's account and the commonsensical argument that the person responds because he thinks it would be unpleasant to die, and he fears the mugger will kill him if he does not give up his money? There is none: The two are equally uninformative.

It was very important to neobehaviorists that a response be elicited by a physically present stimulus, which was possible in the laboratory because the experimenter could make the stimulus happen at will. It is from this physical presence that the term "stimulus" derived the great objectivity Skinner claimed for it. But if this is necessary in language, Chomsky asks, how can we explain people's use of words and statements to refer to objects that are not only not present, such as *Eisenhower* and *Moscow,* but perhaps never have been, such as *unicorn.* Where might the stimulus be that elicits the statement, *This is war*? In fact, if the stimulus must be present to exert its effect, then Skinner's system fails to account for the overwhelming majority of language use. And if it need not be present, it has lost its laboratory objectivity.

Chomsky's review was devastating, and was not answered for 13 years (MacCorquodale, 1970). By that time Chomsky's attack on Skinner had been extended, and there was widespread disdain for behavioristic approaches to language among serious students of the subject. MacCorquodale's retort was ignored, for the new psycholinguistics emphasized aspects of language that had simply never figured in neobehavioristic accounts. For example, Chomsky's followers focused on *syntax,* the rules that govern a language's permissible word combinations and word orders. This led to a completely new view of how remarkable it is that children learn language so readily.

Given a finite number of experiences with language, of which some are grammatical and some are not, and without anyone telling the child which is which, he nevertheless learns in 6 or so years all the rules he needs to make grammatical sense of virtually any sentence he hears. Another change in our thinking concerned the units of language. Before Chomsky, psychologists seldom studied sentences, preferring instead to deal with words. On those rare occasions when they did try to explain how sentences are understood, it was always by reference to the understanding of individual words. No neobehavioristic psychologist ever seriously tried to develop a theory of grammar. That would have required the recognition that rules, as well as words, were an integral part of language, and the neobehaviorist paradigm did not cope well with rules.

Neobehaviorists defined themselves as students of behavior, and they placed great store by the study of observables. As a result of their contact with linguistics, however, many psychologists came to believe that satisfactory theories of language would never emerge from studying what people *do* unless we also attempt to explain what they *know* about language that enables them to do it. This was Chomsky's argument for the study of *competence*—what people know about language, rather than language performance. Most of the sentences you hear, you have never heard before. You could not have learned them by past association with some stimulus situation that gave them meaning. Consider this sentence:

> The catsup bottle was being used as a weight to hold the money down, but when the ace of spades fell from his right sleeve, the bottle became a lethal weapon.

You have probably never heard it before, but you understand it. You could not possibly have a learning history associated with that whole sentence. While you have learned the individual words, what is it that you know that makes this novel combination of them understandable to you? Language is an astonishingly creative business; the number of possible sentences in a language is infinite. How many objects do you suppose there are in the universe that are smaller than a bread box and weigh between 8 ounces and 5 pounds? You could substitute any of them for "catsup bottle." How many people do you suppose there are, have been, and will be? You could give ownership of the money weight to any one of them:

> Little Johnny Bostlethwaite's handmade ashtray was being used as a weight to hold the money down, but when the ace of spades fell from his father's right sleeve, the ashtray became a lethal weapon.

You could substitute any card in the deck for the ace of spades. You could invent other uses for the catsup bottle. And you could combine and recombine all these substitutions into an extraordinarily large number of understandable sentences describing the regrettable outcome of a poker game! When you consider the other possible things you might talk about instead, and realize that each other sentence has similar possibilities, you can see that you are truly capable of inventing and understanding a potentially infinite number of sentences in your language.

This infinite potentiality poses an insuperable difficulty for any explanation of language that relies on repetition and practice, as S–R conditioning theories ultimately do. But if we posit that speakers learn more than words, that they also learn rules for combining them into grammatical sentences, the difficulty disappears. The speaker's knowledge of these rules and words constitutes his *competence*. While competence is not reflected perfectly in actual behavior, it must be accounted for if a satisfactory theory of language is ever to be achieved. Although psychologists might have attempted to study how competence was conditioned, those committed to the information-processing approach did not do so. They had rejected the adequacy of the conditioning model as an approach to human higher mental processes on too many other grounds. Although linguists provided strong logical arguments against S–R accounts of language acquisition (e.g., Bever, Fodor & Weksel, 1965a, 1965b) these were probably not needed to convince most information-processing psycholinguists that the rules of language must be acquired some other way.

You may be thinking, "I speak a language, and I don't know the rules. I was awful at grammar." But the linguist's concept of grammar does not require that the language user be able to state the rules explicitly, only that he behave as if he knows them. As an example, consider English pluralization. You may think the rule is simply "add an *s*." It is more complicated than that, however; and your language behavior reflects its complexity, even though your explicit statement, "add an *s*," does not. If we asked you to articulate the plural forms of *blit, blib,* and *blish,* you would respond with a hard *s* sound added to *blit,* giving *blits;* with a soft *z* sound added to *blib* giving *blibs;* and with an *iz* sound added to *blish,* giving *blishes.* This reflects your implicit knowledge that English pluralization depends on the final consonant: hard consonants such as *t, p,* and *k* require *s;* soft consonants such as *d, b,* and *g* require *z;* and sibilants such as *s* and *sh* require *iz.* You also know irregular plurals, such as *mice, oxen,* and *Seraphim.* You should understand, in addition, that linguistic grammaticality is not the correct speech your fourth-grade teacher worried about. Unprestigious speech, such as the use of *ain't* and double negatives, may be quite grammatical. It is only necessary that the speaker speak in a consistent, rule-governed way. People who use *ain't* do use rules; they will say, for example, *He ain't much of a violinist,* but they will never say *He much of a violinist ain't* unless they are trying to be funny. Thus, from the viewpoint of cognitive psychology, a grammar is the model of one's own language that one carries around in his head. To a linguist, that model is the speaker's competence.

So the linguists gave psychological students of language a new focus and a new conceptualization. Language is an abstract system, governed by rules, and people behave as if those rules are guiding their behavior. To understand language behavior, we must understand the language itself. We must know the structure and rules people use as they speak and understand a potentially infinite number of novel sentences.

It follows that the child who learns his language must learn not only words and their meanings but also the rules that govern their combinations—a seemingly amazing intellectual feat for a child. The rules that govern natural languages are so complex that linguists have yet to work out a full account of even one; yet the 6-year-old child behaves as though he has mastered a full set. How can he learn so complex a system in so short a time? Unbound as they were by behavioristic environmentalism, linguists found the answer to be obvious and simple: In human beings, important aspects of language are innate. Just how innate, and just what aspects of language might be innate, was not fully agreed on, but the majority of psycholinguists became convinced that language is at least *species-specific*. That is, they believed that evolution has equipped human beings to learn and use language the way it has equipped birds to fly—they come into the world predisposed to do it, and they need only minimal environmental assistance for it to emerge. It is therefore not learned in the same way as bike riding, ballroom dancing, or watchmaking. This idea is quite consistent with other commitments of information-processing psychologists. They believe that humans arrive with a set of inborn capabilities with which environmental events are interactively processed, stored, and retrieved.

It is probably true that most psycholinguists still consider language to be species-specific. However, a defense of this claim is more complex now than it was 10 years ago, because several psychologists have elicited remarkably language-like behavior from nonhuman primates (Gardner & Gardner, 1971, 1975; Patterson, 1978; Premack, 1970). While their achievements are modest by human standards, these apes have far exceeded the performance most linguists and psycholinguists would have expected. We review their accomplishments in our chapter on psycholinguistics.

At the same time he was attacking the behaviorist position, Chomsky was formulating his own linguistic theory, called *transformational grammar*. A linguist's job is to write a grammar; that is, to construct the set of rules that govern the language he is trying to explain. Linguists have disagreed on the best way to build grammars, but Chomsky argued persuasively for an approach he called *generative*. His approach is best illustrated by example. Suppose you are given three sets of elements: Set A consists of the letters *x, y,* and z. Set B consists of the letters j, k, and l. Set C consists of p, q, and r. There are 819 strings of three or less (for instance, xyl and pj) that could be made out of these letters. Now you are given two rules for picking *permissible* strings: Rule 1 states that a permissible string is any A followed by either a B or a C, but not both. Rule 2 states that a permissible string is (either) any C followed by any A followed by j (or) any C followed by any B followed by y. These rules enable you to select all the permissible strings:

xj	*xp*	*yj*	*yp*	*zj*	*zp*	*pxj*	*qxj*	*rxj*	*pjy*	*qjy*	*rjy*
xk	*xq*	*yk*	*yq*	*zk*	*zq*	*pyj*	*quj*	*ryj*	*pky*	*qky*	*rky*
xl	*xr*	*yl*	*yr*	*zl*	*zr*	*pzj*	*qzj*	*rzj*	*ply*	*qly*	*rly*

If this seems like quite a few possibilities for only three sets of three elements each plus two rules, consider that 785 possibilities are excluded! This set of rules, in conjunction with its sets of elements, can be said to "generate" the set of permissible strings; that is, anyone with the rules and the elements can construct the set of permissible strings, or decide for any string whether it is or is not permissible. For Chomsky, an important function of a grammar was to state the rules that generate a language's acceptable sentences. A successful grammar generates only those sentences a speaker of the language finds acceptable. As we show in Chapter 10, a well-designed generative grammar also provides a *structural description* of the sentences it generates. That is, in the course of generating a sentence, the grammar can indicate which rules have determined its organization. It can also indicate which parts of the sentence are related and specify the nature of the relationship. These capabilities of a generative grammar were extremely important to Chomsky.

A grammar is a sort of theory of the language user: The grammar is assumed to be part of the speaker's competence. Additional theory is needed to explain why people sometimes have slips of the tongue, make false starts, forget what they were going to say, and the like. But the grammar provides the abstract ideal that characterizes their speech in the absence of factors which cause deviations from it. Mathematics provides an analogy. If you want to understand what a mathematician does, the first thing you would want to know is mathematics itself, the system he works with. The mathematician performs imperfectly: He makes errors. But the ideal mathematical system is still the best explanation of his activity. Eventually, you may wish a specific theory of his errors; but until you have a clear picture of the ideal system that guides him, you will not know which behaviors are errors and which are not; so you could not construct a theory of error. In this case it is apparent that a theory that treats both correct and erroneous behaviors in the same fashion will be incomplete, and so it now seems with language. It seems that the best way to understand speech is to characterize the abstract system that guides the speaker. Ancillary theories can then be devised to explain deviations.

Grammars are a formal way of representing theories of language. Cognitive psychologists devoted considerable effort to testing Chomsky's particular theory, called *transformational grammar*. For example, according to tranformational grammar, certain sentences are related because they mean the same thing: *My dog bit someone* and *Someone was bitten by my dog,* or *It is easy to please John* and *John is easy to please.* Because neither psychology nor linguistics had a satisfactory theory of sentence meaning, it was not as easy as it might look to write explicit rules of how one of these sentences is transformed into the other. However, Chomsky proposed and described a system that accomplished this goal without relying on meaning. His system included *transformational rules* that could relate these and other pairs of sentences, and psycholinguists spent considerable time trying to determine whether the transformational rules had "psychological reality." That is, they sought to find out whether these rules were used by people to relate sentences in the way Chomsky's grammar related them. They tried to predict the effects of the mental processing of these rules on such psychological phenomena as memory and perception. We present some of the highlights of this line of research in Chapter 10.

Linguistics also resurrected intuition. Around the turn of the century, much psychological theory was built on intuition. A psychologist would study the workings of his own mind by thinking about his thought processes. This approach was markedly unproductive and often led to unresolvable controversies that degenerated into fruitless polemicizing. Behaviorism developed in part as a reaction to these essentially philosophical squabbles, and behavioristic psychologists banished any appeal to intuition, as well as other mentalisms. They came to believe that intuition was not only useless, but downright misleading. In the heyday of behaviorism it was a great triumph to give a laboratory demonstration of some "counter-intuitive" finding. Its counter-intuitiveness was taken as additional support of its validity. For the linguist, intuition is an indispensable tool of the trade. Linguists typically decide whether a sentence is grammatical, or acceptable, or ambiguous, by asking themselves whether they as native speakers find it so. They demonstrate the necessity for a given rule by deciding for themselves whether sentences that violate the rule are anomalous. If they are unsure in their own mind, they may ask a spouse or a colleague for their intuitions. Psycholinguists found this practice much less objectionable than behavioristic psychologists had. They welcomed it as a means of generating hypotheses, and have sometimes devised experiments in which subjects report their intuitions about grammaticality and other properties of sentences.

What has happened since the initial meeting of psychology and linguistics? At first, they had something of a honeymoon. Discouraged by the progress of behaviorism in illuminating language, psycholinguists borrowed the paradigm and theory of Chomsky whole. It provided a new way of looking at language, a way that was consistent with the rest of the budding information-processing paradigm. So, at first, Chomsky's approach seemed incredibly promising. But time has cooled the earlier optimism, and psycholinguistics is less heavily reliant on our sister discipline than was once the case. As research proceeded, we developed a clearer idea of which parts of the linguistic paradigm we could use most profitably and which parts are likely to be psychologically useless. What is more, events have moved on in linguistics: Chomsky's theory is no longer unrivalled.

What have we retained from our contact with linguistics? We have accepted its major arguments against S–R associationism and rejected that approach as a viable way to the study of language. Although today's psycholinguists seldom mention the competence–performance distinction, most of them appear to accept it implicitly. Their work suggests that they are trying to discover the psychological processes or mental operations that underlie linguistic performance, and that the kind of knowledge Chomsky called "competence" will be an important part of these operations. Although the ape research has raised some question about the species-specificity of language, most psycholinguists believe that language as humans use it is a result of evolutionary specialization. We have also concluded that the novelty and productivity of language is characteristic of other cognitive activities as well, including perception, memory, thinking, and understanding (Weimer & Palermo, 1974).

Some of what we took from linguistics, we first modified. For example, some linguists, and even a few psychologists, seemed to favor substituting intuition for laboratory research. We have not done that. Most information-processing psychologists conduct their research in laboratories: They believe that is the best way to verify scientific theory.

Interest in transformational grammar has waned. The honeymoon is over. Ten years have passed and, though we have progressed, a complete explanation of language is nowhere near at hand. Psychologists and linguists are both dissatisfied with the status of meaning in Chomsky's work. While it purports to relate sound and meaning, his theory actually relegates both to peripheral positions. The main focus of the theory is syntax. Semantics, or meaning, is a poor relation. There have been efforts to mesh semantic theory with the syntactic aspects of transformational grammar, but the fit has been unappealing to psychologists. It appears today that translation of Chomsky's theory into psychological theory would be very awkward. The reason is that Chomsky's prime effort went into developing a theory of syntax, while psychologists are becoming more and more committed to the study of meaning. In linguistics, a new group calling themselves "generative semanticists" is mounting a vigorous attack on Chomsky's transformational grammar, which had been so unopposed for 15 years as to be called "the standard theory." The generative semanticists believe, with many psychologists, that meaning should play a more central role in theories of language. But they have expressed their alternatives to transformational grammar in logical formalisms that are familiar in linguistics, but outside the paradigm of most psychologists. This has inhibited communication, and until someone translates these new linguists' formalisms into cognitive psychologists' paradigmatic language, we will not know whether linguists will continue to change our paradigm. Its impact has already been altogether profound. It has given us new ways of looking at language and thought that will remain with us even though the specifics of Chomsky's linguistics have fallen by the wayside.

4 The Information-Processing Paradigm

ABSTRACT

I. *Introduction: The Concept of Intelligent Action*
The concept of intelligence was treated in American psychology as a personal trait, and there was more interest in its measurement than its explication. One of the earliest efforts to deal with intelligent behavior in nonmeasurement terms was the notion of hierarchical plans developed by Miller, Galanter, and Pribram (1960). Intelligent behavior is a major domain of cognitive psychology.

II. *The Influence of Computer Science on Cognitive Psychology*
A. *Conceptual Origins in Mathematical Logic* Around the turn of the century, issues were raised in metamathematics concerning the related problems of computability and proof. Working on these issues, Turing (1936) developed the mathematical concept of a Universal Machine. A Universal Machine is a mathematical system that, with very few properties and capabilities, can perform any logical or mathematical procedure that can be fully specified. Although the Universal Machine was an abstract mathematical automaton, it is realized in present-day computers, which work with the basic capabilities of Turing's Universal Machine.
B. *Concrete Symbol Manipulation: The Link Between Formal Logic, Computer Science, and Psychology* The Universal Machine was conceived as a symbol-manipulating system; these developments in mathematics concretized the processes involved in symbol manipulation with important consequences for psychology. Newell and Simon (1972, 1976) had the critical insight that the mind might be considered a general symbol-manipulating system as well. If so, then *some* mental processes could be described in the precise, concrete, objective terms of mathematical logic rather than by intangible abstractions. They held a series of conferences to disseminate their ideas, and many important psychologists attended. Their seminal meta-

theoretical contribution has had a much greater impact than their own work on problem-solving, which did not produce a strong normal-science tradition.

C. *The "Third Metaphor": The Nature of the Computer Analogy* Although some psychologists understand and use the formal concepts of general-purpose symbol-manipulating systems, assuming that both people and computers are instances of such general systems, others work with a somewhat looser analogy between human information processors and computer programs. They note important similarities that recommend the metaphor to them.

1. *Generality of Purpose* Unlike other machines, the computer can follow any instruction put in proper symbolic form. It is therefore more general in capability than other machines; in fact, it can simulate any other machine.

2. *Algorithms, Subroutines, and Compilers* Computers store instructions and groups of instructions. One of the computer's great strengths is its ability to take the instructions comprising an algorithm and use them all at once. When whole sequences can be called at once, they are known as *subprograms* or *subroutines.* Computers also need compilers to translate programming languages into the small set of operations that constitute the machine's basic capabilities.

3. *Conditional Instructions and Decision Making* An important feature of computers is their ability to follow conditional instructions.

4. *Programs and Internal Storage* One of the most important features of computers is the fact that they store programs and data in the same symbolic form. This means that any operation they can perform on data can be performed on their own programs. Coupled with conditional decision-making, this characteristic means that programs can conditionally change their own instructions, which is part of the meaning of recursion.

D. *Computer Science and Psychological Theory*

1. *Computer Simulation* Because a Turing machine, which underlies computer capabilities, is so universal, it can imitate other machines. A program to accomplish this imitation is a kind of theory of the imitated system. If a program can be written to imitate some aspect of human behavior, the programmer must have a theory of how that behavior is effected. The steps in the program, consequently, constitute a behavioral theory. Each run of the program is like an experiment, whose outcome can be compared to actual behavior. Computer simulation of well-developed and underdeveloped systems is useful for different reasons. Psychological processes are underdeveloped systems.

2. *Structural Theory* Just as computer scientists put programs and flowcharts between input and output, psychologists now put hypothetical cognitive processes between input stimuli and output responses. This is a departure from functionalist and behaviorist views of psychological theory.

3. *Levels of Abstraction* Computer programs constitute one level of description of the internal activities of the machine. There are others, but no one level is the most right or scientific for all purposes. Computer science has suggested to psychologists the appropriateness of describing internal mental processes at the "program level." This is the level of the computer analogy. It concerns the logical capabilities of humans and

computers, not the physical hardware of computing machinery and biological brains.

4. *Theories of Language and Knowledge*   Efforts to communicate with the computer by means of natural language have pointed up the close relationship between language and world knowledge. This has stimulated psychological theory in the area of knowledge of the world. The computer has also been an invaluable resource in developing theories on this perennially intractable topic.

III. *An Information-Processing System*
An account of the formal capacities of a general information-processing system as proposed by Newell and Simon (1972).

IV. *The Information-Processing Paradigm*
A summary statement of the commitments of the contemporary paradigm and the forces that shaped it.
A. *Intellectual Antecedents*
B. *Pretheoretical Ideas*
1. *Symbol Manipulator*   The human is a general-purpose symbol manipulator; a few basic symbolic computational operations may ultimately be able to account for intelligent human behavior.
2. *Representation*   Since the very function of symbols is to represent, the concept of representation has taken on great significance in the information-processing approach.
3. *Systems Approach*   The paradigm is generally sympathetic to a "systems" view of the human as an interrelated set of capacities.
4. *Constructive/Creative Processes*   The human is viewed as an active information seeker; internal events change input information and literally create new knowledge.
5. *Innate Capacities*   Human behavior is generally considered to result from the interaction of innate capacities and learning experiences.
6. *Mental Chronometry and the Isolability of Subsystems*   Temporal measures are widely used to determine the time course of information processing and to decouple subsystems for study.
7. *Sufficiency Conditions*   There is a growing reluctance to study capacities that are unique to the laboratory. Increasingly, information-processing psychologists want theories that encompass behavior in its normal context.
C. *Subject Matter*
D. *Analogies*
E. *Concepts and Language*   Many terms have been borrowed from computer science, information theory, and linguistics. These are not mere terminological changes, but represent different concepts of the things the terms designate. Some familiar terms that are still used have different meanings for us than they had for our predecessors.
F. *Methodology*   The overall strategy is to develop structural theories of mental events, events that cannot be directly observed. To infer such processes, we use convergent validation. Many of our studies are intended to decouple mental events. We often represent our theories as flowcharts. Temporal measures are very prominent in information-processing psychological research.
G. *The Conventional Commitments in a Glance*

I. INTRODUCTION:
THE CONCEPT OF INTELLIGENT ACTION

Charles Sanders Peirce wrote in 1887, "Precisely how much of the business of thinking a machine could possibly be made to perform, and what part of it must be left to the human mind, is a question not without conceivable practical importance; the study of it can at any rate not fail to throw needed light on the nature of the reasoning process." Though quaintly worded, Peirce's statement was prophetic. It anticipated developments that began about 1950, for it was only then that the business of thinking was seriously implemented on a machine. Peirce was right: To get a machine to act as though it were thinking, its creators must have some idea what "thinking" actually is. There is no question that the development of computers, and the intellectual climate that permitted it, has profoundly enriched our understanding of human cognition.

"Computer science" is actually a family of loosely related subspecialties, including algorithm theory, numerical methods, automata theory, programming languages, and artificial intelligence. The relationship between these subspecialties and contemporary cognitive psychology is an intimate one indeed. The two fields have evolved in tandem. Both are derived from seminal work in mathematics that occurred during the first half of the twentieth century, and both are centrally concerned with the nature of intelligent behavior. Consequently, we have chosen to present the influences of computer science on cognitive psychology in this chapter, together with our summary of the information-processing paradigm itself.

Before the development of computational machinery, and the source of ideas it provided, American psychology had already given much attention to the concept of "intelligence." However, most of this attention was directed to the *measurement* of intelligence rather than to developing theories of its nature. The measurement approach, together with the pervasive influence of neobehaviorist pretheory, had several implications. For one thing, it tended to emphasize individual differences rather than human commonalities in intellectual functioning. Intelligence came to be viewed as some kind of personal characteristic, of which some people have much and others little; however, what it consisted of was never adequately specified. In fact, it was not long ago that students were told that human intelligence is "whatever the intelligence test measures." This facile answer served only to evade, rather than illuminate, a legitimate and centrally important psychological question. It might have been better to acknowledge that the notion of intelligence, like all our scientific psychological concepts, is in a state of evolution and development. Consistent with the then-dominant neobehaviorist paradigm, it was reasonable enough to give the circular, operational definition of "whatever the test measures." But this should have been recognized as a makeshift solution, to serve until our ideas and knowledge developed further, rather than presented as an end-state of psychological thought of the nature of intelligent behavior.

As long as intelligence was defined primarily by reference to a measuring instrument, scientific progress was seriously curtailed. First, the generality of the concept was restricted—infants, infrahumans, and machines were excluded from the concept's domain, because they could not take the tests. Most important, such a closed definition did not create an intellectual atmosphere that would encourage the effort to define the concept of intelligence in terms of underlying mechanisms.

The appearance of computing machinery, and the conceptual foundations on which it rested, provided an alternative way of looking at human intelligence. This new approach, because it was unconcerned with different people's *relative* intelligence, emphasized commonalities among all human beings whether bright or dull. Viewed this way, intelligence underlies most cognitive behaviors. Intelligent action—in some sense not yet fully understood—has something to do with the essential nature of mankind. It designates the ability to pose and solve problems without prior specification of the problem domain or the range of acceptable solutions. Human beings, even rather slow-witted ones, can solve problems even if they have never faced problems of similar structure. How do they accomplish this feat? One of the first psychological proposals that was not rooted in the measurement tradition came from Miller, Galanter, and Pribram (1960). They suggested that humans solve problems by using a variety of strategies that can be conceptualized as *plans*. They described plans as hierarchical arrangements of goals with embedded subgoals and specific behaviors at the base (see Fig. 4.1). Hierarchical plans of action have the virtue of grouping salient aspects of the internal processing steps underlying behavior into organized patterns aimed at particular goals, subgoals, and so on.

Miller, Galanter, and Pribram's (1960) book, in which the notion of plans was introduced and developed, constituted one of the opening shots in the neobehaviorist/information-processing paradigm clash. The plan concept sorted badly with neobehaviorist approaches to such complex behavior as thinking and problem solving. However, there is a considerable affinity between hierarchical plans and computer flowcharts; such flowcharts show the flow of information between the components of a program and the passage of control between programs, subprograms, and subroutines (Bower, 1975). There is no doubt that Miller, Galanter, and Pribram's work reflected the growing influence of computer science on cognitive psychology.

Information-processing theory has since gone beyond the concept of hierarchical plans to provide a much deeper analysis of intelligent behavior. This analysis relied on theoretical developments in computer science, which in turn relied on important advances in mathematics. These advances

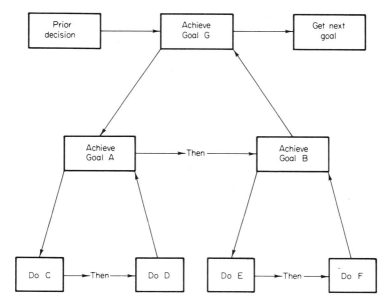

FIG. 4.1. A hierarchical arrangement of subgoals embedded within a primary goal. (After Bower, 1975.)

culminated in the abstract concept of an *information-processing system*. This concept, which may be central to any theory of intelligent action, was developed and refined for human cognitive systems by Newell and Simon (1961, 1972). Their collaborative effort (Newell & Simon, 1976; Simon & Newell, 1964), which we describe shortly, lies on the boundary between computer science and psychology. Artificial intelligence (a subfield of computer science) and cognitive psychology share such concepts as information-processing systems and physical symbol systems, because the objects they study (intelligent machines and human beings, respectively) both appear to be describable by such concepts. The basic concepts of *symbol systems, information-processing systems,* and *internal symbolic mechanisms* are subtle pretheoretical ideas, but they are central to the way many information-processing psychologists think about cognitive processes. At their core, these concepts may entail the mechanisms whereby a system— human or artificial—*creates new knowledge.*

As central as they have become to the paradigm, the concepts of general information-processing systems and symbol systems were not imaginable until important improvements had occurred in the field of mathematical logic. To trace these developments, we must step back a few years and examine the state of the art as it existed then.

II. THE INFLUENCE OF COMPUTER SCIENCE ON COGNITIVE PSYCHOLOGY

A. Conceptual Origins in Mathematical Logic

The requisite improvements began around the turn of this century, and concerned the twin notions of mathematical proof and computability. Mathematical arguments had relied on proof for perhaps 2000 years; however, there had never been a formal development or deep understanding of the nature of proof—it remained a largely intuitive concept. In 1899 a mathematician named Hilbert posed a series of unsolved problems in the foundations of mathematics. A major set of these questions concerned the nature of proof and the issues of computability, completeness, and consistency in formal axiomatic systems such as geometry, arithmetic, logic, and the like. In a complete and consistent mathematical system, any problem that can be posed can be computed, and equivalent computations will yield the same outcome. A related set of issues investigated was: Are there computable solutions to specific classes of problems? The fundamental task was how to show that a system, such as arithmetic or geometry, is both complete and free of inconsistencies. In other words, is it possible to *prove*, within the axioms of a system, that: (1) any statement formulated within the system can be determined true or false by inference from the axioms; and (2) no statement that can be formulated within the system will ever be determined to be both true and false by inference from the axioms? These fundamental problems remained unsolved even after a monolithic effort by Whitehead and Russell (1910–1913) to supply an axiomatic system from which arithmetic—and indeed all systems of pure mathematics—could be derived. Eventually, Gödel (1931) discovered that no nontrivial system of axioms could possibly be formulated that could be used to prove its own completeness and consistency. In other words, the matter of computability of particular mathematical problems could not be decided in terms of the axioms of the same system in which the problems are formulated.

Shortly after Gödel formulated his "incompleteness theorem," a young mathematician named Turing (1936) published a paper in which he approached the problems of completeness and computability somewhat differently. Turing analyzed the properties of an *effective procedure*—a procedure of specific steps or behaviors that lead to the solution of solvable logical problems. The idea of an effective procedure is quite similar to the idea of an *algorithm*: a set of steps that, if performed, will inevitably lead to the solution of a problem. The question is, how may we be sure that a proposed "effective procedure" is really complete? How may we know that it is so fully specified that no creative intelligence is required to carry it out? In other words, how may we be sure that it is fully automatic? Obviously, if a simple machine, without human intellect, can follow each step and invariably achieve a solution to the problem, the procedure is completely specified. However, Turing (1936) defended the reverse thesis: Any effective procedure that can be accomplished and characterized by human problem solvers can be achieved by a "machine" having only a small number of properties and capabilities. "Machine" in this context does not have its usual meaning. It can be understood as an abstact mathematical system, or an abstract process, whose states and changes of state can be described by four or five elementary operations. The abstract properties of this sort of "machine," or automaton, are potentially realizable as an actual machine. In fact, the formal information-processing approach to cognition makes the explicit assumption that both computers and aspects of biological organisms can be considered real-world implementations of such an abstract machine or automaton.

The abstract system that Turing proposed is called the "universal machine" or "Turing machine." With a very small set of primitive operations, this system could solve a formidable range of mathematical problems. Despite the simplicity of the Turing machine, the logico-mathematical arguments for its problem-solving versatility are lengthy and are not presented here. Suffice it to say that, despite 40 years of subsequent mathematics, no effective procedure for solving a logical or mathematical problem has yet been described that cannot be simulated on a Turing machine (Minsky, 1967). Turing's paper contained fundamental ideas foreshadowing the invention of the modern digital computer; in fact, everything actual computers can do is reducible to the fundamental capabilites of Turing's universal machine.

Because of the universal character of a Turing machine, it is possible to classify subtypes of machines (automata) by restricting the universal machine in various ways. The nature of a Turing machine and its subtypes can thus be used to define classes of complex systems and to prove claims about such classes. And, clearly, the Turing machine and the concepts of effective procedures and computability can be used to support statements about proof and solvability. A procedure for solving a problem that can be implemented with a Turing machine is, ipso facto, fully specified; no leap of human intuition is required to accomplish the solution.

Turing's discovery was echoed in two other mathematical papers published the same year (Church, 1936; Post, 1936). Turing showed the equivalence of his work to Church's concept of "effective calculability." This technical concept had been used in a classic paper on absolutely unsolvable problems (Church, 1936) to relate the intuitive concept of "effectiveness" to formal logical processes. And in the same year, Post (1936) also described the concept of effective calculability in yet another form. Thus, the year 1936 saw three formulations of the universal machine and the concept of effective calculability, which have been shown to be isomorphic or functionally equivalent (Minsky, 1967). These discoveries stemmed from the challenge posed by Hilbert, and by the existence of absolutely unsolvable mathematical problems. The field of pure mathematics opened by this work is called the theory of recursive functions, or automata theory in its wider applications. Among the various classes of abstract automata, four are of particular interest: finite, pushdown, linear bounded, and Turing machines. For each of these, there exists a formal grammar that is isomorphic with its corresponding automaton, in most important respects. The "in principle" arguments made earlier by linguists and psycholinguists specifying the absolute limitations of S–R theory were based on one or more of these formal theories of automata.

For psychology, the importance of the developments in mathematical logic is that they provided a concrete basis for characterizing abstract mental operations. The Turing machine accomplished these abstract processes in a very concrete way. It may seem paradoxical that the Turing machine is characterized as both "abstract" and "concrete." In fact, it is both. It is abstract in the sense that the logical operations involved are not tied inextricably to any particular physical implementation. They can be realized in a wide range of physical devices, including a variety of electronic systems and, we believe, in some biological systems. However, certain mathematical proofs, as well as symbols and the processes that operate on them, are concrete in the sense that there *are* physical devices—even man-made ones— that can effect these operations; no ineffable appeal to the intangible or mysterious processes of human reasoning is required to reproduce them. The same can be said of symbol-manipulating systems, which are abstract and concrete in just the same way as the Turing machine.

B. Concrete Symbol Manipulation: The Link Between Formal Logic, Computer Science, and Psychology

The formulation of the universal machine was one culmination of a drive toward formalization of logic and mathematics that began before the end of the last century. The discoveries of Turing and others were to have profound impact on the study of cognitive psychology, because they effectively concretized the processes involved in symbol manipulations. Mathematical logicians were able to demonstrate that symbols and the operations performed on symbols could be described in terms of explicit, concrete processes rather than intangible abstractions. The abstract symbols of formal logic could be copied, transformed, rearranged, and concatenated in much the same way as physical things. Moreover, formally objective standards of validity and consistency could be applied to these processes. Symbols, and symbol-manipulating processes, became tangible objects of study. This opened the way to showing that at least some human ideas could be represented symbolically, and that these symbolic representations could be meaningfully altered by precisely defined symbol-manipulating processes.

The significance of these developments is best understood against the background of general intellectual history and the psychology of the time. For at least two centuries, the mind and material body had been considered forever disparate. It seemed that the stuff of thought—"ideas"—could never be understood in the same kind of theoretical terms that described the biological substances of the nervous system or the physical universe. The "mind–body problem," as it was called, was solved during the behaviorist and neobehaviorist days by casting "mind" out of psychology. The discoveries in mathematics and formal logic provided an alternative resolution with potential revolutionary consequences. Mathematical logicians showed that certain ideas could be exactly represented by symbols, and that the operations on the symbols could be specified precisely. If the potential of this achievement was recognized, psychology could have the wherewithal to construct rigorous theoretical statements for hypothetical mental processes. Mental activities could be described in terms at least as real and concrete as the atoms and molecules of physical chemistry.

It remained for someone to have the insight that the mind might be formally construed as a symbol-manipulating system. This insight, which was fundamental to information-processing psychology, is owed largely to Allen Newell and Herbert Simon (Newell & Simon, 1972, 1976). However, even before this insight occurred, real computing machinery became widely available around 1950. A whole new field, computer science, developed to deal with a host of new problems and concepts. By the time Newell and Simon conceptualized aspects of the human mind and the computer as separate instances of the same kind of system, a great deal was known about computers and their properties; and many features of the computer, such as internal programs, compilers, buffers, and the like, were available as analogies for human mental processes. Moreover, the computer provided us a tool to implement and test theories that were cast in the languages of formal logic. These languages are under continuous development, as is their application in psychological theory (see Chapter 12 on global models).

Although the physical computer was immediately recognized as a realization of a Turing, or universal, machine, it was first viewed primarily as a mathematical device—a number manipulator. However, very early in the history of computer science, the computer was reconceptualized as a general-purpose symbol manipulator. Simon and Newell were among the first to recognize this essential fact, and even to widen the conception of the universal machine, the archetype of real computers. Where it had once been viewed primarily as a mathematical instrument working with numbers, it became possible to think of the universal machine as a symbol-manipulating system. Simon and Newell set to work on implementing their insight that the internal workings of both machines and minds could be treated as *systems of symbol-manipulating processes*, or *symbolic computational systems*. This idea is quite central in the complex of pretheoretical ideas underlying the information-processing paradigm and is more completely described later in this chapter.

How did Newell and Simon's metatheory come to have such impact? Much of it came about through a series of conferences they held to help disseminate their pretheoretical ideas on information processing and their research on problem solving. The most important of these conferences was held in 1958. The basic pretheoretical ideas of information-processing psychology were explained at the conference and in a paper published the same year (Newell, Shaw, & Simon, 1958). "The heart of the approach", they stated in that article, "is describing the behavior of a system by a well specified program, defined in terms of elementary information processes." The explanation of behavior is given by "a program of primitive information processes that generates this behavior." The conferences were attended by many of the leading psychologists of the time and by some who became prominent later, including George Miller, Richard C. Atkinson, Roger N. Shepard, and others. These psychologists are among the giants of information-processing psychology, and their work makes up large sections of our content chapters. The pretheoretical ideas of information processing, presented at the conferences, were superimposed on the problem areas occupying psychologists in 1958, such as verbal learning, memory, and perception. The consequence was the emergence of normal science traditions in these areas based on the ideas of information processing. Linguistics, which had been influenced by the same mathematical advances that inspired Newell and Simon, contributed related conceptions. The resulting normal science research comprises most of the content chapters of this book.

Newell and Simon's metatheoretical work has thus been profoundly influential in shaping our current paradigm. They developed core concepts, simulation techniques, root analogies, and the central notion of information-processing symbol systems. They also applied these ideas to their own psychological investigations of problem-solving behavior. It is interesting that, despite the powerful impact of Newell and Simon's metatheoretical contribution, their theoretical and empirical work on thinking has had relatively less direct impact in psychology. Although their metatheory inspired many normal science traditions in psychology, none has emerged directly from their own work in problem solving (although it generated a massive literature in the field of artificial intelligence). The reasons have to do with the discipline-related preferences mentioned in Chapter 2. Most cognitive psychologists study groups of subjects, using classical techniques of Fisherian research design. Newell and Simon, by contrast, studied the thoughts of individual subjects, who described their thinking as they attempted to solve problems. Newell and Simon collected and analyzed individual protocols with the objective of formulating and testing computer simulation theory. Moreover, Newell and Simon's own research involves specialized computer languages that most cognitive psychologists find too burdensome to master. Consequently, the Newell and Simon approach to problem-solving did not produce a flurry of related experiments by other cognitive psychologists, and problem solving never became a central research area in information-processing cognition. This is, in fact, the main reason our book contains no chapter on problem solving. Newell and Simon's conceptual work, however, formed a cornerstone of the information-processing approach, along with such contributions as those of Broadbent (1958), Miller, Galanter, and Pribram (1960), and Chomsky (1957). These fundamental contributions launched the information-processing approach, which became dominant after Neisser's (1967) classic work incorporating many of their ideas. In 1978, Herbert A. Simon received the Nobel Prize in economics for his work on decision processes. This suggests the broad applicability of this approach in all social sciences.

C. The "Third Metaphor": The Nature of the Computer Analogy

Computers take symbolic input, recode it, make decisions about the recoded input, make new expressions from it, store some or all of the input, and give back symbolic output. By analogy, that is most of what cognitive psychology is about. It is about how people take in information, how they recode and remember it, how they make decisions, how they transform their internal knowledge states, and how they translate these states into behavioral outputs. The analogy is important. It makes a difference whether a scientist thinks of humans as if they were laboratory animals or as if they were computers. Analogies influence an experimenter's choice of research questions and they guide his or her theory construction. They color the scientist's language, and a scientist's choice of terminology is significant. The terms are pointers to a conceptual infrastructure that defines an approach to a subject matter. Calling a behavior a *response* implies something very different from calling it an *output*. It implies different beliefs about the behavior's origin, its history, and its explanation. Similarly, the terms *stimulus* and *input* carry very different implications about how people process them. As a consequence of coming to know computer science, cognitive psychologists now theorize about human capacities and behavior using concepts such as input, output, storage, buffer, executive processor, and system architecture.

It is not unusual for a psychologist to reflect the influence of computer science in his work without a detailed understanding of Turing machines, general-purpose symbol manipulators, or for that matter computers themselves. Information-processing psychologists vary widely in the precision with which they apply the computer analogy, or what George Miller

(1974) has termed "the third metaphor." For some, it is more than an analogy: They explicitly assume that some aspects of computers and humans *are* instances of the same kind of system, and that system has quite specific capabilities and properties. Others go little further than a loose comparison between human mental processes and the flow of information in a computer program. And most fall somewhere in between, making use of the notion of general-purpose symbol manipulator, or information-processing system, without the formal logical apparatus that can accompany these concepts.

If some information-processing psychologists are unaware of the formal basis for the computer analogy, what recommends the analogy to them? The answer is that parallels to human functioning can also be drawn on an informal, nontechnical basis. Let us consider some of the capabilities of the computer that many psychologists feel may have parallels in the human mind.

1. Generality of Purpose

Most people know that computers follow instructions, but that does not set them apart from other machines. Here we mean "machines" in the everyday, nonmathematical sense. In some ways all machines, from a kitchen blender to a Boeing 747, follow directions. The difference is that the blender and the Boeing have extremely limited repertoires, while the computer can follow any instruction put in proper symbolic form. Symbolically, the computer can perform the function of both the blender and the aircraft and, in principle, of any other artifact. It is possible to instruct the computer to "chop" a symbolic carrot of specified size, density, moisture content, shape, and initial position. If you appropriately program the computer to process all the important features of a real blender, such as the shape, size, sharpness of its blades, the shape of its container, and the power of its motor, the computer can provide an exquisitely detailed account of carrot particles after blending for any specified period of time. Given the relevant conditions of temperature, pressure, load, speed, instrument settings, and the initial conditions of the aircraft, the computer can be programmed to report any feature of interest in the progress of an imaginary flight of a Boeing 747—the amount of bow in its wings, for example, or the amount of fuel it has used—at any designated moment in time. Moreover, it can do an unlimited number of other tasks, many of which are particularly interesting to psychologists. It can solve logical problems somewhat like a mathematician, and answer some questions like a college sophomore. This enormous range of "behaviors" is possible because the computer is a general-purpose symbol manipulator. The assumption we make is that there are relevant commonalities between people and computers by virtue of their corresponding symbol-manipulating capacities.

Computers can deal with any event, concept, or aspect of a system that can be represented in symbolic form and for which successive states can be specified, at least to a first approximation. As its input, the computer takes symbolized facts, ideas, and conceptions. Inside the computer, these symbols are transferred, combined, eliminated, saved, and transformed in various ways, and ultimately the computer can "output" an incredibly detailed account of the performance of a blender, an airplane, or a person. A computer can, in principle, carry out any instruction that its human programmer can specify exactly, no matter how complex the system represented by its input; the only limitations are set by the time it may take and the amount of storage space the computer has. The success of the enterprise—how similar the computer's output is to the actual performance of the blender, the plane, or the man—will depend on how well the programmer has supplied all the variables that significantly affect performance and how well his instructions to the machine compare with the actual manner in which the blender, the Boeing 747, and the person perform. You can see, then, that the programmer's instructions are also a theory of the relevant variables affecting performance and the manner in which the simulated system works. The theory can be tested by comparing the output of the computer program to that of the simulated system. We presently have more to say about computer simulations as theories of psychological processes.

2. Algorithms, Subroutines, and Compilers

Computers process and store *algorithms*. For example, a series of steps is performed to find the mean of a set of numbers. Another series of steps is performed to find the square root of a number. These sets of steps are called algorithms. An algorithm enables the production of specific output information from given input information. One of the great strengths of the computer is its ability to take the instructions comprising an algorithm and recall and use them all at once. It is thus possible in one program to repeatedly instruct a computer somewhat as follows: "Whatever number you have now, find its square root. Locate the instructions you filed under the label SQRT." This class of capabilities is called *subroutines* or *subprograms*.

If you have ever taken a course in computer programming, you know how detailed your instructions must be. The amount of detail, however, depends on the programming language and will vary considerably. Actually, even the statements and instructions that the programmer writes in a typical higher-order language are much grosser than the internal commands that the machine follows. Computers actually perform very few operations: They can store a symbol, retrieve a symbol, compare two symbols and determine which is the larger, replace a symbol with another one, and perform the basic arithmetic operations. Computers perform a relatively small number of these fundamental operations although the operations can be packaged into complex combinations. Computer programs are seldom written as series of commands to do the most basic operations. Special languages are available, such as FORTRAN and COBOL, that allow the programmer to instruct the computer in terms more similar to natural language; his instructions are then translated into the fundamental operations by the computer's *compiler*. The only function of a computer's compiler is to translate the programmer's language into the machine's language, into commands it can read and execute. The computer's enormous capability results, in part, from its ability to recombine its small set of operations into new sequences. Even more important, it can use its decision-making capability to generate a potentially endless number of new strings of instructions.

3. Conditional Instructions and Decision Making

Another important way in which the computer achieves its excellence is in its capacity for following conditional instructions. States of the computer's symbolic world can be specified so that it will act differently for each state. In a program simulating the flight of an aircraft, for example, we could include an instruction that said, in effect: "Take a look at the wings. Are they bowed more than 10° from the center position? If not, continue with what you were doing. If so, print out the message, EMERGENCY! WINGS BREAKING!"

Conditional instructability alone does not set the computer off from other machines. Thermostats operate conditionally on ambient temperature; some street lamps operate on ambient light. However, in combination with its ability to symbolize any specified variable, the computer can predicate its next act on a specific state of any variable or combination of variables— provided that an initial state was provided for each at some earlier point. This capacity equips the computer with a much greater versatility than other machines. It need not be festooned with heat, light, and humidity sensors to act conditionally on various levels of heat, light, moisture, and so on. Like the human mind, it can operate on symbolic representations of states of the world. Thus, its complex decision-making capability is an important property that reeommends it as an analogue of human thought processes. However, there is still another property of computers that, when coupled with symbolic capacity and conditional instructability, makes the computer unlike any other artifact. That is its capacity for *recursion*, which derives from the way the computer stores its own programs.

4. Programs and Internal Storage

A program, as generally conceived, is a linear order of instructions that specifies, at some level of abstraction, all operations to be performed and their sequence. An important characteristic of the computer is that programs are stored internally in terms of the same symbol systems that represent data. The computer is "blind" to the status of symbols in its information flow and treats programs like any other data. Programs can thus operate upon themselves as data—this is part of the meaning of recursion. Combined with conditional instructability, recursive capacity means that the program can conditionally change its own instructions. In the airplane example given earlier, a computer can accommodate the following more elaborate instructions: "Take a look at the wings. Are they bowed more than 10° from the center position? If not, continue with what you were doing. If so, scan the wings for hairline cracks. If cracks are present, print out the message WINGS BREAKING. If not, increase the criterion by 2°." It is possible to have the program re-check the wings periodically; in this example, the next check will not result in a search for cracks unless the wings are bowed 12° or more. If no cracks appear at 12°, the third check will only scan for cracks if there is 14° or more of bow, and so on.

Technically, a program is a set of difference equations for each possible state of the computer that determines what discrete operation it will next execute. Simon (1976) defines it thus: "If $S(t)$ defines the state of the computer at time t, $I(t)$ is its input, and P is its program, then we may describe its behavior by:

$$S(t + 1) = P[S(t), I(t)]."$$

In summary, then, the computers and the human mind, in some respects, are both instantiations of a general-purpose machine. They achieve their excellence by their ability to symbolically represent and manipulate anything that can be specified in symbolic form—from states of the world to their own functions—and to combine a relatively small set of basic operations into complex, high-speed sequences guided by conditional decision making. The information-processing paradigm includes the idea that human cognition, too, involves the symbolic representation and manipulation of events, and the concatenation of a finite set of basic capabilities into a potentially infinite range of behaviors, in situations that are familiar or unfamiliar.

The concepts of stored programs, subroutines, and compilers have insinuated themselves into research and theory on language comprehension, memory, perception, and even motor skills. Johnson-Laird (1977), for example, has proposed a theory of semantics based on a direct analogy between natural and computer programming languages. The concept of compiler and compilation has been suggested by Miller (1974) as the appropriate metaphor for human understanding of language. Understanding a question, in this view, is directly comparable to the compilation of a program to answer it. Davies and Isard (1972) have expanded the details of this analogy, at least preliminarily.

Computer science also deals empirically and theoretically with the problem of data structures—how information is organized in a storage system. Types of data structures are as varied as the imaginations of theoreticians and programmers. Broad classes of storage structures include strings, lists, trees, and graph networks. They include elements like nodes, links, and pointers. Many of these concepts have also been imported into cognitive psychology. They are encountered in the several chapters covering semantic memory and language.

A major postulate in the pretheory of information processing is that scientific theories of human mentation and behavior can be represented in a program, or by program-like codes. For this reason, psychological theories are often represented as computer simulations, or at least as flowcharts that could be developed into actual computer programs.

D. Computer Science and Psychological Theory

1. Computer Simulation

There are many kinds of computer programs. However, from a psychological point of view, one of the most interesting is a program that *imitates.* Because the computer is an instance of a "universal machine," it can in principle imitate the performance of any other machine. Because computers must be programmed by people, someone must supply the instructions on how to achieve the imitation. It follows that the instructions are a kind of theory of how the imitated system works and what variables are relevant to its performance. When a computer is made to behave like a thinking human, its program is a theory of human cognition. Expressing theories as computer programs is called *computer simulation.*

A computer-simulation theory of human cognitive behavior is a program that describes changes in the cognitive system through discrete intervals of time. It characterizes exactly each new state of the organism as a function of the immediately preceding state. In a sense, this state of affairs—knowing every step involved—is an ideal goal that is the long-range end state of theory construction. Information-processing psychologists, in general, consider a proper theory of a behavioral system to involve relatively complete specification of the steps occurring between an initiating event and an observable response.

Because a computer is so literal, it will only perform like a person if the programmer has given it the equivalent of every step the person carries out in executing some behavior. Cognitive psychologists are nowhere near able to do this, even for very simple cognitive behaviors. Nevertheless, computer simulation can be helpful in improving our theories. For one thing, it can help us to identify gaps in our understanding. When we attempt to specify a series of steps leading from input to output, we may find a place in the sequence where we have no idea what happens next. The program, however, must be told what to do. Research can then be focused on the gap in an effort to develop hypotheses as to plausible "next steps."

A second contribution of simulation is to provide an output that can be compared to human behavior and used to modify the theory implemented in the simulation. This output allows us to cast our hypotheses in a previously unavailable form. We can ask, "If our theory were correct, what should the output be like to resemble that of humans given the same task and input?" When the program gives output that differs from that of people, the nature of the differences can be used to diagnose where the theory needs correction. In this sense, each run of the program is a sort of experiment.

Finally, a proper simulation is capable of "predicting" behaviors that are based on interactions of states whose complexity precludes unaided prediction by a theorist. Used this way, the computer becomes an intellectual prosthetic device. Although we may understand a set of basic concepts, and their step-by-step implementation into a program, when the sequence of steps becomes very long, very complicated, and set up to deal with a large number of contingencies, we may simply be unable to predict what the program will do until it runs. Anyone who has taken a course in computer programming knows how surprising the results of a seemingly straightforward computer program can be. When we are expressing our theory in the form of a computer program, these surprises can be extremely informative. By examining the program's operation, we can sometimes see which instructions—which aspects of our theory—are clearly inappropriate or insufficiently explicit. Having simulated a process, we can examine aspects of our computer program to learn about our theory of the process. This is a powerful tool in extending our understanding.

Computer simulations deal with two types of systems: well-developed and underdeveloped ones. The distinction is loosely related to the earlier one we drew between relatively finished and unfinished sciences. A well-developed system is one whose laws and principles are known. We know the variables that permit perfect prediction of system outcomes. Then why simulate well-developed systems? There are two reasons. Such systems often are so complex that a human being cannot keep track of all the possible values of the variables; so he cannot make even one really confident prediction. Examples include ticketing systems, manufacturing processes, designing new aircraft, or predicting the orbits of spacecraft. Simulation work in such areas has been extremely successful, for the simulation model can take account of all variables that significantly influence performance. Consider for a moment the use of simulation in the building of aircraft. Unlike Wilbur and Orville Wright, today's aircraft designers do not build their plane, take it onto the runway, and hold their breaths to see whether it will fly; they know perfectly well that it will. They can be certain because the important parameters of currently flying planes, such as wing span, engine thrust, surface areas, and so on, are worked out in a simulation, a theoretical model of flying machines. The manufacturers can consider new planes as modifications of old ones. When considering a modification, the simulator feeds new values of the variables into his model to represent the proposed modification. The modified, as-yet-unbuilt airplane is then "flown" on the computer. The computer's output supplies information on the new plane's performance, its speed, safety, and other capacities or properties. An example of such preflight simulation is the Saturn first-stage booster that took our astronauts to the moon and permitted man to walk on the lunar surface for the first time. Before the Saturn was built, a digital computer program was created to study the manufacturing and assembly processes involved in producing the rocket. The output from the model told the engineers which of the hundreds of proposed scheduling procedures would enable completion of the rocket in the least time and at the most economical cost. Long before the astronauts were launched, the computer simulation of their flight had virtually guaranteed the success of their mission under normal anticipated conditions. Simulation of well-developed systems is facilitated if the system can be described in mathematical terms, using soluble equations. However, this is not essential; simulation is also useful for systems that operate in uncertainty, that are ill-structured, and that defy mathematical description. The major feature of a well-developed system is that the variables that influence it and its major states are well known.

As you might have anticipated, psychological processes are not well-developed systems. We are still discovering the variables that influence their operation. Nevertheless, computer simulation of behavior processes can still be useful for the reasons we mentioned previously. Computer simulations have alerted us to the complexity of processes previously taken for granted, and have also shown us the inapplicability or irrelevance of certain variables. For example, a simulation program called EPAM (Simon & Feigenbaum, 1964) revealed some unexpected information about paired-associate learning. EPAM produced learning rates comparable to actual data—but without reliance on the experimental variables of similarity, familiarity, and meaningfulness. Despite their use in hundreds of experiments, these variables were not important in the task. Instead, EPAM showed that stimulus units must exist as an integrated chunk in memory before learning begins.

When psychologists first started borrowing from computer science, the claims for how quickly simulation would give us a relatively complete understanding of thinking were somewhat overblown. As it became apparent how complex the task is, disillusionment set in, and computer simulation was sometimes depreciated. Nevertheless, many brilliant scientists are still using simulation to make important advances in the understanding of human cognition (e.g., Anderson, 1976). Even more common than actual simulation programming is the flowcharting of theoretical information-processing sequences. A flowchart describes the main features of a computer program, but without the detail required for an actual run on a machine. Implicit in a flowchart is the potential for constructing a running program, although many psychologists do not actually complete this final step.

2. Structural Theory

In addition to such valuable techniques as the simulation of cognitive processes, computers have helped give cognitive psychologists a changed conception of the nature of scientific explanation. It has changed many of us to mental structuralists, whereas there used to be many more "black-box theories." A black-box theory does nothing but relate the input of a system to its output, without specifying, at any level of abstraction, the processes that intervene between the two. It does not theorize about what happens between input and output. Such theories fail to give an account of what is happening, at either the logical or physical level, between input and output. This failure limits their utility as explanations and accounts for the designation "black-box theories." They leave the insides of the box, whose output they attempt to predict, unilluminated. A structural model, on the other hand, describes at least at a logical level the inner workings of the "box" whose output it seeks to explain. Before the advent of computer concepts, psychology used the functionalist approach extensively, particularly in verbal learning. Much research on perception and concept learning was also functionalist. There was minimal speculation about the internal processes involved in these cognitive activities. The introduction of concepts from computer science stimulated a lively resurgence of structural theorizing.

Information-processing psychologists began to put cognitive processes between people's input and output, just as computer scientists put programs and flowcharts between the computer's input and output. As more verbal-learning psychologists became familiar with computer science, many gradually dropped their functionalism for a concern with what goes on between input and output. They came to ask, What is the nature of the stored code? Are there several kinds of memory stores? Is there a temporary memory, like the buffer that holds the inputs to a computer until the central processor can work on it? When someone retrieves something from memory, how does he know where to find it? Is it "content-addressed" so that he can go directly to it? Or does he search all of the elements in his memory until he runs across what he is looking for? Does he search only some of the elements in his memory? If so, what principles determine which elements he will search? Can he search in parallel, or must he proceed serially? Such questions would almost never occur to a functionalist. But to a "computerized" structuralist, they are priority matters. Concrete examples of the research and theory motivated by these questions occur throughout our data chapters. The Atkinson–Shiffrin model, analyzed in Chapters 7 and 8, directly illustrates the impact of the computer analogy. As we mentioned earlier, Atkinson was a participant in the Newell and Simon 1958 seminar, which served as a focal point for dissemination of information-processing ideas in the prelude to the cognitive revolution.

3. Levels of Abstraction

In structural models of a computer, we can represent the flow of information and its modification at several different levels of abstraction. This is also true of the flow of information inside people. To understand what is meant by a "level of abstraction," take any piece of reality—this textbook, for example. Like any other system in nature, we can single it out for investigation and description. The book can be accurately described at many levels of abstraction. It could be characterized in terms of the atoms or molecules it contains, and their activity. Or it could be described by reference to the chemical composition of its pages and ink, or its geometry—volume, size, and so on. Still another investigator might render a complete description of its typeface, print size, page tint, and ink color. The book could be described more abstractly by counting its punctuation marks, articles, and conjunctions. Mathematical equations could be written for estimating the frequency of occurrence of these elements on each page. Or the book could be described in terms of its content. None of these levels of description is any more "scientific" or "right" than any other. Despite the rigorous appearance of equations describing the book at the level of atomic particles, such equations would tell us nothing about its content. If it is the content we want to know about, we need to work at a higher level of abstraction. The content could be described mathematically, too, in terms of set theory, and put into the form of equations. But that would be totally inappropriate if we were interested in the geometry of the book. The point is that the appropriate level of abstraction depends on what one wants to know about the system one is studying. No level provides *the* complete and correct characterization. Systems in nature are so complex and multifaceted that we need descriptions at many different levels of abstraction to understand them. No single level has absolute priority over any other. We can theorize about computers at the level of the transfer of electronic pulses; but that level of theory is useless as an explanation of machines as general-purpose symbol manipulators. In order to simulate natural or even manmade systems on the computer, we must move from the level of physical description to the level of logical description, where we theorize in terms of the transfer and manipulation of symbols. This is the only level at which the computer provides an analogy with the human mind, and herein lies one of the most prevalent misconceptions about the computer analogy.

Perhaps because of the popular use of the term "electronic brain" in the early days of computers, many people think that when scientists liken people to computers they mean to say that the machine's physical parts are the same as parts of the human brain. This is not so. Early in the development of the modern digital computer, von Neumann (1958) demonstrated that its physical characteristics determine its logical organization in ways that make it completely unlike a biological brain. When we draw the computer analogy, it is not to parts of the brain, but to human competence and capacities of the mind. We do not refer to the hardware from which the computer is built, or its electrical parts, but to certain of its functions. The analogy is between functions created by appropriate programming and human cognitive processes.

4. Theories of Language and Knowledge

Computer science, and in particular its subfield of artificial intelligence, has substantially advanced psychological theories of language, of the organization of human knowledge, and of the relationship between them. The development of computer science has parallels in linguistics. Linguists were strongly influenced by Post (1936), who made discoveries about computability and solvability equivalent to those of a universal machine at about the same time as Turing. The concept of a generative grammar (Chomsky, 1957) is related to that of an "effective procedure"—it is an effort to specify a set of rules that will automatically produce just the legitimate sentences of a natural language. There has been a continuing dialogue between linguistics and artificial intelligence for many years (see Bobrow & Collins, 1975; Hays, 1967). In fact, the fields of computer science and linguistics intersect in a subfield called "computational linguistics." Many information-processing psychologists are also interested in language. Some closely resemble computational linguists, even though some linguists (Dresher & Hornstein, 1976) and computer scientists (Weizenbaum, 1976) find these developments alarming.

Efforts to communicate with the computer by means of natural language have pointed up the importance of human knowledge in language use. There was great optimism, when computers were first built, that they could translate languages. But it turned out that translation cannot be done mechanically. The sentences of one language cannot be matched to sentences in another language by any system, human or artifact, that cannot comprehend the thoughts expressed by the sentences. Translation depends on world knowledge, which is not contained in sentences. This fact is illustrated by the following (possibly apocryphal) story. In an early program designed to translate from English to Russian, the machine was given the sentence *The spirit is willing, but the flesh is weak*. The Russian translation it produced ran something like this: *The vodka is fine, but the meat is tasteless*. Examples like this show that the computer will require a programmed representation of human knowledge before it will be able to render satisfactory translation.

Unfortunately, psychology had no theories of how people know what they know. However, the development of computer methods also reawakened psychological interest in the problem of how human beings know and understand. While it may seem obvious that psychologists should be interested in human knowledge, for many years there was essentially no research on this important question. It defied all efforts to approach it empirically; and with the explicit unwillingness of neobehaviorists to study mental events, the question of how people know things seemed inappropriate to many psychologists. Others recognized meaning and understanding as centrally important, but despaired of being able to deal experimentally with issues of such enormous complexity. When development of sophisticated computer methods provided a way to represent knowledge symbolically in the machine, interest in human knowledge returned, and there arose a renewed optimism that answers to ancient questions might be attainable. Efforts to write programs to answer questions alerted us to the large number of ways humans use their knowledge, and it suggested hypotheses. Further, the method of computer simulation gave us means, in addition to traditional experimentation, for trying out the hypotheses and evaluating them. These areas of work are flourishing in contemporary information-processing psychology; we present them in our chapters on semantic memory, comprehension, and global models.

The impact of computer science on cognitive psychology, then, has been profound on several dimensions. First, it supplied us with a new set of ideas on symbolic processes, a new methodology, and a new way of expressing our theories: computer simulation. The importance of this contribution will be most evident, we believe, in how we ultimately understand human language and the role of knowledge in human activities. Second, computer science opened up new research areas that were neglected because of the previous dominant paradigm. Third, it provided new ways of looking at old problems; it moved the study of memory out of a functionalist tradition into a more structural, theory-building one. It supplied concepts by which theories of internal events could be developed—for example, storage, retrieval, buffer device, executive control, and the notation of graph networks. It gave us a new perspective on the human organism, in which man is viewed as a general-purpose symbol manipulator of fascinating complexity and considerable efficiency. As you study this book, you will see again and again the concepts that have been imported and refined from computer science to serve us well in the study of the human mind.

III. AN INFORMATION-PROCESSING SYSTEM

We have now discussed the concept of a Turing machine and various properties of computers. In this book, human beings have been characterized as belonging to this genre and have repeatedly been designed as information processors. What, then, is a general information-processing system? At the most basic level, the system proposed by Newell and Simon (1972) is diagrammed in Fig. 4.2. The essence of such a system is its ability to represent things symbolically, and to manipulate the symbolic representations. The two "things" it must be able to represent are events in the external environment and its own set of operations.

Events, including objects, in the environment are represented by symbols and symbol structures. Symbol structures are configurations of single symbols connected by relations; for example, an A may be a single symbol, while a word such as CAT is a symbol structure. An information-processing system that can process the Roman alphabet must be able to represent an A and to recognize a new instance of an A whenever one impinges on its receptors. If such a system is to read the word CAT, it must recognize this particular configuration of letters when it is encountered, and distinguish this order from others such as TAC and ACT. An information-processing system can only "recognize" if it has a memory. It must retain some prototype (*type*, in Newell and Simon's terms) in its memory so that when a new instance (*token*, as such instances are called) of the prototype reaches the receptors, the system can say, in effect, "Ah, yes; CAT again."

The system must also be able to process the symbols, and hence must have a set of elementary information processes such as reading (inputting), encoding, recognizing, storing, and so forth. These can be concatenated into complex routines to achieve the greatest versatility of performance. What is more important, however, is that such processes—like environmental events—can be represented in symbolic form. With such a capability, an information-processing system can perform elementary information proc-

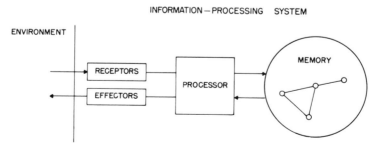

FIG. 4.2. An information-processing system. (From Newell & Simon, 1972.)

esses upon symbolic representations of its own capabilities. It can process its own processes just as it can process the external environment! This feature of the system may be an essential requirement for intelligent behavior.

Although it may be hard to believe, the general information-processing system is an instance of a simple Turing machine. It can be effected with only a very few "primitive" capacities. It must be able to designate environmental events and its own processes by means of symbol structures, and it must be able to produce responses designated by its symbol structures. It must be able

TABLE 4.1
Definitions and Postulates of an Information-Processing System[a]

1. There is a set of elements, called *symbols.*
2. A *symbol structure* consists of a set of *tokens* (equivalently, *instances* or *occurrences*) of symbols connected by a set of *relations.*
3. A *memory* is a component of an IPS capable of storing and retaining symbol structures.
4. An *information process* is a process that has symbol structures for (some of) its inputs or outputs.
5. A *processor* is a component of an IPS consisting of:
   (a) a (fixed) set of *elementary information processes* (eip's);
   (b) a *short-term memory* (STM) that holds the input and output symbol structures of the eip's;
   (c) an *interpreter* that determines the sequence of eip's to be executed by the IPS as a function of the symbol structures in STM.
6. A symbol structure *designates* (equivalently, *references* or *points to*) an object if there exist information processes that admit the symbol structure as input and either:
   (a) affect the object; or
   (b) produce, as output, symbol structures that depend on the object.
7. A symbol structure is a *program* if (a) the object it designates is an information process and (b) the interpreter, if given the program, can execute the designated process. (Literally this should read, "if given an input that designates the program.")
8. A symbol is *primitive* if its designation (or its creation) is fixed by the elementary information processes or by the external environment of the IPS.

The indefinite term *object* is used in the definitions above to encompass at least three sorts of things:
1. symbol structures stored in one or another of the IPS's memories, which are often usefully classified into
   (a) data structures, and
   (b) programs (see item 7 in the list above);
2. processes that the IPS is capable of executing;
3. an external environment of sensible (readable) stimuli. *Reading* consists in creating in memory internal symbol structures that designate external stimuli; *writing* is the inverse operation of creating responses in the external environment that are designated by internal symbol structures.

[a]From Newell & Simon, 1972, pp. 20–21.

to compare instances of symbols and symbol structures, and classify them as the same or as different. It must be able to store and retrieve symbols and symbol structures. The system must be able to create new symbol structures by modifying existing ones, and it must be able to create a new symbol to stand for a symbol structure. Thus, for example, the system that reads the Roman alphabet must be able to designate instances of the letter A by a symbol, and it must be able to tell whether two input symbols, such as A and A or A and B, belong to the same category. It must be able to concatenate several symbols, such as those standing for C, A, and T and those standing for order information, into a symbol structure (e.g., C-A-T); and then it must be able to create a new symbol standing for CAT. Conversely, the system must be able to "recover" the parts of such structures; in the preceding example, it must be able to work back from CAT to access the more elementary symbols C, A, and T and their order. Perhaps the capacity that gives the system its "flavor" is the ability to act contingently. It must be able to execute different sequences of information processes depending on the symbol structures it deals with. That is, it must be able to execute a different sequence of processes when it encounters CAT from when it encounters something else, such as DOG. It is this feature that makes the system responsive to content—to the actual events (external and internal to the system) that it is capable of representing in symbolic form.

Newell and Simon (1972) have developed the description of these capacities more fully than our presentation here; however, the foregoing set of capacities is essentially sufficient for the functioning of a general symbol-manipulating system. Actually, no unique set of processes is required; a number of equivalent sets exist that will do the job. However, all the sets have the essential features just mentioned incorporated into their elementary capabilities in one way or another. These elementary information processes, when coupled with the axiomatic system described by Newell and Simon, can produce an enormous range of performance—all the intelligent performances of which computers are capable, and perhaps most of which humans are capable as well. For the interested reader, the axioms of Newell and Simon's general information processing system are presented in Table 4.1. It is striking how much of the pretheory of the information-processing approach to human cognition is derivative from this elegantly simple formulation. It is now time to describe and summarize the main aspects of that pretheory; then we look at data.

IV.   THE INFORMATION-PROCESSING PARADIGM

Information-processing psychology has entered a period of normal science. Its revolution has been over since around 1970. The conventional beliefs of its practitioners are stable but slowly evolving; there is no serious challenge as yet. Paradigmatic commitments are quietly guiding research decisions, and cognitive psychologists are relying on a rich set of pretheoretical ideas. Subgroups have identified their various subject matter interests. They have an elaborate language and network of concepts with which to characterize their work. They have a robust analogy. These various facets of their paradigm guide the researchers' selection of what data to collect and help them to formulate theories. We describe many such experiments and theories that organize their findings in the next part of this book. Most of these experiments reflect some aspect of the information-processing paradigm, and we frequently point out the connection. But first we summarize the paradigm and the forces that shaped it.

At the end of Chapter 1, we described key features of scientific paradigms. Paradigms could be told apart by their intellectual antecedents, their pretheoretical ideas, their subject matter, their language, their analogies, and their research methods. We now characterize the complete paradigm, using the foregoing features as an outline. It should be clearly understood that there never was and never will be complete agreement on any single paradigmatic attribute or small subset. The cohesive force that holds us together is the overlapping or intersection of intellectual commitments. Finally, we recognize that not all cognitive scientists view their commitments as conventional, ideological, and value-laden methodological judgments, but prefer to view them more like some kind of eternal truth.

A. Intellectual Antecedents

Table 4.2 summarizes the contributions to the information-processing paradigm from each of six intellectual ancestors of cognitive psychology. On the left, it lists what cognitive psychology has accepted from each ancestor, and on the right it lists what has been rejected.

B. Pretheoretical Ideas

There is an ideology—a set of beliefs—that characterizes the information-processing paradigm. Some of these beliefs have come to us through our history as a discipline and from our own teachers, some by way of other disciplines, and some as a reaction to the state of affairs in psychology before the information-processing approach was born. The bedrock of the approach is the view that human beings in certain cognitive tasks act like an information-processing system.

1. Symbol Manipulator

A few relatively basic symbolic computational operations, such as encoding, comparing, locating, storing, and the like, may ultimately account

TABLE 4.2

The Scientific Ancestry of Cognitive Psychology

Six Ancestors	What They Gave to Cognitive Psychology	What Cognitive Psychology Rejected
A. Neobehaviorism	1. Nomothetic explanation as its goal 2. Empiricism as the main method of proof 3. Laboratory experimentation as its main mode of research 4. Operationism for describing experiments 5. The rational canons of natural science	1. All-encompassing behavior theory 2. Explanation by extrapolation from a small set of learning principles 3. Animal experimentation as a source of basic principles 4. Learning as the central psychological problem 5. Conditioned associations 6. Logical positivism as a philosophy 7. Radical environmentalism 8. Antimentalism
B. Verbal Learning	1. Memory as a key problem 2. Part of the data base of verbal learning 3. Laboratory procedures and measurement techniques 4. Productive scientists	1. Neobehavioristic leanings 2. Verbal learning as a central problem 3. Fruitfulness criterion for research
C. Human Engineering	1. Analogy of man as decision maker and information transmitter 2. Information transmission limits 3. Theory of signal detectability 4. Access to concepts from engineering and physical sciences 5. Sophisticated instrumentation 6. Attention as a key problem	1. Focus on applied problems

(continued)

TABLE 4.2 (continued)

Six Ancestors	What They Gave to Cognitive Psychology	What Cognitive Psychology Rejected
D. Communication Engineering	1. Analogy of communication channels 2. Limited channel capacity 3. Coding to overcome limits 4. Serial vs. parallel processing 5. Information theory 6. Concepts of uncertainty and information 7. Inclination to mentalism 8. Inclination to structuralism	1. Mathematical axioms of information theory 2. Information measures based on the number of physical alternatives were rejected in favor of measures based on the number of mentally inferred alternatives.
E. Computer Science	1. Man as symbol-manipulating system 2. The computer analogy 3. Computational concepts 4. Explanation by specification of underlying mechanisms 5. Simulation techniques 6. Focus on complex, intelligent behavior 7. Sufficiency conditions 8. Clarification criterion instead of fruitfulness	1. Brain–machine analogy
F. Linguistics	1. Reasons to reject neobehaviorism 2. Reasons to reject animal model 3. Biological and evolutionary explanations 4. Focus on language 5. Interest in creativity and ruliness 6. Competence/performance distinction 7. Intuitive hypotheses	1. Intuition as data 2. Denigration of performance 3. Syntax as central 4. Applications of transformational grammars

for human intelligence and the capacity to create knowledge, novelty, and perhaps expectations about the future. The human mind is thus viewed as an instantiation of a general-purpose machine. A central idea is that the technical conception of an information-processing system will be adequate to the complexity of human beings and ultimately account for their intelligence and most of their cognitive processes. Not all cognitive psychologists explicity share this pretheoretical idea. Some are so immersed in day-to-day normal science that they may not be cognizant of this assumption. Others are neutral regarding the abstract parallel of symbol systems and accept only the computer analogy as a source of concepts for various aspects of cognition and as a source of working hypotheses. Still, the technical conception of mankind as a symbol-manipulating system is implicit in many of our paradigmatic beliefs and much of our normal science.

2. Representation

The concept of representation has always been implicit in most work on perception, memory, and language. However, the pretheoretical ideas that the human mind is a general symbol-manipulating system explicitly sweeps representation to center stage. The very function of symbols is to represent things—environmental objects and events, other symbols, and processes. Cognitive representation is essential to the paradigm: Information processes must operate on something, and part of that something is an internal representation of reality.

At the metatheoretical level, representation refers to the theoretical elements and processes on which information-processing mechanisms operate. At the ontological or referential level, the concept refers to the internal mechanisms that represent any and all aspects of our world knowledge. Theorists do not always distinguish metatheoretical from ontological usage, and it is not always evident how "real" they intend their notion of representation to be. However, efforts to develop and clarify the concept are under way (Palmer, in press).

3. Systems Approach

In general, information-processing psychologists view humankind as a natural system, and are sympathetic to the "systems" approach. We view intelligent behavior as emerging from the interactions among a system of components. We think of human capacities and activities as interrelated both with each other and with representations of the environment. In studying any one human characteristic, many of us find it, in principle, useful to imagine how we would go about building a machine or writing a computer program to fully relate it to people's many other properties and characteristics.

4. Constructive/Creative Processes

Many of us believe that the human being is an active information-seeker. People do not wait passively for an environmental stimulus to provoke an automatic response. Rather, we view people as hungry for information, as constantly scanning their environment in search of relevant developments. This may have been necessary for survival, and a consequence of evolution. We think, however, there are always many things going on inside the human mind, even when we cannot observe overt behavior; the environmental events that impinge on the mind are not merely reflected but are also changed and amplified by internal processes. Consequently, we are struck by the constructive nature of human information processing. Unlike the behaviorists, whose paradigm sensitized them primarily to the repetitive elements in human behavior, we find novelty and productivity everywhere evident—in language, perception, and memory. You will find these pretheoretical beliefs reflected in the questions we ask, the justifications we offer for some of our assumptions, and the directions we take in our search for answers. For example, in our study of attention, we ask how the human organism singles out some aspects of the environment to attend to and not others. If we assumed that the organism was passive, we would not even wonder—it would be the environment that stimulated him. But because we view our organism as active, we suppose that the impetus for selective attention to the environment comes partly from inside the person.

The pretheoretical idea of constructive processes originated early in the empirical development of psychology (Bartlett, 1932) and is currently in vogue (Cofer, Chmielewski, & Brockway, 1976). An information-processing system, by virtue of its capacity to create new symbol structures, can, in principle, accommodate constructive processes and creativity.

5. Innate Capacities

Another pretheoretical belief concerns the importance of innate abilities. We do not believe in postulating mysterious "instincts" to account for otherwise unexplainable behavior, but we do feel that everything the human does is the result of inborn capacities, as well as of learning. We give innate capacities more significance than behaviorists did. We think part of the job of explaining human cognition is to identify how innate capacities and the results of experience combine to produce cognitive performance. This leads us, especially in the area of language, to suppose that some aspects of cognition have evolved primarily or exclusively in humans. These capacities, consequently, can never be illuminated by the study of animals lower than primates. We do not yet know which aspects of comprehension and reflection are species-specific, and which are not; but we strongly suspect that those responsible for metalinguistic capacities exist in the human alone.

6. Mental Chronometry and
the Isolability of Subsystems

The pretheoretical assumption that a subset of processing stages can be isolated underlies much research on the time course of the flow of information in the organism (Posner & Rogers, 1978). This leads to extensive use of reaction-time measures, although conventional accuracy measures are so widespread.

In classical physics, virtually all theories posited three spatial coordinates in which physical events occurred. A fourth was time. Time is also an important coordinate of biological and psychological events. Psychological processes unfold over time. For some things we study, our sophistication allows us to measure only how long a process takes; but ultimately we want to pinpoint the nature of the events that occur during that time. A concrete example may illustrate the approach. Suppose a person is looking at a screen when the letter E is projected. If the E is projected for an extremely short time, such as 1/1000th of a second (1 millisecond), the viewer will not be aware that he was shown anything. In other words, perception is not instantaneous. Following a somewhat longer exposure, say 5 milliseconds, the person will know he has seen something, but he will not know what it is. This shows that even when perception occurs, identification is not inevitable. It is also possible to project an E long enough for a person to know that it is not O or Q, but briefly enough so he will still be uncertain whether it was E or F or K. Thus, we can determine the minimum interval necessary for complete identification, partial identification, or even the subjective experience of having seen anything at all. The assumption that perception is an accumulative business that seems to involve specific, identifiable, and describable stages leads us to do chronometric studies.

Much information-processing research intends to discover and describe the stages of processing that underlie various psychological events—how long they take and what happens when they occur. The view that psychological events occur in time is characteristic of information-processing psychology. This interest is not characteristic of our associationistic predecessors. Because they were uninterested in internal events, it stands to reason that they would not think of speed as an index of occurrence of events inside the head.

7. Sufficiency Conditions

The paradigm is giving rise to a new set of values in research and theory. We generally are committed to the value that a cognitive theory should have the capacity to predict, or better yet to perform, the cognitive tasks in its domain of application. This means that it is also important to understand human capacities in their normal context. All members of the paradigm rely on laboratory verification, but some of us are inclined to worry about the generality of our findings. That is, we do not want to study capacities that are unique to the laboratory. We mention this because much research in many disciplines is designed to answer questions about previous experiments, rather than about the natural system the discipline presumably seeks to understand. Perhaps there were conflicting outcomes in different studies, uncertainty whether the outcome would be the same under somewhat modified conditions, or ambiguities in the conclusions that could be reached. So other studies would be designed to explain the conflicting outcomes. A progression sometimes develops, in which lines of research eventually arise that have very little to do with the natural system of original interest. Under such circumstances, even obvious questions about the original natural system may come to seem peripheral—even sophomoric—to the professional investigator. Believe it or not, such developments have not always been regarded as a deficiency. The ability to generate more studies—"fruitfulness" —has sometimes been regarded as a hallmark of successful science. Indeed, at one time most published psychological studies ended with the cliché, "More research is needed." Recently, an awareness has arisen that an unlimited number of experiments could be done to resolve such issues. And there could be countless variations on standard experimental arrangements. There is a growing feeling that these endless studies are unproductive and that they may distract researchers from tackling the intransigent, but central, questions about the system under study. For this reason, some information-processing psychologists have begun to impose sufficiency conditions on their work (Anderson & Bower, 1973; Newell & Simon, 1972; Norman, 1973). A commitment to sufficiency conditions means that scientists will give the highest priority to doing their theorizing and research in such a way as to discover mechanisms capable of performing the cognitive tasks people do naturally.

C. Subject Matter

The information-processing paradigm has proved most attractive to researchers of the higher mental processes. This is generally considered to include such subjects as thinking, perception, problem solving, concept formation, memory, language, and learning. There is little agreement on which of these are the more basic processes, and cognitive scientists have concentrated in varying degrees on all of them. Learning is treated in this book, but it comes indirectly under the headings of memory, knowledge, and language comprehension. Thinking is here, too, but it is seldom mentioned explicitly by name. The study of memory has occupied a central position in the paradigm for over a decade, and it occupies a large share of this book. The emphasis on memory may be giving way somewhat to the kind of interests reflected in our chapters on semantic memory, comprehension, and global models. These chapters concern knowledge, meaning, and understanding, which are present in most cognitive acts and are ubiquitous in human affairs. During the revolutionary phase of cognitive psychology, "meaning" was barely visible as subject matter. Now, the importance of meaning and the various cognitive roles it plays thread their way through all of the later chapters of the book.

D. Analogies

Although the computer analogy is pervasive in information-processing psychology, it should be clear by now that the computer is more than just a metaphor. For some cognitive psychologists, those human properties that involve symbol manipulation are instances of the same theoretical abstraction that serves as the conceptual prototype for digital computers. At the same time, many information-processing psychologists view their theorizing as analogical rather than instantiational.

Either way, the computer and its properties have had a profound influence on psychological research and theory. The likening of the mind to a computer program has provided us with very many productive ideas, and it promises more as computer science progresses. While the lode of ideas provided by the computer analogy seems far from exhausted, the analogy of the mind with a limited-capacity communications channel appears to have been pushed to the end of its usefulness. We still use some concepts provided by the communications-channel analogy, such as limited capacity and efficiency in human cognition. However, little recent research has relied directly on this analogy for hypotheses.

E. Concepts and Language

Some of the terms used by information-processing psychologists are the same as those of other paradigms, but they usually have a somewhat different meaning for us. For us, *stimulus* and *response* are laboratory terms, defining laboratory operations. A stimulus is whatever we present to the subject in an experiment, and his response is whatever he does that we measure. These terms are not as all-encompassing for us as they were for neobehaviorism. When we speak of information processing in a theoretical vein, we are likely to use the terms *input* and *output*. Does this represent a mere terminological change, a new jargon? Are these new-sounding terms merely synonyms for *stimulus* and *response*? Only in the sense that *bastard* is a synonym for *foundling*, *jock* for *athlete*, and *dine* for *eat*. These terms carry very different connotations and implications. They are part of a scientific vocabulary that is paradigm-determined.

A term that we still use but whose meaning has changed is *association*. As we have mentioned, human comprehension must involve the apprehension of relationships between things. But for many years, the association was the S–R unit formed by conditioning. In our use, the term has no such restrictive meaning. For many of us, to "associate" objects or events is to know what they have to do with one another. Such knowing is not an automatic process; it does not require contiguity between environmental events; it can occur totally within the mind of the thinker. For the neobehaviorist, the most important thing about a person's associations—for example, of *drink* to *water* and of *black* to *white*—was their strength, usually indexed by the number of people who gave each associate. For us, the important thing is the *kind* of relationship or meaning between the terms, not just the strength of the relationship. "Drink" is a relational act with "water," the object of the act. The "black–white" association reflects the relation "opposite of," and perhaps the relation "extremes on a continuum" where the continuum is brightness. Neither "opposites" nor "points on a continuum" are relational acts; so it seems inappropriate to think of *drink–water* as the same sort of association as *black–white*, even if their strengths are equal.

Terms that have entered our scientific lexicon from computer science include to *store*, which means to take some environmental input and hold it somewhere in the mind, and to *retrieve*, which means to get back again something that was stored. Computers have a central processing unit, which is where the symbol manipulation occurs or where it is controlled, and buffer devices, which hold information until the central processor can get to it. These concepts are used in analogous fashion in information-processing psychology. *Buffer*, for example, refers to any system that is the basis or locus for certain very brief memory activities. Your ability to recall the last few words you heard when you are asked to, even though you were not paying any attention to the speaker, implies buffer storage for aspects of the speech stream.

Modern computer hardware really includes interrelated systems of several machines working together in harmony to process information. The organization of the system is guided by a principle of economy: The goal is the maximum processing of information for the lowest cost in time, energy, and other resources. Biological systems, including the human mind, may operate on similar principles. In the computer system there is a *systems program*, one part of which is called the *executive control system*. It keeps the different machines—tape drives, card readers, drums and disks, central processor, and their various parts—all working in harmony. We have adopted this concept and such others as *subroutine, mainline,* and *pushdown stack* from programming technology to describe certain workings of the human mind, and they are defined in the text when appropriate.

Some of the terms we use derive from the communications-channel analogy. Terms like *limited capacity, serial processing* and *parallel processing, signal,* and *noise,* are still in wide use in information-processing psychology. We also borrowed from information theory the concepts of *filter* and *bandwidth*. In communications technology, a particular range of frequencies is called a bandwidth; and it is possible to filter a sound signal so that only some frequencies are allowed to pass. This happens in poor-quality, low-fidelity speakers, which transmit neither very high nor very low notes. Such speakers act as a sort of filter to exclude certain frequencies from the transmitted signal. The same can be done intentionally and with much more precision by a bandpass filter. Information-processing psychologists have used the term *filter* in theories of attention, in which something seems to narrow down the range of environmental information so a person is consciously aware of processing only part of what goes on about him.

Among the concepts we have borrowed from linguistics are *competence, grammar, rule-governed behavior*, and *hierarchical structure*. The meaning of some of these concepts was gradually expanded to satisfy the requirements of a psychological approach to language. Many new concepts also have been generated in the paradigm's main fields of interest. We leave them to our data chapters.

F. Methodology

Like other scientists, we make observations and measurements; we do laboratory experiments; and we develop theories. However, the measurements we make and the experiments we do differ in several important respects from those of our predecessors. Our overall scientific strategy is different, and so is the combination of techniques we use. Taken one at a time, our scientific methods are not unique to our paradigm, nor even to our discipline. Taken together, they comprise a constellation of methodological preferences and procedures that give information-processing research much of its special character. We speak here first of the overall strategy and then of particular techniques or tactics that tend to set our paradigm apart from others.

Our research strategy is largely dictated by the fact that we are interested in mental events, in addition to directly observable behavior. The very meat of our theories concerns what occurs in the mind, between input and output. First and foremost, we seek to understand the mental mechanisms underlying human behavior. In this regard, we see an appropriate parallel between our science and that of the cell endocrinologist who likened his work to that of an industrial spy. Sitting on a hillside above a factory with field glasses, he watches railroad cars arrive with raw materials. They are taken into one end of the factory, while at the other end trucks pick up completed products. The spy's job is to figure out what transpires in the factory. Every once in a while he can send in a car of materials he has selected, and later he can see what comes out; but he cannot take a trip through the factory. We are in a similar position with respect to human mentation. We cannot observe it directly. We must infer what happens inside by watching what goes in and what comes out.

You may wonder how we validate our inferences, and how we confer scientific status on our theoretical statements, which are, after all, about unobservables. We do it much as physical scientists do, for a big part of their subject matter is also unobservable. The temperature of the sun, for example, or the activity of molecules, atoms, and electrons, cannot be known directly. Nevertheless, scientists have detemined that the surface temperature of the sun is about 11,000°, and the interior temperature is about 25,000,000°. The key to the problem is that several phenomena that *are* observable place constraints on the possible interior temperature of the sun. In cognitive psychology, we endeavor to make observations that place constraints on the possible workings of the mind. In both cases, properties of the system under study give rise to observable data, even though these properties are not themselves observable. Interlocking inferences then permit construction of valid, factual statements about the unobservable properties. This technique is sometimes called *convergent validation* (Garner, Hake, & Eriksen, 1956); when data of several different kinds converge on a conclusion, the conclusion is convergently validated.

Beyond providing convergent validation, our research strategy must allow us to "decouple" mental mechanisms from the system in which they normally operate. Decoupling was never a central concern of neobehaviorism. They were not guided by their paradigm to imagine that a complex mental system was always at work when their subjects did their experimental tasks. But according to our paradigm, the mind is a system and its various parts work in concert. To be certain that we are observing the effects of one part of the system and not the products of various interacting parts, we must design our experiments to separate the process we are studying from others. At the very least, we must minimize and stabilize the effects of other mental mechanisms. You might think of our decoupling efforts, which we describe in later chapters, as damming up a creek to see what its bed does when there is no water in it. Or, you might think of us as using a dam to regulate the flow of water through the creekbed so that its effects do not vary and contribute "noise" to our observations of the bed itself. There are in fact several kinds of decoupling, but they all depend on the possibility of preventing the mental subsystem that any experiment studies from interacting with other subsystems.

By now you should have a good feeling for our scientific ideology, the goals of our theorizing, and what our scientific theories are about. You should also understand how we express our theories, which is often done by using flowcharts. These are ubiquitous in the information-processing literature. As mentioned earlier, a flowchart is a graph that presents the stages of processing, either internal to a system or inherent in the solution of some problem. Flowcharts use symbols to represent operations, information flow, component processes, and transformations of information. For information-processing psychologists, the goal of a flowchart is to specify as completely as possible, at some desired level of abstraction, what happens to an input after it enters the cognitive apparatus. Flowcharts, in a way, have the same status for us that operational definitions had for our predecessors. Whereas they were concerned with completely specifying the conditions of their experiments, we are concerned with a detailed and rigorous specification of the workings of the mind. Drawing flowcharts is a reasonable way to express our conception of the system we study so that we can design intelligent experiments and communicate our theoretical claims.

Figures 4.3 and 4.4 show examples of flowcharts. Figure 4.3 is not a conventional cognitive flowchart, but it is included to show how information and physical flow can quickly be apprehended in *any* system by flowchart graphics. Figure 4.3 illustrates one representation of the flow of information and patients into and out of a hospital. It expresses our understanding of the hospital intake and release system. Among other things, it says that there are only three ways to enter the system (hospital), and that there are two ways to exit, dead and alive. It is impossible to leave alive unless two conditions are met: (1) information, in the form of a medical release, comes from the record

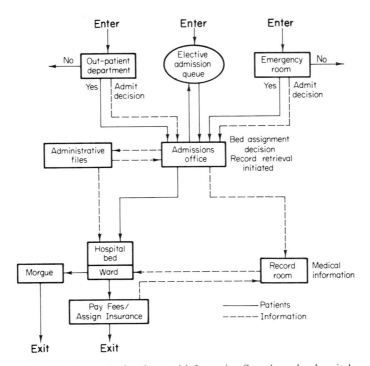

FIG. 4.3. A model of patient and information flow through a hospital.

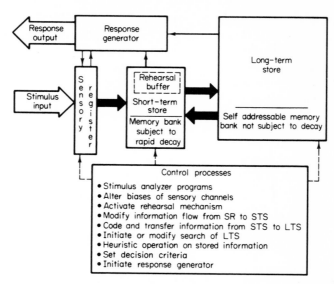

FIG. 4.4.   An information-processing model of human memory. (After
Shiffrin & Atkinson, 1969.)

room; and (2) the cost of the hospital stay is either paid or assigned to an
insurance carrier.

One use of flowcharts in cognitive psychology, as we have indicated, is to
present the conceptual infrastructure of a formal theory. Figure 4.4 is an
example of that type of information-processing flowchart. Suppose that we
were using the theory to describe someone trying to remember a phone
number between looking it up in a drugstore phone book and reaching a pay
phone across the street. The phone book is the environment. The receptors
(eyes) see the phone number, which is encoded into a representation that is
held in the sensory register. Control processes, currently not understood, may
operate on the contents of the sensory register, using information retrieved
from the long-term memory. Meanwhile, the encoded information is moving
from the sensory register to the short-term store. If the person is saying the
phone number aloud while running across the street, the information in the
short-term store is passed to mechanisms that produce the oral responses,
uttered by the mouth, and the person hears them himself. His vocal response
has become part of the environment, and the whole process can start over
again because the receptors (now his ears) can take it in—the information is
cycling. The flowchart can accommodate a variety of other information-
processing sequences, as well. For example, someone listening to a lecture
and trying to understand it takes information in through the receptors, holds
it in the sensory register and the short-term store, uses information from the
long-term store to interpret and condense the information in the short-term

store, and then transfers the condensed version into the long-term store until it is needed again—perhaps to make sense of tonight's textbook chapter, or perhaps to write a test.

Although the flowchart is a characteristic representation for the conceptual core of information-processing theories, it should not be mistaken for a formal theory. The formal components of cognitive theories are represented by various formal calculi: propositional logic, mathematical equations, computer simulation, graph theory notation, and grammars. As we see later, well-developed formal theories use a variety of different calculi as part of the formal implementation of their conceptual core.

Finally, let us turn to the nuts-and-bolts aspect of our paradigm—some of the laboratory methods we favor and the variables we most commonly measure. While information-processing psychologists are willing to measure almost anything at all that will advance understanding of the human organism, they have a few specially favored techniques. Among the most prominent of these is the measurement of reaction time, which reflects the interest of information-processing psychologists in the temporal aspect of cognition. We know that performance can be explained in terms of the temporal duration of the underlying mental processes responsible (Chase, 1973). Consequently an inventory of chronometric methods has evolved (Posner & Rogers, 1978). Under appropriate circumstances, we infer that a task that takes more cognitive time also takes more cognitive activity. The original version of this idea was suggested many years ago by Donders (1868/1969). He was a nineteenth-century Dutch experimenter who observed that a subject responds more quickly when there is only one signal and one response (simple reaction time) than when there is more than one signal and more than one response (choice reaction time). In the first situation, the subject simply responds as quickly as he can when a stimulus occurs; in the second, he must decide which stimulus has occurred and select the appropriate response. Donders suggested that the time difference represented how long it took for the subject to identify the signal and choose a response. While the situation turned out to be somewhat more complex than Donders supposed, his original analysis of the problem had merit. The general approach taken by Donders underlies many reaction-time experiments, although considerable effort has gone into extending and refining the technique (e.g., Taylor, 1976).

G. The Conventional Commitments in a Glance

We told you at the end of Chapter 1 that you could make a great deal of sense out of any research science by grasping aspects of its paradigm. To make that job manageable, we singled out six features of paradigms, and suggested that you approach each new science with an eye to isolating them. You can regard everything we have said since then as illustrating that these features do in fact characterize sciences; in our case, cognitive psychology. But you surely want and need a more succinct characterization! You might even want to see our paradigm at a glance. We gave you a sort of one-glance view in Table 4.2, where we summarized the ancestry of the information-processing approach to cognitive psychology. Table 4.3 provides another view at a glance. It describes present-day cognitive psychology in terms of its pretheoretical ideas, its subject matter, its analogies, some of its concepts and language, and its chief methodological strategies. We believe it will repay you to carefully examine it.

TABLE 4.3
The Information-Processing Paradigm in a Glance

Pretheoretical Ideas

1. Some human behavior is viewed as an instantiation of the *symbol-manipulating* capacity of a *general-purpose machine*.
2. The resulting information-processing theory will be adequate to human competence and complexity.
3. The concept of *representation* is essential to the paradigm.
4. The human mind has parts, and they interrelate as a *natural system*.
5. Man's cognitive system is constantly active; it adds to its environmental input and literally *constructs* its reality.
6. *Innate capacities*, some of which evolution has given to man alone, combine with experience to produce cognition.
7. Cognitive processes are noninstantaneous—they take *time*; their duration is informative.
8. Some processing *stages* can be isolated.
9. *Sufficiency* conditions require that cognitive theory have the capacity to predict or perform the requisite tasks of its domain of application—in or out of the laboratory.

Subject Matter

1. At the highest level of abstraction, our subject matter is man's *mental processes*.
2. Man's basic mental capabilities are *attention, perception, abstraction, problem solving, learning, memory*, and *language*.
3. Memory has always been a focal problem. *Meaning, comprehension* and *knowledge* have recently emerged as tractable problems.

Analogies

1. Humankind as an *information-processing system* is not a metaphor but an instantiation of an abstract automaton.
2. But research and theory are guided mainly by the *comptuer analogy;* we liken the function of mind to some functions of computer programs.
3. The analogy of *limited-capacity communication channels* was once important, but it is now used infrequently as a guide to theorizing and the design of experiments.

(continued)

TABLE 4.3 *continued*

Concepts and Language

We use the terms *stimulus* and *response* to define laboratory operations. When we speak of *associations,* we are more interested in their meaning entailment than in their strength. Like computer scientists, we use the concepts *to store, to retrieve, buffer, systems architecture, executive processor,* and so on. From communication engineers, we have taken the concepts of *signal, noise, channel, capacity, filter, bandpass,* and *serial-parallel processing.* From linguists, we have borrowed and modified the notions of *competence, grammar,* and *hierarchical structure.* Many new concepts and terms originated in the paradigm and are found in the data chapters.

Methodology

1. We make inferences to underlying mental processing mechanisms by designing multiple experiments and by using *convergent validation* techniques.
2. We employ various techniques to *decouple* cognitive processes from their natural system in order to see their unique functions.
3. Flowcharts are used to represent the conceptual core of our theories.
4. The formal component of cognitive theories include *computer simulations, propositional logic, mathematical models,* and *grammars.*
5. We frequently, but not exclusively, measure *reaction time.* This has produced an inventory of mental chronometry.

5 Reaction Time: The Measure of an Emerging Paradigm

ABSTRACT

I. *Introduction*
Choice reaction time (CRT) is one favorite dependent variable of cognitive psychologists, and historic changes in the use of reaction time illustrate the rise of the information-processing paradigm.

II. *Preview: A Brief History of Reaction-Time Research*
Interest in human reaction time predates scientific psychology. During the nineteenth century, Donders used subtraction of reaction times to decouple mental processes from one another. In the heyday of behaviorism, reaction-time research declined. During the 1960s, mental processes again became the focus of reaction-time research. Today, many kinds of cognitive research use CRT methods.

III. *Information Theory*
Interest in efficient transmission of messages over limited communication channels led to experiments in which the human was the limited channel.
A. *Information Theory and Choice Reaction Time* Shannon (1948) defined information mathematically in terms of the number of alternatives and the probability of each. Merkel (1885) found that CRT increased linearly with the number of alternatives. Hick (1952) and Hyman (1953) related the increase to the amount of information transmitted.
B. *Binary Decisions* Information theory is built on a logarithmic metric, which implies underlying binary decisions. Leonard (1958) tried to see whether people used binary mental decisions to solve CRT tasks, but his data indicated that they do not.
C. *Cognitive Inference and Information* Fitts and Switzer (1962) found that CRT depends on the number of stimuli people infer to be present more than it does on the actual number employed by the experimenter.

IV. *Engineering Psychology*

    A. *Man/Machine Compatibility*   The need for cognitive concepts was highlighted by research on CRT and man/machine compatibility. The question was how to best tailor machines to fit people's capabilities, and trying to answer it showed that some of these capabilities are cognitive. Fitts and Seeger (1953) showed that the response arrangement producing the fastest reaction time depended on the stimulus arrangements used.

    B. *Psychological Refractory Period*   One limit on how people perform is revealed when they are required to make two responses in succession; the second response is typically slower.

V. *Decomposing Mental Processes*

By the mid-60s, CRT research included information theory experiments, engineering studies with utilitarian purposes, functionalist investigations of stimulus and response variations, studies of skills that demanded sophisticated cognition, and high-powered mathematical theorizing about CRT results. Smith (1968) moved psychology importantly toward the information-processing approach by integrating all of these sorts of research into a single stage-analytic framework, which reflected the influence of a computer analogy. He argued that four underlying processing stages are all reflected in CRT: stimulus preprocessing; stimulus categorization; response selection; and response execution.

    A. *Sternberg's Serial Exhaustive Model*   Elegant reaction-time research by Sternberg (1966) stimulated much psychological interest in mental processes.

        1. *Sternberg's Task*   Sternberg's item recognition task requires people to memorize a short list of digits and to then respond *Yes* or *No* as to whether a test digit is one of the digits in the memorized set.

        2. *Exhaustive Scanning*   *Yes* reaction times increase linearly with the number of items in the memory set. Reaction times for *No* responses parallel those for *Yes*es: Memory scanning is exhaustive.

        3. *High-Speed Scanning*   People scan their memories at the rate of about 38 milliseconds per item, which is about 25 items per second.

    B. *Additive Factor Method*   Sternberg (1969b) improved upon Donders' subtraction methods by developing the method of additive factors. It attempts to isolate distinct information-processing stages of cognition. Sternberg's task and his additive factor logic have been used in hundreds of experiments.

    C. *Criticisms of Sternberg's Model*   Because they have been scrutinized by so many experimenters, Sternberg's task and model have been criticized frequently.

        1. *Alternate Models*   Theories have been developed to explain Sternberg's data with mental mechanisms that are basically different from those specified by Sternberg, and there is no compelling reason to reject any of them.

        2. *Unpredicted Results*   Modifying Sternberg's procedure in any of several ways produces results that his theory cannot accommodate. This shows that his model is an elegant theory of a particular sort of performance, but it is not a general theory of human performance.

    D. *Sternberg's Contribution*   The elegance of Sternberg's research inspired many psychologists to study cognition from an information-processing point of view. The additive factor method provided a powerful tool for convergent validation of cognitive processes.

VI. *Speed–Accuracy Trade-Off*
The logic of many reaction-time experiments requires that their subjects make
no errors, but they make some nevertheless. Fitts (1966) showed that errors and
reaction time can be changed by paying subjects for one or the other. People will
trade speed for accuracy or vice versa.

A. *Sternberg Again*   Speed–accuracy trade-off accounts for some data that
are inconsistent with Sternberg's model.

VII. *Signal Detection Theory*
Situations where a person must detect a faint stimulus in noise were treated as
problems in sensory psychophysics—defining the energy level that produces a
response. However, powerful decision processes and motivational components
were discovered. Signal detectability theory was developed to separate true
sensory factors from decision processes. It soon proved to have wide
applicability in cognitive research beyond the original task.

A. *Hits and False Alarms*   When someone is trying to indicate whether or not
a signal is present, he scores a Hit when he says *Yes* and the signal is there.
He has made a False Alarm when he says *Yes* but the signal is absent.

B. *D-Prime (d') and Beta (β)*   Whether a person scores a Hit or a False Alarm
depends both on his sensitivity, called d', and his biases, called β.

C. *ROC Curves*   By varying payoffs (or certain other factors), one can
construct a Receiver-Operating-Characteristic (ROC) curve. From the
ROC curve, one can estimate d' free of bias (β). ROC curves have helped to
solve complex problems in several areas of cognitive psychology.

D. *CRT and Signal Detection Theory*   Atkinson and Juola (1974) applied
signal detection theory to account for both Sternberg's CRT data and many
findings that his theory does not encompass.

E. *Caveats*   We have presented only the main concepts and general outlines of
signal detection theory. The theory highlighted internal decision processes:
Active cognitive mechanisms came to be used in the analyses of human
perceptions and reaction, replacing the passive information theoretic
analogy.

VIII. *Serial or Parallel Processing?*
A. *Neisser's Work*   Although Sternberg typically found support for serial
processing, Neisser (1964) used a visual search task that suggested parallel
processing. This apparent conflict stimulated much research.

B. *Egeth's Approach*   Elegant designs by Egeth (1966) to resolve the conflict
using multidimensional stimuli did not provide unequivocal support for
either serial or parallel processing.

C. *The Current Views of Serial and Parallel Processing*   It now appears that
the early stages of pattern recognition are parallel and that the serial
processing observed by Sternberg may be due to later stages of processing
present in his task but not in the tasks of other investigators. The current
view is that very early pattern-recognition processes are mostly preattentive,
automatic, nonstrategic, and parallel. Later processing stages are mostly
attended, flexible, strategic, and serial.

IX. *The Status of CRT in 1979*
Choice reaction time has become a ubiquitous dependent variable rather than a
topic area. This is possible because of the well-developed theoretical framework
that researchers have established for the CRT task. Reaction-time measures are
now used in all areas of cognitive psychology.

I.   INTRODUCTION

To do an experiment, one must choose a dependent variable. He must decide what to measure. A scientist's paradigmatic allegiance can often be inferred from his dependent variables. If a psychologist measures the number of tries (which he calls *trials*) it takes to learn something, it is a good bet that he has been influenced by neobehaviorism. Nowadays, measuring reaction time often indicates a commitment to the information-processing paradigm. That was not always so; long before the computer and the information-processing paradigm were invented, reaction-time measures were used for diverse psychological purposes. Changes in reaction-time research illustrate well the rise of cognitive psychology. In this chapter we describe the origins of reaction-time research, show how it contributed to the growth of the information-processing paradigm, and describe some of what we have learned about cognition by measuring reaction time.

Consider first an experiment that measures simple reaction time. You are seated before a light, and your right index finger is resting on a key, rather like a piano key. When the light comes on, a clock starts. When you press the key, the clock stops. Your task is to press the key as soon as you can after the light comes on. The typical reaction time is about 190 milliseconds, about a fifth of a second. (A millisecond is 1/1,000 second). According to Keele (1973), *Sports Illustrated* measured and published the reaction time of Muhammad Ali, the longtime heavyweight boxing champion of the world. Ali was renowned for his quick movements, his ability to duck punches and to jab with lightning speed. But his simple reaction time was about 190 milliseconds, the same as the rest of us. Ali's evident quickness in the ring was not due to the speed of his movements. Rather, it stemmed from his ability to anticipate and predict his opponent's moves, and required sophisticated and quick decision.

Such decision processes can be studied in reaction-time experiments by giving people a choice between two or more stimuli and two or more responses. Most cognitive psychologists have studied choice reaction time rather than simple reaction time. *We use the abbreviation CRT for choice reaction time.* The CRT measure is sensitive to differences in high-speed processes: More difficult information processing takes longer. To paraphrase Ben Franklin, who said *Time is money,* we can say, *Time is cognition.*

II.   PREVIEW: A BRIEF HISTORY OF REACTION-TIME RESEARCH

Psychologists became interested in reaction time late in the nineteenth century because of an earlier problem in astronomy (see Boring, 1957). Early astronomers measured the transit time of a star by watching it travel between two cross hairs in a telescopic field while counting the beats of a clock. Today, we would consider this a complex information-processing task, but it seemed then to be direct, natural, and easy to do. At Greenwich, in 1796, an astronomer named Maskelyne fired his assistant for coming up with times that were different from his own (by 0.8 seconds). Later, it became evident that each astronomer estimated heavenly events differently. Each astronomer had a "personal equation" that gave his amount of measurement "error" as compared to someone else's. This human element in scientific measurement prompted much study of reaction time during the 1800s. By far the most important contribution was made by Donders (1868/1969), a Dutch physiologist who in 1868 devised methods for studying what he called the "Speed of Mental Processes."

Donders distinguished three reaction-time tasks. The A task is what we called simple reaction time. There is a single stimulus and a single response. The B task is more complex; it is called CRT. You have to make a decision if you are a subject in a CRT task. Suppose there are two lights and two keys. If the light on the left comes on, you press the left key; if the light on the right comes on, you press the right key. The time it takes you to press the correct key is your choice reaction time, or the time for your type-B reaction. In the type-B task there are two stimuli and two responses, but any number of stimuli and responses can be used. Donders' C task has multiple stimuli, but only one response. For example, there might be two lights. If the left light comes on, you press the key; but if the other light comes on, you do nothing. Donders' tasks are summarized in Table 5.1.

Donders was not a psychologist, and he was not caught up in any psychological paradigm. However, he contributed greatly to subsequent psychology when he hypothesized that reaction time could be used to estimate the speed of internal cognitive processes. For example, he thought the B reaction involved three processes: (1) the simple reaction—the time to respond to a stimulus; (2) Stimulus Categorization, the time needed to decide which stimulus had been presented; and (3) Response Selection, the time needed to select the right key. Notice that the A reaction is a component of the

TABLE 5.1
Donders' Three Reaction-Time Tasks

Task	Number of Stimuli	Number of Responses	Mental Processes Measured
A	One	One	Simple reaction time
B	Many	Many	Simple reaction time Stimulus categorization Response selection
C	Many	One	Simple reaction time Stimulus categorization

B reaction. CRTs (Donders' B reactions) are longer than simple reaction times (A reactions) because two extra cognitive processes are involved. The C reaction requires the subject to make the same stimulus categorization decisions as the B reaction, but does not include a response-selection stage. By comparing performance in these various tasks, we can obtain estimates of the time needed for two decision processes. To find out how long it takes to categorize a stimulus, A reaction time is subtracted from C reaction time. Similarly, response-selection time can be obtained by subtracting C from B:

$$\text{Stimulus-categorization time} = C - A \qquad (5.1)$$
$$\text{Response-selection time} = B - C \qquad (5.2)$$

These equations illustrate Donders' subtraction method, which is an example of the decoupling of mental processes described earlier as part of the information-processing paradigm. We show later how the logic of Donders' methodology has been extended to provide important insights about cognitive processes.

Reaction-time research nearly died with the advent of behaviorism. Two forces, engineering psychology and information theory, eventually revived it. During World War II, engineering psychologists became interested in performance of well-learned skills and in promoting maximum performance from workers, pilots, and soldiers. To them, the reaction-time task seemed a pure measure of error-free performance—one that truly measured the limits of people's performance. If a person was performing as fast as he could, any factor that slowed him down could truly be said to limit him, and such limiting factors were precisely what interested engineering psychologists. Information theory was also concerned with factors that limit speed; in their case, speed of information transmission over a limited-capacity channel. Viewing the lights on a reaction-time apparatus as a source of information, the human subject as the transmission channel, and the response key as the receiver, information theory predicted that human reaction time would vary with amount of information transmitted. The study of choice reaction time under varying information-transmission conditions became a popular kind of research in the 1950s: The telecommunications problem became a psychological problem. For psychologists, the communication channel was the human, and the question was the human's maximum capacity.

Information theorists and engineering psychologists shared the contemporary information-processing interest in human performance, but their research had a definite functionalist flavor. Much of their reaction-time research catalogued the effects of stimulus parameters on response speed. In this, they shared aspects of the paradigm of verbal learning. Human engineers concentrated on variables that would increase performance. Information theorists concentrated on the quantification of the stimulus parameters and viewed people as if they were passive channels. Like verbal-learning psychologists, human-performance researchers eventually dropped functionalism and discovered structure. They were among the first psychologists to see the value of the computer analogy. As the computer became more widely used, the theorizing of human-performance psychologists became more structural. They designed experiments to find out about internal processes. They revived Donders' subtraction methods; they became information-processing psychologists.

Today, reaction time wears two hats in information-processing psychology. It is still considered a laboratory analogue of rapid decision making; and it is one of our more ubiquitous dependent variables. We turn now to some major reaction-time experiments. Almost all studied choice reaction time.

III.   INFORMATION THEORY

Communications engineers are interested in the nuts and bolts of communications. How can a message be sent through a physical medium, such as a telephone wire? First, the message has to be translated at its source so that it can be represented electrically. Such coding was discussed in Chapter 3 and we discuss it further in Chapters 7 and 8. For now, note that communications engineers, who are interested in sending information most efficiently, must define information concretely. It may be all right in a psychology lecture to talk vaguely about meanings or messages, but the telephone wire has to know what you mean in a very electrical way. So what is information?

You will recall our discussion in Chapter 3 of Claude Shannon, a mathematician at Bell Laboratories who defined information precisely in 1948. Shannon's mathematical theory of communication showed psychologists how to quantify information exactly. That was a profoundly important contribution. For science, the invention of a pertinent measuring device is as important as a theoretical breakthrough.

Shannon saw that information is related inversely to uncertainty. Measuring one amounts to measuring the other. When we tell you that $2 + 2 = 4$, we are not communicating: You already knew that. You had no uncertainty, so we transmitted no information. Information is communicated only when the receiver is uncertain about the content of the message. The more uncertain the receiver, the more potential there is for information transmission.

How, then, can we define amount of uncertainty? Isn't it all or none? You either know it or you don't? No, some things are more uncertain than others. In November of 1975, you did not know who would be elected President of the USA in 1976. There were many candidates and great uncertainty. In November of 1975 Jack Anderson listed 8 potential Republican nominees and 16 Democrats (Anderson & Whitten, 1975). On election eve 1976, there was less uncertainty. Two candidates remained: Ford and Carter. The difference between November 1975 and November 1976 was in the number of candidates who could be elected. The more alternatives there are, the more uncertain the outcome. The more uncertainty, the greater the potential for information transmission.

Shannon quantified information in terms of the number of alternatives. He expressed the metric—which is called a *bit*—in logarithmic terms. Whenever you double the number of alternatives, you increase the uncertainty by 1 *bit*. With 2 alternatives (e.g., flipping a coin), there is 1 bit of uncertainty. With 4 alternatives (e.g., pick one suit at random from a deck of playing cards), there are 2 bits of uncertainty. Eight alternatives yield 3 bits, and so on. Uncertainty can be computed with the following formula:

$$U = \log_2 k \qquad\qquad (5.3)$$

where k = the number of alternatives.

The general idea should be emphasized: The more things that might happen, the more bits of uncertainty. But uncertainty depends not only on the number of alternatives, but also on the probability of each. If all alternatives are equally likely (as in the coin and card examples), then equation 5.3 is appropriate. But in our presidential example the probabilities were unequal. Unequal probabilities reduce uncertainty. Consider the case in which one of several possibilities has a .99 probability; there is hardly any uncertainty.

Table 5.2 lists the 16 leading candidates for the Democratic nomination for President, as of November 1975. The effect of the primary campaigns was to reduce our uncertainty as to who would be the nominee. In other words, the nominating process communicated information. How much information? One might suppose that because there are 16 alternatives, the uncertainty was 4 bits ($\log_2 16 = 4$). But according to Jimmy the Greek, as reported by Anderson and Whitten (1975), the probabilities were unequal (see Table 5.2). There was less uncertainty than 4 bits. Shannon derived a measure of uncertainty to correct for unequal probabilities:

$$U = -\Sigma\, P_i \log_2 P_i \qquad\qquad (5.4)$$

where p_i represents the probability of each alternative. According to this formula, there were 3.5 bits of uncertainty as to who would be nominated by the Democrats; this is somewhat less than the 4 bits that would be obtained without correcting for probability. The lesson is that uncertainty depends on two things: (1) the number of alternatives, and (2) the probability of each.

The relationship between uncertainty and information is counterintuitive to some students; so here is another example. Suppose you are a lookout for a

TABLE 5.2
Democratic Candidates for President
as of November 1975[a]

Candidate[b]	Probability of Nomination (p)	$-p \log_2 p$
Humphrey	.25	.5000
Jackson	.15	.4105
Carter	.10	.3322
Kennedy	.07	.2686
Bayh	.05	.2161
Bentsen	.05	.2161
Church	.04	.1858
Sanford	.04	.1858
Shapp	.04	.1858
Udall	.04	.1858
Wallace	.04	.1858
Glenn	.04	.1858
Muskie	.04	.1858
Harris	.02	.1129
Shriver	.02	.1129
McGovern	.01	.0664
	$U = 3.5363$ bits (see Equation 5.4)	

[a]Adapted with some modification from Anderson and Whitten, 1975.

[b]If you have forgotten some of these candidates (Milton Shapp?), you have a lot of company. We did not make up these names.

team of bank robbers. You are on the third floor of an apartment building across from the bank late at night. One of the robbers inside the bank is watching for you to signal if trouble develops. Your job is to watch and signal if necessary. Your signal system or code will depend on what you want to communicate. To communicate one of two possibilities (*all clear* or *trouble*), all you need is a simple on–off signal. You leave your window dark as long as the coast is clear, and you turn on a flashlight if there is trouble. But you might want a more informative signal. You could arrange with your accomplices to place the light in a different one of the window's four corners depending on the direction from which the trouble was coming. Then, the same light in the same window would communicate more information, because there are more alternative possibilities. In information theory, the structure of the situation—its possibilities—is what matters. These define both uncertainty and information. Table 5.3 elaborates our example.

TABLE 5.3
An Example Illustrating That Information Transmission is
Determined by the Structure of the Situation

You are the lookout for a band of robbers. You are to signal danger with a flashlight from a window across from a bank.

Here are three codes you might use. Notice that the Message (Signal) does not change, but its meaning does.

		Message	*Meaning*
1. *Code*		Steady light in	There's trouble
Light *off* if all is clear		upper right-hand	
Light *on* if trouble		corner of window	
2. Light *off* if all clear			
Light *on* if trouble			
Placement of light in			
window tells direction			
from which trouble is			
coming:			
upper left	= north		
upper right	= east	Steady light in	Trouble is coming from
lower left	= south	upper right-hand	the east
lower right	= west	corner of window	
3. Light *off* if all clear			
Light *on* if trouble			
Direction of trouble:			
upper left	= north		
upper right	= east		
lower left	= south		
lower right	= west		
If police: Steady light			
If someone else: Flashing light			
		Steady light in	The police are coming
		upper right-hand	from the east
		corner of window	

Moral: The light transmits different amounts of information for the three codes because of the number of alternative signals in each, because of their uncertainties.

A. Information Theory and Choice Reaction Time

Long before Shannon's information theory, Donders had shown that the time needed for a B reaction increased with the number of alternatives (Donders, 1868/1969). Similarly, Merkel (1885) found that CRT increased logarithmically with the number of alternatives. The relevance of these data to psychology was established in the 1950s when two investigators, on opposite sides of the Atlantic, performed essentially the same experiment to test information theory. A scientific law was named for the one who published his data first.

According to Hick's law, choice reaction time increases as a logarithmic function of the number of alternatives. Hick (1952) used himself as a subject and varied the number of lights from 1 to 10, using up to 10 fingers for reaction-time responses. His data are plotted in Fig. 5.1 against an abscissa (horizontal axis) showing the number of alternatives (n) plus one. These numbers are spaced logarithmically, and the CRT data fall on a straight line. In other words, CRT is a linear function of informational uncertainty. By using Formula 5.3 you could compute the uncertainty in bits from the number of alternatives (n).

Hyman's (1953) contribution was to demonstrate that CRT is a function of the amount of information, not simply the log of the number of alternatives. He did this by varying uncertainty in three ways. In Experiment I, he varied the number of equally likely alternatives, as Hick had done. In Experiment II, some alternatives were more probable than others because they were presented more frequently. Recall that uncertainty changes with the alternatives' probabilities (equation 5.4). Experiment III varied probability by sequential dependencies; subjects knew that certain alternatives were more likely to occur after certain sequences. Figure 5.2 shows Hyman's results for four separate subjects. The abscissa shows informational uncertainty in bits as computed appropriately from the different experiments. Notice that all four subjects show about the same relationship between CRT and information. It is information, not the sheer number of alternatives, that controls CRT.

Despite their simplicity, the experiments by Hick and Hyman became cornerstones of the information-processing paradigm. They chipped away at the associationistic tenets of neobehaviorism and set the stage for important new advances from other reaction-time experiments. To see how Hick and Hyman undermined associationism, consider the puzzle that results from viewing the speed of CRT response as the result of learning an S–R

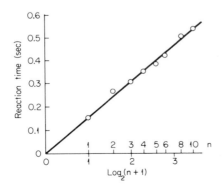

FIG. 5.1. Data from a choice-reaction experiment by Hick (1952).

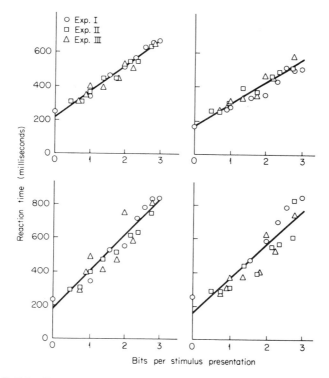

FIG. 5.2.   Four people's reaction times plotted against stimulus information (expressed in bits). Information is varied differently in each experiment (Hyman, 1953).

connection. There is no doubt that the people who participated in Hick's and Hyman's experiments learned stimulus–response relations. And they were given considerable practice, which assured strong associative bonds. But the S–R analysis had nothing to say about the effect of information itself. This can be seen by comparing two-choice and four-choice CRT tasks as in Fig. 5.3. In the four-choice task, when light number three comes on, the subject responds with the right index finger. This same stimulus–response relation occurs in the two-choice task. The puzzle is why in the four-choice task the response is slower. Information theorists resolved the puzzle with the notion of uncertainty. Response speed depends on what could have happened, but did not. This was a new idea for experimental psychology, and associationism had difficulty incorporating it.

The fact that CRT increases with information load was viewed by information theorists as evidence that people have limited channel capacity. Because the relationship between uncertainty and CRT is linear, the implication is that people process a fixed amount of information per unit of

TWO ALTERNATIVES

2 STIMULI
(LIGHTS)

2 RESPONSES
(KEYS)

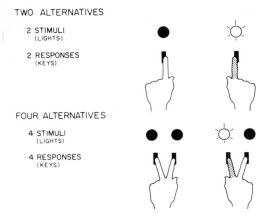

FOUR ALTERNATIVES

4 STIMULI
(LIGHTS)

4 RESPONSES
(KEYS)

FIG. 5.3. Illustration of CRT tasks with two and four alternatives. The same stimulus is lighted in both tasks, and the correct response is made on the same key with the same index finger. The difference in reaction time for the tasks is due to the number of alternative stimuli and responses that could have been tested.

time, and that fixed amount is their channel limit. Also, the information theory approach exemplified by Hick and Hyman viewed the human as a passive information channel, which amounted to a denial that interesting processes go on internally. Therefore, much information-theoretic reaction-time research emphasized precise quantification of the stimulus and determination of the limits of the human transmission channel. These are functionalist emphases. Welford (1976) criticized this functionalism when he argued that the information metric "has proved a convenient unit for describing and comparing a wide range of experimental conditions and performances, without having any truly explanatory value [p. 57]." By Welford's view, true explanation would require abandoning the idea of a passive channel in favor of the idea that people actively process information. By about 1960, many reaction-time experimenters had abandoned the passive channel analogy in favor of the active computer analogy. We illustrate this evolution with two of the many sorts of CRT research that came after Hick (1952) and Hyman (1953).

B. Binary Decisions

Leonard (1958) turned the information theory formalism for calculating uncertainty into a hypothesis about cognitive decision making. He reasoned that if CRT increased by one unit every time the alternatives were doubled, then perhaps people make high-speed binary decisions, each of which rules out half of the alternatives. Suppose you were confronted with a string of eight lights and the seventh light from the left came on. In order to decide which of eight keys to press, you might first determine whether it should be one of the four on the left or one of the four on the right. Then among the four on the right, you might decide whether the first two or the second two are correct. When you have narrowed it down to two, you could make one last decision to arrive at the correct response. Thus, there are three hypothetical decisions—and also 3 bits of uncertainty. The idea that people often think this way now sounds implausible, but it seemed worth testing when information theory was a dominant guide to psychological research. Notice that 6 years passed after Hyman's work before Leonard translated the information-theory formalism into an experiment to seek a psychological process. Most psychologists were not yet looking for cognitive mechanisms.

Leonard (1958) began by comparing three-choice to six-choice stimulus displays, much as Hyman did. In the three-choice situation, three lights came on and then one went off. The subject had to give the response that corresponded to the light that went off. The six-choice situation was very similar. Six lights came on, one went off, and the subject had to give the correct signal response as soon as possible. A correct CRT took .294 seconds in the three-choice condition and .339 seconds in the six-choice condition. As the alternatives doubled from three to six, the CRT increased by .045 seconds. If Hick's law were due to successive binary decisions, then .045 seconds would seem to be the time needed for a single decision. The novel part of Leonard's experiment tested this idea.

To determine whether people solve CRT problems with binary decisions, Leonard employed a condition whose purpose was to eliminate the need for one of the hypothetical decisions. First, six lights came on, then three went off, then one more went off. In other words, the hypothetical binary decision between six and three lights was made for the subject by the experimenter. Because the earlier portions of this experiment indicated that each binary decision took .045 seconds, Leonard allowed just that amount of time between the onset of six lights and the turning off of three of them. If his hypothesis about binary decisions underlying CRT was correct, he should have found that CRT measured from the time when the three lights were turned off was the same as the CRTs in the original three-light condition. This was not the case: People performed more slowly in this successive condition than in the simple three-alternative condition. The logic of Leonard's experiment is not airtight, but his results do not support the idea that people employ underlying binary decisions to solve CRT problems.

Leonard's experiment is an early illustration of the use of hypotheses about internal cognitive processes to guide psychological experimentation. The fact that Leonard failed to isolate any such mechanism is less important than the fact that he tried to. His effort is illustrative of an important step along the road toward the information-processing approach to cognition. It is an example of reaction-time researchers seeking cognitive explanations for their data.

Notice that Leonard's results do not invalidate Hick's law. They simply show that his law applies to the structure of information rather than to the mental processes that handle that information. This lesson is reemphasized in our consideration of psycholinguistics. Scientists can and should build formal systems for characterizing the structure of situations, as Chomsky did for language and Shannon did for communication. But there is no guarantee that those formal descriptive systems will also describe the mental processes that people use in the situations.

C. Cognitive Inference and Information

Fitts and Switzer (1962) moved the field closer to the contemporary information-processing approach by illustrating the flexibility of cognition, thereby questioning the passive channel idea. In their CRT experiment, subjects watched for and then named numerals as quickly as possible. Fitts and Switzer used three stimulus conditions. In the first condition, the subjects watched for the digits 1 and 2. The second condition also had two digits: 2 and 7. Condition 3 had eight digits: 1–8. Note that the numeral 2 occurred in all three conditions and that the first and second conditions had 1 bit of uncertainty, but the third condition had 3 bits.

Fitts and Switzer's results are shown in Fig. 5.4. On the vertical or Y-axis, we show reaction time to name the critical item, 2. Note that we have the same stimulus and the same response in all three conditions. The X-axis shows the effect of practice: All participants served in three experimental sessions. In the first session, the reaction time to a 2 was no faster in the 2 and 7 condition than it was in the 1–8 condition. Although there were only two alternatives, subjects responded as if there were eight. CRTs were significantly faster in the 1 and 2 situation. With practice, CRT in the 2 and 7 condition speeded up, and approached the speed of the 1 and 2 condition. The inference is that people began the experiment believing that the 2 and 7 set was larger than two digits; they treated it mentally as if it were a set of eight items. As the experiment progressed, they learned to treat the 2 and 7 condition as if it had fewer digits. The conclusion is that the effects of uncertainty depend not on how large the stimulus set actually is, but rather on how large the subjects infer it to be. Such results question the fixed channel notion and put the interesting psychological questions inside the head of the subject, not in the careful quantification of stimulus parameters.

Figure 5.4 shows that Fitts and Switzer's subjects never decreased their CRTs in the 2 and 7 condition all the way to their CRTs in the 1 and 2 condition. Data from Mowbray and Rhoades (1959) indicate that more practice would have eliminated the remaining difference. They gave one heroic subject 45,000 trials on two- and four-choice reaction time tasks. The experiment began in January and ended in May, and even after 5 months of practice on this simple task, the subject's performance continued to improve.

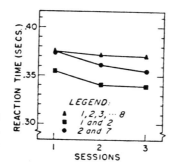

FIG. 5.4. Reaction times to the numeral 2 when it occurred as a member of three sets of numerals (Fitts & Switzer, 1962).

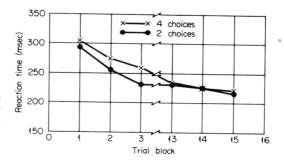

FIG. 5.5. Mean choice reaction times for two choices and four choices as a function of the number of trials (Mowbray & Rhoades, 1959).

The results are summarized in Fig. 5.5. Each data point on the graph is a mean of 500 CRTs. It is clear not only that CRT continued to improve with practice, but also that the difference between two and four choices disappeared.

Mowbray and Rhoades' (1959) major conclusion was that the "human observer is adaptable [p. 22]." This notion of flexible processing is inconsistent with the analogy of man as a passive communication channel, but it later found a congenial home in the computer analogy. Their data also suggest that Hick's law holds only for unpracticed subjects. That conclusion has been disputed, for under some conditions no amount of practice seems to eliminate the uncertainty effect. But the point stands that there are conditions under which skills follow different principles after much practice. The implication for psychological research is captured in this question: Could it be that everyday language skills, which are highly practiced, operate according to different principles from those studied in the laboratory after only a little practice? Of course! That likelihood is one of the factors that dictate the caution and care that cognitive scientists exercise in the interpretation of their experiments. Their conservatism, which can frustrate and confound laymen and students, has a factual basis.

IV. ENGINEERING PSYCHOLOGY

To trace the development of the information-processing paradigm further, we turn now to engineering psychology, which grew out of psychologists' involvement in World War II. Engineering psychology is concerned with the general problem of the human/machine interaction. Machines need to be designed to maximize the efficiency of the human operator. The machine must capitalize on human information-processing strengths, and accommodate itself to the limitations of the human operator. As our society has become increasingly technological, more psychologists have worked to accommodate machines to people. They generally call themselves Human Factors Engineers. They work in the communications industry, for automobile and airplane manufacturers, for medical instrumentation firms, and so on.

For an example of human factors engineering, consider your telephone. The top panel in Fig. 5.6 shows how a telephone looked before World War II. It had both letters and digits inside the finger holes. Such a dial was undesirable, because much of the information was difficult to see at various visual angles. The middle panel shows an experimental dial that solves this problem. The digits and letters have been put next to the holes and are easy to

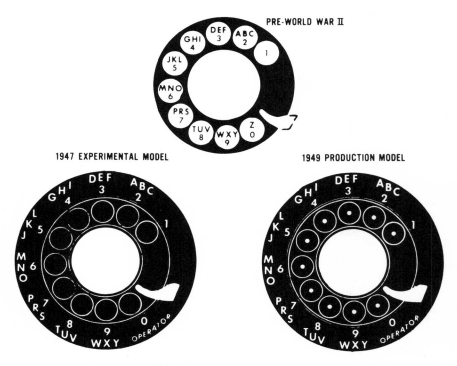

FIG. 5.6.   Three telephone dials.

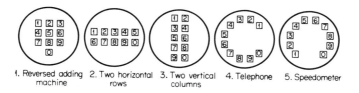

1. Reversed adding   2. Two horizontal   3. Two vertical   4. Telephone   5. Speedometer
   machine   rows   columns

FIG. 5.7.   Push-button arrangements of telephone key sets used experimentally. On the basis of combined considerations of keying time, errors, and expressed preferences of subjects, the first design was selected (Deininger, 1960).

see. However, the experimental dial has another problem: It consumes a second longer to dial a number than the earlier version. A second may at first seem to be very short and inconsequential, but multiply it by the number of calls you make in your lifetime. The phone company must multiply that second by the 500,000,000 calls that are made on an average business day. That figures out to about 140,000 hours and would necessitate the addition of extra transmission capacity. Taking a second off of the dialing time would save time for people and save money for the phone company. J. E. Karlin of Bell Telephone Laboratories performed an evaluation of dialing and proposed that the dial be redesigned as shown in the bottom panel of Fig. 5.6. The change is both simple and elegant: White dots were put in the finger holes. The dots give the dialer a target to aim at while the dial is spinning. They allow anticipation of the next number to be dialed. The effect is to reduce dialing time by one second.

The conversion of telephones from dials to push buttons created problems, too. The basic configuration of the touch-tone telephone is likely to be with us for many years. Is it the best of all possible configurations? To answer this question, Deininger (1960) conducted research at Bell Laboratories. He tested several configurations, shown in Fig. 5.7. He measured speed of touch dialing, number of errors, and people's preference. Configuration 4 was fastest, and configuration 3 caused fewest errors. But configuration 1 best combined speed, accuracy, and preference. Deininger's results will affect us for years to come. Consider, now, how human factors research advanced psychology toward the information-processing paradigm. It did so largely by studying choice reaction time.

A. Man/Machine Compatibility

Whenever humans interact with machines, there is the question of how well they go together. Sometimes the compatibility question can be answered intuitively. It would be silly to design an automobile so that turning the steering wheel clockwise made the car go left. Common sense also says that the windshield wiper control should be within reach of the driver. Subtler

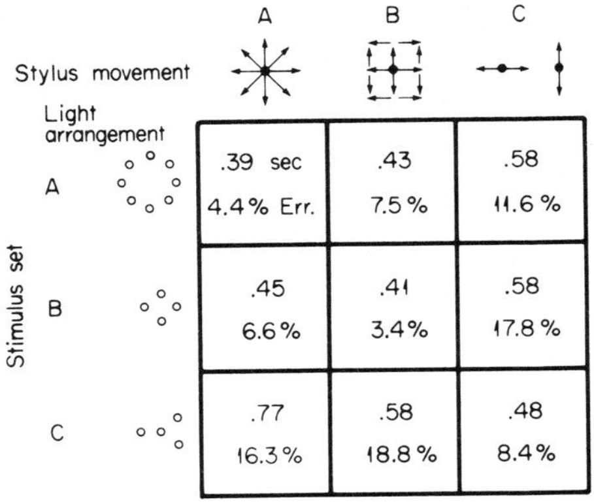

		A	B	C
Stimulus set	A	.39 sec 4.4% Err.	.43 7.5%	.58 11.6%
	B	.45 6.6%	.41 3.4%	.58 17.8%
	C	.77 16.3%	.58 18.8%	.48 8.4%

FIG. 5.8. Reaction time and percent errors for different combinations of stimuli and responses (Fitts & Seeger, 1953).

relationships require laboratory study, partly because of a consideration highlighted by Fitts and Seeger's (1953) CRT experiment on compatibility.

Fitts and Seeger gave their subjects the 9 combinations of three stimulus sets and three response sets illustrated in Fig. 5.8. Across the top are three different ways of responding by pressing a lever to stop the reaction-time clock. Response A required the subjects to move the lever outward to one of eight points on a circle. This response is most compatible with the A configuration of lights. Response B, however, fits stimulus set B the best. For that set the lever had to be moved in one of four directions. Response C required the movement of two hands and worked best with stimulus configuration C. The table shows CRT and error percents for the various combinations. The data show no one best stimulus configuration and no best response pattern. Optimal performance for a response set depends on which stimulus is used.

The notion of compatibility has a deeper meaning than the fit between different stimulus and response patterns. Welford (1968) restated the compatibility problem as one of translation. Internal cognitive translation intervenes between stimuli and responses. Some translations seem built-in; others are learned and initially require much attention and thought—such as typing or driving a car. Either way, the study of cognition is necessary for understanding human skills (Welford, 1968). Recognizing this was a part of the evolution of cognitive psychology.

B. Psychological Refractory Period

Skills such as steering an automobile require constant readjustment on the basis of feedback. They require numerous successive decisions. Human engineers have studied the dynamics of such successive responding by giving people two reaction-time tasks in rapid succession. One stimulus and its response is followed by a second stimulus, requiring a different response. The response to the second stimulus is usually slower than it would have been without the first. This slowing is called the psychological refractory period. Research on the refractory period began early (Craik, 1948, 1949) and continues to this day.

The psychological refractory period seems to reflect an internal or central limit on human performance. Even with extended practice and highly compatible stimulus–response arrangements, the phenomenon shows itself (see, Smith, 1967). Whenever two stimulus presentations are timed properly, people respond more slowly to the second one, suggesting an inherent human capacity limit. The notion of human limits remains central to cognitive psychology, and it arose partly out of human engineering research.

V. DECOMPOSING MENTAL PROCESSES

In 1968, E. E. Smith published a remarkable integration of research on choice reaction time. He reviewed diverse studies and fit them together. Looking back, we can see that Smith's basic facts came from information theory experiments, human engineering studies, straightforward functionalist research, and sophisticated mathematical modeling experiments. His synthesis was an information-processing framework that encompassed all of these disparate elements. Though out of date in certain respects, Smith's (1968) paper still repays study. He conceptualized a sequence of mental events intervening between CRT stimulus presentation and response. The sequence had four stages:

1. The raw stimulus is *preprocessed*, making a clear representation for later processing;
2. The stimulus representation is compared with items in memory until it is *categorized*;
3. The categorization is used as a basis for *response selection*;
4. The subject then programs his *response execution*.

Smith's division of the CRT task into four discrete mental stages illustrates the essence of information-processing psychology. His paper is an excellent example of how the computer analogy can clarify theoretical ideas. Suppose we gave you a computer program and asked you to tell how it works. Your best strategy would be to divide it into components. You could then analyze each subprogram, and understand the overall process by combining the components. When a computer executes a program, no matter how rapidly, it goes through a sequence of operations. These sequences can be divided into stages or subprograms in order to make the complete program understandable. Smith's CRT framework illustrates how cognitive psychologists can use this strategy to understand people's information processing.

A. Sternberg's Serial Exhaustive Model

Sternberg's research provided an important impetus to the information-processing analysis of choice reaction time. His experimentation was an important factor in the increasing psychological concern with the study of mental processes.

1. Sternberg's Task

Sternberg first described his deceptively simple task at a convention in 1963 (he called it an item recognition task). On a typical trial he gave the subject a small group of digits to memorize; these are called the positive set, and different positive sets have different numbers of digits. He then presented a single digit, called the test stimulus, for the subject's reaction. If you were the subject, and if the test stimulus was a member of the positive set, you should respond *Yes*. If the test stimulus was not from the positive set, but rather was a member of the negative set, you should respond *No*. People are cautioned to perform this task as fast as they can without making errors. To gain a feel for the task, have a friend give you the four trials in Table 5.4.

If you actually served as a subject in a Sternberg experiment, you would feel that your responses were almost instantaneous. Especially after a little

TABLE 5.4
Four Trials of the Sternberg Task from a Subject's Point of View

	Trial 1	*Trial 2*	*Trial 3*	*Trial 4*
Positive set (Hold this list in memory.)	2,7	9	3,7,6	8,5,2,9,1,3
Test stimulus (Did this item occur in the positive set?)	2	8	7	4
Correct response (You indicate your response by pressing one of two keys.)	YES	NO	YES	NO
Typical CRT (See Fig. 5.9 for real data.)	480 msec	440 msec	520 msec	640 msec

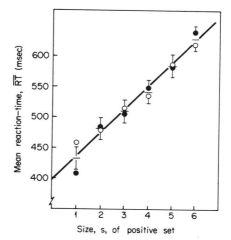

FIG. 5.9. Results from item-recognition experiment (Sternberg, 1966). Mean latencies of positive responses (filled circles) and negative responses (open circles) as functions of size of positive set.

practice, the task seems to tap automatic processes. But Sternberg's results show that the processing takes time. Typical results are shown in Fig. 5.9. Reaction times in milliseconds are shown along the ordinate (vertical axis), and the size of the positive set is plotted on the abscissa (horizontal axis). Notice first that CRT increases with the size of the positive set. Second, CRT is a linear function of positive set size. For every digit added to the positive set, there is a fixed increase in CRT. Third, CRT is much the same for *Yes* and *No* responses. In Fig. 5.9, positive and negative responses are designated by the closed and open circles, respectively. Because the *Yes* and *No* responses took about equally long, they have been averaged together to derive a single best-fitting line.

2. Exhaustive Scanning

To explain his results, Sternberg postulated an exhaustive memory search, during which a mental representation of the test digit is compared serially and very rapidly to memorial representations of each digit in the positive set. Sternberg called the search *exhaustive* to indicate that people compare the test digit to all of the items in the positive set before responding. Here is his logic. People respond very accurately to item recognition tests. In order to say *No* accurately, they must check a negative test item against each positive item, because they are never told the items in the negative set. Because it takes them as long to say *Yes* as to say *No*, they evidently also search all of the items when the test digit comes from the positive set. The idea that people search completely through a memory set, instead of stopping when they locate the item they are looking for, does not seem to square with common experience. If you were looking for a book in a library, surely you would stop when you found it. You would not examine every book unless the one you were seeking was the last one you looked at, which would hardly ever be the case. Exhaustive scanning seems contrary to ordinary intuition, and that accounts in part for psychologists' fascination with Sternberg's findings. Well-documented counterintuitive findings attract careful attention.

Exhaustive scanning seems to involve memory comparisons that are unnecessary, but Sternberg argued that the speed of the scanning process made its exhaustiveness more efficient than the self-terminating alternative. He would have called the memory scan self-terminating if, as in the book-seeking example, it stopped when the test item was found in the positive set. How did he infer the speed of the scan?

3. High-Speed Scanning

If each positive set is scanned exhaustively, then the increase in recognition time from smaller to larger positive sets can be used to estimate the speed of scanning a single item in memory. Figure 5.9 shows that each time the positive set is increased by one item, an additional 38 milliseconds of processing time is added. That is, the slope of the straight line relating reaction time to size of the positive set is 38 milliseconds. (The convention is that slopes are expressed as the amount of change on the ordinate per unit on the abscissa.) Given a scan rate of 38 milliseconds per item, approximately 25 items are scanned per second. Sternberg (1966) argued that this rate of scanning far exceeds the rate of deciding whether a scanned item matches a test item. That is, Sternberg supposed that deciding whether a test item matches an item in the positive set takes more time than scanning an item, so that it would be inefficient to decide one at a time for each item in the positive set. It would be more efficient to scan them all rapidly (38 msec per item) and then make one decision about matching at the end. Indeed, some computers for telephone switching employ such exhaustive scanning precisely because it is faster (see Sternberg, 1975). And there are other examples of mechanical and physiological processes running on longer than seems necessary. When a propeller-driven airplane lands, the pilot does not stop its engine immediately. He lets his engine slow gradually, because it would require more energy to stop it quickly than is used by letting it run down. The bodily arousal occasioned by fright, as when one narrowly avoids an automobile accident, often persists well after the danger has passed. So, while exhaustive memory scanning seems counterintuitive, it does have analogues outside of the cognitive domain.

B. Additive Factor Method

Sternberg's inference that memory scanning takes 38 msec per item illustrates Donders' subtraction method. Given a CRT of 434 msec for a one-item positive set and a CRT of 472 msec for a two-item set, the estimate of 38 msec per item is obtained by subtraction. Using the slope of the CRT function to estimate comparison times is a subtractive procedure.

Sternberg (1969a, 1969b) pointed out that the assumptions of the subtraction method are often invalid, particularly the assumption of pure insertion. In Sternberg's experiments, the assumption of pure insertion amounts to supposing that varying positive set size influences scanning alone, and that it has no influence on rate of stimulus preprocessing or response execution. The general idea is that each experimental variable affects only one kind of cognitive process, and this assumption is often wrong (Pachella, 1974; Teichner & Krebs, 1974). Therefore, equation 5.1 is not generally valid.

Sternberg's alternative to the subtractive method is the additive factor method. Its goal is to convergently validate the existence of distinct information-processing stages, rather than to determine the speed with which the various processes work, which was the goal of the subtractive method. Massaro (1975) suggested, and we agree, that abandoning the effort to precisely quantify processing speed is no great sacrifice. It seems more important to determine the nature of psychological processes than to measure how long they take.

Like Donders' subtractive procedure, Sternberg's additive factor method depends on the notion of stages of information processing. He posits four sequential stages, which are similar to those proposed by Smith (1968). Sternberg's four stages are shown in Fig. 5.10. When a test stimulus is presented, it is first encoded. The encoded representation is then compared to memory representations of the items in the positive set. This memory scan is said to be serial and exhaustive. Following the scan comes a *Yes–No* decision as to whether the test item was from the positive set. The final stage is to translate the decision into a performable response.

Specifying a stage model, like the one in Fig. 5.10, is a prerequisite of the additive factor method. Another is to identify the hypothesized stages with different dependent variables and with different experimental manipulations. Thus, stage 2 of Sternberg's model, the memory scan, is identified with the slope of the line relating set size to reaction time, a dependent variable, and with the size of the positive set, an experimental manipulation. The remaining three stages—stimulus encoding, binary decision, and response organization—are reflected in the times for all positive sets. They add together with scanning time to determine reaction time. To estimate how long these three stages take together, the line connecting all positive set sizes is extended to the

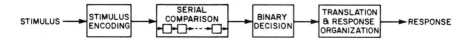

FIG. 5.10.   Sternberg's serial exhaustive model of item recognition.

left, until it hits the vertical axis of the graph, which is located at the zero point on the horizontal axis. The vertical or Y-axis is theoretically located at the point where no memory scanning takes place; so the place where the slope function intercepts the Y-axis provides an estimate of how long it takes to encode a test stimulus, make a binary decision, and organize a response. In Fig. 5.9, the Y-intercept is equal to about 400 msec. The mechanics of the additive factor method are illustrated by the ways in which Sternberg worked to decompose this conglomerate Y-intercept value into its component stages and to separate them from memory scanning. He identified different experimental manipulations with his different processing stages, and examined their effects on the slopes and Y-intercepts of the resulting CRT functions.

A visually degraded stimulus takes longer to react to than a clear one. Sternberg (1967) reasoned that this could be due to the increased difficulty of encoding a visually distorted image. If so, and if people encode the stimulus before beginning their memory scanning, then distorting the test stimuli in a Sternberg task should elevate the Y-intercept but not change the slope of the function relating RT to set size. If, on the other hand, people try to compare the distorted or incompletely encoded stimulus to their memory representations of the undistorted items in the positive set, then the effect of distortion should be to slow down the scan time for each memory comparison, resulting in a steeper slope of the function relating set size to RT. These two alternative possibilities are depicted in Fig. 5.11. In the left panel, the slope of the line for degraded test stimuli is steeper than the slope for undegraded stimuli. These slopes are an example of nonadditive effects. The effect of stimulus degradation is not simply to add a constant to each positive set size. The larger set sizes have more added to them than the smaller ones. In the right panel, the two functions are parallel. Only the Y-intercept is affected. Stimulus degradation increases RT equally for each set size, and this is an example of additive effects.

Sternberg (1967) performed an experiment in which he compared the reaction times of people to distorted and undistorted test stimuli. His findings

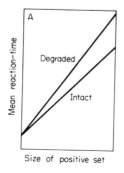

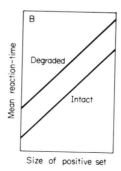

FIG. 5.11. Two possibilities for the effect of test-stimulus quality on the reaction-time function. (A) Quality influences comparison stage only. (B) Quality influences encoding stage only. (From Sternberg, 1969b.)

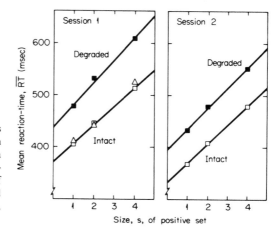

FIG. 5.12. Effect of stimulus quality on item recognition. Mean reaction times, based on pooled data from positive and negative responses as a function of size of positive set for intact and degraded test stimuli. (From Sternberg, 1969b.)

for the first and second sessions of this experiment are shown in Fig. 5.12. The data on the left are from the first session. There is a clear intercept effect, indicating that degraded stimuli take longer to encode. But there is also a slope effect. The slope is steeper for degraded stimuli, suggesting that test stimuli were not encoded completely before the memory scan. These data are not additive. But during the second session (right-hand panel of Fig. 5.12), the slopes for degraded and intact stimuli were the same. With practice, stimulus degradation affected only the Y-intercept. By the logic of the additive factor method, different processing stages can be inferred when experimental variables have additive effects. During session 2, the effects of stimulus degradation and positive set size did add simply together, allowing the conclusion that stimulus encoding and memory scanning are distinct and successive stages of processing.

Varied application of the additive factor method allows convergent validation of different cognitive processes. The idea is to show that various manipulations combine additively. As a general rule, when two variables have additive effects, they are acting on different stages of processing.

Sternberg (1971) stresses the generality and power of the additive factor method, arguing that it can be applied to a wide range of psychological problems. For example, much of the experimental research on psychopathology can be summarized by saying that abnormal people do worse than normal ones. While some psychologists would consider this an unfair characterization of an important research area, it is true that research on abnormal behavior has not been as analytic as it might have been. But Checkosky (see Sternberg, 1975) has shown the power of the additive factor method and the relevance of information-processing approaches to clinical psychology. He administered Sternberg's task to hospitalized schizophrenics and alcoholics. In Fig. 5.13, their performance is compared to that of normal

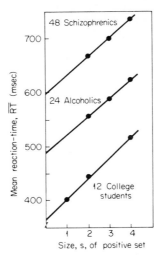

FIG. 5.13. Results from item-recognition experiments with three groups of subjects. Overall mean reaction times as functions of size of positive set, and lines fitted by least squares. Data for schizophrenics (average hospitalization, 15 months) and alcoholics (average hospitalization 8 months) from a study by S. F. Checkosky (Sternberg, 1975).

adults. The abnormal people performed worse overall, but the slopes of the three CRT functions are remarkably similar. High-speed memory scanning is evidently not one of the cognitive processes adversely affected by psychopathology; and by manipulating variables known to affect the other processes in Sternberg's model, one could gain a more analytic view of the cognitive effects of schizophrenia and alcoholism.

C. Criticisms of Sternberg's Model

Over the past decade it has sometimes seemed as though half of the cognitive psychologists in North America were devoting themselves to testing Sternberg's theory. His basic results have been replicated many times, but the mass of data has also provided bases for much criticism of his notions. In this section we give you the flavor of the criticisms that have been directed at Sternberg's model, while trying to avoid belaboring minor squabbles of transient interest.

1. Alternate Models

Several scientists have proposed mathematical models to explain item recognition with concepts directly opposed to Sternberg's. One of Sternberg's notions is that the memory scan is serial, rather than parallel, by which he means that each memory representation is scanned completely before the scan of the next begins. In an earlier chapter we illustrated the distinction between serial and parallel processing in telegraphy. You may also think of the construction of a house. Building a foundation and putting up walls are necessarily serial, for one cannot be done until the other is completed. But putting in the electrical wiring and plumbing, as well as shingling the roof, can all go on simultaneously—that is, in parallel. Sternberg concluded that item-recognition memory searches are serial because each one-item increase in set size results in the same increase in RT. His conclusion seems reasonable, for if there were some parallel scanning, each additional item added to the positive set should result in successively smaller increases in RT. But because there is no direct evidence on the matter, it is possible to dispute this inference, as Townsend (1974) has. He described a number of models of underlying cognitive processes, all of which account for Sternberg's data, and one of which assumes parallel processing. Similarly, Theios (1973) built a simulation of the processes underlying performance on Sternberg's task. The model incorporated a self-terminating mechanism, rather than Sternberg's exhaustive mechanism. The point is that many theoretical views might account for any particular collection of data, and judgmental considerations determine which model is used. For the findings we have so far described, the preponderance of the evidence seems to fit best with Sternberg's theory (see Fig. 5.10). But there are other findings.

2. Unpredicted Results

Here are a few findings not easily accounted for by Sternberg's model: (a) If the items in the positive set are words from different conceptual categories, people search exhaustively within categories—stopping with the category containing the item, instead of searching every category in the positive set (Naus, Glucksberg, & Ornstein, 1972). (b) If people are given extensive practice recognizing simple multidimensional stimuli, the slope of the CRT function is reduced to zero (Dumas, 1972). (c) When the probability of tests for items in the positive set is unequal, reaction times are faster to more probable items (Theios, Smith, Haviland, Traupman, & Moy, 1973). (d) When an item is repeated in the positive set, reaction times to it are unusually short (Baddeley & Ecob, 1973).

Some of these results can be handled by modifying Sternberg's theory. For example, Biederman and Stacy (1974) argue that probability effects can be explained as changes in response selection, which leaves intact the main feature of Sternberg's model—serial-exhaustive scanning. We also see in the next section how Baddeley and Ecob's (1973) results can be incorporated into a model that encompasses Sternberg's (Atkinson & Juola, 1974). Nevertheless, Sternberg's serial-exhaustive model is not general. Under one set of experimental circumstances, it works well, but when Sternberg's basic task is varied, his model breaks down. This does not mean the theory is valueless. Humans process information differently in different experimental situations, just as they do in different natural situations. No theory has yet been built to encompass behavior in all situations. The challenge to psychologists is to formulate rules that specify the situations to which particular theories of underlying processes are relevant.

D. Sternberg's Contribution

Within its domain, the serial-exhaustive model of memory scanning is an elegant theory. Its elegance excited large numbers of experimental psychologists, and it encouraged them to believe that mental processes could be measured with reaction time. Sternberg's research methods and theories prompted much research that depended not at all on neobehavioristic presuppositions. It depended instead on a simple computer analogy and the notion that unobservable cognitive states could be rigorously studied. And by elaborating the additive factor method, he demonstrated a widely applicable technique of convergent validation.

VI. SPEED–ACCURACY TRADE-OFF

The research of Sternberg and others shows that even seemingly simple tasks, like those studied in CRT experiments, depend on complex cognitive processes. And the story is even more complicated, as people like Paul Fitts have shown. Fitts established the area of investigation now called the study of human performance. He founded the Human Performance Center at the University of Michigan, where some of today's most prominent information-processing researchers obtained their doctoral degrees. One of his many experiments (Fitts, 1966) showed that people balance speed and accuracy against one another when they perform reaction-time tasks, which vastly complicated the interpretation of CRT research. It also vastly broadened cognitive psychologists' conception of how cognition works. Fitts (1966) gave different instructions to three different groups of people before giving them a reaction-time task. People in the *speed* group were told they would earn extra money for fast responses, while people in the *accuracy* group were to be paid extra for being correct. People in the third group were given ambiguous instructions and paid a flat rate. People in the accuracy and speed groups were given immediate feedback on their performance; the control group was not. The reaction-time and error data are summarized in Fig. 5.14. The speed group was fastest, but made the most errors. The accuracy group was slowest, but made the fewest errors. The control group was intermediate on both speed and accuracy.

Fitts' experiment, like many others, shows that people adjust their performance cognitively. If money is involved, they go faster. Or they go more slowly, if that is what you are buying. But notice that increasing speed costs

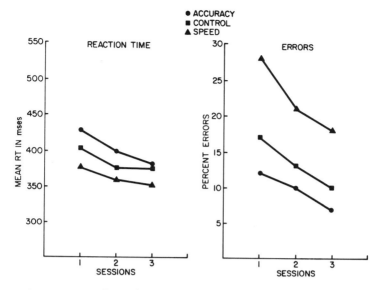

FIG. 5.14.   The effects of speed and accuracy instructions on reaction time and errors in three experimental sessions (Fitts, 1966).

errors, and increasing accuracy costs time. People trade off time against errors, and vice versa. Where they place the balance between time and accuracy depends on motivation, bias, belief and so on. Fitts (1966) called these things together *cognitive set*.

Pachella (1974) summarized the speed–accuracy relation graphically. Along the abscissa of Fig. 5.15 he plotted reaction time (for no experiment in particular). Consider the value marked "fast" to be something like 100 msec, and the value marked "slow" to be 2 seconds. On that time line it is

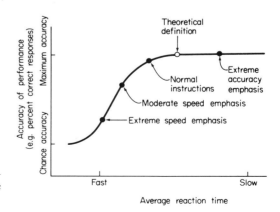

FIG. 5.15.   An idealized speed–accuracy operating characteristic (Pachella, 1974).

theoretically possible to have a CRT of zero. That is, you could anticipate the stimulus on a trial and respond just as it occurs. It is also possible to go to the other extreme. You could take half an hour to decide which button to push. Which you do will influence your accuracy, shown on the ordinate of Pachella's graph (Fig. 5.15).

Pachella's graph is called a speed–accuracy operating characteristic (Pew, 1969). It shows an idealized relationship between speed and accuracy: As speed decreases (left-to-right), so do errors (bottom-to-top). We are sure that this aspect of Fig. 5.15 squares with your experience. Suppose you were trying to find *Dear Abby* in the morning paper. Flipping through the pages at top speed would get you there quickest, unless you went so fast you missed the column and had to start over again. Going through the paper slowly and methodically, checking each page thoroughly, may make you late for lunch, but you will find Abby the first time through. College tests require that you make speed versus accuracy decisions. What do you do when there are more questions than you can answer in 50 minutes? Answering as fast as possible may be best, if all that matters is number correct. But if the professor penalizes errors, you may have to go more slowly to maximize your grade.

From the vantage of CRT researchers, the most important aspect of Pachella's graph is the discrepancy between reaction time to normal instructions and the theoretical definition. Normal CRT instructions call for people to respond as fast as they can without making any errors. The theoretical definition is the point of fastest responding when no errors are made; it is the point that represents people's processing limit. The two are not the same. In response to normal instructions, people are typically 97% correct. Pachella's graph shows an appreciable reaction-time difference if accuracy drops only 3% between 97% and 100% (remember that 100% accuracy is the theoretical ideal). Are actual experimental conditions close enough to the ideal? (Would we ask, if they were?) Pachella's graph shows that normal CRT instructions result in reaction times that overestimate people's capacity, which estimation was the purpose of much CRT research.

The absolute value of any reaction time has to be interpreted with respect to its associated error rate, which markedly complicates the work of researchers who wish to interpret CRT differences in terms of information-processing mechanisms. The problem is to rule out the possibility that observed CRT differences are the result of the various factors that cause speed–accuracy trade-offs. Only after ruling out that possibility can the experimenter attribute CRT differences to changes in the information-processing mechanisms his conditions were intended to influence.

Table 5.5 shows four different CRT and error patterns that might result from three different experimental conditions. In example A there is a CRT difference between the three conditions that cannot be attributed to the speed–accuracy trade-off. Accuracy is the same in all three conditions. With results like this, an experimenter can safely conclude that his conditions affected some process other than those that determine the speed–accuracy trade-off. If he chose his conditions well, he should be able to attribute his observed differences to particular cognitive processes. Example B shows the same CRT data as example A, but they are not interpretable as anything other than speed–accuracy effects. Example B's condition 3 is the slowest, but it is also the most accurate. Condition 1 is the fastest, but it has the most errors. Condition 2 is intermediate. This is the pattern of results summarized by Pachella's speed–accuracy operating characteristic (Fig. 5.15). To determine whether these three conditions produced interpretable CRT differences, one would have to correct the CRTs of conditions 1 and 3 by however many milliseconds are equal to four percentage points of error. He would have to combine CRT and error information.

Information theorists (e.g., Hick, 1952) use a complex formula for combining CRT and error information. It measures information transmitted. We do not present the information-transmission metric as a solution to the speed–accuracy problem. It is based on the conception that humans are passive communication channels, which they are not. A more promising approach is to construct speed–accuracy operating characteristics, by varying people's mental set and deriving empirical functions similar to the idealized one presented in Fig. 5.15. Having done that, one can estimate the theoretical ideal from his data. But this process is time-consuming and, for some purposes, unnecessary.

Consider the data in example C of Table 5.5. The fastest condition is the most accurate; the slowest is the least accurate. This relationship between speed and accuracy is exactly the opposite of the one that would result from trading speed for accuracy. It is a rather common finding in psychological

TABLE 5.5
Hypothetical CRT Data With Associated Error Rates

	Condition		
	1	2	3
A. CRT increases	500 msec	600 msec	700 msec
Errors are constant	5%	5%	5%
B. CRT increases	500 msec	600 msec	700 msec
Errors decrease	9%	5%	1%
C. CRT increases	500 msec	600 msec	700 msec
Errors increase	1%	5%	9%
D. CRT increases	500 msec	600 msec	700 msec
Errors constant at zero	0%	0%	0%

experiments. Experimental conditions that interfere with cognition often slow responding and increase errors at the same time. Conversely, those that facilitate cognition often speed responding and reduce errors. So the experimenter whose CRT data fall like those in example C can safely infer that his conditions have influenced cognition rather than changed the speed–accuracy trade-off. However, he cannot conclude anything from the *size* of his CRT differences. From the data in example C it would be perfectly legitimate to conclude that conditions 2 and 3 created different cognition, but it would not be appropriate to conclude that the cognitive differences were worth exactly 100 msec in processing time. Such a conclusion would be warranted only when the subject had no errors and was performing at maximum possible speed—that is, at the idealized point on Pachella's graph. Example D in Table 5.5 shows CRT differences with a constant error rate of zero. This does not solve the trade-off problem, for there can be wide variations, due to mental set, in CRT at 100% accuracy.

A. Sternberg Again

Reconsider Sternberg's (1966) data, as shown in Fig. 5.9. CRT is a linear function of the size of the positive set, and error rate is uniform at 1–3%. But many investigators have failed to find such linearity. Rothstein (1973) listed 39 experiments that show significantly nonlinear functions between RT and set size. Many of these results stem from varying important aspects of the Sternberg task, but differential error rates account for some of the nonlinearities.

Figure 5.16 shows data that might come from an item recognition experiment of the Sternberg type. The error rates are shown as bars along the abscissa and refer to the right ordinate. The CRT data are not linear. They are negatively accelerated, which means that the slope increases less as the function moves from left to right. These data differ from Sternberg's (1966). But consider errors, which increase with set size. What if the error rates had

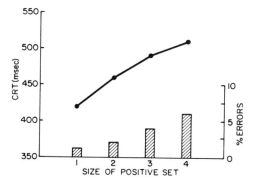

FIG. 5.16. Hypothetical data showing possible effect of errors on CRT in item-recognition experiment.

been the same for all set sizes? It is likely that, for set size 4, people would respond more slowly to be as accurate as they were for set size 1. Lowering error rate would push up CRT, making the function more linear. Perhaps the data in the hypothetical experiment of Fig. 5.16 would be linear if the error rates were low and equal.

Considerations like these have led Sternberg (1975) to say that "the rate of memory scanning is about 38 milliseconds for each item in the positive set [p. 3]." The key word is "about." It recognizes that one can draw quantitative conclusions on the basis of reaction times only when there is a perfect trade-off between speed and accuracy. People would have to have exactly zero errors at the minimum reaction time in order for Sternberg to infer the precise rate of memory scanning. The additive factor method is a powerful tool for exposing processing stages, but it does not seek quantitative assertions that are complicated by varying error rates. It is more relaxed about precision than Donders' methods.

VII. SIGNAL DETECTION THEORY

The discovery that people so flexibly trade speed for accuracy opened psychology's door to important advances made by human engineers. The speed–accuracy trade-off implied rapid decision making in CRT experiments, and engineering psychologists had developed a theoretical framework with which to view decisions. It was called signal detection theory, which grew from sensory psychophysics and the study of man/machine problems in World War II. We turn now to a description of signal detection theory, and then return to how it was applied in CRT experiments. That application also moved psychology further toward the information-processing approach to cognition. We see later that signal detection theory is used to this day to account for short-term and semantic memory phenomena.

It used to be thought that sensations were discrete; you either heard something or you did not. There were thought to be sensory *limens* or *thresholds*. If a sensation was strong enough, it passed a barrier and you heard or saw it. If the stimulus was too weak, it was imperceptible. Sensory detection and perception were determined by characteristics of the stimulus and by fixed sensory capacities of the observer. But people were inconsistent. In psychophysical experiments, identical signals would be detected at one time, but not at others. So limen and threshold were defined statistically. The threshold was defined as the stimulus intensity detected 50% of the time. The theory of signal detectability builds on the idea that thresholds are defined statistically. It is a sophisticated statistical theory of sensation and perception.

Consider the submarine's sonar operator. He depends on sound patterns to detect nonvisible objects in his vicinity. His equipment is imperfect; it always produces some static or noise. To detect an enemy, he must notice some change in the pattern of otherwise irrelevant background stimulation. It is important that he detect the enemy while he is far away; but the further away he is, the more the enemy's signal will be like the normal background noise of the sonar system. Under these conditions, detecting signals is complicated, and signal detection theory was developed to reduce the complications.

The problem for both the sonar operator and the subject in a CRT experiment is one of error. It is difficult to perform perfectly, and people's errors are not determined solely by stimulus parameters and sensory acuity. People's responses to signal detection problems also depend on their response biases: Some sonar operators bias their responses toward more intense signals, other operators toward less intense signals.

A. Hits and False Alarms

Imagine yourself in a signal detection experiment. You are staring at a dim translucent screen onto which a spot of light is sometimes projected. The light is faint and hard to see. In this situation, there are two states: (1) the screen shows visual noise alone, and there is no signal; and (2) the signal is on the screen, but against a noisy background. So there will be either noise alone (N), or a signal plus noise (SN). You can make either of two responses: (1) *Yes, I see the signal;* or (2) *No, I do not.* The possibilities are shown in Table 5.6.

If there is a signal and you say *Yes*, you have scored a correct response, called a Hit. The percentage of Hits could be a poor measure of your performance, however. You could say *Yes* every time you were asked to respond, giving you 100% of all possible *Hits.* But you would also have said *Yes* every time there was no signal. Such errors are called False Alarms. Hits and False Alarms must be considered together to give a good indication of your performance. The other possibilities in the experiment are for you to say

TABLE 5.6
Names of the Possible Responses in
a Signal Detection Experiment

		State of the World (What the Experimenter Actually Presents)	
		Noise Alone	Signal Plus Noise
Detection response of the subject	Yes	False alarm	Hit
	No	Correct rejection	Miss

No either correctly or incorrectly. Saying *No* in the absence of a signal is called a Correct Rejection. Saying *No* when the signal is there is a Miss. Correct Rejections and Misses are usually ignored by experimenters, because Hits plus Misses add up to 100% for the signal-plus-noise trials, and False Alarms plus Correct Rejections equal 100% for noise alone trials. Hits and False Alarms tell all there is to know about accuracy of responding in a signal detection experiment.

B. D-Prime (d') and Beta (β)

People's responses to a signal detection task are affected by their perceptual sensitivity and their response biases. The goal of signal detection theory was to give a pure measure of sensory sensitivity, uncontaminated by response bias. It will help you to see how signal detection theory tried to realize this goal if you think back to our submarine's sonar operator. His world comes through his earphones as a continuously changing spectrum of sound, and his job is to divide that spectrum accurately into signal and noise. The noise is always present, but it is not a fixed quantity. The intensity of the noise varies; sometimes his sonar system has more static than at other times. The signals he hopes to detect are also sounds; so they add together with the noise. Moreover, the signal's intensities also vary. On the average, the intensity of the sound heard by the sonar operator will be greater when a signal is present than when it is absent. But because the intensity of both the noise and the signal vary, the sum of the signal and noise may not always be greater than the intensity of the noise alone. There will be two ranges or distributions of sound intensities. One range is for noise alone, and one is for noise plus signal. If the average signal is weak or its range of intensities large, or if the average noise is strong or its range large, then the distributions of noise and signal-plus-noise will overlap, markedly complicating the sonar operator's chore. Refer now to Fig. 5.17.

Figure 5.17 illustrates the signal detection model. Its abscissa (horizontal axis) reflects what the observer observes, which in the sonar example is sound intensity. The intensity or amount of what is observed (called Observation in the figure) increases from left to right. On the vertical axis is the number of observations. That is, Fig. 5.17 illustrates a large number of observations, showing how they are distributed along some observational scale. The two bell-shaped curves correspond to observations that contain noise alone and to those that contain signal and noise. The peaks of these curves correspond to the most frequently observed value. Because the observations are distributed symmetrically around these peaks, the peaks also correspond to the average or mean value of the two sets of observations. The figure says that the mean of the Noise distribution is lower than that of the Signal-plus-Noise distribution, but the two distributions overlap.

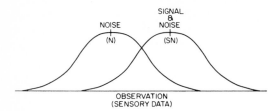

FIG. 5.17. Assumptions of the model of signal detection theory.

To describe the sensitivity of an observer, one must consider both the difference between the means of the Noise and Signal-plus-Noise distributions and the amount of overlap between them. Signal detection theory does this by subtracting the means of the two distributions from one another and dividing the answer by a measure of the range or variability of the two distributions. The variability measure used by signal detection theory is the average standard deviation of the two distributions. The resulting statistic is called d' (pronounce it d-prime). The d' statistic is a measure of observer sensitivity, and it is calculated by subtracting the means of two distributions and dividing the resulting difference by the variability of those distributions. Thus, if the Noise distribution had a mean of 10 and the Signal-plus-Noise distribution had a mean of 30, and the standard deviation of the two distributions was 5, d' would equal $[(30-10)/5 = 4]$.

Figure 5.18 should help you interpret different values of d'. Figure 5.18 shows 3 hypothetical situations for which d' might be calculated. Situation A asks you to imagine that you are in a room with a running buzz saw (Noise) trying to detect the sound of a mosquito (Signal-plus-Noise). Impossible, right? Figure 5.18 reflects this by showing almost complete overlap between the Noise and Signal-plus-Noise distributions. The sensory stimulation is just about the same in both cases: The value of d' is nearly zero because the means of the two distributions are so similar. In situation B you are a physician trying to hear a slight heart murmur (Signal-plus-Noise) through a stethoscope against a background of innumerable bodily sounds (Noise). Figure 5.18 represents this task with moderately overlapping distributions: d' is equal to about two standard deviation units. Situation C is an extreme case. You are in the library, hearing its usual quiet (Noise), when a gun is fired (Signal-plus-Noise). You have no trouble detecting the gun's report, for there is no overlap between the distributions. The value of d' is more than 8 standard deviation units. The next question is how d' relates to Hits and False Alarms.

In the gun-shot example (Situation C of Fig. 5.18), it would be a simple matter to recognize all Hits and all False Alarms. To distinguish between the two, one has only to adopt a criterion of sound intensity that falls some place in the large gap between the Signal and Signal-plus-Noise distributions. Any sound above that criterion is a Hit, and any sound below it is a False Alarm. In that situation, there are no sounds between the two distributions. But what about detecting a heart murmur? The Noise and Signal-plus-Noise distributions overlap (Example B in Fig. 5.18), and there is no gap between them. In order to maximize Hits and minimize False Alarms, signal detection theory shows that the observer should set his criterion of when to respond at the point where the two distributions intersect. Figure 5.19 illustrates this idea, and it shows the consequences of setting the criterion at other points.

In Fig. 5.19, as in signal detection theory, the criterion is signified by the Greek letter β (beta). The criterion is the point above which a signal is called, giving a Hit, and below which it is not called, giving a Miss. In example A, d' is equal to 3, and β is set 1.5 standard deviations above the mean of the Noise distribution and 1.5 standard deviations below the mean of the Signal-plus-Noise distribution, which is the point at which the two distributions intersect. By calling every sound that falls above β a Hit, the subject would have a Hit rate of .93; he would miss .07 of the true signals. He would have a False Alarm rate of .07; he would call that proportion of the noise a signal. (Given d' and β, the exact proportions of Hits and False Alarms can be determined from z tables, which are reproduced in most statistics books.) What happens when β is set somewhere other than where the Noise and Signal-plus-Noise distributions intersect, and why would anyone ever set it elsewhere?

It is not always a good idea to set a detection criterion to maximize Hits while minimizing False Alarms. Sometimes a Miss is too expensive, and sometimes a False Alarm has unacceptable consequences. By setting β lower, one can increase his proportion of Hits, but he will also have more False Alarms. By setting his criterion higher, he can reduce his False Alarms, but he will have fewer Hits. Consider example B in Fig. 5.19. It says your job is to watch a radar screen for missiles that will destroy North America if not stopped. If you report a signal, it will be checked very carefully. In this setting, a Hit would be important; a False Alarm would not, because they happen all

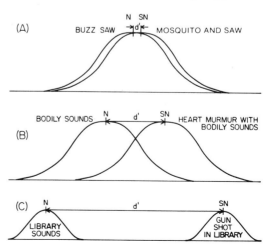

FIG. 5.18. Illustration of d' for three detection tasks.

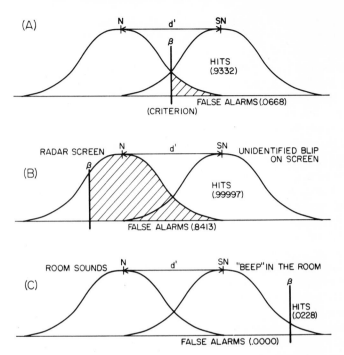

FIG. 5.19. The effects of setting beta at different locations relative to Noise and Signal-plus-Noise distributions.

the time. A Miss would be catastrophic for North Americans; a Correct Rejection would count for nothing. If you were a radar operator for the Strategic Air Command, you would set your criterion to maximize Hits, even at the price of many False Alarms. In Fig. 5.19, we have set β at four standard deviations below the mean of the Signal-plus-Noise distribution, which would produce a Hit rate of 100%. Notice, however, that the false alarm rate (shaded area) would be 84%. This criterion assumes that the commanding officer is not bothered by checking False Alarms. What if the commanding officer were irritated by errors?

Situation C in Fig. 5.19 assumes that you have been kidnapped by someone who makes you play a grisly game. He keeps you in a room and creates a faint beep every few minutes. You are paid $5 every time you report the beep, a Hit. The penalty for a False Alarm is instant death. You might play this signal detection game prudently, adopting a criterion five standard deviations above the mean of the noise distribution. You would make no False Alarms, but your hit rate would only be 2.3%. Some captives would move β off the graph to the right, never saying they heard the beep. (They would have missed the chance to pick up a few bucks.)

C. ROC Curves

Recall now that the goal of signal detection theory is to give an unbiased estimate of observer sensitivity. Bias means setting β somewhere other than midway between the peaks of the Noise and Signal-plus-Noise distributions, and we have seen that the observers do so readily. The problem for signal detection theory is to estimate sensitivity from information about Hits and False Alarms. Because the rate of Hits and False Alarms is determined by both d' and β, determining these two rates for a single set of conditions will not allow an unbiased estimate of sensitivity (d'). The experimenter must be able to assess the influence of bias—that is, where β is set—in order to arrive at an unbiased estimate of d' (sensitivity). This is done by manipulating bias and making multiple determinations of Hit rate and False Alarm rate. In a typical signal detection experiment, the subject's criterion (β) is manipulated by a system of payoffs, much as Fitts (1966) did in his CRT experiment. Hits and False Alarms are determined for each payoff condition. For example, Table 5.7 shows hypothetical data for five different conditions of payoff. The Hits column of Table 5.7 tells the proportion of signals reported by the subject. The False Alarm column tells the proportion of times when the signal was absent that the subject said it was present. Having collected data like these, we must next plot them against one another, as in Fig. 5.20. The ordinate is Hit Rate, and the abscissa is False Alarm rate. The five data points from Table 5.7 are connected by a smoothed curve in Fig. 5.20. That smooth curve is called a Receiver Operating Characteristic (ROC) curve. An unbiased estimate of d' can be derived from a comparison of the ROC curve to the diagonal line, also shown in Fig. 5.20.

The diagonal represents the data that would result if people had no sensitivity ($d' = 0$). Thus, the lower left-hand point on the diagonal represents a condition in which people never produce either a Hit or a False Alarm. Is it intuitively obvious that this represents insensitivity? The upper right point represents the condition in which people make 100% Hits, but they also make 100% False Alarms, which is another form of insensitivity. It is the sort of insensitivity you would show by responding true to every item on a true–false test, which you could do without reading any of the questions. Whenever Hit rate equals False Alarm rate, $d' = 0$, and the diagonal represents all cases where Hits equal False Alarms. The further the data points depart from the diagonal, the more sensitive the observer. A perfectly sensitive observer would make no False Alarms and 100% Hits, so that his data would fall in the extreme upper left-hand corner of Fig. 5.20, the furthest from the diagonal one can get.

According to signal detection theory, bias reduces sensitivity, and where sensitivity is highest, bias is absent. Having created an ROC curve, one can calculate the point of its maximum separation from the diagonal. The

TABLE 5.7
Hits and False Alarms for Five Different Payoff Conditions
(These hypothetical data are plotted in Fig. 5.20)

	Hits	False Alarms
1. Strict criterion (High cost for false alarms. Little payoff for hits.)	.28	.08
2. Somewhat strict criterion (High cost for false alarms. Moderate payoff for hits.)	.52	.20
3. Intermediate criterion (Costs and payoffs well balanced between the hits and false alarms.)	.68	.32
4. Somewhat loose criterion (High payoff for hits. Moderate cost for false alarms.)	.88	.64
5. Loose criterion (High payoff for hits. Little cost for false alarms.)	.96	.84

Note: These data represent *one* particular signal to noise ratio—that is, *one* value of d', the observer's sensitivity.

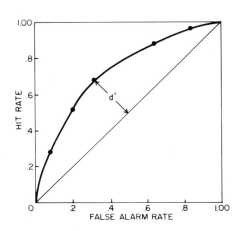

FIG. 5.20. ROC curve for the hypothetical data in Table 5.7.

difference between that point and the diagonal, where $d' = 0$, is the subject's unbiased d', as shown in Fig. 5.20.

To round out this introduction to signal detection theory, we need mention only one more thing. A typical signal detection experiment varies the intensity of its signal and its noise, as well as its payoffs. One cannot learn enough about observers' sensitivity by studying one signal intensity and one noise level. He must vary the two to see how sensitivity increases and decreases with changes in the Signal-to-Noise ratio. And for each Signal-to-Noise ratio, the experimenter must vary the payoffs so as to eliminate bias in the d' estimate for each ratio. Thus, the typical signal detection experiment creates a family of ROC curves, one for each combination of signal and noise.

D. CRT and Signal Detection Theory

We introduced the theory of signal detectability as a way of approaching CRT speed–accuracy trade-offs. The question was how to measure CRT unbiased by errors. ROC analysis and the concepts of d' and β provide a way to do so. Consider that alcohol interferes with driving. Because alcohol is a depressant, we might assume that it causes accidents by slowing reaction time. Jennings, Wood, and Lawrence (1976) studied the effects of alcohol on reaction time, creating a speed–accuracy operating characteristic. They found that drinking decreased performance; the more alcohol, the worse the performance. But the performance decrement did not always show up in the reaction times. Rather, error rates were affected. As they become more intoxicated, people can maintain their reaction times, but at the cost of increased errors. Evidently, alcohol may modify people's decision criteria, not their movement speed.

Earlier we mentioned some item recognition data that Sternberg's model does not handle. For example, if a positive-set item is mentioned twice when the positive set is presented, it earns an unusually fast CRT when it is the test item (Baddeley & Ecob, 1973). Similarly, Rothstein and Morin (1972) compared CRT using 10 words over and over again to form the positive and negative sets (much as Sternberg uses the same digits over and over again) to CRT using many words so that none was used in more than one positive set. The reaction times were much faster in the latter condition. Atkinson and Juola (1974) used signal detection theory to create a model that handles both the foregoing results and Sternberg's typical findings. Their model incorporates Sternberg's theory as a special case, justifying the claim that their theory is more general than his. It also shows that signal detection theory is not limited to situations in which the observer's problem is to identify the presence of a sensory event. The principles of detection theory can also be applied to decisions based on non-sensory attributes of stimuli. In Atkinson and Juola's model, the relevant non-sensory attribute is the familiarity of the test items in a recognition experiment. According to this model, a test item's familiarity is determined by how often and how recently it has been experienced, and sometimes a person can determine whether the test item came from the positive set by how familiar it is, without searching his memory of the positive set.

Reconsider Rothstein and Morin's (1972) experiment. Under one of their conditions, every recognition trial was composed of unique positive and negative sets, but as in all item recognition tasks, only the items in the positive set were presented for study. Therefore, test items from the negative set had never before been presented during the experiment and should have been unfamiliar, whereas test items from the positive set had just been studied and should have been familiar. Under these conditions, people might have decided whether a test item was from the positive or negative set by assessing its familiarity alone. The distributions of familiarity of the positive and negative sets would have had substantially different means (d' would be large), and a familiarity criterion (β) could be set so that it would be unnecessary to scan memory to respond correctly. Because scanning takes time, people might respond more quickly by attending to familiarity and not scanning. What about Rothstein and Morin's other condition? It was like Sternberg's standard item recognition task. Every positive and negative set was drawn from the same 10 words. Over the course of the experiment, all test items would have become comparably familiar to the subjects, because they were all presented many times. The positive and negative familiarity distributions would overlap considerably (d' would be small), and no β could be set to accurately separate positive and negative items. People would be unable to decide from the item's familiarity; so they would have to scan their memories, taking longer to decide whether the item came from the positive or negative set. Consistent with this analysis, Rothstein and Morin found much longer reaction times for the standard Sternberg procedure than for the condition with unique positive and negative sets.

Now reconsider Baddeley and Ecob's (1973) experiment. Their task was like Sternberg's, except that some items in the positive sets were repeated. Thus, a five-item positive set might have no repetitions (5 1 7 3 9), one repetition (5 1 5 3 9), or two repetitions (5 1 5 3 5). Notice that the repeated item is necessarily from the positive set. As in the standard Sternberg procedure, there would have been substantial overlap between the familiarity distributions of the positive and negative sets, but the item that was repeated on any particular trial would be at the upper end of the positive set's distribution. It would be possible, then, for people to establish a positively biased β to recognize repeated items without scanning, but they would have to scan in order to decide about the unrepeated items. Consistent with this analysis, Baddeley and Ecob found faster CRT to repeated items, and the more repetitions, the faster the response. Turn now to Atkinson and Juola's (1974) model, which is schematized in Fig. 5.21.

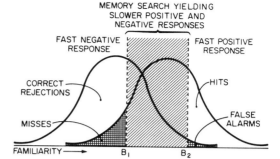

MEMORY SEARCH YIELDING
SLOWER POSITIVE AND
NEGATIVE RESPONSES

FAST NEGATIVE
RESPONSE

FAST POSITIVE
RESPONSE

CORRECT
REJECTIONS

HITS

MISSES

FALSE
ALARMS

FAMILIARITY ⟶ B_1 B_2

FIG. 5.21.   Distributions of familiarity values for distractor items and target items. (Adapted from Atkinson & Juola, 1974.)

   The abscissa of Fig. 5.21 represents the familiarity of recognition test items. Familiarity increases from left to right. The distribution on the left represents the familiarities of test items from the negative set. Compared to the average item from the negative set, the average item from the positive set, represented by the distribution on the right, is more familiar because it was studied and put into memory immediately before the test item was presented for recognition. But under the usual item recognition conditions there is great overlap between the familiarity distributions of the positive and negative sets. Still, the overlap is not complete, so that by setting two criteria it is possible to identify some correct negative items and some correct positive items on the basis of familiarity alone. Atkinson and Juola thus specified two criteria, which are indicated as β_1 and β_2 on the abscissa. β_1 is an *un*familiarity criterion, and any test item falling below this value is said by the subject to be a member of the negative set. Most such items are from the negative set, and in Fig. 5.21 they are called Correct Rejections. A few of these unfamiliar-feeling items are from the positive set, and they are called Misses. β_2 is a familiarity criterion, and test items that fall above it are said by the subject to come from the positive set. Most such items are from the positive set, and in Fig. 5.21 they are called Hits. A few highly familiar items are from the negative set, and they are called False Alarms. According to this model, items that fall below β_1 and above β_2 are responded to very quickly, because they require no search of memory. But items that fall between the two criterion cannot be responded to on the basis of familiarity alone. These items are indicated by the shaded area in Fig. 5.21, and according to Atkinson and Juola's model, they are responded to only after a relatively time-consuming memory search of the sort specified by Sternberg.
   Atkinson and Juola's (1974) model can also be represented by a flow chart, as in Fig. 5.22. It is read from the top down. The ellipse at the top represents the presentation of a test item in a Sternberg task. The arrow from the ellipse to the rectangle indicates that the subject first encodes the item and assesses its familiarity. He next uses the familiarity of the item to decide whether to respond. If the item falls below some criterion of unfamiliarity, the person

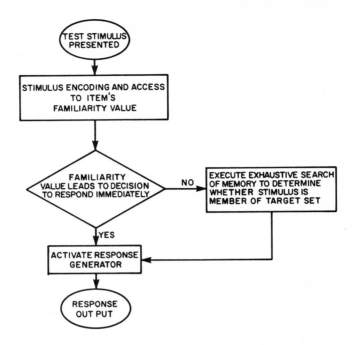

FIG. 5.22.   Flowchart representing the memory and decision stages involved in recognition. (Adapted from Atkinson & Juola, 1974.)

decides immediately to respond negatively. If the item falls above some criterion of familiarity, the person decides immediately to respond positively. The arrow labeled Yes indicates that either decision leads directly to a response-generation system that leads in turn to an output (overt Yes or No response). If the test item is neither below the unfamiliarity criterion nor above the familiarity criterion, the subject decides to execute an exhaustive search of memory. This is indicated by the arrow labeled No, which leads to a box representing Sternberg's view of memory searching. When that search leads to a decision as to whether the item was in the positive set, the response generator is activated and an overt response is made.

E. Caveats

The preceding presentation of signal detection theory has omitted many details, particularly mathematical ones. It has presented concepts only. The mathematical details of the theory are modified for each particular application. Researchers use what is helpful to them and discard the rest of the theory. Still, signal detection theory has markedly influenced cognitive psychology. It played a key role in the research that showed the inadequacy of information theory's analogy to man, the passive communication channel. It highlighted the flexibility of cognition even in simple reaction-time experiments, thereby enhancing the acceptability of computer analogies and the study of exceedingly complex cognition.

We should also emphasize that there is far more to cognitive psychology than signal detection theory. Many scientists feel that d' and β are not useful concepts for many research undertakings. Nevertheless, the concepts of signal detection theory are used in several areas of contemporary cognitive research, and we discuss them further in subsequent chapters of this book.

VIII.   SERIAL OR PARALLEL PROCESSING?

Contemporary choice reaction-time research grew out of efforts to resolve one of the first theoretical disputes intrinsic to cognitive psychology. The question was posed: Is human information processing serial or parallel? This seemingly simple question had to be rephrased immediately, because it has no single answer. People can do some things simultaneously, but they have to do others one at a time. As research proceeded, the rephrasing took many forms, and different investigators worked to solve different facets of the complex issues that grew from the question. But at first, most scientists understood the question to be about stimulus identification as measured by choice reaction time.

Recall Smith's (1968) four-stage analysis of CRT performance (p. 149). Smith called his second stage *stimulus categorization*. Stimulus categorization or identification is fundamental to human perception and cognition. How do we identify things? Smith's idea, which is shared by many psychologists, is that we match stimulus inputs against memories. We know an A is an A because we have stored in memory an idea of what an A is. The process of identification consists of making a match between the stimulus A and our stored representation of A. In other words, whenever we recognize or identify something, we have categorized it. Could the CRT methodology tell us how we match inputs with memories? Sternberg's research suggested that it could, at least in part.

Sternberg first reported his findings on memory scanning in 1963. His results, you will recall, suggested a serial process, involving the comparison of an item in a visual display with a variable number of items held in memory. Notice the similarity of this comparison process to the notion of categorization. Sternberg's data fit well with the idea of channel capacity brought from information theory to psychology, in part through the efforts of Broadbent (1958). As you know, Sternberg's serial processing theory became one of the more exciting ideas in the early history of cognitive psychology.

EHYP	ZVMLBQ
SWIQ	HSQJMF
UFCJ	ZTJVQR
WBYH	RDQTFM
OGTX	TQVRSX
GWVX	MSVRQX
TWLN	ZHQBTL
XJBU	ZJTQXL
UDXI	LHQVXM
HSFP	FVQHMS
XSCQ	MTSDQL
SDJU	TZDFQB
PODC	QLHBMZ
ZVBP	QMXBJD
PEVZ	RVZHSQ
SLRA	STFMQZ
JCEN	RVXSQM
ZLRD	MQBJFT
XBOD	MVZXLQ
PHMU	RTBXWH
ZHFK	BLQSZX
PNJW	QSVFDJ
CQKT	FLDVZT
GHNR	BQHMDX
IXYD	BMFDQH
QSVB	QHLJZT
GUCH	TQSHRL
OWBN	BMQHZJ
BVQN	RTBJZQ
FOAS	FQKLXH
ITZN	XJHSVQ
VYLD	MZRJDQ
LRYZ	XVQRMB
IJXE	QMXLSD
RBOE	DSZHQR
DVUS	FJQSMV
BIAJ	RSBMDQ
ESGF	LBMQFX
QGZI	FDMVQJ
ZWNE	HQZTXB
QBVC	VBQSRF
VARP	QHSVDZ
LRPA	HVQBFL
SGHL	HSRQZV
MVRJ	DQVXFB
GADB	RXJQSM
PCME	MQZFVD
ZODW	ZJLRTQ
HDBR	SHMVTQ
BVDZ	QXFBRJ

FIG. 5.23. Examples of visual scanning tasks (Neisser, 1964). The letter K is the target in the list at left. A more difficult task is to search for an item that does not include a specified letter. In the list at right, for example, there is only one item that does not include a Q.

A. Neisser's Work

Ulric Neisser also published in 1963, but his data ran counter to Sternberg's. Neisser had worked in the field of artificial intelligence, trying to invent a computer program that could recognize printed letters (Selfridge & Neisser, 1960). The problems encountered in that enterprise gave him a healthy respect for the scope of the pattern recognition problem. His experiments were designed to provide "preliminary information about the depth, breadth, and flexibility of the processes involved in recognizing printed letters [p. 376]." In his research, Neisser stressed the enormous complexity of recognition processes. He found evidence for parallel processing in a task involving visual search. This data, at first blush, appeared to directly contradict Sternberg's theory.

Neisser studied visual search with a procedure illustrated in Fig. 5.23. Your task as subject is to find the letter K as fast as possible. The whole display of 200 letters is presented, and a reaction time clock is started. When you find the K, you press a button, which stops the clock. Your reaction time will depend on where the K is located in the display. Its location is varied from trial to trial; so it is necessary for you to start each time at the top and read serially through all the letters until you find the one you seek, called the *target letter*. Your rate of visual search is calculated from your reaction times on many trials. The typical search rate is about 10 lines per second for well-practiced people. That translates into a serial search rate of approximately 25 milliseconds per letter, which agrees well with Sternberg's estimate of memory search rates.

Neisser's (1964) most important finding concerns searching for more than one letter at a time. Given the same visual display (Fig. 5.23), people searched for either a K or Z, pressing the reaction-time key when either was found. To perform this task accurately, subjects must compare each item in the visual display against each item in the memory set until a match is found. When you have twice as many targets to look for, you have twice as many comparisions to make. Does the process take twice as long? Strangely enough, it does not. Highly practiced subjects find either of two targets as fast as they find one. Pressing the issue, Neisser had people search simultaneously for up to 10 targets. He found that after several days of practice, people search for 10 targets as rapidly as for one.

Neisser's results demonstrate parallel processing. For the skeptics, Neisser supplemented his findings with several arguments. He pointed out that letter scanning does not require conscious perceptual analysis. The processes involved in pattern recognition are rapid and seemingly automatic. Introspection is not a satifactory way to question his experimental data. He also pointed out that some electronic data-handling systems process in parallel. And Neisser cited real-world support for his conclusion. News-clip companies hire people to read newspapers and clip articles for many clients. For example, a senator from Ohio might want a clipping of every article in Ohio newspapers that mentions his name. An oil company might want all articles about gasoline, depletion allowances, oil embargoes, its pricing policies, trends in the size of automobiles, and the like. People hired by news-clip agencies scan stacks of newspapers each day, and they do so very rapidly. They simultaneously search for many different targets for many different clients. After prolonged practice, they scan more than 1000 words per minute. And their rate does not seem to change as they pick up new clients.

Here was a tantalizing puzzle. Both Sternberg and Neisser appeared to be studying the same process—matching an input stimulus to a stored representation. But one found clear evidence for serial processing, while the other found equally clear evidence for parallel processing. Sternberg's and Neisser's tasks were analyzed to see if differences between them could account for their differing results. However, careful experimental tests of differences in the display size (Nickerson, 1972) and amount of practice (Burrows & Murdock, 1969) failed to explain the discrepancies.

B. Egeth's Approach

Egeth attempted to resolve the controversy by using a stimulus set that differed from the digit or letter stimuli used by Sternberg and Neisser. Egeth's research was based on the fact that digits and letters are themselves bundles of perceptual features. In order to recognize an A as an A, you have to attend to its defining properties. Unlike H, A has a closed top and its vertical lines are not parallel. The letters O and Q differ by a single distinguishing feature. In other words, letters and digits can be broken down into elementary components called *features*. Egeth asked whether these features are processed in series or in parallel.

To answer the question, Egeth constructed multidimensional forms whose features he could define and control simply. Figure 5.24 illustrates his stimuli. The stimuli vary on up to three dimensions: (1) form: square or circle; (2)

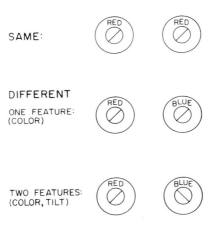

FIG. 5.24. Examples of the stimuli used by Egeth (1966). Where we have written color names, Egeth's stimuli were actually colored.

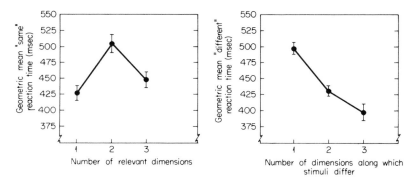

FIG. 5.25. Average "Same" and "Different" reaction times from Egeth (1966).

color: red or blue; (3) tilt: left or right. People in Egeth's experiment were shown pairs of stimuli to judge as *same* or *different*. Consider trials on which the stimuli differ. Will the number of features on which they differ affect reaction time? A serial model predicts Yes, a parallel model, No. Simultaneously examining all of the possible differences among the stimuli would lead equally quickly to a judgment of *different* no matter how many ways the stimuli differ. Examining the possible differences one at a time will lead to quicker responding the greater the number of differences, assuming that the person responds as soon as he or she finds any feature that is not the same for the two stimuli. How about trials on which the stimuli are the same? Serial models predict longer CRTs for stimuli with more possible differences, because each feature will have to be checked before a confident decision of sameness can be made. Each feature would also be checked in the case of parallel processing, but because all comparisons are made simultaneously, the number of necessary comparisons will not affect CRT.

Despite the elegance of Egeth's reasoning and design, his experiment did not resolve the serial/parallel issue. Figure 5.25 shows the CRT results for both *same* (left figure) and *different* judgments (right figure). The data for *same* responses supported neither theoretical view. The *different* responses support a serial model according to which people self-terminate when they discover any different feature. Egeth's results were equivocal with respect to an absolute dichotomy of serial vs. parallel in *overall* processing.

C. The Current Views of Serial and Parallel Processing

Even though Egeth's results were equivocal, they figured in the contemporary resolution of the puzzle. Bamber (1969) followed up the anomaly in Egeth's data, that *same* and *different* responses yielded different conclusions about cognition. He noted yet another oddity: In studies using multidimensional stimuli, *same* responses are generally faster than *different*. But judging sameness requires testing all the features, whereas judging difference does not. Bamber concluded that different processes underlie *same* and *different* responses in these tasks.

But if various responses within the same experiment could reflect different processes, it is surely possible that different processes could operate in tasks as dissimilar as Sternberg's and Neisser's. Today, it is generally believed that this is the case. Egeth, Jonides, and Wall (1972) anticipated the contemporary view in a paper that also reported a number of experiments supporting parallel processing. They noted that pattern-recognition processes appear to take place in parallel; however, certain factors may initiate serial processing. In particular, they mentioned unfamiliar or arbitrary stimulus–response mappings. For example, in Sternberg's experiments, a particular digit might be a target on one trial and a nontarget on another trial. Egeth, Jonides, and Wall suggested that this might occasion a kind of response conflict, to which the subject reacts by adopting a serial processing strategy. Their basic explanation has been somewhat reinterpreted since then, but their major point is generally accepted. That point is that Sternberg's serial outcomes reflected a somewhat later portion of the information-processing sequence than Neisser's (and Egeth et al.'s) parallel outcomes. The analysis generally made today is in terms of the amount of automaticity and directed attention that various components of the task require.

It seems to be the current majority view that there is a set of pattern-recognition processes that occur very early after the onset of a stimulus. These are considered to be automatic, not subject to strategic control, and pre-attentive—they do not require conscious attention to be accomplished. In general, these early processes are thought to operate in parallel. Another set of processes occurs somewhat later in the information-processing sequence. These are considerably more under the subject's conscious control and require more attention; they are also generally thought to be serial. Recent textbook treatments of the Neisser and Sternberg studies place them in different chapters. For example, Rumelhart's (1977) excellent book considers Neisser's research to involve pattern recognition, but Sternberg's experiments are covered as examples of primary memory phenomena that occur after the pattern recognition process is completed. Serial and parallel processing still appear as research issues; however, researchers are more likely to ask the question about newly isolated information-processing stages rather than about a globally defined performance such as "pattern recognition" or "retrieval." Recently, Anderson (1976) has argued that it may in principle never be possible to decide if a cognitive process is truly parallel or serial. This position raises fundamental metatheoretical issues on the nature of scientific evidence and corroboration. We treat the problem in our final chapter.

IX.   THE STATUS OF CRT IN 1979

Choice reaction time is no longer an active research area in cognitive psychology, but that does not mean it is gone. In fact, it is more in evidence than ever. It appears in every remaining chapter in this book. However, it has shifted its status from that of a research topic to that of a methodological tool. This shift reflects the fact that we have a rather extensive understanding of CRT and a well-developed theoretical framework for it. Similar shifts have occurred outside psychology, as well. For example, lasers are now used to measure interplanetary distances. Previously, the properties of lasers per se were the major focus of study. Once their theoretical properties were well-understood, they could become potent research tools. Often, one cannot fully understand studies using lasers as tools without understanding the theories explicating lasers themselves. This requires learning some ideas that may have been known to physical scientists for some time. In the same way, to understand the many uses of CRT in psychological experimentation, a student must know the theories of CRT. Imparting that knowledge has been one of the goals of this chapter.

In later chapters, you will find reaction-time studies of memory, psycholinguistics, semantic memory, pattern recognition, and speech perception. Why is reaction time such a popular dependent variable? We have already mentioned how congenial Donders' approach was to psychologists who viewed cognition as a series of mental events unfolding over time. But now that psychological research has yielded a well-developed technology of reaction time, there are even more reasons favoring its use. Posner and Rogers (1978) show the power of reaction time "chronometric analysis" applied to either mental or neuropsychological events. They indicate that it is useful in isolating independent subsystems, mental or physiological. When some experimental manipulation changes the time required for one response while leaving unchanged the time required for some other response, the two responses must arise, at least partially, from independent systems. Posner and Rogers also note that chronometric analysis can illuminate "psychological pathways." A person is naming stimuli, for example, and an identical one is repeated: The response to the second is usually faster than the first. This can be taken as evidence that the person is capitalizing on an already-activated "pathway" in making the second response. The logic of mental chronometry permits many experimental arrangements that yield inferences about pathways involved. For example, a pair of presentations should result in a slowing, or inhibition, of the second response if the pathway must operate serially, but not if it works in parallel. Posner and Rogers suggest numerous possibilities for using chronometric analysis to: (1) infer properties of psychological pathways; (2) distinguish automatic from attended processes;

and (3) relate processing models to introspective reports of visual experiences such as illusions.

Wickelgren (1977) suggests a further refinement on the basic reaction-time technology. Because people can trade speed for accuracy, experimenters must draw inferences cautiously. It might not be the case that the condition which produces the shortest latencies is the easiest, or least complex. This conclusion is reasonable only if the fastest condition produces the lowest error rates. But if short latencies are accompanied by high rates of error, the condition may not be "easy"—it may have some characteristic that changes the subject's relative tolerance for slow responses and for errors. To avoid this pitfall, Wickelgren recommends that latency data be supplemented by speed–accuracy trade-off functions—that is, by noting error rates at various levels of response speed. There are several methods for obtaining such information, such as differential payoffs for speed and accuracy, instructions to emphasize either speed or accuracy, and partitioning of reaction times. An added virtue of this approach, Wickelgren notes, is that it permits scrutiny of the observed process at various states of completion. That is, when a subject follows instructions strongly emphasizing speed at the expense of accuracy, his or her responses will be given before processing is "complete." Neutral instructions will yield more "complete" responses; whereas accuracy-biased instructions should encourage full completion of the relevent information-processing sequence before a response is made. Comparison of data under these different weightings of speed and accuracy may yield valuable processing information.

The current state of CRT has moved from a topic of study to a methodological tool. It has a well-developed theoretical framework, and its properties are rather clearly understood. Because it is so useful, it is used in virtually every area of cognitive psychological research. An important consequence of the ubiquitousness of reaction-time measures is that relationships between separate research areas are likelier to be detected. It has been some years since Haber (1969) observed that the discontinuity between "perception" and "memory" was disappearing in the information-processing paradigm. We describe in Chapter 8 an exciting new theory that relates work in the several areas of pattern recognition, memory, and attention (Schneider & Shiffrin, 1977; Shiffrin & Schneider, 1977). The theory is directly responsive to the sequence of developments described in this chapter, and reaction-time data is featured extensively in its formal arguments. Theoretical integration of diverse areas is an uncommon occurrence in psychology; but the Shiffrin and Schneider theory is such an event. Students who have mastered the contents of this chapter and the next two on attention and memory will share a deep appreciation of the Schneider–Shiffrin theory and others that follow.

6 Consciousness and Attention

ABSTRACT

I. *Introduction*
Scientific psychology began as the study of consciousness. The method was analytic introspection, but introspection was unreliable and analysis destroyed the richness of conscious life. Introspective methods fell from favor and were replaced by the conditioning procedures of behaviorism. The study of consciousness was ignored for many years.

II. *Attention as Consciousness*
Broadbent's studies of attention, reported in his 1958 book, *Perception and Communication,* brought the study of consciousness back into experimental psychology.
   A. *Experimental Basis of Filter Theory* Broadbent's filter theory of attention was based on two ways of studying attention to auditory input.
      1. *Shadowing* Cherry played different stories to the two ears, requiring listeners to repeat the message to one ear as it was heard. As a rule, people did not remember the unrepeated messages. Changes in meaning, such as a switch from English to German, went unnoticed, whereas a change in voice pitch was picked up.
      2. *Split-Span Experimentation* People readily recall six digits in their presentation order, when the digits are given one at a time. But when the six are divided into pairs, and one each is presented to the separate ears, people recall accurately only when they say back the digits to one ear before saying the digits to the other ear. Broadbent explained this finding by arguing that people can attend to only one ear at once. Accordingly, they hold the digits to the other ear in a buffer memory, from which they recall only after recalling the digits from the attended ear. A filter mechanism allows attention to only one of the two channels (ears) at a time.
   B. *Broadbent's Filter Theory* Broadbent's theory identifies attention with consciousness, which can handle only one input at a time. To see that only

pertinent input enters consciousness, the theory posits a tunable filter that screens incoming information according to its physical features but not according to its meaning. A buffer temporarily holds information that does not pass the filter, so that after inputs that do pass have received conscious processing, the filter can be retuned to allow earlier inputs to receive conscious processing. The filter theory accounted for all of the early results from split-span and shadowing experiments.

C. *Treisman's Filter-Attenuation Theory*   Because the split-span and shadowing procedures allowed ready variation of stimulus conditions, much experimentation was done to test Broadbent's theory. Before long, Moray (1959) and Treisman (1960), among others, showed that the meaning of material to both the attended and unattended ears determined whether material to the unattended ear was noticed. Treisman liberalized Broadbent's conception of the filter, arguing that it never completely blocked any stimulation but that it was tuned by perceived meanings to attenuate some materials less than others. In Treisman's view, perception was still limited to one thing at a time.

D. *Evaluation of Filter Theory*   Broadbent's theory and research brought the study of consciousness back into experimental psychology by highlighting common-place situations in which it played important functions, by illustrating simple experimental procedures for its study and by offering a concrete analogy, the electromechanical filter. His theory has been largely abandoned because it does not allow adequately for the ways in which meaning determines perception. He gave too small a role to long-term memory as a determinant of what becomes conscious.

III. *Memory Processes in Selective Attention*
Gray and Wedderburn (1960) used Broadbent's own split-span procedure to show that the meaning of materials determines recall order, thereby fully undermining filter theory.

A. *Selective Response Theory*   Deutsch and Deutsch (1963) offered a radically different view of selective attention, which held that all inputs were analyzed fully, but only some were responded to. This view implicitly emphasized the role of long-term memory.

B. *The Semantic Basis of Selectivity*   Deutsch and Deutsch wrote at the beginning of the information-processing revolution, so their account of selective attention implicated little in the way of internal processes. Norman (1968) spelled out such processes by giving great emphasis to the role of semantic memory in determining attentional selectivity. Whereas Broadbent emphasized processes that go on shortly after stimulus input, the Deutsch–Norman view emphasized what happens relatively long after stimulus input.

C. *A Two-Process Theory: Analysis by Synthesis*   Neisser (1967) formulated a view of attention that accommodated both the data-driven phenomena emphasized by Broadbent and the conceptually driven phenomena emphasized by Norman. Like Norman, Neisser made attention a matter of degree, he postulated extensive unconscious processing, and he made consciousness a matter of the amount of processing given to input. In Neisser's theory, complex preconscious processes guide the focusing of conscious attention.

IV. *Attention as Processing Capacity*
When the role of unconscious processes in determining attention was acknowledged, attention could be viewed as processing capacity as well as consciousness. To study the limits of processing capacity, psychologists

performed experiments requiring people to do more than one thing at a time. People were asked to do two simple things at once, and the focus was upon how the characteristics of the two tasks influenced one another (Posner & Boies, 1971).

A. *Kahneman's Model of Attention Allocation*   Kahneman (1973) provided a model that conceived of attention as a resource whose allocation was influenced by unconscious rules (Enduring Dispositions) and conscious decisions (Momentary Intentions) as well as by task difficulty.

B. *How Much Attention Does Shadowing Require:*   Zelniker (1971) showed that shadowing does not use a person's total attentional capacity.

C. *Increasing Capacity by Reducing Difficulty With Practice*   Underwood (1974) showed that extensive practice increases the amount of attention allocated to the unattended ear in shadowing experiments .

D. *Promoting Parallel Processing*   Spelke, Hirst, and Neisser (1976) showed that with practice people come to take dictation on one subject while reading about another, with no apparent loss in comprehension on either task. This and other findings raise the possibility that attention viewed as processing capacity has no limits though conscious attention does.

E. *Routinization, Flexibility, and Consciousness*   The specialized functions of conscious and unconscious processing are discussed.

V. *Reprise*
The chapter is summarized, and special emphasis is given to whether linear, flowchart models will continue to be useful in the study of attention.

I.   INTRODUCTION

Scientific psychology began as the study of consciousness. William James studied it at Harvard in the last century. At about the same time, Wilhelm Wundt established the first psychology laboratory, at Leipzig, Germany, in 1879. Wundt believed that psychology should be concerned with consciousness, which he set out to study with introspection—the self-reporting of personal mental states. E.B. Titchener, one of Wundt's students, returned to the United States after training in Germany, and by the turn of the century he was a dominant figure in the structuralist paradigm of early American psychology. In his laboratory at Cornell, as in other labs around the country, students introspected about their experience. They did such things as record their sensations and feelings as they watched calibrated variation in color stimuli or as they sipped lemonade. But introspections were unreliable. Different people claimed different sensations and feelings in response to the same stimulus, and there was no way to objectively evaluate their discrepant claims.

Psychology began as a subdiscipline of philosophy, and to establish its independent existence as a science, its early practitioners correctly believed it necessary to be objective and rigorous. They were profoundly influenced by the achievements in chemistry of the last century. As a result, they greatly emphasized *analysis,* the breaking down of phenomena into their component parts. Tied to introspection, unfortunately, analysis destroyed the regularities to be discovered in mental life. Being both unreliable and impoverished, the introspective study of consciousness had reached a dead end by the time behaviorism came along. However, scientists do not switch paradigms lightly. Scientific revolutions require not only a breakdown of normal science, like that which gave rise to widespread disenchantment with introspection, but also an attractive alternative. An alternative to introspection was provided by the Russian physiologist Ivan Pavlov, who conditioned the "psychic reflexes" of dogs, thereby giving inspiration and an objective method to behaviorism. The failures of structuralism convinced John B. Watson that consciousness was not a proper subject of scientific study. Most American psychologists agreed, and the behavioristic revolution proceeded. The study of consciousness was one of the casualties.

To this day, few psychologists claim to study consciousness. Instead, they study attention, but that includes much of what most people mean by consciousness. Like consciousness, attention connotes awareness. To attend is to be conscious of something. Attention also implies selectivity; when we pay attention to something, we have selected it and ignored other things. Attention also means alertness. A person must be awake to pay attention, and alertness influences information processing.

This chapter summarizes some of what we know from experiments about attention, which is a fundamental concept for cognitive psychology. Attentional mechanisms have been postulated to explain experimental results on reaction time, short-term memory, and pattern recognition, to mention only a few. We emphasize two views of attention that are not necessarily inconsistent with each other: attention as consciousness and attention as processing capacity.

II.   ATTENTION AS CONSCIOUSNESS

Just as the birth of scientific psychology is dated from the opening of Wundt's laboratory, for the purpose of studying consciousness the birth of cognitive psychology can be dated from Donald Broadbent's report of his studies of attention. Broadbent's (1958) book *Perception and Communication* brought the study of consciousness back into experimental psychology. In the book, the mind was likened to a communication channel whose capacity is limited by the number of things to which attention can be given. In Broadbent's 1958 theory, attention was treated as analogous to an electromechanical device, and because psychologists knew that there is no magic in the workings of such devices, from which telephone systems were then built, it seemed to them that consciousness could be studied objectively.

Broadbent's book, which he wrote while doing research with British Royal Navy recruits on matters of vigilance and attention, became a major force in the information-processing revolution. His approach was atypical for the period, and its success established the study of attention as a major normal-science topic of information-processing research.

Before studying attention and vigilance, Broadbent studied in England, with F.C. Bartlett, who taught him very few behavioristic principles. Bartlett marched to his own drummer. You will see that Bartlett's theory of constructive memory processes, which is described in Chapter 12, anticipated many of the pretheoretical commitments that are now widely held in cognitive psychology. Broadbent's research also grew out of problems created by the explosive growth of aviation during World War II. Consider, for example, the difficulties confronted by air traffic controllers as they guide airplanes coming and going from busy airports. Their job is the prototype of dealing with an overload of information. They must attend selectively, but if they do not also attend judiciously, planes will collide. Broadbent's experience with problems like theirs gave him a deep interest in attention. Broadbent was also influenced by information theory and its emphasis on capacity limits. The idea of limited capacity seemed particularly pertinent to human attention, for no one can attend consciously to all of the information in his environment. Moreover, the reason for this inability is psychological. People's eyes and ears take in far more information than they can attend to. These facts are illustrated by two types of data on which Broadbent built his theory: data from *split-span experiments* and from *shadowing experiments.*

A. Experimental Basis of Filter Theory

Because attention is supposed to be accomplished in the brain and not with the senses, studies using visual stimuli should give the same results as those using auditory stimuli; and indeed, they generally do. But it is easier to study attention by ear than by eye, because different messages can be presented to the two ears. When this is done, both messages will get to the brain, and selectivity can only be accomplished there, centrally. There is an uninteresting peripheral way to screen out one message when different ones are presented to the two eyes; it is to close one eye. Consequently, researchers like Broadbent have worked mostly with auditory stimuli, and most of the research we describe will concern attention by ear. Still, there has been enough attentional research with vision to make us confident that some principles discovered in auditory research apply generally and not to a single sensory mode.

1. Shadowing

Cherry (1953) studied what happened when people had to listen to more than one thing at a time. His most interesting experiments concerned what he called the "cocktail party effect." At most cocktail parties, people sip alcoholic drinks, and several groups of people talk simultaneously about different and mostly meaningless matters. When confronted with the din of several simultaneous conversations, people attend to one and ignore the others, even after several cocktails. They use central processes to do this, because the sounds at the ear do not change as one tunes in particular conversations, except in minor degree from turning one's head to reorient one's ears.

Cherry (1953) simulated listening at a cocktail party by using earphones to send different messages to the two ears. This technique is called *dichotic* presentation. The messages were usually stories, and the listener was instructed to attend to one and ignore the other. To force selective listening, Cherry required the listener to repeat the message as it arrived in the attended ear. In other words, the subject "shadowed" the information to one ear, while ignoring the other. When the shadowed message comes in rapidly, people claim they do not hear the message to the unshadowed ear, and when questioned afterward, they usually have no memory of the information presented to the unattended ear. It makes no difference which ear is attended to, and some marked changes in the unattended message go unheeded. For example, people do not notice changes in the language (English to German) in which the unshadowed message is spoken, nor do they notice if the tape recording to the unattended ear begins to play backward. On the other hand, a change in the pitch of the speaker's voice, as for example a switch from a male to a female speaker, is noticed, as is a tone or beep. Broadbent (1958) used these findings by Cherry as well as findings of his own to build a comprehensive theory of attention.

2. Split-Span Experimentation

Broadbent (1954) required people to listen to digits through headphones. The digits came dichotically, three to each ear, in simultaneous pairs presented at half-second intervals. Figure 6.1 illustrates the procedure, which shows that a list of digits, like those used to study memory span, is split and presented one half to each ear. The first two digits come at the same time (7 to the right ear and 2 to the left), followed quickly by the next pair (6 left, 9 right) and then the last (1,5). Immediate recall of 6 successively presented digits is easy, but it is exceedingly difficult to recall three dichotically presented digit pairs in their order of presentation (7,2,6,9,1,5 or 2,7,9,6,5,1). People perform much more accurately when they recall the three digits from one ear, then the three from the other (7,6,1,2,9,5 or 2,9,5,7,6,1). Left to their own devices, this is the way people do the split-span task, and they do it accurately.

From Broadbent's perspective, the ears are separate channels that can be attended to only one at a time. People cannot attend to two things at once; we are serial processors. But we have compensating capacities, such as a "buffer"

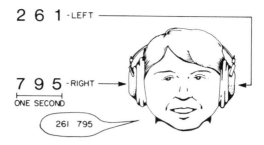

FIG. 6.1.   Illustration of split-span procedure.

memory that stores raw sensory information for a few seconds. The buffer allows us to hold information from one ear while we attend to information from the other, following which we can retrieve the information held in the buffer and attend to it. Thus, a time-limited process, the buffer, compensates for a size-limited process, attention.

Even the simple chore of recalling six digits thus shows that there are conditions under which people cannot do two things at once. Of course, there are other conditions under which people can do two or even more things at once. Attention theorists must also deal with the fact that some behaviors do go on simultaneously, as we shall see.

B. Broadbent's Filter Theory

Contrary to the then dominant paradigm, Broadbent claimed the mind was like a communication channel and therefore eminently researchable. He viewed communication channels somewhat differently than information theorists, who saw them as passive devices. Broadbent conceived of communication channels as active devices that are flexible processors as well as transmitters of information.

Broadbent was probably the first psychologist to describe cognitive functioning with a flowchart, and his theory of attention is outlined in that form in Fig. 6.2. It depicts cognition as a flow of information through the organism. The several streams of arrows to the senses, the short-term store, and the selective filter are intended to suggest that people receive more information than they process. The job of the selective filter is to block unwanted input, letting through only those messages that merit full cognitive analysis. The selective filter can be variously "tuned" so that at any one time it only relays messages that pass certain physical tests. Between the senses and the filter is a buffer to hold much unanalyzed information briefly, allowing it to be attended to later. According to Broadbent's theory (Fig. 6.2), only information that becomes conscious (passes through the limited-capacity channel) enters long-term memory and becomes part of or modifies our world knowledge. The filter thus controls what we know. We note in passing

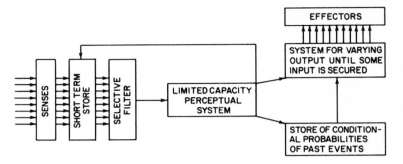

FIG. 6.2.   Broadbent's information-flow diagram for the organism.

similarities between Broadbent's flow diagram and Atkinson and Shiffrin's model of memory, which came 10 years later and is described in the next chapter. Broadbent's "buffer" became Atkinson and Shiffrin's "sensory register," and his "limited-capacity channel" became their "short-term store."

Broadbent's theory accounted for the data from split-span experiments by tuning the selective filter to one ear. Information to that ear passes through the filter to the limited-capacity channel and is used to generate a response. The information to the unattended ear is temporarily blocked by the filter and held in the buffer until the first digits sent to the attended ear have been reported. Then the filter is tuned to the information from the other ear, allowing it to be processed by the limited-capacity channel.

Broadbent's theory posited strict serial processing. His theory explains apparent parallel processing (watching TV and doing crossword puzzles at the same time) as *time sharing*, or *multiplexing*. Two or more tasks are done by simply switching attention back and forth between them, as between the ears in split-span experiments. Thus, according to the theory it should be impossible to do two things in parallel if they both require continuous attention, and all of the parallel processing observed in everyday settings must involve tasks that can go unattended from time to time.

Broadbent's (1958) theory also accounts for Cherry's results. During shadowing, the filter is tuned so that it passes the unique aspects of the message to be repeated. The message's location (left or right ear) is presumably the main tuning feature in shadowing experiments, but the gross features of all input are monitored. Because only the gross physical characteristics of the unattended input pass through the filter, its meaning will usually not enter consciousness. Therefore, a tape played backward or a switch from one language to another will go unnoticed. But changes in the gross physical features of the message will be noticed, as are voice pitch or a tone. This account indicates that Broadbent's theory allows some unconscious perceptual analysis of unattended input, but these analyses are very crude and do not concern meaning.

C. Treisman's Filter-Attenuation Theory

The split-span and shadowing procedures allowed ready manipulation of stimulus materials; so the work by Broadbent and Cherry stimulated much experimentation. For example, Moray (1959) used the shadowing technique in several tests of filter theory. Some of his findings were consistent with the theory, as when he repeated the same few words 35 times in the unshadowed ear. Recognition of the repeated words was quite poor only 30 seconds after their final repetition. Had the repeated words been attended, they would have been recognized perfectly long after presentation. On the other hand, some of Moray's findings did not square so well with filter theory. He showed that people often recognized and attended to their own names when the names were presented to the unshadowed and presumably unattended ear. This contradicted Broadbent's contention that the filter does not respond to meaning, only to gross physical features. Moray's results suggest that all inputs are analyzed for some aspects of their meaning before they are kept from becoming conscious.

Additional contrary evidence came from an experiment by Treisman (1960). She told people to shadow what they heard in one ear and to ignore what they heard in the other. As they shadowed a story (call it story 1), it was switched to the unattended ear, whose story (call it 2) was dropped out of the experiment when the switch was made. Simultaneously, story 3 came in the attended ear, replacing story 1. If people attended according to Broadbent's filter theory, they should not have noticed that story 1 was being continued in the unattended ear, and they should have taken right up shadowing story 3. But when the first words that arrived in the unattended ear from story 1 made more sense, in view of what had preceded them, than the first words of story 3 in the attended ear, people shadowed a few words from the unattended ear before taking up story 3. Fifteen of Treisman's 18 subjects did this, indicating that the meaning context from the attended ear determined whether the words in the unattended ear were shadowed. This finding, like some of Moray's, suggested that unattended input receives some analysis for meaning, which is inconsistent with Broadbent's argument that the selective filter works on gross physical features alone and that it does its work before the extraction of meaning from incoming signals.

To explain her findings, Treisman (1964a, 1964b) liberalized Broadbent's conception of the filter. Broadbent had made the filter more active than the communication channel of information theory, but Treisman made it more active yet. According to her view, the filter sometimes passes information solely on the basis of its gross physical features, as Broadbent claimed, but on other occasions it passes information according to more abstract properties, even as abstract as its meaning. She argued that the filter is selective across a whole continuum of input characteristics, and that its tuning at any moment is determined by the character of the information that has most recently entered consciousness. As her analogy for the filter, Treisman called on signal detection theory, according to which an observer's criterion determines whether a particular signal is noticed against a particular background of noise. The looser the criterion, the more likely a signal will be detected. According to Treisman, the meanings in consciousness feed back on the selective filter, loosening and tightening its criteria. Thus, words that fit an attended context will be more easily detected, even in an unattended ear, because the context will have loosened the selective filter's criteria for the sorts of words that fit the context. By this analysis, the filter never completely blocks any incoming stimulation. It simply attenuates it, making it more or less perceptible.

The only way in which Treisman modified Broadbent's theory was to liberalize its conception of the filter. Broadbent (1971) has accepted this modification, and his theory remains focused on the limits of perception that result from consciousness being a single-channel process. The main argument of his current theory is that perception is limited to one thing at a time, as a consequence of which the conscious registration of input is strictly serial, and switching between input channels is mandatory. An experiment by Axelrod and Guzy (1968) seems to justify this argument.

Participants in this experiment heard series of brief clicks either monotically (all to one ear) or dichotically (alternating between the ears). The rate at which the clicks came was varied in order to see whether the speed of their presentation influenced subjects' estimates of how many clicks were presented. If only one ear is monitored at a time, as Broadbent's theory says, then the speed of switching from ear to ear should limit estimation accuracy in the dichotic condition. A presentation rate should be reached that exceeds the rate of switching between ears, so that some clicks would not be heard. The subject would be attending to one ear, while clicks came in the other, and the number of clicks presented would be underestimated. Because the monotic condition requires no switching, estimated rate should not vary with presentation speed as it does for dichotic presentation. As predicted, people grossly underestimated the number of clicks in the dichotic condition when the presentation rates were very rapid. In another experiment, subjects estimated whether monotic or dichotic clicks were faster. As Broadbent would predict, they reported that the rate was slower in the dichotic condition. These results support Broadbent's notion of a filter with limited ability to switch between the ears. Processing of the dichotic clicks is serial, which illustrates that attention is limited.

D. Evaluation of Filter Theory

Broadbent's theory and the research on which he based it served to bring experimental psychologists back to the study of consciousness, which earlier they had good reason to abandon. Broadbent showed that those reasons no longer justified neglecting the study of consciousness. He reawakened interest in consciousness, first by highlighting commonplace situations in which it functioned in remarkable ways: the cocktail-party effect. Second, he fashioned experimental procedures that were readily extended by others: the split-span technique. Third, he advanced an analogy that was admirably concrete: electromechanical devices like those used to filter out unwanted sounds in audio equipment. Psychologists could use this conception without sacrificing their commitment to objective methods. For these contributions, cognitive psychology is deeply indebted to him, some say for its very birth. But his theory has not survived.

To accommodate the discrepancies between her data and Broadbent's theory, Treisman had made a seemingly modest change in the theory. She made the filter flexible. It no longer blocked inputs, it simply attenuated them. One effect of this seemingly modest change was to highlight the importance of people's knowledge, because their knowledge seemed responsible for tuning the filter. In highlighting the importance of knowledge, Treisman anticipated by several years cognitive psychology's subsequent great interest in the contents of long-term memory, which is discussed at length in subsequent chapters. No form of long-term memory (the repository of knowledge) was clearly depicted in Broadbent's model. Moreover, he allowed only for information going to long-term memory, not for the contents of that memory to influence attention to incoming information. This is perhaps the main reason that Broadbent's theory has not survived. We turn now to how psychologists came to two-process theories of attention that consider both what happens to sensory input and what people add to perception from stored memories.

III. MEMORY PROCESSES IN SELECTIVE ATTENTION

Moray (1959) and Treisman (1960) both used Cherry's shadowing procedure. Their findings with this task undermined Broadbent's view that selective attention is due to the filtering of information solely on the basis of crude stimulus properties. But shadowing experiments were only one mainstay of filter theory. The other was Broadbent's own finding, with the split-span procedure, that dichotically presented digits are recalled by the ear to which they come rather than by the order in which they come. Gray and Wedderburn (1960) undermined this mainstay with a simple variation on Broadbent's split-span experiment. Rather than present only digits, they presented both words and digits, mixed across ears, so that people received messages like these:

	Left Ear	*Right Ear*
Pair 1	Mice	8
Pair 2	2	Eat
Pair 3	Cheese	5

According to Broadbent's theory of selection by channel, such messages should have been recalled by ear, just as digits are, giving a recall order like this:

Mice 2 Cheese, 8 Eat 5

Instead, people recalled like this:

Mice eat cheese, 825

A. Selective Response Theory

Findings like these by Gray and Wedderburn (1960) led Deutsch and Deutsch (1963) to propose an alternative to Broadbent's view of perceptual analysis. The difference between the views is illustrated in Fig. 6.3. According to Broadbent's filter theory, multiple inputs are registered and held briefly, but only one message is analyzed perceptually. The reason is that perceptual analysis requires attention, which is limited to one input at a time. Thus, for filter theory, attention is a bottleneck that limits perception. Moreover, attention operates very soon after sensory input. According to response selection theory (Deutsch & Deutsch, 1963), all inputs are registered and held briefly, and all are analyzed perceptually. Perceptual analysis is unconscious, it is not limited by attention, and the results of perceptual analyses are all stored in memory. The bottleneck created by limited attention comes later in

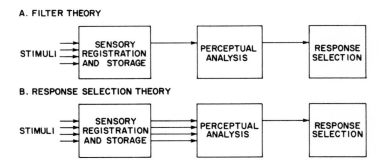

FIG. 6.3.   Two models of selective attention.

the information-processing chain, when the results of perceptual analyses must be retrieved from memory in order to execute a response. Thus, in the experiment by Gray and Wedderburn, subjects would have perceived all six input items and would have stored the results of their perceptual analyses of those items in memory. Those perceptual analyses would have given access to the meanings of the items, which are also stored in memory. When a response is required, the subjects would retrieve the items from memory. Because they have already fully recognized the items and know their meanings, they organize their response around meaning rather than around ear of arrival. According to this view, what seems to be selective perception is actually selective responding. Both views agree that attention is a limited process that forms a sort of bottleneck in the cognitive system, but the bottleneck comes at different places in the two views, and perceptual analysis is differentially complete in the two. Also, response selection theory gives a far greater role to meaning and knowledge than does filter theory.

B. The Semantic Basis of Selectivity

Deutsch and Deutsch wrote near the beginning of the information-processing revolution, well before the current interest in meaning and semantic memory had developed. Consequently, while they rejected Broadbent's idea that selective attention occurs soon after information input, they had little to say about the mechanisms that might account for semantically motivated selectivity later in the processing chain. Rather, they spoke about stimuli and responses and the difficulty of discrimination. These concepts, of course, were consistent with behaviorist modes of explanation. The congeniality of their basic argument to information-processing theorists is shown, however, by the fact that most textbooks refer to their theory together with Norman's (1968), treating the two singly as the Deutsch–Norman theory. Norman did couch his explanation of selective attention entirely in information-processing terms, and he gave long-term semantic memory a crucial role in all perception. Semantic memory, which has a full chapter later, is the repository of meaning and world knowledge.

According to Norman (1968), sensory inputs (auditory or visual) must receive extensive automatic and unconscious processing before they enter consciousness. This processing relies on information that is permanently stored in semantic memory. The sensory features of a stimulus automatically provide access to a person's knowledge of the stimulus by directing his cognitive system to a pertinent "address" or location in semantic memory. Thus, every word-like bundle of speech sounds yields an address in semantic memory. If the bundle of sounds is a word, that address will yield its meaning. If the sounds are not a word, the addressed location will be empty—telling you, for example, that *mantiness* is not a word. Notice that by Norman's

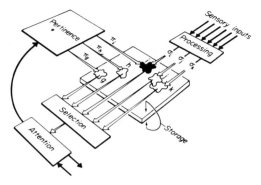

FIG. 6.4. A model of selective attention. (After Norman, 1973.)

account, no search of memory is needed to make a decision that a word-like sound is not a word. Also, attended and unattended inputs both access semantic memory effortlessly. Selective attention comes later. Figure 6.4 shows three inputs, i, j, and k (toward upper right), all of which are processed unconsciously until they activate their representations in semantic memory. Whether i, j, or k will be selected for attention depends on their pertinence to current cognitive activities. Pertinence is determined by the context of the inputs, and it operates by activating locations in semantic memory. The activation of addresses or *nodes* in semantic memory activates related addresses. This type of theorizing is currently used in semantic memory—for example, in the spreading activation model of Collins and Loftus, which is described in detail in Chapter 9. Thus, when an input is referred to an address that has been activated by prior accessing of semantic memory, that input is more likely to be selected for attention. Perceptual selectivity is based on the summation of semantic memory activation from both current sensory inputs and contextual pertinence. Consciousness is the end product of several unconscious memory processes.

Norman's (1968) theory readily handles the data on semantic selectivity that were so troublesome for filter theory. For example, Treisman's (1960) finding that highly probable words to the unattended ear are shadowed can be explained as an effect of context-determined pertinence. And a good deal of other evidence supports Norman's conception. Lewis (1970) measured the time between the presentation of a word to an attended ear and the point at which the subject said (shadowed) the word. Simultaneously occurring words in the unattended ear were related associatively, semantically, or not at all to the attended words. Even though people remembered none of the unattended words, the time it took to say a shadowed word was greater when a semantically similar word came simultaneously to the unattended ear. That is, the unattended words unconsciously slowed the processing of attended words, just as Norman would predict. The same point was made by Corteen and Wood (1972), Von Wright, Anderson, and Stenman (1975), and

Treisman, Squire, and Green (1974), all of whom conditioned subjects to respond physiologically to particular words. Presenting these words in the unattended ear produced physiological responses, even from subjects who reported that they did not hear the unattended words.

Compared to Broadbent's theory, those of Deutsch and Deutsch and of Norman suggest that the selective effects of attention come relatively long after stimulus input. But unlike Broadbent, Deutsch and Deutsch argue that all stimuli are analyzed completely, which opens their theory to the criticism that the cognitive apparatus is unlikely to be so inefficient. Why should people analyze all stimuli completely, regardless of whether they will later be attended to and given further processing? Norman (1968) avoids this criticism by arguing that perception is a matter of degree: "The automatic matching of a stimulus with its stored representation does not imply knowledge of everything related to that stimulus (p. 528)." In Norman's theory, unattended inputs are only partly analyzed. Attended inputs receive more processing and are remembered longer. This aspect of Norman's theory relates it to the "levels of processing" views of memory, which we describe in Chapter 8. Treisman's filter-attenuation theory also makes attention a matter of degree, and much current work on attention builds from this assumption of hers and Norman's.

C. A Two-Process Theory: Analysis by Synthesis

Broadbent's filter theory accounted well for selective listening based on physical cues and gross sensory analysis. But it could not accommodate experimentally demonstrated intrusions from the meaning of things that were supposedly ignored. Norman's theory focused entirely on the semantic effects and had little to say about data that filter theory accounted for. Both views are incomplete; what is needed is a theory of attention that accounts for sensory effects as well as for effects of people's semantic knowledge. Perceptual analysis can evidently be driven either by data (sensory input) or by concepts (world knowledge). The distinction between "data-driven" and "conceptually driven" perception was drawn by Norman and Bobrow (1975), but we use Neisser's (1967) theory to illustrate how both sorts of processes can be combined.

Neisser's theory has similarities to both Treisman's and Norman's, but he expressed his ideas differently, perhaps because he looked primarily at visual attention. His visual search experiments were described earlier. After practicing his subjects extensively, he had them scan through large arrays of letters, looking for a particular target letter. While looking for a target letter, people see only a blur until it jumps into sight. Nontarget letters are like the unattended channel in dichotic listening experiments. Just as Moray (1959) found no memory for unattended input, Neisser (1964) reported that people do not recognize a list of letters they have recently searched. But the unrecognized letters must have been processed to some extent, for if they were not, the person would not find the target letter. Nontarget letters are evidently rejected by a gross analysis of their sensory features. To account for this, Neisser made some aspects of his theory like Broadbent's (1958).

Unlike Broadbent, however, Neisser made attention a matter of degree, because it takes longer to search for the letter Z in a list of angular letters (e.g., X, M. W) than in a list of rounded letters (e.g., O, C, Q). In the former case, more perceptual analysis is required. Neisser (1969) also found intrusion of semantic information from visually unattended input. People who were instructed to read every other line of a text (the lines were printed alternately in red and black) did not remember information from the unattended lines and denied having seen them. Still, they noticed their name when it appeared in an unattended line. (You may have had a similar experience yourself, seeing your name or the name of your home town jump from a page of newsprint.) Therefore, Neisser (1967) postulated preattentive processes that function for vision as Treisman's filter does for audition. Preattentive processes monitor unattended inputs for important information, and they use stored semantic information unconsciously, in the fashion of Norman's concept of partial analysis and Treisman's adjustable filter.

Consciousness—or, as Neisser would say, focused attention—is a byproduct of full constructive processing. In his view, people do not simply convert environmental information directly into percepts. Rather, they *construct* their percepts by supplementing sensory inputs with what they already know. This constructive analysis *is* the perceptual process, in Neisser's view. The fuller the analysis, the more likely a perception is to come into awareness. The difference between attended and unattended input is a matter of degree of processing. Unattended stimuli are not blocked out or attenuated. They have simply not been fully processed.

An experiment by Neisser and Becklen (1975) aptly illustrates Neisser's view of consciousness. They showed people two superimposed scenes. One showed two men slapping each other's hands. The other showed three males moving around and throwing a basketball. Figure 6.5 shows an outline of what the subjects saw. They were instructed to follow one scene and to ignore the other. They easily did so. While focusing on the basketball scene, they pressed a button whenever the ball was passed. For the slap game, they recorded the number of slaps. The tracking of neither scene was affected by the presence of the other, even when odd events were put into the unattended one. Infrequently, the basketball players stopped to shake hands, but people did not notice and they expressed surprise when told this had happened. Neisser and Becklen also showed that performance did not change when the two scenes came to different eyes. The eyes did not act as separate channels; consciousness is central, as well as being the consequence of degree of processing.

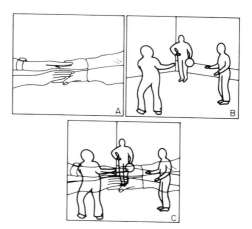

FIG. 6.5.   Illustration of Neisser and Becklen's (1975) experiment.

You can have an experience something like Neisser and Becklen's subjects had by looking out a window at dusk from inside a lighted room. When the lighting is proper, you can either see out or you can see reflections from the interior of the room. You can switch back and forth between the images by focusing your attention. You will not need to practice, for this exercise uses your normal perceptual processes. Like the people in Neisser and Becklen's experiment, you will be constructing your perception by preattentively selecting stimulus images. As Neisser and Becklen put it: "What defines one episode and distinguishes it from the other is not its distance or clarity, or the sense organ involved, but its intrinsic properties . . . what is seen guides further seeing [p. 491]." The unattended inputs need not be "blocked" or "attenuated"; they simply are not picked up for further processing.

In Neisser's view of selective perception, complex preconscious processes guide our focusing of conscious attention. This guidance uses stored knowledge actively. By this view, it is meaningless to ask questions such as, "Does selective attention occur before or after perception?" In a left-to-right flowchart model like Broadbent's, such a question makes sense. But in a two-way conception of interaction between stimulus information and stored knowledge, selectivity occurs in no one place. There are degrees of consciousness depending on how actively an input is processed.

IV.   ATTENTION AS PROCESSING CAPACITY

So far, we have considered research and theory about the selectivity of attention. We have considered several different views of how and where selectivity enters the attentive process, culminating in Neisser's theory of analysis-by-synthesis. By about 1970, Neisser's view or close variants on it came to dominate psychologists' conceptions of attention's selectivity. On this issue, his theory still dominates, and since 1970 research has concentrated on other aspects of attention. We turn now to research on attentional limits and how that work has changed the view that attention is limited to a small, fixed number of inputs. Attention turns out not to have fixed limits, and it may have no limits at all, though consciousness surely does. This suggests that consciousness is not identical with attention. Although conscious experiences must be attended to, not all attention is necessarily conscious.

In Broadbent's theory, attention was fixed and limited, and either all or none of it was allocated, one task at a time. The buffer that held sensory information until it could be attended to also was thought to have fixed limits. In this theoretical framework, little research was directed at the amount of attentional capacity available. Rather, the interesting question was how the small amount of available attention was allocated. But then the idea of all-or-none allocation broke down, as a consequence of experiments on the influence of the meaning of presumably unattended stimuli. Evidently people could allocate various amounts of attention to several things at a time, even those they believed themselves to be ignoring. Moreover, more researchers came to believe that much unconscious processing influences what becomes conscious. It was a small step to the inference that people can attend without awareness, where attention means processing information. And if attention need not be conscious, then our intuitions about the limits of consciousness need not apply to attention. Viewing attention as processing capacity led psychologists to ask about its limits by studying how much processing people can do. It led them to ask how many activities, of what kinds, people can spread their attention over.

The essence of experiments for studying attentional capacity is illustrated by observations you can make for yourself (see Kahneman, 1970). Take a walk with a friend, and when you are moving briskly along, ask her to multiply 17 times 46. Your friend will probably stop walking while trying to calculate. You may not have thought of walking as demanding attention, but it does, as you can see if you and your friend try to cross a busy street while you are talking. The conversation will thin as you make your way to the other side. Or notice your professors as they lecture. Some are pacers, but as they talk at you, they do not run into objects. They monitor their movement while they lecture, and this requires at least some attention from them. For most of us, driving an automobile is so automatic that we do not think of it as cognitive, but it requires attention even though we can listen to the radio or hold a conversation while we do it. Notice, the next few times you ride in a car, who does more talking—the driver or the passenger.

When the sorts of observations suggested in the preceding paragraph are brought into the laboratory, they spell themselves out in experiments, such as one by Posner and Boies (1971). These investigators required people to do

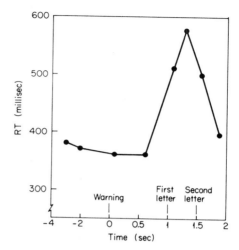

FIG. 6.6. Results from Posner
and Boies (1971).

two things at once. One was a letter-matching task in which a warning signal
preceded the visual display of a letter (e.g., *A*) by one second. After another
half-second, the next letter appeared, and the subject had to judge whether it
was the same as the first. Responses in the letter-matching task were made
with the right hand, but the left hand provided the data of interest. While
performing letter-matching responses with their right hands, subjects listened
for a tone, and whenever they heard one, they pressed a key left-handedly.
This task was used to assess the attention (processing capacity) consumed by
various aspects of letter naming. The tone came at unpredictable times
throughout the various phases of letter naming. Reaction times to the tones
are shown in Fig. 6.6. From shortly before until immediately after the
warning signal, reaction time remained constant. The inference is that
perceiving the warning signal takes little or no attention. But reaction time
jumped sharply during the interval between the two letters, when the subject
was attending to the first one in preparation for responding to the second.
Measuring the effects of one sort of processing on a second thus can show how
much attention the first one requires. Among other things, this technique has
been used to study the attentional requirements of various memory processes
(e.g., Griffith, 1976; Johnson, Greenberg, Fisher, & Martin, 1970).

A. Kahneman's Model of Attention Allocation

Experiments like the one by Posner and Boies (1971) reveal the limits of
attention by observing changes in its allocation. They seek to estimate the
limits of processing capacity by examining how it is distributed across various
activities. Kahneman (1973) provided a model of attentional allocation that

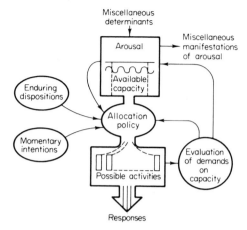

FIG. 6.7.   Kahneman's (1973) model of attention allocation.

clarifies what it means to study attention as a processing capacity. The model views attention as a limited resource that can nevertheless be quite flexibly deployed. The model (Fig. 6.7) incorporates the idea of flexible attentional deployment by indicating that people change their Allocation Policy from moment to moment. They focus all of their attention on only one of their Possible Activities (see Fig. 6.7), or they divide it among a number of activities. Allocation Policy is governed by well-learned or innate unconscious rules (Enduring Dispositions), such as *pay attention when someone says your name,* as well as by conscious decisions (Momentary Intentions), such as *I will read this book and ignore that barking dog.* Allocation Policy is also determined by task difficulty (Evaluation of Demands on Capacity). We allocate more attention to more difficult tasks.

Notice that Kahneman's model is not a flowchart. Instead of information flow, it shows a model of the mind, which is rather like Freud's, as Kahneman (1973) explained:

An important notion of Freud's view was that the total quantity of attention cathexis available at one time is limited, and that the amount of attention demanded by an object of thought or perception depends on how it is elaborated in cognitive activity. This view implies that the limitation on what man can perceive depends on how he perceives and on what he does with his percepts [p. 128].

Though not concerned with the flow of information, Kahneman's model does treat attention as processing capacity, and it does organize research based on that view. The model suggests questions like the following: How fully does a task use people's attentional capacity? Does shadowing use it all? Because task difficulty affects attentional allocation and tasks become easier with practice, does practice increase attentional capacity? With practice, can several tasks, each of which originally consumes all of one's attention, be done simultaneously? Might people read and take dictation at the same time? We now present the research on each of these interesting questions.

B. How Much Attention Does Shadowing Require?

Shadowing experiments meet the requirements of studies of divided processing capacity: People can be viewed as doing one thing with their attending ear and another with the nonattending ear, though this is not how the filter theorists viewed it. They assumed that shadowing occupied attention fully, so that the unattended ear was doing nothing. But viewing attention as processing capacity rather than as consciousness prompts one to ask whether people do assign all of their capacity to the attended ear. Zelniker (1971) showed that they do not. She combined shadowing with a situation called delayed auditory feedback. As people said what came into their attended ear, she tape-recorded their voices and played them back a fraction of a second later to their unattended ear. It is known that delayed auditory feedback to both ears seriously disrupts speech and causes stuttering. (Many tape recorders allow you to demonstrate this for yourself. Simply set the machine to record and speak into a microphone while wearing headphones. It will be difficult to speak normally.) But Zelniker provided delayed feedback only to the unattended ear, so that if filtering were perfect, there would be no stuttering. An interesting feature of this procedure is that people find delayed auditory feedback very unpleasant; so they should have been more motivated than under standard shadowing conditions to allocate all of their attention to the shadowed ear.

Zelniker's subjects were adults and children, and her experiment included a hard and an easy shadowing task. The average proportion of stutters per shadowed word is shown in Table 6.1. There were fewer stutters when the shadowing task was hard than when it was easy. This makes sense; a hard task consumes processing capacity, and there is little left over for the unattended channel and the disruptive effects of delayed auditory feedback. When

TABLE 6.1
Mean Stuttering Frequency as a Function
of Age and Attention Conditions

Group	Attention Condition	
	Easy	Hard
Adults	.046	.020
Children	.124	.069

shadowing is easy, however, people apparently allocate their spare capacity to the ear receiving the disruptive feedback. Processing capacity is shared between tasks, and shadowing does not always use attention fully. How fully it uses attention depends on its difficulty, as is true of other tasks also.

C. Increasing Capacity by Reducing Difficulty With Practice

Underwood (1974) showed how practice changes the allocation of attention in shadowing. Neville Moray was his subject. Moray, as you recall, performed many dichotic listening experiments and published two books on selective attention (Moray, 1969, 1970). In the course of conducting his experiments, he became one of the world's great shadowers. In Underwood's experiment, Moray listened to lists of 16 pairs of rapidly presented letters, shadowing those presented to one ear. He was required to say when a digit was substituted for one of the letters. The digits came unpredictably to either ear, one per list of letters. Under normal shadowing conditions Moray did only a little better than unpracticed subjects (88% vs. 72%) at detecting letters in the shadowed ear. But with his unshadowed ear, Moray far outstripped unpracticed people (67% vs. 8%). Evidently, practicing a task reduces the processing capacity it requires, thereby increasing the amount of attention that can be devoted to something else. Moray had plenty of attention for the unshadowed channel. Similarly, Ostry, Moray, and Marks (1976) showed that practice increases the detection of unshadowed items that relate meaningfully to shadowed items.

D. Promoting Parallel Processing

Whether cognition is parallel or serial was one of the first questions to be hotly researched by information-processing psychologists, but it turned out to be not one but many questions, each of which has been pursued in its own right. In the present context, parallel processing might occur whenever the combined processing capacity of several tasks is less than a person's total attentional supply. Until processing capacity is exceeded, tasks might be performed concurrently with no loss of efficiency for any of them. One might show parallel processing by using several tasks that require little processing no matter who performs them, or one might practice his subjects on more demanding tasks until performing them requires little attention. The former approach is illustrated in an experiment by Shiffrin and Grantham (1974), and the latter is illustrated by Spelke, Hirst, and Neisser (1976).

Shiffrin and Grantham (1974) asked people to respond to three stimuli, any one of which might occur at any time. The stimuli were in different modalities: a faint light, a faint tone, or a gentle vibration on the skin. They were difficult to detect: When each was used by itself, it was noticed only 75% of the time. Shiffrin and Grantham asked whether it is as easy to attend to three sensory modalities at once as to attend to one. In this experiment, it was as easy. People were as accurate when they divided their attention among three modalities as when they focused on one. The inference is that none of the tasks required very much attention. Another experiment made the same point: Shiffrin, McKay, and Shaffer (1976) asked people to detect a dot, which might appear any time at any of 49 locations. Accuracy was not increased by advance knowledge of which location would be used next. Both of these experiments show parallel processing without accuracy loss. People have the attentional resources to perform these tasks simultaneously. There are other activities that supposedly cannot be done in parallel, because their attentional demands exceed people's resources. Reading and taking dictation seem to be such tasks, but Spelke, Hirst, and Neisser (1976) showed that they need not be.

Spelke et al. trained two people to read and take dictation at the same time. Throughout the experiment, both people were forced to understand what they read and what they wrote: Following each session they were given a comprehension test on what they read and a recognition test for the words they took in dictation while reading. At first, performance while dividing attention between the tasks was far worse than when either task was done alone, but after 6 weeks of practice, the two read and wrote as well simultaneously as separately. Then the dictation task was changed. Instead of writing the words that were dictated, the people had to write the category name of the words. Thus, to the word CHAIR, they should have written FURNITURE. At first, their reading suffered, but gradually they came to read as well while categorizing words as when reading alone. The authors concluded that the subjects were simultaneously reading for meaning and extracting meaning from the material they were listening to.

Had Spelke et al. not practiced their subjects extensively, their experiment would have seemed to give different results from the one by Shiffrin and Grantham. The different outcomes might have been explained by a distinction made by Norman and Bobrow (1975). Although people perform as accurately when monitoring three sensory modalities as one, accuracy can be decreased for any modality by reducing the intensity of the stimuli: A light can be made so dim that a person never sees it. Shiffrin and Grantham used this fact to set the intensities of their stimuli so that no one of them could be detected all of the time, even when the other two were not being presented. Evidently, this sort of performance is limited by the quality of the stimuli—or, as Norman and Bobrow would say, it is data limited. People have the attentional resources to do the job, if the stimuli are sufficient. For the experiment by Spelke et al., performance was not data limited, because people's improvement depended on their own practice rather than improvements in the stimuli. In that situation, the limit was people's resources. At first, the two subjects did not have the attentional capacity to read and take dictation at the same time. But because they eventually did, with no loss in accuracy, the notion of strictly limited attentional resources is compromised. People have the processing capacity to do both, once they have learned how.

There is as yet no satisfactory way to identify tasks that require so much processing capacity that they cannot be done simultaneously, except to ask people to try to do them simultaneously. This is because we do not understand what controls attentional resources. More devastating, it is beginning to look as if the notion of limited resources is invalid. It is intuitively and experimentally true that people's conscious awareness is limited, but it may not be true that their attention is limited. When attention is viewed as processing capacity, and when they are given sufficient opportunity to practice, limits seem to recede. Notice that this argument is not a claim that all things can be done in parallel, if only you try long enough. Processing capacity is a central resource available for different perceptual and sensory mechanisms. Even if that capacity is unlimited, a person cannot do two things simultaneously if they require the same bodily part to work in different ways. One person cannot sing and recite poetry at the same time (although some are reputed to talk out of both sides of their mouths). Treisman (1969) has extended this idea of incompatability to perceptual analysis, arguing that parallel processing is possible between different analyzing mechanisms, but serial processing is required when two inputs compete for the same mechanism. Treisman and Davies (1973) tested this idea, and found support for it, but others have not found such support (e.g., Shiffrin, 1975).

Research on attention has produced many conflicting data on issues like serial and parallel processing, capacity limits, and so on (the details of which we have spared you). The inconsistencies are partly the result of subjective commitments of scientists. Researchers do not do just any experiment as if all data were equally informative. Choosing a research question takes great "savvy," which not even graduate training guarantees. Few scientists ask exactly the questions that others want answered. Moreover, designing an experiment requires many arbitrary decisions. Particular materials, procedures, and subjects need be chosen. Subjects must be instructed, motivated, and practiced. These things are rarely done the same way in different laboratories. A positive result of these differences is increased generality when various researchers reach the same conclusions. A negative consequence is conflicting claims that are due to varying beliefs about how to do research and to inexplicit differences among experiments.

E. Routinization, Flexibility, and Consciousness

Despite inconsistencies, the literature shows that attention and consciousness are not the same, which for Broadbent they were. The top panel in Fig. 6.8

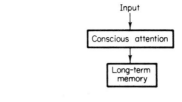

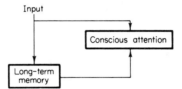

FIG. 6.8.   Two views of the place of long-term memory in attention.

shows the role of consciousness in his filter theory. It was to select from all of the input one receives a part that would influence long-term memory. If information did not become conscious, it did not enter long-term memory, nor was its processing influenced by the contents of long-term memory. Consciousness has the same role in the memory model of Atkinson and Shiffrin (discussed in the next chapter), though they called it the short-term store. We have seen, however, that people can perform complex cognitive tasks unconsciously. Consciousness is not necessary for information processing. It is an optional characteristic that sometimes accompanies information processing and sometimes does not, as shown in the lower part of Fig. 6.8. What function does consciousness serve?

Posner has argued that consciousness is a processing bottleneck (Posner & Klein, 1973; Posner, Klein, Summers, & Buggie, 1973; Posner & Snyder, 1975) that is usually bypassed. Through practice and experience, cognition becomes routinized so that it proceeds without the limits of consciousness. Most of what we do goes on unconsciously. Consciousness is reserved for special processing. For one thing, consciousness inhibits extraneous perceptions (Posner & Snyder, 1975), so that we can work without distraction, which otherwise would occur automatically. Shallice (1972) expressed a similar idea: Consciousness also allows us to direct our behavior to particular goals. It allows for flexibility and creativity in mental processes (Mandler, 1975). It is the exception, not the rule, when thinking is conscious; but by its very nature, conscious thought seems the only sort. It is not the only sort; it is the minority. It is as great a challenge to explain routinized, unconscious thought, as to explain flexible conscious thought. There are many forms of life whose information processing is accomplished entirely without benefit of consciousness. Unconscious processing is phylogenetically prior and constitutes the product of millions of years of evolution. Conscious processing is in its evolutionary infancy; but it is probably responsible for all of the cultural and intellectual achievements of mankind.

V.   REPRISE

The study of consciousness was scientific psychology's first undertaking, but its investigation has been inconstant. William James and Wilhelm Wundt started the process—James with incisive phenomenological descriptions and Wundt with analytic introspections. Wundt's way dominated, but his method yielded inconsistent conclusions, and subjective analysis destroyed the phenomena. Behaviorism was born when it became clear that introspection was not the way to divorce psychology from philosophy, nor the way to scientific achievement and assumed scientific respectability for psychologists. So introspection fell from favor, and conditioning took its place. Consciousness went unstudied for many years, for it seemed to many no more tangible than the soul. But it came back to the laboratory under the rubric of attention, which assumed center stage at the birth of cognitive psychology. The work of Cherry and of Broadbent was responsible. Their shadowing and split-span procedures allowed ready investigation of seemingly real-life phenomena, and Broadbent's theoretical analogies were sufficiently mechanistic to avoid the criticism of spiritualism. His filter theory eventually floundered, but before that happened, the study of attention was firmly re-established.

We have considered the work on both attention as consciousness and attention as processing capacity. Though there are many seemingly irresolvable inconsistencies in the research literature on attention, some facts are certain. Consciousness is severely limited, and it can fairly be called a processing bottleneck. But consciousness is not necessary for effective cognition. In fact, most cognition goes on outside of awareness, though it is nevertheless exceedingly complex. Moreover, the limits of unconscious processing capacity are uncharted, and there is reason to suspect that any observed limits can be transcended by the automaticity that follows extensive training. With practice, people come to do seemingly incompatible tasks simultaneously with no loss in accuracy. Also, unconscious processing draws nearly instantly on our entire corpus of mental knowledge, so that perception is both data driven and conceptually driven. This has created theoretical dilemmas, which may eventually require changes in the information-processing pretheoretical framework.

Cognitive psychologists like Norman and Bobrow (1975) appear ready to abandon the stage-analytic approach, to which the information-processing paradigm has been deeply committed. Norman sees no further value in trying to localize attention in or between any of the processing boxes of flowcharts. Whether his pessimism is anything more than an overreaction to the complexities of attention cannot yet be said. The problem may not lie in the limits of flowcharting, but in the complexity of the processes to be charted; and, if so, abandoning the effort may not serve the science well. In any event, other investigators continue to pursue the stage-analytic approach. Massaro (1975), for example, argues that we simply need further analysis of the various stages of processing. He believes that when each processing stage is sufficiently understood, we can assess the limits of each, by holding the others constant. The chore will be complicated, however, by the virtual certainty that some processing stages operate in parallel. The end of the scientific study of attention is not at hand.

We return to attention after describing the study of short-term memory. Some of the most current research has attempted to integrate theories of attention with those of memory to reflect the integrated operation of those processes outside the laboratory.

7

Some Structural Features of Human Memory: The Episodic Memory System and Its Parts

ABSTRACT

I. *Introduction*
   People notice the situations in which they forget, and they judge them to require memory. Cognitive psychologists see memory wherever information is maintained over time. We are as interested in the processes that underlie remembering as those that cause forgetting.
   A. *The Episodic–Semantic Distinction*   Tulving (1972) distinguished episodic from semantic memory. Episodic memory is autobiographical; it preserves the temporal and spatial features of a person's past experience. Semantic memory preserves people's general knowledge of symbols, concepts, and the rules for manipulating them. This chapter is concerned only with how people remember episodes from their own past.
   B. *Structural Features and Control Processes*   This chapter is organized around Atkinson and Shiffrin's (1968) account of the episodic memory system. It describes the evidence for various structural features of that system. By structural features, Atkinson and Shiffrin mean the permanent aspects of memory over which people exercise no voluntary control, and which they use unvaryingly from one situation to another. By control processes they mean memory routines or strategies that are selected, constructed, and used at the option of the person, depending on the characteristics of the situation facing him.

II. *Three Memory Stores*   According to Atkinson and Shiffrin, the basic structural features of episodic memory are three memory stores, called the *sensory register*, the *short-term store* and the *long-term store*. The three stores are said to be structurally distinct because they preserve information in different formats, for different durations and for different purposes, and because they lose information in different ways and have different anatomical bases.

A. *The Sensory Register*   Environmental information enters the memory system through the various senses, and it goes first to the sensory register. Information in the sensory register is an unconscious, nearly literal, and complete record of its sensory image, but it is lost from the register very rapidly. It either decays spontaneously, just dissipating with the passage of time, or new information from the senses writes over already registered information, erasing it. The purpose of the sensory register is to hold information long enough for the cognitive system to run off routines that select from its sensory inputs those that will be further processed. When Atkinson and Shiffrin wrote, there was experimental evidence for a visual register only.

B. *The Short-Term Store*   The short-term store is a working memory where conscious mental processes are performed on information from both the sensory register and the long-term store. Information can be maintained indefinitely in the short-term store, provided it is given constant attention. As soon as attention is shifted from information in the short-term store, it begins to decay, and it will be gone completely in 15 to 30 seconds. The purpose of the short-term store is to briefly hold small amounts of carefully selected information from the sensory registers and the long-term store in order for people to execute the optional conscious processes necessary to tailor their behavior to the changing demands of their environment. When Atkinson and Shiffrin wrote, there was experimental evidence for only auditory–verbal–linguistic information in the short-term store.

C. *The Long-Term Store*   Information enters the long-term store from the short-term store and perhaps also from the sensory register. From the short-term store, transfer can be effected either consciously, by using control processes to relate its contents to those of the long-term store, or unconsciously, by processes that are not understood. Long-term store contains an unlimited amount of information coded in many forms. It loses information in several apparently different ways: by decay, by disruption from new inputs, and by efforts to retrieve for recall. The purpose of the long-term store is to keep information and the rules for its processing when they are not being used.

D. *Historical Antecedents of the Three-Store Model*   Atkinson and Shiffrin's view of memory is typical of the views of other information-processing psychologists, like Broadbent and Neisser. It also reflects the thinking of earlier workers like James and Hebb. Waugh and Norman proposed a similar theory.

III. *Experimental Reasons for Positing a Sensory Register*
Research on sensory memory for visual information is called the study of *iconic* storage. Experimentation on auditory sensory memory is called the study of *echoic* storage.

A. *Iconic Storage*

1. *The Prototypic Phenomenon*   Sperling (1960) used a partial report procedure to show that people can see far more in a brief glance than they can report when they are required to tell everything they saw. He found evidence for a brief visual storage system, called the *icon*, of all the letters. The icon faded rapidly, and Sperling estimated that it was gone completely in 250 msec.

   a. *Repeatability of the phenomenon*   Averbach and Coriell (1961) were among the first to establish the repeatability of Sperling's demonstration that a relatively complete and raw visual image persists after the offset of brief visual displays, and that it fades completely in about .25 seconds.

    b. *A converging operation*   Haber and Standing (1969) used a very different method for estimating the duration of the icon, but they too obtained an estimate of 250 msec. Haber and Standing also showed that the icon exists centrally, in the brain, not peripherally, in the eye.

  2. *Visual Masking*   Visual masking experiments present two brief stimuli in rapid succession to see how the second, masking stimulus affects perception of the first, target stimulus. Cognitive psychologists have distinguished icon formation from icon identification, called its *readout*.

    a. *Disrupting icon formation*   Sperling (1960), Eriksen (1966), Spencer (1969), and Smith and Schiller (1966) employed a bright flash of light as their mask. In sum, they showed that (1) brightness masks disrupt perception maximally when they coincide with target presentation; (2) the disruption occurs equally for masks that precede and masks that follow the target; but that (3) the effect falls off rapidly as the mask is delayed, disappearing completely for delays of 100 msec; and (4) no disruption occurs when target and mask are presented to separate eyes. These results show that icon formation occurs peripherally and is completed in 100 msec.

    b. *Disrupting read-out of the icon*   Averbach and Coriell (1961), Smith and Schiller (1966), and Spencer and Shuntich (1970) used patterned masks. They found that: (1) pattern masks disrupt perception maximally at 100 msec delay; (2) after 100 msec the brightness of the mask is irrelevant; and (3) disruption is as great when the pattern and mask go to different eyes. These results show that icon read-out occurs centrally and that it can be interrupted by the arrival of a second icon.

  3. *Decoupling and Operationism*   We explain how studies of iconic memory illustrate the decoupling of one cognitive subsystem from another, and how they justify a focus upon underlying processes rather than on the operational features of experiments alone.

B. *Echoic Storage*   Is there an auditory analogue to the iconic store?

  1. *Storage Capacity, Rate of Decay, and Form of Stored Information as Shown by Auditory Partial Report*   Darwin, Turvey, and Crowder (1972) performed an auditory analogue of Sperling's partial report experiments. Their findings suggest an echoic store with a relatively large capacity for raw auditory information but with a slower decay rate than iconic storage. They estimated a 2-second decay rate.

  2. *Attempts to Find Convergence*   A chief interpretive question is whether the partial-report technique overestimates the echo's duration due to its failure to incompletely decouple the auditory sensory register from the short-term store. Several converging operations have been used in efforts to answer this question.

    a. *Estimating the echo's duration*   Efron (1970a, b, c) used a procedure like Haber and Standing used for visual stimuli. His estimate of 130 msec is much briefer than the 2-second estimate of Darwin, Turvey, and Crowder.

    b. *Recall of unattended input*   Glucksberg and Cowen (1970) studied recall accuracy for unattended verbal materials. Their estimate of the echo's duration was 5 seconds.

c. *Auditory recognition masking* Massaro (1970) used tones in a masking procedure to arrive at an estimate of 250 msec for the echo's duration.

3. *Conclusions* The research on echoic storage supports the idea of an auditory sensory register that preserves the temporal pattern of sounds long enough to allow higher-level cognitive processing. The failure to find full operational convergence on an estimate of the echo's duration probably resulted from a failure to separate echoic memory from the short-term store.

IV. *Characteristics of the Short-Term Store*

Looking up a new phone number and trying to dial it under various conditions is used to illustrate the space and time limits of the short-term store.

A. *Space Limit* Miller's (1956) analysis of the limits of short-term memory at 7 ± 2 items is described. Informal experiments that a student can perform are suggested to demonstrate that the limit on the number of items applies regardless of their size.

B. *Time Limit* Peterson and Peterson (1959) demonstrated that items are lost from the short-term store about 20 seconds after attention is withdrawn from them. Murdock (1961) showed that this rate of loss applies regardless of the size of the items from which attention is withdrawn. Bjork's (1972) findings on intentional forgetting illustrate the adaptive value of a relatively rapid loss of information from the short-term store.

C. *The Modalities of Short-Term Storage*

1. *Auditory-Verbal-Linguistic* Atkinson and Shiffrin posited only an auditory-verbal-linguistic mode of operation for the short-term store. Conrad's (1964) findings support this position. He showed that recall errors for visually presented letters were based on acoustic confusions.

2. *Visual Storage* Brooks (1968) and Shepard and Metzler (1971) showed that visual information can also be held in the short-term store.

V. *Differentiating the Long-Term Store From the Short-Term Store*

A. *Clinical, Anatomical Findings* Clinical reports by Shallice and Warrington (1970) and Milner (1959, 1966) suggest different anatomical bases for short- and long-term memory.

B. *Experimental Evidence* Glanzer has shown that the serial position curve for free recall is a discontinuous composite of two underlying curves, one reflecting output from a long-term store and one from a short-term store. Craik's (1970) use of final free recall to separate the short- and long-term stores is cited as an elegant example of psychological experimentation.

VI. *A Reminder*

This chapter described data that are consistent with the model by Atkinson and Shiffrin. Data collected in the 1970s led psychologists to other views of episodic memory.

I.   INTRODUCTION

People are most likely to notice their memories when they forget. They decide that an activity requires memory when forgetting keeps them from doing it. Cognitive psychologists say that people are aware of the results of their memory processes, not of the processes themselves. And people are aware of the results primarily when they are unsatisfactory: They notice largely when memory fails, not when it succeeds. Still, they cannot tell you how they forget, nor how they remember. Cognitive psychologists want to investigate the processes that underlie remembering and forgetting.

People do know the situations in which they forget, and they use that knowledge to judge which situations require memory. Consequently, they judge that recognizing well-known things, like familiar faces, does not involve memory, but only knowledge. They judge that immediately reproducing something, as when parroting what was just said for someone who did not hear, depends simply on hearing or perceiving, not having remembered. Cognitive psychologists view memory more broadly. They see it wherever information is maintained over time, regardless of whether the maintained information is ever forgotten by anyone. The duration of the maintained interval may be as short as a fraction of a second, or as long as a lifetime.

Cognitive psychologists assume that memory is a cognitve system. Noting that, and recalling what was said in Chapter 1 about analyzing natural systems, you might expect an early question to be about the memory system's parts. To study the memory system, we must identify its subsystems; we must specify its structure. This chapter primarily concerns the results of experiments that cognitive psychologists have relied on to evaluate one influential theory of the structure of memory. That theoretical view was advanced by Atkinson and Shiffrin, in 1968, and we consider experiments that led them to it.

From our opening paragraphs, you might have observed that information-processing psychologists have blurred the distinction between perception and memory, by seeing memory even in activities that are so brief that people usually think of them as matters of perception. You should expect, therefore, that this chapter considers experiments that track the time-course of very rapid happenings. And it does, when describing work on iconic and echoic memory. What you could not have anticipated is that this chapter deals with memory for personally experienced events or episodes, not with semantic memory.

A. The Episodic–Semantic Distinction

What are the differences between episodic and semantic memory, and why do we distinguish between them? Tulving (1972) formalized and clarified the distinction between episodic and semantic memory. The distinction has many facets, but chief among these is that a person's episodic memories are personal. They refer to his own past. They are autobiographical, and can usually be translated into the form: "I did such and such, in such and such a place, at such and such a time." The essence of an episodic memory is that it recaptures the temporal and spatial context of a person's past experience. To illustrate, Tulving gave the following examples:

1. I remember seeing a flash of light a short while ago, followed by a loud sound a few seconds later.
2. Last year, while on my summer vacation, I met a retired sea captain who knew more jokes than any other person I have ever met.
3. I remember that I have an appointment with a student at 9:30 tomorrow morning.
4. One of the words I am sure I saw in the first list I studied was LEGEND.
5. I know the word that was paired with DAX in this list was FRIGID.

Examples (4) and (5) are hypothetical comments about experiences with verbal-learning experiments. Tulving's use of these examples indicates that verbal-learning experiments should be construed as studies of episodic memory, which in turn suggests that the roots of the episodic–semantic distincton lie in psychology's intellectual ancestry. In fact, the research that led to the distinction began with Ebbinghaus.

Semantic memory, in contrast, is not autobiographical. It contains a person's knowledge of words and symbols, their meanings and referents, knowledge of the relations among words, and the rules or algorithms for manipulating words, symbols, and the relations among them. Of course, people learn these things, but in their semantic memories there are seldom records of the situations in which they learned any particular word, concept, or rule. Thus, accuracy of semantic memories cannot be judged against particular past experiences, as the accuracy of episodic memories must be. Here are the examples that Tulving uses to illustrate semantic memory:

1. I remember that the chemical formula for common table salt is NaCl.
2. I know that the summers are usually quite hot in Katmandu.
3. I know that the name of the month that follows June is July, if we consider them in the order in which they occur in the calendar, or March if we consider them in alphabetical order.
4. I know that the uncertainty of an event having five equiprobable outcomes is 2.322 bits.
5. I think that the association between the words TABLE and CHAIR is stronger than that between the words TABLE and NOSE.

Each of these illustrative statements refers to its speaker's general knowledge, to knowledge that is divorced from particular episodes in his past and from the context in which the knowledge was acquired. The statements are linguistic translations of general concepts and their relations. Nevertheless, they are definitely memory statements, because they could not be made if semantic information had not previously been stored in the speaker's mind. Notice that you can judge the accuracy of these statements without knowing the speaker_or his past. You could not do that for episodic memory statements.

Tulving distinguished episodic from semantic memory in order to clarify a complex cleavage among memory investigations. Among other issues, the cleavage concerns the value of laboratory experiments that use verbal-learning techniques. As the information-processing paradigm spread, so did its pretheoretical commitment to clarifying human cognition in its normal context, and cognitive psychologists increasingly asked whether verbal-learning experiments tapped processes that operate in everyday situations. Most verbal-learning procedures are unlike the things people normally do, and this fact led some to question the importance of verbal-learning experimentation. On the other hand, semantic matters are directly relevant to such everyday activities as reading, writing, and classroom learning. Thus, learning what schools have to teach has little to do with remembering personal experiences, but it has much to do with learning generalized concepts and how to use them. The study of episodic memory thus seems to say little about it. As insights like these occurred to cognitive scientists, and as they were swept up in their new techniques for studying semantic memory, there arose among some a disdain for the more traditional laboratory experimentation of the verbal-learning type. Still, many others continued the older style of research, and the cleavage grew.

Tulving's clarification of the differences between episodic and semantic memory helped reduce the potential divisiveness of this cleavage, and it heralds relative peace among students of memory. It highlights the fact that people have autobiographic memories and that these serve indispensable human functions. People need to know whom they have seen and what they have done, when they saw them and when they did their activities, and where. Otherwise they could not know what they have left to do and whom they must see, or likely will see again. They could not remember the name of the boss's wife whom they met only once at a cocktail party. The study of episodic memory can therefore amount to the study of typical cognition. In a serial learning experiment, one receives no credit for remembeing SHRUB when he studied BUSH, just as he receives no credit for recalling the boss's wife as OPAL when her name is RUBY. Given the information-processing psychologist's commitment to laboratory investigation, the use of verbal-learning procedures to study episodic memory is paradigmatically acceptable. Most information-processing psychologists can likewise agree that it is important to study semantic memory.

Tulving therefore helped add a pretheoretical idea to the information-processing paradigm—namely, that the episodic and semantic memory systems are distinct from one another. Not all cognitive psychologists accept the distinction, but many do. It fits the rest of their system of assumptions, and it legitimizes a division of labor: Some scientists study semantic memory, while others study episodic memory.

Generally, paradigmatic commitments guide science, they are not tested by it. Pretheoretical commitments provide the occasional exception to this rule, because they are sometimes put to experimental test. It is too soon to tell whether this will be the case with the notion that the episodic and semantic memory systems are distinct from one another. Presently, many studies make the distinction as an assumption rather than a hypothesis. At present, the separation is a paradigmatic decision, which cannot yet be justified by citing experiments. Even so, the distinction will be maintained as long as no compelling evidence accumulates against it and no competing view serves better to organize research findings and support formal theories.

We would not be surprised to find the semantic-episodic memory distinction put to experimental test. Since most memory experiments tap both episodic and semantic memory, cognitive psychologists who use the distinction will want to know how the two combine to produce performance in their experiments. To find out, they will have to think about how to distinguish the two systems experimentally. If anyone finds an agreeable way to do this, the idea may be elevated to explicit theoretical status. Subsequent experiments testing the distinction may prove supportive, or they may not. If a great weight of evidence accumulates against the distinction, psychologists will make less and less use of it. However, all this is in the realm of the future. No one has yet worked out a way to put the semantic–episodic memory distinction to direct empirical test. For now we treat them separately, because we find the distinction useful. We have been able to make a comfortable division in our chapters between work that is primarily concerned with episodic memory and that with semantic memory. In this chapter we discuss proposals and evidence for structural features of episodic memory. In the next chapter we consider control processes that work in episodic memory and alternatives to the structural approach. Then we turn to semantic memory.

B. Structural Features and Control Processes

When Atkinson and Shiffrin (1968) advanced their view of episodic memory, they distinguished its structural features from its control processes. By structural features they meant relatively stable information-processing sequences over which people exercise no voluntary control, and which they use unvaryingly from one situation to another regardless óf the content of the information coming in. By control processes they meant memory routines or strategies that are selected, constructed, and used at the option of the person, depending on the characteristics of the situation facing him. Control processes are sensitive to the content of incoming data.

For the reader familiar with computer programming, the following analogy should serve to illustrate the distinction. Consider the flow of information in a computer program. Some sequences, such as unqualified READ, direct GO TO, and fully specified DO loops will always be executed, regardless of the specific content of the symbolic material that the program is processing. Such instructions are therefore analogous to structural processes in psychological theory. In contrast, there are contingent decision-making statements; some READ, GO TO, and DO instructions are only carried out when the symbolic material being processed takes on specified values. These contingent instructions are analogous to control processes. When the programmer, in time-sharing or interactive computing, interrupts the flow of information to change some instruction, this is equivalent to conscious intervention in human control processes.

For those readers unfamiliar with computer programs, the following illustration makes essentially the same point. Automatic rapid transit systems, such as San Francisco's BART, have aspects analogous to structural processes. For example, the routes do not change; there are fixed sequences of stops; there are some express and some local trains; and so on. These features of the system are impervious to activity going on within the system, such as the number of passengers, the spacing between cars, and such. Systems like BART also have features analogous to control processes. For example, if cars get too close together or too far apart, speeds are automatically adjusted to improve their spacing. Some automatic systems may even adjust themselves to the number of passengers; trains may automatically enter or leave the tracks if the number of passengers increases or decreases to some criterial level. Such systems also have a counterpart to human conscious intervention. They have control centers, where human operators monitor the system's activity. If there is an emergency, the human operators can override many of the usual control processes by making trains speed up, slow down, stop altogether, bypass stations, or change routes.

Structural features can be theoretically valid and useful whether or not distinct anatomical or physiological correlates are found for them. Such evidence would, of course, be powerful support; however, knowledge of how brain physiology relates to behavior is still minimal. It may be a long time before the science of neurophysiology supplies much usable information to psychologists. Instead, the most common method of studying structural features is to attempt to identify memory functions that operate similarly across many apparently different situations. Control processes are more likely to be studied by showing that they are used differently by different people or that they operate uniquely in particular contexts.

II.   THREE MEMORY STORES

According to Atkinson and Shiffrin, the basic structural features of episodic memory are three memory stores, which they call the *sensory register,* the *short-term store,* and the *long-term store.* These stores are said to be structurally distinct because they preserve information in different formats, for different durations, and for different purposes, and because they lose information in different ways. In principle, they may also be distinguished on anatomical grounds. The purpose of this chapter is to describe the experimental findings that justify and test these assertions. It is to show why the three-store model was accepted in the first place, and to prepare the way for explaining why many scientists have recently questioned Atkinson and Shiffrin's three-store theory. This latter purpose is pursued in the next chapter.

In Chapter 4 we showed a flowchart of Atkinson and Shiffrin's model (Fig. 4.4). It included a response generation system and control processes, as well as the three memory stores. Here, we are concerned only with the three stores, and they are represented more completely in Fig. 7.1 than they were in Fig. 4.4.

A. The Sensory Register

Figure 7.1 indicates that external information enters the memory system through the various senses, and that it goes first to the sensory register, which we define below. You can see in Fig. 7.1 that Atkinson and Shiffrin provided for the possibility of separate sensory registers for each sense modality. But they explicitly labeled only the visual register, because when they described their model in 1968, there was no experimental proof that the other senses, such as audition, had register memory functions. In their view, information in the sensory register is a nearly literal record of its sensory image. It is not recognized, categorized, or identified until after it has passed through the sensory register. Moreover, they considered that the entry of information into the register is passive. Entry cannot be avoided if the senses are functioning properly. No control processes are involved. But while the register accepts all sensory information in a complete and raw form, it does not keep it for very long. The information is lost from the register in less than a second. Sensory information is lost in either of two ways. Either it decays spontaneously, simply dissipating with the passage of time; or new information from the senses writes over already registered information, erasing it.

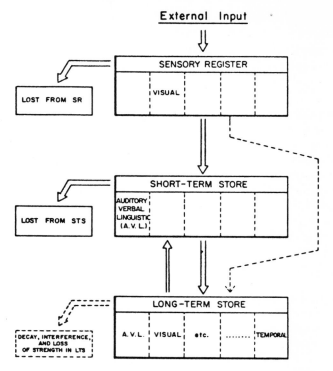

FIG. 7.1. Flow diagram of the three memory stores in Atkinson and Shiffrin's (1968) model of episodic memory.

You may wonder about the function of sensory memories. What value do they have? One answer is that people cannot attend simultaneously to all the information that impinges on their senses. They must be selective, as the data on attention show. According to Atkinson and Shiffrin, that selectivity seems to come during the process of reading information out of the sensory register into the short-term store, which can preserve it longer than the sensory register can. Like all cognitive processes, this selective read-out takes time. The function of the sensory register, then, is to preserve incoming information long enough for it to be selectively transmitted further into the memory system. Without a sensory register, the argument goes, people would be totally absorbed trying to keep up with their sensory inputs. The sensory register holds information long enough for the cognitive system to run off subroutines that select from its sensory inputs those that will be further processed. While Atkinson and Shiffrin have little to say about these selective subroutines, they do argue that their outputs can be attended to (a control process), and that if they are, they enter the short-term store.

B. The Short-Term Store

Atkinson and Shiffrin represent the short-term store as a "working memory," by which they mean that *conscious* mental processes are performed there. As you can see from the arrows in Fig.7.1, its inputs come from both the sensory register and the long-term store. Atkinson and Shiffrin argue that information cannot be consciously processed in either the sensory register or the long-term store: Consciousness is a unique function of the short-term store. For conscious manipulation, information must be copied into the short-term store. This kind of formulation reflects the computer analogy, for computers transfer information by copying it from one register to another. Notice that this transfer by copying does not remove the information from its source store. If it came to the short-term store from the long-term store, it is present in both locations until it leaves the short-term store. Unlike the sensory register, information can be maintained indefinitely in the short-term store, provided it is given constant attention. As soon as attention is shifted from information in the short-term store, it begins to decay, and it will be gone completely in 15 to 30 seconds.

Figure 7.1 shows that Atkinson and Shiffrin provided for the possibility of several kinds of information in the short-term store, just as they provided for each sense modality in the register. But they explicitly labeled only one form of information, which they designated *auditory–verbal–linguistic*. It might seem puzzling that they specified only visual information in the sensory register, and only auditory–verbal–linguistic information in the short-term store. The sensory register is a major source of input for the short-term store, and you might reasonably have expected Atkinson and Shiffrin to specify the same sorts of information for both. That they did not illustrates the sort of anomaly that pervades unfinished sciences. The data available at the time they wrote allowed Atkinson and Shiffrin no alternative. No research had yet been done to show sensory memories outside of the visual modality. There has subsequently been such research, and Atkinson and Shiffrin could now fill in the box they left for an auditory sensory register (see Fig. 7.1). But that would still leave a puzzle, because they had no evidence for visual information in the short-term store. What happens to visual information on its way from the register to the short-term store? Evidently it is converted into an auditory–verbal–linguistic or speech mode. Thus, a word presented visually in a verbal-learning experiment will be converted into a speech-like form after it leaves the sensory register and before it enters the short-term store. It seems highly unlikely that this happens to all visual information, but when Atkinson and Shiffrin wrote, none of the available experimental data allowed them to rule out this possibility. Practically all of the relevant experiments had used linguistic materials, for which a conversion from visual to speech form on the way to the working memory would make sense. The easiest way to work on linguistic materials may be to think of them as speech. Whether this is so or not, it is clear that the character of information in the short-term store is not necessarily the same as its form when it arrived at the senses. Information can be cognitively transformed between its sensory registration and its conscious manipulation. This kind of transformation from one format to another is the type of operation computers can perform; and it is another example of the sort of mental process that is suggested by a computer analogy.

Why should people have short-term stores? What is their function, as contrasted with the functions of the sensory register and the long-term store? We see two keys to answering these questions. The first is that the sensory register and the long-term store are both large-capacity memories, while the short-term store has a small capacity. You can provide a kind of evidence about this assertion for yourself. Ask yourself: Of the probably unlimited number of things you know, how many can you attend to at once? Very few. Evidence about the capacity of the sensory register is harder to come by, but we show shortly that it holds far more information than the short-term store. The second key is that the short-term store allows for conscious work on information, while the sensory registers and the long-term store do not. The function of the short-term store, then, is to briefly hold small amounts of carefully selected information from the sensory registers and the long-term store in order for people to execute the optional conscious processes necessary to tailor their behavior to the changing demands of their environment. In this view, conscious information processing is necessary for people to function effectively. To coordinate their behavior with the world around them, they must consciously bring together a few relevant pieces of information from both their sensory experience and their long-term knowledge stores.

C. The Long-Term Store

The arrows in Fig. 7.1 indicate that information flows into the long-term store from the short-term store and perhaps also from the sensory register (the arrow of dashes). From the short-term store, transfer can be effected either consciously, by using control processes to relate its contents to those of the long-term store, or unconsciously. Conscious transfer occurs, for example, when one commits a telephone number to memory by inventing a mnemonic. However, it was necessary to postulate unconscious transfer because people know things that they almost certainly did not acquire deliberately. For example, many people will be able to tell you how many windows are in their living room—or even how many there were in a house they moved away from long ago. For reasons like these, and more technical ones too, Atkinson and Shiffrin postulated an unconscious mechanism for the transfer of information from the short- to the long-term store. They did not specify the character of this mechanism, but they did specify one of its results: The longer information remains in the short-term store, the more strongly it is represented in the long-term store. It is as if some automatic transformation is performed on information as long as we are conscious of it, as long as it resides in the short-term store. That transformation makes the information we are conscious of compatible with the storage style of the long-term store. Furthermore, it is as if these transforms of information in the short-term store are automatically passed on to the long-term store, and the extent of this transfer seems determined by how long the information is in the short-term store. These transformation and transfer processes remain mysterious, but Atkinson and Shiffrin found it necessary to posit them.

Figure 7.1 shows that Atkinson and Shiffrin specified several forms of information in the long-term store. This seems to suggest that when they wrote, there was a greater variety of research on long-term memory than on sensory or short-term memory, but that is not true. Most research into long-term memory had been done in verbal-learning laboratories with linguistic materials. This research constrained and guided Atkinson and Shiffrin with respect to the sensory register and the short-term store. However, they had little research to guide them in long-term memory; so they had to rely on common sense and their own personal experience when it came to positing its content. Everyone is able to recognize tastes, smells, faces, voices, and so on, and such recognition is by itself sufficient reason to believe that every sense has its own mode of long-term storage. This is even true for what Atkinson and Shiffrin call temporal storage (see Fig. 7.1). Temporal patterning is not uniquely associated with any sense modality, but we can and do readily recognize temporal patterns.

We have already mentioned that the capacity of the long-term store greatly exceeds that of the short-term store. As far as we know, its capacity is unlimited. We cannot conceive of cataloguing all its contents. But its great capacity does not mean that information is never lost from long-term storage. On the contrary, it is lost, and in several apparently different ways. Here we will just mention the names of those ways: decay, interference by disruption when new information is transferred to the long-term store, interference by changes in the form of old information when new information contacts it in the long-term store, and interference during attempts to search for or retrieve information from the long-term store.

What is the function of the long-term store? To do their mental work, people must have recourse to a vast repository of information, and they must be able to call on many mental rules. The function of the long-term store is to keep information and the rules for its processing when they are not being used. This sort of storage need not be conscious, because we do not use all of our knowledge nor all of our cognitive subroutines all of the time. But these things need to be maintained so they can be called up to the short-term memory when they are needed.

D. Historical Antecedents of the Three-Store Model

Table 7.1 summarizes most of what we have said about the characteristics of the three memory stores. It shows what Atkinson and Shiffrin had to say about how long each store holds information, the form of the information held in each, their sources of information, their capacities, and how information is lost from them. Before we describe experiments justifying the characterizations presented in Table 7.1, we should reiterate that all scientific ideas have histories. The three-store model did not jump unprompted into the heads of Atkinson and Shiffrin. Rather, in stating their model, they drew on the thinking of many scientists.

A main notion embodied in the three-store model is that there are different kinds of memory functions. Information is stored in a variety of forms, for different durations and different purposes. As early as 1890, William James formalized this idea by distinguishing primary from secondary memory. By primary memory, James meant the contents of consciousness, and he noted that people could report what they were conscious of with great accuracy. By secondary memory, he referred to the recall of information that was no longer in consciousness, and he noted that this kind of memory was not always highly accurate. These two memory functions bear similarities to Atkinson and Shiffrin's short- and long-term stores. More recent writers also drew the distinction between short-term and long-term memory (e.g., Hebb, 1949), and perhaps the most important antecedent to Atkinson and Shiffrin was Waugh and Norman (1965). These authors mathematized the distinction between short-term and long-term memory, and showed how the distinction explained well-established laboratory phenomena. Atkinson and Shiffrin probably would not have distinguished three memory stores if it were not for the work of Waugh and Norman, and psychologists would have been far less likely to have accepted the distinction.

For years, verbal-learning psychologists differentiated memories according to how long they lasted. Thus, they spoke of very-short-term memory, short-term memory and long-term memory. This distinction, too, finds expression in the Atkinson and Shiffrin model. But understand that Atkinson and Shiffrin do not mean the same thing by short- and long-term *store* that verbal-learning psychologists meant by short- and long-term *memory*. In verbal learning, the distinction was largely a descriptive one, referring to the time interval over which particular memories lasted. For Atkinson and Shiffrin, the distinction is a structural one, referring to different parts of the cognitive system. This is an important difference when it comes to explaining any particular memory phenomenon. Thus, when Atkinson and Shiffrin account for forgetting that occurs in a matter of minutes, they can invoke functions associated with their long-term store as well as ones associated with

TABLE 7.1

Structural Features of the Three Episodic Memory Stores

Memory Store	How Long Information Is Held	Form of Information	Source of Information	Information Capacity	How Information Is Lost
Sensory register	For less than 1 second	Visual and auditory	The senses	Unknown, but large	Decay, erasure by overwriting
Short-term store	As long as it is attended to, and for 15 to 30 seconds if not attended to	Auditory–verbal–linguistic (A.V.L.)	Sensory register and long-term store	Small	Decay
Long-term store	Indefinitely, and often permanently	Visual, A.V.L., olfactory, temporal etc.	Short-term store and, perhaps, the sensory register	Unlimited	Decay, interference of various sorts

the short-term store. Verbal-learning psychologists, on the other hand, could hardly explain forgetting that occurs in minutes by talking about forgetting that takes weeks or months. Of course, one need not take a structural view to invoke a variety of underlying mechanisms when explaining forgetting that happens in only a few minutes. Psychologists can posit strictly functional mechanisms whose combined effects they invoke to account for memory phenomena; and, in fact, some have. You should expect, therefore, to find some researchers who question the structural distinctiveness of the memory stores. When they interpret the experiments that Atkinson and Shiffrin used to justify their argument that the three stores are structurally separate, they see only functional differences, not structural ones.

As you may remember from our discussion of Newell and Simon's influence, Atkinson was one of the psychologists who attended the important 1958 conference. The Atkinson–Shiffrin model clearly reflects the utilization of the computer metaphor. The differentiation between structural storage systems and control processes, the transfer of information through different stores with different formats, and the conversion of information from one format to another are all derivative from computer systems and their workings.

Even the notion of three memory systems did not originate with Atkinson and Shiffrin. For example, 10 years earlier, in 1958, Broadbent had argued for the separate existence of a very brief storage system, an active perceptual system and a long-term storage system. The properties he ascribed to these three systems are very similar to those ascribed by Atkinson and Shiffrin to the sensory register, the short-term store, and the long-term store (see Chapter 6). In 1967, Neisser also proposed three distinct storage systems. Neisser's and Broadbent's writings have had massive impact on cognitive psychologists, as have Atkinson and Shiffrin's. We have relied on Atkinson and Shiffrin's memory model in this exposition, rather than the others, only because their model is so thoroughly typical of the approach of cognitive psychologists to episodic memory during the 1960s and early 1970s. Of course, things are somewhat different now, as is shown in the next chapter.

III. EXPERIMENTAL REASONS FOR POSITING A SENSORY REGISTER

Research on sensory memory was originally concerned with visual phenomena, though there has subsequently been more study of auditory phenomena. We begin with the visual work—or, as Neisser called it, the study of iconic storage. Then we describe research on echoic storage.

A. Iconic Storage

1. The Prototypic Phenomenon

The prototypic experiment on iconic storage was performed by Sperling for his doctoral dissertation. He published his report of this experiment in 1960. Sperling began with the question: How much can be seen in a single brief exposure? His was not the first experiment in which people saw very short visual displays, but it improved importantly on earlier ones. The value of Sperling's study was that it objectively measured what earlier such experiments only elicited from their participants as incidental verbal reports. Some participants in earlier experiments insisted that they saw more than they had been able to report to the experimenter. Sperling hypothesized that people could not tell all of what they saw in a brief glance because their visual record, which we now call the icon, faded too rapidly. He suggested that people could record a great deal of visual information, but that they could not talk fast enough to describe much of that record before it faded away. The general idea of such a brief visual storage system was not new. Wundt advanced such a notion in 1899, and there is anecdotal evidence for it. For example, if someone waves a lighted cigar in a dimly lit room, it appears to leave a trail; part of the visual experience persists where the cigar no longer is.

Sperling's experiment succeeded in a way that earlier ones had failed, because it used a partial-report technique. Earlier experimenters had asked people to report everything they saw in each brief visual display. Sperling, too, asked for whole reports some of the time; but sometimes he asked that people tell him about only part of what they saw in each display.

Sperling showed people visual displays of 12 letters similar to the display in Fig. 7.2. The letter displays were shown for 1/20th of a second, or 50 msec. In the first part of the experiment, he asked the people to write down as many of the letters as they could, beginning immediately after the display. Using this "whole-report" method, Sperling's people averaged about four or five letters correct. This average, which is called the "span of apprehension," is typical for

				Pitch of tone
Z	Q	B	R	High
M	C	A	W	Medium
T	K	N	F	Low

FIG. 7.2. Sample visual display from Sperling's (1960) partial report experiment. The pitch of a tone following display offset indicates which row people were to report.

experiments using such short exposures. The span of apprehension in Sperling's experiment thus amounted to 30 or 40% of the letters shown.

Once he had determined his subjects' span of apprehension by the whole-report method, Sperling asked them for partial reports. After he presented each display of letters (see Fig. 7.2), he sounded a tone to signal which row of letters should be reported. A high-pitched tone called for recall of the top row, a medium tone for the middle row, and a low tone for the bottom row. The row to be reported from any one display was selected randomly, so that the subjects had no way of anticipating which row it would be. Notice that the tone came on only *after* the letters had been displayed. Physically, the letters were gone. Notice, too, that Sperling asked people to recall only four letters from any one display, and that four letters was within their span of apprehension. Therefore, any failure to recall a letter would not be due to having required too long a report, as it might have been in complete recall. And because the people never knew which row was to be reported, Sperling could take the percentage of items recalled from the rows as the percentage of the total display that people might recall if only they could report rapidly enough. Thus, Sperling could use people's partial reports to see how many letters were available to them through iconic storage—that is, in their sensory register. If, for example, a person could report 75% of the letters in a randomly selected row, Sperling could infer that his sensory register still held 75% of all the letters in the display at the time the tone sounded. As you can see, the logic of the partial-report technique is like the logic of college tests. An instructor tests on an unpredictable part of the material that he assigned. A student who answers 75% of the questions is judged to know about 75% of all the course material, even though the student was tested only partially.

Sperling varied the time between the offset of the letter displays and the occurrence of the tone indicating which row was to be reported. In some cases, the tone came on just as the display went off. In other cases he delayed the tone either .15, .30, or 1.00 seconds. He did this in order to see how many letters would be recalled at each delay interval. He wanted to see how rapidly information was lost from iconic storage. He reasoned that as the icon faded, his subjects would be able to report fewer and fewer items.

Translating Sperling's purpose into experimental terms, we can say that it was to see how the dependent variable—percentage of correct items in the partial report condition—changed with the independent variable—delay of indicator tone. Sperling's findings are shown in Fig. 7.3. By referring to the vertical axis on the right, you can see that people averaged about 40% by whole report. The curve that falls going from left to right gives percentage correct with partial report. At brief delays of tone, accuracy was very high, exceeding 80% at no delay. That is, when the tone came immediately after the visual display, people had 80% of the display available to them. This amounts

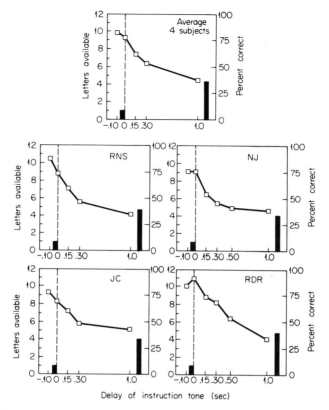

FIG. 7.3.   Sperling's (1960) findings on decay of icon for 12 items. Top graph is average of bottom four, each of which depicts findings for a single person.

to about 10 out of the 12 items in the display. But at the 1-second delay interval, there was no advantage of partial over whole report. At 1 second, people recalled only four or five of the 12 letters.

Sperling's results demonstrate the existence of a visual storage system that holds far more than we might believe from the usual span-of-apprehension experiment. It also shows that the contents of the iconic store decay very rapidly with the passage of time. By 1 second, the icon may be totally gone. In fact, most of the useful information in the icon has deteriorated by .30 seconds. Sperling's novel findings verify the observation that subjects can see more than they can report, and it identifies the reason why the span of apprehension is so limited. The limit is a verbal one, not a visual one. The number of letters reported depends on the speed with which the subject can read them off a fading icon.

a. Repeatability of the Phenomenon.   The scientific community often views novel findings with great skepticism. When novel findings conflict with their conventional beliefs, scientists scrutinize them especially closely. They are apt to express doubts about new findings until they are convinced that they conform to the rational rules for evaluating scientific evidence. A main purpose of the rational rules of science is to ensure that only real findings are taken seriously. By "real," the scientist means findings that are reliable. There are many statistical techniques for determining whether data are reliable, but in the final analysis, reliability means repeatability. So scientists will often withhold judgment on new data until it has been shown that they can be repeated by other investigators in other laboratories.

Sperling's findings were not met with great skepticism, but they have nevertheless been subjected to the test of repeatability. They have passed that test. For example, in 1961 Averbach and Coriell reported a variation on Sperling's experiment that used a different sort of letter display and a different kind of partial report technique. Figure 7.4 illustrates their displays, in which 16 letters were arranged in two rows of eight letters each. Where Sperling had used an auditory signal to indicate which part of the array was to be reported, Averbach and Coriell used a visual signal.

Following the offset of the letter display, they showed a vertical bar next to where one of the letters had appeared. This was the person's signal to report one letter from the display, the one next to where the bar appeared. Thus, at the top of Fig. 7.4, you can see that, first, 16 letters were presented. A brief period—called Display Off in the figure—followed this presentation, and then there was an indicator bar. In the case illustrated in the figure, the vertical indicator bar came on immediately above where the Q had been in the letter display. The people who participated in this experiment had to tell Averbach and Coriell the name of only one of the letters, the one nearest the indicator (Q in the case illustrated in Fig. 7.4). The location of the indicator bar was unpredictable from trial to trial, so that people never knew which of

Display on :   A X Q P N B L M
                  V T C H R E V K

Display off :

Indicator on :   ∎

At test, person sees :   A X Q P N B L M   FIG. 7.4.   Example of the Aver-
                         V T C H R E V K   bach and Coriell (1961) partial
                                              report procedure.

the eight positions in which row they would have to report. Moreover, while the displays were always two rows of eight letters, the letters were in unpredictably different positions in different displays.

Averbach and Coriell reasoned that people would correctly report the indicated letter only if their iconic record of the original display was still available in their sensory register when the indicator bar came along. If the icon was still present, Averbach and Coriell reasoned that their subjects would see the display and the indicator together, in some fashion like the one indicated at the bottom of Fig. 7.4, and would be able to report correctly. Like Sperling, Averbach and Coriell varied the interval between offset of the letter display and appearance of the partial report indicator. As in the Sperling experiment, percentage of correct recall declined as delay of the indicator increased. The data indicated that after about a quarter of a second, most of the information in the icon was gone, which agrees well with Sperling's findings.

b. A Converging Operation.   Once scientists have determined that a new phenomenon is reliable, they often become skeptical about it in a different way. They ask whether its interpretation is correct. Thus, following experiments like Sperling's and Averbach and Coriell's, the skeptical question became: Do these reliable data mean that people have a rapidly decaying visual icon, or do they mean something else? Is there some other way to account for the findings?

In 1970, Holding argued that Sperling's results were due to his subjects' ability to sometimes guess in advance which row they would be asked to report. By this view, the partial-report technique yielded greater accuracy than the whole-report technique only because people were sometimes able to anticipate which items they would have to report. Interpretive issues of this sort are resolved in cognitive psychology by the use of converging operations. The idea is to use a variety of techniques in order to rule out interpretations that are peculiar to any particular experimental procedure, and thereby to make a single-process interpretation more reasonable. The results of several different kinds of experimental operation do converge on the interpretation that Sperling gave for his findings. Perhaps the most elegant converging evidence comes from experiments by Haber and Standing.

Haber and Standing (1969) reported the results of experiments in which they successively presented circles that lasted for 10 msec and that were separated by brief intervals. The people to whom they showed the circles had only to say whether the preceding circle had faded completely before the next came on. By varying the time between circle presentations, Haber and Standing found that if the interval between them was less than .25 seconds, people reported that they could still "see" the last circle when the next came on. But if the interval was greater than .25 seconds, they reported that the first circle had disappeared before the next circle came on. The interpretation is that the icon persisted for about .25 seconds. This estimate of the duration of the icon agrees well with those of Sperling and of Averbach and Coriell. Because Haber and Standing's task was so simple, and not subject to possible guessing bias, the fact that their results converge so neatly on the earlier findings gives us great confidence in the conclusion that there is an iconic memory system from which visual information decays very rapidly.

The findings that we have described so far justify some of what Atkinson and Shiffrin said about the sensory register (see Table 7.1). They justify the assertions that the sensory register has a large capacity, and that information is lost from it rapidly by decay. We turn now to evidence about another aspect of what Atkinson and Shiffrin said about the sensory register; namely, that information was lost not only by decay, but also by erasure from other incoming information. We show that there are two kinds of erasure: one that occurs centrally (in the brain) and one that occurs peripherally (in the eye).

2. Visual Masking

The experimental technique for demonstrating that one visual image can destroy another is called *masking*. It amounts to presenting two different stimuli in rapid succession and determining what the subject sees. Haber and Standing used a procedure like masking, except that they presented a single stimulus twice, rather than presenting two different stimuli.

The possibility of using masking to understand iconic storage occurred to both Averbach and Coriell and to Sperling. Sperling used a bright flash of light as his mask. He gave people his usual brief presentation of multiletter displays, as in Fig. 7.2. Soon after each display went off, Sperling shined a bright light in the observer's eyes. Under these conditions, people experienced great difficulty in seeing the letters that had been presented. The number of letters they could report depended on how soon the brightness mask came on. The sooner the mask came on, the fewer letters people reported. In this experiment, the brightness mask always came within .15 seconds after the offset of the letters. Sperling knew from his earlier work that without the mask, the icon would be very informative less than .15 seconds after stimulus offset. With the mask, it was not. Sperling concluded that the brightness mask somehow interfered with the process of obtaining information from iconic storage.

Averbach and Coriell (1961) used quite a different mask. Figure 7.5 outlines their procedure. The subjects were briefly shown two rows of letters. Soon after letter offset, a ring appeared where one of the letters had been. If the letter was still available in iconic storage, people might have seen it with a ring around it. But they did not. Instead, they saw only the ring. They failed to see the letter! Presentation of the ring 100 msec after the letters seemed to

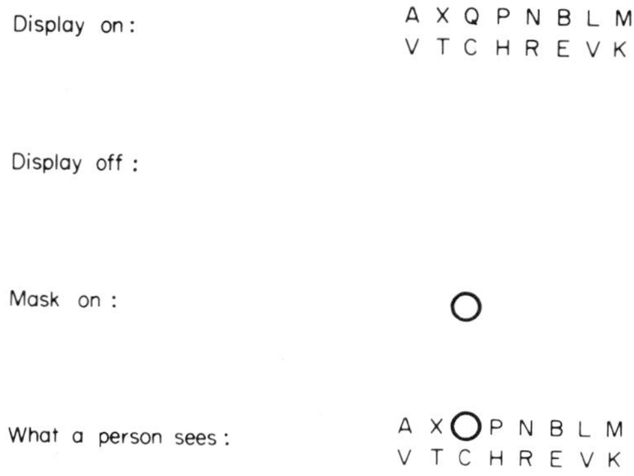

Display on:
A X Q P N B L M
V T C H R E V K

Display off :

Mask on :

O

FIG. 7.5. Example of the pattern
masking technique used by Aver-
bach and Coriell (1961).
What a person sees :
A X O P N B L M
V T C H R E V K

"erase" a letter. Averbach and Coriell knew from their earlier results that the letter would have been seen 100 msec after the display if it were not for presentation of the ring. They concluded that the ring mask caused the premature destruction of the icon.

These experiments have an air of paradox about them. The principle of causality says that one event can influence another only if it precedes or occurs simultaneously with it. But in these experiments, the mask, which comes after the letters, influences the letters' perception. Scientists certainly cannot abandon the principle of causality, because their whole enterprise is built on it. It is a cornerstone of the rational rules of science. The answer to the apparent dilemma is that the mask only *seems* to exert a backward influence. Actually it does not. It affects processes that are happening when it occurs. Cognitive processes, even such simple ones as perceiving a letter, take time. In these experiments, perception continued after the offset of the briefly exposed display, and the masks interfered with the continuation of the perceptual process.

Notice that there are at least two stages in the process of iconic storage during which a mask could have its disruptive effect. It could interfere with the formation of the icon, or it could interrupt the identification of the letter while the person attempts to read it off the icon. Remember that, according to Atkinson and Shiffrin, the icon is a raw sensory image, and that identification of the image occurs only following its formation. By pursuing the implications of this view and applying information-processing techniques, cognitive psychologists have shown that both kinds of disruption occur.

a. Disrupting Icon Formation. How might we distinguish disruption of an icon during its formation from disruption during its identification? First, icon formation should precede its identification. Therefore, we might look to see whether one kind of disruption occurs earlier than another—that is, closer to the offset of the stimulus display that initiates the icon. Second, because formation and identification are supposed to be different processes, we should be able to show that they are disrupted by different kinds of events. Therefore, we might expect earlier and later effects to be produced by different kinds of masks. Finally, because stimulus identification occurs later in the information-processing chain than icon formation, we might expect the two to take place in different parts of the nervous system. For instance, icon formation might be a more peripheral event than stimulus identification. Recall, in this regard, Atkinson and Shiffrin's argument that the sensory register works automatically, provided only that the senses are intact. Here are some experiments that show that a brightness mask has a peripheral effect which occurs only within 100 msec of a brief visual display. They define the phenomenon of disrupting a forming icon.

Eriksen pointed out in 1966 that the eye has limited resolving power. If two inputs come to the eye in very close succession, it adds them together and treats them as the same event. If one of those inputs was a bright flash of light and the other was a letter against a white background, then adding the two together might make the letter fail to stand out from its background. Eriksen called this the "luminance summation–contrast reduction hypothesis." He pointed out that if this hypothesis was correct, then a brightness mask should have its greatest effect when it coincided precisely with the presentation of a letter, and that the effect of the mask should be the same when it preceded the letter as when it followed it. He performed an experiment that confirmed these expectations. Spencer (1969), working in Eriksen's laboratory, showed in addition that a brightness mask has no effect after a delay of 100 msec. This means that the icon of a visual display is formed in the first 100 msec after the display's presentation, and that once the icon is formed, it cannot be disrupted by a brightness mask. Recall our previous suggestion that icon formation might be a peripheral process. Evidence to this effect was presented by Smith and Schiller (1966). They presented visual displays to one eye and brightness masks to the other. Under these conditions, the mask had no effect, regardless of how rapidly it followed the displays. We can conclude that brightness masks have their effects at the periphery, in the eye.

b. Disrupting Read-out of the Icon. Brightness masks have their largest effects when they coincide with display presentation, and they have no effects when they come 100 msec or longer after display termination. Pattern masks exert their influence later than brightness masks. For example, the ring used by Averbach and Coriell has *no* effect when presented simultaneously with the letters. Its maximum effect occurs at about 100 msec after display termination, but some disruption occurred even when the delay exceeded 100 msec. Our interpretation is that pattern masks affect the read-out of information from iconic storage.

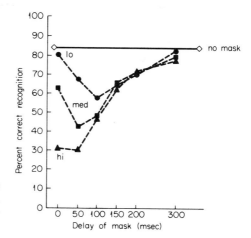

FIG. 7.6. Recognition accuracies obtained by Spencer and Shuntich (1970) with pattern masks of three different intensities.

The effects of pattern masks occur centrally, not in the eye. Smith and Schiller (1966) showed this by presenting a visual display to one eye and a pattern mask to the other. The pattern mask disrupted perception of the display. Unlike the effects of a brightness mask, the pattern mask affects central information processing and not peripheral visual processes. Spencer and Shuntich (1970) made the same point with a different experimental operation. They presented subjects with a 12-letter display followed by a pattern mask. They varied the intensity of the mask as well as its delay. During the first 100 msec of delay, the intensity of the mask differentially affected the perception of the letters, as you should expect from Spencer's 1969 findings. But as you can see in Fig. 7.6, the intensity of the mask has no differential effect after 100 msec. After 100 msec, all masks, regardless of their intensity, interrupted equally. This result should make the "ring" effect found by Averbach and Coriell more comprehensible. Students usually have difficulty understanding how a see-through ring could erase a visual image. The answer is that it does not directly erase the letter. Rather, the registration of a new input causes the perceptual processing of the earlier stimulus to stop, so that the process can start over again on the second stimulus (the mask). The first stimulus is not erased; it just receives too little perceptual processing to allow identification.

3. Decoupling and Operationism

The foregoing research on iconic storage justifies Atkinson and Shiffrin's assertions about sensory registers. It also illustrates what cognitive psychologists mean by decoupling and why they focus on underlying processes instead of operational features of experiments. Consider decoupling first.

All of the experiments on iconic storage that we have described required subjects to report what they were conscious of having seen. According to Atkinson and Shiffrin, consciousness is a unique property of the short-term store. Obviously, then, the experiments previously described could not have completely decoupled the visual sensory register from the short-term store. In what sense *did* they decouple the two stores? Long before Sperling's work, psychologists recognized the limits of consciousness, which they often acknowledged by speaking of the span of apprehension. Also before Sperling, it was generally believed that there was another cognitive limit on how much people could see in a single glance. Sperling showed that these were the same limits, that much more could be seen than could be reported. By using a partial-report procedure to show that the capacity of the visual register was greater than the capacity of the short-term store, he effectively decoupled two sets of processes. In other words, he held constant the effects of the limit of the short-term store and kept it from obscuring the capacity of the sensory register by requiring people to report only numbers of items that were smaller than their span of apprehension. You can see, then, that cognitive psychology's commitment to decoupling cognitive subsystems does not mean completely separating one part of the cognitive apparatus from others. It means using experimental arrangements that keep the properties of other cognitive subsystems from obscuring the characteristics of the system they are studying in any particular experiment. Clearly, decoupling is possible only when the scientist has a reasonably good picture of the functions of each cognitive system that affect the performance measures he is using to study any particular system.

We argued in earlier chapters that cognitive psychologists focused on underlying processes rather than on the operational features of their experiments. The findings of experiments on iconic storage partly explain this focus. Before they knew that perceptual processing continued after stimulus termination, psychologists performed experiments whose interpretation depended on the assumption that stimulus processing stopped when brief visual displays were turned off. But experiments on iconic storage show that we cannot control perception simply by controlling the duration of stimulus presentation. To understand what is happening in experiments that use very brief visual presentations, we must appreciate that processing continues following visual display, unless we use appropriate masking to terminate the processing. From the information-processing psychologist's viewpoint, findings like this dictate a focus on underlying processes, rather than on the operational features of experiments alone.

B. Echoic Storage

Neisser coined the term "echoic storage" for the auditory analogue of the visual sensory register. In 1967, when his book was published, there had been no research to clarify the characteristics of auditory sensory memory. Because Neisser had to rely on studies that had other purposes, he could build only an indirect case for the existence of an auditory analogue to iconic storage. Here we summarize subsequent experiments that have been more directly designed to unravel the role of the "echo" in sensory memory.

Echoic storage should be similar to iconic storage. It should preserve sensory input in fairly raw form for later analysis. Its contents should be neither categorized nor identified. The echoic store should have a large capacity, but a brief duration. Moreover, one might expect the same sorts of research strategies in the study of echoic storage as were used in the study of iconic storage. Specifically, one could anticipate that a major goal of these experiments is to decouple the echoic store from the short-term store. Recall in this regard that Atkinson and Shiffrin specified the form of information in the short-term store as auditory–verbal–linguistic. You might expect from this that decoupling the echoic store from the short-term store will be trickier than decoupling the iconic store from it, because there will be a greater similarity in the form of the information in the echoic and the short-term stores. In addition, you should not expect the iconic and the echoic stores to have identical characteristics. Vision is more spatial than temporal, while audition is more temporal than spatial. A main purpose of the icon is to preserve spatial relationships, while a main purpose of the echo is to preserve temporal patterns.

1. Storage Capacity, Rate of Decay, and Form of Stored Information as Shown by Auditory Partial Report

Darwin, Turvey, and Crowder (1972) performed an auditory version of Sperling's (1960) partial-report experiment. Their purpose was to show that there is a large-capacity sensory store in the auditory mode, just as Sperling showed in the visual mode. Sperling had used a visual array of rows and columns, but that is impossible in the auditory mode. Darwin, Turvey, and Crowder threw their auditory displays, which contained nine items, into a spatio-temporal matrix, after the fashion used earlier by Moray, Bates, and Barnett (1965). People listened over stereo earphones to tape recordings, which successively presented three groups of three simultaneously spoken digits and letters. The procedure is illustrated in Fig. 7.7. Each column in the figure corresponds to a simultaneously presented group of items. Thus, the

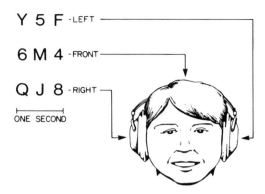

FIG. 7.7.   Illustration of stimulus presentation procedure for auditory partial report experiment by Darwin, Turvey, and Crowder (1972).

listener-participants in the experiment would first hear Y,6,Q, all at once. The items were presented so that the Y was heard only in the left ear, the Q was heard in only the right ear, and 6 was heard equally in both ears. To the listeners, the Y seemed to have come directly from the left, the Q directly from the right, and the 6 directly from the front. A third of a second after the presentation of Y,6,Q, the listeners heard 5,M,J, all at once, and then F,4,8. All nine items were thus presented within 1 second, and the item array was specified spatially (left, front, right) and temporally (first, second, third).

As in Sperling's experiment, participants could not report all of the items. When asked to recall by whole report, performance was poor: The vertical bar at the right of Fig. 7.8 shows that people recalled an average of fewer than half of the nine items. Like Sperling (1960), Darwin, Turvey, and Crowder used a partial-report procedure to see whether the subjects had more auditory information available to them than revealed by whole reports. At intervals of 0, 1, 2, or 4 seconds after stimulus presentation, a visual signal indicated whether the listener was to report the left, front, or right items. In Fig. 7.8, you can see that partial reports yielded higher recall accuracies. The superiority of partial over whole report was greatest for the shortest delay between stimulus

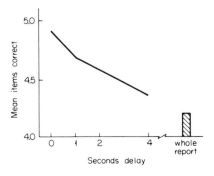

FIG. 7.8.   Results of auditory partial report experiment by Darwin, Turvey, and Crowder (1972). Maximum possible correct is nine.

presentation and partial-report indicator signal. At 4 seconds there was no advantage for partial report.

Qualitatively, these auditory partial-report results are the same as those found for iconic storage. But quantitatively, the effect is much smaller, as you can see by comparing Fig. 7.8 to Fig. 7.3. The findings of Darwin, Turvey, and Crowder do show a rapid decay of the echo, but its useful duration seems to extend out to 2 seconds, rather than to the .25 seconds usually found for iconic storage.

In addition to decaying rapidly and having a larger capacity than the short-term store, sensory registers are said to hold information in a relatively raw form. To determine whether this was true of echoic storage, Darwin, Turvey, and Crowder performed a second experiment. Recall that their items were both digits and letters. To distinguish between digits and letters, a person has to identify them, and the identification process is said to come after formation of a sensory image. If their partial-report procedure reflects the operation of an auditory sensory register, then requiring people to recall either digits or letters should not result in an increase in accuracy over whole report, even though recalling only one or the other of the two types of items amounts to partial recall. The reason is that to make this kind of partial report, people will have to have identified the items, and they can only do that in their short-term stores, not in their sensory registers. Consequently, these partial reports should be limited by the capacity of the short-term store, which is the same thing that limits whole reports. Darwin and his colleagues performed a second experiment to test this prediction. They found no increase in accuracy over whole report when people had to report only digits or only letters. This is consistent with the idea that the auditory sensory register contains only raw, unidentified echoes.

2. Attempts to Find Convergence

a. Estimating the Echo's Duration.   The chief interpretive question about the experiment by Darwin, Turvey, and Crowder is whether it satisfactorily decoupled the echoic store from the short-term store. A main reason for asking this question is that the auditory partial-report technique suggested that the duration of the echo was about 2 seconds, whereas the earlier work on vision suggested that the duration of the icon was about .25 seconds. It is possible, of course, that echoes last longer than icons, but it is also possible that people in the auditory partial-report experiment used information from their short-term stores, rather than relying on sensory memory alone. Recall in this regard that the size of the increase of auditory partial over whole report was not as great as in Sperling's visual experiments. We can ask the interpretive question this way: Are the echoic, partial report findings due to preconscious sensory processes alone, or do they result in part from operations of the short-term store? Darwin, Turvey, and Crowder sought to guarantee that their results were due to preconscious processes by presenting so much auditory information that it could not be consciously processed in the short time allowed. Efron (1970a, 1970b, 1970c) used techniques like those employed by Haber and Standing (1969) in order to rule out the possibility that conscious processes nevertheless contributed to the 2-second estimate of the duration of echoic storage found by Darwin and his colleagues. Recall that Haber and Standing's estimate of icon duration converged precisely on the estimates from partial-report experiments by Sperling (1960) and by Averback and Coriell (1961). The question for Efron's experiments is whether they converge precisely on the estimate of echoic duration found by Darwin, Turvey, and Crowder. They do not.

Efron found in three separate experiments (1970a, 1970b, 1970c) that the perception of auditory stimuli, in the form of tones and hissing noises, takes about 130 msec. Efron's subjects were asked to adjust the interval between the offset of a brief auditory stimulus and the onset of a light so that the light onset coincided precisely with the disappearance of the fading echo left by the preceding tone. He systematically varied the duration of the brief auditory tone. When the tone was shorter than 130 msec, his listeners always adjusted the light so that it came on 130 msec after the onset of the tone. Thus, if Efron presented a 20-msec tone his listeners would adjust the onset of the light to come 110 msec after the tone's offset. If he presented a 60-msec tone, they would adjust the light to come on 70 msec after tone offset. This leads to the conclusion that there is an echoic store that guarantees that an auditory stimulus will persist for at least 130 msec. The inference is that 130 msec is the shortest time required for the perception of an auditory stimulus. This estimate is appreciably shorter than 2 seconds, suggesting that the procedures of Darwin, Turvey, and Crowder did not satisfactorily decouple the echoic store from the short-term store. Alternative converging operations are called for.

  b. Recall of Unattended Input. In 1970, Glucksberg and Cowen reported another approach to separating preconscious sensory processes from conscious short-term store processes in the auditory mode. They asked people to attend to one auditory input and to ignore another. By definition, the attended input would be in the short-term store. Moreover, because sensory memory functions are supposed to be automatic, Glucksberg and Cowen assumed that the unattended input would be represented in echoic storage, though not in the short-term store. Both the attended and unattended auditory inputs were prose passages. One passage was spoken into one ear, and the other into the other ear. To guarantee attention to one passage but not the other, people in the experiment had to "shadow" one by repeating aloud the passage to one ear, as it was presented. The prose in the unshadowed ear was to be ignored. From time to time, the unattended passage contained a spoken digit. Occasionally the listeners were cued to report the digit from the unattended passage. The independent variable of interest was the delay between the occurrence of the digit and the cue to recall it. This delay ranged from a small fraction of a second to over 20 seconds.

Glucksberg and Cowen found a steady decline in accuracy of reporting the unattended digits over the first 5 seconds of cue delay. After 5 seconds, there was no evidence of echoic storage; however, up to 5 seconds there was increased recall accuracy, which might be attributable to echoic storage. Can we conclude that the echo lasts 5 seconds? No. We cannot be certain that the shadowing task was totally attention-absorbing. Glucksberg and Cowen practiced the participants in their experiment until they could perform the shadowing task without error. Only then did they collect their data on recalling information from the unattended passage. Because their participants were so accomplished at shadowing, it may not have required all of their attention; as you recall from the last chapter, practiced shadowers can allocate some attention elsewhere. Glucksberg and Cowen's listeners may have been able to devote some attention to the presumably ignored passage, and the experiment provided no way to evaluate this possibility.

Lindsay and Norman (1972) argued that if Glucksberg and Cowen had made the shadowing task so difficult that practiced people continued to make about 10% errors, they could have evaluated whether their participants ever attended to their ignored ears. Here is their logic. When people are performing any cognitive task perfectly, we have no ready check on how much of their information-processing capacity the task consumes. The shadowing in Glucksberg and Cowen's task may have consumed all of their participants' attention, or it may have consumed only part of it. If it consumed only part, then they could occasionally atttend to the unshadowed ear without reducing the accuracy with which they shadowed. If, on the other hand, Glucksberg and Cowen had guaranteed that all of the participants' attention was used up, by making the shadowing so difficult that they could not do it perfectly, then any shifts of attention to the unshadowed ear would have reduced their shadowing accuracy. Accuracy decreases could then have been used to evaluate whether people gave any attention to the unshadowed ear. This argument is a particular manifestation of a general point often made by behavioral scientists, which is that their measurements are only sensitive when people are performing neither perfectly nor at chance on the task giving rise to the measurements.

No one has yet taken up Lindsay and Norman's suggestion. Consequently, data from experiments like Glucksberg and Cowen's are equivocal. They seem to provide additional support for the existence of an acoustic sensory register, but their estimate of how long it retains acoustic information may be significantly inflated. We now have three different estimates of the duration of echoic storage: Efron's 130 msec; Darwin, Turvey, and Crowder's 2 seconds; and Glucksberg and Cowen's 5 seconds. We return to this discrepancy after a brief consideration of some experiments on auditory masking.

    c. Auditory Recognition Masking.   Earlier we described how masking techniques reveal characteristics of the visual sensory register. Massaro has used similar methods to study echoic storage. In an experiment reported in 1970 (Massaro, 1970), he first taught people to identify one tone as high in pitch and another as low. He then introduced masking tones: After the first tone, he presented a second, masking tone. He varied the interval from the offset of the first tone to the onset of the second, so that it ranged from 0 to 500 msec. The participants' job was to recognize the first tone as high or low.

    The results for one of Massaro's experiments are shown in Fig. 7.9. A different curve is shown for each of three people, but all three curves have similar characteristics. The worst a person could do on this task would be 50% correct recognition, for he could be right half the time by guessing which of two tones had come first. All three people represented in Fig. 7.9 did nearly as poorly as the worst possible performance when the masking tone came within 40 msec after the to-be-recognized tone. Their recognition accuracy increased up to an interval of 250 msec, after which they made no further improvements. Massaro's results suggest two things about auditory recognition. First, the recognition process is completed in 250 msec, so that a raw image of the auditory stimulus need not be preserved any longer than that. Second, an auditory mask can interfere with perception of a tone during the one-quarter-second interval *after* it has been presented. The latter finding strongly implies that an auditory image of the tone persists after input, and that recognition of the tone is based on an analysis of this raw auditory configuration. According to Massaro (1972), the echoic storage of

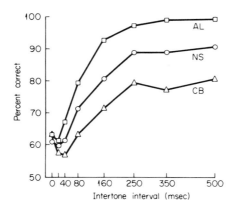

FIG. 7.9.   Massaro's (1970) findings for backward masking of tones. Each curve represents a different person.

information is necessary because it provides the time needed for higher level processing of the input. Echoic storage preserves the temporal pattern of the input, and the subsequent recognition process consists of an analysis of features that are extracted from the auditory image. His estimate of the duration of echoic storage, while differing from other estimates, agrees remarkably well with most of the iconic estimates. Moreover, Massaro (1975) has performed experiments in which a masking tone at 250 msec prevented recognition judgments between the masked and an earlier standard tone, providing good convergence on his estimate of the echo's duration.

3. Conclusions

The research on echoic storage supports the idea that there is a sensory register for auditory input. The purpose of the echoic store is to preserve the temporal pattern of sounds long enough to allow higher-level processing, such as recognition and categorization. By definition, the echo is precategorical. But the various experimental procedures used to study echoic storage have produced substantially different estimates of its useful duration. This failure of operational convergence requires explanation, because the technique of converging operations is one of cognitive psychology's main tools for increasing confidence in scientific inferences.

Is the failure of convergence on a single estimate of the duration of echoic storage due to imperfect methods, or are there basic flaws in our conception of the sensory register? Our judgment is that some of the methods are imperfect: Procedures like those of Darwin et al. and Glucksberg and Cowen fail to satisfactorily separate the echoic store from the short-term store. They have other problems, too (Lindsay & Norman, 1972; Massaro, 1975). Consequently, these investigators' estimates of echoic persistence are probably inflated. Massaro's estimates of 250 msec and Efron's of 130 msec are perhaps closer to the "true" values of the duration of echoic storage.

IV.   CHARACTERISTICS OF THE SHORT-TERM STORE

You have undoubtedly had the experience of looking up a telephone number and then forgetting it before you could dial it. In this little frustration you experienced all the major characteristics of the short-term store. A seven-digit phone number is very close to the capacity of the short-term store. For most people, remembering a phone number the first time they look it up is mentally strenuous, and they would never succeed the first time if the number was much longer than seven digits. It is also clear that you have to dial a newly found number rapidly, or else you will forget it before you dial it. If you have used both the older dial phone and the newer push-button one, you may have gained a direct appreciation of how rapidly the short-term store loses information. Pushing in a number is just enough faster than dialing one to largely overcome the time limit of the short-term store; most people make fewer forgetting errors with push-button telephones. Another characteristic of the short-term store is that it loses information particularly rapidly when you stop attending to it. Thus, if you look up a phone number and then hear someone call your name, you may very well forget the number and have to look it up again. On the other hand, you can make information persist in the short-term store. Thus, when you must pause between looking up a number and dialing it, you can hold it in your short-term store longer than usual. You can do this by repeating it to yourself, or *rehearsing* it.

Many other tasks also rely on the short-term store, but not as obviously. Sentence comprehension is a good example. Comprehending a sentence word by word is inefficient and results in many errors (Miller, 1962). In both reading and listening, comprehension lags behind initial perception. By holding the first part of a sentence in the short-term store, the human information processor can comprehend the idea behind the sentence all at once. The following sentence is easy to comprehend: *The window was broken.* You probably cannot appreciate the role of the short-term store in your reading of this short sentence. But as sentences become longer and more complex, you begin to notice your reliance on the short-term store. Thus, in the following sentence, you should be aware that you are holding some information in short-term storage until you receive further information: *The boy who lives across the street was caught stealing.* Still other sentences can seem incomprehensible because they overload the capacity of short-term storage: *The man who said that a cat that the dog chased killed the rat is a liar.* These examples show that we need a short-term store to help us decode the syntactic relations of sentences. Once the sentence is comprehended, we attend to its meaning and quickly discard the syntactic information (Sachs, 1967).

The usefulness of the short-term store is not confined to verbal material, such as numbers and words. We have already said that most people can answer the following simple question, even though they have never stored the answer in long-term memory: "How many windows do you have in your living room?" People's typical strategy for answering this question is to construct a visual image of their living room from information in long-term memory. Then, holding the image in consciousness—that is, in the short-term store—they simply count the windows. Notice that the answer to the question cannot be retrieved directly from the long-term store, because it was never stored there. The answer to the question is arrived at by a manipulation of information in working memory. The working memory, which we are calling the short-term store, is thus not confined to verbal material, but can contain visual images as well.

By the mid-1960s, much research had seemed to verify the structural features of the short-term store highlighted by the foregoing examples. It had shown that conscious memory has both space and time limits. It is a sort of bottleneck in the information-processing system. Research had shown that information can be lost rapidly from the short-term store, and that to maintain it requires constant attention or rehearsal. It had shown that it can work on both auditory-linguistic and visual information.

A. Space Limit

In 1956, George Miller summarized a vast literature on the span of immediate memory by concluding that short-term memory is limited to seven (plus-or-minus two) items. He found the limit to be exceedingly general. It applied to all kinds of people, various stimulus materials, and numerous test procedures. Accordingly, Miller (1956) coined the term the "magical number seven" to characterize people's short-term memory capacity. Notice that this functional limit is on short-term memory, not on the short-term store. Thus, Mandler (1967) has argued that the short-term store has a capacity of fewer than seven items, probably four or five. Such disagreements on its precise capacity notwithstanding, no cognitive psychologist who accepts the idea of a short-term store disputes the notion that it is severely limited in the number of items it can hold.

You can perform informal versions of the kinds of experiments summarized by Miller, and doing so will quickly illustrate the approximate limits of the short-term store. Arrange six digits in an unsystematic order, and read them to a friend whom you have told to repeat them immediately. Your friend's recall will probably be perfect. Now, repeat your test with nine digits. Your friend will almost certainly make errors. The effect is strikingly reliable, and it demonstrates a fundamental limitation on human memory. The limit on the space available in the short-term store is perhaps the strongest evidence for distinguishing it as a separate memory subsystem.

The space limit in immediate memory is on the number of items, not on the amount of information. Miller summarized many experiments that make this point, but you might simply recall our earlier example of how much easier it is to learn four dates than 16 digits: 1,4,9,2,1,7,7,6,1,9,8,4,2,0,0,1. You might try slowly reading these 16 numbers to your friend for immediate recall. If you read them with the same accent on each, without calling attention to groups of four, her recall will be terrible. But if you then tell her to think of them as four important dates, her recall should become perfect, because four items is within the limits of the short-term store. A variant on this demonstration is to slowly read the following 16 letters for recall: N,E,P,O,L,I,A,S,T,A,O,B,W, E,R,C. Your friend will not remember many of the letters. But if you point out that each group of four letters spells a simple word, in reverse, then on a slow reading she should easily say OPEN SAIL BOAT CREW, one letter at a time. And with scarcely greater effort, she will be able to repeat the letters in the order given, by spelling the four words backwards. Using dates, or backwards words, or any other simple grouping procedure, you should be able to show that your friend can remember up to 4 × 7 = 28 digits or letters. The number of items recalled is still about seven, but the item is four times as large. As far as we know, there is no limit on the size of the "item" or on how much information it can contain. The limit of the short-term store is on the number of items, regardless of their size.

B. Time Limit

The short-term store is limited not only by the number of items it can hold, but also by how long it can hold them. Peterson and Peterson (1959) elegantly showed this. They had people try to remember only three consonants, such as *X R V*. This number of items is well within the memory span, and could be remembered indefinitely if people were free to rehearse them while they waited for their recall test. But the Petersons kept them from rehearsing. Immediately after showing three consonants, called a *trigram*, Peterson and Peterson presented a three-digit number—722, for example. Starting with the number, the participants had to count backwards by threes. Their counting was performed in time to a metronome beating every half-second. After a variable retention interval (filled by counting), a participant was signalled to recall the trigram. The experiment's procedure is outlined in Fig. 7.10, and its results are shown in Fig. 7.11. When rehearsal is prevented, forgetting occurs within several seconds. People recalled the trigrams very accurately with short retention intervals, but they recalled practically nothing after 18 seconds.

Murdock (1961) showed that the time limit on items in the short-term store applies equally, regardless of their size. He repeated the Petersons' procedure

Experimenter presents trigram :	X Q J
Experimenter presents number :	247
Person counts backwards :	244
Counting rate is	241
two numbers per second	238
	235
	232
Person tries to recall trigram :	X — J

FIG. 7.10. Illustration of Peterson and Peterson's (1959) procedure. In this example, the counting interval is 3 seconds long, and the subject has forgotten the "Q".

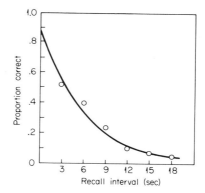

FIG. 7.11. Peterson and Peterson's (1959) results.

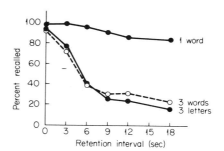

FIG. 7.12. Murdock's (1961) results using Peterson and Peterson's technique with different size units.

with three kinds of items: three letters, like the Petersons' (e.g., DQX); one three-letter word (e.g., DOG); and three three-letter words (e.g., CAT, BAR, RIG). The important thing to notice about these conditions is that the first and the last have the same number of *items*, while the first and second have the same number of *letters*. If the time limit of the short-term store applies to items regardless of their size, then recall should fall off equally rapidly for the first and third conditions, but not for the second. Figure 7.12 shows that to be the case. In the short-term store, the size of the memory unit has no effect on how rapidly it is forgotten, just as it has no effect on how many units can be retained.

To estimate the duration of information in the short-term store, we must prevent rehearsal, for rehearsal will increase the persistence of information. In the Peterson and Peterson procedure (often called the Brown/Peterson procedure, because Brown [1958] introduced a similar version), rehearsal prevention is accomplished by having people count backwards, which raises an interpretive problem. Counting backwards should cause new information (the numbers) to enter the short-term store, and that information might displace the trigram whose persistence in the store is being studied. In fact, the usual interpretation of results in the Brown/Peterson task is that the short-term store loses information by displacement; and this means that the procedure cannot provide suitable evidence from which to infer how long the original information stays in the short-term store if it is neither rehearsed nor displaced. There is no question that information leaves the short-term store quickly in a Brown/Peterson procedure, but there is a question as to whether that leaving has anything to do with time per se. Psychologists cast the question this way: Is the mechanism of information loss from the short-term store decay (time per se) or is it displacement? Reitman (1974) has shown that decay and displacement mechanisms are both needed to account fully for the time limit of information in the short-term store.

While the time limit for information in the short-term store is severe, it serves an adaptive function. As a working memory, it is desirable for the short-term store to purge itself of information that is no longer useful. Otherwise, outdated information could interfere with new mental operations. The results of most operations of our working memories do not need to be retained for very long. Thus, Bjork (1972) has pointed out that the *intentional* forgetting of information in the short-term store is probably more common than its intentional remembering. As Bjork puts it: "We overhear conversations, we see things in newspapers and store windows, we add up numbers, we dial phone numbers, we pay attention to advertisements, and so on—nearly all of which we have no use for beyond the point at which we attend to them [p. 218]." Bjork and his associates have performed many experiments demonstrating that people can selectively purge information from working memory, and that doing so increases their recollection of other information. The rapid loss of information from the short-term store should not be viewed as an unfortunate aberration. Rather, it is a structural feature that is adaptively suited to the demands placed on a working memory. Moreover, people use many memory control processes (such as rehearsal) to overcome this limit. Now, we turn to the question of the form of information in the short-term store.

C. The Modalities of Short-Term Storage

1. Auditory-Verbal-Linguistic

As you have seen, Atkinson and Shiffrin posited only an auditory-verbal-linguistic mode of operation for the short-term store. They were accommodating what was known at the time they wrote. Until then, investigators had focused on the translation of visually presented material into an auditory format for short-term storage. Thus, Sperling had shown that the fading visual icon was rapidly translated into an auditory form. When people recalled an incorrect letter in his partial-report experiment, the recalled letter sounded, rather than looked, like the one they should have reported. For example, they might say a *V* for *B*, rather than *R* for *B*, or an *S* for *F*, rather than *E* for *F*. Findings reported by Glanzer and Clark (1962, 1963) also suggested that the short-term store was basically auditory. They showed that people's recall of visual figures was influenced more by names given to them than by the shapes of the figures. Perhaps the most definitive experiment on the translation of visual information into auditory form was reported by Conrad (1964).

Conrad presented letters visually in a memory span experiment, and he performed a careful analysis of the recall errors that people made. Like Sperling, he found a strong tendency for people to make errors of *acoustical* confusion. Even though the letters were shown, not spoken, people did not make visual confusion errors. Evidently, information was stored in working memory according to its sound characteristics. Conrad further confirmed this hypothesis with a converging experiment on speech perception. He required people to identify letters spoken against a background of noise. Their identification errors were the same as for the short-term memory experiment, providing strong evidence that short-term storage operates in an auditory mode.

2. Visual Storage

Experiments like Conrad's, and many others performed in the 1960s, seemed to support the view that the short-term store was entirely auditory. But toward the end of the 1960s, after the experiments on iconic storage, suspicion grew that the short-term store only seemed to be exclusively auditory because of the kinds of procedures used to study it. It was noticed, for example, that the vast majority of experiments on short-term storage had used verbal materials, even though they were visually presented. If people preferred an auditory mode for verbal material, then these experiments would mistakenly suggest that the short-term store was only auditory. Perhaps the form in which information is entered into the short-term store is under people's control. Reasoning like this led in the late 1960s to experiments that showed that the short-term store can operate on visual information when the experimental arrangements demand it.

Brooks (1968) reported an experiment that highlights the difference between auditory and visual storage in the working memory. He asked people to visualize a letter *F*, like the one depicted in Fig. 7.13. While holding the *F* in mind, half of the people were required to make an auditory report of its visual characteristics. They had to categorize its corners as to whether or not they were at the extreme top or bottom. The correct sequence for the *F* in Fig. 7.13 would be: *Yes, Yes, Yes, No, No, No, No, No, No, Yes.* The other half of the people performed the same task, but had to report spatially: They had to point to the correct series of YESs and NOs on a sheet of paper. For this

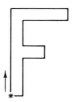

FIG. 7.13. Example of stimuli used by Brooks (1968).

simple task, pointing was much more difficult than the verbal report. How does that show visual storage? According to Brooks, holding a visual image in working memory is interfered with by other visual processing. In other words, the working memory can only concentrate on so much information from any one modality at a given time. Recall the space limit on the short-term store. When people are given competing tasks within the visual modality, this limit reduces their accuracy. But if they can report in an auditory mode, there is no conflict, and performance is more accurate. Brooks strengthened this conclusion by showing opposite effects when people are required to hold verbal information in working memory. He asked people to remember a sentence like: *A bird in the hand is not in the bush.* Then he required them to report *Yes* or *No* as to whether each word was a noun. (The correct sequence for the foregoing sentence is: *No, Yes, No, No, Yes, No, No, No, No, Yes.*) In this case, verbal report was more difficult than spatial report. Speaking the YESs and NOs conflicted with the auditory storage of the sentence. In a series of experiments with much the same logic, Segal and Fusella (1970) showed that, when holding a visual image, people detected visual signals less

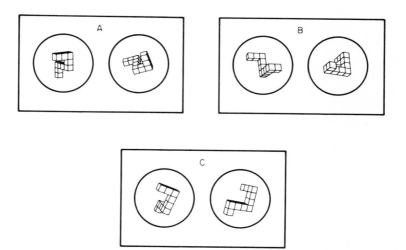

FIG. 7.14.   Examples of stimuli used by Shepard and Metzler (1971).

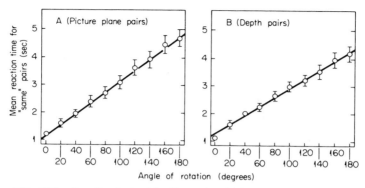

FIG. 7.15. Results obtained by Shepard and Metzler (1971) when stimuli were rotated in a plane at right angles to viewer and when they were rotated in depth.

accurately than auditory ones. The opposite was true for people holding an auditory stimulus in working memory.

Another striking example of visual information-processing in the short-term store comes from an experiment by Shepard and Metzler (1971). They asked people to make judgments that required mental rotation of three-dimensional figures. Examples of the materials to be mentally rotated are shown in Fig. 7.14. People were shown two figures, such as those shown in Panel A, and were required to make a rapid judgment of whether they were the same. Those in Panel A are the same, but they are represented as 80 degrees different in rotation. The same is true for Panel B. The two figures in Panel C, however, are not the same. The independent variable of major interest was the degree of difference in physical rotation between the figures when they were in fact the same. The subjects' reaction time was measured for the same–different judgment. The results for the *same* judgments are shown in Fig. 7.15. There is a linear increase in reaction time as a function of the degree of rotation of the figures. The results show a remarkable correlation between the physical characteristic of spatial figures and the mental operations performed on their visual images in the short-term store. Clearly, subjects have the capability of storing and manipulating visual information in working memory.

V. DIFFERENTIATING THE LONG-TERM STORE FROM THE SHORT-TERM STORE

As their names imply, a basic difference between the short- and long-term store is how long they retain information. In contrast to the dramatic loss of information in a matter of seconds from the short-term store, people remember things for years. That different structures underlie these duration differences is suggested both by clinical evidence from brain-injured people and by experimental data.

A. Clinical, Anatomical Findings

Shallice and Warrington (1970) reported the case of a patient who had normal long-term memory, but a severe deficit in short-term memory. The patient (KF) had a memory span of only two items, as opposed to the normal seven. His performance on the Brown/Peterson task was uniformly low, whether the retention interval was 0 or 15 seconds. KF also had a deficit in the ability to rehearse. His normal long-term memory, combined with his abnormal short-term memory, makes it very difficult to account for KF's performance without postulating different short- and long-term mechanisms.

Milner (1959, 1966, 1967) has reported more extensive clinical evidence. In her words:

> Bilateral surgical lesions in the hippocampal region, on the medial aspect of the temporal lobes, produce a remarkably severe and persistent memory disorder in human patients, the pattern of breakdown providing valuable clues to the cerebral organization of memory. Patients with these lesions show no loss of preoperatively acquired skills, and intelligence as measured by formal tests is unimpaired, but, with the possible exception of acquiring motor skill, they seem largely incapable of adding new information to the long-term store. This is true whether acquisition is measured by free recall, recognition, or learning with savings. Nevertheless, the immediate registration of new input (as measured, for example, by digit span and dichotic listening tests) appears to take place normally and material which can be encompassed by verbal rehearsal is held for many minutes without further loss than that entailed in the initial verbalization. Interruption of rehearsal, regardless of the nature of the distracting task, produces immediate forgetting of what went before, and some quite simple material which cannot be categorized in verbal terms decays in 30 seconds or so, even without an interpolated distraction. Material already in long-term store is unaffected by the lesion, except for a certain amount of retrograde amnesia for preoperative events [Milner, 1966].

Like all clinical data, these findings are open to various interpretations. For example, the patients described by Milner were abnormal before the operation whose effects she describes. We might dismiss her descriptions as atypical of normal people. But experimental evidence also leads to the conclusion that the short- and long-term stores are structurally distinct.

B. Experimental Evidence

To make a compelling case for two distinct memory stores, one has to demonstrate a discontinuity in performance in memory tasks. The discontinuity must be sharp to compel the conclusion that two different storage mechanisms are at work. Evidence for such discontinuity is available, and most of it is the result of a systematic research program conducted by Glanzer and his associates (Glanzer, 1972; Glanzer & Cunitz, 1966).

Glanzer's work is based on the serial position effect obtained in free-recall experiments. In free recall, a person is given a long list of words to recall in any order he wishes. People typically remember the words presented at the end of the list (presented immediately before recall) far better than any others, though they recall the first words better than the middle ones. Figure 7.16 illustrates the effects. It shows that for each of three different list lengths, the main characteristics of the serial position curves are the same. There is a primacy effect: People do well at the beginning of the list, at the so-called early serial positions. But there is an even greater recency effect: People recall extremely accurately at the last few serial positions. But accuracy for items from the middle of the lists is poor. According to Glanzer, recall accuracy throughout most of the long lists reflects output from the long-term store. Long-term storage is exceptionally good for early items in the list (for reasons that are not important here) but reaches a low at the middle. The recency effect, however, is due primarily to output from the short-term store. It is this discontinuity in accuracy near the end of the list that Glanzer uses to justify the distinction between short- and long-term storage. Theoretically, he argues, the serial position curve for free recall is actually a composite of two curves, reflecting output from two memory systems.

The way psychologists convince themselves that distinct underlying mechanisms are at work is by showing that different environmental arrangements affect the supposedly distinct mechanisms. In Glanzer's case, the argument is that the recency portion of the serial position curve reflects short-term processes, while the initial and middle portions of the curve reflect long-term processes. To convince the psychological community, he should

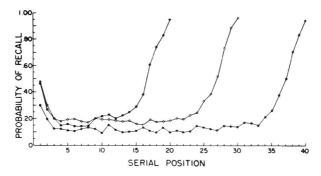

FIG. 7.16.   Free recall serial position curves for three different list lengths as reported by Glanzer (1972).

show that various environmental arrangements have different impacts on these different portions of the serial position curve. He should show that some operations lower the recency portions of the curve without affecting the remainder, and that other operations raise the primacy and middle portions without affecting recency. He has successfully done that.

As you learned earlier, Peterson and Peterson have shown that short-term recall is quickly and markedly reduced by a brief period of counting backwards. Glanzer and Cunitz (1966) took this as a starting point. They reasoned this way: If output from the short-term store is reflected only in the recency portion of free-recall curves, then counting backwards after a long list should reduce the recency effect and leave accuracy unchanged in the earlier serial positions. To test this hypothesis, Glanzer and Cunitz had people free recall lists of 15 words following either 0, 10, or 30 seconds of counting. With no counting they should have observed a strong recency effect. With 10 seconds, recency should have been markedly reduced, and with 30 seconds it should have been eliminated. These figures are drawn from the Brown/Peterson task. Recall that it took 18 seconds, according to Peterson and Peterson, for the contents of the short-term store to be lost completely. The data shown in Fig. 7.17 confirm these expectations precisely. Moreover, no amount of counting produced any systematic changes in recall at the early or middle serial positions. Glanzer has isolated other variables that affect only the recency portion of the free-recall curve. For example, simply presenting the

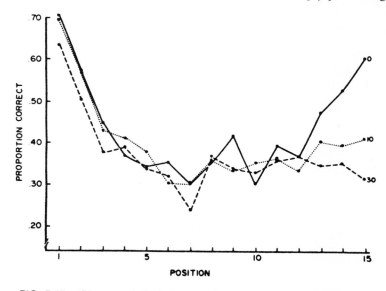

FIG. 7.17.   Glanzer and Cunitz's (1966) findings on the effects of different amounts of counting backwards upon the recency portion of free recall serial position curves.

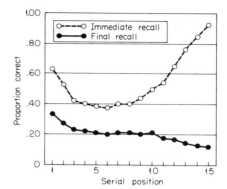

FIG. 7.18. Craik's (1970) comparison of immediate and final free recall.

words in rhythmic groupings increases recency while not affecting recall from earlier parts of the list. He has isolated a host of variables that change accuracy at the early and middle serial position without affecting recency. These include the rate at which the words are presented, the semantic relationships among the words, and whether they are repeated more than once in the list. In the mid-1960s, the evidence due to Glanzer alone justified the distinction between the short- and the long-term stores. And there was more.

Scientists look upon experiments as certain men look upon women. They scan many, find beauty in some, but they see elegance in few; they call upon the elegant whenever they can. Craik reported an experiment in 1970 that we cite for its simple elegance as a demonstration that the recency effect in free recall is due to the short-term store, while the remainder of the curve reflects long-term storage. He first performed a basic free-recall experiment. He had people immediately recall 10 lists of 15 words, after the fashion of hundreds of investigators who needed a standard of comparison for some manipulation, like counting backwards before recalling. Then, he simply asked these people to tell him as many of the words as they could from the 10 lists they had already recalled. This additional or final free recall, as it is now known, could necessarily reflect only information that people had transferred to their long-term stores. So if the recency effect reflects output from the short-term store, then accuracy during final recall should show no recency effect, but it should show a primacy effect.

Craik's results are shown in Fig. 7.18. Notice first the shape of the serial position curve for immediate free recall. It has both primacy and recency effects, with recency being much the larger. Final free recall is lower overall, showing forgetting from both the long-term store and the short-term store. But notice how much greater the difference between immediate and final free recall is for items near the lists' ends. The recency effect in final free recall is not only gone, it is negative. Whereas in immediate recall, people remembered more items from the final serial positions than from the middle ones, in final recall they remembered fewer. This "negative recency effect" can only be accounted for by positing two separate memory systems. In preparation for immediate recall, people rely on their short-term store for the last few items, and do not therefore transfer them to the long-term store. They do transfer the early and middle items to the long-term store. Consequently, at final recall they not only show no recency, they show less accuracy than they would have if they had relied on their long-term stores for all serial positions. This last assertion assumes that accuracy at the middle position is a good estimate of the accuracy due to long-term storage.

VI.   A REMINDER

This chapter is not the last word on episodic memory. The Atkinson and Shiffrin model has not endured in its initial formulation; no theory in a dynamic science does. In the next chapter, you will see how the theory has been modified, why some cognitive psychologists have moved away from structural models like the one by Atkinson and Shiffrin, and what they have substituted instead.

8

Flexibility in the Episodic Memory System: New Directions for Multistore Models

ABSTRACT

I. *The Current Status of Multistore Models*
   A. *Change in the Context of Normal Science*   The expectations of memory theorists were that the Atkinson–Shiffrin model would be extended and the characteristics of the stores firmed up. This did not happen, and the central characteristics of multistore formulations are no longer the primary interest of memory researchers. This change took place within the context of normal science, not revolution.
   B. *The Fall of Theory*   Theory can be abandoned without change in the six facets of a paradigm. This is a gradual process, which can be tracked in scientific journals as articles appear criticizing the theory followed by a lack of interest in either the theory or its criticism. To explain why this happened to Atkinson and Shiffrin's theory, we consider what attracted researchers to it, and how scientists decide to retain or abandon theory.
      1. *Three Dimensions of the Atkinson–Shiffrin Model*   Theory consists of a conceptual core, a formal implementation, and a domain of intended applications. The conceptual core of the Atkinson–Shiffrin model comprised the three stores and their properties; the formal implementation was drawn from mathematical learning theory; and the domain of intended applications was to a range of traditional verbal-learning data. Each of these aspects of the model attracted a constituency.
      2. *What Influences an Experimental Psychologist's Choice of Theory?*   Psychologists differ. Some are highly committed to successful experimental testing; others are more committed to sufficiency. In the case of Atkinson and Shiffrin, both types of psychologist found reasons for dissatisfaction with the model.
   C. *Experimental Problems With Multistore Models*
      1. *Coding*   Although each store was supposed to accept a unique type of code, experiments indicated that they were more flexible than that.

2. *Forgetting Functions* Researchers were unable to establish stable estimates of the forgetting rates from the stores.
3. *Capacity* Capacity estimates also turned out to be unpalatably variable.
D. *Conceptual Problems With Multistore Models* Some psychologists were dissatisfied with the model because it was so tied to verbal-learning experimentation. They made the metatheoretical judgment that it could not be extended to the kind of meaningful human information processing that interested them. They would have abandoned it on these grounds, however the experiments came out. Some turned to semantic memory research.

II. *Alternatives to Multistore Models of Human Episodic Memory*
A. *The Current State of Episodic Memory Research*
1. *What Remains of the Multistore Approach?* The data that multistore models were intended to organize still compels episodic memory research: iconic memory and limited capacity in particular. However, current approaches emphasize flexibility.
2. *The Heterogeneous Nature of the Contemporary Field* No single theory has come to replace multistore models. At present, there are a number of loosely related problem areas in episodic memory research. We describe those that involve a relatively large number of researchers, transcend particular laboratory tasks, are relatively theory-oriented, and are most likely to have a continuing impact on cognitive psychology.
B. *Levels of Processing*
1. *The "Levels" View of Memory* Levels of processing were introduced by Craik and Lockhart (1972) as a metatheoretical alternative to stores or stages. Since then, there has been an effort to develop a precise theoretical account of levels.
2. *Some Typical Experiments*
3. *Theoretical Extensions* Besides attempts to systematize "levels" into a coherent theory, there have been demonstrations of its extensibility to sentences, paragraphs, and theories of semantic memory. Nevertheless, "levels" is most successful in the context of episodic memory studies. It remains to be seen if it will generalize successfully.
C. *Encoding Specificity*
1. *The Encoding Specificity Phenomenon* It is easier to remember something if the same cues are present when one tries to remember as were present when the event initially occurred.
2. *The Generality of Encoding Specificity* Although it was introduced in word memory studies, parallel outcomes have occurred in studies of memory for sentences, faces, and tones.
3. *Further Research Questions Suggested by Encoding Specificity* Several researchers are attempting to determine what makes a particular cue "salient" at encoding and retrieval.
D. *Analogue Memory* Although much episodic memory research involves words, letters, and digits, a major memory function is the storage of perceptual (e.g., visual) experience. What is the coding format of such "analogue" memory, and what is its relation to more abstract memory function?
1. *Evidence for Analogue Memory* People claim to be able to form mental images, and yet for a long time psychology ignored this fact. There is now good experimental evidence that people can use images to help them remember and that they can manipulate these images mentally.

2. *Multiple Coding*   Paivio (1969, 1971) has suggested that people have two codes available: one for perceptual inputs, one for linguistic inputs. Much research evidence supports this idea. However, the characterization of the perceptual code as an "image" is controversial. Many theorists consider this metaphor too photographic.

III. *Extensions of Multistore Models*
Both Atkinson and Shiffrin have developed models that are built on the foundation of the original multistore theory. However, both emphasize the flexibility of human episodic memory, and the three stores are not necessarily essential to either one.

A. *The Atkinson–Juola Theory*   The conceptual core of this theory retains the three stores, but the role of short-term storage is different and there has been considerable development of the nature of the long-term store. Two kinds of codes are considered available: perceptual and conceptual. The major focus of the model is how people compare input information to stored memory information in a memory-scanning task similar to that of Sternberg. The Atkinson–Juola account incorporates the mathematics of signal detection theory.

B. *The Shiffrin–Schneider Theory*   The new model authored by Shiffrin and Schneider emphasizes two fundamental capabilities: automatic detection and controlled search. They hope to bring together under one theoretical umbrella the research on memory scanning and other episodic memory tasks, and existing work on attention. The domain of intended applications, and the type of experiments offered by the authors, is primarily a modified version of Sternberg's memory-scanning tasks. The theory is potentially of great significance.

IV. *Conclusions*

I. THE CURRENT STATUS OF MULTISTORE MODELS

A. Change in the Context of Normal Science

The previous chapter was organized around Atkinson and Shiffrin's multistore model of episodic memory. It and several similar models (e.g., Norman, 1970; Waugh & Norman, 1965) are called "multistore" because they posit two or three separate memories: a short-term and a long-term store, and sometimes a sensory register. Some also posit a set of control processes for transferring information among memory stores. Such models have successfully organized various research findings, have suggested many straightforward research questions, and have guided a comfortable period of normal science. For several years, it looked as though only the right experiments were needed to answer the important questions about memory. The most important questions seemed to be about the properties of the three stores and the control processes that passed information among them.

Consider how the scenario might have developed. First, the main properties of the three memory stores might have been firmly established. Experimentation might have shown how the stores differed with respect to coding, retention, and capacity. Had all gone according to the early indications, experimental data from a wide variety of tasks would have accumulated to show that the sensory register codes and holds sensory information, the short-term store holds acoustic information, and the long-term store holds semantic information. Other differences among the stores also would have been discovered. Anomalous experimental data—for instance, those suggesting that visual as well as acoustic coding occurs in the short-term store—would have been accounted for without damage to the model. Also, stable and reliable estimates of forgetting rates from the three stores would have emerged from laboratory investigation. The mechanism of forgetting from the short-term store would have been found to be decay, displacement, or a clearly specified combination of the two. The nature of the short-term store's capacity limit would have been clarified: The limit would turn out to be either on the amount of information that the store holds or on the number of rehearsals possible in a given time, or both. Tactile and olfactory analogues to the icon and the echo would be found, thereby extending the concept of the sensory register to new sense modalities. The character of the long-term store would have been elaborated more fully: Researchers would have discovered its contents and mechanisms. Finally, the promissory note on control processes would have been cashed, and the mechanisms of transfer from store to store would have been discovered.

Needless to say, this happy scenario was never enacted. The multistore approach to memory guided much research, as it does to this day, but no precise version of such models has survived. All multistore models have lost their credibility, and many theorists find even their general features wanting. To explain the demise of the Atkinson–Shiffrin model and its relatives, we must add to our account of scientific change.

In Chapter 1, we spoke of revolutionary and normal science. We emphasized the stability of normal science and the change of revolutionary science. But some change does occur during normal science, and stability can be found in revolutions. For example, the Einsteinian revolution shows that some scientific concepts can remain unchanged despite sweeping changes in others. Einstein showed that basic concepts such as "space" and "motion" were incorrectly conceived by Newton. Nevertheless, aspects of Newton's theory of celestial mechanics accounting for local conditions in our solar system remained useful, as they had been for two centuries. They were subsumed or incorporated into Einstein's otherwise completely new theory. There also are numerous instances in all branches of science of the decline or revision of major theories in the absence of an accompanying revolution. One example is the demise of multistore models in cognitive psychology.

Whether a change in science is called revolutionary depends on how rapid, sweeping, and fundamental it is. Gradual, cumulative change in a science's accepted body of facts is characteristic of normal science, as is the occasional discarding of a theory, such as Atkinson and Shiffrin's. Such nonrevolutionary changes rarely have an impact beyond the discipline in which they occur. The popular media seldom report them, and the lay public is unlikely to hear of changes in normal science. In contrast, revolutions often have impacts beyond the science in which they occur (Segal & Lachman, 1972). Normal-science changes take place without altering the six facets of paradigms introduced in Chapter 1: pretheoretical ideas, intellectual antecedents, data base, language and concepts, analogies, and major research methods. Scientific revolutions change all or most of the six elements. A theory can be rejected without changing any of these paradigmatic matters, which is what happened when the conceptual basis for the multistore models was abandoned. This took place as a part of normal science, not as part of a revolution.

We realize that the foregoing arguments blur the distinction between revolutionary and normal science, but they also make it more like other distinctions. Few are entirely categorical. Logicians and philosophers of science seem to lose interest in distinctions whose boundaries are fuzzy, but as long as there are clear cases, unclear boundaries do not keep a distinction from extending our thinking, simplifying theories, and facilitating discussion. Thus, it is useful to distinguish fair from foul weather, even though some days are neither, but are a mix, such as "partly sunny." The distinction between normal and revolutionary science is similarly useful.

B. The Fall of Theory

Acceptance and rejection of a theory in the course of normal science are usually gradual affairs, which can be traced in the scientific literature. As the theory gains acceptance, it is cited more and more frequently in scientific writings, and the majority of articles reporting experimental tests of the theory support it. Eventually, negative outcomes are reported, and when these outnumber the positive findings, the theory may start to decline. If so, there begin to be fewer articles describing experimental tests of the theory. Citations of the theory diminish, but citations of articles critical of the theory increase, until eventually even the critical articles suffer reduced citation. When a theory generates so little interest that even its critics are ignored, the theory has been effectively rejected. The rejection of a theory may or may not be accompanied by a simultaneous shift in the character of some paradigmatic analogy or by the introduction of new concepts. It may be accompanied by nothing but silence. In any case, the six fundamental factors of its field's paradigm remain essentially unaltered when a theory dies a normal-science death.

What happened to the Atkinson–Shiffrin model and its relatives is a good example of theory change during normal science. To examine the matter more closely, we look first at what originally attracted researchers to the model and then at some of the reasons experimental psychologists revised their theoretical views.

1. Three Dimensions of the Atkinson-Shiffrin Model

Atkinson and Shiffrin (1968) developed their model when information-processing psychology was new and when its intellectual antecedents still emphasized discernibly separate parts of cognitive psychology. Atkinson and Shiffrin's model reflected the pluralism that then prevailed in experimental psychology. This can be seen in the model's conceptual core, its formal propositions, and in the problems to which it was applied. All theories can be viewed as having these three facets: a conceptual core; part of the core expressed in formal or mathematico-logical statements; and a range of intended applications (Stegmuller, 1976). What these terms mean should become clearer in the following discussion. In the case of the Atkinson–Shiffrin model, each of these three elements came from a different intellectual ancestry, and each therefore gave the model a different constituency of psychologists.

The *conceptual core* of the theory likens human memory to the structure of typical digital computers. When Atkinson and Shiffrin wrote, cognitive psychology was growing increasingly fond of the computer analogy, and they invoked it heavily to explain their conception of memory. At the very outset, they distinguished structural components from control processes. This distinction came straight from computer science. In fact, Atkinson and Shiffrin themselves mentioned using a computer analogy to explain such structural components of their theory as memory stores, registers, and buffers, and such control processes as voluntary coding, rehearsal, and memory searching. They clearly adopted the pretheoretical view that the relevant human information handling is an instance of information handling by automata. Theirs was the first detailed use of this pretheoretical view to build a theory of memory. Most earlier theories of memory had been expressed in the language of verbal learning, which carried only associationist pretheoretical assumptions. Atkinson and Shiffrin's conception was a radical departure from associationist approaches to memory, and it attracted a following of psychologists who were committed to structural, computer-inspired approaches to human information processing. As to the *math-*

ematico-logical component, Atkinson and Shiffrin stated their theory formally in the language of mathematical learning theory, which attracted another sort of constituency to their cause—namely, the many psychologists influenced by Estes' (1959) quantitative work. Estes had shown earlier that mathematical theories could be applied to a broad range of learning data. Moreover, his work stimulated the construction of many other mathematical models. Some of these techniques were further developed by Atkinson and Crothers (1964), who used mathematical formulations to handle data from paired-associate experiments. When Atkinson and Shiffrin developed the three-store memory model, they capitalized on the recently developed mathematical methods to supply precise predictive power to the new model.

There can be considerable maneuvering room in the matter of selecting problems to which a theory applies. All theorists hope that their models will explain a broad range of phenomena. Some probably entertain pleasant dreams of their theory applying to all of psychology, winning them the adulation of their colleagues, job offers at the world's most prestigious universities, and scientific awards. When advancing a new theory, authors usually express more modest intentions than these; but they try to suggest the broadest range of application that seems plausible. So it was with Atkinson and Shiffrin. The conceptual core of their model featured control processes, suggesting that the theory would apply to the coding of information during input and to voluntary strategies for learning and retrieving information. Also, Atkinson and Shiffrin suggested that permanent knowledge of the world and language reside in their long-term memory store. These things seemed to give the theory a wide applicability, but all eight of the experiments originally reported along with the model used standard verbal-learning techniques. None dealt with control processes nor with permanent memory. Atkinson and Shiffrin knew their way about the highly technical world of the verbal-learning laboratory, and they probably believed, reasonably enough, that it was important to establish that their model could account for the most rigorously collected data psychology had to offer. Extending their theory to other sorts of behavior could come later. When Atkinson and Shiffrin wrote, it was widely accepted that verbal-learning studies represented people's out-of-the-laboratory capacities. Although this assumption is much less widely accepted today, it was widely held in 1968. Nevertheless, the immediate applications of the model consisted entirely of verbal-learning studies.

The fate of the model can be analyzed in terms of these three components and the constituency each attracted: the computer analogy that lay at the core of their theoretical conception, the mathematical expression of their main ideas, and the application of the conceptual core to laboratory data of the verbal-learning type.

2. What Influences an Experimental Psychologist's Choice of Theory?

The answer depends on the psychologist. Even researchers who share a paradigm are not of one mind. Among other things, they differ in the importance they attach to experimentation as compared to theorizing. All professional researchers give great weight to experimental failures in evaluating a theory, and persistent failures of experimentation will convince nearly all of them that a theory deserves rejection. However, the opposite is not always true; persistent experimental success does not ensure universal acceptance of a theory. Some psychologists are attracted most to a plausible and sufficient theory, regardless of whether it generates elegant experiments. For them, it is pointless to test a theory that is rationally insufficient; the time would be better spent broadening the theory's range of application than testing it in narrow and "uninteresting" ways. Other psychologists value technically flawless experimentation as if it were an end in itself. They may find value in theories that suggest a large number of elegant studies, whether or not these studies bear directly on any incontestably central human ability.

While this dichotomy of researchers may seem tasteless, its validity can be seen in the many articles in psychological journals decrying either too much theory or too much research. The two types of researchers who author these different kinds of articles tend to keep each other honest. Those who prize experimentation attack or (worse) ignore loose theory. Those who value sufficiency ignore or recommend against publication of self-perpetuating experimentation. The result is a dynamic balance: They often keep each other from going to extremes.

Different scientists may reject a theory for different reasons, which is what happened in the case of the multistore models of memory. Researchers from the verbal-learning tradition were most put off by the model's numerous failures to predict the results of experiments designed to test it. Consistent with their tradition, they have kept their interest in the theory's domain of application: the problems the theory was originally applied to. Though they have abandoned the model, many are still engaged in the same kind of research that was done to test the model and call it into question. Some researchers were most influenced by the model's lack of sufficiency. For them, it was important that psychological models account for a suitably broad range of human competencies, including symbolic behavior people display outside the laboratory. Information that was supposed to be in the long-term store seems central to such activities, but the concept of the long-term store was never successfully developed by multistore modelers. The subsequent work of psychologists who rejected the multistore models for this reason is found in later chapters of this book, which have very little to do with episodic memory. Finally, a few researchers are still working to develop more adequate multistore models.

Experimental failures of theory are part of the public record. Such failures of the multistore models have been summarized by Craik and Lockhart (1972) and by Postman (1975). Some of these failures are presented in the next section. Judging the failure of a theory to explain central human capacities is a more private affair, involving scientific values as well as data. Although documentation of such judgments is harder, we presently illustrate how particular scientists eased multistore models out of their writing, apparently because of the models' limited applicability to human capacities that they be judged to be fundamental.

C. Experimental Problems With Multistore Models

The heart of a multistore model is the notion that information moves through several (usually three) distinct and separate memory systems. Without distinct memory stores, there would be no model. In theory, the stores were distinguished from one another by how information in them was coded, by their capacity, and by their forgetting rates.

1. Coding

It was generally considered that only the long-term store could maintain semantic information—that is, meaning-based codes. The short-term store was held to accept only acoustically coded information. However, experiments by Shulman (1970, 1972) suggested that semantic codes could also be held in the short-term store. In Shulman's studies, subjects were presented with a list of ten words. Following this list, a "probe" word was presented, and the subject's task was to say whether it was identical with one of the list items, a synonym, or a homonym. To understand the logic of Shulman's studies, remember from the last chapter that the short- and long-term stores were thought to make distinctive contributions to the serial position curve (Glanzer, 1972). Accuracy of recalling the last few items was supposedly an index of the contents of the short-term store, while recall of the earlier items supposedly came only from the long-term store. Shulman assumed that correct identification of a homonym requires the use of acoustic information —presumably from the short-term store. Similarly, he assumed that correct identification of a synonym requires the use of semantic information—which, according to multistore theory, should only be available from the long-term store. If all this were true, homonym probes should have been judged more accurately for the later items than for the earlier ones. Synonym probes should have been judged more accurately for earlier than later items. These predictions from the three-store model were not supported by Shulman's data. The serial position effects were quite similar for homonyms and synonyms, and a pronounced recency effect for synonyms suggested that people retrieve semantic information from the short-term store as well as from the long-term store, if in fact the two are separate at all.

Shulman's studies are cited as evidence against a distinction between the short- and long-term stores (Craik & Lockhart, 1972; Postman, 1975). Even though a defender of multistore models could reasonably discount his data, Shulman's studies were persuasive because the three-store formulation was in trouble on other grounds as well. Though the short-term store was supposed to hold acoustic codes alone, Kroll, Parkinson, and their associates found evidence that it held visual codes (Kroll, 1972; Kroll & Kellicutt, 1972; Kroll, Parks, Parkinson, Bieber, & Johnson, 1970; Parkinson, 1972; Parkinson, Parks, & Kroll, 1971; Salzberg, Parks, Kroll, & Parkinson, 1971). Their subjects were asked to remember a letter while repeating other letters that were spoken to them—that is, while shadowing the other letters. The three-store model says that the to-be-remembered letter should be transferred to the short-term store for rehearsal, and that this transfer requires conversion to an acoustic code regardless of how the letter is presented. If that were true, shadowing ought to have had the same effect on memory for letters presented visually as for those presented aurally. The experiments by Kroll and Parkinson showed that shadowing interfered less when the to-be-remembered letter was presented visually. This suggests that visually presented letters are not recoded into pure acoustic information.

The original claim of three-store theory was satisfyingly strong: The short-term store required an exclusively acoustic code. By 1972, the data required that the claim be hedged. In addition to acoustic codes, the short-term store had to accept semantic and visual codes, and there was evidence for articulatory coding as well (Levy, 1971; Peterson & Johnson, 1971). Because a distinguishing characteristic of the short-term store was said to depend on its acceptance of acoustic codes alone, the suggestion that it accepted semantic, visual, and articulatory codes as well cast doubt on the idea that it was a separate entity at all. This doubt might have been dispelled by further experimentation, but the other two reasons for postulating separate stores were also called into question. Consider now the outcomes of studies testing whether the stores had different rates of forgetting.

2. Forgetting Functions

Early experiments suggested that information was lost from the sensory register in a second or less, and that the short-term store could hold information for about 15 seconds, without rehearsal. The long-term store was supposed to hold information indefinitely.

The earliest studies of the icon (Averbach & Coriell, 1961; Sperling, 1960) seemed to converge on about ¼ of a second as its duration. The Peterson & Peterson (1959) experiment provided the initial estimate of 15 to 20 seconds for the short-term store. Regrettably for multistore models, subsequent experiments yielded widely different estimates of the duration of both the icon and the short-term store. For the icon, Posner (1969) estimated up to 1.5 seconds, Murdock (1971) estimated 6 seconds, Phillips and Baddeley (1971) 10 seconds, and Kroll, Parks, Parkinson, Bieber, and Johnson (1970) pushed it up to 25 seconds. It is possible that the latter studies were manipulating visual images, not icons. Nonetheless, the relevant point here is that the theory provided no guidance to separate these two processes. Also, while the methods of estimating icon duration are very different, all the techniques required people to maintain literal, nonverbal information over some period of time. In the three-store model, the only system for such maintenance is the sensory register. Therefore, the different techniques can fairly be said to be estimating its duration. Variability in estimation of this magnitude is a classic experimental anomaly. Worse, some of the estimates clearly overlap with those of the duration of the short-term store, which eliminates retention duration as a basis for distinguishing between the two systems.

Researchers fared no better at determining a solid estimate of the forgetting function of the short-term store. Whereas Peterson and Peterson (1959) found complete loss from the short-term store following 15 to 20 seconds of no rehearsal, studies using different interpolated tasks (Reitman, 1971; Shiffrin, 1973) found no forgetting at all after 15 seconds. In a critique of multistore models, Craik and Lockhart (1972) report that some estimates of the short-term store's retention far exceed 20 seconds. As Craik and Lockhart put it: "If memory stores are to be distinguished in terms of their forgetting characteristics, a minimal requirement would seem to be that the retention functions should be invariant across different paradigms and experimental conditions [p. 674]."

The failure of different methods to yield similar estimates of the forgetting rate of either the sensory register or the short-term store might have been explainable within the framework of the three-store model. The various procedures used to make the estimates might have been contaminated to different degrees by information from a store other than the one the researcher wanted to study. Or, there might have been reasonable explanations in terms of processes of transferring information between stores. Nevertheless, most researchers concluded that convergent validation of the duration of information retention in the various stores would not be forthcoming, and the idea that there are distinct stores suffered accordingly. It was entirely unacceptable for the estimates of the icon's duration to be as great as that of some estimates of the duration of information in the short-term store.

3. Capacity

The third main difference among the three hypothetical stores was said to be their capacity. The sensory register was considered to have a large capacity, and that of the long-term store was considered unlimited, but the capacity of the short-term store was thought to be quite small. This limit is extremely important for the multistore models, because it explains forgetting during input. Not everything that enters the sensory register can enter the short-term store, because the short-term store works serially, allowing much information in the sensory register to decay before it has an opportunity to move to the short-term store. Moreover, the short-term store presumably passes information to the long-term store. It does this by rehearsal, but its rehearsal capacity is also said to be small. Thus, two kinds of forgetting are said to result from the capacity limits of the short-term store. Forgetting occurs either because an item is lost from the sensory register before it is encoded for the short-term store, or because the capacity of the short-term store does not allow an item to be passed on to the long-term store by rehearsal. Considering how important the short-term store's capacity was for explaining forgetting, and considering how central the study of forgetting was to experimental psychology, a stable estimate of this store's capacity was an important first step for research guided by the three-store model of memory.

Like forgetting rate, experimental estimates of the short-term store's capacity turned out to be highly variable. Depending on the kind of material used, the short-term store seemed capable of maintaining anywhere from two to 20 words (Craik & Lockhart, 1972). Two words is implausibly low (Postman, 1975). Twenty is unacceptably high. The usual explanation for variations in estimated capacity was that information in the short-term store could be "chunked." That is, while the subject might appear to be retaining 20 *words* in short-term memory, he might be retaining considerably fewer functional *units*, by grouping the words, perhaps into familiar phrases. While plausible, this explanation calls for direct experimental tests of chunking, and none were done by the multistore modelers.

Two theoretical questions about the capacity limit of the short-term store were never satisfactorily resolved (Peterson, 1977). One of these questions, lucidly discussed by Postman (1975), is that the mechanism by which the store loses information was never clearly established. Some adherents of the three-store view (Waugh & Norman, 1965) argued that the information is lost by displacement. As they saw it, each new item entering the short-term store pushed out one already there. Other theorists (Atkinson & Shiffrin, 1968) viewed loss as a combination of displacement and decay. For them, failure to rehearse resulted in loss through decay, but the number of units that could be maintained by rehearsal was strictly limited. The second unanswered question was whether capacity limits stemmed from an inability to *hold* more than a fixed number of items at *one* time, or an inability to rehearse more than a fixed number of items during any *given* time (Craik & Lockhart, 1972). Undoubtedly, these questions would have received considerable research attention in the cheerful scenario described earlier in the chapter. But the empirical problems associated with distinguishing the stores from each other discouraged more and more practitioners. Research inspired by the three-store model became unsatisfying before these questions were addressed. Moreover, many researchers were discouraged by broad conceptual problems, having to do largely with the conceptual insufficiency of the long-term store.

D. Conceptual Problems With Multistore Models

The foregoing objections to the Atkinson–Shiffrin model are public criticisms based on empirical findings. A more private metatheoretical objection to multistore models is that they deal effectively only with data from list-learning experiments. The models do not account for human activities that have *meaning* at their core. That is, the models are seriously limited in their application to such complex but normal activities as conversation, understanding the implications of a visual scene, reading a book, and comprehending the intentions of a TV actor. The objection is not that multistore theory was applied first to verbal-learning experiments. In time, the theory might have been extended to other domains. The objection is that the models *cannot* be extended to account for people's meaning-laden activities. Some cognitive psychologists believe that the multistore models are insufficient *in principle*, others believe that extending them is impractical and hopelessly complex. Usually, such judgments are made in silence, unlike empirical criticisms, which rely on the rational rules of science and are the approved, impersonal way to reject a colleague's theory.

Objections because of sufficiency and similar grounds are based on personal values and conventional judgments. They are the kinds of judgment that amount to saying that the scientist who spends his/her career collecting data to test a theory of low sufficiency is wasting his/her time. While a number of cognitive scientists think exactly that about testing multistore models of memory, most are reluctant to say it in so many words. Their pretheoretical assumptions must be inferred from their overt scientific decisions. Pretheoretical judgments, such as those about the sufficiency of multistore models, may be made suddenly, with a flash of "insight." On the other hand, convictions about appropriate topics for scientific study may develop over a number of years.

Consider the work of a prominent cognitive psychologist, Donald Norman. He collaborated in the formulation of one of the earliest and most influential multistore models (Waugh & Norman, 1965; 1968). Later, he developed a more elaborate, mathematically fine-tuned, multistore model (Norman & Rumelhart, 1970). Like Atkinson and Shiffrin, Norman and Rumelhart reported only verbal-learning experiments as tests of their theory. Although the theory contained a more detailed account of perceptual mechanisms and structures than was usual for memory models, it still remained a multistore approach. Two years later, Norman and his colleagues (Rumelhart, Lindsay, & Norman, 1972) published the first installment of an entirely new, global theory. Unlike any of the multistore models, it emphasized the contents and structure of long-term memory. While its authors used the theory partly to account for the results of list-learning experiments, their main purpose was to account for what people know and how they use their world knowledge in whatever they do. This was a major difference between the new theory and multistore models, for the latter had little to say about long-term memory and nothing about the actualization of knowledge. With later versions of the theory—called LNR or Elinor— Norman and Rumelhart made hardly any effort to account for data from verbal-learning studies. The 430 pages of the most recent version (Norman & Rumelhart, 1975) contain no mention of any multistore model nor of any verbal-learning data. Norman put the cap on it a year later when he explicitly rejected all multistore models (Norman & Bobrow, 1976).

Between 1968 and 1975, Norman's work showed a movement away from the multistore approach, which he fully rejected in 1976. The evolution of his theorizing is best viewed as the result of a gradual change in judgment about what cognitive theory should account for. In 1968, Norman worked squarely in the tradition that viewed memory for recent events as the main thing to be explained by a theory. From this verbal-learning perspective, questions about perception and permanent knowledge were interesting primarily insofar as they influenced episodic memory. By 1976, Norman judged that the main thing to be explained by a cognitive theory was permanent knowledge and how it is used to process incoming information. The short-term store was no longer conceived of as a separate entity, but rather as portions of permanent memory (called schemata) that people use for active processing at any given moment. This is evident from Fig. 8.1 and Norman and Bobrow's (1976) description of it:

> Incoming data and higher-order conceptual structures all operate together to activate memory schemata. Short-term memory consists of those schemata that are undergoing active processing. There is no set of sequential stages; the limits on processing capability are set by the total amount of processing resources

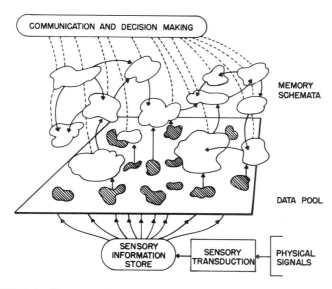

FIG. 8.1.   Norman and Bobrow's (1976) conception of episodic memory.

available to the system. . . . We believe that the aim of cognitive processes is to form a meaningful interpretation of the world. That is, the sensory information available to a person at any moment must be gathered together and interpreted in terms of a coherent framework. We assume that past experience has created a vast repertoire of structural frames or schemata that can be used to characterize the propositional knowledge of any experience. The problem of the perceptual processes is to determine the appropriate schema and to match the present occurrences with the frame provided for them [pp. 118–119].

This quote shows that rejection of multistore models is now complete for at least one theorist, and Norman is not alone. The work of J. R. Anderson displays the same conceptual reorientation (Anderson, 1972; Anderson, 1976; Anderson & Bower, 1973), and others could be mentioned as well (e.g., Restle, 1974). Some memory theorists did not have to change their attitude toward the multistore models, for they rejected the entire approach to start with. For example, Collins and Quillian (1972) approached human memory from an artificial intelligence perspective. That perspective selects human language, comprehension, and question-answering as central problems for the psychology of memory. For this group of theorists, the main research questions concern the internal representation, modification, and use of knowledge. Their approach produced the semantic memory models and global models of comprehension covered in later chapters.

II. ALTERNATIVES TO MULTISTORE MODELS OF HUMAN EPISODIC MEMORY

A. The Current State of Episodic Memory Research

1. What Remains of the Multistore Approach?

While multistore memory models no longer organize and guide most memory research, many of the notions incorporated in those models are still frequently used. For example, there is still general acceptance of the idea that information enters the memory system through some sort of sensory "buffer." The facts that established the existence of iconic and echoic storage were not discounted, as was the belief that further research would reveal fixed properties of buffer storage systems. Also, the findings that gave rise to the concept of a limited-capacity short-term store are still regarded as sound: Any credible theory of memory must account for the fact that people can consciously process only a limited amount of material at once. A current alternative to accounting for this by positing a short-term store is to consider that conscious processing is done in long-term memory, by somehow activating small portions of it (Atkinson & Juola, 1974; Craik & Jacoby, 1975; Shiffrin & Schneider, 1977). Used this way, the notion of short-term memory somewhat resembles the everyday concept of "consciousness," and theorists who adopt this view often call it "working memory." Baddeley (Baddeley, 1976; Baddeley & Hitch, 1974) has developed the notion of working memory to a considerable degree. In his view, it is a limited-capacity work space that must be allocated among two types of storage and ongoing processing. One type of storage is a phonemic buffer for a limited and ordered amount of speech-like responses or rehearsals, such as a telephone number that is being repeated to oneself. This phonemic buffer is passive, and it makes no demands on processing space unless its capacity is exceeded. If its capacity is exceeded, rehearsal routines are set up by an executive routine, which is part of working memory's processing component. Recoding routines can also be called into play by the executive, and these can convert sequential phonemic material into smaller units. The smaller units can be stored in the other, more central storage component of the working memory.

Despite the markedly diminished influence of multistore models, the facts that once suggested the existence of a sensory register, short-term store, and long-term store are not in question. What has been questioned is the utility of explaining these facts by postulating separate storage locations with fixed, invariant characteristics, through which information flows serially. A belief is growing that remembering over brief intervals is the result of flexible processes. In fact, they seem too flexible for a theory with the fixed architecture of multistore models.

2. The Heterogeneous Nature of
The Contemporary Field

Three research trends have emerged since the wane of multistore theory. Some researchers have returned to their laboratories to do experiments without benefit of general theory. Others are attempting to develop alternative theories. And some are attempting to develop and extend the three-store concepts to accommodate the flexibility of episodic memory. No alternative to multistore models has captured the imagination of a majority of episodic memory researchers. Without an organizing theme, the field has become increasingly heterogeneous.

A search through recent journals reveals that within the three trends there are a large number of small-scale research programs, each devoted to rather specific questions. Researchers are trying to explain certain reliable phenomena without reference to any broad integrative theory. Some of the phenomena seem quite task-specific. For instance, there is still a considerable amount of research on proactive interference, the rapid forgetting found with the Brown–Peterson task (e.g., Charness, 1976; Ellis, 1977; Pollatsek & Bettencourt, 1976; Radtke & Grove, 1977; Warren & Warren, 1976). In this task, a subject memorizes a trigram of consonants and tries to hold them in memory while counting backwards by threes. One version of this task produces the "Wickens effect" (Wickens, 1970), in which rapid forgetting is attenuated by shifting to new stimulus materials (Schendel, 1976; Wickens, Moody, & Shearer, 1976). A large group of studies concerns the free recall of unrelated lists of words, and many studies still compare recognition and recall memory. There is no easy way to relate these groups of studies to one another nor to tell the student what is important about them, even though some of the experiments seem extraordinarily elegant and creative.

The remainder of this chapter focuses on four research topics. Each involves many researchers, each aspires to explain several sorts of laboratory performance, each seems pointed toward the construction of a theory that might be as broad as the Atkinson–Shiffrin model, and each concerns how people use their understanding and knowledge. The topics are: (1) levels of processing; (2) encoding specificity; (3) analogue memory; and (4) efforts to improve on multistore models.

B. Levels of Processing

The first sweeping criticism of multistore models was that published by Craik and Lockhart (1972), who argued for an approach to episodic memory called "levels of processing" and, sometimes, "depths of processing." Their criticism contributed importantly to the abandonment of the multistore approach, and their view of levels of processing has gained many adherents, though not near as many as the multistore models lost (Cermak & Craik, 1978). This may be because Craik and Lockhart did not make levels of processing into a concrete theory. Rather, they advanced it as a conceptual orientation that emphasizes the role of memory processes instead of the multistore models' emphasis on structure. The general process orientation suggested by Craik and Lockhart has achieved a reasonable degree of acceptance. There is much more interest now in the dynamic aspects of memory, and much less interest in fixed structures, than there was a few years ago. Since introducing the "levels" framework in 1972, Craik and his colleagues have worked to turn the concept of levels into a theory (Craik & Jacoby, 1975; Cermak & Craik, 1978; Jacoby & Craik, 1978).

1. The "Levels" of Memory

Craik and Lockhart's basic claim is that information does not pass through a series of transformations by moving from store to store. Instead, the internal nature of incoming information is determined by operations performed during input. The input operations are called perceptual–conceptual analysis, which may include analysis not only of the sensory aspects of stimulation, but semantic analysis as well. The sort of perceptual–conceptual analysis performed is said to be determined by the person's intentions. If a person intends to remember an input for all time, he/she will perform a different analysis on the input than when his/her intention is simply to decide whether a stimulus is present or absent. The outcome of perceptual–conceptual analysis is coded stimulus information, and each sort of analysis yields a different sort of code. Whatever its character, the code created by the initial perceptual–conceptual analysis constitutes the only thing about an input that is available for further processing. Therefore, it is a memory code as well as a perceptual code. According to the levels view, memory depends on the nature of the code, not on the properties of memory stores. Different codes have different permanence. Codes of the sensory aspects of an input, such as appearance, are short-lived. Hence, a person who looked at a word to decide whether it was printed in red or green would not remember the word's name very long, because his coding would have emphasized color, not meaning. In contrast, a person who looked at a word to decide whether it was a synonym for some other word would form a semantic code, and he/she would remember the name of the examined word for quite a while.

Another aspect of levels of processing is that the life of a given code can be lengthened by "recirculating" or updating it. A code that might last only a few seconds without recirculation might be maintained for several minutes by continued updating. According to Craik, updating does not change the level of processing because that is fixed by the nature of the input code. Nor does recirculation improve later memory of the input, as rehearsal was said to do by multistore theories. Recirculation simply extends the life of a code while it is updated. Repetition of a telephone number while waiting to dial it is an example of recirculation. When the number is read, perceptual analysis extracts an acoustic code that does not persist unless it is updated. Repeating the number to oneself amounts to recirculating its acoustic code, thereby lengthening its normal life. If a person were to form a mnemonic while recirculating the number, so that he could remember it far into the future, Craik would say that he had reperceived or reconceptualized the number at a semantic level. He would say that the recirculation itself contributed nothing to the increased memorability of the number.

The levels view also includes a distinction that is superficially similar to the one between the short- and long-term store. Craik and Lockhart spoke of primary and secondary memory. Unlike the short-term store, primary memory is not a way station that information passes through on its way from somewhere to somewhere else. Instead, it is like conscious attention. Whatever is being actively processed is said to be "in" primary memory. Secondary memory contains records of past analyses, and comprises what the person knows without thinking about it.

2. Some Typical Experiments

When they introduced their ideas about levels of processing, Craik and Lockhart (1972) showed that much existing data were consistent with their views. They attempted to account for the results of studies of selective attention, iconic storage, free recall, serial position effects, repetition, and rehearsal. However, the main evidence for levels of processing comes from new studies of incidental learning, such as those reported by Craik and Tulving (1975). Subjects were told that the experiments were about perception and speed of reaction, though Craik and Tulving were actually studying memory. The misleading instructions were necessary to make the studies concern incidental rather than intentional learning. On each trial, subjects saw a word for 200 msec. Prior to a word's exposure, the subject was asked a question that he was to answer by looking at the word. The questions were designed to produce different levels of processing. Table 8.1 shows the kinds of questions asked and the level and type of processing each question set was intended to produce. After each word was presented, the subject answered its preceding question either *yes* or *no* by pressing one of two keys. Thus Craik and Tulving measured both accuracy and latency of question answering. After many such question-and-answer trials, the subjects were tested for their memory of the words. Some subjects were given a recall test, others a recognition test.

The main prediction for such studies is that people will recall more words that were processed deeply than words processed shallowly (see Table 8.1).

TABLE 8.1

Typical Questions and Responses Used in
Experiments by Craik and Tulving (1975)

		Answer	
Level of Processing	*Question*	*Yes*	*No*
Structural (shallow)	Is the word in capital letters?	TABLE	shark
Phonemic	Does the word rhyme with WEIGHT?	crate	MARKET
Category	Is the word a type of fish?	SHARK	heaven
Sentence (deep)	Would the word fit the sentence:		
	"He met a _____ in the street"?	FRIEND	cloud

Craik and Tulving's findings supported that prediction. Moreover, the data allowed them to rule out a competing explanation of their results. The *total time hypothesis* (Bugelski, 1962) holds that retention increases with processing time: The longer a person processes an item, the better he should remember it. This is a functionalist hypothesis, for it says nothing about what the person does during the total time to enhance recall. Nevertheless, it was still necessary for Craik and Tulving to reject "total time" as an account of their findings. In one of their studies, there was a shallow task that took longer to perform than an easy deep one. Memory was better for the deeper task, allowing rejection of encoding time as an explanation of the effects of levels of processing.

Craik and Tulving also found that people recalled more accurately when the answer to the question about words was *yes* than when it was *no*, except when the questions were about the word's physical characteristics, the shallowest questions asked. The researchers took this as a clue to what happens in deep processing to improve memory. They hypothesized that answering "yes" might require a more elaborate and detailed coding of the target word. For example, suppose you were asked whether a word fit the sentence, *The boy met a _____ on the street.* If the word was FRIEND, you might code it by integrating it into your detailed conception of what makes a person a friend. More "internal computing" would occur, in the symbol-manipulating sense. On the other hand, if the word was SPEECH, you would be less likely to integrate it into your knowledge of speeches, because "speeches" do not walk around streets. If this were the explanation for recalling "yes" words more accurately than "no" words, then it would be plausible to say that deep processing results in better retention because it induces the subject to form more elaborate and detailed encodings of the target word. Moreover, this explanation is consistent with the fact that the shallowest level of processing did not show the *yes–no* difference. More elaborate codes are not required for *yes* than *no* responses when the only decision is whether the word is printed in upper- or lower-case letters.

To test their hypothesis that the *yes–no* difference resulted from greater elaboration, Craik and Tulving constructed experimental materials to induce deep but symmetrical semantic processing. For example, subjects were asked to judge whether a button or a jewel was more valuable than $10. Saying *no* to button should require as much time and as much elaborative coding as saying *yes* to jewel, because both require reference to knowledge of value. Craik and Tulving predicted that the *yes–no* difference would not appear with such materials. It did not, leading the experimenters to conclude that semantic elaboration might be the mechanism by which deep processing results in better retention.

3. Theoretical Extensions

Efforts have been made to extend the levels of processing approach in two directions. Craik and his colleagues have striven for theoretical refinements that would let their position encompass findings from various studies of episodic memory conceived largely as list learning (Craik & Jacoby, 1975; Cermak & Craik, 1978; Jacoby & Craik, 1978). Seemingly, their goal has been to give their theory experimental support beyond that provided by their own studies of incidental learning. Other investigators have sought to extend the levels-of-processing view to situations involving something more like everyday cognition. We now describe these efforts.

In studies of incidental learning, deeper processing means more semantic analysis. In other words, people have been shown to recall more words after being directed to a stimulus word's meaning than after being directed to its appearance or its sound. However, it seems intuitively clear that people process words sometimes deeply and sometimes shallowly. When someone is trying to talk to us while we are reading, we can respond appropriately with "Mmhmm," or "No, indeed," when their voice stops. But the semantic processing that allows us to do this seems shallow compared to the way we listen, for example, to a spicy bit of gossip about a prominent individual or a colleague. Several studies have investigated the possibility that even semantic processing may be deep or shallow. One such study exploited a property of ambiguous sentences. Ambiguous sentences have more than one meaning, such as, *They are shooting stars*, which could mean that stars are falling or being shot. Ambiguous sentences usually take longer to comprehend than unambiguous ones. Mistler-Lachman[1] (1972) presented both ambiguous and unambigous sentences in tasks at three different depths of processing. At the shallowest depth, subjects viewed target sentences and simply judged whether or not each target sentence was meaningful. At the intermediate depth, subjects judged whether a target sentence reasonably followed a context

---

[1]Now using the name Janet L. Lachman.

sentence. In the deepest task, they made up a sentence to follow the target sentence itself. Mistler-Lachman reasoned that ambiguity should slow performance most when the subject was trying to understand the meaning deeply enough to generate a sentence to follow the target. Ambiguity should have the least effect on time to judge simple meaningfulness, because a person should be able to decide that a sentence means something without having to determine precisely what that something is. True to this reasoning, ambiguous sentences had least effect on time to judge meaningfulness and most on time to generate a second sentence that semantically followed a preceding sentence.

Schallert (1976) used reasoning similar to Mistler-Lachman's in a study of prose recall. She constructed ambiguous passages, such as this one:

> In the last days of August, we were all suffering from the unbearable heat. In a few short weeks, our daily job had turned from a game into hard labor. "All we need now," said the manager in one of his discouraged moods, "is a strike." I listened to him silently, but I could not help him. I hit a fly. I suppose things could get even worse," he continued. "Our most valuable pitchers might crack in this heat. If only we had more fans, we would all feel better, I'm sure. I wish our best man would come home. That certainly would improve everyone's morale, especially mine. Oh well, I know a walk would cheer me up a little [pp. 621–622].

For such paragraphs, Schallert supplied titles that suggested different meanings: *Worries of a Baseball Team Manager* or *Worries of a Glassware Factory Manager*. She varied level of processing four ways: Subjects counted four-letter words, they counted personal pronouns, they rated the passages' ambiguity, or they tried to learn the passages. Following these experimental tasks, the subjects were given an unexpected recall test. Finally, they were given a multiple-choice test about the paragraphs. Among the multiple choices, two answers were completely wrong, one was right for the "Baseball" interpretation, and the other was right for the "Glassware" interpretation. Schallert expected people to remember more of the passages they tried to learn than of passages whose words they counted, but she also reasoned that the effect of the title should depend on the depth of the *task*. In other words, people who were counting words should not be as influenced by the title as those who were judging the ambiguity of the passage or trying to learn it. Her expectations were supported. The findings of Mistler-Lachman (1972, 1974) and Schallert (1976) are consistent with the idea that there are levels of processing, even for semantic material. However, these studies preclude the conclusion that semantic processing is necessarily deep, since shallow semantic processing appears possible. The outcomes are more consistent with the idea of a continuum of semantic elaboration, as proposed by Craik and

Tulving (1975). The more semantic elaboration coding an input receives, the better its recall should be.

Anderson and Reder (1978) have found the concept of semantic elaboration compatible with a major model of comprehension. The model, Anderson's (1976), posits a structure for permanent memory information, which is discussed in Chapter 12. Anderson and Reder showed that a more elaborate semantic code could establish more retrieval cues in the permanent memory structure, thus leading to better recall.

Despite these extensions to language processing (Mistler-Lachman, 1972, 1974; Scallert, 1976) and permanent memory (Anderson & Reder, 1978), levels of processing has been applied mainly to episodic memory research. The incidental learning experiment remains just about the only way to study levels, which raises the troublesome possibility that the view does not generalize to other situations. Indeed, Bransford, Franks, Morris, and Stein (1978) and Tulving (1978) have implied that the main claim of the levels approach can apply only to verbal-learning experiments. They argue against the idea that deep or semantic encoding produces better or stronger memory traces than other kinds of encoding. Both Bransford et al. and Tulving point out that conditions of retrieval influence memory just as the conditions of encoding do. They conclude that whether a memory trace is good depends on what one needs to do with it at retrieval time. The implication is that deep processing is simply the kind that enables an experimental subject to do well on recognition or recall tests—that is, on the kinds of tests given in verbal-learning experiments. Shallow processing might enable the subject to do well on other sorts of tests, which just happen not to be used in typical verbal-learning experiments. To see the point more clearly, imagine a study in which subjects perform the four orienting tasks shown in Table 8.1. In Craik and Tulving's (1975) version of such a study, people recalled and recognized words from the semantic encoding condition better than words from the other conditions. But suppose that instead of recalling or recognizing the initial stimulus words, people had been given a new list of words and were asked to check off ones that rhyme with the original words. Then, the shallower rhyming task of Table 8.1 might produce more accurate performance than the deeper semantic task. As a matter of fact, Morris, Bransford, and Franks (1977) found just such a result, which seriously questions that "deeper" processing is necessarily better, unless one restricts his view to typical verbal-learning studies. Bransford et al. (1978) suggested that the notion of *transfer-appropriate processing* is a more valid idea than *levels of processing*. The former notion captures the idea that no particular encoding is always better than any other; rather, different encodings are better for different retrieval tasks. Tulving (1978) argued the same point. Moreover, he claimed that levels-of-processing experiments can be explained fully with his principle of *encoding specificity*, which we discuss after summing up our discussion of levels of processing.

There was a time when a good theory of recognition and recall performance would have been a smash hit, but cognitive psychologists are becoming more concerned with generality and sufficiency, as can be seen in the waning of multistore models. If Bransford et al. and Tulving are correct, the levels view will not explain performance outside the verbal-learning laboratory, and it will not attract many adherents. It will be abandoned sooner than is typical of normal-science advances. Even if that happens, Craik and Lockhart will have contributed importantly to the metatheory of cognitive psychology. Their arguments dramatized the flexibility of the memory system, and to a considerable degree undermined the static view of memory processes suggested by multistore models. Regardless of whether levels of processing ever develops into a viable theory, its authors have reached their metatheoretical goals. They have helped change the conventional paradigmatic beliefs of many cognitive psychologists.

C. Encoding Specificity

1. The Encoding Specificity Phenomenon

You have undoubtedly met a familiar person out of his usual context, and found it hard to recall his name or anything about him. It can be very hard to identify the parish priest, for example, if one sees him in colorful clothes at a discothèque. Such experiences are mirrored in the laboratory by the phenomenon known as encoding specificity. Tulving and Osler (1968) and Thomson and Tulving (1970) were the first to show that the recallability of an event depends on how similar the context of retrieval is to the context of encoding.

The idea that retrieval is easier if the acquisition context is reinstated may seem sufficiently intuitive to make you wonder why anyone has regarded it as a hypothesis worth testing experimentally. But, when Tulving and Osler (1968) first introduced evidence for encoding specificity, at least one anonymous editorial reviewer found the conclusion "vehemently objectionable." To understand the objection, we must recall the conventional beliefs of the verbal-learning tradition. That tradition emphasized acquisition—the formation of associations that would allow the items in a list to be retrieved automatically at recall. The hypothesis of encoding specificity shifted the emphasis to retrieval processes and context. Also, verbal-learning researchers placed great importance on the power of natural associations between words, such as the high-frequency connection between WHITE and BLACK or between OLD and NEW. Encoding specificity highlighted the flexibility of the encoding system, suggesting that such well-established associations would not influence recall in all encoding contexts. A determined experimenter could make powerful associations irrelevant to recall, overriding their effects with those of the acquisition-retrieval context relationship. Because many episodic memory researchers traced their intellectual antecedents to verbal learning, these conclusions were not as intuitively obvious to them as they might be to someone in artificial intelligence; rather, they were objectionable. Both earlier data and their conventional beliefs suggest other "intuitions" to many verbal-learning researchers.

Tulving and his colleagues have presented powerful evidence for encoding specificity. Thomson and Tulving (1970) presented their to-be-remembered list items in contexts consisting of either weak or strong associates. For example, the word COLD might be presented along with "hot" (a strong associate) or with "blow" (a weak associate). Then, the experimenters used the associates as cues in a recall test. A subject who studied "hot-COLD" would receive either "hot - ?" or "blow - ?" as a test item, and a subject who studied "blow-COLD" would receive either "blow - ?" or "hot - ?" at test time. Thomson and Tulving compared recall under such arrangements to recall when there was no context at input and when the contexts were not used as cues at output. Strong associates were very helpful recall cues, when they had been presented with the list items. Strong associates also helped subjects who received no context with the original list items. However, strong associates were not helpful when weak associates had been the context. People who studied COLD in the context of "hot" or in no context at all were greatly aided by the cue word "hot." But people who studied COLD in the context of a weaker associate, "blow," were only helped when "blow" was a cue. Thomson and Tulving concluded that a cue word is only effective insofar as it re-establishes encoded aspects of the acquisition context.

2. The Generality of Encoding Specificity

Despite its inconsistency with the verbal-learning emphasis on acquisition and associative strength, encoding specificity has turned out to be quite general. It occurs in various episodic memory tasks (Thomson & Tulving, 1970; Tulving, 1978; Tulving & Osler, 1968; Wiseman & Tulving, 1976). Baker and Santa (1977) found encoding specificity when words were given context by placing them in sentences. Some of the word–sentence combinations were highly congruous (e.g., The TRUCK carries milk from Dallas to New York), somewhat congruous (e.g., The TRUCK was parked on top of the high school), and incongruous (e.g., The TRUCK was making pancakes when the phone rang). When subjects later viewed the capitalized words in either the same or different sentences, they had to decide which capitalized words had occurred previously and which were new. Subjects recognized the fewest words in new sentences, as predicted by the encoding-specificity hypothesis. In addition, the advantage of old sentences over new ones depended on congruity between the sentence and the to-be-remembered word. The most congruous old sentences were the best ones for recall.

Encoding specificity has also been demonstrated in memory for faces (Watkins, Ho, & Tulving, 1976; Winograd & Rivers-Bulkeley, 1977) and for tones (Dewar, Cuddy, & Mewhort, 1977). Because of its generality and reliability, the encoding-specificity procedure has also been used to study topics such as word meaning (e.g., Anderson & Ortony, 1975), as we see in our chapter on comprehension.

3. Further Research Questions Suggested by Encoding Specificity

A major job left for research on encoding specificity is to discover what determines which cues are encoded during study and used during recognition and recall. The data collected so far show that recall is better when aspects of the encoding context are present at retrieval, but the entire encoding context need *not* be perfectly reproduced for retrieval to occur. Only "relevant" aspects of the encoding situation need be reinstated to facilitate memory performance. The job is to show what aspects are relevant and why.

Several suggestions have been made. Salzberg (1976) emphasized that a cue's concreteness is an important determinant of whether it is encoded and, hence, is a good prompt. Spyropoulos and Ceraso (1977) concluded that stimulus classification is an integral part of encoding. The original classification given a stimulus determines the cues that will be effective retrieval prompts. For example, if a person classifies a red triangle as simply a triangle, then triangularity will be a more effective retrieval cue than redness. Conversely, if the person classifies the stimulus as a red object, then redness will be the more effective cue.

Stein (1977) has argued that the uniqueness of the relation between an event and a contextual cue determines that cue's effectiveness as a retrieval prompt. This seems hard to square with results obtained by Thomson and Tulving (1970) and by Baker and Santa (1977), but it can be reconciled by considering the details of these experiments and the one by Stein. During input, Stein's subjects had to invent a relationship between pairs of words; their task was to treat the words as similes. Productive activity of this sort greatly aids memory, presumably because it is very easy for a person to regenerate an idea he generated by himself (Bobrow & Bower, 1969; Mistler-Lachman, 1974). When one of the words in Stein's experiment was supplied as a retrieval cue, it would be very easy for the subjects to recall their own uniquely invented relationship, and hence the other member of the pair. But in Thomson and Tulving's and Baker and Santa's experiments, described earlier, people were shown weakly associated cue words or an incongruously related sentence.

While these seem to be unique cues, the passive nature of their presentation may have made people more dependent on experimenter-supplied retrieval cues to reinstate the to-be-remembered item than Stein's subjects were.

Clearly, there is much speculation in the efforts so far made to isolate those aspects of an encoding context that will serve as effective retrieval cues. A substantial research effort will be required before a clear answer can be given to the main question raised by the encoding-specificity hypothesis. It is likely that the research will be done. Encoding specificity is an attractively robust phenomenon and may relate to memory outside the laboratory. The hypothesis, moreover, is consistent with the current trends toward study of flexibility of memory processes. Furthermore, the encoding-specificity hypothesis seems to have generality beyond the episodic memory experiments for which it was originated (Weingartner, Adefris, Eich & Murphy, 1976; Parker, Birnbaum & Noble, 1976).

D. Analogue Memory

Most episodic memory experiments have studied recall or recognition of such abstract symbols as letters, digits, and words. But people also remember perceptual experiences. From the information-processing view, it is important to know the form or code in which such experience is stored.

Perceptual episodes might be stored in several ways. The person could maintain a direct "copy," rather as the film in a camera records a direct copy of light patterns and thereby maintains specific spatial relationships. This view is often ascribed to theorists who argue for mental imagery. Another possibility is that perceptual experience is "translated" into linguistic descriptions that capture salient aspects of events. Another possibility is "multiple coding": A stable, long-lived code with perceptual properties is formed and stored, and at the same time a linguistic description of the experience is generated and stored. Finally, retention (transient and permanent memory storage) might depend on a single, unitary code into which both perceptual and linguistic experience are transformed, but which is more abstract than either vision or language. Cognitive psychologists are not yet able to select among these possible modes of storage. However, considerable information has accumulated on what we shall call *analogue memory* (see Kosslyn & Pomerantz, 1977; Palmer, in press; Pylyshyn, 1973). By analogue memory we mean memory for perceptual (usually visual) events, as contrasted with memory for the abstract mental operations that the perceptual event might have initiated.

1. Evidence for Analogue Memory

You have no doubt formed images in your mind of past events. For example, in order to recall who was at a party, some people re-create an image of the room where the party took place, and then scan the image to identify the party-goers. To most people, such experiences are so compelling that it is hard to believe that anyone would deny them. However, for a time in American psychology, images were denied. To behaviorist psychologists, images were too subjective and mentalistic for science. Those who did not actually deny their existence believed images were too subjective, inferential, and difficult to manage experimentally (e.g., Deese, 1965).

Paivio (1969, 1971) may have contributed more than any other psychologist to reintroducing imagery into psychology. His achievement was due to two factors. For one thing, he accompanied his arguments for imagery with many well-designed and carefully controlled experiments. His evidence was collected in full compliance with the rational rules of science and the conventional precepts of the verbal-learning tradition. At the same time, the information-processing revolution created a climate more congenial than behaviorism to mentalistic concepts.

Paivio's studies (Paivio, 1969, 1971; Paivio & Csapo, 1969) showed that memory for concrete, imageable words is far better than memory for abstract, difficult-to-image words. MARKET, for example, is a concrete term for which most people can readily create a mental image. SOUL is abstract and difficult for most people to image. Lists of words like MARKET are considerably easier to learn than lists of words like SOUL. Of course, other psychologists have also studied imagery. For example, Bugelski (1968) taught people how to use imagery in order to remember a list of words. His subjects first learned a noun that rhymed with each of the numbers one through 10: one-BUN, two-SHOE, and so on. They used these nouns to learn other lists of 10 words. For each word in a list, they formed a mental image with a number-rhyming noun. For example, if the first word were LADY, a person might form an image of a lady in a bun as though she were a hot dog. If the second word were SCISSORS, a possible image would be of a pair of scissors cutting a shoe in half. Using this technique, subjects were able to memorize 10-word lists in only one presentation. Similar results were obtained by Bower and Reitman (1972). Such verbal-learning experiments actually deal with imagery storage during learning.

Other studies produce imagery manipulation. Data reported by Cooper (1975), Cooper and Shepard (1973), and Shepard and Metzler (1971) show that people can do in their minds some of the same things they do to objects that are physically present. For example, Shepard and Metzler (1971) showed people drawings of two pairs of two-dimensional forms (see Fig. 7.14, p. 250) and asked them whether they were rotations of each other. Subjects claimed that they could decide by mentally rotating the objects, and the data supported this introspection: How long they took to make their decisions was a linear function of the degree of rotational separation of the pairs. Figure 7.15 (p. 251) shows that the more rotation there was between the pairs, the longer it took to decide whether they were identical. Experiments of this type strongly support the view that an analogue code is directly available in short-term memory, and that it preserves much of the information in a visual scene. Moreover, a subject can apparently generate and manipulate an analogue representation even when a stimulus is absent.

2. Multiple Coding

Paivio (1969, 1971) has advanced a dual-coding hypothesis to account for data on imagery. According to this hypothesis, there are separate representational systems for verbal and nonverbal information. An analogue system is specialized for encoding, transforming, and processing information about concrete objects and events; it contains perceptual knowledge. There is a verbal system to deal with linguistic units. The two systems can be accessed independently—one by pictures, the other by language. But they communicate, because words can be transformed into images and images into words.

Much data support Paivio's reasoning. For example, it has been known for a long time that recognition memory for pictures is far better than memory for words (Shepard, 1967; Standing, 1973), which suggests that they are represented differently. Nelson (1978) found that people who had learned paired associates maintained information about the physical characteristics of the input even though the task did not require it. Kolers (1978) has done many experiments in which people read typed materials whose letters are reversed or upside down. Even after long periods of time, people have better-than-chance memory for the typeface in which a distorted message was printed. Another sort of evidence for multiple coding comes from interference studies. Baddeley, Grant, Wight, and Thompson (1975), Brooks (1967, 1968), Kroll, Parks, Parkinson, Bieber, and Johnson (1970), and Kroll (1975) all showed that retention of visual material is hampered more by an interfering visual task than by a verbal one, and that retention of verbal material is more subject to interference from a verbal than a visual task. These results can be intepreted to mean that separate systems are involved in the different types of tasks, and tying up one of them does not compete with activity going on in the other.

Few psychologists have difficulty accepting the idea that people code events both linguistically and perceptually, as long as the perceptual code is characterized as analogue (Anderson, 1978; Kosslyn & Pomerantz, 1977). However, Paivio has been criticized for referring to perceptual coding as an imagery system. To many psychologists, imagery connotes a literal internal copy of perceptual experience, which is unacceptable both on cognitive and neurophysiological grounds. Pylyshyn (1973), for example, has argued persuasively that a subject's description of a mental image is in many ways *unlike* a description of an actual scene. When an image is incorrect or incomplete, its missing parts are not close together, as they would be if one tore pieces from a photograph. Instead, people forget or misrepresent classes of information, such as the relative size of objects or the clothes people were wearing. Such classes are not the raw stuff of visual input. They are interpreted categories. Pylyshyn concludes that images are the product of an interpretive system. He argues that the imagery metaphor suggests too "photographic" a view of the perceptual code.

Posner (1969) accepted the distinction between analogue and linguistic representation. He reviewed his earlier experiments on letter matching and concluded that two codes are available and may be accessed simultaneously. His earlier experiments showed that people more rapidly judge two physically identical letters (A and A) to be the same than they judge two linguistically similar (same name) but physically different letters (A and a) to be the same. Moreover, when the second letter was delayed, the match had to be made on the basis of a memory code; but the superiority of a physical match persisted, showing that the physical characteristics of the first letter were maintained in the memory code, and were available to facilitate the match.

In later publications (Posner, 1973; Posner & Rogers, 1978), Posner reached other similar conclusions. First, there were at least three types of codes—visual, verbal, and motor (see also Bower, 1972; Paivio, 1971). Second, each code endures; they are not transient leftovers of stimulation. Third, people differ in their propensity to use each type of code (Neisser, 1967; Paivio, 1971). Fourth, the codes are parts of separate memory systems that can be isolated in the laboratory.

The foregoing data and conclusions indicate that an adequate theory of memory will have to include a mechanism for storing and retrieving nonverbal information. It will have to account for how perceptual information is maintained for later use. Moreover, there is reason to think that perceptual information passes through an interpretive—not necessarily linguistic—system on its way to permanent storage, because what is available for later recall is not a literal copy of what was initially perceived. This will need to be explained too.

III. EXTENSIONS OF MULTISTORE MODELS

There are three main reasons that many cognitive psychologists have forsaken multistore models. One is that those models emphasized cognitive structure at the expense of flexible processing. Second, the models did not give sufficient due to people's knowledge—that is, to the contents of the long-term store. Finally, the models applied to a narrow range of laboratory phenomena rather than to many of people's cognitive skills. But you will recall that Atkinson and Shiffrin allowed for both structure and process when they distinguished structural features from control processes, and they did posit a long-term store to hold people's permanent knowledge. While it is true that Atkinson and Shiffrin said very little about either control processes or the long-term store, this neglect might be remedied. The multistore approach might be extended so that the criticisms of too much emphasis on structure, too little attention to knowledge, and too narrow a range of application would no longer be valid.

Atkinson and Shiffrin have both worked to extend the multistore approach, though they have taken different approaches to solving its problems. Atkinson and a former student, James F. Juola, have developed a theory that retains the conceptual core of the original model (Atkinson & Juola, 1973, 1974; Juola, 1973; Juola, Fischler, Wood, & Atkinson, 1971; see also Atkinson, Herrmann, & Wescourt, 1974), but they have de-emphasized the invariant properties of the stores and formalized the flexibility inherent in subjects' strategies. At the same time they have extended the model to account for recognition memory as well as list-learning experiments. Shiffrin, in collaboration with Schneider, has retained far less of the initial Atkinson–Shiffrin conception (Schneider & Shiffrin, 1977; Shiffrin, 1978; Shiffrin & Schneider, 1977). The main emphasis of Shiffrin's new model is flexible processing, and at its core is a distinction between subject-controlled memory search and automatic attention-focusing during information retrieval. Shiffrin also intends his new model to apply to a broad range of phenomena.

A. The Atkinson–Juola Theory

Atkinson and Juola have kept Atkinson and Shiffrin's (1968) structural assumption of three stores, but they have given greater breadth and flexibility to their memory system (cf. Chapter 5, p. 171ff). First, they postulated two kinds of coding: perceptual and conceptual. Second, they elaborated the content of the long-term store and divided it into two substores, which resemble Tulving's (1972) semantic and episodic memories. Third, they extend the theory's domain of application to memory-scanning tasks of the kind originally developed by Sternberg. According to Atkinson and Juola, physical stimulation enters the memory system via an appropriate sensory register (see Fig. 8.2). Then, pattern recognition routines turn each stimulus into an uninterpreted *perceptual code*—that is, a code that is not linked to the meanings of the stimulus. The perceptual codes are made up of primitive features, such as lines and curves, and the perceptual codes are linked to *conceptual codes*. A conceptual code consists of attributes that combine to make up the meaning of a concept. Thus, the attributes of the concept Bird might be that it has wings, feathers, a range of sizes; lays eggs; probably sings; and so on. Each conceptual code is linked to several perceptual codes. For example, the sight of a bird, the printed word BIRD, and the spoken sound

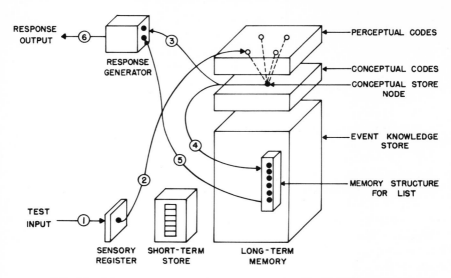

FIG. 8.2.   Memory structures and processes postulated in the Atkinson and Juola (1974) and the Atkinson, Herrmann, and Wescourt (1974) extension of the Atkinson–Shiffrin (1968) theory. The diagram illustrates the stages of processing in determining whether a probe stimulus is a member of a "large" list of words stored in long-term memory. "Component processes are as follows: (1) input of test stimulus to sensory register; (2) pattern-recognition process leading to a mapping of test stimulus onto a perceptual code, and in turn access to the conceptual code; (3) immediate decision to respond based on familiarity; (4) selection of code to be scanned against memory structure in the Event Knowledge Store; (5) decision to respond based on scan of the list's memory structure; (6) response output" (Atkinson et al., 1974).

/bɔrd/ each activate a separate perceptual code, but each is linked to the same conceptual code.

Perceptual and conceptual codes, which are acquired through genetic endowment and learning, are stored in long-term memory, which is partitioned into an event-knowledge store and a conceptual store. The conceptual store corresponds to semantic memory. It contains "nodes" corresponding to perceptual as well as conceptual codes. In Fig. 8.2, all of the codes connected by dotted lines form a single node. The nodes hook incoming perceptual information to permanently stored conceptual information. The event-knowledge store corresponds to episodic memory, and its contents are called *memory structures*. When patterns of stimuli, such as a list of words, enter the system, copies of the perceptual and conceptual codes that they activate are linked together and become a memory structure in the event-knowledge store. Memory structures represent environmental events and episodes, including word lists learned while participating in an experiment.

The short-term store (see Fig. 8.2) is a limited-capacity structure that contains the "current state of consciousness." Although this short-term store resembles its predecessor in the Atkinson–Shiffrin model, it does not have fixed coding characteristics (i.e., acoustic–articulatory).

Atkinson and Juola intend their theory to account for data from memory-scanning experiments of a sort originated by Sternberg (1966), but modified for the study of long-term memory. In the Sternberg experiment, the subject is told to keep in mind a set of items (e.g., the letters B, F, and K). He/she is asked to indicate as rapidly as possible whether a probe stimulus (e.g., J) is a member of the memory set. (In this example, the subject would respond *no*.) The main dependent variable is the subject's response speed. Atkinson and his co-workers (Atkinson, Herrmann, & Wescourt, 1974; Atkinson & Juola, 1973, 1974; Juola, 1973; Juola & Atkinson, 1971; Juola, Fischler, Wood, & Atkinson, 1971) have reported several memory-scanning experiments that confirm predictions from the theory by Atkinson and Juola. The studies used words and pictures as well as letters for stimuli, and an important variable was the size of the memory set. Small memory sets contained from two to six items. Atkinson and Juola assumed that small sets were held in the limited-capacity short-term store, so that comparing the probe item with a small memory set would not involve the long-term store. Large memory sets contained from 10 to 60 words, which the subject usually memorized the day before the reaction-time task. Large memory sets should exceed the capacity of the short-term store, and Atkinson and Juola assumed that each large set was held as a memory structure in the event-knowledge part of the long-term store (see Fig. 8.2).

The central claim of the Atkinson–Juola theory concerns the way a subject compares and decides whether a probe matches an item in the memory set. The idea is that memorizing a list increases the familiarity of its items. Information about familiarity is said to be stored with an item's conceptual node. When a stimulus probe is presented, the subject first encodes it and accesses its conceptual node—and the familiarity information it contains. If the conceptual store's node yields a very low familiarity value, the subject can reject the probe rapidly, without mentally scanning his memory set. Likewise, if the familiarity value is very high, the subject can rapidly confirm the probe, without scanning memory. But intermediate familiarity values lead to slow reaction times, because the subject must resort to an internal scan of the stored list whenever the probe is neither very high nor very low in familiarity. The theory thus proposes two stages of search and decision, with the outcome of the first stage determining whether the second stage is needed. Decisions made after the first stage alone, whether *yes* or *no*, are fast. They are also subject to error, because familiarity is not perfectly correlated with list membership. Decisions made after the second stage are slower but exceedingly accurate.

The Atkinson and Juola theory has several testable implications. For example, after the subject has learned a memory set, but before testing has begun, incorrect or distractor probes should be very unfamiliar. Therefore, the subject should be able to produce a correct *no* response on the basis of the first-stage familiarity judgment, without the second-stage memory scan, and *no* responses should be fast. However, if the same distractor probes are repeated several times during the experiment, their familiarity should increase. The correct answer would still be *no*, but the subject should have to execute the second-stage memory scan when familiarity has risen, so that a distractor probe cannot be rejected on the basis of familiarity alone. Therefore, as the experiment proceeds and distractor items are repeated, reaction time to reject them should lengthen. The opposite should happen for probes that belong to the memorized list. As the experiment begins, the subject will have studied the target items and they will have intermediate familiarity. The subject should make a *yes* decision relatively slowly, because a scan of the list is necessary for items with intermediate familiarity levels. However, as these items are repeatedly probed, their familiarity should increase. When they become very familiar, a *yes* response will be possible during the first stage, without memory scanning; therefore, reaction times to target probes should become faster as the experiment proceeds. In line with these predictions, Atkinson and Juola (1974) found that *no* responses are fast at first, but become slower, and *yes* responses are slow at first but become faster as the experiment proceeds.

The modifications and extensions of the Atkinson–Shiffrin model by Atkinson and Juola (1974) illustrate nicely how theories evolve during normal science. Ten years ago, the vaguest parts of the theory were the control processes and the long-term store. The most specific detail and the heaviest research attention concerned the sensory register and the short-term store. The only control process that was given any attention at all was rehearsal. Now the least specific part of the theory is encoding by sensory registers, and the short-term store has lost most of its specified properties. The recent theory has a detailed long-term store and decision processes that lend flexibility to memory performance. Rehearsal is barely mentioned in recent theoretical statements. The control processes of interest now are the automatic recognition decisions based on familiarity and the second stage thorough search of memory contents. Notice, too, that flexibility was added to the model by incorporating earlier developments by Sternberg and ideas from signal detection theory, which also illustrates how normal science is cumulative.

In 1977, Atkinson was appointed by President Carter to the post of Director of the National Science Foundation. The National Science Foundation provides, by a 1950 Act of Congress, a major portion of the support for basic science of all kinds in the United States. The directorship of this agency is an extremely important and time-consuming position. It is unlikely that Atkinson will participate soon in the further development of this model, which leaves it to others, like his colleague Juola. The model of Atkinson and Juola requires further specification of how perceptual codes are formed and what they consist of, how perceptual and conceptual codes are linked, and the nature of conceptual codes. Without such developments the model will be unable to account for the recognition of imperfect or degraded perceptual inputs; and it will not be extendable to more cognitively demanding activities than memory set scanning, which is a relatively modest variation on the sorts of list learning the original model was designed to explain.

B. The Shiffrin–Schneider Theory

Shiffrin and Schneider have also modified the Atkinson and Shiffrin theory. Their (Schneider & Shiffrin, 1977; Shiffrin & Schneider, 1977) revisions are so extensive that they view theirs as a new theory; and it is very different from the original model. Although the origins of the new theory are unmistakable, it is more ambitious than either the model by Atkinson and Shiffrin or its extension by Atkinson and Juola (1973, 1974). Shiffrin and Schneider are trying to bridge the gap between the theoretical processes involved in selective attention and in memory scanning. There are many experiments on both selective attention and memory scanning, and even a successful first step toward integrating them would be a significant development in the cumulative normal science of cognition.

According to Shiffrin and Schneider, attention and memory scanning both reflect two processes: *automatic detection* and *controlled search*. Automatic detection is the apprehension of stimuli by means of previously learned routines that are in long-term storage. These automatic routines control information flow, focus attention, and generate responses, but they are so well learned that they do not require conscious effort, and they use none of the limited capacity of short-term memory. Controlled searches are deliberate and novel sequences of processing steps. Such sequences are not stored as unitized strategies in long-term memory. They are not automatized. Their value is that they can be changed and adapted to new circumstances, but such flexibility has its price: Controlled processes use short-term memory, and they may require conscious effort. Controlled searches are frequently conscious, and they can be manipulated by verbal instructions. Nevertheless, serial comparisons in short-term memory may occur too quickly to enter consciousness, even though they use short-term memory and require attention. Whether these processes are conscious or not, Shiffrin and

Schneider consider that they can be initiated or terminated by the subject. In contrast, automatic detection is resistant to alteration and is difficult to ignore or suppress once set into motion by a stimulus.

Here is a real-life example. Suppose you have arrived in an unfamiliar city to attend a university. You have found a place to live and are ready for your first visit to campus, so you ask directions. Your initial trips using your instructions will require controlled search. For each turn you must make, you have to watch carefully for cues: the second stoplight, the large red house, another half-mile and the rectangular contemporary house, a gas station, an empty lot, and so on. Detecting these cues will use your attentional and short-term memory capacities. During your first drive to the university, you will find it difficult to participate in a conversation unrelated to the business of detecting landmarks. You will not be able to process the news broadcast on your radio as fully as you will months later, after you have made the trip many times. But eventually, you will use automatic detection processes to locate the campus. You will make the required turns smoothly at the second stoplight, the large red house, the rectangular modern one, the gas station, and the empty lot. You will do this without using up attention and short-term memory, which will become available for other things. Pretty soon you can carry on a lively conversation about practically anything, listen to the news, examine pedestrians and unusual cars, rehearse your studies, or plan for your evening date—all the while flawlessly executing the necessary moves to get you to the campus. You may even become unsettled one day by "coming to" in the parking lot with no memory of the drive there, or its various stops and turns.

This illustration contains a point that is important to Shiffrin and Schneider. Visual cues are of two sorts: same category and mixed category. Suppose you are to turn left at a small contemporary house near a corner in a residential neighborhood. The house would be a same-category cue, because the distractors—the other houses—are similar to it. On the other hand, if the cue is a gas station in a residential neighborhood, it is a mixed-category target. The gas station and private dwellings among which it must be sought belong to previously learned categories that are different. As you might expect, same-category cues are harder to detect, take more time, and produce more errors than mixed-category cues.

Shiffrin and Schneider's laboratory analogue of finding your way somewhere is a version of Sternberg's memory scanning task, in which the memory set items are sought in visual displays; but Shiffrin and Schneider varied size of the display as well as size of the memory set. That is, subjects were shown visual displays containing one, two, or four items, and their task was to determine whether any one of several display items was the same as any of the memory set items. They used both same-category and mixed-category displays. In other words, a subject might have a memory set of J and D. He must report *yes* if the display contains either a J or a D, and it might consist of

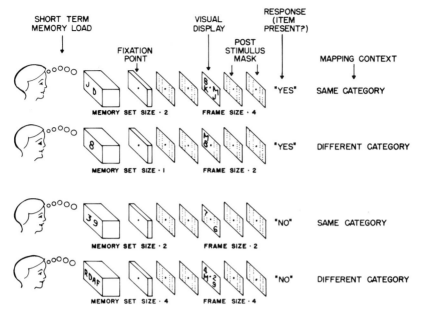

FIG. 8.3. Two examples of a positive trial and two of a negative trial in a single-frame scanning study with reaction time as the dependent variable. The subject is first shown the memory set that is held in short-term storage. A fixation dot comes on, followed by dot and mask frames, the target frame, and two postmask frames. The stimulus is visible for 160 msec (Schneider & Shiffrin, 1977).

one, two, or four items. In a same-category condition, all display items would be letters. In the mixed-category condition, some of the items would be digits. The same-category condition is analogous to looking for a particular house in a residential neighborhood; the mixed-category condition is analogous to looking for a gas station in a residential neighborhood. Figure 8.3 shows several examples of Shiffrin and Schneider's conditions. Their dependent variable was reaction time.

Still another variation was to present a whole series of displays. Instead of one frame containing from one to four items, Shiffrin and Schneider did experiments in which 20 frames were presented in rapid succession, and the subject had to indicate whether any item from the memory set had appeared in any of the frames. Thus, their experiment varied size of display, same or mixed category, and rate of frame presentation. In experiments using 20 frames, the experimenters usually measured accuracy rather than reaction time.

The reaction times in Fig. 8.4 come from an experiment in which the subjects sought the targets in a single frame. The size of the memory set was

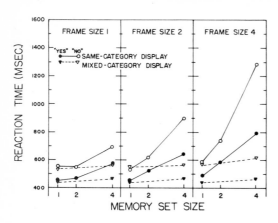

FIG. 8.4.   Mean reaction time for correct responses as a function of short-term memory set size and visual display frame size. "YES" responses are correct when a symbol in the memory set is found in the display frame. "NO" responses are correct when no member of the memory set is to be found in the display set. (After Schneider & Shiffrin, 1977.) Same category and different category treatments are illustrated in Fig. 8.3.

either one, two, or four letters or digits, but not both. The size of the display was likewise either one, two or four. However, the display could be either same or mixed category. A subject whose memory set contained letters might seek the target among other letters or among digits. For instance, a subject in the same-category condition with the letter *J* in memory might see a display containing *X, F, J,* and *B*. A subject in the mixed-category condition might see *2, 9, J,* and *4*. In Fig. 8.4, the reaction times in the mixed-category condition are indicated by the dashed line, and those in the same-category conditions are indicated by the solid line. As you can see, there is very little effect of display size in the mixed-category condition. A subject can detect a target letter among digits just about as quickly as he can detect it if it is presented alone. You can see this by comparing the pairs of dashed lines across the three panels. Display size makes a substantial difference in the same-category condition, as you can see by comparing the solid lines across the three panels. The open circles and triangles represent conditions in which a target is absent, and the filled circles and triangles represent the case where a target is present. It takes longer to determine that a target is absent, because the subject must search the entire memory set before responding *no*. Unlike Sternberg, Shiffrin and Schneider assume that the subject can stop searching when he finds the target; therefore, *yes* decisions can be made faster on the average than *no* decisions.

It is Shiffrin and Schneider's view that the mixed-category condition permits automatic detection, whereas the same-category condition requires controlled search. This is because the subject can reject items that come from a category different from the target by using category information that he has practiced through his lifetime, and which is stored in his long-term memory. He does not have to consider consciously whether a *3* or a *6* or a *5* is a *B*— automatic detection routines reject them out of hand because they come from a different category. The subjective impression in the mixed-category condition is that display items from the same category as the memory set "pop out" of the display for immediate comparison with the memory set. The experimental outcome for mixed categories validates this impression; regardless of the number of distractors, they do not influence the length of the comparison process. In contrast, when the subject must search for a B in a display containing several letters, or any other letter, no item "pops out." Hence, the number of letter distractors present in the display determines how long the search process will take.

What takes the time in controlled search? It is the comparison to items in the memory set of those items that cannot be rejected on the basis of category information. According to the theory, a given memory symbol is cycled for comparison through all the items in the display, and if no match is found, the search is switched to the second memory symbol. Of course, if there is only one memory symbol, the procedure can terminate with a *no* response. The search continues until there are no more items in the memory set and a *no* response can be made, or until a match is found and a *yes* response can be made. Each switch from memory symbol to memory symbol takes time, as does each comparison of a memory symbol to a display item. Shiffrin and Schneider have developed precise predictions for their experiments, by estimating these times.

Shiffrin and Schneider expressed their theory as a mathematical model for the serial, self-terminating search-and-comparison processes assumed for controlled search situations. The model yields precise predictions of both reaction time and accuracy data from their memory scanning experiments. This is a significant achievement. W. K. Estes pioneered mathematical psychology, and he now edits psychology's most prestigious journal, the *Psychological Review*. He understands more fully than most that mathematical models make a major contribution to psychology when they reveal relationships between processes or sets of data that are not otherwise apparent (Estes, 1975a). With their mathematical model, Shiffrin and Schneider are able to do exactly that. Perhaps this is why Estes has accorded them 170 pages in the *Psychological Review* to present their model and report their experimental results (Schneider & Shiffrin, 1977; Shiffrin & Schneider, 1977). Few theoretical papers are given more than 20 to 30 pages of journal space.

Although the actual experimental tests of Shiffrin and Schneider's theory have been primarily the kind of memory scanning studies we have described, its intended range of applications is extremely wide. Shiffrin and Schneider established relationships between their theory and previous theories of memory scanning and attention, and they showed that their theory accounts for or is consistent with a sizable portion of the existing literature. They conclude the performance deficits due to divided attention (see Chapter 6) arise from the limited rate at which serial comparisons can be made during controlled search. They believe that divided attention does not result in deficient performance if the target symbol and the distractors come from different categories, because this permits the use of automatic detection routines.

Shiffrin and Schneider have embedded their notions of controlled processes and automatic detection in a multistore theory of information processing; however, their multistore theory is unlike its predecessors in many significant respects. Its long-term store is an elaborate collection of interrelated and interassociated information, which is normally dormant. Most of their long-term store is passive most of the time. As in Atkinson and Juola's model, short-term memory is the currently active information in long-term memory. A flowchart of the system would show short-term storage as a small box contained completely within the larger box of long-term memory. Information stays in the short-term store (stays active) only briefly, and forgetting over the short term amounts to a return of inactive information to the long-term store. In addition, Shiffrin and Schneider's controlled processing takes place in the short-term store, which directs attention to selected aspects of information extracted from the environment. Thus, their short-term store has two functions: It holds for a brief interval information that is currently important to the organism, and it is a working register for decision processes, thinking, and any other control processes of which the system is capable. Therefore, control of the entire system's operation is effected by directing information into and out of short-term memory.

IV.   CONCLUSIONS

Each of the several directions that episodic memory research has taken shows the evolution of normal cognitive science. Some theorists are attempting to correct and extend the multistore hypothesis.

The levels-of-processing approach has undermined the original multistore models and suggested a new direction for the field of memory research. Most current theorists, including multistore modelers such as Shiffrin and Schneider, have incorporated elements of the levels-of-processing approach. The work on encoding specificity promises to withstand the ravages of time, and general memory theory may eventually incorporate its principle. The same may be true of dual-coding theory. A few theorists, like Norman and Bobrow, have completely rejected multistore models and abandoned the study of episodic memory. They have turned their interest to semantic memory, language capacities, and the role of meaning and knowledge in human behavior.

The heterogeneity of the present study of episodic memory does not indicate a fragmentation of the field. Neither does it indicate an incipient revolution. We say this because there are patterns and emphases that characterize the field now, just as they did when Atkinson and Shiffrin first conceived their model. Working memory is still treated as a limited capacity system, even though it is now viewed more often as an activated portion of long-term memory than as a separate store. All theories allow some mechanism for transferring information from short-term to long-term storage, even though few now emphasize rehearsal. All theories still accept some modality-specific and automatic process to serve the function of the sensory registers. Such changes are too subtle to be called revolutionary. What has happened is a shift from emphasis on structure to emphasis on process, which is a far less radical change than the shift from the neobehaviorist approach to the information-processing approach.

9
Semantic Memory

ABSTRACT

I. *Introduction*

The information-processing paradigm has re-awakened interest in the questions: What is it to know, understand and believe? In information-processing language, these become questions of how information and world knowledge are stored, represented, maintained, and accessed by the human processor.

II. *Formation of the Field of Semantic Memory*

More than any other field in cognitive psychology, the study of semantic memory reveals the blending of intellectual forces that shaped the information-processing approach to cognition. This was possible partly because researchers in several areas converged on a very similar cognitive task—that of speeded classification and verification. Variations on these tasks have been used in the vast majority of semantic memory experiments.

A. *Influences from Experimental Psychology* Prior to their concern with semantic memory, psychologists used the speeded classification or verification task for many purposes and interpreted their outcomes from other viewpoints. An information-theoretic use is illustrated in an experiment by Pollack (1963), a neobehavioristic use by Schaeffer and Wallace (1969), and an information-processing use by Landauer and Freedman (1968).

B. *The Merging of Artificial Intelligence and Experimental Psychology*

1. *Quillian's Model: the "Teachable Language Comprehender" (TLC)* Working within the orientation of artificial intelligence, Quillian built a computer simulation designed to learn from text and answer questions. The memory contained a set of hierarchically interconnected concepts called *nodes*. These were connected to information about their characteristics by property *links*, and to information about their superordinate and subordinate categories by superordinate links. A feature of the model was cognitive economy: It could infer information not directly stored.

2. *An Empirical Test of Quillian's Model*   Collins and Quillian (1969) performed the first semantic memory experiment as a test of TLC. They predicted that the time required for people to verify assertions would be related to the number of links that TLC would have to traverse to verify the same assertions. When the sentences were true, the predictions were confirmed, but false sentences contradicted predictions from TLC.

III. *The Normal-Science Study of Semantic Memory*

   A. *Are Structural Notions Necessary?*   Schaeffer and Wallace were among the first to respond to the Collins and Quillian paper. They argued that it was unnecessary and unparsimonious to make structural assumptions about how semantic memory is organized to predict latencies in the speeded classification/verification task. They also showed that the semantic distance between concepts predicts reaction time, a finding that necessitated revision of the Quillian model.

   B. *Are All Instances of a Category Equal?*   According to Quillian's theory, every instance of a superordinate category should give equally rapid access to that concept; all instances have equal status. Wilkins (1971) varied what he called *conjoint frequency* and showed that all instances were not equal. Some could be more rapidly categorized than others. This outcome seriously questioned the hierarchic character of Quillian's model of semantic memory structure.

   C. *How Economical is Semantic Memory?*   Conrad (1972) showed that some properties led more quickly to their associated concepts than others. This means that the strong form of cognitive economy cannot apply to semantic memory but not that there is no cognitive economy at all. Elimination of all cognitive economy would be tantamount to eliminating inferential capability.

   D. *Conjoint Frequency, Semantic Distance, or What?*   Rips, Shoben, and Smith (1973) showed that verification times differ depending on normatively indexed relationships between the words in the assertions to be verified. With the other norms that predict reaction times, these raise the question of what the norms measure: semantic relatedness, instance dominance, conjoint frequency, or what? Which best describes the organizational principles of semantic memory? So far, no experiment has supplied an answer.

   E. *Typicality and Base Level*   Rosch (1975) found that some category instances are "better" exemplars than others. These are verified faster; typicality may underlie the relationship measured by the norms. Rosch and her colleagues also discovered a level of specificity, called *base level*, which appears especially psychologically salient.

   F. *Summary*

IV. *Two Models of Semantic Memory*

   A. *Overview*   Two models are discussed in detail, although several more have been proposed. We describe the Theory of Spreading Activation (Collins & Loftus, 1975), which is a revision of Quillian's TLC, and a two-stage feature comparison model by Smith, Shoben, and Rips (1974).

   B. *The Spread of Activation*

      1. *Structural Assumptions*   Collins and Loftus (1975) revised Quillian's model of how semantic information is organized. They abandoned the hierarchic network in favor of a network organized around semantic distance. They also added superordinate relationships not used by Quillian.

2. *Processing Assumptions*   The model posits that a concept node is activated when a person sees or thinks about a concept. The activation spreads to adjacent nodes. The path between two nodes supplies the information to evaluate a proposition about concept pairs.

3. *Decision Assumptions*   Collins and Loftus postulate five kinds of evidence that enter into the decision whether a proposition is true or false.

C. *A Feature Comparison Model*   Smith, Shoben, and Rips believed that the difficulties with TLC were so great that it made better sense to start over. Their model contains two stages. The first is used when two concepts are very related or very unrelated; the second is added when the concepts are moderately related.

1. *Structural Assumptions*   Concepts in the semantic memory are structured as sets of features. Some features are defining; others are only accidental. Features vary in their centrality to a concept's definition.

2. *Processing and Decision Assumptions*   Smith et al. proposed a two-stage model. Stage 1 makes decisions on the basis of an aggregated value calculated from all of the features of concepts to be compared. Stage 2 uses only defining features. The first stage makes quick, approximate decisions, and the second stage makes slower, more exacting decisions about how two concepts are related.

D. *Summary*

V. *Word Production*

A. *Overview*   Sentence verification procedures show how people use their world knowledge to comprehend language. Word production studies are designed to see how people draw on their world knowledge to produce language. In studies of word production, people are asked to name pictures, and their naming times are related to characteristics of the pictures' names or to characteristics of the pictures themselves. Whereas a main goal of verification studies is to understand how concepts are organized in semantic memory, the goal of production studies is to understand how words are organized. Every major model of semantic memory assumes that words and concepts are stored separately.

B. *Word Frequency*   Oldfield and Wingfield (1964, 1965) showed that naming latency increases as the frequency with which the word is used in written English decreases. Pictures with infrequent names take longer to name.

C. *Codability*   Oldfield and Wingfield studied the naming of pictures with a single commonly accepted name. Many objects have no single agreed-upon name (Lachman, 1973). Poorly-coded pictures, which elicit many names, are named more slowly than well-coded pictures, which elicit few names (Lachman et al., 1974).

D. *Age of Acquisition*   Carroll and White (1973) found that some low-frequency words were named quickly. These words were likely to be those that children learn early. Further research led Carroll and White to conclude that frequency effects reduce to the effect of acquisition age.

E. *Word Frequency, Codability, or Age of Acquisition?*   A study by Lachman, Shaffer, and Hennrikus evaluated effects of all three variables. All appear to contribute to naming latency.

VI. *Comparison of Word Production and Sentence Verification Studies*
The two kinds of research have been done very differently, and the studies in the two areas of work have not addressed the same variables. Consequently, it is

impossible to give a direct answer to the question of whether lexical information and conceptual information are stored in separate systems in permanent memory. However, indirect evidence and logical considerations strongly suggest that they are.

I. INTRODUCTION

We turn now to semantic memory, which was distinguished from episodic memory in Chapter 7. Episodic memory was characterized as preserving the temporal and spatial features of people's experience. Semantic memory was described as preserving people's general conceptual information, world knowledge, and linguistic abilities. Exactly how this abstract formulation translates into concrete particulars can be seen after you first understand this sentence:

More Americans have been killed by firecrackers than were killed in the Revolutionary War.

The processes that allow you to understand sentences and utterances are what cognitive psychologists who study semantic memory want to explain, and it will clarify their goal if you think about what you know and do to understand the preceding sentence. You know that shooting off fireworks is a customary part of the annual American celebration called the Fourth of July, a holiday that commemorates independence of the United States from Great Britain, the independence that was one outcome of the Revolutionary War. You know that firecrackers are explosive devices that can cause injuries leading to death. You know many of the biological differences between living and dead people. All of this knowledge, and much more, allows you to understand our sample sentence, and to judge that this one means the same thing:

The War for Independence did not result in as many deaths of United States residents as fireworks have.

This paraphrase uses very few of the same words as the earlier sentence, showing that meaning is in the mind of the reader or listener, not in utterances and sentences themselves. Semantic memory is fundamentally a matter of internal cognitive events. The extent to which semantic memories are in people's heads can be hinted at by paraphrasing the foregoing sentences to more fully exhaust their meaning:

More Americans, who are people living in the United States of America, a country between Mexico and Canada on the continent of North America, have had their hearts' beating stopped, as a consequence of which their voluntary activity has ceased, from being struck or pierced in vital parts of their bodies by pieces of firecrackers, which are small devices containing gunpowder, which when exposed to heat expands rapidly and causes its container to break into pieces that travel with great force through the air, and which Americans have a tradition of igniting, thereby exposing them to high temperatures, at certain times each year, one of which is the Fourth of July, in order to celebrate momentous occasions like the Revolutionary War, which took place....

One of the points of this exercise in paraphrase is that speakers strive to include enough in their utterances to be understood, but they leave out information that the listener can infer from what is given. Inferential processes are thus a part of the study of semantic memory. Other parts are people's funds of knowledge, and how those funds are organized.

Broadly conceived, the study of semantic memory encompasses age-old questions. What is it to know? to understand? to believe and intend? Couched in the language of information processing, these become questions of how knowledge of the world is represented, stored, transformed, and accessed by the human symbolic processing system. Semantic memory concerns the human capacity to construct an internal representation of reality—to take in and interpret perceptual experiences, to combine them with the products of previous experiences, to draw inferences and implications and make predictions from them, to attribute causality, and to reshuffle old ideas into novel combinations without benefit of new perceptual inputs. These human activities, and all the derivatives of them, are the province of semantic memory. It should not surprise you that cognitive psychology has not yet explained them. The effort is new, and the goal is awesome.

The goal is to give an unambiguous description of the specific sequences of processes underlying the human's unique semantic talents. The scope of these talents is very broad indeed. Accounting for all of them with one theory now seems impossible, but that is not a major source of grief for contemporary information-processing scientists. After the fashion of all scientists, they are conquering the complexities of their subject by dividing it into manageable parts. They have largely agreed which semantic memory abilities are representative, prototypic, and fundamental. Despite the fact that the field of study called semantic memory came into being rather recently, it has already become a part of normal science. Methods have been settled upon for studying the abilities that the information-processing paradigm suggests operate in all situations requiring semantic memory. Foremost among these methods are classification and verification tasks, whose primary function is to provide latency differences from which to infer the structure of semantic memory.

II. FORMATION OF THE FIELD
OF SEMANTIC MEMORY

The study of semantic memory, which we treat in this chapter and Chapter 11, reflects more clearly than any other the blending of intellectual forces that have shaped the information-processing paradigm. We can see in today's research and theory about semantic memory the influence of information theory, decision theory, and verbal-learning transmitted by earlier experimental psychologists; the impact of artificial intelligence; and the influence of linguistics. These influences converged to produce the field of semantic memory, partly because of the reliance of scientists from each of these different traditions on the same method—the study of speeded classification. It is interesting to compare different researchers' reasons for studying speeded classification and to contrast their interpretations of results. These are different indeed, and they illustrate how the same facts are viewed differently by scientists with different conceptions of reality.

Speeded classification procedures have two defining features: They yield measures of response speed; and people must use their everyday knowledge of how events and things are categorized in order to respond correctly. It is this latter feature that makes the procedures seem prototypic of semantic memory. Just as you had to draw on your knowledge of American history, folk customs, and biology to understand the two sentences at the beginning of this chapter, so people making speeded classifications have to draw on their knowledge.

A typical speeded classification experiment requires a person to indicate whether a given word is a member of a specified category. In some studies, subjects are shown words and required to give their category names. For instance, a person might have to say either *animal* or *plant* to words like GOAT, ROSE, DOG, TREE, HORSE, and BUSH. In other studies, the subject might say *same* or *different*, or he might press buttons to signify *same* or *different*, depending on the category membership of paired words. Thus, GOAT-HORSE should evoke a *same* response, because they are both animals; but GOAT-TULIP should evoke a *different* response. Sometimes the subject says *yes*, if the first word belongs to the category named by the second word. For example, the sequence RED-COLOR should be answered *yes*, but the sequence RAZOR-VEHICLE should be answered *no*. Another arrangement requires people to respond *true* or *false*, either orally or by pressing switches, to statements like *A typhoon is a dwelling* or *A watermelon is a fruit.*

Whichever arrangement is used, the cognitive demands of the task are the same: People must use their knowledge of concepts and categories in order to respond. This requirement can also hold when no category is mentioned. For example, the sentence *Canaries are related to finches* does not mention birds, but a person could not verify that assertion without knowing that canaries and finches are both birds.

Many semantic memory experiments have required people to say *true* or *false* to propositional expressions that have the form Subject-Verb-Predicate. For purposes of this chapter, it is sufficient to consider propositions as the underlying meaning, or content, of various surface sentences. The technical use of propositions to represent declarative knowledge is developed extensively in the chapter on global models. The *Subject* and *Predicate* of Subject-Verb-Predicate expressions are category names. The conceptual classes, thus represented, may have relatively few members (e.g., COLLIE) or very many (ANIMAL) or somewhere in between (DOG). The *Verb* may designate property relationships with a familiar verb, such as HAS in *A canary has skin.* Or it may be a verb-like concept that explicitly identifies subset–superset relations; this concept has no exact English equivalent, but has the technical name ISA. ISA actually functions as a verb in the proposition *dog isa animal,* which is expressed in English as *A dog is an animal.* By this analysis, which is justified on linguistic grounds, both *A canary has skin* and *A dog is an animal* are propositions of the form Subject-Verb-Predicate. When an experimental subject is required to judge them true or false, he is *verifying* the propositions.

In the foregoing examples, the proposition is explicitly stated. It may also be implicit in the experimental instructions. For example, a subject who says *yes* to the pair DOG-ANIMAL has implicitly verified the proposition *A dog is an animal.* The view of semantic memory researchers is that all speeded classification and speeded verification procedures depend on the same underlying cognitive structures and processes. Since about 1970, variations on these procedures have been used in the vast majority of semantic memory experiments. The dependent measure is usually reaction time. Reaction times have been used to justify inferences about such matters as the distance between elements in the layout of semantic memory, about the operations involved in the retrieval of those elements, and about the relationships among these operations.

A. Influences from Experimental Psychology

Pollack (1963) studied speeded classification well before the field of semantic memory was established. Because Pollack came from the information-theory tradition of experimental psychology, he justified his use of speeded classification as an effort to understand the effects of stimulus and response diversity (or uncertainty) on reaction time. His sole purpose was to document a functional relationship between variables. He stated his purpose tersely and without speculating about the structures that a functional relationship might reflect: "The classification task . . . provides a critical examination of stimulus and response factors in human information processing . . . it permits us to ask whether the speed of information processing is primarily determined by: (a) the number of different response categories that S must employ; or by (b) the number of different examples per category . . . [p. 159]." Following this lean introduction, Pollack moved directly to an account of his method. He asked nothing about how meaning is stored in memory. He raised no questions about cognitive systems that control word classification; no questions about perceptual mechanisms, the mind or consciousness, decision processes, or the language system. These things, which Pollack did *not* mention, are preceisely what interest today's users of the speeded classification task.

Like Pollack, Schaeffer and Wallace (1969) conceived their work as free of structural assumptions, but they expressed their purposes and interpretations in neobehavioristic rather than information-theory terms. To show that the semantic similarity of words influences the judgment that the words belong to the same category, Schaeffer and Wallace presented words two at a time. Their subjects judged whether both words in a pair were the names of living things (e.g., LION-TULIP or LION-ZEBRA), nonliving things (e.g., ZINC-NYLON or ZINC-STEEL), or one of each (e.g. ZINC-LION). If both were living or both were nonliving, the subject pressed a button marked *same*. If one was living and the other nonliving, he pressed a button marked *different*. Schaeffer and Wallace predicted that "same" judgments would be made more quickly when the two words were semantically similar, a factor that they varied by the use of subcategories. Thus, LION-ZEBRA were considered more semantically similar by virtue of both being animals (a subcategory of living things) than LION-TULIP; and therefore the experimenters predicted a faster "same" response for LION-ZEBRA than for LION-TULIP. Schaeffer and Wallace's (1969) prediction was based strictly on association-istic considerations:

The prediction is based on the assumption that associations are activated when a given word is understood. Two semantically similar words can be more readily judged equivalent than can dissimilar ones because they activate many of the same associations and these provide cues of similarity. Two similar words can be less readily judged different because the cues of similarity provided by their common associations interfere with the difference judgment [p. 343].

When their prediction was confirmed, their interpretation was also couched in neobehavioristic terms: "the associations common to similar words evoked an implicit 'same' response that facilitated the 'same' button press [p. 346]." The necessity to postulate an "implicit 'same' response" derives from the insistence of neobehavioristic thinkers that behavior results from sequences of stimulus–response associations. By the time Schaeffer and Wallace wrote, it had become acceptable to describe stimuli and responses as implicit and covert, but many psychologists still clung to the conditioning model. For them, it seemed more acceptable to emphasize the role of stimuli and responses than to invoke other explanations, such as memory searches or internal structures.

Landauer and Freedman (1968) were the first to explicitly phrase the classification question in information-processing terms:

> This paper is addressed to the general problem of how information is retrieved from human long-term memory. Given that an individual has at some time in the relatively distant past learned something, how does he manage to produce this information in the present? An interesting and potentially instructive case of this retrieval process is the identification of an instance as belonging or not belonging to a particular class. When one sees a sparrow and decides that it is a bird, or sees a dog and decides that it is not a bird, one has in some manner consulted a store of memories and determined that the stimulus is or is not one of those for which the class name is appropriate [p. 291].

Their version of the speeded classification task varied the size of the categories about whose instances subjects had to make timed decisions. The size of many categories is known: The category size of *Sex* is two, *Seasons* four, *Days of the Week* seven, *Months* 12, *States in the U.S.A.* 50. Even when people do not know the exact number of instances in a category, they may know their relative size, if the categories are nested. For instance, while few people know how many types of dogs there are (e.g., collie, chow, etc.), or how many animals, practically all people are confident that there are more types of animals than of dogs. Nearly everyone agrees that the following categories are listed in the order of their size: *Dog, Canine, Mammal, Animal, Living thing.* Landauer and Freedman used such nested categories to vary their relative size in order to study whether the search through long-term memory is serial or parallel.

Landauer and Freedman relied heavily on the computer analogy for developing their approach in 1968. A computer program written to respond "yes" or "no" to a question such as *Is a dog an animal?* must have stored (memory) information on which to base its answer. Programmers typically build the necessary memory so that various elements are stored with each word. For example, the programmer might include with "dog" the information "barks," "has four legs," "is an animal," "is a pet," and so on. When asked the question "Is a dog an animal?" the program will retrieve all the elements stored with "dog" to see whether "is an animal" is one of them. If the machine was programmed to act as if all the comparisons are made simultaneously, it would not matter how long a list of characteristics the programmer had stored with "dog"; but if the search was serial, it would take the machine longer to respond if the list is long than if it is short. The computer analogy suggests that the time people take in similar tasks will give clues to the way memory is organized. This was the perspective brought by Landauer and Freedman to the speeded classification task. It differs completely from the perspectives of Pollack (1963) and of Schaeffer and Wallace (1969).

Landauer and Freedman reasoned approximately that if verification time increased with category size, then subjects must scan their memories serially rather than in parallel, because very few parallel models predict time differences for searching long versus short lists. Thus, because there are fewer types of dogs than of animals, it should take less time to judge *Collie is a Dog* than *Collie is an Animal* only if semantic memory searches have a serial component.

Landauer and Freedman gave their subjects words such as *Collie* to classify into a larger category such as *Animal,* and, at some other time, into a smaller category such as *Dog.* They found that it took longer to classify the words into larger categories. This finding has been replicated in some studies (Landauer & Meyer, 1972; Meyer, 1970; Meyer & Ellis, 1970) but not others, particularly those requiring subjects to verify whole sentences (Rips, Shoben, & Smith, 1973; Smith, Shoben, & Rips, 1974). There have also been disagreements as to whether Landauer and Freedman varied something besides category size— perhaps one or more variables that changed systematically with category size. Two possibilities are *typicality* and *semantic distance.* If people are asked to rate how typical a particular instance is of a category, there is considerable agreement. For example, most people consider *Potato* more typical than *Garlic* of the category *Vegetable,* and *Robin* more typical than *Chicken* of the category *Bird.* Collective ratings of typicality are predictive of reaction time to classify such instances into categories (Rosch, 1973, 1975). It is also possible to ask people how "closely related" various word pairs are and to obtain considerable consensus. The pairs can be the names of category instances and their superordinates, such as *Dog-Animal.* Whether they have this hierarchical relationship or not, however, ratings relatedness also predict reaction times to make various decisions about the word pairs. It is possible that Landauer and Freedman inadvertently varied typicality and/or semantic distance with category size, and these factors may be responsible for the reaction-time differences they found. Because of these criticisms, the category size effect has not influenced any of the major models of semantic memory. Their contribution was the explicitness with which they stated the central problem for semantic memory theory—the problem of how information is structured in long-term memory and retrieved therefrom.

So far, we have seen that speeded classification was used by experimental psychologists for a variety of purposes, before it was used to study the structure of semantic memory. Pollack (1963) used it to study functional relationships of the information-theory sort. Schaeffer and Wallace (1969) used it to study semantic variables from a neobehaviorist perspective.

Landauer and Freedman (1968) used it to see whether retrieval from long-term memory is serial or parallel, a distinction originally drawn from communications engineering. This flexible experimental tradition seemed to prepare psychologists to accept speeded classification as the major way to test notions about memory structure. At any rate, they gave such acceptance; and the occasion for them to do so came indirectly from a theorist by the name of Ross Quillian. His dissertation, described presently, was done in the intellectual environment of the Newell and Simon research program and reflects their approach.

B. The Merging of Artificial Intelligence and Experimental Psychology

Quillian (1968), whose background was greatly influenced by artificial intelligence, authored a computer theory to answer questions. To do this, he had to select a memory structure; that is, he had to represent the information that would be the source of the answers, in an absolutely unambiguous way. For his computer program, he had to function as nature has for man—of all the possible ways one might represent knowledge, he had to pick exactly one. Then, given this structure, he had to work out exactly how the information in it was to be used, and specify each step of the process. It is, of course, certain that Quillian's decisions about structure and process were not independent; he developed them to be as efficient as possible and mutually compatible. As we have mentioned before, when one has written a program of this sort, it becomes a psychological theory as soon as one asserts that it functions *like a human being* in carrying out its task. It was a short step from Quillian's (1968) original artificial intelligence program to the psychological theory of human question-answering that was proposed and tested in the important work of Collins and Quillian (1969).

1. Quillian's Model: The "Teachable" Language Comprehender"

The model developed by Quillian (1969), called the Teachable Language Comprehender, was conceived as a theory of language and expressed in a computer simulation program that aspired to the comprehension of English texts. This work is described in some detail because much in the global models chapter is derived from it. To continue, Quillian hoped (as he said):

> to develop a computer program that could comprehend newspapers, textbooks, encyclopedias, and other written text. That is, the program should be able to extract and somehow retain meaning from natural language text it has not seen before, at a level of skill comparable with that of human readers. TLC is in the

development stage, and so far it only works on certain isolated phrases and sentences. Together, these constitute a theory of what text comprehension is and how to achieve it . . . . We also happen to believe that, given the present state of psychological theories, almost any program able to perform some task previously limited to humans will represent an advance in the psychological theory of that performance [p. 459].

Quillian's theory defined comprehension as the relating of input assertions to information previously stored in memory as general world knowledge. Each piece of information, or "element," had to be represented in a precise, unambiguous code. Yet there had to be sufficient flexibility to permit the code to be extended to represent any concept expressible in natural language. The structure Quillian used was a data structure called a *network of finite automata*, a portion of which is shown in Fig. 9.1. The network consists of interconnected elements called *nodes*, which are represented by dots in the figure. Each node is connected to at least one other by a *link*, or pointer, which designates the relationship between the pair of nodes. Although this may look complicated—and it is at the level of actually writing a program—the general principles are rather straightforward. All that is meant by the diagram in Fig. 9.1 is that the programmer sets up the computer's memory so that whenever it has *Bird* represented in its central processor, it also has all the necessary instructions to retrieve the information that a bird has feathers, can fly, has wings, and is an animal. Once this related information is retrieved, new concepts are available to the central processor—that is, *Feathers, Fly, Wings, Animal.* Their availability supplies the necessary instructions to retrieve any

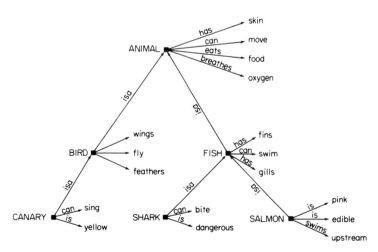

FIG. 9.1.   A representation of part of semantic memory according to the hierarchical structure of Quillian (1968).

information stored with (linked to) these concepts, and so on until the central processor reaches a concept that has no further linked concepts. The representation of knowledge as a hierarchical network makes it possible to incorporate the important capacity of inference in the model. Quillian was explicitly attempting to build inferential ability into his program. Indeed, when we know that a bird has skin because birds are animals and animals have skin, we have made an inference; and this was how the Teachable Language Comprehender was designed to "know" more than it had explicitly stored in memory.

Quillian set up the semantic memory so that the first link of a concept node is connected to the node representing its immediate superordinate. The other links connect the concept with its properties, or attributes—these correspond to adjectives, possessions, and other predications, such as *is dangerous, has wings, swims upstream*. Quillian distinguished between the semantic memory and the natural language lexicon; in other words, these nodes were *not* intended to represent the words in a person's vocabulary, but the concepts in his mind. Quite often, of course, there are words that represent the concepts, such as *Robin, Tulip, Park, Hippie,* or *Beauty*. However, there can be concepts that have a single node in the memory, but no single-word name in English. For instance, an art historian's semantic memory might contain a single node for "French impressionist painter," even though English has no single name for the concept. The semantic network, which is the part we are most interested in, was designed to represent the conceptual knowledge system. So, while all the nodes in Fig. 9.1 are labeled with words, in Quillian's theory they do not represent words: They represent concepts. Semantic memory concerns meanings, not words.

The knowledge structure selected by Quillian incorporates a feature called *cognitive economy*. According to the principle of cognitive economy, properties shared by a number of concepts are stored with their common superordinate. Thus, a *Shark* and a *Salmon* both have fins, both can swim, and both have gills; but these properties are not stored with the concept for *Shark* nor are they stored with the concept for *Salmon*. Instead, *has Fins, can Swim* and *has Gills* are stored with *Fish*, which is the immediate superordinate of both *Salmon* and *Shark*. The economy is realized by having such properties represented only once, instead of storing them with the node for every particular fish.

Recall now that a chief difference between episodic and semantic memory is that semantic memory depends on inference, while episodic memory does not. By giving his hierarchical network cognitive economy, Quillian provided a specific mechanism for inference. If the computer were asked to verify the statement *Sharks can swim,* the node corresponding to *Shark* and the pointers associated with it would be tested. Because the information that *can Swim* is not one of *Shark's* property pointers, the computer would traverse

Shark's superordinate pointer, which would lead it to access the node for *Fish,* one of whose property pointers is *can Swim.* Because Shark *is a Fish,* the computer would infer that *Sharks can swim,* and it would verify the input assertion as true. Inference is thus a derivative of tracing pointers, which is required in turn by the property of cognitive economy.

In this example, the inference that *Sharks can swim* required the tracing of only one superordinate link. But the tracing of many links might be required, depending on the nature of the assertion and on the structure of memory. Quillian's memory scheme incorporated the principle that all nodes are connected, albeit complexly and indirectly in many cases. For example, in Fig. 9.1, *Shark* is connected to *Fish,* which is connected to *Animal.* A more complete drawing than Fig. 9.1 would also show *Animal* linked to *Living thing* linked to *Physical object.* Someone whose memory was structured in this way would be able to verify that *Sharks are composed of matter,* even though he had never thought about sharks in this way before.

2. An Empirical Test of Quillian's Model

When Quillian built his Teachable Language Comprehender he had no way of knowing the structure of people's knowledge. He went ahead anyway, specifying a structure on a priori grounds. Very soon, Collins and Quillian (1969) experimentally tested structural aspects of Quillian's theory. To do this, they assumed that some unknown psychological process corresponds to the traversing of links, and that this process takes time. Accordingly, they predicted that the time required by people to verify assertions would be predicted by the number of links that would have to be traversed by Quillian's computer program, if it were asked to verify the assertions. The more links the program had to traverse, the longer it should take people to verify the assertion.

The concepts in Quillian's theory have specific, concrete meanings expressed in a computer programming language. But when those concepts are applied to people, they become more abstract. Although Quillian's computer simulation may be interpreted as a psychological theory, it would be unreasonable to view it now as even approaching an exact specification of the mechanisms people use to comprehend language. However, Quillian's theory can be viewed as a precise shorthand way of expressing arguments like these: Perhaps people represent a concept like animal by keeping together in their memories the information directly relevant to particular animals they know of, such as the facts that they can move, breathe, eat, and so on. Perhaps when people are asked about animals, they bring into their working memories constellations of related information, which permits them to answer the question. Similarly, we may say that someone has "accessed a node," even though the terms *node* and *access* have at present no definitive psychological meaning. Such theoretical concepts can only be understood by analogy to the mathematical systems or computer programs from which they are borrowed, or as first approximations to inferred mechanisms. Quillian's model, therefore, can be used as an approximate way of understanding part of the obscure cognitive system, provided only that we keep in mind that the theory is not now a precise statement about how people work. This is the sense in which Collins and Quillian compared data from people against predictions from the Teachable Language Comprehender. The question was whether the theory was a generally valid approach, not whether it immediately specified precise mechanisms.

Collins and Quillian (1969) timed people as they verified statements about the superordinate relationships and about the properties of nouns. They varied both the superordinate and property relationships with respect to the number of links or nodes people should have had to access. The number of links varied from zero to two. Thus, referring to Fig. 9.1 again, a *true* property-0 relationship might be represented by *A shark is dangerous,* and a *false* property-0 by *A shark is harmless.* A *true* superordinate-2 relationship might be represented by *A canary is an animal.*

With respect to *true* assertions, the results were straightforward (see Fig. 9.2). The greater the number of links specified in theory, the longer it took to verify *true* propositions. Moreover, the relationship between verification time and number of links tended to be linear, suggesting that the process associated with traversing a link, whatever it might be, consumed about 75 msec. Also, the curve relating number of links to reaction time was much higher for assertions about properties than for assertions about superordinate relationships. This follows from Quillian's structural assumptions, for a person must

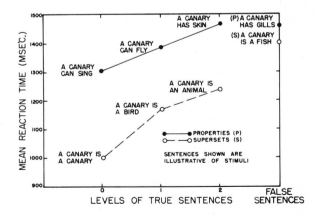

FIG. 9.2.   Average reaction time to confirm or deny sentences designating set inclusion or property nodes at varying hierarchical distance. (After Collins & Quillian, 1969.)

first traverse a superordinate link before gaining access to a property link. It should take longer to verify that *Salmon can swim* than *Salmon is a fish*, even though one must trace the superordinate pointer from *Salmon* to *Fish* in order to verify both of these propositions.

The results for false sentences do not readily support any single plausible hypothesis. Collins and Quillian considered several, including the *contradiction hypothesis*. One might think that contradictory information at a node, when found, would suffice to falsify a sentence. For example, if a subject is deciding about *A canary is purple,* he should be able to respond *false* as soon as he comes to the contradictory memory information *Canary* (node) - *is* (link) - *Yellow* (node). The trouble is, that is exactly the information necessary to respond *true* to *A canary is yellow.* The two judgments should thus take an equal, or at least similar, amount of time. However, the *false* judgment is much slower. Other plausible explanations of false sentence processing were considered by the authors, but all suggested contrary predictions to what actually happened. It may be that different individuals handle false sentences in different ways, and that complex formulations will be necessary to predict the data (Glass & Holyoak, 1975). This depressing possibility is rendered all the more likely by Collins and Quillian's observation that people were more variable in their response times to false sentences than to true ones. Furthermore, falsity is quantitatively asymmetrical with truth: An infinity of possible false statements can map on falsely to a given state of the world, whereas only a small number of true statements map on truthfully. Falsity seems sometimes a matter of degree, and therefore subject to idiosyncratic variations, to a greater extent than truth—*A canary is brown* does not seem quite as false to some people as *A canary is purple.*

III.   THE NORMAL-SCIENCE STUDY OF SEMANTIC MEMORY

A. Are Structural Notions Necessary?

The publication of the seminal paper (Collins & Quillian, 1969) stimulated a rash of studies. Among the first responses was one by Schaeffer and Wallace (1970). They asked whether it is necessary to theorize about memory structure. To make their point that it is not necessary, they chose to study the verification of false statements. It took no killer instinct to see that this was where Collins and Quillian were most vulnerable; but Schaeffer and Wallace missed the jugular on the issue of structure, even though they did demonstrate a relationship that must be accounted for by any theory of semantic memory.

Before the research by Collins and Quillian, Schaeffer and Wallace (1969) had defined semantic similarity in terms of category membership. Two animals are more semantically similar than an animal and a plant. They had shown that semantic similarity speeds up *true* judgments, and they gave a neobehaviorist interpretation to this finding. In 1970, after Collins and Quillian published, Shaeffer and Wallace studied the influences of semantic similarity on *false* statements. They gave their subjects four categories: trees, flowers, birds, and animals. The subjects then looked at pairs of words. They pressed one button if the two words belonged to the same category (both birds or both animals). They pressed another button if the words belonged to different categories. The categories themselves fit into superordinate relations: Trees and flowers are both plants. This allowed the calculation of reaction times for two sorts of *different* response: those in which the two words belonged to the same higher-level superordinate (both plants, but not both flowers) and those in which the higher superordinate was different (one plant and one animal). Schaeffer and Wallace found that semantically similar word pairs were judged *different* more slowly. It took longer to judge that PARROT and GIRAFFE were *different* than to judge PARROT and ELM *different*.

To account for these and their earlier results on *same* judgments, Schaeffer and Wallace proposed that semantic similarity facilitated *same* judgments and retarded *different* judgments. They moved out of an associationist framework in suggesting a decision-theoretic model, which is somewhat more congenial to information-processing psychology. Unfortunately, some of the values they carried with them from their previous tradition prevented them from developing their model into the kind of structuralist theory that is now quite common. They couched the model in the most general terms possible and then contrasted it with Collins and Quillian's (1969), arguing that their own was preferable because it made no structural assumptions about the organization of permanent memory or the retrieval processes involved in comparing concepts. This type of argument—and similar ones based on the doctrine of parsimony—are made more often than analyzed. We take a moment here to point out some of its flaws.

First, investigators sometimes confuse ignorance of their assumptions with absence of assumptions. In other words, their assumptions may be so intuitive and automatic that they do not realize they are making any at all. Schaeffer and Wallace, in using taxonomic categories to vary semantic similarity, assumed that their own intuitions about what constituted semantic similarity were the same as their subjects'. This is tantamount to a claim that the organization of subjects' semantic and associative categories corresponded to the experimenters'—a structural assumption, albeit a familiar and defensible one. But a familiar, defensible assumption is an assumption nevertheless.

Second, investigators may also confuse vagueness with an absence of assumptions. Thus, Schaeffer and Wallace (1969) postulated that "concepts are composed of elements [p. 145]," and that "the overlap between the concepts lion and elephant is greater than that between the concepts lion and daisy [p. 145]." These claims have implications for the organization of memory, even though they are phrased so vaguely that it is hard to turn them into predictions. What are the "elements"? What is "overlap"? What overlaps: Elements? Properties? Features? Evidently something does, but the failure to specify what overlaps is not a lack of structural assumptions so much as vagueness of assumptions. Schaeffer and Wallace argued for their model in these terms:

> The model does not argue for a particular form of retrieval but only argues that the product of retrieval be a concept. . . . In addition, the model does not demand that the information in concepts, the elements and their possible relationships, be represented in a particular form . . . the model does not insist . . . that the elements of concepts be ordered in any particular way or that they be wordlike [p. 145].

This is a valiant effort to make vagueness a virtue, but it falls short. One cannot describe a theory by saying what it is not, even though the data that one thereby avoids predicting cannot be handled by the particular structural model of Quillian. Schaeffer and Wallace's findings on semantic similarity stand as evidence that Quillian's a priori structuring of semantic memory does not fully capture the complexity of the organization of people's world knowledge. But their data argue for some structural theory other than Quillian's; they do not argue for nonstructural theory. Schaeffer and Wallace (1969, 1970) were the first to document one of the most powerful and reproducible principles in the field of semantic memory: Semantic relatedness controls the time required to compare concepts. The question is, what sort of structural theory will explain this finding? We return to this question later.

B. Are All Instances of a Category Equal?

According to Quillian's theory, the first link of any concept leads to its immediate superordinate. *Canary, Sparrow, Chicken, Ostrich* and *Stork* all link directly to the superordinate *Bird.* There is no reason in Quillian's theory why any bird should be categorized faster than any other, because all are instances of the superordinate *Bird.* But Wilkins (1971) was able to show that there are systematic differences in classification speed for different category instances. Some are more typical of a category than others and were consequently judged faster. The concept of typicality (Rosch, 1975) is discussed shortly. The latency differences between category members were predictable from normative data concerning the instances people think of when they are given a category name.

The normative data used by Wilkins were similar to those collected by Battig and Montague (1969), who gave category names to a large number of students at the Universities of Maryland and Illinois, asking them to write as many instances of the category as they could. They were given 30 seconds per category to write instances. Their responses were listed in order of frequency. For example, Table 9.1 shows the data for the category BIRD. The first column shows the number of people who gave an instance, and in parentheses the number who gave it first. Thus, 377 people gave *robin* as an instance of BIRD, and of those, 189 wrote *robin* first among the birds they gave. By contrast, only 10 people wrote *stork,* and only one listed it first.

These norms give an indication of the relationship between a category and its instances. Wilkins called the relationship conjoint frequency, but it has also been called semantic distance, category dominance, production frequency, and typicality. Whatever it is called, it suggests the same prediction to many researchers: Items high in the list, such as *robin, sparrow,* and *cardinal,* should be easily classified as birds, while items low in the list, such as *warbler, pelican,* and *stork,* should be harder to classify.

Wilkins selected items high and low in conjoint frequency. He found that subjects assigned high conjoint frequency words to their appropriate categories in 589 msec; words of low conjoint frequency took 632 msec. In other words, high conjoint frequency combinations were verified faster than low conjoint frequency combinations. This shows that level in a hierarchical network like Quillian's will not account by itself for verification time. In some sense, a *Robin* and a *Sparrow* are "better" *Birds* than *Warbler* or *Pelican,* even though Quillian's theory says that they all are at the same hierarchical level relative to the concept *Bird.* To account for such findings, Quillian's theory needs additional modification.

TABLE 9.1
Category Norms for Verbal Items[a]

	Category: A Bird		
Response	Total Freq. (1st)	Illinois Freq.	Maryland Freq.
1. robin	377(189)	155	222
2. sparrow	237(27)	104	133
3. cardinal	208(38)	104	104
4. blue jay	180(7)	70	112
5. eagle	161(18)	62	99
6. crow	149(11)	64	85
7. bluebird	138(17)	61	77
8. canary	134(12)	48	86
9. parakeet	115(11)	36	79
10. hawk	111(3)	41	70
11. blackbird	89(6)	37	52
12. wren	83(7)	46	37
13. oriole	77(19)	19	58

(continued)

TABLE 9.1 *continued*

Category: A Bird

Response	Total Freq. (1st)	Illinois Freq.	Maryland Freq.
14. parrot	72(5)	23	49
15. pigeon	56(5)	16	40
16. hummingbird	50(4)	14	36
17. starling	49(1)	20	29
18. woodpecker	46(2)	19	27
19. vulture	44(3)	17	27
20. swallow	41(3)	13	28
21. chicken	40	18	22
22. dove	36(3)	17	19
23. duck	36(4)	17	19
24. owl	36(1)	13	23
25. redbird	36(10)	8	28
26. sea gull	32(3)	5	27
27. thrush	31(1)	10	21
28. falcon	28	9	19
29. jay	24(3)	9	15
30. pheasant	22(1)	12	10
31. finch	20(2)	10	10
32. mockingbird	19(2)	3	16
33. buzzard	17(1)	3	14
34. ostrich	17(2)	9	8
35. flamingo	16(2)	7	9
36. lark	15(2)	6	9
37. peacock	15(1)	5	10
38. turkey	15	4	11
39. penguin	14	9	5
40. purple martin	14(1)	14	—
41. raven	14	5	9
42. swan	14	6	8
43. crane	13	8	5
44. geese	12	5	7
45. chickadee	11	4	7
46. pelican	11(2)	5	6
47. stork	10(1)	4	6
48. warbler	10(1)	3	7

[a]After Battig & Montague (1969).

C. How Economical is Semantic Memory?

Wilkins studied Collins and Quillian's superordinate relationship. Conrad (1972) studied the property relationship. She cast her work as a test of the notion of cognitive economy. Her belief was that some attributes come to mind more quickly than others. She began by asking college students to write descriptions of concepts such as *Animal, Bird, Shark, Canary,* and *Airplane.* She ordered the responses according to the percentage of subjects supplying each. For example, over 75% of her subjects supplied *can move* as a property of *Animal,* but only 12% supplied *has ears.* Having collected such norms, Conrad conducted an experiment paralleling Collins and Quillian, timing her subjects as they verified such sentences as *An animal can move* and *An animal has ears.* She found that her norms predicted verification times. Frequently given properties took 1080 msec to verify, while infrequently given ones took 1140 msec.

Conrad argued that her results contradicted Collins and Quillian's assumption of cognitive economy, the strong form of which is expressed in this quote from Conrad: "Properties which do not uniquely define a word but are also properties of the word's superordinate are stored only in the configuration which defines the meaning of the superordinate [p. 149]." This strong form of the assumption of cognitive economy has several unbelievable implications, quite apart from its difficulty with Conrad's data. For example, if we told you that *An aardvark has skin,* you need not store that fact if you operated by Quillian's model, because the information that animals have skin would already be present at your superordinate node for *Animal.* But if you do not know whether an aardvark is an animal, a vegetable, or a fruit—all of which have skin—what do you do with the fact AN AARDVARK HAS SKIN, while waiting to learn its proper category? Furthermore, if you find out that ALL REPTILES HAVE SCALES after you have learned that SNAKES HAVE SCALES, the strong hypothesis of cognitive economy requires that you erase *has scales* from SNAKE and restore it with REPTILE. Erasure is an uncongenial notion. On the other hand, the cognitive economy with which Quillian supplied the Teachable Language Comprehender was in effect its inference-making capacity. Rather than storing *eats food* with both *Animal* and *Canary,* it was only stored at the superordinate node; thus, verification of *A canary eats food* required an upward search of properties in the superordinate hierarchies of the network (see Fig. 9.1).

Conrad's experiment showed that sentence verification data that might support the strong form of cognitive economy failed to control for differences in property frequencies at different levels in the hierarchy. Her argument was based on the fact that when a particular property showed high production frequency in her norms, verification reaction times were fast no matter how many hierarchical levels intervened between the subject node and the predicate node where the property ought to have been stored for maximum efficiency. This observation certainly supports the inference that properties can be stored at more than one node, and therefore suggests that the strong assumption of cognitive economy is wrong. However, the fact that properties *can* be stored at more than one node does not mean that they must be stored at *every* node, as Conrad mistakenly concluded: "This suggests that properties are stored in memory with every word which they define and can be retrieved directly rather than through a process of inference [p.154]." Thus, having found evidence contradicting the strong form of cognitive economy, she rejected the weak form as well.

However, some form of cognitive economy is suggested both by logical considerations and by Conrad's own data. It is implausible to conceive of a system in which every imaginable or inferrable fact must be directly represented. People can verify a potentially infinite number of such statements as *Richard Nixon has a backbone, Harold's wife has skin, Joan of Arc had thumbs,* and falsify an infinite number such as *Plato drove a Mercedes-Benz* and *Marion's mother had 8,862 children by Caesarean section.* Without inferential capability, every single property conceivable of *Homo sapiens* must be stored with every instance of the category about whom the person knows anything at all. This would require an infinite storage capacity. Although human retrieval capacity is in principle infinite, storage capacity is not. Conrad's norms, moreover, support the idea that certain properties are *not* stored at certain nodes—the weak claim of cognitive economy. The property *is liquid* is given by 50% of her subjects for the concept *Drink,* but not at all for *Coca-Cola, Coffee, Lemonade,* or *Beer.* Similarly, every one of her subjects supplied *has wings* for *Bird,* but none of them supplied it for *Canary, Owl,* or *Ostrich.* It is puzzling that Conrad's interpretation was so widely accepted, for it denies the organism an inference-making capacity. Sufficiency considerations absolutely demand an inference capacity irrespective of the outcome of any given experiment.

D. Conjoint Frequency, Semantic Distance, or What?

What do the production frequency norms of Wilkins (1971) and Conrad (1972) measure? Whatever it is, it seems to be a powerful predictor of reaction time in classification tasks. Rips, Shoben, and Smith (1973) named it *semantic distance.* They operationalized the concept of semantic distance in two ways. In one experiment, they used norms that indicate the frequency with which instances are given for categories, such as *Animal, Mammal, Bird, Vehicle,* and *Car.* As predicted by Quillian's model, instances such as *Cardinal, Eagle,* and *Robin* were verified as *Birds* faster than as *Animals.* But the *Mammal* category was inconsistent with predictions from Quillian's theory. *Mammal* should be at the same level as BIRD, but people verified *Bear, Cat, Cow,* and *Deer* faster as *Animals* than as *Mammals.* This suggests that the logical taxonomic categories of Quillian's hierarchic model are not the categories that people use. Rips et al. also observed considerable variation for the decision times of hierarchically identical propositions; for instance, *A pig is a mammal* took considerably longer (1476 msec) to verify than *A cow is a mammal* (1258 msec).

In their second experiment, Rips, Shoben, and Smith defined semantic distance in terms of norms collected explicitly to determine how far people judged category instances to be from their superordinate category name. People were asked, for example, to rate the distance between the concept *Mammal* and its various instances, such as *Cow, Goat, Horse,* and so on. The obtained ratings were excellent predictors of reaction time to verify statements such as *A cow is a mammal, A goat is a mammal* and *A horse is a mammal.* They also determined that these distance ratings appeared to reflect organization along two dimensions, size and predacity, for both mammals and birds. Birds and mammals that were unusually large or small, or unusually predatory or meek, tended to be rated as more distant from the category name than those of intermediate size and predacity. Rips et al. interpret their results as contrasting with hierarchical distance models such as Collins and Quillian's, and interpret them in the context of the Smith, Shoben, and Rips (1974) model to be presented in detail among the contemporary models.

E. Typicality and Base Level

The studies we have just described represent several ways of operationalizing semantic distance—from experimenter's intuitions to normative measures reflecting the judgments of large pools of subjects. However collected, the norms have some common dimensions. All correlate in varying degrees with the time needed to classify subordinates and properties or verify subject–predicate propositions. What are these norms measuring? An interesting view is represented in the work of Rosch (1973, 1975). Rosch originally approached the problem from a different perspective than semantic memory theorists usually do. She wanted to discover the principles people use in dividing up the perceptual world. But her work quickly extended to the study of natural-language concepts, or categories, such as those commonly used in semantic memory studies. Rosch argued that speakers of English living in urban America know how *typical* an instance is of its superordinate category. They know, for instance, that *Bed* is more typical of the category *Furniture* than is *Hammock,* and that *Robin* is a more typical *Bird* than is a *Penguin.* This observation was unlike previous psychological research in concept formation, in which natural categories were usually treated as all-or-none. Rosch proposed that most natural categories are actually *analogue* in nature; by this she meant that a category's internal structure represents the degree of relatedness of various category members to the category itself. The category members, in other words, are organized around prototypical instances, and vary in their proximity to the prototype. The organization exists *in the minds* of the people of common cultural background who use the category.

Rosch also distinguished prototype and nonprototype members for some categories. Prototype category members are the clearest cases, or most typical instances; *Chair, Bed,* and *Table* are prototype members of the category *Furniture,* while *Ashtray, Drapes,* and *Vase* are nonprototype members. Nonprototype members vary in their degree of typicality. *Lamp* and *Stool* are "better" examples of furniture than *Ashtray* and *Picture.*

The prototype structure of natural-language semantic categories has been called *typicality.* Rosch has shown that people can reliably rate how typical the various members of familiar categories are. Their ratings also predict various aspects of performance in a task requiring people to match words or pictures (Rosch, 1975). It is also possible to make up artificial categories, in which some category members are more typical than others; when this is done, the more typical instances are easier to learn (Rosch & Mervis, 1975).

These data support Rosch's proposed analogue typicality structure of superordinate semantic categories. However, Rosch (1975) states that her research "was not intended either as a model of semantic memory or as a verification or refutation of any particular theory of semantic memory [p. 225]." Still, her results will be difficult to incorporate in any theory of semantic memory that posits sharp category boundaries, such as one proposed by Glass and Holyoak (1975). The findings are much more compatible with theories positing flexible conceptual structures. One such theory, that of Smith, Shoben, and Rips (1974), is presented in the next section of this chapter.

Rosch has recently made another very significant contribution to psychological semantics. She discovered a *base level* type of category membership (Rosch, Mervis, Gray, Johnson, & Boyes-Braem, 1976). Most objects fit into a hierarchy of categories having increasing generality. For example *Colonial kitchen chair* is less general that *kitchen chair,* which is less general than *chair, furniture, artifact (man-made object), inanimate object,* and *physical object.* Rosch observed that many such hierarchies contain one level that is special in terms of descriptive salience. At this level, people can describe what you do with the object, what actions can be performed on it, draw a silhouette, and supply its characteristics. At higher levels, they cannot do these things, because the category is too abstract; and at lower levels there is no difference in what they can say about the object. For example, it is possible to draw a silhouette of a chair, but not of furniture; it is possible to describe what you do with a Colonial kitchen chair, but this is no different than what you do with chairs in general. For this hierarchy, *Chair* is at the base level; it is the highest level in the hierarchy that is descriptively salient.

Rosch suggested that most object properties may be stored at the base level. While her work is still too new to be included in current theories of semantic memory, it has partly motivated a new approach to the general concept of psychological similarity. Tversky (1977) has described a set-theoretic approach to similarity that encompasses the Rosch data as well as people's similarity judgments of faces, personality traits, and other semantic and perceptual stimuli.

F. Summary

After 90 years of research on episodic memory, psychologists became interested in the structure of semantic memory. By 1969, new attitudes toward the human organism, the renewed interest in structural theory, and beginning attention to sufficiency had laid groundwork within psychology for a model with the broad ambitions of Quillian's. Its acceptance and ability to stimulate research would have been highly unlikely 10 years earlier. As late as it appeared, it still seems to us that the Collins and Quillian (1969) paper was a part of the information-processing revolution. Questions about the organization and access of permanent knowledge were ripe to be asked; in fact, Landauer and Freedman (1968) were formulating the focal question even as Collins and Quillian were developing a tentative answer.

Collins and Loftus (1975), in their recent defense of the Collins and Quillian model, consider that many of the studies purporting to undermine the basic framework of the Quillian theory greatly overstated their case. They consider that it was not fundamentally incorrect as originally formulated, but incomplete; their up-to-date revision incorporates the recent data. The Collins–Loftus–Quillian Spreading Activation Theory is as viable as its competitors. As we have said before, psychology is a dynamic research science, and none of the models can begin to do justice to *all* the data, nor are all the relevant data yet known. It is a considerable advance to be asking the right questions.

Semantic memory research is at present in a stage of normal science. Our next section describes several of the current models of semantic memory that place heavy reliance on data from studies of speeded classification and sentence verification. There is considerable consensus among the authors of these models as to what the right questions are, how to formulate hypotheses, and how to test them. There is also considerable agreement regarding the basic set of empirical facts that must initially constrain the models.

First, all attempt to accommodate the semantic distance or typicality effect. When two items are semantically close, people classify them *same* more quickly than *different*. For semantically distant items, the reverse is true. This generalization has held up in many studies using different versions of the speeded classification task (Conrad, 1972; Rips, Shoben, & Smith, 1973; Schaeffer & Wallace, 1969, 1970; Wilkins, 1971). One major exception has been discovered by Glass and Holyoak (1975). They provided a taxonomy of "false" sentences and demonstrated that certain types are judged *false* quickly despite the semantic similarity of the subject and predicate. All models must be able to explain such anomalies.

Second, all must determine what properties are stored with which concepts. From Conrad's (1972) data, as well as logical considerations, it is reasonable to assume that properties can be stored at more than one location, but they are probably not stored with every instance of every category to which they apply. There is some cognitive economy. It is therefore a plausible assumption that some properties are stored with more than one concept—but how many and which ones? And what are the principles determining multiple storage, and choice of location?

There has been considerable support for the hierarchical portion of the Quillian model, and it is almost certain that at least some of the permanent memory is organized hierarchically. However, Collins and Quillian assigned too much importance to logical hierarchies, as the data by Rips et al. (1973) on the *Mammal* category suggested. Most theorists in the field treat subordinate-superordinate as only one of a number of relations that may obtain between stored concepts.

IV. TWO MODELS OF SEMANTIC MEMORY

A. Overview

Out of at least six contemporary models of semantic memory, we describe two. They have sufficient empirical corroboration and formal explicitness to justify a detailed characterization. The models are relatively small in scale. They are primarily supported by speeded verification data, with a lesser emphasis on such other research as multidimensional scaling of semantic relatedness. Global models of world knowledge, language, and understanding are presented in a later chapter.

The first model we describe is the Theory of Spreading Activation, an updated version of Quillian's model. Collins and Loftus (1975) modified Quillian's model to make it account for the effects of semantic distance and to allow the storage of properties at multiple nodes. Also, they modified the structure of the knowledge network, and spelled out processes that search for information within the network. The second model is that of Smith, Shoben, and Rips (1974). They concluded that the semantic distance effect damaged Quillian's model so completely that it made more sense to start over. Their model was formulated as an explicit alternative to Quillian's; so it is also a direct competitor to the Collins and Loftus Spreading Activation Theory.

Of the several related models we do not discuss in detail, two have not yet inspired efforts at experimental refutation. One is by Glass and Holyoak (1975), the other by Fiksel and Bower (1976). It is too soon to tell how influential these two will become. A third, Meyer's (1970, 1973) model, is older, and it illustrates many of the features of contemporary information-processing theory. But his model had a more specific focus than those of Quillian, Collins, and Loftus or Smith et al. Meyer used a version of the speeded classification task including *quantifiers* in his stimulus sentences, such as *all, some, no,* and the like. Based on data from experiments in which subjects verified such statements as "All stones are rubies" and "No men are nurses," Meyer formulated a two-stage category search model that was initially quite different from Quillian's approach. However, Meyer had to modify his model to take account of experimental refutations and later data, including the semantic distance effect. The most recent formulation of it (Meyer & Schvaneveldt, 1976) is much more like Collins and Loftus' (1975) than the original earlier version. Because the early Meyer model is of primarily historical interest and the later one is similar to Collins and Loftus, we do not detail Meyer's work in this chapter.

As we discuss the models, we consider their *structural, processing,* and *decision* assumptions. The distinction between structural and computational or processing hypotheses appears in the literature on both semantic memory and artificial intelligence (Shoben, Rips, & Smith, in press; Smith, 1978; Winograd, 1975). Structural hypotheses concern the layout or configuration of information that is prestored in memory. They address the representational problem: How is knowledge represented in memory? Computational hypotheses concern processes that locate, transform, transfer, relocate, compare, modify, and rearrange symbols in the memory structure.

In a sense, a road map represents a structural statement about a city. We have found it useful to divide computational assumptions into two types, processing assumptions and decision assumptions. Charts of traffic motion and flow constitute the processing statement corresponding to the road map. If some agent at a central facility can control traffic lights, that process would correspond to decision processes. Decision processes involve comparisons between symbols and such decisions about them as "same as," "equal to," "different from," "more than," "includes," and the like. All other suppositions about the handling of symbolic information are processing assumptions and hypotheses.

B. The Spread of Activation

1. Structural Assumptions

Collins and Loftus (1975) expressed their revision of Quillian's model as a network of linked concept nodes, but their revision does not assume hierarchical organization as the basic structure. Instead, concept relatedness —that is, semantic distance—is the central organizational principle of the new memory network. Comparing Fig. 9.3 with Fig. 9.1 should show the differences between the structural assumptions of Quillian's theory and the theory of spreading activation. In Fig. 9.3, the length of lines connecting concept nodes indicates the strength of association between concepts. For example, OSTRICH and CANARY are both instances of BIRD, but OSTRICH is further from BIRD than CANARY, thus indicating that canaries are semantically closer to the concept BIRD than ostriches are. Of course, the length of the lines will vary somewhat with how semantic distance is measured. The distances in Fig. 9.3 are based approximately on the norms of Battig and Montague (1969), though we might have used Rosch's (1975) measures of typicality, or other normative ratings of semantic distance. Deciding how to measure semantic distance is a primary challenge for semantic memory models, and especially for the Spread of Activation Theory. The method used to estimate link strength determines how well a model can fit reaction-time data. Even if a model was correct in all other respects, a poor measure of link strength would cause it to predict reaction times poorly. The theorist who solves the problem of how to determine which nodes are linked, and how strongly, will significantly influence the direction

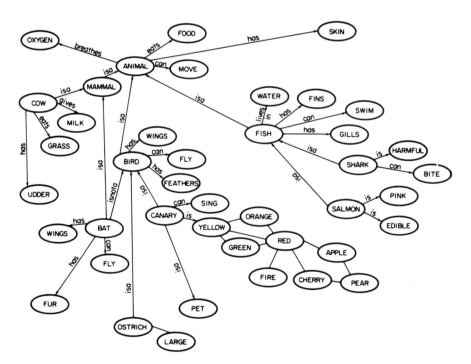

FIG. 9.3.   A piece of conceptual memory as it might be represented by the theory of spreading activation.

of semantic memory research and see the solution incorporated into all viable theories of semantic memory.

Like the original Quillian model, the semantic memory network of Collins and Loftus links concepts, not words. Words are located in a lexicon, which is a separate system in the Spreading Activation Theory, as it is in Quillian's theory. Each name in the lexicon is linked to one or more concepts in the semantic memory. This assumption, that conceptual and lexical information is in different systems and differently organized, is not unique. Other semantic memory theorists (e.g., Lachman, 1973; Loftus, 1976, 1977; Rumelhart, Lindsay, & Norman, 1972) have also felt that the conceptual and vocabulary knowledge must reside in separate systems. Aphasics may lose vocabulary information and yet respond in a clearly appropriate way to objects they cannot name. Normal people in a "tip-of-the-tongue" state may be unable to produce the name of some concept they have clearly in mind. Prelinguistic infants and even many animals recognize familiar events (i.e., have semantic memory representations of them) and behave appropriately to them even though they have no vocabulary with which to express their knowledge of these events. These facts argue for different systems containing conceptual and linguistic information; however, there must be some interface or hook-up between the two systems so that each concept can be easily paired with the name a person has learned to use for designating the concept. In Spreading Activation Theory, each name in the lexicon is linked to at least one concept in the semantic memory. The lexicon is also a network structure, but it is organized differently from the semantic memory. Proximity of word-nodes in the lexical network is primarily determined by how similar the words sound. This organization is justified partly by the work of Brown and McNeill (1966), who showed that people have systematic memories for certain aspects of the sound of a word that they cannot quite recall, but have "on the tip of the tongue."

Collins and Loftus also used concept links that Quillian did not. For example, they use a negative superordinate link that we have called *isnota* in Fig. 9.3, as between *Bat* and *Bird*. One reason is the finding of Holyoak and Glass (1975) that many *false* decisions are made faster than would be possible by inference. Evidently, some category exclusions are directly available, which agrees with the intuition that some negations are directly learned and need not be inferred. Some examples are *A bat is not a bird, A whale is not a fish,* and *An eel is not a snake.*

2. Processing Assumptions

The easiest way to appreciate the processing or computational assumptions of the model of spreading activation is to think of a roomful of identical tuning forks. When you strike a fork, it will vibrate and ring. Its intensity will be greatest right after it is struck, following which its ringing will decrease until it eventually becomes silent. Forks near the one you strike will also vibrate, but less intensely, and the intensity of the ringing of the nearby forks will also decrease over time. In a roomful of tuning forks, vibration will spread outward from the one you strike. Now think of concept nodes as acting like the tuning forks.

According to the model of Collins and Loftus, a concept node is activated when a person sees, hears, reads, or thinks about a concept. The meaning of activation is best understood by its hypothetical effects. Activating one node activates its adjacent nodes, which in turn activate their adjacent nodes. Thus, activation spreads through the memory structure, and like the vibration of the tuning forks, node activation decreases over time and distance. Thus, when the node *Fish* is activated, the adjacent concepts *Water, Fins, Gills, Shark, Salmon,* and *Animal* are also activated in proportion to their distance from *Fish*. According to Fig. 9.3, *Water* would be more strongly activated by *Fish* than *Salmon* would be. *Shark* would be activated, too, as would *Harmful* and *Bite*, though less strongly than *Shark*. *Fish* would activate *Salmon*, which would more weakly activate *Pink* and *Edible*. For all nodes, activation fades over time.

The spread of activation through the memory structure permits the verification of propositions. Consider the case in which a subject is asked to verify the Subject-Verb-Predicate proposition *A fish eats food*. FISH is read first, so the node for *Fish* is activated first. As a consequence, activation begins to spread from *Fish* to adjacent nodes. An instant later, the predicate FOOD is read, and activation begins to spread outward from its node. Activation from the nodes *Fish* and *Food* intersect at the node for *Animal*, at which point a decision must be made as to whether the relationship represented by the links connecting *Fish* and *Food* is consistent with the verb *EATS* in the proposition *A fish eats food*.

To evaluate a proposition, we require a decision mechanism, which must be able to determine where the spreading activation originated and how it has spread through the memory structure, because all nodes are interconnected. To accomplish this record-keeping, Collins and Loftus assumed that as activation spreads, it leaves "tags" at intervening nodes. These tags had to be assumed for the model to work. Otherwise, when *Animal* was stimulated in the foregoing example by activation emanating from two sources, the evaluating mechanism would no longer know where the stimulation had come from or what proposition to evaluate.

The model also assumes that the activations, such as those spreading from *Fish* and *Food*, sum together; it is greater from both than it would be from either alone. A further assumption is that the activation level at an intersection node must exceed a decision threshold; if it does not, it is ignored. Because everything in semantic memory is linked by some path to everything else, the system must be able to ignore activated intersections that are so weak as to be irrelevant.

3. Decision Assumptions

So far, we have spoken of the structural and computational assumptions of Collins and Loftus. We turn now to the decision assumptions of their model of spreading activation.

As we have already said, deciding whether an assertion is true requires keeping track of the concept nodes along the paths of activation initiated by the assertion. The relations specified in the memory structure between activated Subject and Predicate nodes must then be compared to the Verb in the assertion to be evaluated. The problem is to decide whether the relations specified by the superordinate or property pointers in semantic memory are the same as or different from the relation specified by the Verb in the assertion to be verified. Both positive and negative sources of evidence enter into this decision. An *isa* superordinate, for example, provides strong positive evidence for propositions of the form *Subject ISA Predicate,* while an *isnota* superordinate provides strong negative evidence.

According to the theory, each source of evidence is considered. The values or strengths of the negative bits of evidence are summed, in proportion to the degree of activation of their associated nodes. Similarly, the values of positive bits are summed. *True* and *false* decision criteria are set, and when the summed values exceed one or the other, a *true* or *false* response is made. Thus, locating an *isa* superordinate would push the positive evidence over the criterion for a *true* response, if the assertion had the form Subject *isa* Predicate. For that same assertion, an *isnota* superordinate would push the negative evidence over criterion.

In the graph theory notation, length of the lines representing relational links indicates the strength of the link. Links contribute evidence about the truth of propositions in proportion to their strength. For instance, strong positive evidence for *A canary can sing* is contributed by the link between *Canary* and *Sing* because that link is strong (the line is short). It is strong, at any rate, according to Conrad's (1972) norms: 88% of her subjects gave *can sing* as a property of *canary.* For the proposition *A salmon is edible,* weaker positive evidence is supplied by the link between *Salmon* and *Edible.* Only 57% of Conrad's subjects mentioned that salmon can be eaten. A mismatch on a strong link constitutes strong negative evidence. For instance, a person should be able to reject *A bird cannot fly* on the basis of the strong *can* link between *Bird* and *Fly.* Another source of negative evidence, according to Collins and Loftus, is finding that two subsets have the same superordinate in semantic memory, which strongly implies an *isnota* relation between the subsets. Thus, *A mammal is a fish* may be negated by the fact that *Mammal* and *Fish* are separate subsets of the superordinate *Animal.*

Altogether, Collins and Loftus describe five kinds of evidence that may be used, alone or in combination, by the semantic decision system. The resulting configuration of possible bases for decisions is complex. This is a desirable feature of an information-processing theory: It is consistent with the paradigm in its effort to encompass a large number of human capacities by combining and recombining a very small group of basic operations. As theorizing matures, there will undoubtedly be more effort to identify the minimum set of elementary decision rules that will handle the range of semantic judgments people make.

Collins and Loftus (1975) describe a wide variety of reaction-time data with which their model copes well. Like other models in this chapter, the Theory of Spreading Activation does best with data from the speeded verification task. It will be enhanced as a general theory if it can be extended to accommodate different kinds of tasks that people rely on their semantic memories to perform.

C. A Feature Comparison Model

Smith, Shoben, and Rips (1974) built another kind of model to account for semantic memory findings. They did so in large part because they believed that Quillian's theory could not be changed enough to handle the effects of semantic distance. People sometimes judge very quickly whether two words are related. The speed with which they sometimes make such judgments suggested to Smith and his colleagues that inferential processes are sometimes not required, while at other times inference is necessary. So they built a two-stage model. The idea is that when people are asked to judge simple sentences, they first make a global comparison between their stored knowledge of the sentence's Subject and Predicate nouns. If the concepts corresponding to the Subject and Predicate are highly related, or if they are related very little, a decision about the proposition is made immediately. But if Subject and Predicate are just moderately related, a second sort of processing is used: A more complete and systematic comparison of the features of the concepts is made.

1. Structural Assumptions

According to Smith et al., concepts are stored in semantic memory as sets of *features*. The concept *Robin,* for example, is represented by the extent to which it is avian, winged, red-breasted, common, and so on. Smith, Shoben, and Rips regard features as the values the concept has on each of several dimensions. Thus, the features of *Robin* would be its values on the dimensions *Avianness, Wingedness, Red-breastedness, Size, Commonness,* and so on. The features, in turn, are ordered, or weighted, by their importance to the definition of the concept. The features we mentioned for *Robin* are all central to its definition, so they have high weights. Such features are called *defining.* But *Robin* includes other, less-defining features as well: *Is undomesticated, Is edible, Eats bread.* Such features have low weights; they are characteristic, but not defining, features of robins. These are called *accidental*. Smith et al. consider that semantic memory contains a feature list for every concept, and that the weight associated with each feature indicates how central it is to a concept's definition. The memory also contains a cutoff level for weights, above which features are called defining and below which they are called accidental. Let us now consider Smith, Shoben, and Rips' computational and decisional assumptions.

2. Processing and Decision Assumptions

Figure 9.4 shows the two decision stages postulated by Smith, Shoben, and Rips for the speeded verification of such Subject-Is-Predicate statements as *A robin is a bird*. In Stage 1, a global comparison is executed to determine the semantic relatedness of Subject and Predicate terms. This is done by retrieving all the features, both defining and characteristic, of the two concepts and comparing the two feature lists in toto. The comparison yields a *similarity index* for the two feature lists. The exact set of features that define a concept, as well as the importance of various features to the definition, may vary between individuals (and even in the same individual from time to time). Consequently, the similarity index will not be identical every time it is computed. In fact, the model assumes that the value of the similarity index for any given pair of concepts will be normally distributed—sometimes higher, sometimes lower, but falling most of the time around some characteristic mean level. The Stage 1 decision processes are based on signal detectability theory for recognition tasks, as is the Atkinson and Juola (1974) model described in Chapter 8.

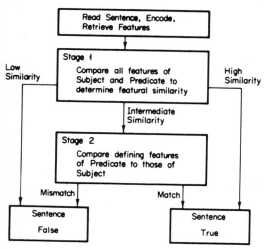

FIG. 9.4. The Feature Comparison Model of Smith, Shoben, and Rips (1974).

Once the similarity index has been computed, it is compared to two decision criteria. One criterion distinguishes high from moderate similarity, and the other distinguishes low from moderate similarity. If the similarity index falls above the high criterion, the subject immediately responds *true*. This will typically happen for such sentences as *A collie is a dog* and *A shark is a fish*. If the similarity index falls below the low criterion, the subject immediately responds *false*. This will probably happen for such sentences as *A banana is a mountain* and *A rabbit is a computer*. When the Subject and Predicate are neither highly related nor highly unrelated, the similarity index will fall between the high and low criteria. When that happens, Stage 2 is executed before the person responds.

Whereas Stage 1 decisions are based on an aggregated value calculated from all of the features of the compared concepts, Stage 2 uses only defining features. If some defining features of the Subject have values that fall outside the range of allowable values for defining features of the predicate (as in *A man is a woman*) the subject can respond *false*. Otherwise, the defining features of Subject and Predicate are compared. A *true* response is made if all defining features of the Predicate are also defining features of the Subject, as in *A chicken is a bird*. Likewise, a *false* response is made if some defining features of the Subject are not defining features of the Predicate, as in *A bat is a bird*. Smith and his colleagues point out that Stage 1 is holistic, intuitive, and error-prone, because it considers similarity of feature lists as a whole without taking into account *which* features are similar. It is possible that a fast *true* response could be made in Stage 1 to *A bat is a bird*, for example. Stage 2 is selective, logical, and relatively error-free. Smith et al. suggest that these two stages correspond to the two ways people understand subset relations, which might be described as "loosely speaking (a bat is a bird)" and "technically speaking (a chicken is a bird)."

Smith, Shoben, and Rips' theory was initially formulated to deal with subset and disjoint relations, and this it does well. It predicts the outcomes of most extant experiments in the field, including many we have not presented. The theory can predict most effects of typicality, semantic relatedness, and category size. It uses a single mechanism, feature weights, to account for verification latencies and behavior in normative tasks involving production or rating.

The theory suggests the basis for common errors in the verification task—namely, the overlap of accidental features. Because the decision making in Stage 1 does not select out the defining features, but makes its judgment on the overall similarity index, there will be an occasional fast but erroneous judgment when accidental features are misleading. The result may be a fast (but incorrect) *true* response to propositions like *A porpoise is a fish*. In the case of erroneous *false* responses, the model accommodates Rosch's (1975) typicality data. Atypical instances of a category (e.g., *penguin* in the case of *bird*) may share defining features, but too few accidental features to push the similarity index above the low criterion. The result may be a fast *false* response to *A penguin is a bird.* The theory also accommodates category size effects, which are subsumed under semantic distance. Smith, Shoben, and Rips (1974) experimentally justified this subsumption in a study showing that category size effects vanish when semantic distance is controlled.

Will the Smith, Shoben, and Rips theory be extensible to encompass other tasks besides sentence-verification of category-membership sentences? Rips (1975) has shown that the theory does a better job of predicting reaction times to quantified sentences than Meyer's, which was designed explicitly for that purpose. Beginnings have been made in extending the theory to the study of analogies and the verification of definitional properties. It remains to be seen whether the sentence verification task is truly prototypical of knowledge retrieval; and the extensibility of the model will depend on the extent to which it is.

The model of Smith, Shoben, and Rips has been criticized on grounds that it is incomplete. It is true that several mechanisms in the theory are either completely unspecified, or remain amenable to several different specifications. For example, the model does not specify the mechanism for partitioning a word's semantic features into *defining* and *accidental*. Some critics argue that philosophers have tried for centuries to separate the defining and characteristic features of concepts to determine their meanings; they suggest that the task must be impossible. This criticism misses the mark, however. Smith et al. are not building a philosophical model whose purpose is to instruct us what the proper meaning of a well-defined concept *should* be; they are constructing a theory to reflect how people actually make judgments of category membership. The model need not suggest *the correct* decision rule; it only need capture the ones people use. A psychologically acceptable decision rule can be probabilistic, as are elements of the theory by Smith et al. There will never be an everlasting philosophic answer to such questions as: When does a bird stop being a bird? When you kill it? When you pluck its feathers? When you cook it? Eat it? Digest and assimilate it? But there can be a satisfactory psychological answer. In terms of this theory, the more highly weighted the features you remove, the less likely people are to consider the remainder a bird; and feature weights, as well as the difference between defining and accidental features, can be estimated from property ratings, similarity ratings, typicality ratings, and production norms.

A second incompleteness in this model concerns the formula for computing the similarity indices used in Stage 1. Smith, Shoben, and Rips suggested some constraints that they feel should guide the choice of a formula, but the constraints are very loose. How this incompleteness is judged will probably depend on one's view of how quantitative the theoretical effort should be. It seems to us that theory should ultimately be completely quantitative; but, for now, even crude qualitative distinctions are informative. Accordingly, we are not bothered by the current lack of precise formuli.

D. Summary

The structural, processing, and decision assumptions of two models were considered. The spreading activation model by Collins and Loftus assumes a network structure in which all concept nodes are connected, either directly or indirectly. The feature of complete connectedness is a major departure from the purely hierarchic character of Quillian's model. Another change from a simple hierarchical structure is the provision of different strengths or lengths of connections between nodes that are directly connected. Directly connected nodes are related in proportion to their semantic distance from one another. Smith et al. used another structural arrangement that also departed from the hierarchic feature of Quillian's model. Concepts in the newer model are collections of features, and concepts are not so much connected as they are similar with respect to the values of their defining and nondefining features. Of the models that we did not describe in detail, all employ some network view of the structure of semantic memory; so there seems a consensus that network models are more appropriate. Whether this consensus will be sustained is not certain, because efforts to model semantic memory are so new. It does seem clear, however, that network models handle some data more readily than feature comparison models. For example, Smith's model has great difficulty accounting for the verification of certain kinds of false sentences, such as *All birds are sparrows* (Holyoak & Glass, 1975).

The models of both Collins and Loftus and of Smith, Shoben, and Rips assume that a concept's representation is accessed whenever a person reads, hears, or sees an instance of the concept. Beyond this commonality, their processing assumptions are very different. Collins and Loftus presume that accessing a concept node sends activations spreading throughout the memory network. Smith et al. presume that each concept has a characteristic but fluctuating pattern of feature values that distinguishes it from other concepts. The decision assumptions of Collins and Loftus concern comparisons between the relational requirements of statements to be verified and relations traced by the spread of activations through the memory network. The decision assumptions of Smith et al. concern the similarity between feature values of concepts in statements to be verified. Neither model is a complete specification of the structures and processes required to verify propositions, despite the fact that both have emphasized verification studies. Both seem committed to the view that the way to general theory is to develop models that account for the exact details of performance in narrowly defined experimental situations.

A reasoned choice between the theories is not possible now. The two theories, however, are imaginative and fit well to substantial sets of data. Both are excellent examples of how the problem of psychological semantics has been approached within the constraints of the information-processing paradigm. The values of the paradigm will guarantee a continuous output of theory and data on psychological semantics. Each new theory will very probably take either the Feature Comparison Model, the Spreading Activation Model, or both as a point of departure. In this regard, Glass and Holyoak (1975) formulated a theory specifically as a rival to Smith, Shoben, and Rips. Glass and Holyoak emphasized *false* verification times, since these are not the strongest suit of the original models.

A second recently formulated theory (Fiksel & Bower, 1976) was intended as a formalized competitor to the developments based on Quillian's original work. The Fiksel and Bower model was, like the Teachable Language Comprehender, developed as a question-answering automaton. The model was specifically formulated for the data we have covered in this chapter; it incorporates mechanisms for these tasks that are designed to predict the outcomes we have described. It goes beyond Quillian's (1969) model in that it specifies conceptual and mathematical properties of *nodes* and *links* in considerable detail. The model also formalizes the details of signal propagation through a network, and includes a path intersection method for answering questions and verifying propositions. It was developed to handle most of the extant data on sentence verification, including quantification and negation. It also allows for the storage of transient, episodic information and the interaction of semantic and episodic information.

Semantic memory theories are in a state of rapid growth and transition. Nevertheless, their details are well worth learning. Many of the characteristics of the current models will be maintained in future theories, and consequently these models provide excellent background for understanding their successors.

V.   WORD PRODUCTION

A. Overview

Most models of semantic memory distinguish the storage of concepts from the storage of the concepts' names. The concept store, which we might call the mind's encyclopedia, is said to be separate from its word store, which we might call its lexicon, so that the two might be structured differently. Indeed, there are reasons to believe that they are, even though the only organizational principles we have so far spoken of concern the encyclopedia. You might also notice that all of the experiments described in this chapter have used written stimulus materials. Obviously, there are other ways to activate concepts. The concept of *Robin* can be accessed by reading its name, as in the experiments described, or by hearing its name, or by reading or hearing a description—such as "a bird about the size of a bluejay with a chestnut-red breast and belly"—or by seeing a robin or a picture of one. These different ways of activating a concept involve three distinct access channels: a visual analogue channel, a lexical channel, and a semantic–descriptive one. People can translate from one channel to another: Given a picture, they can provide a name; given a name, they can provide a description. It follows that various channels lead to the same concept node, which implies several things. First, there must be connections between the concept and the channels that access it. Second, in processing stages leading to a concept node, there must be separate cognitive systems for visual analogue representations, for descriptions, and for names, including both their pronunciation and their spelling. Furthermore, each of these systems must have its own code and organization, because people do not confuse sources and types of stimulation. You do not wonder while thinking about robins whether you saw one or heard it mentioned. Considerations like these, along with data from aphasiology, imagery, and scanning studies, have convinced a number of investigators (Atkinson, Herrmann, & Wescourt, 1974; Collins & Loftus, 1975; Lachman, Shaffer, & Hennrikus, 1974; Paivio, 1971) that semantic memory has either two or three separate underlying systems: conceptual, lexical, or visual analogue.

In all of the experiments so far described in this chapter, the first network accessed is the lexical one: Words are the input in these experiments. Sentence verification is thus an analogue of comprehension. Another class of laboratory procedures, called production tasks, are more analogous to speaking than to comprehending. Instead of starting with the lexical network, these tasks end with it. For example, subjects are shown a picture or given a description of a concept, and their job is to produce its name. Thus, Brown and McNeill (1966) gave people definitions and asked them to produce the words they defined. Lachman (1973) and colleagues (Butterfield & Butterfield, 1977; Lachman, Shaffer, & Hennrikus, 1974) gave people pictures and asked for names.

Not many years ago, production and comprehension seemed closely related. For example, Neisser's (1967) influential theory of analysis by synthesis held that people understand an utterance by going through the steps they would use to produce it. Hardly anyone subscribes to that view anymore. Surely there must be some connection between processes we use to comprehend and the ones we use to produce speech, but now the view that if we explain one we will have explained the other is generally rejected. We now assume that there is internal processing common to both but, more important, that there are independent comprehension and production processes. To comprehend, we must use a word to find a concept, while to produce a word, we use a concept or analogue representation.

The point is that our understanding of the structure of semantic memory will remain seriously incomplete until we explore the organization of the lexical and visual analogue systems, and until we compare their structure to the structure of the conceptual system. To be sure, there have been studies of the lexical system, using production rather than comprehension tasks, but the astonishing thing is how different those studies are from studies of the conceptual system.

You might imagine that the first question would be whether the organizational principles of the two systems are the same. That is, a reasonable starting point would be to ask whether the variables that seem to index conceptual structure also index the structure of lexical memory or visual analogue memory. If the same variables influenced both production and verification, then rational arguments to justify the distinction between the conceptual and lexical systems would seem invalid. With the exception of Loftus's (1977) work, verification and production studies tend to examine different variables.

Production researchers have studied word frequency, codability, and age of acquisition, while verification researchers have studied semantic similarity, sentence quantifiers (e.g., *All, Some, Many*, and the like), and subject–predicate relations. Verification studies have either ignored or controlled, but not varied, word frequency, codability, or acquisition age (e.g., Wilkins, 1971). When word frequency has influenced verification speed, it has been explained away as a consequence of semantic similarity (e.g., Smith et al., 1974). The use of production norms in verification studies biases them toward high-frequency words, for people tend to give high-frequency responses in the procedures used to collect norms. The stimuli in production tasks, by contrast, involve systematic variation of frequency, codability, and acquisition age. As yet, no one has studied the verification of sentences with low-frequency words, such as *All perambulators are conveyances.* It is not clear what the effect of low-frequency words like these might be on sentence verification, nor how reductions in frequency might change the effect of semantic distance. There are obviously experiments to be done. For now, let us examine some word production studies.

B. Word Frequency

As far back as 1963, Professor R. C. Oldfield of Oxford University estimated that an average educated person uses 75,000 words (Oldfield, 1963, 1966). Yet, people talk at the rate of about two words per second. Oldfield argued that people could not talk so fast unless their lexical memory stores were efficiently organized and indexed for ready retrieval. His reasoning required several suppositions. Suppose that words were stored randomly and that the search for them to produce speech was not guided. Assume, moreover, that it took only 500 msec to consider each of the 75,000 words when one was needed for ongoing speech. Then, it would require over a year to deliver a lecture that professors give in 50 minutes. The representation of words in memory must be organized in some efficient way, but how?

Some words are used much more frequently than others. Therefore, one way to reduce the time to retrieve words would be to group them in memory according to how frequently they are used, and to search the most frequently used ones first. This would reduce the *average* retrieval time, while making rare words take longer to retrieve than frequent ones. Oldfield and Wingfield (1964, 1965) sought to test whether the lexical store is organized by word frequency. Because people can read words that they do not know, it was necessary to use a procedure that required words to be found, but did not use words as stimuli. Naming pictures satisfies this requirement. Oldfield and Wingfield used line drawings of objects whose names varied over the entire frequency range of English words (Thorndike & Lorge, 1944). The time it took people to name the pictured objects fell sharply as the frequency of the objects' names increased (see Fig. 9.5). Naming latency is a linear function of the name's logarithmic frequency. The range of frequency in Fig. 9.5 is 100 occurrences per million words (-log 4) for words like BOOK and CHAIR to about one occurrence per million words (-log 6) for words like BAGPIPE and STETHOSCOPE. The range of latencies in the data is from 600 to 1300 msec. The largest differences—on the order of 700 msec—are much larger than differences obtained in speeded verification studies.

To account for the data in Fig. 9.5, Oldfield proposed that lexical memory is divided into eight or 10 "storage bins," or subsets of words of similar frequency. According to Oldfield's proposal, a person who is shown an object first estimates its frequency, and then does a binary search through the names in the corresponding bin. The search ends when the correct name is found or all names in the bin have been searched and rejected. This proposal proved too simple, as we see below, but Oldfield and Wingfield's data have proven

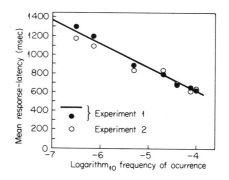

FIG. 9.5. Naming reaction time as a function of name frequency. (Adapted from Oldfield and Wingfield, 1965.) Experiment 1 had 80 pictures and 5 subjects, Experiment 2 had 26 pictures and 12 subjects.

highly reliable: Objects with frequently used names are named quickly (Carroll & White, 1973; Lachman, 1973).

C. Codability

Oldfield and Wingfield (1965) studied the naming of pictures with "a single commonly-acknowledged name [p. 277]," but they did not say how they established that a picture had only one name. This prompted one of us (R.L.) to hypothesize that frequently encountered objects, such as *book, chair, shoe,* and *key,* are more likely to be given a single, commonly acknowledged name than are low-frequency objects, such as *stethoscope, gyroscope, bagpipe,* and *syringe.* To check this possibility, Lachman showed college students pictures and asked them to write the first name they thought of for each. Sure enough, as the frequency of the dictionary name went down, the number of names the students supplied went up. For example, everyone responded *book* to a picture of a book; but to a gyroscope, they supplied *spinner, top, machine, whirler, circumrotator, rotator,* and *gyroscope.* This led Lachman (1973) to findings that undermined Oldfield's explanation of his word frequency observations. Lachman found that when high-frequency names were given to low-frequency objects, the naming latencies were indistinguishable from low-frequency names to the same objects. Thus, reaction times to the picture of a gyroscope were the same whether the subject called it *gyroscope,* which is low-frequency, or *machine,* which is high-frequency. Something about the pictures or the concept represented by a picture, rather than the frequency of the names given to them, was determining reaction time. Lachman considered that something to be the concept's codability (Lachman, 1973; Lachman et al., 1974).

Codability concerns the extent of agreement among people about the correct name for a thing. Brown and Lenneberg (1954) introduced the notion to account for the naming of colors. They began by asking people to name colored patches, and they found considerable differences in the number of words in the labels supplied, the amount of agreement between respondents, and the likelihood that a person would give the same name when asked on two separate occasions. When colors were given short names (e.g., *red, sky blue*), different people gave them the same names, and people gave the same name each time they saw the colors. They were termed *highly coded.* When color patches were given longer names (e.g., *dark mustard-colored yellow, green like dry summer grass*), the names supplied were often different from one respondent to the next, and even from the same respondent from test to test. These were called poorly coded. Brown and Lenneberg found that highly coded colors were named faster and remembered better than poorly coded ones. Highly coded colors were also communicated more accurately; listeners more often selected the correct patch out of a number of patches when the description they heard was of a highly coded color (Lantz & Stefflre, 1964).

Now consider the communicative significance of codability. People's descriptive powers far exceed their vocabulary of single-word names. Some events can be described by single words, but many cannot. What determines whether a piece of the environment has a short, efficient, frequent, shared, single-word descriptor or a longer, more idiosyncratic description? No one knows for sure, but it seems likely that those things that people have to talk about often will have efficient codes—one-word names. Parts of reality about which there is infrequent communication are less likely to have simple, agreed-upon names. Moreover, each person who refers to such infrequent subjects may select different descriptors. For example, pueblos are not often discussed nor are they terribly central to the lives of most college students, and different students will give different names to a picture of one, including *Indian village, adobe, huts, buildings, houses,* and *Hopi village.* On the other hand, all college students see, use, and discuss books, pens, and chairs, and all call pictures of those objects by the same name.

Lachman's examination of the frequency effect reported by Oldfield and Wingfield showed that the speed with which people retrieve the names of pictures probably cannot be accounted for solely in terms of the names themselves. Properties of the concept displayed in the pictures must be taken into account as well. Lachman chose to study the effects of pictures' codability upon the speed with which they are named. He reasoned that codability is an important determinant of how words are mapped onto reality, and that by understanding the effects of codability he might be in a better position to determine the structure of the lexical network. Notice his dilemma; it is the same as all cognitive psychologists'. No aspect of the problem that interested him is well understood. We know little of how either reality or the lexicon is structured, but both must be taken into account if we are to understand either. Codability seems to lie at the intersection between the structure of reality and the structure of the lexicon, so that is what Lachman studied.

Lachman began by determining how many names students gave to each of many pictures. To quantify the pictures' codability, he used the measure of uncertainty as a descriptive statistic, computing the uncertainty of the distribution of names supplied for each picture. Zero or low uncertainty in *bits* reflected good codability, and was obtained for pictures such as *apple, glove,* and *table,* to which everyone supplied the same name. High uncertainties were obtained for poorly coded pictures, such as *pueblo, gondola,* and *ram,* because many different names were given to these pictures. Between the extremes of codability, there was a substantial range; so

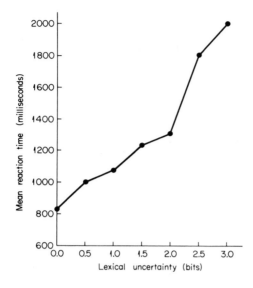

FIG. 9.6. Latencies for naming 105 pictures varying in uncertainty (codability). The pictures were named a second time (Trial 2) after approximately 45 minutes. (After Lachman, Shaffer, & Hennrikus, 1974.)

Lachman was able to select many pictures from each of seven uncertainty levels. He ordered these randomly and asked people to name each as quickly as possible.

The results are plotted in Fig. 9.6, which shows a steady increase in reaction time with uncertainty. This fact can be attributed to two factors. First, the lexical network (but not the semantic network) is structured partly on the basis of codability. The surface features of words (their sound and spelling) are stored according to the codability of their referents, so that the names of well-coded things are accessed most quickly. Second, when uncertainty is very high (i.e., when one must name a poorly coded event), there is an abrupt increase in reaction time, suggesting that complex decisions may be required to select a name, which adds to an already long access time.

A complication with Lachman's data is that codability is related to two other variables, frequency (which we have already discussed in connection with Oldfield and Wingfield) and age of acquisition (which we discuss in the next section). As uncertainty increases, frequency goes down and the age at which most people learn the name goes up. Consequently, one cannot attribute the latency increase in Fig. 9.6 uniquely to codability (uncertainty). It may instead be due to frequency or acquisition age. To rule this possibility out, Lachman selected highly uncertain pictures. Their frequency was determined, and a matched-frequency low-uncertainty item was chosen as a control for each high-uncertainty picture. The final set of stimuli included high- and low-uncertainty pictures, which were equal in mean frequency. When people named these as quickly as possible, the effects of uncertainty remained. Highly coded pictures were named from 300 to 700 msec faster than poorly coded pictures. By matching high- and low-uncertainty pictures for age of acquisition, Lachman also showed that codability has effects over and above those of acquisition age.

D. Age of Acquisition

As Lachman studied codability, Carroll worked to extend the findings of Oldfield and Wingfield on word frequency. Carroll and White assembled 103 pictures, including those used by Oldfield and Wingfield, and their data precisely replicated the earlier work. However, Carroll spotted a striking anomaly in the data. Certain words such as *clown* and *zebra* were named much too fast for their objective frequency in the English language. He recognized that most of these words are learned at an early age.

As a result of this observation, Carroll undertook further studies to determine whether word frequency or age of acquisition was the more important determinant of naming latency. He used a statistical procedure called regression analysis. This technique allows inferences about the relative influence of each of several independent variables, such as frequency and age of acquisition, upon a single dependent variable, such as naming latency. Carroll and White (1973) concluded that word frequency has no influence on naming latency separate from the effects of acquisition age. Put the other way around, of the two independent variables, age of acquisition alone influences naming latency. But Lachman had shown that codability influences naming latency over and above the effects of both word frequency and acquisition age. So Lachman (1973) and Lachman et al. (1974) used regression analysis to further examine the influence of word frequency, codability, and acquisition age on naming latency. It is not a simple puzzle they tried to solve.

E. Word Frequency, Codability, or Age of Acquisition?

A child is likely to hear frequent words before infrequent ones, because they occur more often. Also, frequent words are more likely to refer to highly coded events, because they are important to everyday living. In fact, there is a strong inverse correlation between frequency and acquisition age—the higher its frequency, the earlier a word is learned. And we have already mentioned the correlation between codability and frequency.

If these three variables—codability, age of acquisition, and frequency— were perfectly correlated, there would be no point trying to isolate the unique influence of any of them. They would simply be different measures of the same thing and it would not matter what the thing was called nor which measure of it was used. But the variables are not perfectly related, only strongly related. Under those circumstances it is important, though difficult, to determine whether all or only some of the variables determine some other performance, such as picture naming latency. At issue is the nature of the organizational scheme of lexical memory. Is it organized around frequency or codability or what?

We argued earlier that it would soon be necessary to make direct comparisons of the possible organizing principles of conceptual information in semantic memory. Such tests have not yet been made, and the problems that will arise when at first they are is shown by the findings of Lachman et al. with respect to lexical memory. Whereas Carroll and White found that word frequency had no explanatory value when compared to age of acquisition, Lachman et al. found that both of these variables, and codability too, contributed independently of each other to the prediction of naming latency. Where does the truth lie? Is frequency important or not? Carroll and White say no. Lachman et al. say yes. Is age of acquisition *all* important? Carroll and White say yes. Lachman et al. say no.

For nearly all questions of this sort, truth may lie in better methods. Consider the problems of measuring age of acquisition. One can ask college students to estimate when they learned a word, but how accurate can such estimates be? One can go to records of when children typically use particular words; but children learn some words before they speak, and very few children have been observed systematically enough to provide adequate estimates of when they speak any particular word. Moreover, the children who have been observed are not necessarily typical. Many have been the offspring of linguists or their students, who have a way of being unusually verbal people. Even if there were good records of when the typical child speaks particular words, what is to guarantee that the adults who participate in naming latency studies were typical children? Under conditions like these, it is far easier to call for better methods than to use them. But that is where we stand: calling and hoping for better ways to study semantic memory.

Until more satisfactory methods are devised, we must rely on the most comprehensive available evidence, which was collected by Lachman et al. (1974). To assess the structure of lexical information in semantic memory, these authors related three variables to naming latency. The variables were the codability of the pictures and the frequency and acquisition age of the names applied to them. As in studies of the structure of conceptual memory, the assumption of this investigation was that a variable will predict reaction time only if it reflects an organizational principle of semantic memory—in this case the organization of the lexical store. Unlike studies of the conceptual store, which have examined one variable at a time, the work of Lachman et al. measured several variables around which memory might be organized. The authors then compared the predictive validity of those measures. Word frequency, age of acquisition, and codability all contributed uniquely to the prediction of naming latency, and the magnitudes of their predictive validities were not very different.

There are two ways to view this outcome. One conclusion is that the lexical store is structured around several principles, which can be used separately or in combination to retrieve a word. This conclusion is congenial to the view that the cognitive system incorporates alternative and redundant mechanisms to do its work, so that when one mechanism fails, another may do as well. This view has intuitive appeal, because such an organizational scheme would fail to retrieve a sought-for word less often than a unitary organization. It is easier to find one of many paths out of the woods than to find the only one. However, such an organization would create complications for the cognitive researcher, because multivariate and redundant organizational schemes are far more difficult to characterize fully. The rules for when one has completed his job are unclear. How does one know when he has found all of the paths, or which one of an unknown number was used on any particular trip? A second conclusion that could be drawn is that a single factor, not yet discovered, accounts for naming latency. It is the nature of unfinished science that investigators have no rational ways to select among such alternative conclusions.

VI.   COMPARISON OF WORD PRODUCTION AND SENTENCE VERIFICATION STUDIES

Word production studies appear to tell most about the lexical system, while sentence verification studies seem to tell most about the semantic or conceptual system. This assumption is reflected in separate treatment of the two kinds of research. There is still no direct evidence against which to evaluate the assumption that separate systems are implicated in the different tasks used. Among the sources of indirect evidence are studies of aphasic people (Gardner, 1974). Many aphasics behave appropriately to objects they cannot name, suggesting that their impairment is specific to lexical abilities. Because aphasia frequently results from strokes, it can be inferred that conceptual information resides in a different organization of the brain than lexical information, which argues for theoretical distinctness of the functions as well as for their physiological separation. The "tip-of-the-tongue" phenomenon also justifies the separation of the lexical and conceptual store. That is, people can often say what they know about a concept or object, including the fact that they know its name, but may still be unable to say the name.

To justify the assumption of separate lexical and semantic stores directly, someone will have to study the effects of the same variables on both sentence verification and word production. As yet, no one has studied the verification of sentences composed of low-frequency words; so we do not know what their effects on sentence verification time might be, nor how reductions in frequency might change the semantic distance effect. The same is true of codability. Poorly coded objects often represent fuzzy, ill-defined concepts and categories, making it difficult to guess how people's categorization strategies would be affected in judging such sentences as *All pagodas are churches*. The production studies, being concerned with access of individual words, have not studied semantic distance.

Another difference between the study of word production and the study of sentence verification is that model building has proceeded further for the study of sentence verification. Still, semantic memory models are incomplete, particularly with respect to specifying the relationships between concepts. For network models, the problem is to specify a small number of concept links between nodes that will simulate the large number of conceptual relationships people actually use.

Semantic memory supplies the content of thought, and consequently underlies what people talk about. How do they manage to express their ideas in linguistic form? This topic is the province of the area of study called psycholinguistics, to which we turn in the next chapter. As you will see, semantic memory studies have influenced psycholinguists far less than the theories of syntax developed by linguists.

10 Psycholinguistics

ABSTRACT

I. *Introduction*
Neobehaviorists and linguists differed in their views of language development. Neobehaviorists took words as the prime units of language, focused upon its repetitive aspects, and concluded that language is learned according to stimulus–response principles. Linguists took sentences as the unit, focused on their novelty, and concluded that language is innate. Today, most cognitive psychologists believe at least that language is specific to the species *Homo sapiens*. Primate research may yet modify this conviction.
  A. *The Species-Specific Nature of Language* The reasons for believing in the species-specificity of language are its:
  1. *Universality Among Humans*
  2. *Relationship to Physiological Factors*
  3. *Relationship to Other Measures of Intelligence*
  4. *Developmental Regularities*
  B. *Animal Communication* Language is distinguished from communication, and the evidence concerning communication among bees, dolphins, and apes is considered. The evidence does not damage the claim that language is specific to people, but it fits neatly into an evolutionary view of language and cognition.

II. *Neobehavioristic and Information-Theory Approaches to Language*
Contemporary accounts of language are built on reactions to both the behaviorist and information theory approaches.
  A. *Neobehaviorist Accounts*
  1. *Classical Conditioning* Osgood (1953) offered an explanation of word meaning in terms of classical conditioning.

    2. *Instrumental (Operant) Conditioning* Skinner (1957) and Staats and Staats (1963) gave book-length accounts of how operant learning principles might account for word and sentence meanings.

    3. *Mediation* Conditioning theory was applied to various aspects of language by extending the concepts of stimulus and response to covert events that might mediate complex relations between observable stimuli and responses.

B. *Linguists' Reactions to Neobehaviorist Accounts of Language* Linguists invented many sentences that embarrassed neobehaviorist theory, and psycholinguists brought some data to the argument against neobehaviorism (Brown, Cazden, & Bellugi, 1969). The data were probably less important in the demise of neobehaviorism's approach to language than were judgments based on pretheoretical beliefs.

C. *Information-Theory Approaches to Language* Following World War II, information theory was used as a guide to psychological research on language. The amount of information in linguistic strings was shown to influence memory and perception. However, the information metric could not be applied precisely to sentences or longer strings, and a more attractive alternative to neobehaviorist accounts came from new developments in linguistics.

III. *The Influence of the Linguist Noam Chomsky*

While he was a student of linguistics, Chomsky studied both behaviorism and information theory. He rejected both as approaches to language. Neither dealt satisfactorily with the fact that sentences are hierarchically organized, since both depended on left-to-right chaining. His arguments for an alternative view produced a new paradigm for linguists and gave them new theories.

A. *Chomsky's Paradigm* Chomsky distinguished language performance from language competence. Performance is what people *do* with their language; competence is what they *know* about their language. Chomsky argued that linguistic theory should explain competence, not performance. He took sentences as the units of linguistic theory, and he took the construction of sentences from smaller elements as the fact to be explained by theory. He offered generative grammar as the appropriate sort of theory, and advanced the criteria of elegance and agreement with speakers' intuitions for evaluating theory. He gave syntax the primary emphasis in theory, arguing that it could be understood without reference to the meaning conveyed in the sentences under study.

B. *Some Adjunct Importations From Linguistics* In order to test Chomsky's ideas, psychologists had to learn not only his concepts but also the notational conventions and style of argumentation used by linguists. Pertinent ones of these for psychologists are described.

    1. *Notational Conventions*

    2. *Major Concepts*

C. *Chomsky's Theoretical Positions*

    1. *Phrase Structure Grammar* Chomsky's transformational grammars were built on a simpler model, called *phrase structure grammar,* which is described here.

    2. *Transformational Grammar* Chomsky built two transformational grammars, both of which were intended to do more justice than phrase structure grammar to intuitions of native speakers about their language. The first transformational grammar included the notions of kernel

sentence and transformation rule, both of which prompted considerable psychological experimentation. The second transformational grammar substituted the notions of deep structure and surface structure for the notion of kernel sentence.

IV. *The Psychology of Syntax*
   A. *The Psychological Reality of Grammar* Psychologists designed experiments to show that syntax and grammaticality influence memory and perception.
   B. *The Psychological Reality of Phrase Structures* Psychologists did research to see whether phrase structure units are used to organize sentences for perception and memory.
   C. *The Psychological Reality of Grammatical Transformations* We describe studies designed to show that the operation of transformation rules in Chomsky's theory corresponds to psychological processes. The experiments were intended to show that a sentence is stored in memory as a kernel plus transformational information, that these are forgotten independently, and that transformations take cognitive time and use up memory.
   D. *The Psychological Reality of Deep Structures* It was proposed that deep structures are the storage mode of sentences, while surface structures are maintained only long enough to allow deep structure extraction. A number of memory studies show that deep structure information lasts longer than surface structure information. Experimenters also used deep structure diagrams to predict which words from a sentence would best prompt its recall; their results were mixed.

V. *Semantics and Pragmatics*
   While studying syntax, psychologists discovered that many experimental results can only be explained by reference to extralinguistic factors such as context, subjects' expectations, and their knowledge. The effects of syntax are overridden by context and subject focus. Imagery was proposed as an alternative to deep structures as a storage mode for sentences, and experiments have not ruled it out.

VI. *Case Grammar*
   Fillmore, a linguist, proposed a transformational-generative grammar called *case grammar* as an alternative to the standard theory. Case grammar uses a semantic form of deep structure representation. It is attractive to psychologists, who have incorporated it in several models of comprehensive and semantic memory. Despite its intuitive appeal, it has resisted empirical test.

VII. *Summary*
   We emphasize conclusions that seem well-established after 20 years of psycholinguistic research.

I. INTRODUCTION

Newborn humans gurgle and cry, but they do not talk. By 6 months they babble vigorously, and by 1 year most utter a few words. The average 2-year-old works words or word-like vocalizations into short utterances; 3-year-olds speak in childish ways, which they ultimately refine into adult forms of speech. These are the facts of the matter. How should we explain them? Linguists and behaviorists took different tacks.

Linguists' bread and butter was writing rules to characterize languages, and they found it exceedingly difficult. Yet, 6-year-olds behave as if they largely know the rules of their language. How do they do it? It seemed obvious to linguists that conditioning was not the answer, because it relies on repetition. Linguists focused on sentences: Because nearly every sentence is novel, and 6-year-olds produce and understand a theoretical infinity of them, any theory relying on repetition is inadequate. It seemed impossible to linguists that practice would allow children to do this by so young an age; the child must have help from nature. Language must be innate.

In contrast, neobehaviorist learning theorists were struck by how gradually language is learned. Six years did not seem so short to them, nor were they impressed by the novelty of language. They found no special magic in sentences; words were their conventionally accepted units of analysis, and young children do use their words repetitively. Neobehaviorists saw no reason to discard stimulus–response theory. They considered that it explained other kinds of learning; it could explain language learning as well.

Neither learning theorists nor linguists compromised. Their differing paradigmatic commitments were at stake. Behaviorists and neobehaviorists assumed that all learning was due to experience, and they devoted themselves to studying the effects of experience in the laboratory with animals. If adult language use could not be understood as the outgrowth of early experience, these theorists' whole enterprise would be seriously qualified. Linguists studied the grammars of the world's languages, and they were committed to the belief that every particular grammar is a variant of a single universal grammar. By their view, only humans have an innate predisposition to acquire this universal grammar, without which they could not master the language they are exposed to. By this view, no amount of studying animal learning could explain language development, and if it could, the linguists' whole enterprise would be seriously threatened. It is not surprising that the debate between the linguists and the learning theorists was sometimes shrill [see, for example, the exchange between Braine (1963a, 1965) and Bever, Fodor, & Weksel (1965a, 1965b)].

Time is the arbiter of paradigmatic disputes, and concerning the innateness of language, the linguists prevailed. The consensus of information-processing psycholinguists (the majority in psychology today) is that language is in some measure an innate capacity or predisposition of the human infant. Beyond this consensus, there is disagreement about how much language the infant has at birth. McNeill (1970) made one of the most sweeping claims for innateness. He argued that the infant is born with a language acquisition device (LAD), which contains knowledge of the universal forms of grammar, such as that all human languages use sentences that are constructed by transforming an underlying linguistic rule system. According to McNeill, each child acquires his language by formulating and successively testing hypotheses about how his innate language knowledge is actualized in the speech of his community. A less sweeping claim about linguistic innateness is that a disposition to acquire language is part of the newborn infant's behavioral repertoire. This claim amounts to saying that language is specific to the species *Homo sapiens*. Most linguists and psycholinguists accept this claim at least. Here are some of the reasons they are convinced that language is species-specific.

A. The Species-Specific Nature of Language

1. Universality Among Humans

Every human society, however primitive in other terms, has a language. All normal infants acquire language spontaneously, with no special tutelage. Even most deaf and mentally retarded children learn some language. In contrast, no nonhuman species, however intelligent, has linguistic ability, despite claims to the contrary for bees, dolphins, and some apes. These claims are discussed later, to show why we say that no convincing demonstration of language has been made for any nonhuman species.

2. Relationship to Physiological Factors

Language apparently depends on the left hemisphere of the brain. Because of this hemispheric lateralization, damage to the left hemisphere, or its removal, is far more likely to impair an adult's language than similar trauma to the right hemisphere. Furthermore, certain regions of the left hemisphere are more involved in language function than others. This suggests biological prerequisites for language. There also appears to be an age past which a human being who has not been exposed to language will not learn it (Lenneberg, 1967). This critical age seems to end between 10 and 14, which is when developmental changes in hemispheric lateralization of brain function also seem to cease.

3. Relationship to Other Measures of Intelligence

Lenneberg (1967) has argued that linguistic ability correlates better in humans with milestones of motor development than with chronological age, or such measures of intelligence as IQ and mental age. According to Lenneberg, children usually take their first steps and speak their first recognizable words within a few weeks of each other, regardless of how old or intelligent they are when they do these things. Moreover, the milestones of motor development (e.g., grasping, thumb opposition, standing, crawling, and walking) emerge in an invariant order, suggesting an innate maturational timetable for physical skills. The fact that language relates more closely to motor development than to intellectual development suggests a parallel unfolding of a physiologically based maturational language sequence.

Between species, as well, presence or absence of language is relatively unrelated to differences in intelligence, as best we can measure it so as to compare different species. One rough-and-ready measure of intelligence in different species is brain size. Lenneberg pointed out that some humans with language have smaller brains than nonhumans without language. In particular, nanocephalic dwarfs are normally proportioned people who grow only 2½ to 4 feet tall. These individuals have smaller than average heads, and their brains are small, too—smaller than the average chimpanzee's. Their brain cells are of normal size, and though they have fewer than the average-sized person, they are usually adequately fluent. They learn language spontaneously, as do other human beings. The average chimpanzee, with a larger brain, does not. A more refined measure of interspecies intellect is the ratio of brain weight to body weight, but it is also not a reliable predictor of language possession. The average adult female chimp has about the same brain-weight-to-body-weight ratio as a 13-year-old human boy. These facts also suggest that language has its own biological principles.

4. Developmental Regularities

There is also a striking regularity and universality to language development. Whatever language they are acquiring, all children seem to go through the same stages. Babbling is followed by a stage of single-word utterances, followed by a period of two-word utterances. Children produce even longer sequences of words before they master all of their language's sounds and its rules for combining them (i.e., their language's phonology). This sequence seems universal among children, but it is not the order in which adults typically learn a foreign language. Adults usually try to master phonology and to speak in complete grammatical sentences from the beginning. They restrict what they talk about to the things they can speak of correctly, while children speak in abbreviated sentences and imperfect phonology about anything they can.

Language acquisition thus seems to have its own rules, which, along with its universality among humans, its absence among nonhumans, its physiological correlates, and its relative independence of intellectual development, suggests species specificity or innateness. Indeed, information-processing psychologists are generally convinced that the capacity for language is part of the genetic heritage of *Homo sapiens* and is distinct from intelligence or the ability to learn. But, you may ask, what of bees, birds, dolphins, and talking apes, about whom much has lately been written? Do they not communicate? Do they not have language?

B. Animal Communication

Communication should be distinguished from language. Communication covers more. A plant may communicate need for sun or water, but we would not attribute language to the plant in order to account for its turning brown and drooping its leaves. Dogs communicate with their owners, and some owners may be convinced that their dogs use language. Nevertheless, the communicative behaviors of dogs and humans are so different that it masks important distinctions to call both language. All animals probably communicate with other members of their species. Birds have special calls for danger, mating, and so on, and they are responded to appropriately by other birds. Bees (von Frisch, 1962, 1967) perform an apparently communicative dance to describe the discovery of a nectar source for other bees in their hive. The form of the dance conveys information about the distance, direction, and quality of the discovered nectar. Apes in the wild make a variety of gestures and sounds that seem to be interpreted correctly by other apes. But none of these creatures seems to use its signals as productively as people use speech. Compared to the communication behaviors of other species, people are enormously flexible, because the elements of human language can be combined and recombined productively, in novel and unique ways. Apes and birds label and signal a fixed few states of affairs. An ape who might wish to distinguish for his companions danger from one lion and danger from several could not do so. A bee who wished to bring home information about nectar, besides its direction, distance, and quality, could not invent a dance to do so, nor could the other bees interpret such a dance. No such restrictions constrain people, who will talk about anything they conceive.

What about the dolphins? Has it not been shown that they have as complex a communication system as human beings? No. Only a little research has been done with dolphins, and this has not established the flexibility or versatility of dophins' communication. It has been established that dolphins cannot imitate human speech. They whistle and make clicks, but nothing more. The clicks are used like sonar, to locate objects and other creatures by reflected echoes. The functions of the whistles are unknown, and may never be; because even the U. S. Navy, which has been the chief patron of dolphin research, finds its cost too high. Those who are inclined may thus continue to believe that dolphins have language, but the evidence necessary for a balanced decision has not been produced. There is much more evidence about teaching language to apes, and it has been given much play by the press and television. You may wonder about the results of efforts to teach language to chimps, and quite recently to a gorilla.

In the 1930s, a couple named Kellogg (Kellogg & Kellogg, 1933) began the effort by raising Gua, a female chimpanzee, along with their son. Their son learned to speak normally, but Gua never produced a recognizable word. Although she communicated with gestures, she understood only a few words, and they had to be spoken by one of the Kelloggs. In 1951, a very similar enterprise was begun by a couple named Hayes (Hayes, 1951). Their chimp, Viki, was given more careful linguistic instruction. Eventually she learned to produce three words (mama, papa, cup) in a guttural croak. Though these words were used appropriately, only the Hayeses readily understood them. Viki understood far more than three words, and a few word combinations, but only after extensive drills of a sort that normal humans never receive.

Language and speech are separable: Many humans who cannot speak nevertheless use language. Perhaps the failure of Gua and Viki to acquire language was only a failure to speak, which was precluded simply by the shape of the ape's vocal apparatus (Lieberman, 1975; Lieberman, Crelin, & Klatt, 1972). Perhaps if speech were not required, chimps would do better.

To answer this question, the Gardners raised their chimp, Washoe, to use a visual language. Gardner and Gardner (1969,1975) tried to teach Washoe to use American Sign Language, a system of hand movements used by many deaf people. They gave Washoe her own living quarters, and she spent nearly all of her time with a human who communicated in American Sign Language. Washoe learned many words, and in addition she produced novel combinations of them to express complicated ideas. For example, she has combined the signs for "go" with the signs for "in" and "out"; while near a locked door, she produced "open key" and, at the barking of an unseen dog, "listen dog." To anyone who has seen Washoe, it is clear that the Gardners have elicited remarkable behaviors from her. But are they language?

The Gardners believe that Washoe's language is comparable to that of a young child. But others are not so sure; they doubt whether Washoe's behavior proves much about language. After 8 years of training, her communication skills were inferior to those of an average 3-year-old. The Gardners acknowledge Washoe's deficiencies, but they believe they are not due to her being a chimp. They think different training will allow other chimps to do better. Washoe's trainers were not native speakers of American Sign Language, and they may not have been good models. Washoe was a year old when her training began, and she may have done better if she had started earlier. To remedy such difficulties, the Gardners have recently begun training several baby chimps from the first days of their lives. Their trainers are deaf people whose native language is American Sign. The Gardners hope to accomplish more with these babies than they did with Washoe. They also hope that their male and female babies will mate, have babies of their own, and perhaps teach the signing system to their infants. They hoped this would happen with Washoe, but she seemed to believe herself superior to the uneducated males to whom she was introduced, and she refused to associate with them.

The Gardners strive to give their chimps a natural learning experience that resembles as much as possible the situation in which human children acquire language. Premack uses an altogether different approach to studying the language capabilities of chimpanzees. Premack (1971) restricted the chimp Sarah to a laboratory cage. He gave her a carefully programmed sequence of tasks to learn, using behavioristic principles to shape her behavior. Premack's tasks were not designed to give language to Sarah, but rather to determine whether she possessed the prerequisites that underlie language. Premack sought evidence that Sarah could name objects, use syntax, and grasp such relations as *if . . . then, same–different,* and so on. For "words," Sarah uses metal-backed plastic chips shaped so that they do not look like the objects they represent. Sarah's job is to arrange the chips on a magnetic board in order to earn food and other rewards. For example, to study Sarah's labeling, Premack might lay five word chips in front of her, and then show her an object named by one of the chips. In this situation, Sarah's task is rather like that of a student in a multiple-choice test: She must select the correct chip and place it on the board.

Seemingly more complex capacities can be studied with similar techniques. For example, Premack studied whether Sarah used the concept *is the name of* by placing an object (e.g., apple) and the word chip that names the object near one another on a table. He gave Sarah several chips, including one meaning *is the name of,* and he rewarded Sarah for placing this chip between the chip for *apple* and the real apple. Similarly, he has used a chip meaning *is not the name of,* whose use he rewarded Sarah for when the chip for *apple* was placed on the table with a real banana. Sarah was given this task many times with different chip–object pairs. She came to the point of being correct on the first test of new pairs about 80% of the time. This degree of accuracy indicates fair understanding of the linguistic concept, *is the name of.* Premack has used similar techniques to show that Sarah can use many concepts of the sort that human language use relies on. Sarah's performance, like Washoe's, is fascinating, and it demonstrates a remarkable complexity and variety of abilities that seem linguistically relevant.

Another impressive performance has been turned in by a different ape species. Patterson (1978) has achieved remarkable results with Koko, a female gorilla. Patterson's approach was informal, but intensive American Sign Language training—more like the Gardners' work with Washoe than Premack's work with Sarah. Patterson reports that Koko, by about age 4 years, exhibits a wide variety of language-like behaviors that can be compared to those of human deaf children learning sign language. She signs to herself while looking at magazines, displays the same types of semantic categories as human children at a roughly comparable stage of language acquisition, and commonly produces (spontaneously) over 150 signs per day. Her first unequivocal combination of signs occurred at 15 months, when she signed "more" followed by "food." Patterson reports this rather remarkable exchange between Koko and an assistant:

K: You chase me.
B: My name is Barbara.
K: Barbara chase.
K: You tickle me.
B: Where?
K: Tickle arm. (leading companion to refrigerator)
K: You me there. (indicating refrigerator)
B: What want?
K: Eat drink.
B: Eat or drink, which?
K: Glass drink.
B: That? (gets out juice)
K: That.

Unlike Washoe, Koko shows consistent word order. She uses about 75% correct word order in such constructions as "tickle me" and "Penny sit," putting the actor first and the recipient of the action last.

Koko also has shown some creative combinations. For example, she was given a stale sweet roll, and signed "cookie rock"; and when shown a mask she signed "eye hat." An interesting dimension of Koko's training was that she received both visual and auditory inputs from her trainers. As they signed to her, they also spoke aloud. Koko now gives evidence of considerable spoken-language comprehension.

What is the implication of these ape studies for the claim that language is species-specific to humans? We think that the claim is still mostly valid, although it now seems more interesting to ask which linguistic capacities are specialized in *Homo sapiens* and which are not. Actually, the findings of the Kelloggs, the Gardners, Premack, and Patterson fit well into an evolutionary perspective, and they make good sense when one views apes and human beings in their evolutionary relationship to each other. Most psycholinguists and other information-processing psychologists endorse the notion that contemporary apes and contemporary humans share a distant ancestor. Because only humans demonstrate spontaneous, flexible, and highly complex language use, at least some specialization for it must have occurred after *Homo sapiens* branched off from the other primates in the evolutionary tree. But the evolution of language surely required conceptual prerequisites that might well have been possessed by the common ancestor of apes and humans. Washoe's and Sarah's accomplishments stand more reasonably as contemporary evidence of historic evolutionary changes in conceptual abilities than as evidence against the assertion that much language function is specific to *Homo sapiens*.

One implication of species-specificity is that little about human language can be learned from the study of apes. We still believe this is true, at least for contemporary human language use. The reason is that, as information-processing psychologists, we are concerned with the internal processing mechanisms underlying behavior. These mechanisms are surely different in humans and nonhuman primates. Even if there is overlap between language-relevant capacities, the partial specialization of human language provides mechanisms that apes do not share. The chimp and the gorilla must achieve their performance without them. Consequently, the internal activities of the chimp, the gorilla, and the human child cannot be the same. When Koko signs "cookie rock," her internal processing mechanisms are at best only analogous to those of a human child saying the same thing, and may in fact be altogether dissimilar.

To emphasize this point, consider another skill at which apes excel, but humans do only with difficulty. Infant apes spontaneously acquire the ability to swing expertly through the air by their hands. No special tutoring is necessary. Some humans, through intensive training and practice, can swing through the air by their hands—trapeze artists do so much better than most people, if not so well as the clumsiest chimp. To achieve a poor imitation of the chimp, human trapeze artists must certainly rely on some characteristics that they share with other primates—arms, fingers, balance, and so on—although these are much better designed for swinging in nonhuman species. But there are great differences in motivation, ease, and naturalness. The cognitive activities that characterize a human trapeze artist and those of the wild chimpanzee must be very different. The human must concentrate and maintain his skills through practice. He must consciously anticipate falls and judge distances, aspects of tree-swinging that are second nature to a chimp. The question is, then, what can be learned about the tree-swinging skills of chimpanzees by studying humans—even trapeze artists? The answer to this question will also suggest what can be learned about human language by studying nonhuman primates—even the most accomplished. Such studies are by no means worthless; much can be learned about the conceptual prerequisites for language and the limits of skills common to both apes and humans. However, the scientific utility of teaching language-like behaviors to apes should not be naively overestimated just because it is remarkable.

One facet of the neobehavioristic paradigm was a commitment to animal research. One way linguists contributed to the relative eclipse of neobehaviorism and the rise of the information-processing paradigm was by their successful championing of the claim that language is specific to humans. Linguists, particularly Chomsky, contributed to the information-processing approach in other ways as well.

Chomsky was influenced by both behaviorism and information theory. His program of studies included information theory as well as linguistics, which at the time was influenced by behaviorism. Thus, he understood both behavioristic and information theory accounts of language, and he rejected both. After briefly reviewing both earlier approaches to language, we examine what he put in their place and why.

II.   NEOBEHAVIORISTIC AND INFORMATION-THEORY APPROACHES TO LANGUAGE

One of the most remarkable aspects of the first 60 or 70 years of American experimental psychology is how little concern it gave to language. Pavlov, who discovered the conditioned reflex, thought that the principles of conditioning would help explain how language is used (Pavlov, 1927), and there was some Russian experimentation toward that end (e.g., Volkova, 1953). But language fell largely in the cracks between the subdisciplines of American psychology. Gestalt psychologists studied perceptual and memory organization. Verbal-learning psychologists studied rote acquisition, and from their viewpoint, natural language habits were sources of contamination to be eliminated from their experiments. Neobehaviorists viewed language as a complex configuration of the simple processes they studied in the animal laboratory, and, before 1950, accounting for language seemed to them a job for the future.

A. Neobehaviorist Accounts

By the mid-1950s, the neobehaviorist paradigm was relatively complete, optimism ran high, and conditioning theory seemed ready for extension to new problems. It seemed that the time had come when tasks previously left for the future might be profitably addressed. Here, we provide only a few examples to give the flavor of the neobehaviorists' extensions of their theories to language. Staats and Staats (1963) provide a superb and much longer account of the various aspects of language that were addressed from a neobehavioristic point of view, including speech development, semantic differentiation of word meanings, acquisition of word meanings, and word associations, grammar, and communication, among other things.

1. Classical Conditioning

Osgood (1953) provided one account of how word meanings might be learned by classical conditioning which was extended by Staats and Staats (1963). Consider a baby crawling toward the television and reaching for the dial. Mother slaps the baby's hand, forcefully saying, "No." By Osgood's account, the slap is an Unconditioned Stimulus (UCS), and the word NO is a Conditioned Stimulus (CS). Hand-withdrawal by the baby is an Unconditioned Response, (UCR), which eventually becomes a Conditioned Response

(CR) through classical conditioning. Thus, after several repetitions of the approach–withdrawal sequence, it will suffice for the mother to say "No." She will not need to slap the child's hand at the same time, because hand-withdrawal will be elicited by the word alone, just as a dog eventually salivates (CR) to a bell (CS) without food (UCS).

2. Instrumental (Operant) Conditioning

According to Staats and Staats (1963) correct speech is instilled in the young child by successive approximations. Parents respond positively to the first word-like sounds of the baby. At first, they reward gross approximations of the adult form; for instance, they may respond to WAHWAH by supplying a drink of water. As the child grows older, the parent will require closer and closer approximations—WAHDA, WATAH, and finally WATER—before supplying the drink. In this way, some of the child's vocalizations are selected for reinforcement. Those that are not reinforced supposedly drop out and the rest are shaped by conditioning to resemble the adult form.

3. Mediation

The foregoing examples illustrate neobehaviorists' efforts to account for the learning of individual words and their meaning. Adding the concept of mediation to conditioning theory was an important step in neobehaviorist attempts to explain other aspects of language. To grasp the idea of mediation, imagine someone in a paired-associates experiment trying to learn the response FOD to the stimulus BAK. To mediate this association, a person might associate BAK with the word *backward* and FOD with *forward*. Because *backward* and *forward* are already associated in most people's minds, our imaginary subject should be able to use a chain of covert stimulus–response associations to mediate learning of BAK-FOD (see Fig. 10.1). Note that to neobehaviorists these covert associations are not

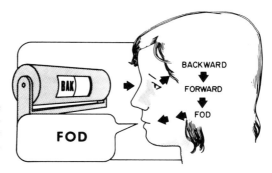

FIG. 10.1. Hypothetical sequence of associations in a subject who mediates BAK–FOD with the previously learned associates BACKWARD–FORWARD.

qualitatively different from other stimulus–response bonds. They are simply invisible to the experimenter.

The extension of conditioning to include covert responses allowed an explanation of word meaning and sentence comprehension that violated no precepts of the neobehaviorist paradigm. Thus, Osgood (1953) proposed that some of the responses to an object that are conditioned to its name (as a consequence of repeated association of the object with its name) became covert and constitute its meaning. For example, a child has many responses to a hammer, such as pounding and grasping, happiness, and so on. By classical conditioning, the simultaneous occurrence of the word HAMMER with these responses results in their being conditioned to the word. Some of these overt responses will later be extinguished; for instance, grasping and pounding may not prove rewarding, because they interfere with other activities. But internal equivalents of the overt responses to HAMMER will last for the rest of the person's life, constituting his meaning of HAMMER (Staats & Staats, 1963).

Mowrer (1954) built this view of word meaning into an explanation of how sentences might be understood. Suppose you had known someone named TOM for several years. His name would have been associated with his appearance and his acts many times; so it would have meaning for you. Then suppose someone you trust told you, "Tom is a thief." You know the meaning of THIEF; covert responses have been conditioned to it just as they have been conditioned to TOM. According to Mowrer, hearing *Tom is a thief* causes covert responses previously conditioned to THIEF to occur contiguously with covert responses to TOM. This amounts to a conditioning experience, which results in the formation of new associations between TOM and THIEF. These new associations are part of your understanding of the sentence. They allow you to respond to Tom somewhat as you respond to thieves; you may now hide the silverware when Tom comes to your parties, whereas before you would not have dreamed of using plastic forks and paper plates.

B. Linguists' Reactions to Neobehaviorist Accounts of Language

The foregoing few examples, along with the description in Chapter 3 of Skinner's approach, should give you the flavor of the behaviorist and neobehaviorist approaches to language. They focused on explaining the acquisition of words, particularly nouns, words' meanings, and the understanding of simple sentences. They emphasized the role of both classical and operant conditioning, and they cited much laboratory data to bolster their arguments. You should recall from Chomsky's criticism of Skinner (Chapter 3) that linguists were convinced that these approaches did not do justice to language, and that the basis of their skepticism was largely a matter of differing pretheoretical beliefs.

Here are a few other linguistic reactions to the neobehaviorist account of language, which further illustrate the character of paradigmatic clashes. Linguists cited few laboratory data. Instead, they produced examples of words and sentences that seemed impossible to explain without doing violence to the methodological commitments of the neobehaviorists or the basic requirements of conditioning theory. For example, Fodor (1965) pointed out sentences that Mowrer's (1954) theory did not encompass. *Tom is NOT a thief* would require the hearer to delete some conditioned responses, which is not possible in conditioning theory. Conditioning theory offered no mechanism for the learning of articles; so Fodor argued that *Tom is a thief* and *Tom is the thief* should be understood identically. *Tom is a perfect idiot* should be completely incomprehensible, because the contradictory associations to *perfect* and *idiot* would presumably all become attached to *Tom*. Chomsky (1959) noted that the neobehavioristic conception of how meanings are acquired could not account for the understanding of words like *Moscow* and *Eisenhower*, by people who have never personally experienced either. Homonyms (e.g., BERRY and BURY) and ambiguous words such as FLY raise problems, too. It is difficult to know how a single word can elicit now one response, then another.

Some data were brought to the fray. Brown, Cazden, and Bellugi (1969) observed parents interacting with their young children. If parents use reinforcement to shape pronunciation, they should use it to teach grammar also. But Brown et al. found that parents reinforce the truth of their children's productions, not their grammaticality. Thus, one child said about her mother, "He a girl," and the mother responded, "That's right." Another child said, "There's the animal farmhouse," but was corrected because it was a lighthouse. Brown et al. note the paradox for behaviorism that such training produces adults whose speech is highly grammatical, but not notably truthful.

Such arguments and findings persuaded many psychologists. By the end of the 1960s, psycholinguistics was an established discipline, and it completely ignored the principles of learning based on conditioned associations. Nor did it incorporate information theory, which at one time seemed a viable alternative to associationist accounts of language.

C. Information-Theory Approaches to Language

The advances that occurred in information theory after World War II attracted the attention of psychologists interested in language. You may recall from Chapters 3 and 5 that information theory is concerned with the amount of information transmitted, not with the content of the transmission. This was dictated by engineers' concern with maximizing the efficiency of telecommunications. The amount of information that can be transmitted depends on the number of possible messages and their probabilities. High-probability events transmit less information than low-probability ones. These information-theory notions were applied in many ways to the study and conceptualization of language. We begin with some simple applications and build gradually to some more sophisticated experiments that were inspired by information theory.

It should seem intuitively obvious that letters transmit less information than words, words less than phrases, and phrases less than sentences. This is entirely consistent with information theory's expectation from the numbers of these units. In English, there are 26 letters, hundreds of thousands of words, incalculable numbers of phrases, and an infinite number of sentences. From the fact that there are 26 letters, we can calculate that each would carry about 4.5 bits ($\log_2 26$, Equation 5.3), if each letter appeared equally frequently and if the occurrence of each was independent of previous letters. The letters do not appear equally often: Compare the number of E's and X's on this page, or refer to Table 3.1. What is more, some sequences are far more frequent than others. The sequence PV does not even appear in English, but PR (as in proof) and PL (as in plug) do. Factors like these reduce the information carried by any single English letter to about 1 bit, which, compared to the possibility of 4.5 bits, indicates the great redundancy (about 80%) of English orthography. You might appreciate the redundancy by reading the following sentence, from which all vowels have been deleted:

MST PPL CN RD THS SNTNC.

It is not possible to calculate the uncertainty of the average English word, because of the great number of words and the difficulty of estimating the frequency of all of them. It is clear that some words are used far more frequently than others. From a carefully selected sample of 1,014,232 words from running English text, there were only 50,406 different ones (Kucera & Francis, 1967). The 10 most frequent words (and the number of times each occurred) were: *the* (69,971); *of* (36,411); *and* (28,852); *to* (26,149); *a* (23,237); *in* (21,341); *that* (10,595); *is* (10,099); *was* (9816); and *he* (9543). The word *she* occurred only 2859 times (Kucera & Francis, 1967), and we can only speculate about how much this male-to-female imbalance in pronoun use has been corrected by the recent awareness of the sexist implications of such language patterns. In German, the 30 most frequent words constitute almost one-third of all written words (Meier, 1964), and the situation is similar in English. While it is impossible to calculate the exact uncertainty of words in any language, it is possible to study how the words in any language sample are used. Consider the matter of the relative use of words that vary in their frequency.

From a speaker's or writer's viewpoint, the approach requiring the least effort would to be to use the most frequently occurring words as often as possible, but that would complicate the listener's or reader's job. It would require the receiver to work harder to extract subleties of meaning, because the sender's vocabulary would be small and impoverished. Do communication patterns suggest lazy receivers or lazy senders? Research by Zipf (1949) suggests that we humans have reached a compromise. Zipf counted the frequency of words used in a sample of American newspapers and words used by James Joyce in the novel *Ulysses*. He ranked the words according to their frequency, and then plotted each word's absolute frequency against its rank. An interpretation of this kind of data is that speakers and writers would have it easier if frequency fell off more slowly for the highest-ranking words than for lower-ranking words. This would imply heavy use of relatively few words and minimal use of the remainder. Listeners and readers would be favored by a more rapid fall-off of absolute frequency for the highest ranking words and a slower fall-off for the ones ranked lower; this would imply more diversity in word production on the speaker's or writer's part. Spreading the communication load equally would result in an equal decrease in frequency across the whole range of frequency ranks: The function relating frequency and rank would decrease linearly. Figure 10.2 shows these three possibilities and Zipf's findings for *Ulysses* and the sample of newspapers. For both newspaper stories and Joyce's novel, word frequency was a linear function of word rank, even though Joyce used less frequent words overall than journalists. This linear relationship is called *Zipf's law*.

Miller, Heise, and Lichten (1951) performed one of the earliest experiments guided by information theory. (Zipf's was an observational study, not an experiment. He did not control what Joyce wrote.) Miller worked with

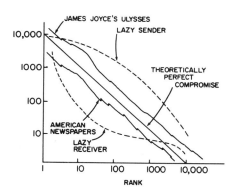

FIG. 10.2. Zipf's law relating absolute word frequency to rank frequency. (From Cherry, 1966.)

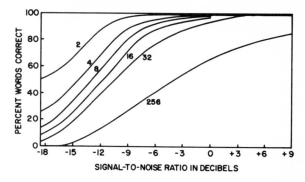

FIG. 10.3.   Word identification accuracy as a function of number of words to be identified and signal-to-noise ratio. (After Miller, Heise, & Lichten, 1951.)

telecommunications engineers during World War II and was one of the leaders in the movement to apply information theory to psychological problems. In his experiment with Heise and Lichten, he sought to determine whether the amount of information contained the language materials affected identification of the individual language units against a background of noise. If you were a subject in such an experiment and you knew that the only word you would hear was *RIVER*, then you would only need to determine that a word had been spoken to identify it correctly. If you knew that there would be two words, *RIVER* and *CALENDAR*, you could identify them correctly by hearing well enough to estimate the number of syllables, by picking up the first letter, by detecting the presence of a *V* or an *I* sound, and so on. When there are two words, you will be more dependent on the stimulus than when there is one, and the task should become harder and harder the more alternative words there are. Miller et al. varied information in just this way: Subjects were told which words would occur, and their task was to identify the words, which were presented against a noisy background. Conditions ranged from one bit (two words) to eight bits (256 words). Figure 10.3 shows the percent correct identification for each condition from two to 256 words under each of several signal-to-noise ratios for the experiment by Miller et al. The greater the information transmitted per word (the greater the number of possible words), the louder the signal had to be relative to the noise for the subjects to achieve comparable identification accuracies.

So far, nearly all of our illustrations of information theory's application to language have concerned the effects of uncertainty due to distributions of letters or words. Such examples represent much of the language research inspired by information theory, but they have little to do with the essence of language, which lies in sequences of words, not in the words themselves. We should tell you now that the computations of information theory apply to sequences, too, and therein lay the greatest possible pertinence of the theory to language. It was the possibility of quantifying the informational properties of sequences that created much of the early hope for the application of information theory to language. An experiment by Miller and Selfridge (1950) shows where the hope ultimately led.

Miller and Selfridge studied how the information content of word strings influences their memorability. They varied information content by creating lists of words that varied in their approximations to English discourse. For their zero-order approximation, Miller and Selfridge made lists by choosing words randomly from a dictionary. In their first-order approximation, the words were ordered randomly, but their likelihood of being in the list reflected their actual frequency of occurrence in written English. For higher order approximations to English, Miller and Selfridge asked people to help generate lists. For the second-order approximation, they gave a person one word chosen according to its frequency and had that person suggest a word that might follow it. Then, they gave the first person's suggested word to a second person, and so on until a list was complete. Third-order approximations were obtained by giving successive people pairs of words and asking them to supply a third, and so forth up to sixth-order approximations (five words to suggest a sixth). Miller and Selfridge also used actual English texts. Examples of the various sorts of lists are given in Table 10.1.

People memorized lists like these that were 10, 20, 30, 40, or 50 words long. The results obtained by Miller and Selfridge are shown in Fig. 10.4. For every list length, the percent of words recalled increased with the order of approximation to English. For a variety of technical reasons, little can be made of the subject's failure to recall text better than fifth- or sixth-order

TABLE 10.1
Examples of the Materials Used by Miller and Selfridge (1950)

Zero-order:	crane therewith egg journey applied crept burnish pound precipice king eat sinister descend cab Idaho baron alcohol equality Illinois
1st-order:	house reins women brought screaming especially much was said cake love that school to a they in is the home think with are his before
2nd-order:	the book was going home life is on the wall of you are ready to the waltz is I know much ado about it was a dog when it was
3rd-order:	happened to see Europe again is that trip to the end is coming here tomorrow after the packages arrived yesterday brought good cheer at
4th-order:	the first list was posted on the bulletin he brought home a turkey will die on my rug is deep with snow and sleet are destructive add
5th-order:	go it will be pleasant to you when I am near the table in the dining room was crowded with people it crashed into were screaming that they
6th-order:	won't do for the members what they most wanted in the course an interesting professor gave I went to at one o'clock stopped at his
Text:	Archimedes was a lonely sort of eagle as a young man he had studied for a short time at Alexandria Egypt where he made a life-long friend

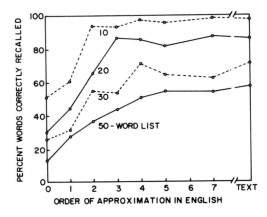

FIG. 10.4.   Results obtained by Miller and Selfridge (1950).

approximations (Coleman, 1963). Nevertheless, Miller and Selfridge arrived at the remarkable conclusion that it is not meaning per se that contributes to memorability. Rather, it is the short-term sequential dependencies that characterize the known structure of English. This conclusion was surely too sweeping. If paraphrase rather than literal recall is required, and when much material is presented, people will recall the gist of the message quite well. Even in sixth-order approximations to English, there is no coherent gist; so certainly the conclusions of Miller and Selfridge do not apply to situations such as studying, recalling conversations, capsulizing a novel, and so on. At the same time, there is little doubt that the predictability of language material importantly influences its perception and memory. If your mother says basically the same thing every time you call her up, you will be able to understand her even if the phone connection is poor. And it will be much easier to study, understand, and recall the contents of a textbook that makes substantial use of things you already know to explain things you are supposed to be learning. Both these examples show that information theory applies at least loosely to situations from which you must extract meaning for later recall.

One final example of the influence of information theory on psycholinguistic research concerns patterns of speaking. Goldman-Eisler (1968) used the concept of information to explain the location of hesitations in people's speech. She transcribed spontaneous speech and found that speakers were most likely to pause just before they uttered words of low predictability. Notice that these are the points of highest information-transmission. Goldman-Eisler also found that fluency was positively related to redundancy; more redundant speech is more fluent.

The foregoing examples do not exhaust the language research stimulated by information theory, but they are representative. Language research from an information-theory viewpoint never became very widespread in psychology. Measuring the informational value of language sequences was exceedingly difficult, and psycholinguists came to focus more on internal processes of the language user than on characteristics of the language itself. The main legacy of information theory for the contemporary study of language concerns the influence of predictability. Most psycholinguists consider predictability an important determinant of the strategies people use for such language-related activities as speech production and perception, comprehension, and recall. Psycholinguists still take care to control the predictability of their experimental materials, in order to increase the precision of their findings concerning other factors. While information theory was vitally important to some psycholinguists, it never became a dominant part of the conventional commitments of psychologists who study language. Instead, the informational properties of language became variables to reckon with in psychological research. By the time the more dominant neobehaviorist approach was superseded, the grammatical structure of language seemed more important than its informational properties. In large part, this was due to Chomsky's influence on psychology. Chomsky was a student of Zellig Harris, a linguist who had been influenced by the behaviorist ideas of Leonard Bloomfield. Chomsky also studied information theory, and he felt both approaches were inadequate.

III.   THE INFLUENCE OF THE LINGUIST NOAM CHOMSKY

Chomsky argued that both behaviorist and information-theory approaches were too closely tied to the sequential aspects of language. From Chomsky's perspective, both of these approaches missed the point that languages' grammatical structures are hierarchic, not sequential. The argument went like this. Neobehaviorists tried to explain language by treating it as chains of words, each of which is the stimulus for its follower. With this treatment, syntax—the rule system by which words must be put together to form grammatical sentences—is an accidental byproduct of sequential associative chaining. Chomsky claimed that information theory, despite its different terminology, explained sentence production in the same way as neobehaviorism. It substituted sequential probabilities for stimulus–response associations, but it relied on the same left-to-right chaining of words to form sentences.

Chomsky pointed out that many syntactic rules pertain to nonadjacent words. For instance, *if...then* are related, and the occurrence of *then* is predictable from a previous occurrence of *if*, even though these two words may be separated by many intervening words. In addition, many grammatical sentences have no high-probability sequences. Chomsky's famous example was *Colorless green ideas sleep furiously.* This sentence is semantically anomalous and unlikely to be spoken spontaneously, but most English speakers would agree that it is grammatically proper. It certainly is better than *Sleep ideas green furiously colorless*! Chomsky (1957) argued that, if one were listing all grammatical English sentences, the former sentence ought to be in the list even though it is semantically bizarre. Neither neobehavioristic nor information-theoretic accounts provide a mechanism by which to judge that such sentences are grammatical, and Chomsky considered that to be one critical failing of these approaches.

Trenchant criticisms can be extremely important to a science, and Chomsky's were. But criticisms provide no foundation for new approaches, though they may destroy old ones. They may create the need for new advances, but the advances themselves depend on new ideas, not the destruction of old ones. Chomsky's cardinal contribution was to provide novel ideas upon which a new style of linguistics was built. This new linguistics, in turn, came to the attention of psychologists searching for more viable ways to study language. Perhaps the revolution Chomsky created in linguistics would have had little impact on psychology had it not been for earlier developments: anomalies within the explanatory framework of neobehaviorism; information theory and the birth of computer science; human engineering; and so on. In any event, Chomsky's views also contributed importantly to the information-processing revolution within psychology.

Chomsky gave linguistics a paradigm and two theories. His paradigm consisted of new guidelines for constructing and evaluating linguistic theories. His two theories—his original transformational grammar and the later revision—both followed his paradigmatic precepts; but distinguishing them from his paradigm is necessary. Chomsky himself abandoned the original version of transformational grammar, and his revised version has been seriously challenged, even though the essentials of his paradigm are still accepted by most linguists. We presented some aspects of Chomsky's paradigm in Chapter 3. Here we review its highlights and fill in some additional details before turning to his theories and the psycholinguistic research done to test them.

A. Chomsky's Paradigm

Chomsky argued that linguistics should account for language competence, not merely performance. The job was to explain knowledge about language, not about speech. Linguistic theories should account for all of the potential language behavior of which any speaker is capable, not just actual language behavior. This was diametrically opposite to practices in both linguistics and psychology when Chomsky proposed it in his book, *Syntactic Structures* (1957), which may account for the difficulty he had finding a publisher for the book. (Publishers rely on the advice of other scholars when they decide whether to accept a manuscript for publication.) Chomsky proposed that linguists should explain the ideal language knowledge that a person has in his head by writing generative grammars. A generative grammer is a set of rules that, when applied systematically and exhaustively, generates a list of all the grammatical sentences and no nonsentences in a particular language. You may recall from Chapter 3 that generating sentences is not the same as producing utterances. As Chomsky conceived it, sentence generation is a logico-mathematical activity performable by abstract automata equipped with the elements of a language and rules for combining them. It deals with abstract, potential productions—in short, with competence. Producing utterances, on the other hand, is a matter of the performance of real people saying real things in concrete situations. It is neither logico-mathematical nor abstract; it is psychological and concrete. Chomsky argued that such performance cannot be explained completely by competence theories, but an explanation of grammatical competence is a necessary part of any psychological theory that explains language behavior.

Chomsky considered that the basic fact to be explained was how elements (such as words) are strung together or concatenated grammatically. Any concatenation of words is a string, but not every string is a sentence. The rules that make some strings sentences and others nonsentences are the grammar of a language, and it is the linguist's job to induce a language's grammar from knowledge of its sentences. The induced grammar should be so complete that no prior knowledge of the language is needed to use the grammar to generate all the sentences that native speakers of the language judge to be well-formed without generating any that they reject as improper. Because native speakers of what is apparently the same language do not always agree about the grammaticality of particular sentences, you may wonder how linguists decide which sentences to use when inducing a grammar and how they decide whose opinion to take when judging a grammar's output. What do they do about the fact that some American speakers of English accept this sentence as proper, but others do not: *I might go fishing tomorrow, or either I might go swimming.* First, linguists recognize that all languages have dialects, each of which has a somewhat different grammar. Thus, the foregoing sentence is acceptable only to those people who speak Southern American English. Second, they recognize that despite dialect differences, there is a large central core of sentences on which all speakers of a language will agree, and it is quite enough for the time being to build grammars for a language's overlapping segment, reserving dialect variations for future modifications of the basic grammar. Linguists are not committed to the idea that there are only a few grammars. Rather, they believe that a grammar can be written for each and every community of speakers who do agree. They recognize, too, that each person may have his own idiolect, so that ultimately there might be as many grammars as speakers, though no linguist seriously expects that so many grammars will ever be written.

Chomsky recognized that many rule sets might generate all and only the well-formed sentences of a language community. With any mathematical approach such as Chomsky's, there are alternative proofs or derivations. When there are alternative grammars, how is one to decide which is best? For one thing, he should choose the most elegant solution. Other things equal, the preferred grammar is the simplest one that will produce all and only the sentences of the language. To illustrate this point, consider that one grammar of English might be a very long list, containing all permissible sentences. To generate the set of English sentences, the automaton would read the list. Even if this were possible, it would be most inelegant. It would be more elegant to write rules to cover particular sentence types, such as *John loves Mary, Albert likes pie, Wilbur fears rats*, and so on. Even if this simple sentence type took 20 or 30 rules, it would still be more efficient than listing all such sentences, of which there must be a very great number.

Chomsky also suggested other criteria for evaluating grammars. He argued that the preferred grammar is one that more closely reflects the intuitions of native speakers about their language. For example, if speakers sense a relationship between two sentences, they should be generated in part by the same rules. Thus, various alternative rule sets could be devised to generate the following pair of sentences (among many others):

Milton solved the problem.
The problem was solved by Milton.

Because most native speakers of English view these sentences as paraphrases of each other, a grammar that generated them with partly overlapping rules would be preferable to one that generated each from different rules.

A final criterion for evaluating alternative grammars is that a good one should have features that apply to many languages. Chomsky could make this demand only because he felt that there are universal rules that apply to all human languages. This is a manifestation of the idea that aspects of language are innate: A feature is unlikely to hold for all of the thousands of languages in the world unless it is due to some innate property of the human species. It follows that Chomsky placed heavy emphasis on language acquisition, because if anyone must rely heavily on their innate language abilities, it is children who are learning their parents' tongue. Linguistic commonalities that are discovered among young children seem most apt to signal universal features of languages, and hence also to signal those features that ought to characterize the most adequate grammar.

In his early work, Chomsky (1957) also argued for the independence of syntax and meaning. He asserted that it was possible to theorize about the form of language without reference to its content. In this respect, Chomsky was perpetuating the tradition of Harris and Bloomfield, who also wished to avoid the difficulties of characterizing meaning. Chomsky himself moderated this position in later work (Chomsky, 1965). It does appear to be an overstatement that grammatical form can be understood without reference to content. Experimental studies show that the effect of syntactic variables depends on their communication context, the beliefs and expectations of the experimental subjects, their knowledge of the world, and so on. These influences are here termed semantic factors, a usage that is somewhat broader than is conventional among linguists and certain linguistically trained psychologists.

Chomsky's ideas precipitated a scientific revolution in linguistics. In psychology, they influenced a revolution that was already taking shape. The influence is seen most concretely in psychological research undertaken to assess the psychological reality of various elements in Chomsky's theories. Psychologists tried to show that linguistic constructs could be treated as independent variables that yield predictable effects on perception, memory, and reaction time.

B. Some Adjunct Importations From Linguistics

As will happen when one science borrows ideas from another, psychology got more from linguistics than Chomsky's ideas. Chomsky wrote for linguists, and to understand him, psychologists had to learn linguistic notational conventions, concepts, and style of argumentation. Having learned these things, they used them.

1. Notational Conventions

The linguistic notational conventions used in this chapter include the use of an asterisk to indicate an unacceptable string, the conjoining of elements with the + sign, and the way we enumerate sentences. Thus, when we introduce an example sentence that will be mentioned again, we set it off with a number, thus:

(1) Psychologists borrow formalisms from linguists.

Later, this particular example will be referred to as Sentence (1). If the exemplary sentence is ungrammatical, it will be preceded by an asterisk:

(2) *Psychologists linguists from borrow formalisms.

According to the rules of English, Sentence (2) is not well-formed, as you can see. When we wish to show the conjoining of several components to make a string, the + sign is used, as in:

NP + VP

which should be read "Noun phrase followed by verb phrase."

2. Major Concepts

Some linguistic concepts have become part of the everyday vocabulary of psycholinguists, and to understand psycholinguistics one must know the terms. Most of us learned some of the terms in high-school English. These include the notions of *syllable, phrase, clause*, and *complex sentence*. Other terms are less familiar. For example, *verb complements* include such usages as the italicized portion of "I persuaded the young man *to return the stolen book*." Also, sentences can be *embedded* within other sentences. For example, *The kid you invited to lunch is here* contains the sentence *You invited a kid to lunch* within the sentence *The kid is here*. This is an example of *center embedding*, which should be distinguished from *left branching* and *right branching*. The direction of branching—left or right—depends on whether the embedded sentence refers to a word at the beginning or end of the superordinate sentence. Consider two ways of compounding the simple sentence *The dog chewed the rug*. We could add more information about the dog (left branching) or more information about the rug (right branching). Thus, *The dog that your sister who lives in Cleveland gave to your brother chewed his rug* exemplifies left branching, as does the children's poem called The House That Jack Built. *The dog chewed the rug that your aunt who lives in Cleveland gave to your brother* branches right.

A number of linguistic units figure in psycholinguistic research. The *morpheme* is the smallest unit of meaning, and includes words as well as meaningful suffixes and affixes. A *morph* is a single word. Thus, *GIRL* is both one morph and one morpheme, while *GIRLS* represents one morph and two morphemes, *GIRL* and *-S*. *WOMEN* is also one morph and two morphemes (*WOMAN* and plural morpheme). *UNHAPPINESS* contains three morphemes, and so on. Whereas a morpheme is a unit of meaning, a *phone* is a unit of sound. *Phonetic transcription* specifies how a segment of language should be pronounced. Many of the symbols used in phonetic transcription resemble the English alphabet, but there are others as well (see Table 10.2). Such transcription is usually placed between slashes. For example, /mēt/ designates the pronunciation of *meet*. There are a number of physically different sounds that may be identically interpreted by the language user. For instance, in English, the initial sound of *pepper* is not the same as the sound in the middle. The first phone (sound) is an *aspirated p* (represented [p^h] in phonetic transcription), while the middle phone is unaspirated. You can notice the difference in pronunciation if you hold your hand in front of your lips as you say "pepper." English does not distinguish meaning on the basis of whether or not *p*s are aspirated; if you pronounced *pepper* without aspirating the initial phone, you would be understood (although your listeners might think you were affecting a French accent). Alternative representations, such as aspirated and unaspirated *p*, are called

TABLE 10.2

Jakobson, Fant, and Halle's Analytic Transcription of the Phonemes of English[a]

	call ɔ	father a	men ɛ	book ʊ	fun ə	pin ɪ	long l	sing ŋ	virgin ĵ	version ẑ	king k	chip k̂	ship ŝ	good g	man m	friend f	put p	van v	bay b	now n	so s	thin θ	top t	zoo z	there ð	dull d	how h	glottal stop #
1. Vocalic/Nonvocalic	+	+	+	+	+	+	+	−	−	−	−	−	−	−	−	−	−	−	−	−	−	−	−	−	−	−	−	−
2. Consonantal/Nonconsonantal	−	−	−	−	−	−	+	+	+	+	+	+	+	+	+	+	+	+	+	+	+	+	+	+	+	+	−	−
3. Compact/Diffuse	+	+	+	−	−	−	−	+	+	+	+	+	+	+	−	−	−	−	−	−	−	−	−	−	−	−	+	−
4. Grave/Acute	+	+	−	+	+	−		+	−	−	+	−	−	+	+	+	+	+	+	−	−	−	−	−	−	−		
5. Flat/Plain	+	−		+	−																							
6. Nasal/Oral								+							+					+								
7. Tense/Lax (voiced/unvoiced)									+	+	−	−	−	+	+	−	−	+	+	+	−	−	−	+	+	+		−
8. Continuant/Interrupted									−	+	−	−	+	−		+	−	+	−		+	+	−	+	+	−		
9. Strident/Mellow									+	+		+	+			+		+			+	−		+	−			

[a] Adapted from Malmberg (1967, p. 188).

allophones of the same *phoneme* in English. A phoneme is a group or combination of phones with a common meaning. In some languages, aspirated and unaspirated *p* constitute two phonemes: You could not freely substitute one for the other without changing the meaning. In the Thai language, for example, /pʰay/ means *danger* and is spoken like the English word *pie*. However, /pay/ is a different word, meaning "to go." In Thai, aspiration is a *distinctive feature*—a property of sound that distinguishes one phoneme from another (Jakobson & Halle, 1956). Distinctive features are usually defined in articulatory terms; that is, in terms of the speaker's act in producing the sound. Aspiration is not a distinctive feature in English; however, *voicing* is. Voicing is the only difference between the English phonemes /p/ and /b/, for instance, or /t/ and /d/. When you pronounce /p/ your vocal cords do not vibrate, but when you pronounce /b/ they do. Otherwise, your mouth, tongue, lips, and vocal apparatus are in the same position. The same is true of /t/ and /d/, as well as /k/ and /g/. There are other distinctive features in English; Table 10.2 gives the analysis offered by Jakobson, Fant, and Halle (1963).

C. Chomsky's Theoretical Positions

Chomsky's theory, which he called transformational grammar, was first presented in 1957. It was considerably revised in 1965; the 1965 version has been elaborated in minor ways, and the resultant theory is known in contemporary linguistics as *the standard theory*. Each of the two versions of transformational grammar set off a wave of psycholinguistic research. The following sketch of transformational grammar is by no means complete; we have omitted details that have not figured importantly in psychological research and in the thinking of psycholinguists.

Both versions of transformational grammar were lists of rules intended (if properly extended and completed) to generate the well-formed strings of English morphemes. Chomsky never explicitly claimed that the sequence of rule applications that generated a particular string necessarily bore any resemblance to the mental processes a person might execute in order to utter the same string, although he sometimes seemed to imply it. Whatever Chomsky intended, it is important not to confuse the formal operation of a grammar with the psychological operations of the mind. Chomsky's approach to grammars was that of a linguist, not a psychologist. When psychologists used his theories to guide their experimentation, it was to satisfy their curiosity, not to test Chomsky's explicit psychological claims. The reason that psychologists were curious about grammatical theories was that such theories were based on what people know about their language, which should enter into how they use it. Most of the experiments we describe in this chapter sought to determine whether, how, and to what extent the linguistic knowledge people have (as presented in linguistic theories) influences how they perceive, produce, understand, and remember language inputs.

1. Phrase Structure Grammar

Transformational grammar is an elaboration of the somewhat simpler phrase structure grammar. Unlike associationistic or information-theoretic systems, phrase structure grammar represents the groupings of sentence elements, or *constituents*, in hierarchical order. Chomsky argued that the goal for a grammar was to generate all of the sentences of a language. Presumably, then, a grammar of English should generate, among others, this one:

(3) The patio resembles a junkyard.

If the explanatory apparatus of information theory, or neobehaviorism, were re-cast as generative grammar, this sentence would have to be produced by probabilistic chaining of the adjacent words. But phrase structure grammar works differently. A sentence is generated from phrase structure grammar by applying a series of *rewrite rules*, which subdivide large units into successively smaller and smaller ones, down to the level of the morpheme. Figure 10.5 shows a subset of the rules of a phrase structure grammar of English that would be used to generate Sentence (3). Panel A shows the rules themselves. The symbol → means that whatever is on the left *may be rewritten as* whatever is on the right. Thus, rule 1 in Panel A means "A sentence may be rewritten as a noun phrase followed by a verb phrase." Panel B shows how successive application of the rules yields Sentence (3). Other paths through the rules would generate slightly different sentences, such as *The patio resembles the junkyard, The junkyard resembles the patio,* and so on. Panel B is a *derivational history* of Sentence (3). Panel C shows how the same information can be illustrated graphically with a tree diagram, which is the most useful way to express the relationships involved, and Panel D shows how some of the information can be expressed by using brackets. This latter mode of representation takes the least space, but reading such representations requires great familiarity with the system. You should notice that phrase structure grammar characterizes the hierarchy of word groupings we intuitively feel in Sentence (3). You very likely feel that there is a close relationship between *the* and *patio;* you could replace these two words with one, *it.* You should not feel such a close relationship between *resembles* and *a.* This difference is captured in phrase structure grammar by the fact that *the* and *patio* belong to the same

A. Rewrite Rules

```
1.  S(entence)  ⟶  NP (Noun Phrase)   +   VP (Verb  Phrase)
2.  NP          ⟶  D(eterminer)       +   N(oun)
3.  VP          ⟶  V(erb)             +   NP
4.  N           —   patio, junkyard, . . .   etc.
5.  V           ⟶  resembles,. . . . . .    etc.
6.  D           ⟶  the, a,. . . . . . . .   etc.
```

B. Sentence generation by Rule (Derivational History)

```
S ⟶ NP + VP                                   (by  Rule  1)
S ⟶ D + N + VP                                (by  Rule  2)
S ⟶ D + N + V + NP                            (by  Rule  3)
S ⟶ D + N + V + D + N                         (by  Rule  2)
S ⟶ the + N + V + D + N                       (by  Rule  6)
S ⟶ the + patio + V + D + N                   (by  Rule  4)
S ⟶ the + patio + resembles + D + N           (by  Rule  5)
S ⟶ the + patio + resembles + a + N           (by  Rule  6)
S ⟶ the + patio + resembles + a + junkyard    (by  Rule  4)
```

C. Tree Diagram

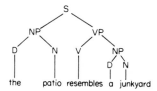

D. Bracket Equivalent of Tree Diagram

((The patio) (resembles (a junkyard)))

FIG. 10.5.   Use of phrase-structure rewrite rules and alternative schematizations.

small constituent (the Noun Phrase), while *resembles* and *a* belong to the
same constituent only higher up in the diagram (earlier in the derivational
history).

Students often wonder about the relationship between the tree structures of
phrase structure grammar and the kind of diagramming many of us did in
school. The difference lies in their relative ability to represent word order and
certain kinds of semantic information. For example, consider Sentence (4),
which is represented both ways in Fig. 10.6:

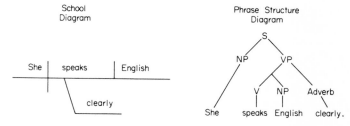

FIG. 10.6.   Comparison of school diagram and phrase structure diagram.

(4) She speaks English clearly.

You cannot tell whether the school diagram is of Sentence (4) or of the alternative, *She clearly speaks English*. No such doubt exists in phrase structure grammar, which provides a different analysis for *She clearly speaks English*. On the other hand, school diagrams supply some semantic information. For sentences such as (4), school diagrams show which noun is the subject and which is the object, whereas phrase structure grammar only specifies which comes first.

2. Transformational Grammar

The rules that generate Sentence (4) are only a few of the phrase structure rules that would be required to generate all the sentences of English, and that whole set will never be written. The reason is that there is no point in writing all the rules for any grammar, once it has been shown to have insuperable difficulties generating some kind of acceptable language constructions. Chomsky himself showed that phrase structure grammar needs substantial modification in order to generate some sentences in ways that square with speakers' intuitions. For instance, a grammar should relate sentences that people believe are related, and separate sentences that people believe are unrelated. For a generative grammar, relating and separating pertain to the amount of overlap in the rules that generate different sentences. For instance, Sentence (3) should be derived from very similar rules as such other sentences as, *The child resembles the father, Your cat resembles my cat,* and so on. If the derivational histories (series of rules) for different sentences are identical, except for the last couple of rules (see Fig. 10.5), the sentences are related. But if only the first rule or two are the same, the sentences are not related by the grammar.

Chomsky noted that phrase structure grammar relates some sentences that people find very different, and separates some that people consider to be related. For example, if a sentence is two-ways ambiguous, the grammar should generate it twice, from two different rule sequences, providing two structural descriptions that can be drawn as tree diagrams. Phrase structure grammar succeeds with some kinds of ambiguity, but not with others. The ambiguous sentence shown in Fig. 10.7 is an example of the kind of ambiguity with which phrase structure grammar copes well. It supplies two different diagrams for the sequence of words *They are shooting stars*. This sentence has *surface structural ambiguity*, because its two readings result solely from the different ways the words can be grouped. When the source of ambiguity is alternative word groupings, phrase structure grammar does well. Other examples that show this are *They had cooked eggs for breakfast*, where *cooked* describes either the type of eggs they ate or what they had done to prepare them, and *All old men and ladies are excused from calisthenics,*

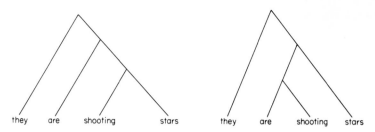

FIG. 10.7.   Two phrase structure diagrams of an ambiguous sentence.

where the phrase *old men and ladies* may or may not include young ladies.

Phrase structure grammar does not cope with other kinds of ambiguity. Even though native speakers report multiple meanings, only one structure is assigned by the grammar for Sentences (5) and (6):

(5) Visiting relatives can be boring.
(6) The mayor had to remind the police to stop brawling.

Sentence (5) could mean either that relatives who visit are boring or that it is boring to visit relatives. Sentence (6) could mean either that the police were brawling or that they were letting others brawl. You would not see these ambiguities if your linguistic competence were fully described by phrase structure grammar. It gives only one constituent structure for each of these sentences.

Phrase structure grammar also fails to match speakers' intuitions about relationships like those between Sentences (7) and (8):

(7) Soldiers are easy to shoot.
(8) Soldiers are eager to shoot.

They have the same constituent structure in phrase structure grammar, but most speakers of English recognize immediately that there are very important differences between the two sentences, differences that may determine whether one wants to side with the soldiers or not. In this case the grammar relates sentences the people consider unrelated. Phrase structure grammar also does the opposite, as these examples show:

(9) The chairman does the hard work.
(10) The hard work is done by the chairman.

Sentences (9) and (10) are considered by most people to be closely related, but phrase structure grammar takes no account of the relationship between an active sentence and its passive form; entirely different rules are required for actives and passives.

You may wonder why phrase structure grammar could not be modified by adding a rule such as, *The chairman does the hard work → The hard work is done by the chairman.* In fact, Chomsky considered such a rule, but it did not solve the problems of phrase structure grammar. The logic of rewrite rules requires that only one symbol appear to the left of the arrow. Rewriting more than one symbol (as in the proposed rule) muddies the constituent information generated by phrase structure grammars. Chomsky solved the problems of phrase structure grammar by adding a new set of rules that could be applied to several elements at a time. Chomsky called the second set *transformation rules.* Unlike the rewrite rules of phrase structure grammar, transformation rules generate nothing from single elements. They apply to already generated strings—reordering some elements, deleting others, replacing others with yet different ones, and so on. In Chomsky's transformational grammar, the generative process became a two-step sequence: Phrase-structure rules generated basic strings; transformation rules changed them around. The basic strings were simple, active, affirmative, and declarative. They were called *kernel sentences.* Complex sentences, passives, negatives, and interrogatives resulted from the transformation of kernel sentences, and were called *transforms.* Figure 10.8 shows how this system works, using the passive transform as an example.

So far we have considered the syntactic component of Chomsky's transformational-generative grammar. The entire system included semantic and morphophonemic components as well. Once the syntactic component had generated a string of morphemes forming a grammatical utterance, the

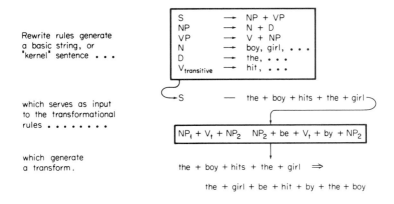

FIG. 10.8.   Generative sequence of a kernel sequence and passive transform in Chomsky's transformational-generative grammar (1957 version).

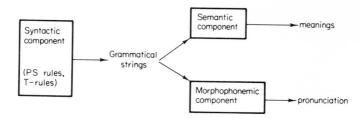

FIG. 10.9.   Illustration of the several components of Chomsky's transformational grammar.

semantic component interpreted it for meaning and the morphophonemic component indicated how it should be pronounced. Figure 10.9 shows how these components work together to perform the ideal function of a grammar. It shows the relationship between sounds and meanings.

Adding transformational rules to the phrase structure grammar resolved the problem of relating active and passive versions of sentences. They became members of the same family of sentences. Their derivational history in the syntactic component is identical except for the last step, the transformation rule. The same is true for negatives, interrogatives, and so on. Recall that phrase structure grammar assigned only one structure to Sentences (7) and (8). In transformational grammar, these sentences are generated by different rules, and belong to different families. Sentence (7) belongs to the same family as Sentence (11), and Sentence (8) belongs to the same family as Sentence (12).

(11) It is easy for someone to shoot soldiers.
(12) Soldiers are eager to shoot someone.

The ambiguity problem of phrase structure grammar is solved in a similar way. For example, Sentence (5) is generated twice by transformational grammar, once as part of the same family as (13) and once as part of the family of (14).

(13) It is boring to visit relatives.
(14) Relatives who visit can be boring.

Transformational grammar seemed to solve all of the problems that phrase structure grammar solved and some problems it failed. Of course, Chomsky did not write out all of the rules required for transformational grammar to generate the sentences of any language. Producing all of the rules in a transformational grammar of even one language would take armies of linguists working for years, even assuming they all agreed with each other—

which is no more likely for linguists than for cognitive psychologists. The absence of a completely worked-out rule system did not bother psychologists, however, for it was the broad outlines and paradigmatic implications of Chomsky's theory that attracted them. Psychologists used the broad outlines of Chomsky's theory to generate researchable hypotheses about the effects of syntax, phrase structures, and grammatical transformations on psychological processes. They did experiments to find out whether grammatical relations influenced the perception and recall of language strings. They studied whether people perceive sentences by grouping the words in ways suggested by phrase structure analyses, and whether they recall words in the groups generated by phrase structure grammar. Psychologists asked whether transformations resulted in sentences that were psychologically more complex than the kernel, whether people stored sentences in memory as kernels plus transformational tags, and whether the time to transform sentences could be measured.

No sooner had psychologists discovered the excitement and promise of transformational grammar than Chomsky overhauled it, creating what is now known as the standard theory. His reasons for revising transformational grammar were linguistic rather than psychological, but two aspects of the revised theory were important to psycholinguistic researchers. These two aspects were the replacement of the kernel sentence by *deep structures*, and a new way of representing words. A new role was given to rewrite rules in the standard theory. Instead of generating kernel sentences, as do the rewrite rules of the original transformational grammar, the rewrite rules of the standard theory generate abstract symbol strings called deep structures. Deep structures contain no words. They become sentences through the application of further rules, some of which insert words into the deep structures and some of which reorder the deep structures into acceptable sentences, called *surface structures*.

The representation of the vocabulary, in the standard theory, is quite different from that of the earlier transformational grammar. Rather than incorporating vocabulary into the phrase structure rules by grammatical class, such as Noun, Verb, and so on (see Fig. 10.5), the standard theory uses a separate lexicon. Each word (lexical item) is listed separately, along with information about its grammatical class and some semantic information governing how it may combine with other lexical items. Adding this sort of lexicon put semantic information in the syntactic component of the theory, which was a major change. The change was prompted by the intuitions of native speakers, who distinguish levels of acceptability for strings such as (15), (16), and (17):

(15) Friendly young dogs seem harmless.
(16) *Colorless green ideas sleep furiously.
(17) *Dogs harmless seem friendly young.

The original transformational grammar generates both (15) and (16), which Chomsky considered equally grammatical in 1957. But some native speakers do not accept (16), and the semantic information that Chomsky incorporated in the lexicon of the standard theory prevents its generation. Items in the lexicon contain *semantic markers*. Thus, the word *ideas* is marked as an abstraction, while *sleep* is marked as a verb whose subject must be concrete and animate. The rules that generate surface structures (called T-rules) take account of these markers, and do not generate sentences having the noun *ideas* as the subject of the verb *sleep*. Similar restrictions preclude sentences in which both *colorless* and *green* modify the same NP, and neither can modify abstractions, only concrete objects.

Figure 10.10 shows in schematic fashion how the standard theory can operate. Phrase-structure type rules generate the symbol strings of the deep structure, and *lexical insertion rules* select the vocabulary items that can legitimately fit each structure. Lexicalized deep structures are called *base strings*. Then the T-rules operate to produce *surface structures*, which include all the sentences of the language. The semantic component interprets the meaning of the deep structures, and the morphological component specifies the pronunciation of surface structures.

The standard theory prompted a whole new realm of research questions for psycholinguists. Every sentence in the standard theory has both a deep and a surface structure; so it was asked whether people store sentences as deep structures, retaining deep structure representations and forgetting surface structure as soon as the deep structure had been extracted. In deep structure trees, some lexical items are more central than others, and psychologists asked whether these items serve as pivots around which sentence memory is organized. The rules governing lexical insertion suggested that some words are relatively free of restrictive markers so that they could be inserted in many sentence types, while other words are multiply marked to exclude many uses. Psycholinguists wondered whether more marked terms were psychologically

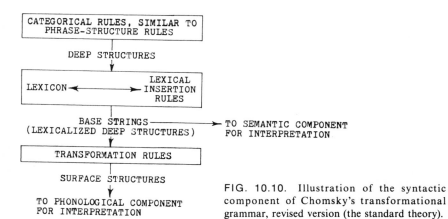

FIG. 10.10. Illustration of the syntactic component of Chomsky's transformational grammar, revised version (the standard theory).

more complex. In the remainder of this chapter, we describe research intended to answer such questions. The people who did this research are psycholinguists in the information-processing tradition. The basic attitudes of information-processing psychologists are reflected in their work, as are the considerable influences of linguistics.

IV. THE PSYCHOLOGY OF SYNTAX

The general question to which psycholinguistic research was addressed, beginning in the 1960s, was whether the notions incorporated into linguistic theory had what is called "psychological reality." Did linguistic theory, whose purpose was to account for language competence, specify factors that controlled language performance? Would people's behavior follow the patterns linguistic theories do?

A. The Psychological Reality of Grammar

In one of the earliest studies of grammaticality, Epstein (1961) showed that the syntactic structure of verbal material facilitates its recall over and above the effects of meaning or informational considerations. To show this unequivocally, Epstein required people to memorize two kinds of material, grammatical and ungrammatical, that were identical with respect to other variables known to influence recall—for example, sequential dependencies, frequency, and meaningfulness. Epstein gave people nonsense materials either with or without grammatical tags, like those of Jabberwocky. In one condition, people memorized strings like these:

> deebs haky the um flutest reciled pav a tofently dison
> cligs seping a wur rad un moovly glers the un vasing

In another condition, capital letters and periods were added to make the strings resemble sentences:

> A haky deebs reciled the dison tofently um flutest pav.
> The glers un cligs wur seping un vasing a rad moovly.

In a third condition, the grammatical endings and articles were removed from the pseudowords, and neither capitals nor periods were used.

> haky deeb um flut recile pav tofent dison
> clig sep wur rad un moov gler un vas

These nonsense materials all had zero frequency, meant nothing, and had no sequential regularities in the preexperimental experience of Epstein's subjects.

The easiest lists to learn were those that most closely resembled Jabberwocky (the second condition). The hardest were those without grammatical endings, even though removing the articles made these shorter than the other lists. Epstein concluded that these differences in memorability were due to the differences in grammatical information, because meaningfulness, predictability from sequential information, and frequency were all equated at zero. Syntax has some psychological reality.

Miller, who had so enthusiastically advocated information-theoretic approaches to language, also became an enthusiastic advocate of research on grammar. He and Chomsky were colleagues in Boston at Harvard and MIT, and their interaction contributed greatly to the infusion of linguistic ideas into psychological research. Miller became a major bridge between the two disciplines. He and his collaborators provided several experimental demonstrations of the importance of grammar to psychological processes. In these experiments, they independently varied the extent to which their stimuli violated the grammatical and semantic requirements of English. They began with five-word sentences like these:

Rapid flashes augur violent storms.
Pink bouquets emit fragrant odors.
Fatal accidents deter careful drivers.
Melting snows cause sudden floods.
Noisy parties wake sleeping neighbors.

They created ungrammatical strings by scrambling the words of such sentences—for example, *Rapid augur violent flashes storms.* They created anomalous strings by mixing the first word from the first sentence with the second word from the second sentence, and so on: *Rapid bouquets deter sudden neighbors.* Scrambling violated syntactic constraints, and mixing violated semantic constraints. Scrambling the words of the mixed sentences produced strings that violate both semantic and syntactic requirements: *Rapid deter sudden bouquets neighbors.* By comparing recall of such materials, it was possible to assess the importance of syntax and semantics separately.

Marks and Miller (1964) presented several such strings to people, and tested for recall. Memory was best for the original sentences, next best for the semantically distorted strings, third best for the grammatically distorted strings, and worst for the doubly distorted strings. Using similar material, but without the doubly distorted condition, Miller and Isard (1963) obtained parallel results for the perception of sentences. They tested how accurately people reported strings heard against a noisy background. The normal sentences were reported most accurately; ungrammatical strings were the worst; and semantically anomalous strings fell in between. Such experiments showed that there are behavioral facts whose explanation requires the concept of grammaticality. Because psychologists were not expert in syntax, they looked to linguistics for ideas about grammar, and the stage was set for further research to see whether linguistic accounts of grammar were psychologically useful. This boiled down to several years of research designed to see whether Chomsky's (1957, 1965) accounts of grammar had psychological reality, for by this time Chomsky was the dominant figure in the field of linguistics.

B. The Psychological Reality of Phrase Structures

Because the foundation of Chomsky's theory was phrase structure rules, a sensible first question for psychologists was whether people organize the words of sentences into groups as phrase structure grammar does. To answer this question, psychologists turned naturally to studies of memory and perception. Johnson (1965) tested the question of whether phrase structure grammar predicted memory groupings. He used the well-established method of paired-associates learning for the new purpose of seeing whether phrase structure constituents serve as memory units. People were required to learn stimulus–response pairs in which the stimuli were digits and the responses were words that formed a sentence, like this:

Stimulus	Response
1	the
2	tall
3	boy
4	saved
5	the
6	dying
7	woman

Johnson presented many such lists to his subjects to assess where forgetting occurred. If sentence constituents form units in people's minds, then the words of different constituents should be forgotten or remembered together; all or none should be recalled. People should remember all the words, *the tall boy*, or they should forget them all. They should not remember *the* and *tall*, but forget *boy*. However, people might remember *the tall boy* and forget *saved*. This prediction stems from the constituent structure assigned the sentence by phrase structure grammar, which is shown in Fig. 10.11. Johnson used transitional error probabilities to show how likely someone was to forget a word, given that they had recalled the word preceding it. Thus, Johnson computed the probability of forgetting *tall* for those subjects who

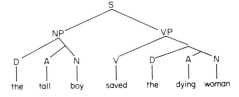

FIG. 10.11. Phrase structure diagram of illustrative sentence studied by Johnson (1965).

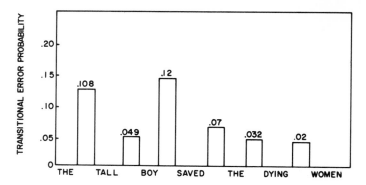

FIG. 10.12.   Transitional error probabilities from experiment by Johnson (1965).

remembered *the*. Then he computed the probability of forgetting *boy* for those subjects who remembered *tall*, and so on through the sentence. He found that transitional error probabilities were highest at the phrase breaks. Thus, forgetting *saved* was more likely for people who remembered *boy*, than forgetting *boy* was for people who remembered *tall*. Figure 10.12 shows Johnson's results, which support the notion that phrase structure has psychological reality. Using a variety of methods, other experimenters (Fodor & Bever, 1965; Garrett, Bever, & Fodor, 1966; Marks, 1967; Mehler & Carey, 1967) have found support for the claim that phrase structure grammar does capture aspects of how people organize sentences for memory and perception.

C. The Psychological Reality of Grammatical Transformations

Chomsky's theory also featured the concept of a grammatical transformation—a rule governing how a whole string may be converted. While Chomsky did not design his system as a psychological model of how speakers and hearers actually produce or understand utterances, he often implied that his system might have psychological reality. Psycholinguists picked up this implication and subjected Chomsky's theory to the sort of behavioral test that Chomsky, as a linguist, would not perform himself. The results of such tests are not critical to whether Chomsky's theory is linguistically sound, but they are critical to its utility for psychologists.

One of the earliest studies of the psychological reality of grammatical transformations was done by Miller, McKean, and Slobin (reported in Miller, 1962). This is the same Miller who worked in the information-theory tradition and who demonstrated the importance of grammaticality to both sentence perception and sentence recall.

Miller and his associates studied the effects of relationships among families of sentences, such as those shown in Fig. 10.13. Each edge of the cube represents one grammatical transformation. The number of edges that must be traversed to move from one sentence to another equals the number of grammatical transformations required to convert either sentence to the other. Thus, from kernel (K) to negative (N) involves only one transformation; only one edge must be traversed to get from K to N in the diagram. To go from the kernel to the passive negative (PN) requires two transformations. The maximum number of transformations is three, as from the kernel to the passive negative question (PNQ). If people actually perform transformational operations in their heads, each additional transformation should add to the time required to convert sentences from one form to another. For example, the cube suggests that converting a kernel to a negative (*John loves Mary* to *John doesn't love Mary*) should take less time than converting a kernel to a passive negative (*John loves Mary* to *Mary isn't loved by John*). Drawing the sides of the cube all the same length suggests that each transformation takes equally long. If so, changing a kernel to a negative should take about the same time as changing a kernel to a passive. In fact, any conversion requiring only one transformation should take the same time; and any conversion requiring two transformations should take twice as long as those requiring only one.

Miller, McKean, and Slobin tested the foregoing possibilities with an experiment based on Donders' subtraction method (see Chapter 5). They

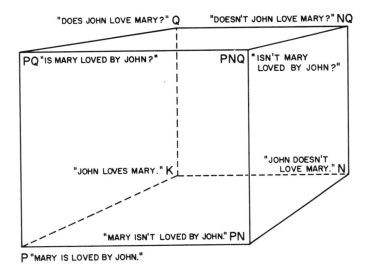

FIG. 10.13.   Illustration of the number of transforms between sentence types (P = passive, N = negative, Q = question, K = kernel).

TABLE 10.3
Example of a Sentence-Matching Test Designed by Miller, McKean, and Slobin
(Miller, 1962) to Study Transformations Between Affirmative-Passive
and Negative-Passive Sentences

—The old woman was warned by Joe	1. The small boy wasn't warned by John
—The small boy wasn't liked by Joe	2. The old woman wasn't warned by Jane
—The young man was liked by John	3. The young man was warned by Jane
—The old woman wasn't liked by Joe	4. The old woman wasn't warned by Joe
—The young man wasn't warned by Jane	5. The old woman was liked by John
—The small boy was liked by Jane	6. The small boy wasn't liked by John
—The young man wasn't liked by Jane	7. The young man wasn't warned by John
—The old woman was warned by Jane	8. The old woman was warned by John
—The small boy wasn't warned by Joe	9. The young man wasn't warned by Joe
—The small boy was warned by John	10. The small boy was warned by Jane
—The young man was warned by John	11. The small boy was warned by Joe
—The small boy wasn't warned by Jane	12. The small boy wasn't liked by Jane
—The small boy was liked by John	13. The young man wasn't liked by John
—The young man wasn't liked by Joe	14. The young man was liked by Jane
—The young man was warned by Joe	15. The old woman was liked by Joe
—The old woman was liked by Jane	16. The old woman wasn't liked by Jane
—The old woman wasn't liked by John	17. The small boy was liked by Joe
—The old woman wasn't warned by John	18. The young man was liked by Joe

gave people lists of sentences similar to those shown in Table 10.3. The
subjects were to read the sample sentences, determine how they were related
to each other, and match the sentence in the left-hand column with the
appropriately transformed sentence in the right-hand column. Different
people were instructed to convert kernels to negatives, kernels to passives,
kernels to passive negatives, passives to passive negatives, negatives to passive
negatives, and negatives to passives. As a control, some subjects matched
identical sentences from the right- and left-hand column, to show how long
matching took when no transformation was necessary. By subtracting the

TABLE 10.4
Results of Experiment by Miller, McKean, and Slobin (Miller, 1962)

	Estimated Transformation Time
Negative transformation only	
K — N	1.1
P — PN	1.2
Passive transformation only	
K — P	1.5
N — PN	1.8
Negative and passive transformation	
K — PN	2.7
N — P	3.5

time required to do the control sentences from the time required to do the experimental sentences, Miller and his associates estimated how much time was attributable to the transformations required for each sort of conversion. They divided this estimate by the total number of sentences matched to estimate the amount of time *per sentence* attributable to the mental operations required by the transformation(s). The estimates so computed are presented in Table 10.4. The more transformations required, the longer people took to perform the matching task. Single transformations took similar amounts of time, whether passive or negative. Two transformations took slightly more than twice as long as one transformation. These results are quite consistent with predictions suggested by transformational grammar, and they are not readily predictable from intuitive considerations alone. Still, these findings do not establish that people perform the transformations in exactly the same way as the rules work in transformational grammar. They simply suggest that the transformation rules of the grammar correspond to some mental operations that take time.

As if to converge on the conclusions of Miller, McKean, and Slobin (Miller, 1962), Clifton, Kurcz, and Jenkins (1965) used a different technique to test the psychological distance between various transforms. They had people study a long list of unrelated sentences, and then gave them other sentences, one at a time, with instructions to press a key for each test sentence they believed to be from the original list. Some of the test sentences were from the original list, some were grammatical transforms of the original sentences, and some were new unrelated sentences. Subjects seldom pressed the key to new unrelated sentences, but they frequently did for transforms; they believed they had seen many of the transforms in the original list. Clifton and associates took frequency of false recognition responses as a metric of the psychological distance between the transforms. This metric yielded results that paralleled those of Miller, McKean, and Slobin, with the exception that negatives and kernels were more psychologically distant from each other than Miller, McKean, and Slobin's work suggested. All in all, we would say that transformational generative theory fared reasonably well in the tests by Clifton and Miller and their associates.

Perhaps because psycholinguistics was a new field, without established methodologies, a host of methods was invented to test the psychological reality of concepts from transformational generative theory. Consider an experiment by Savin and Perchonock (1965), who relied on the idea that immediate memory is of limited capacity. You will recall that in 1965 it was widely held that the capacity of immediate memory was about seven items or chunks of items (Miller, 1956). Savin and Perchonock reasoned that a kernel sentence would be treated as a chunk, so that one kernel sentence and six unrelated words would fill the available spaces in short-term memory. But what if the subject had to recall six unrelated items plus a transformed sentence? Would memory span be exceeded? If the transformation had to be remembered separately from the kernel, more than seven items would have been stored, because the subject must recall six words, plus the kernel, plus the transformation. You might better understand the reasoning of Savin and Perchonock by imagining a trough just long enough to hold seven bowling balls. When an eighth ball is pushed in, the first one falls out. The eighth ball is analogous to a transformational tag that might displace an unrelated word.

Savin and Perchonock asked people to memorize a sentence plus some unrelated words. The sentences varied in number of transformations, and the word lists ranged in length from two to eight. The instructions emphasized the sentence; people were to recall the sentence exactly, and then recall as many words from the list as possible. Savin and Perchonock predicted that the word lists would be recalled less accurately when the sentence to be recalled was more complex. Their subjects' performance confirmed this prediction; more words were remembered in connection with kernel sentences than with transformed sentences. Savin and Perchonock's method has been criticized, but their experiment stands as an example of creative and imaginative scientific investigation.

A number of other methods were used to show that linguistic transformations have psychological consequences. McMahon (1963) found that people could respond "true" more quickly to such statements as *Three follows one* than to such sentences as *One is followed by three*, or *One does not follow three*. This suggested that the active affirmative sentence is internally processed more quickly than the passive or the negative. Gough (1965, 1966) required his subjects to read a sentence. Then he presented a picture, and timed how long was required to judge whether the sentence was true or false, in view of the picture. The sentences were kernels, passives, negatives, or passive negatives. Gough found that active sentences were verified faster than passives, and affirmatives faster than negatives. This was true even if the passive sentences were shortened by deleting the agent phrase beginning with *by*. Slobin (1966) gave this sort of task to different age groups from kindergarten to adult. He included sentences that were reversible and others that were not. A reversible sentence is one that remains meaningful when the subject and object are reversed. For example, *The dog is chasing the cat* can be reversed to *The cat is chasing the dog*; but *The girl is watering the flowers* cannot be reversed to *The flowers are watering the girl*. Slobin's results were essentially the same as those of Gough (1965, 1966), but only for reversible sentences. For nonreversible sentences, syntax (number of transformations) made little difference. Presumably, this was because syntax could affect truth and falsity only for reversible sentences; subjects had to consider who was chasing whom in the case of *The cat is being chased by the dog*. But in the case of *The flowers are being watered by the girl*, a judgment of *true* could be made as soon as the subject found both girl and flowers in the picture, regardless of whether the sentence was expressed in active or passive voice. This outcome was one of the first signals that the psychological effects of syntax might be overridden by extralinguistic factors such as context, the subject's knowledge, expectations and beliefs, and the like. We return to these matters later, when we discuss the research directions taken by psycholinguists when they moved beyond the study of grammar.

So far, we have considered only experiments based on the 1957 version of Chomsky's theory. The results of these and many other psycholinguistic investigations done before 1965 indicated that linguistic theory had much to contribute to cognitive psychology. In 1965, when Chomsky published his revised (standard) theory, psycholinguistics was one of the fastest-growing cognitive research fields. Its major focus was syntax, and while an occasional experimental outcome (e.g., Slobin, 1966; Wason, 1965) suggested that nonsyntactic factors deserved more attention than they were receiving, the ever-increasing number of psycholinguists maintained their enthusiasm for testing linguistic theories. They were struck that in a few years psychology had discovered grammar, acquired a ready-made grammatical theory, and used this theory to predict the outcomes of a host of laboratory experiments. There was little doubt that linguistic theory captured an important part of the truth about actual language processing. Moreover, there was a sense of further progress in the works. Thus, when Chomsky (1965) introduced the revised version of transformational grammar, psycholinguists were quick to derive predictions from it and to subject them to laboratory test. The revised theory's new concept of deep structure received most attention.

D. The Psychological Reality of Deep Structures

Like the other concepts that attracted the early attention of psycholinguistics, deep structures were invented to meet formal requirements of the linguistic paradigm. Such concepts were not designed to explain data from psychological experiments nor to guide such experimentation. Deep structures were pure abstractions. They were part of the derivational history of a concrete surface structure, but they themselves were inexpressible in concrete terms. The deep structure did represent certain meaningful relationships, such as "actor," "acted upon," "acted for," and so on, but there was considerable confusion about how closely deep structure should be identified with meaning. The murkiness of the term *meaning* added to the confusion, and Chomsky himself did little to clear up the issue. Psycholinguists were left to develop a psychological role for deep structures without help from their inventor, and their success was only a very general one. The psychological reality of the specifics of deep structures was never established. Instead, psycholinguists eventually turned their attention to semantics, but first they devised ways to study deep syntactic structures.

Recalling the centrality of memory experimentation to information-processing psychology, you may anticipate the role psychologists suggested for deep structure. Perhaps, they reasoned, deep structures provide a memory code. Although people *extract* information from surface structures (utterances, written matter), perhaps they *retain* information in deep structure format. This hypothesis was consistent with information-processing views of memory, according to which environmental inputs are recoded for processing and storage. The congeniality of this hypothesis to the information-processing approach no doubt explains why so many of the studies done to elucidate the role of deep structure were memory experiments.

Sachs (1967) reasoned that if people store information in deep structure format, memory for deep structure should last longer than memory for surface structure. Someone shown a sentence, and later asked whether another sentence is identical with it, might not notice changes of syntactic form but would recognize changes of the basic relationships among the elements in the sentence, because these relationships are fixed by the deep structure. To test this hypothesis, Sachs (1967) read her subjects stories, for example:

> There is an interesting story about the telescope. In Holland a man named Lippershey was an eyeglass maker. One day his children were playing with some lenses. They discovered that things seemed very close if two lenses were held about a foot apart. Lippershey began experimenting and his spyglass attracted much attention. *He sent a letter about it to Galileo, the great Italian scientist.* Galileo at once realized the importance of the discovery and set about to build an instrument of his own. He used an old organ pipe with one lens curved out and the other in. On the first clear night he pointed the glass toward the sky. He was amazed to find the empty dark spaces filled with bright gleaming stars. Night after night Galileo climbed to a high tower, sweeping the sky with his telescope. One night he saw Jupiter, and to his great surprise discovered near it three bright stars, two to the east and one to the west. On the next night, however, all were to the west. A few nights later there were four little stars [pp. 438–439].

Notice the sentence in italics. Sachs interrupted the story (0, 80, or 160 syllables following presentation of the italicized sentence) to ask whether a test sentence was exactly the same as a sentence from the story. The test sentences were either identical with the italicized sentence, semantically changed, syntactically changed, or formally changed:

Identical: He sent a letter about it to Galileo, the great Italian scientist.

Semantic change: Galileo, the great Italian scientist, sent him a letter about it.

Syntactic change: A letter about it was sent to Galileo, the great
                     Italian scientist.
Formal change: He sent Galileo, the great Italian scientist, a
                     letter about it.

Semantic changes alter deep structure, while syntactic and formal changes alter only surface structure. Sachs predicted the syntactic and formal changes would be noticed only when the test sentence was presented immediately after the target sentence but that deep structure (semantic) changes would be noticed following 80 and 160 as well as after zero syllables. Her results confirmed this prediction. After 80 syllables, subjects were only guessing whether the identical, syntactically changed, and formally changed test sentences were exactly like a previously presented one. But if the change was semantic, they correctly noticed the change about 80% of the time, even after 160 syllables. These results can be taken as evidence of the psychological reality of deep structures, but they can also be cited as evidence that semantic factors are more important than syntactic ones. The source of this indeterminacy is that deep structures can only be manipulated indirectly, by changing semantics; so a question remains as to exactly what the indirect manipulations have accomplished.

Layton and Simpson (1975) tested the hypothesis that people retain surface structure when demands on memory are light, but they recode into deep structures when there is a lot to remember. To test this idea, Layton and Simpson relied on previously established facts: Active-voice questions are generally easier than passives (McMahon, 1963), but when a question is asked about a just-presented sentence, the answer comes most easily if both sentence and question are active or both are passive (Wright, 1972). Thus, the question, *Did the truck hit the car?* is generally easier to answer than *Was the car hit by a truck?* But the passive question is easier if it is asked immediately after a person is told, *The car was hit by the truck.* Layton and Simpson reasoned that agreement in voice (active or passive) between sentence and question should be important if subjects are responding by interrogating surface structures, but only the voice of the question should matter if they are interrogating deep structures. If subjects retain surface structures briefly, and recode to deep structures for longer retention, then voice agreement should be most helpful immediately after presentation of the sentence, whereas actively phrased questions should be most helpful later on. Layton and Simpson found essentially this result. They concluded that subjects respond on the basis of surface structure if they are interrogated immediately, but by the time several sentences have intervened they respond only on the basis of deep structure.

Blumenthal (1967) used the method of prompted recall to get at the role of deep structures. Blumenthal's idea was that some words would be more effective than others as prompts to recall a forgotten sentence. Perhaps, he thought, the most effective prompt word could be predicted from deep structure diagrams. Deep structures are generated by rules similar to those of phrase structure grammar; so it is possible to diagram deep structures. Blumenthal had people memorize lists of sentences, including ones like these:

(18) Gloves were made by tailors.
(19) Gloves were made by hand.

Despite their superficial similarity, Sentences (18) and (19) have very different deep structure diagrams. The word *tailors* is the logical subject in the deep structure of Sentence (18). It is a much more central word than *hand* in Sentence (19). Blumenthal gave his subjects many such sentences, and then prompted their recall with a single word from each sentence. As predicted, *tailors* proved to be a more effective prompt than *hand*. Several other experiments using the method of prompted recall have shown that prompt effectiveness can be predicted from characteristics of deep-structure tree diagrams (Blumenthal & Boakes, 1967; Danks & Sorce, 1973; Wanner, 1974). In some of these studies, the predictions were not at all intuitively obvious.

The positive findings from the foregoing experiments, all of which used memory measures, have been supplemented by positive findings using other sorts of procedures (e.g., Bever, Lackner, & Kirk, 1969; Stanners, Headley, & Clark, 1972). Nevertheless, Chomsky's standard theory has been used less and less often as the basis for psycholinguistics research. Why? We suggest the following reasons for the decreasing reliance of psycholinguists on linguistic theory. Some of them reflect the rational, and others the conventional, component of science.

First, consider the consequences for psychologists of the changed status of kernel sentences in Chomsky's revised theory. In his original theory, kernel sentences were the objects of transformation rules. Phrase structure grammar operated on simple, active, affirmative, declarative sentences to produce other types. In the revised theory, kernel sentences, like all others, are the result of deep structure transformations. When kernel sentences were primary, and passives, negatives, questions, and compounds were derived from them, it could be predicted that people would find simple sentences, actives, affirmatives, and declaratives relatively easier to process than compounds, passives, negatives, and questions. This prediction required no identification of mental processes with the transformations specified in linguistic theory. It only required the assumption that some additional transformation was required for complex sentences that was not required for kernels. But in the second version of transformational grammar, all surface structures, including kernels, result from the operation of transformational rules. The differential ease of processing sentences cannot be attributed to some unspecified additional step. Rather, the complexity of the derivation from deep to surface structure must provide the explanation for the differential ease of these sentence types. Using derivational complexity to predict behavioral data amounts to assuming that the steps in the mathematical formalism of linguistic theory correspond to psychological processes. Such an assumption cannot be made lightly, because formalisms from nonbehavioral theories seldom correspond to cognitive processes. Recall the problems of assuming that cognitive processes work in binary fashion, as the information-theory formalism does (see p. 143). Indeed, when technical properties of the formalism of transformational grammar have been used to make predictions, the results have been inconsistent. Positive findings (Blumenthal, 1967; Blumenthal & Boakes, 1967; Danks & Sorce, 1973; Wanner, 1974) have already been reviewed. But contrary data are about as frequent. For example, Lesgold (1972) determined that the word "aunt" appeared twice in the deep structure diagram of Sentence (20), but only once in Sentence (21). He reasoned that "aunt" should be a more effective prompt for Sentence (20); but in fact it was an equally good prompt for both sentences. Furthermore, a grounds of derivational complexity, center embedded sentences such as (22) should be simpler than right-branching ones such as (23).

(20) The aunt was senile and she ate the pie.
(21) The aunt was senile and Alice ate the pie.
(22) The man the dog the girl owned bit died.
(23) The girl owned the dog that bit the man that died.

But sentences with multiple center embeddings are actually harder to process and harder to recall than their right-branching counterparts (Blumenthal, 1966; Stolz, 1967). In fact, Sentence (22) does not seem like a sentence at all to many people, although it is technically grammatical.

The most successful laboratory tests of transformational grammar have addressed the broad implications of its concepts. Tests based on specific aspects of the formal system have not demonstrated that they have psychological reality. It is safe to conclude from the broadly conceived research that syntax is part of people's linguistic competence and that it determines some aspects of language performance. People use relationships among sentences in various laboratory tests of memory and perception. It seems certain that people apprehend sentences on at least two levels. Perhaps there are psychological processes corresponding to the formal linguistic operations that convert the deep structures to surface structures in the standard theory, but the research has not uneqivocally shown their existence. Nevertheless, the general concepts of deep and surface structure do capture an important dimension of language processing. People appear to make at least two representations of a sentence, one containing the literal content including syntactic form, and one containing the interpreted content, which is more similar to meaning. In general, memory for literal content is more transient than memory for interpreted content.

These conclusions have not long been as obvious as they may now seem. Several generations of psychologists ignored language and its syntactic organization as a research problem. Some rejected syntax outright, preferring to treat its apparent organization as a byproduct of conditioned language behavior. Others regarded the problem as an interesting one, but felt that researching it was impossible. The impact of linguistics on psychology has been altogether wholesome insofar as it stimulated research interest and, with it, the development of adequate scientific techniques for the study of language. This contribution will far outlive the detailed aspects of any particular theory, including Chomsky's impressive and powerful standard theory of transformational grammar, from which the field has already largely turned.

V. SEMANTICS AND PRAGMATICS

Psycholinguists have turned mostly from primary interest in syntactic variables to the study of semantic and pragmatic concerns. The reason lies partly in the frequent discovery that the effects of syntax vary with the experimental context in which they are studied. Experiments designed to assess syntactic variables revealed that their effects depend on nonsyntactic factors.

Recall the experiment by Slobin (1966), which was one of the earlier tests of the psychological reality of phrase structure grammar. Slobin found that passive sentences take longer to verify against pictures than active sentences, but only when the sentences are reversible. Thus, sentences such as *The dog chased the cat* were verified faster than sentences such as *The cat was chased by the dog*. When the sentences were not reversible, there was no difference between active and passive sentences. Such sentences as *The maid drew the curtains* and *The curtains were drawn by the maid* were verified equally fast in Slobin's study. Explaining these results seems to require appeal to people's knowledge of the world. Reference to syntax alone will not do. When the sentences were not reversible, all people had to determine was that the maid and curtains were both in the picture and that the verb was correct: A picture of a maid drawing window curtains would verify either the active or passive sentence, because people knew they need not consider anomalous sentences like *The maid was drawn by the curtains*. For reversible sentences (*The cat chased the dog*) they had to perform the additional step of confirming that the picture corresponded to the particular real-world possibility conveyed by the sentence. In Slobin's study, the effect of a linguistic variable was determined by nonlinguistic factors, which eventually pointed psycholinguists toward the study of semantic factors.

Like Slobin, Wason (1965) also showed the effects of nonsyntactic variables before their time had come. Wason's research showed that contextual conditions determine experimental responses to negative sentences. The use of negation is closely bound to the pragmatic expectations of communicators: There are some contexts in which it makes sense to use a negative and others in which the negative is peculiar. Wason showed that peculiar negatives delay processing. Wason presented stimuli consisting of eight circles, seven in one color and one in a different color. Subjects were given sentence beginnings to complete in such a way that the statement was true (see Fig. 10.14). For example, the subject might be shown a display in which circle 4 was red and the rest were green. Wason timed how long it took to complete sentences beginning either

Circle #4 is . . . (red)   Circle #6 is . . . (green)
Circle #4 is not . . . (green)   Circle #6 is not . . . (red)

The last type of completion was considerably slower than the others. It seemed easier for people to report that the exceptional circle was not green than to report that one of the unexceptional circles was not red. As Wason remarks, it is more informative to say that *A whale is not a fish* than to say, for example, *A herring is not a mammal*. This appears to result, not from

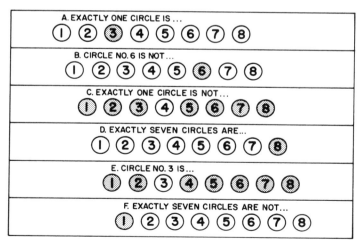

FIG. 10.14. Using the words "dark" and "light," complete the following statements with respect to the accompanying illustrations. Are any of them easier than others?

syntactic factors, but from pragmatic ones; most people know that a whale might be misclassified as a fish, but a herring is unlikely to be misclassified as a mammal. Similarly, it makes more sense to say, *The train was not late this morning,* when the train is usually late than when it is usually punctual.

Slobin (1966) and Wason (1965) reported their findings when psycholinguistics was just beginning to research the effects of syntax and when the field was not ready to wrestle with the problem of extralinguistic context. Later results paved the way more effectively. For example, Olson and Filby (1972) found that passives are sometimes easier than actives. They presented sentence–picture combinations for verification, such as *The truck was hit by the car* followed by a picture of a car hitting a truck. Without context, actives are generally faster than passives in such a task. However, Olson and Filby preceded the presentation of the sentence–picture pair with a passage about either the truck or the car. When the preceding passage was about the logical object of the sentence (in the example given, the truck), passives were verified faster than actives. When the passage was about the logical subject, the reverse was true.

Still another finding emphasizing nonsyntactic factors concerns *marking.* According to transformational grammar, some words should be more complex than others because they are marked. These words are governed by more restrictions on their use, and are less salient semantically than unmarked terms. Bipolar adjectives illustrate the principle. The pair of words *good* and *bad* are bipolar, but they are not entirely symmetrical. *Good* can mean either very good or somewhat neutral; while *bad* must mean bad. Consider the questions, *How good is your physics class?* and *How bad is your physics class?* The latter question presumes the class bad, while the former does not presume it is good. In this pair, the word *bad* is marked, while the word *good* is unmarked. Prepositions can also be marked or unmarked; *above* is unmarked, while *below* is marked. There is some evidence that marked forms are learned later by young children, and in general they are harder to process (Clark & Chase, 1972; Seymour, 1973). Using a picture–sentence verification task, Clark and Chase measured the time to verify such statements as *The star is above the plus* and *The plus is below the star* against the corresponding picture. Sentences containing *above* were verified more quickly than those containing *below*, an outcome that comports nicely with predictions from linguistic theory. However, Clark and Chase (1972) were able to reverse this outcome, obtaining faster response times for *below* sentences, simply by telling subjects to attend to the bottom of the picture. The reference point adopted by the subject—an extralinguistic factor—determined the effect of the linguistic variable.

Another challenge to the primacy of linguistic factors in language processing studies comes from experiments on imagery. Psycholinguists considered linguistic deep structure as a mode of memory storage, but mental images can also be a powerful storage modality (Paivio, 1971). When a person hears the sentence *The truck hit the car*, he could store it as a linguistic deep structure and, upon recall, consult his linguistic representation to produce a correct answer in sentence recognition or verification tasks. Or, he might store a mental image, rather like an internal pictorial representation of a truck hitting a car. Upon request for information about the previously presented sentence, then, the subject may consult a pictorial, not a linguistic representation.

In an effort to resolve this question, Danks and Sorce (1973) used a prompted recall task with full passives such as *Grades were issued by professors* and "agent-replaced" passives such as *Grades were issued by letter*. According to a deep structure analysis, agent-replaced passives are more complex than full passives. Given linguistic storage, full passive sentences should be recalled better than passive sentences with the agent replaced, and indeed this was true. However, Danks and Sorce also varied the imagery value of their prompt words. For example, their sentences might include *Grades were issued by letter* and *Grades were issued by tradition*. It is easier to construct a mental image for the word *letter* than for the word *tradition*, and thus *letter* should prove a better prompt according to an imagery theory. Again, this is what Danks and Sorce found. However, the deep-structure complexity interacted with the imagery value of the prompt word: imagery only made a difference in the relatively complex replaced-agent sentences, and sentence complexity only made a difference in the low-imagery prompt condition. Danks and Sorce concluded that the subject has a choice of strategies. He may encode linguistically, or he may encode imaginally. The choice will no doubt depend on which he perceives to be more difficult in view of the task he thinks he is supposed to perform—in other words, the subject's choice of strategy will be determined by extralinguistic, pragmatic, contextual, and situational influences.

Other findings that highlight semantic and pragmatic matters concern the ordering of the adjectives. There is a conventional ordering, which appears among many languages (Danks & Schwenk, 1972, 1974). As a rule, adjectives ordered in the conventional way are easier to process. It is generally easier to understand someone saying, *The large red Italian car* than someone saying *The red Italian large car*. However, varying contextual factors can make it easier to respond to or produce unconventionally ordered adjectives. If someone is shown four pictures resembling those in the right-hand panel of Fig. 10.15, it is easier to say *The large red car*. However, people shown the four pictures in the left-hand panel will frequently say *The RED large car*. Pragmatic factors override linguistic ones in unusual situations.

Transformational grammar was conceived by Chomsky as a competence model, not a performance model. It described idealized language knowledge. Chomsky realized that additional theories would be needed to explain how

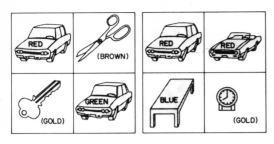

FIG. 10.15.   Illustration of situations in which pragmatic factors override linguistic factors (see text).

people actualize their ideal knowledge in real contexts, like psychological experiments. It should not be surprising that contextual factors influence performance in such experiments. What may be surprising, at least from the optimistic perspective of the early 1960s, is the extent to which context and world knowledge determine the outcomes of language experiments. Experiments designed to study linguistic variables showed their effects to be so contingent on extralinguistic influences that it has become necessary to move on to the building of theories of knowledge. Psycholinguists' research has moved in the last several years toward developing joint theories of world knowledge and language use. This work blends ideas about semantic memory discussed in the last chapter with psycholinguistic insights. This exciting and promising sort of cognitive research and theory are the topics of Chapter 11.

VI.   CASE GRAMMAR

We conclude this chapter by asking whether transformational grammar is the most suitable theory of linguistic competence to guide psychological research. The concepts of deep and surface structure can be accepted without keeping the standard theory's view of the nature of deep structure. At one time, the standard theory was the only available competence theory, but linguists now offer several alternatives. A new generation of linguists, who were educated during and after the Chomskian revolution, are dissatisfied with certain properties of Chomsky's theory. They feel particularly strongly that the generative order of the standard theory is wrong and that its version of deep structure is insufficiently semantic. The standard theory works from syntax to semantics and phonology. The major constraints on its generation of strings are syntactic. Its semantic and phonological components are dependent on its syntactic component for their inputs; they interpret strings generated by an order-oriented rule system. A group of younger linguists, known as *generative semanticists*, have concluded that many rules of syntax are predicated on semantic and extralinguistic considerations. They feel that there is insufficient place in the standard theory for such influences. Consider the correct use of *who* and *which*. Their use is certainly a syntactic matter; but the correct choice of *who* or *which* may depend on extralinguistic beliefs of the speaker. G. Lakoff (1971) supplied these examples:

(26) My cat, who thinks I'm a fool, enjoys tormenting me.
(27) *My cat, which thinks I'm a fool, enjoys tormenting me.

The anomaly of (27) stems from the fact that human intelligence is attributed to the cat, under which circumstance *who* is the correct term. But cats need not always be referred to by *who*, since (28) seems perfectly acceptable:

(28) My cat, which was a birthday present, is a Siamese.

Likewise, Lakoff notes that humanness does not always require *who*:

(29) We have just found a good name for our child, who we hope will grow up to be a good citizen after he is born.
(30) *We have just found a good name for our child, who we hope will be conceived tonight.

The grammatical rule dictating *who* or *which* seems expressible only in terms of the speaker's beliefs. The standard theory precludes inclusion of such rules.

R. Lakoff (1969) noted a similar problem with the terms *some* and *any*. Their use depends not only on the knowledge and beliefs of the speaker, but also on the knowledge and beliefs of his hearer, as well as the knowledge and beliefs attributed to the subject of the utterance. Here are some examples:

(31) John wants to marry that girl, and her name is Betsy.
(32) John wants to marry some girl, and her name is Betsy.
(33) *John wants to marry any girl, and her name is Betsy.

The oddity of (33) is that its *any* implies that the speaker does not think that John has yet selected the girl he will marry; so it is anomalous to mention her name. The word *some* implies that John knows who the girl is, that the speaker knows impersonal facts about her, but the speaker does not know her well; hence the oddity of (34):

(34) *John wants to marry some girl, and she is my sister.

The problem in each of these examples is apparently in the generation of deep structures from syntactic rules. Some contemporary linguists are exploring alternative formulations of deep structure, formulations that imbue the generation of deep structures with greater semantic force. They are working in the tradition of generative grammar and are committed to the concept of deep-to-surface-structure transformations. Thus, no new revolution is under way in linguistics. The field is unified in its commitment to Chomsky's paradigm. It is only his theory that generative semanticists challenge.

There are several current models of generative semantics. None of them solve all the problems raised by generative semanticists, but all are committed to semantically motivated generation of deep structure. The one suggested by Fillmore (1968), called case grammar, is particularly relevant to cognitive psychology, for it has guided some psycholinguistic research and influenced several models of comprehension. The major difference between Fillmore's approach and Chomsky's is their source of deep structures. In case grammar, deep structures do not emerge from phrase structure rules, nor do they contain ordered constituents, such as noun phrase, verb phrase, and adjective. Instead, Fillmore's deep structures contain a modality component and a proposition. The elements of the modality component apply to the entire proposition. They include, for example, mood, aspect, negation, and past tense. The proposition itself, which is the psychologically more interesting part of the structure, consists of a verb and an unordered list of noun phrases. The noun phrases play semantic roles.

In Fillmore's system, deep structure generation begins with a verb. Stored with each verb is a list of the cases that it requires, admits, and precludes. Consider the verb *repair*. Repairing requires an agent to make the repair, and an object to be repaired. There must also be an instrument with which the repair is done. *Repair* thus has three essential cases: Agent, Object, and Instrument. Other verbs require different cases. For instance, *backtrack* precludes an object, while *decay* precludes an instrument. Verb selection is accomplished by a generative process that proceeds automatically through all the verbs in the language. Selection of the verb determines the propositional deep structure. The rules of the system specify that there be a noun phrase for each case required or permitted by the verb.

Look now at Fig. 10.16. The proposition has the deep structure required by the verb *repair*. It has the three noun phrases specified by the verb. Each noun phrase includes a *case morpheme*, which is also determined by the verb, and which indicates the case of each noun: *by* for Agent, *to* for Object, and *with* for Instrument. The next step is application of transformational rules to convert these deep structures into surface structures. One function of the transformation rules is to delete case morphemes where a particular surface structure demands such deletion. Thus, *by* is deleted in the Active transform, but not in the Passive. In our example, *Lisa repaired the doll with tape* reflects the deletion of *by* and *to* in Agent and Object, respectively. The *by* is not deleted in the passive: *The doll was repaired with tape by Lisa*. Transformation rules also permit the deletion of whole noun phrases, as in *The doll was repaired*. It is important to note that the deletion is in the transformation from deep to surface structure. At the level of deep structure,

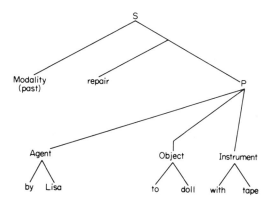

FIG. 10.16. Case grammar diagram of a sentence.

all of the elements are present, whether or not they appear in the surface
structure. Therefore, the deep structure in Fig. 10.16 underlies all of the
following surface structures, as well as a number of others that you can
probably think of:

> Lisa repaired the doll with tape.
> Lisa repaired the doll with something.
> Lisa repaired something with tape.
> Someone repaired the doll with tape.
> Lisa repaired the doll.
> The doll was repaired with tape by Lisa.
> The doll was repaired with tape.
> The doll was repaired by Lisa.
> The doll was repaired.

In case grammar, sentence elements maintain their (deep structure) case
category whatever their form in surface structure. Thus, in the deep structure
of *The janitor opened the door with this key, key* is the instrument, *door* is the
object, and *janitor* is the agent. *Door* and *key* play the same semantic roles in
every surface realization of this deep structure. Despite the variety of
grammatical functions represented by *key* and *door* in the following
sentences, Fillmore's grammar treats all of the sentences as instances of a deep
structure in which *key* is an Instrument and *door* is an Object.

(35) The janitor opened the door with this key.
(36) The door opened with this key.
(37) The door was opened with this key.
(38) This key opened the door.
(39) The door opened.

To get a sense of how different the role of *janitor* and *key* are in sentences (35) and (38), where both are surface structure subjects, consider the two fragments *The janitor opened the door . . .* and *This key opened the door . . .* The former fragment can be completed by *with this key* to yield sentence (35). But the second fragment cannot be completed in the equivalent way to yield *This key opened the door with itself.* Why not? Because one's intuitions are that the Instrument has already been supplied and the completion is redundant; furthermore, this construction attempts to treat *key* as an Agent when it has already been interpreted as Instrument. This kind of test is often used by linguists to reveal hidden differences between sentences that may not be obvious from their surface structure.

Fillmore's system has stimulated two sorts of psychological research. There have been studies of the primacy of the verb and the psychological status of the cases. The verb is central in case grammar, and there is some evidence that it is psychologically primary as well. Glucksberg, Trabasso, and Wald (1973) used a sentence–picture verification task in which the sentences of interest were false. Glucksberg et al. made the sentence false relative to the picture by virtue of either the subject, the verb, or the object. For example, a picture of a car hitting a tree might be paired with sentences such as *The train hit the tree* (subject mismatch), *The car passed the tree* (verb mismatch), *The car hit the pole* (object mismatch). Verb mismatches were detected fastest, which suggests that verbs provide organizational pivots for other elements of the sentence. The success of this experiment led Glucksberg et al. to build a sentence processing model around verb-determined case relations, but not all experimental tests of the centrality of verbs have been so successful. For example, Fillenbaum and Rapoport (1974) failed to find a predicted similarity among certain kinds of verbs. An interesting sidelight of this experiment is that Fillmore himself served as one of its subjects. The data he contributed were no more supportive of his theory than those of the other participants, who were college students.

Shafto (1973) tried to demonstrate the psychological reality of the case relations, Agent, Instrument, Object, and Experiencer (which is the case of the word *Joe* in *Joe suffered.*). Shafto gave his subjects cards, each containing a sentence with an underlined word. The underlined word was either the Agent, the Object, the Experiencer, or the Instrument. Subjects were told to sort the sentences on the basis of the underlined word. Perfect sorting would have meant putting together all underlined Agents, all Objects, and so on; but the subjects were not given case definitions. They were simply told *right* or *wrong* whenever they placed a card with others. Shafto reasoned that if cases have psychological reality, subjects would induce the case relation that underlies all of the words that function as agents, all that function as objects, and so on.

Agent was the easiest case to learn, followed by Experiencer, Instrument, and Object; however, performance was relatively poor and the data did not support the psychological reality of the cases. Furthermore, it appears that Fillmore himself has abandoned the system, partly because of the difficulty of specifying a manageable number of cases. Also, some of his cases apply to many verbs, but others suit only a few. Some verbs require cases that are appropriate to very few other verbs. This inelegance is paradigmatically unacceptable to linguists. They cannot postulate an approximate number of cases; they must name all of them and specify the circumstances of their use. The number should be tractable; thousands of cases will not do. Psycholinguists, on the other hand, are free to test the broader implications of the concept of case. Perhaps this is why psychologists are exhibiting more interest in Fillmore's system these days than he is. Psychologists' uses of case grammar in global models of language, meaning, and memory is discussed in Chapter 12.

VII. SUMMARY

From the 15 to 20 years of psychological research on syntax, we may draw both factual and paradigmatic conclusions. The research establishes these general facts about language and cognition:

1. People know about syntax, and that linguistic knowledge is reflected in their performance.
2. Phrase-structure and transformational-grammar analyses of language are compatible with behavioral data. This does not mean that linguistic theories specify how people perform the mental steps underlying language performances, but it does suggest that theories of such processing will need to incorporate such concepts as deep structure, surface structure, transformation, rule, and constituent.
3. The steps by which transformational grammar converts an active sentence to a passive are probably not the mental processes by which a person does so.
4. There is something special about actives, affirmatives, and declaratives as compared to passives, negatives, and interrogatives that make them generally easier to process—that is, to understand and recall.
5. The literal form of sentences and their interpreted form are partially independent. Memory for the literal form is less permanent than that for the interpreted form; details of syntactic structure are usually forgotten quickly, while semantic content is retained for quite a while.
6. The effects of linguistic variables on performance depends largely on extralinguistic factors.

What paradigmatic conclusions can we draw? It is fair to say that the honeymoon of psychology and linguistics ended sometime after 1970. The relationship between the two disciplines has become less intimate. One reason is the disappointing outcome of the psychological experimentation that stemmed from Chomsky's 1965 theory. Another reason is that, by 1970, both psychology and linguistics had entered a period of normal science. In general, discussion between disciplines is most productive during revolutionary times. As the last scientific revolution recedes further into the past, research and theorizing are determined less and less by broad questions that interest nonspecialists. Research is dictated more and more by the outcomes of previous work. Issues and methods become more and more specialized. After 1970 psycholinguists were working on detailed processing models, and linguists were working on technical details of Chomsky's transformational grammar. The work of both linguistics and psycholinguistics was difficult to understand unless one knew the work of the previous 10 years. For psychologists, using recent linguistic ideas would require mastering a difficult literature, much of which was designed more to meet linguists' formal requirements than to support laboratory research. As the Chomskian revolution receded, the pervasive influence of semantic and pragmatic factors grew increasingly evident, and the study of semantic memory burgeoned. Many psycholinguists concluded that a satisfactory model of how people use their syntactic knowledge will not be forthcoming until we have a theory of how context influences language use. A theory of context, however, is not possible without a theory of how extralinguistic knowledge is represented. The implication of these claims is that language theories and theories of permanent memory and world knowledge ought to interface, and that research questions pertinent to both areas are most important in cognitive psychology. In fact, there is a large body of recent research and theory that concerns both permanent memory and psycholinguistics. We cover this convergence of these two areas in the next chapter.

11

Comprehension From the Psycholinguistic Viewpoint

ABSTRACT

I. *Overview*

Research and theory on comprehension grows from two different traditions. Some of the work comes from the psycholinguistic tradition and is a logical continuation of the work described in the previous chapter. Some emerges from the artificial-intelligence-plus-experimental-psychology tradition begun by Collins and Quillian and described in our chapter on Semantic Memory. This chapter describes the psycholinguistic approach to comprehension.

II. *The Concept of the Synthesized Code*

As interest turned away from syntactic theories and toward semantic issues, the field of psycholinguistics lost the unifying force of Chomsky's theories. Most contemporary researchers are interested in language comprehension, but no powerful model guides research. Several issues have emerged that can be grouped roughly into issues of form and issues of content. Some research concerns the form of a message when it has been understood, and some issues concern the content of the understood message. One relatively comprehensive model of conversational comprehension has been presented.

Information-processing psychologists believe that complex mental processes like comprehension involve a large number of unseen internal events that occur between input and observable response. These events include speech perception, parsing, word look-up, and many other things we have not yet thought of. We call these events, as a group, *input synthesis.* The end product of input synthesis is a representation that is compatible with the contents of permanent memory. We call this end product the *synthesized code.* Much research seeks to explain the form of the code or its contents.

III. *The Form of the Synthesized Code*

The major controversy regarding the form of the synthesized code is whether it is best characterized as a recoded linguistic string (a proposition) or as an analogue of visual experience (an image).

A. *Propositional Theories* Clark has been the major spokesman for the view that the synthesized code is propositional. His first theory (Clark, 1969) relied heavily on Chomsky's ideas and was intended to account for the way people solve reasoning problems. Later versions of the theory made less use of Chomsky's work and were validated by means of the sentence–picture verification task. All these theories conceived of the understanding process as recoding the literal input sentence into an abstract propositional format. Clark's interests have changed, but a descendant of his model has been proposed and defended by Carpenter and Just (1975).

B. *Dual Coding Theory* The main advocate of an imagery code has been Paivio. His position is not a "pure" imagery position but holds that synthesizing an imagery code is the normal strategy for understanding and recalling sentences. But when a sentence is abstract, images may not be available and a verbal code may be all that the comprehension process can extract. This dual coding theory (Begg & Paivio, 1969) has been widely challenged, primarily because the experiments that support the theory use abstract and concrete sentences that are not equally understandable in the first place. This difference in comprehensibility may account for the pattern of results that is taken as support for dual coding. However, the relationship between concreteness and comprehensibility remains an important fact to be explained.

IV. *Content of the Synthesized Code*
A literal account of the contents of an input sentence cannot explain the knowledge a person has as a result of hearing the sentence. Several lines of research converge on this claim.

A. *Constructive Synthesis* People do not accurately distinguish sentences actually heard in an experiment from plausible inferences, recombinations, or paraphrases of those sentences.

B. *The Role of Context* The meaning given to a word depends on the sentential context in which it is embedded. This is a problem for theories of word meaning, because it suggests that there may be no core of meaning that is always salient when the word is heard. On the other hand, it is implausible to suppose that word meanings are totally flexible. Context also supplies meaning to deictic terms such as *this* and *here*.

C. *The Role of Previous Knowledge* People bring their previous knowledge to the comprehension process in several different ways.

1. *Inference* Sentence-recognition experiments show that inferences are as familiar to subjects as the actually presented sentences, although they can distinguish actual sentences from plausible inferences if asked immediately.

2. *Presuppositions* Presupposed information is not evaluated for truth as much as asserted information. This makes it possible for the careful phrasing of questions to manipulate people's memory for events and to cause them to reconstruct events that did not happen.

3. *Nonliteral Comprehension* Sometimes what people extract from a message is not part of its literal content at all. Peculiar sentences are reinterpreted to reflect "what the speaker really meant," and conversational requests are easily understood. However, there is some evidence that

the literal meaning of conversational requests is computed at some point in the comprehension process.

V. *A Model of Conversational Comprehension*
Clark (1976) has suggested that speakers and hearers work within the confines of a sort of contract. Assuming that the speaker will adhere to the contract permits an efficient comprehension strategy in which the hearer locates information already in memory and incorporates new information into it. The theory is very new, but it accommodates much of the data reviewed in this chapter.

I. OVERVIEW

Until recently, very few psychologists studied comprehension, which concerns how permanently stored knowledge is used to interpret new inputs. Bartlett (1932) began to study comprehension several decades ago, but for years no one built on his beginnings, probably because comprehension seemed intractable to some and too mentalistic to others. It was not a respectable topic for research again until the information-processing approach became widespread, but even then it was ignored for a long while. The reason is probably the difficulty of researching comprehension. It is diffuse. Psychologists still have a hard time asking tightly researchable questions about it. No one is even certain how to define it. What does seem certain is that the processes responsible for comprehension are almost unbelievably flexible and many of them are volitionally controlled. Volitional control, in turn, is determined by factors that have usually been considered noncognitive. These include personality and the social situation in which communication takes place. There are thus imposing practical and paradigmatic reasons for cognitive psychologists to have avoided the study of comprehension. We might be avoiding it still, except that the matters we have been concerned with cannot be fully understood until we deal with the conceptual and experimental issues required to explain comprehension.

Psychologists have come to the study of comprehension from either psycholinguistics or semantic memory. Because the research area is so new, these lines are still distinct and largely separate. Some comprehension researchers ask questions and formulate experiments that are similar to those described in our chapter on psycholinguistics. Others have come to the study of comprehension from the study of semantic memory, long-term memory, or computer simulation of memory, and their work is similar to that of the modelers mentioned in Chapter 9. Figure 11.1 shows the intellectual antecedents of these two approaches to the study of comprehension.

This chapter describes the psycholinguistic approach to comprehension, which the figure shows is concerned with coding, context, and the role of previous knowledge. These issues grow from the psycholinguistic tradition described in Chapter 10. We saw there that psycholinguists began by studying syntax as a result of Chomsky's influence. Gradually, they became concerned with semantic and pragmatic determinants of language processing. Many psycholinguists eventually concluded that we will never understand how people process language until we specify the roles of previous knowledge and extralinguistic context on that processing. Accordingly, the views of such generative semanticists as Fillmore, Lakoff, McCawley, and Ross became more influential and the influence of Chomsky's views waned. Psycholinguistic research has moved away from syntax and toward other factors that affect comprehension.

Despite this change in content, the style of earlier psycholinguistic research remains. For example, the focus is still on episodic memory for recent linguistic events, and the sentence is still the most-used unit of stimulus

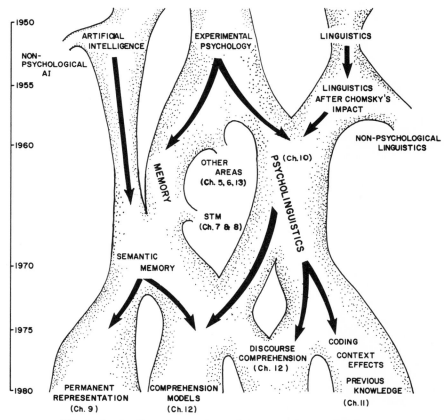

FIG. 11.1.   Intellectual antecedents of the study of comprehension.

materials. Psycholinguists still keep up with developments in linguistics, and these developments often influence their experiments; but linguistics is no longer the dominant force it was in the 1960s. Present psycholinguistic research uses methods that have been popular for 20 years or so. Despite the waning of Chomsky's standard theory, no sweeping model has replaced it. Rather, contemporary psycholinguistic studies are focused on narrowly defined issues rather than on global theoretical accounts of comprehension. Psycholinguistic researchers study permanent memory, but less for its own sake than because it is essential to a scientific understanding of language comprehension. There is no consensus among psycholinguists as to the best model of the structure of permanent memory. Most assume that permanent memory exists and that it is involved in comprehension, but as a group they have not adopted a unitary view of the memory structure.

The other group of scholars who study language comprehension comes from the same tradition as the modelers of semantic memory, and their work is described in the next chapter. As Fig. 11.1 shows, they share the influence of artificial intelligence. However, their models are more ambitious than those described in Chapter 9. The models described there are concerned with the permanent, standing structure of semantic memory. They were not intended as theories of how new information is integrated with old to form new structures. All were based primarily on sentence verification data. The models described in Chapter 12 are concerned with both the permanent memory structure and its modification by new inputs. The tasks they address are much more varied, and the models more comprehensive than the ones already described. We have dubbed them the "Global Models." Some of them are as big as anything the field of psychology has to offer. This chapter deals with the issue-oriented research that stems from earlier work in psycholinguistics, and the next chapter deals with the Global Models.

II. THE CONCEPT OF THE SYNTHESIZED CODE

For most of its early history, psycholinguistic research was heavily influenced by Chomsky's theories, first by his transformational grammar and then by his standard theory. Both, of course, emphasized syntax. As psycholinguists became interested in semantics, pragmatics, and world knowledge, Chomsky's theories provided fewer testable hypotheses. At the same time, linguistics became less unified. The result has been that linguistic theory currently provides fewer experimental hypotheses than it used to. Moreover, psychological theories of semantics are new and poorly developed, so that none of them provides general guidance for psycholinguistic experimentation. Psycholinguistic research is proceeding without an accepted theoretical superstructure, but the field is not in disarray. The information-processing paradigm still serves as a unifying force. In fact, previous research has yielded several general agreements, as summarized at the end of our chapter on psycholinguistics. And Clark (1976, 1973; Clark & Haviland, 1977; Haviland & Clark, 1974) is trying to formalize a precise and researchable theory of conversational language comprehension.

The terms *comprehension* and *understanding* have many meanings. We may understand a language, such as French. Or we may understand things, such as machines. We may understand a sentence, or we may understand the implications and consequences of a sentence. We may even understand whole fields, such as physics. Kochen, MacKay, Maron, Scriven, and Uhr (1964) have detailed the extraordinary range of capacities that are labeled understanding or comprehending. Just which are to be included in theory, and which are to be excluded, is an open matter. As you might guess, the paradigmatic preferences of researchers have determined their choices. Those whose orientation is strongly linguistic are likely to consider that the extraction of literal meaning is the central phenomenon; for them, the objective is to explain how syntax and deep structural relations are computed.

Researchers who are less linguistically motivated include considerably more, such as the determination of the implications of sentences and the drawing of inferences from them. The range of meanings and psychological processes to which comprehension should refer is still a matter of disagreement (see Clark, 1978), and we do not propose to legislate it here. Instead, we note that most psycholinguistic researchers seem to be interested in what we label *input synthesis*. That is, most psycholinguistic research nowadays concerns how linguistic input is converted into a semantically analyzed mental representation of the ideas expressed by the input. Input synthesis includes speech perception, computation of syntax, and the determination of sentential implications.

Comprehension requires the conversion of physical energy (e.g., speech sounds) to semantically analyzed units, such as ideas, thoughts, or beliefs. The physical stimulus is observable, as is the overt linguistic or behavioral response that often ensues. In between come an unknown number of unobservable events—unobservable even by the person in whose mind they happen. Only the consequences of these events can be used to infer the events themselves, and then only if manageable research questions have been formulated about them. The formulation of tractable research problems is greatly aided by knowledge or, more often, assumptions about subdivisions of the unseen events that produce comprehension. As you might guess, it is the paradigm that supplies such a framework of assumptions.

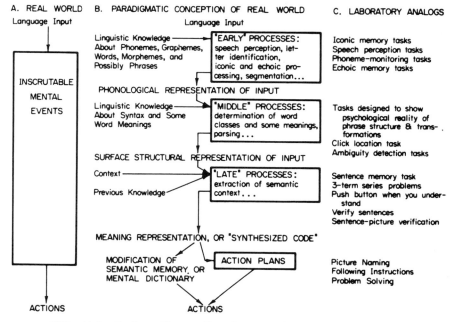

A. REAL WORLD
Language Input

INSCRUTABLE
MENTAL
EVENTS

ACTIONS

B. PARADIGMATIC CONCEPTION OF REAL WORLD
Language Input

Linguistic Knowledge —————▶ "EARLY" PROCESSES:
About Phonemes, Graphemes,   speech perception, let-
Words, Morphemes, and   ter identification,
Possibly Phrases   iconic and echoic pro-
                                  cessing, segmentation...

PHONOLOGICAL REPRESENTATION OF INPUT

Linguistic Knowledge —————▶ "MIDDLE" PROCESSES:
About Syntax and Some   determination of word
Word Meanings   classes and some meanings,
                                  parsing...

SURFACE STRUCTURAL REPRESENTATION OF INPUT

Context —————▶ "LATE" PROCESSES:
                      extraction of semantic
Previous Knowledge   context...

MEANING REPRESENTATION, OR "SYNTHESIZED CODE"

MODIFICATION OF   ACTION PLANS
SEMANTIC MEMORY, OR
MENTAL DICTIONARY

ACTIONS

C. LABORATORY ANALOGS

Iconic memory tasks
Speech perception tasks
Phoneme-monitoring tasks
Echoic memory tasks

Tasks designed to show
   psychological reality of
   phrase structure & transformations
Click location task
Ambiguity detection tasks

Sentence memory task
3-term series problems
Push button when you under-
   stand
Verify sentences
Sentence-picture verification

Picture Naming
Following Instructions
Problem Solving

FIG. 11.2.   Real world, paradigmatic conception of real world, and laboratory analogs designed to infer the properties of various parts of the paradigmatic conception in the area of language comprehension.

Figure 11.2 is our best effort to illustrate how information-processing psychologists (in general) group the unobservable events between linguistic input and output. Panel A is the real world, including the things that go on within the walls of the mind. Panel B is the information-processing paradigm's structuring of that mental domain. The structure is drawn partly from the computer analogy (it is a flowchart), partly from rational and intuitive considerations, and partly from experimental studies of forms of cognition that researchers have deemed relevant. Panel B reflects the paradigmatic view that all cognitive activity involves identifiable subprocesses, each of which takes time. Information-processing psychologists used to be quite confident that such subprocesses could be decoupled experimentally. Today we are less sure, because parallel processing may be more prevalent than was once thought. Parallel processing plays havoc with efforts to decouple processing steps with such measures as reaction time. Therefore, while we can identify many processes that seem required for comprehension, we cannot yet specify their temporal relationships. We are left with identifying groups of subprocesses that do seem to be temporally ordered. The boxes in Panel B of Fig. 11.2 are such groups, and it seems to us that these reflect the intuitions of most researchers and theorists of comprehension.

The top box of Panel B contains activities that seem to be required early in the comprehension process, although we do not know which of them comes first. Reading and listening to speech certainly must, at some time, involve the same iconic and echoic memories that have been found in other kinds of tasks. And speech perception research has identified processes that are apparently unique to the auditory perception of speech. These processes are involved in deciding that a particular sound *is* speech, dividing it into recognizable units, categorizing speech sounds, and so on.

Presumably, the early comprehension processes yield a phonological representation of the input, which feeds into further processing (see Fig. 11.2). That is, the phonological representation is output from the early processes and input to the middle processes. Besides our intuitions, there is some empirical justification for thinking of the phonological representation as an early product of comprehension processing. For example, Green (1975) reasoned that people must consult their mental representations to decide whether a particular word had appeared in a sentence they just heard. If the test word does not appear in the sentence, but rhymes with one of the words that did, people must consult their phonological representation to reject it. But if the test word is synonymous with one of the words actually heard, people must consult their semantic representations to reject it. Green required his subjects either to memorize sentences or to invent continuations for them; he considered inventing continuations to involve more semantic processing than memorization. Following some trials, a word was presented and subjects decided whether it had been in the sentence. For synonyms, rejection took longer when people made continuations than when they memorized. For rhyming words, there was no difference in the subject's latency to reject. This outcome suggests that people formed similar phonological representations for both the memory and continuation conditions, but they formed different semantic representations for the two conditions. These findings are not direct evidence that the creation of a phonological representation precedes the synthesis of a semantic representation, but they can be interpreted that way. The interpretation is based on the notion that, in an efficiently organized system, processes required by many different tasks should be completed before processes that are unique to different tasks.

Strictly speaking, only auditory input should be given a phonological representation, but reading probably requires some analogous sort of representation. For both reading and listening, output from early processes seems required for later syntactic analysis and word meaning determinations. The computer analogy is doubtless influential here. A computer program cannot deal with the structure of elements until the elements have been identified, nor can it look up material associated with the elements until the elements have been isolated and recognized. From this point of view, it is hard to imagine how a language comprehender could determine grammatical structure until he or she has identified such elements as words, morphemes, syllables, or phonemes. It is also hard to imagine how meanings could be sought before the string of input sounds has been divided into words. Despite this logic, many psycholinguists recognize that the ordering illustrated in Fig. 11.2 does not have adequate empirical support, and that it should probably be considered only a rough guide to theorizing about the input synthesis process.

The processes called *late* (Fig. 11.2) may actually begin while the middle processes are still under way. Some late processes may even precede some middle ones, which suggests that early, middle, and late may not be the best designations. The groups of processes shown in the boxes of the figure might better be viewed as differing in their depth, where depth is the extent to which the processes draw on permanent knowledge. The early/late distinction fits the information-processing emphasis on temporal measurements and processing stages, but the depth metaphor (Craik & Lockhart, 1972) better accommodates the notion that much processing goes on in parallel. Whichever designation prevails, there is now sufficient evidence to justify some form of conceptual separation of the groups of processes shown in Fig. 11.2. For example, the products of the later (or deeper) processes are remembered better (Craik & Tulving, 1975) and longer (Sachs, 1967). Thus, people retain a representation of input meanings well after they have forgotten the exact words and syntactic forms from which they derived the meanings. This greater mnemonic permanence warrants the belief that extracting semantic content is a process that can be separated from syntax computation and word look-up. Nearly all students of language comprehension agree that the deep or late processes involve computation of semantic relationships among sentence elements. In addition, many researchers argue that constructive processes such as inference-making and insertion of previously known ideas are an integral part of comprehension.

Completing the early, middle, and late processes produces understanding of an input sentence or utterance. The representation of meaning derived from the various processes of input synthesis is not identical with the linguistic input that starts the process, and the nature and content of this synthesized representation have been the subject of much research. We term this representation the *synthesized code*. Figure 11.2 suggests that the synthesized code sometimes gives rise to action plans, which organize immediate responses. Sometimes the synthesized code is integrated with the permanent knowledge system, thereby modifying it. When such integration occurs, it may result in the loss of memory for where, from whom, and in what situation the idea was originally acquired. In Tulving's (1972) terms, the meaning representation becomes a semantic memory rather than an episodic memory. If it does impact semantic memory, the content it conveys is permanently available and usually easily retrievable. In other words, the synthesized code is an episodic memory for the meaning of an input, but that code may become a permanent representation in semantic memory of the input's meaning.

Contemporary psycholinguistic research seeks to discover the form and the content of the synthesized code. Many researchers are asking, What is the nature and content of the meaning representation of a sentence just after it has been heard (read) and understood? Here is an example to concretize the question.

Imagine yourself eating with a friend, who says:

/ dzentowlmiylæsnaytðetʃIyendIkərgItIŋəpʊdl/

Before this string of sounds is segmented, it is no more meaningful than our phonetic transcription probably appears to you. Although you hear words when people speak, acoustic analyses show very few boundaries in the speech stream. It is continuous sound, which listeners somehow segment. What segments are used is still not known, but this question is being researched by students of speech perception. The paradigm demands some segmentation, because recognition is viewed as the matching of input units to previously stored representational units. Assuming that the units are words, the preceding string of sounds goes into your input segmenter and comes out as a sequence of words:

Jane told me last night that she and Dick are getting a poodle.

To comprehend these words, you must perform syntactic analyses to compute the relationships among them, and you must ascertain the meanings of the words. The result of this mental activity is an appreciation of the import of these word meanings standing in particular relationship to each other. But what is an "appreciation" of something like a familiar couple getting a poodle?

For an information-processing psychologist, explaining this appreciation requires analysis of the sequence of operations and transformations that give rise to it, and transformations of input data do two important things. First, they change the form of the code. This is analogous to what happens when a dictated tape is typed: It is changed from an auditory to a visual code of the same meaning. Presumably, the forms of codes are changed so that they can be used in different ways, by different devices. The eye has a hard time with tape recordings, just as the ear is stymied by a typed page. Second, the contents of the code may be changed. Material may be deleted, added, or altered during recoding. To continue our dictating and typing analogy, the message may be changed by secretarial error during listening and transcribing. A typist's guess about what the dictator intended may be added to the typed version. As sentential input is synthesized, both its form and its content are changed, and these changes are the object of psycholinguistic research on comprehension.

III.   THE FORM OF THE SYNTHESIZED CODE

Viewing information processing as a sequence of transformations and operations on input data requires that the input be continuously represented; otherwise the processing sequence would be broken. It also requires that the input be recoded into a form compatible with the structure of each subsystem that operates on it. An appreciation of an idea is thus some sort of memorial representation, but its form is a matter for research. This view underlies psycholinguistic research, just as it underlies research on the characteristics of episodic memory stages. The assumption of continuous representation by a succession of codes leads us to wonder about the form in which linguistic information is represented at various stages of processing.

What do we know about the form of synthesized code? For one thing, we know that it is more abstract than the original surface structures from which it is derived, because it can often be paraphrased even when it cannot be literally recalled. Furthermore, we know that it is hardy enough to survive the loss of syntax, original wording, and focal attention. A person can use the synthesized code after he has attended to something else for a while. It must also be comparable to the form in which the contents of permanent memory are represented, because by the time a person has synthesized an utterance, he can judge whether it agrees with his pre-existing beliefs. From the information-processing point of view, this could only happen if comparisons of the synthesized code and permanent information were possible. Moreover, a person can manipulate the synthesized input code in accord with rules of logic stored in permanent memory, and can draw implications and inferences from the input sentence.

The synthesized code is a kind of bridge between immediate and permanent memory. It is required for the conversion of information from its transient form, compatible with sense organs and then with working memory, to a form compatible with the structures of semantic memory. Questions of input synthesis are attractive to reasearchers partly because insights into the form of synthesized input may shed light on the way information is represented in permanent memory, because permanent memory representations and synthesized representations must be compatible. Moreover, it is assumed by the paradigm that the form of the synthesized code can be determined experimentally.

A. Propositional Theories

Herbert H. Clark is a central figure in contemporary psycholinguistic research. His career and thinking have paralleled the major trends in psycholinguistics. He attended graduate school in the 1960s, when many psychologists were abandoning associationist explanations of language and turning to Chomsky's theories. Clark's dissertation advisor, Dr. James Deese, was a prominent verbal-learning researcher, who was then beginning to use ideas from linguistics. Clark's education encompassed both the values of verbal learning and a receptive attitude toward linguistics. His work reflects the commitment of verbal-learning psychology to empirical research methods and its strong respect for technically well-designed experiments. Also, Clark took seriously his professors' disillusionment with associationism, which he rejected in favor of the new psycholinguistics. Clark's predilection for borrowing from linguistics may also be partly attributable to his wife and colleague, Eve, who is a linguist. Clark (1969) incorporated Chomsky's ideas into his first comprehension theory. He has continued to make substantial use of ideas from linguistics, but Chomsky is no longer the main source of his ideas. Since 1972, Clark has rarely cited Chomsky.

The first version of Clark's theory was based on data about how people solve three-term series problems, such as this:

(1) If Mary is brighter than Sue, and Ellen is brighter than Mary, who is brightest?

Logically equivalent but semantically different forms of these problems vary in their difficulty. For example, the foregoing version of the problem is easier than this one:

(2) If Mary is brighter than Sue, and Mary is not as bright as Ellen, who is brightest?

Clark treated the solution of such problems as a psycholinguistic matter. He considered that solving the problem required separate understandings of each premise and of the final question, and that the key to the varying difficulty of logically equivalent problems is in the form of the internal representation of these understandings.

Clark proposed that the premise information is represented as base strings, like those in Chomsky's standard theory. In the case of Problem (1), the base strings would be *Mary is bright* and *Sue is bright* from the first premise, *Ellen is bright* and *Mary is bright* from the second premise, along with the comparative information from each as to who is brighter. According to Clark (1969), solution difficulty is attributable to two factors. One is marking. As you may recall from the last chapter, marked and unmarked adjectives differ in semantic salience. A marked adjective such as *bad* does not name the dimension of goodness. *How bad is it?* implies that it is bad, while *How good is it?* does not imply that it is good. Because marked adjectives are considered linguistically more complex than unmarked ones, Clark (1969) argued that solution of three-term series problems is slowed if the adjective in the base strings is marked. Problems containing *shorter, worse, duller,* or other marked adjectives should take longer to solve than those containing unmarked adjectives, such as *taller, better,* and *brighter.* Clark's second important factor was congruity. He argued that if the adjective in the question is the same as that in the base strings, solution will be faster than if it is different. In other words, the question *Who is brightest?* would facilitate solution of Problem (3), while *Who is dullest?* would be easier in Problem (4):

(3) If Mary is brighter than Sue, and Ellen is brighter than Mary, . . .
(4) If Mary is duller than Sue, and Ellen is duller than Mary, . . .

Between 1972 and 1974, Clark revised his theory to account for data from studies of sentence–picture verification. People compared a statement to a picture (usually a configuration of simple geometric designs, such as stars, plusses, circles, lines, and the like in various colors and spatial arrangements) and decided whether the statement was true or false of the picture. Clark believed this task tapped a general comprehension strategy.

As he revised his theory, Clark moved gradually away from Chomsky's base strings. First he changed notation, leaving the deep structural information of transformational grammar only implicit (Chase & Clark, 1972) and representing other kinds of information quite differently from Chomsky. His new notation was more flexible than the base strings and deep structures of transformational grammar. The following examples illustrate Clark's notational system:

Sentence	*Internal Representation*
The plus is above the star.	(true (plus above star))
The plus is below the star.	(true (plus below star))
The star isn't above the plus.	(false (star above plus))

These internal representations contain the *proposition,* or content, of the sentence. The innermost brackets contain the most embedded proposition. The next pair of brackets contains a predication or statement about the embedded proposition. Thus, the representation for *The star isn't above the plus* asserts that the embedded proposition *star above plus* is false.

This propositional representation can be applied to pictures as well as to sentences. A person looking at a picture of a star above a plus may represent its contents as either (true (star above plus)) or (true (plus below star)). According to Clark, task requirements determine which representation will be employed. Chomsky's base strings could only be derived from grammatical sentences, and were unsuitable for representing pictorial information unless one made the implausible assumption that people understand pictures by describing them to themselves in grammatical language. The proposition, however, could be used to represent whatever content people extract from either pictures or sentences. It is desirable to have a form of representation that accommodates both pictorial and linguistic information, because people compare linguistic descriptions and scenes, and doing so requires a similar representational format. If you think you detect the influence of information-processing pretheory in this assertion, you are right. The computer analogy motivates the assumption of a common format. Much of the computer's power comes from its ability to compare elements; but for the computer to do so, the elements must be in the same format.

Clark and Chase assumed that a person encodes the sentence as it is presented. Then the picture is presented, and its encoding depends on that of the sentence. Notice that this picture could be represented as

*

\+

star above plus or *plus below star.* Clark's model asserts that people encode the picture with whichever preposition (*above* or *below*) was used to represent the sentence. Once the sentence and the picture have been represented, comparison proceeds as illustrated in Fig. 11.3. It is assumed that a person begins with a set to respond *true.* That is, if a computer were programmed to do this task, a storage location would be assigned a value corresponding to *true.* The location would be called the truth index, and as information-processing models are wont to do, Clark's model uses this term to describe the subject's set to respond. Having encoded the sentence and picture and set the

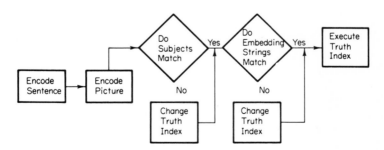

FIG. 11.3.   Sentence–picture comparison process when sentence is presented first. (From Clark & Chase, 1972.)

index at *true,* the subject must next compare (Fig. 11.3) the innermost bracketed propositions (called *Subjects*) representing the sentence and the picture. If they match, the person proceeds outward to the next pair of brackets. If they do not match, the truth index is changed to *false* before proceeding to the next pair of brackets. It is efficient for the subject to encode the picture with the same preposition as the sentence, because then a match or a mismatch in the embedded proposition can be detected as soon as the first term is compared. (As you can see, there is only one way that *star above plus* can match a representation containing *above;* anything but *star* in the first position is a mismatch). Next, the embedding propositions in the outer brackets are compared. In the event of a match, a final response is made on the basis of the current value of the truth index. In the event of a mismatch, the truth index is switched to its opposite value before the final response is made. The following example illustrates one path through the flowchart.

Suppose a person must compare *The star isn't above the plus* with a picture of a plus above a star. The correct response is *true.* The truth index is initialized at *true,* and the person encodes the sentence as *(false (star above plus)).* He then encodes the picture, using the preposition *above: (true (plus above star)).* The first comparison is between the two embedded propositions, *(plus above star)* and *(star above plus).* Because they do not match, the truth index is switched to *false.* The next comparison is between the contents of the outer brackets. These also do not match; one contains *(false (XXXXX))* and the other contains *(true (XXXXX));* so the truth index is switched back to *true.* The person will respond *true,* but because switching takes time, his latency will be relatively long.

Clark's model predicted that response latency should be influenced by time to encode the sentence, time to encode the picture, and number of switches of the truth index. Sentences containing marked terms should take longer to encode than those containing unmarked ones; therefore, *above* sentences should result in generally shorter latencies than *below* sentences. Negative sentences should take longer to encode than affirmative ones; therefore, *The star isn't above the plus* should take longer to verify than *The star is above the plus.* These should add together, so that *The star isn't below the plus* should take considerably longer than *The star is above the plus.* Further increments should result from each change of truth index. Reaction times in an experiment where people verified such sentences and pictures supported the predictions (Clark & Chase, 1972).

Clark's revised model accounted well for sentence–picture verification times, while keeping important features of the earlier model, which accounted for the solution of three-term series problems. The importance of lexical marking was maintained in the later model. The switching of response indexes is an elaborated explanation of the role of congruence in the earlier model. And both models relied heavily on the way the input sentence is encoded (synthesized, in our terms) to explain the differential ease of solving different versions of the same tasks. Clark and Chase (1972) extended the model to account for verification times when the picture was presented before the sentence rather than after. We do not detail this extension, because the topic here is input synthesis, and the extended model is the same as the earlier version in this respect.

Models like the ones offered by Clark (1969, 1974; Clark & Chase, 1972) explain quite well the comprehension of literal content, and for simple statements about spatial relations, literal content seems sufficient. However, much comprehension is not literal. Recently, Clark has moved on to tackle problems of the input synthesis of nonliteral assertions (Clark & Lucy, 1975). However, his students (Carpenter & Just, 1975) have continued to extend his sentence–picture comparison model, explicitly rejecting transformational grammar as a description of the synthesized representation of sentence inputs.

Carpenter and Just were both graduate students at Stanford University, where Clark is a professor; and both coauthored papers with him. They obtained faculty positions at Carnegie-Mellon University, where they have formulated a comprehension model that clearly reflects Clark's influence. Like Clark's, their model explains how people compare sentences with pictures, though it is intended to explain other comprehension tasks as well. People see pictures, such as red dots or black dots, and decide on the truth of such statements as *The dots are red, The dots aren't red, It's true that the dots aren't red,* and so on.

Carpenter and Just's model says that people extract information from sentences and pictures, convert the information into a common underlying form, and then compare the information from sentence and picture to decide whether the sentence is true or false. The form of the information extracted from both sentence and picture is propositional, a term the authors are careful to distinguish from *linguistic.* Like most other comprehension theorists, Carpenter and Just do not say whether they think that people's cognitive codes are propositional or that propositions are simply notationally convenient. We return later to this widespread confusion between psychological, internal representation, and theoretical notation. Also, like many other theorists, Carpenter and Just never say exactly what they mean by proposition. We return to this problem, too, for it plagues many models. Despite these uncertainties, we can see that the propositional notation of Carpenter and Just is more general than base or deep structure notation. Table 11.1 gives some examples. Thus, a sentence such as *The dots are red* is converted to a propositional representation consisting of a *predicate* (red) and one or more *arguments* (in this case the single argument *dots*). Propositions may themselves be arguments, and in the assertion *The dots are red* the proposition (RED, DOTS) becomes the argument of the predicate AFFIRMATIVE. Thus, the entire representation of the sentence, *The dots*

TABLE 11.1
Propositional Representation of Sentences and Pictures
in the Model of Carpenter and Just (1975)

Sentence	Propositional Representation
1. The dots are red.	(AFFIRMATIVE (RED, DOTS))
2. The dots aren't red.	(NEGATIVE (RED, DOTS))
3. It isn't true that the dots are red	(NEG (AFF, (RED, DOTS)))
4. It's true that the dots aren't red.	(AFF (NEG, (RED, DOTS)))

Picture	Propositional Representation
A. (a picture of red dots)	(RED, DOTS)
B. (a picture of black dots)	(BLACK, DOTS)

are red, becomes AFF (RED, DOTS). If this sentence is embedded in another, its entire representation becomes the argument of another proposition. For example, *It's fortunate that the dots are red* is represented as (FORTUNATE (AFF, (RED, DOTS))).

Pictures are represented in the same propositional format—for example, (BLACK, DOTS) or (RED, DOTS). Once this common format is achieved, the person compares the sentence and picture representations element by element until a mismatch is achieved or until all elements have been found identical. The model of Carpenter and Just accounts for sentence–picture verification latencies in a wide variety of psychological experiments.

Clark's models (1969, 1974; Clark & Chase, 1972) and the model by Carpenter and Just (1975) have received some criticism. Anderson (1976, p. 29) and Tanenhaus, Carroll, and Bever (1976) have complained that the representational format is too flexible; it does not specify any unique propositional representation. The criticism is that the theorists change their representational format after the fact to account for particular experimental findings, which has the effect of robbing their models of predictive power. Thus, to account for certain of their outcomes, Carpenter and Just suggest that their subjects varied their coding strategies—for example, by representing *It's true that the dots aren't red* as if it were *The dots are black*. Tanenhaus, Carroll, and Bever argue that such ad hoc flexibility in the model's representational format allows the model to account for any data that might be observed, reducing its predictive power to naught. Clark (1978), Clark and Clark (1977) and Carpenter and Just (1976) have responded that linguists might set the goal for themselves of building an invariant representational format for each sentence, but psychologists cannot. Their job is to find the representations people actually use, which may be partly situationally determined. The trouble is that, if the representational format is assumed in order to test the rest of the model, it cannot be discovered in the course of that test. Alternatively, if the representational format is to be discovered, the rest of the model must be the assumptive framework. This dilemma illustrates how the flexibility of human comprehension processes can increase the difficulty of building a theory, and it is faced by any theory that attempts to specify representation and process at the same time. Obviously, a complete theory will have to include both representation and process, and it will be on firm ground only when it permits advance specification of which representation will be used in a given situation. This objective has not yet been met; however, it is the goal of many comprehension theorists.

Propositional representation is not the only sort that can be imagined. Other theorists have argued for a code that has more in common with perceptual experience and less similarity to linguistic codes than propositions.

B. Dual Coding Theory

The concept of imagery has already occurred in earlier chapters, and it has been suggested that it is an important component of sentence comprehension. You will not be surprised that this position has been energetically espoused by Paivio, who has also shown the importance of imaginal processes in a wide variety of other tasks (Paivio, 1969, 1971).

Other investigators have also found evidence that imagery is important in sentence processing. Jorgensen and Kintsch (1973) found that it is easier to verify sentences that are easily imaged. Instructions to their subjects to use images had no effect on their performance, suggesting that imaging is a spontaneous strategy that subjects will use in sentence verification whether instructed to or not. Jorgensen and Kintsch concluded that sentence verification theories should not restrict themselves to purely semantic operations. Thorndyke (1975) started out to test a linguistic prediction and ended by supporting the role of imagery. He was interested in speed of comprehension and recallability of sentences containing verbs that are relatively complex or relatively simple. His selection of simple and complex verbs was based on the Conceptual Dependency Theory of Schank (1972, 1975). Schank's theory specifies the complexity of different verbs in terms of the complexity of underlying structures into which they can be decomposed. According to Schank, verbs like *watched, angered, surprised* and *hurt* are relatively simple, while those like *obeyed, employed, rescued,* and *resented* are relatively complex. Thorndyke's procedure was straightforward. He presented sentences containing differentially complex verbs, asking people to press a key when they understood the sentence. He collected the comprehension latencies and also asked people to rate how easy the sentence was to image. Then he tested recall of the sentences, giving either the subject or the verb as a cue. It took people longer to understand sentences containing the complex verbs. It also was harder to recall the sentences with more complex verbs if the cue was the sentence subject; however if the verb was the cue, all sentences were recalled equally well. These findings would have been very supportive of the conceptual complexity hypothesis, were it not for one other result: Sentences containing complex verbs were also rated harder to image. Consequently, the difference in comprehension speed and memorability might have been due to imagery, and Thorndyke conducted another experiment in which imagery was carefully controlled. He included high-imagery simple verbs such as *grasped,* low-imagery simple verbs such as *knew,* high-imagery complex verbs such as *rescued,* and low-imagery complex verbs such as *resented.* Thorndyke found that only imagery affected comprehension speed and recallability; verb complexity, the linguistic variable, had no effect.

Evidently, an exclusively linguistic theory of input synthesis is incomplete. On the other hand, linguistic factors such as congruence (Clark, 1969) affect comprehension too. Accordingly, Begg and Paivio (1969) advanced a *dual coding* hypothesis: People sometimes use images and sometimes do not. Although Paivio had long been convinced of the importance of imagery, he also knew that many sentences are understood even though they are difficult to image—for example, *The legislation will be implemented as soon as administrative procedures can be clarified.*

Begg and Paivio tested the hypothesis that people store concrete sentences as nonverbal images, but when a sentence is too abstract to image, they store a verbal form of it. Begg and Paivio offered no explanation of the verbal coding of abstract sentences, but they stated their hypothesis in sufficiently general terms that linguistic theorists such as Clark could fill in the details, if they were inclined. Begg and Paivio tested the dual coding hypothesis with a variant of a technique developed by Sachs (1967). First, they obtained ratings of whether sentences were highly abstract, highly concrete, or in between. They used only those rated as highly abstract or highly concrete (see Table 11.2). They presented five of these sentences, and then asked people whether a sixth sentence was identical with one of the five they had just heard. As in

TABLE 11.2
Examples of Stimuli Used by Begg and Paivio (1969)

	Abstract	*Concrete*
Original:	The arbitrary regulation provoked a civil complaint.	The spirited leader slapped a mournful hostage.
Meaning Change:	The arbitrary complaint provoked a civil regulation.	The spirited hostage slapped a mournful leader.
Wording Change:	The arbitrary regulation provoked a civil grievance.	The spirited leader slapped a mournful captive.

Sachs' work, the test sentences were sometimes identical with one of the five and sometimes were changed versions of one of the five. Sometimes the meaning was changed by interchanging the subject and object of the sentence. Sometimes a word was changed without changing the meaning of the sentence. Table 11.2 illustrates the sentences used by Begg and Paivio, who reasoned that wording changes should be relatively difficult to detect if subjects had stored images. Any accurate description of the stored image should be as acceptable as any other. Meaning changes, on the other hand, should be incompatible with the image and hence easy to detect. On the hypothesis that only concrete sentences are stored as images, Begg and Paivio predicted that meaning changes should be easily detected and wording changes poorly detected for concrete sentences. For abstract sentences, they predicted the opposite. They reasoned that if subjects are storing words, then the same words should look familiar to them. Even if they are in a somewhat rearranged order that changes the meaning, they might not notice the change. On the other hand, a change in wording should be readily noticed, even if it preserved the meaning of the sentence. Their data supported their predictions: Meaning changes were noticed more in concrete sentences and wording changes were noticed more in abstract sentences.

Begg and Paivio's dual coding theory stimulated much research. Klee and Eysenck (1973) tested it by relying on the idea that processing capacity is more limited within a modality than between modalities. They reasoned that an imaginal code should be undisturbed by verbal interference, but should be disrupted by visual interference. A verbal code, on the other hand, should be disrupted by verbal but not visual interference. If concrete sentences are coded imaginally and abstract ones verbally, then visual interference should impede the processing of concrete sentences, while verbal interference should impede abstract sentences. Klee and Eysenck asked people to judge the meaningfulness of sentences, and timed their judgments. Interposed between each word of the sentence was either a visual stimulus or a spoken digit. After judging the meaningfulness of the sentence, the subjects had to report information about the visual stimuli or the digits; this required the subject to hold either visual or auditory information in memory while processing the sentence to decide on its meaningfulness. The auditory task was more disruptive when the sentences were abstract; the visual task was more disruptive when the sentences were concrete. This outcome seems to support dual coding theory, but there are further considerations.

Dual coding theory was offered as a hypothesis about memory. It is taken as relevant to input synthesis, too, because what is remembered is a product of synthesis. But because something will not be recalled if it was not comprehended in the first place, Begg and Paivio's experiment has been criticized on the grounds that abstract sentences may not be understood as well as concrete ones. If so, people's failure to notice meaning changes in abstract sentences may simply reflect the fact that they never grasped the original meaning. Dual coding would then pertain to comprehensible and incomprehensible strings, rather than to concrete and abstract sentences. If that were so, it would be a trivial theory, for its role as a theory of input synthesis is to account for comprehension, not to show that comprehension influences recall. Holmes and Langford (1976) have demonstrated that abstract sentences *are* harder to understand than concrete ones, and Johnson, Bransford, Nyberg, and Cleary (1972) showed this to be true of the particular sentences used by Begg and Paivio. In addition, Johnson et al. collected rating data showing that Begg and Paivio's subject–object reversals changed the meaning of their concrete sentences more than it changed their abstract ones. Therefore, Begg and Paivio's subjects may have noticed these changes more because they were bigger changes, not because of dual coding. Later experiments found some validity for this criticism. Moeser (1974) equated comprehensibility of abstract and concrete sentences by including in her experiments only sentences that were rated equally comprehensible, regardless of how abstract or concrete they were. She was unable to reproduce Begg and Paivio's outcomes, and she concluded that their results did not stem from dual coding.

Before evaluating dual coding theory, it might be a good idea to reconsider what is meant by a representation. Information-processing psychologists assume that an input will not be remembered unless it leaves a record in memory. That record is its representation. It cannot be a literal copy of the input, because what is in the world is different from what reaches the sense organs, and sensations are further transformed and recoded in the course of input synthesis. In general, recoding increases permanence at the cost of detail. Questions about the form of the code, then, are questions about the kind of detail that is sacrificed in the process of recoding.

Dual coding theory is almost certainly correct in this regard: Details of wording are more apt to be sacrificed in some conditions than in others; the human comprehension and memory system has latitude in the kind of detail that is retained and lost. Dual coding theory accommodates such latitude better than models that assume that the synthesized code is completely determined by the content of input sentences. Two other tenets of dual coding theory are less clearly correct. There is considerable doubt that the abstract–concrete distinction characterizes the conditions under which wording details will be maintained or lost. Most data suggest that comprehensibility is the more pertinent dimension. If a sentence is understandable, verbal details will be lost and a more abstract and permanent code will result; but if the sentence cannot be understood, a relatively temporary and literal code that retains verbal detail will be formed. This analysis suggests that comprehension is the translation of literal words into some less literal format, which seems intuitively sensible. To the extent that abstract sentences are harder to understand than concrete ones, it will appear that abstract sentences result in less loss of verbal detail in a fairly immediate test. The second questionable aspect of dual coding theory is its use of imagery as a metaphor for the synthesized code. More verbal detail is lost from imageable sentences, but this may only mean that imageable sentences are more comprehensible and hence more likely to be synthesized in the first place.

Pylyshyn (1973) has made a particularly lucid analysis of imagery and representation, which we mentioned in connection with imagery theories of episodic memory (Chapter 8). He notes that imaginal recall always lacks some details of color, pattern, or aspect of the original event. There are absent, uncertain, or vague perceptual qualities in an image, and they suggest absent conceptual entities rather than missing pieces of a picture. This means that the image must be made up of differentiated and interpreted "perceptual objects" that are actually conceptually represented. Pylyshyn argued that the known properties of visual images are more suggestive of a description of a visual experience rather than a picture of it. He concluded that imagery as a mental representation should be identified with the output of cognitive analyzers rather than the input to them; imagery, in this view, is more like what we mean by knowledge. Knowledge is conceptual and amenable to propositional representation.

Not all investigators accept the implications of Pylyshyn's argument; some still argue for a perceptually based imaginal code. Kosslyn and Pomerantz (1977), for example, believe an image is made of large perceptual units that are themselves stored in memory following their synthesis from aggregates of sensations. It is the perceptual source of the large constituent units that give images their perceptual qualities. But because these units are drawn from memory, their combination should not exactly match any real scene.

Despite the efforts of theorists such as Kosslyn and Pomerantz, most investigators now reject the aspect of the imagery metaphor that suggests that the synthesized code is truly like visual experience, though they may accept the idea that the code is nonlinguistic, holistic, and parallel. Some use the term *analogue* representation, which is freer of visual connotations than the term *imagery*. Others offer no metaphor at all, simply characterizing the synthesized code as a semantic representation, whatever that may be.

Clearly, many questions about the form of the synthesized code remain unanswered. We cannot yet say why comprehensibility and imagery are correlated. It is even puzzling that they should be. Visual recall memory is not so very accurate, so why should comprehensibility and memorability be facilitated by reference to images?

You may wonder whether we can choose between propositional theories and imagery theories. We cannot. Neither kind of theory is sufficiently complete. Propositional theories, such as those of Clark (1974) and Carpenter and Just (1975), have not yet adequately specified how to translate sentences into propositions. Dual coding theory rests too heavily on the assumption that concreteness and imageability are effective because people use mental imagery; there may be other reasons for the facilitating effect of these variables. We are not yet in a position to choose between theories on the basis of their ability to represent reality. Anderson (1978) has argued that an empirically based choice may be impossible in principle (but see our discussion of empirical corroboration of theoretical entities in Chapter 14).

Meanwhile, is there some basis on which to choose? Should we accumulate box scores for propositional and imaginal theories, seeing which is supported by more experiments? Should we assume both are right? These questions have been considered by the global modelers, who want to get on with the business of outlining the whole cognitive system. There is growing consensus among them that there is no fundamental difference between imaginal and propositional representation. Anything that can be represented imaginally can also be represented with propositions. Furthermore, no one knows how to construct a theory of the mind's contents in imaginal format. All the global models are propositional, and several theorists argue that propositions can be used to represent images as well as linguistic forms. It is clear that propositional theories of representation are here to stay, though they will not be able to ignore the importance of imageability. Its importance is too well supported, but how it will be incorporated into propositional theories remains to be seen.

IV.   CONTENT OF THE SYNTHESIZED CODE

We turn now from the form of the representational code that results from input synthesis to research on the contents of the code. The research all supports one point with striking clarity: Input synthesis is a constructive process; knowledge other than that in the sentence itself is used to comprehend the sentence. In one way or another, all experiments on the contents of the representational code make this point, though that is not the purpose of all such experiments. We begin with several experiments designed explicitly for that purpose.

A. Constructive Synthesis

The main demonstrations that input synthesis is constructive are sentence recognition experiments. People are shown a list of sentences. They may be told that they should attend closely to the sentences because they will be asked about them later; or they may be asked questions immediately following each sentence. Later, they are given test sentences and asked which ones are exactly the same as a previously presented sentence. Some of the test sentences contain information a person might construct in the course of understanding the original sentence. If the person identifies these new sentences as ones previously shown, his false recognition is taken as evidence of a constructive process between presentation and test. The most frequently cited study of this type was conducted by Bransford and Franks (1971).

Bransford and Franks were graduate students at the University of Minnesota when they conducted a famous experiment showing that people construct a unified representation of separately presented ideas. They started with four complex sentences:

> The ants in the kitchen ate the sweet jelly which was on the table.
> The rock which rolled down the mountain crushed the tiny hut at the edge of the woods.
> The warm breeze blowing from the sea stirred the heavy evening air.
> The old man resting on the couch read the newspaper in the store.

Each of these complex sentences has four elementary propositions. In the first sentence, for example, the elements are:

> The ants were in the kitchen,
> The jelly was sweet,
> The jelly was on the table,
> The ants ate the jelly.

Bransford and Franks constructed component sentences from these elements. Some component sentences contained one elementary proposition, some two, and some three. These were interspersed with similarly formed component sentences derived from the other complex ones. Thus a subject might hear, among others, sentences like these:

> The ants ate the sweet jelly. (one proposition)
> The ants in the kitchen ate the jelly. (two propositions)
> The jelly on the table was sweet. (two propositions)
> The ants ate the sweet jelly which was on the table. (three propositions)

Subjects never heard the whole four-proposition sentences. They were given an irrelevant task to perform on the sentences as they heard them, and they did not know they would have to remember the sentences; but after all the sentences had been presented they were given a recognition test. Bransford and Franks produced another list of test sentences and asked the subjects to say for each whether it was identical with one that had been presented during the training procedure, and how certain they were of their answer. Bransford and Franks reasoned that it would show that the ideas were integrated into a single unified representation if subjects could not tell the difference between the actual sentences they had been shown and sentences that contained the same idea. That is what happened; subjects' recognition performance was inaccurate. Moreover, people's certainty that they had seen a sentence before (whether they had or not) increased with the number of propositions in the test sentence. The complete four-proposition sentence was given the highest recognition confidence of all, even though it was never presented before the memory test.

This experiment was widely interpreted as evidence that people form an integrated representation from separate ideas. Rather than maintain and use separate representations, they compare the test sentence to their integrated representation. The more similar the test sentence is to the integrated representation, the more familiar it seems. The more propositions in the test sentence, the more similar it is to the integrated representation, and hence the likelier people are to feel that they have heard it before. This conclusion has been supported in several later studies (Franks & Bransford, 1972; Johnson, Bransford, & Solomon, 1973).

Barclay, another graduate student at Minnesota, collaborated with Bransford and Franks. Like them, he advocates the idea that input synthesis is constructive. Barclay (1973) gave people sentences describing ordered arrays, such as those in Table 11.3. Half of the people were told to memorize the sentences. The others were told to figure out the order relationships of the arrays. Barclay's instructions had a decided influence on how his subjects represented the sentences. The Memorizers recreated the arrays poorly (only 10% of them were successful). But in a recognition test, they correctly rejected

TABLE 11.3
Examples of Ordered Arrays and the Sentences
Used to Describe Them[a]

LION   BEAR   MOOSE   GIRAFFE   COW

1. The lion is to the left of the bear
2. The lion is to the left of the giraffe
3. The bear is to the left of the moose
4. The bear is to the right of the lion
5. The moose is to the left of the giraffe
6. The moose is to the right of the lion
7. The giraffe is to the left of the cow
8. The giraffe is to the right of the bear
9. The giraffe is to the right of the moose
10. The cow is to the right of the giraffe
11. The cow is to the right of the bear

[a]From Barclay (1973).

more sentences that were true of the arrays, but had not been presented before. Subjects told to figure out the order recreated the arrays (87% correct), but they erroneously accepted sentences that were true of the array and had not been presented before. Barclay interpreted his outcome, and similar outcomes of several other experiments, as an embarrassment to theories such as Clark's (1969, 1974). Such theories assume that a linguistic analysis of the sentence alone will show what subjects extract from it. But subjects in Barclay's experiment extracted information that was not in the sentences—for example, the true information that the moose is to the left of the cow (see Table 11.3).

Schweller, Brewer, and Dahl (1976) made the same point as Barclay in an experiment on paraphrase. Aptly paraphrasing a sentence depends on knowledge of the world and context. Thus, if one says *I am not paid enough* to a daughter who is asking her father for a new car, a proper paraphrase would be *I can't afford it.* But if the sentence is addressed to one's boss, a better paraphrase would be *I want a raise.* The choice of paraphrase in this example depends on knowledge of the economics of parenthood and the role and power relationships between people, their daughters, and their bosses. Because a representation is like a paraphrase, some of the external nonlinguistic facts implicit in a sentence might be incorporated into its memorial representation. For instance, a person who hears the sentence *The weatherman told the people about the approaching tornado* might include the implication of danger, available because of our knowledge about tornadoes. On a recognition test, one might falsely recognize *The weatherman warned the people about the approaching tornado.* However, if told *The weatherman told the people about the approaching beautiful weekend* one would be unlikely to falsely recognize *The weatherman warned the people about the approaching beautiful weekend,* because our knowledge about beautiful weekends excludes the likelihood of danger. Schweller, Brewer, and Dahl demonstrated such effects. The implication is that the memory representation contains knowledge of facts about the world not conveyed in the sentence itself.

The source of this supplementary knowledge must be the hearer. Hearers must bring knowledge to the comprehension process; otherwise it would take forever to convey the meanings of some sentences; recall our Revolutionary War example at the beginning of the chapter on Semantic Memory. If the hearer did not supply his own knowledge, the brief version of the sentence would be incomprehensible (which it presumably is to a child who does not yet have the relevant knowledge to supply). This suggests that two major sources of information help a listener to synthesize inputs: the context of the utterance, both linguistic and extralinguistic; and his world knowledge.

B. The Role of Context

Situational context and linguistic context both influence the meaning of sentences. Because situational context is hard to study in the laboratory, and because information-processing psychologists have a powerful preference for laboratory research, most work on the effects of context on comprehension concerns linguistic context. Most also adhere to the psycholinguistic tradition of studying isolated sentences. Thus, the study of context has concerned the effect of some words on the meaning of others in a sentence. As it happens, this kind of research addresses an issue of great importance. It shows that words do not have firm, fixed meanings, which markedly complicates the building of models of language comprehension.

The most obvious examples of words with multiple meanings are homonyms, such as *bat*. Context is all-important in determining a homonym's meaning. However, homonyms are theoretically simple, in that their various meanings can be treated as separate words, which accidentally share the same spelling and sound. The far trickier problem is that many words have different senses, or nuances, that are not altogether different meanings. Consider the word *eat* in these two sentences:

(5) The lords and ladies will eat their jellied madrilene with the dainty forks provided.

(6) The starving tramp at the door says he will eat anything you can give him.

Although *eat* has a common core of meaning, it implies considerable differences in speed, urgency, neatness, pleasure, and sociability in these two contexts. Will the real meaning please stand up? No, it will not; and that is a major problem, because information-processing models of comprehension all assume that word meanings are stored in something like a mental dictionary. A hearer is thought to access these meanings when he hears or reads words. But specifying a word's meaning is no easy matter. Because speakers use words so flexibly, it is difficult for theorists to specify what should be stored in a mental dictionary. Many experiments demonstrate the problem, though none has suggested a solution.

Anderson and Ortony (1975) used a cued recall task in their demonstration. They reasoned that they could tell which aspects of a word's meaning are synthesized by noting which words effectively prompt its recall. Suppose a person hears one of these two sentences:

(7) Pianos can be pleasing to listen to.

(8) Pianos can be difficult to move.

A person hearing sentence (7) might encode the musical properties of *piano*, but not that pianos are heavy. The opposite could be true of sentence (8), for which heaviness is more relevant than musicality. If people encode only the relevant aspects of a word, then a prompt word emphasizing music (e.g., *harmonica)* should bring sentence (7) to mind, but not (8). A prompt emphasizing weight (e.g., *sofa)* should work for sentence (8) but not for (7).

Anderson and Ortony constructed sentence sets similar to our example, and found that the meaning of the whole sentence determined which word would be the most effective prompt. Even high associates of words in the sentence were ineffective prompts when the entire sentence focused on some aspect not captured by the associate. For example, you might think that *doctors* would be a good prompt for any sentence about nurses. For some sentences it is—for example, *Nurses have to be licensed.* But for other sentences, it is not so good. *Nurses are often beautiful* is more effectively prompted by the word *actresses,* which is not normally a high associate of *nurses.* Anderson and Ortony concluded that the meaning of the sentence as a whole determines which aspects of a word's meaning are comprehended. Accordingly, they argued against theories that hold that sentence meanings are built up from invariant meanings of their constituent words.

In a similar study, Barclay, Bransford, Franks, McCarrell, and Nitsch (1974) used sentences designed to highlight selected features of their object noun. For example, *The student picked up the ink* emphasizes that ink can be kept in a bottle. In contrast, *The student spilled the ink* emphasizes that ink can be messy. Barclay et al. used phrases as cues to prompt recall of the object nouns in their sentences. Thus, *something that can be messy* and *something in a bottle* were cues for *ink.* Like Anderson and Ortony (1975), they found that the effectiveness of the cue depended on the meaning of the sentence containing the noun. *Something in a bottle* was a better cue for subjects who saw *The student picked up the ink,* whereas *something that can be messy* was better for those who saw *The student spilled the ink.*

Johnson, Doll, Bransford, and Lapinski (1974) further showed that an inappropriate context slows encoding. They gave their subjects sentences that were vague when out of context, such as *The eye is comparatively calm.* Preceding the sentence was a phrase that supplied either inappropriate context (e.g., *geyser)* or appropriate context (e.g., *hurricane).* In a third condition, no context was supplied. Johnson et al. used two rates of presentation, Fast (about 5 seconds per sentence) and Slow (about 11 seconds per sentence). Subjects received 18 such sentences, after which they wrote down as many as they could. Appropriate context gave better recall. When there was plenty of time, as in the Slow condition, inappropriate context did not lead to significantly worse recall than no context at all; but when people had less time, inappropriate context resulted in worse memory than no context. Johnson et al. concluded that trying to relate a sentence to an inappropriate context hampers encoding, and that people need extra time to compensate.

It is easy to see that the meaning of a sentence somehow depends on the meanings of the words it contains. The experiments of Anderson and Ortony (1975), Barclay et al. (1974), and Johnson et al. (1974) illustrate that the reverse is also true, and that the meanings of words somehow depend on the meaning of the sentence that contains them. One of the challenges to students of comprehension is to explain how sentences determine word meanings at the same time that word meanings determine sentences. And the question of how the meanings of words should be represented in our models remains to be answered.

It is not intuitively obvious that words like *ink* and *nurses* take part of their meaning from the surrounding context; so experimental demonstrations that they do are valuable. Other words have meaning only in context. Such words are called *deictic* (from the Greek word deixis, for "pointing"). Pronouns are deictic, as are words like *here, now, yesterday, over there, next week, this,* and *that.* You cannot understand the import of such words unless you know the temporal or spatial context of the utterance.

Brewer and Harris (1974) argued that deictic words are often poorly recalled in psychological experiments because the experimental context renders them meaningless. For example, the typical subject presented with *All of California felt this earthquake* is quite likely to misrecall the word *this.* But suppose the subject received *We hope you are enjoying this experiment.* It is much likelier that *this* would have meaning and that the subject would recall it. Brewer and Harris included sentences of both types in their experiment. In some, the deictic words were relatively meaningless. In others, the time and place of the actual experiment imparted meaning to the deictic words. For instance, their sentence *Marijuana grows wild in this county* is true of the county where the experiment was conducted. The experimenters predicted that deictic words would be recalled as well as nondeictic words, if they appeared in a context that made them meaningful, but that they would be recalled less well than nondeictic words in context that rendered them relatively meaningless. This is exactly what happened. Without suitable context, only about a third of the deictic words were correctly recalled, as compared to about 75% correct for nondeictic words. In the suitable contexts, recall was about equal for deictic and nondeictic words. Verb tense is also a deictic element, in that it specifies time relative to the present; you have to know when a sentence is uttered to know what is past, present, and future relative to it. Verb tenses are also often misrecalled in psychological experiments. Harris and Brewer (1973) showed that verb tenses could be made much more memorable by adding to the sentences such temporal cues as *Next week, Right now,* and *Last month.*

The role of context is important in the study of language comprehension, but not unique to it. Stimuli and context combine in the interpretation of any percept, as for example the *O* in *LOVE* and in *1066*. The literature on encoding specificity, which we described in Chapter 8, concerns a closely related phenomenon. It even uses the same method of cued recall. It is quite possible that the solution to any one of these puzzles will contain the solution to the others.

In summary, context determines which aspects of a word will be encoded, and perhaps whether particular words will be encoded at all. Context may also determine the meaning of the sentence as a whole. The literal content of a sentence is only one determinant of the content of its synthesized code. Context is another, and finally, the hearer's knowledge importantly supplements comprehension of the literal message.

C. The Role of Previous Knowledge

Normal adults rapidly and automatically supplement the linguistic messages they receive with knowledge they already have; if they did not, speakers would never finish their messages. Psycholinguistic research has identified three related ways in which people use what they already know to comprehend what they hear: inference, use of presuppositions, and extraction of the intended meaning (even when it is not exactly what the speaker said).

1. Inference

The recognition memory technique that demonstrated constructive synthesis has also shown that inference is part and parcel of comprehension. Thus, Bransford, Barclay, and Franks (1972) showed that people cannot distinguish actually presented sentences from inferences they made in the course of comprehending those sentences. The following are examples of materials used by Bransford et al.:

(9) Three turtles rested on a floating log and a fish swam beneath them.
(10) Three turtles rested beside a floating log and a fish swam beneath them.
(11) Three turtles rested on a floating log and a fish swam beneath it.
(12) Three turtles rested beside a floating log and a fish swam beneath it.

Notice that Sentence (9) implies Sentence (11). If the turtles were on the log and a fish swam beneath them, it had to swim beneath the log, too. But Sentence (10) does not imply Sentence (12). Although the fish may have swum beneath the log, it need not have. Bransford et al. presented sentences such as (9) and (10), and then asked for recognition of sentences such as (11) and (12).

People who had seen sentences such as (9) were equally confident that they recognized Sentences (9) and (11), even though Sentence (11) was new. Subjects did not confuse Sentences (10) and (12). Bransford, Barclay, and Franks argued from their results (and others in the same published report) that constructive inference is part of extracting the meaning of sentences.

In a similar experiment, Johnson, Bransford, and Solomon (1973) presented materials like the following:

John was trying to fix the birdhouse. He was (pounding/looking for) the nail when his father came out to watch him and to help him do the work.

The word *pounding* was used in the experimental condition, and the words *looking for* were used in the control condition. During a subsequent recognition test, people were asked whether they had seen the sentence *John was using the hammer to fix the birdhouse when his father came to watch him and to help him do the work.* The experimenters expected that this sentence would be falsely recognized more by subjects who had received the word *pounding* in the original paragraph, because most people would infer use of a hammer in pounding a nail. Their expectations were confirmed. As a matter of fact, people were more certain of having seen the plausible inferences than they were of having seen the original sentence! This was not true for the control condition. Subjects who received the words *looking for* in the original paragraph were not especially inclined to falsely recognize the test sentence. Again, the conclusion is that people extract plausible inferences as well as the literal content of messages.

Comparable data have been reported for pictures. Both Baggett (1975) and Jenkins (1977) have shown people pictures of familiar action sequences, such as getting a haircut or drinking tea. In a later recognition test, people distinguish poorly between pictures they actually saw and other pictures that fit the original series but were omitted during the presentation. Professor Jenkins is a faculty member at the University of Minnesota, and was a teacher of Bransford, Barclay, and Franks. The similarity of their interests and approach is more than coincidental.

All these experiments involve delayed recognition for sentences. But what about an immediate test? Do people separate their inferences from the message when they are asked immediately? An experiment by Harris (1974) suggests that they do, but as time passes people confuse what they inferred with what was said. Harris divided his subjects into two conditions. In the Comprehension condition, subjects responded to questions about sentences immediately; in the Memory condition they responded later. The questions concerned the truth value of inferences from complex sentences. For example, *Miss America played the tuba* is a plausible inference from *Miss America said that she played the tuba.* People were asked whether these inferences were definitely true, definitely false, or indeterminate. In the preceding example, truth value is indeterminate, because Miss America could lie about her musical accomplishments. Indeed, subjects in the Comprehension condition tended to judge it indeterminate, in accord with rules of logic. But in the the Memory condition, when asked whether *Miss America played the tuba* was true, false, or indeterminate on the basis of an earlier-presented sentence, people tended to judge it true. In other words, they were more inclined to accept the invited inference as true after some time had passed.

The conclusion is that people analyze the literal content of a sentence as long as the surface structure is still available. But as surface structure is forgotten, people substitute a memory representation that incorporates not only the literal message but also plausible inferences. By the time surface structure is gone, subjects can no longer distinguish between the parts of their memory representations that are based on literal content and the parts that are based on their own inferences.

2. Presuppositions

Sentences presuppose knowledge. Many sentences—perhaps all—both assert some information that the speaker thinks is new to the hearer and presuppose some information that the speaker thinks the hearer already knows. In certain kinds of construction, the presuppositions are easy to identify. For example, *Gloria has stopped getting drunk every night* presupposes that at one time Gloria got drunk every night, and asserts that she has stopped doing so. *Conrad failed to see the stop sign* presupposes a sign's existence, and asserts that Conrad failed to see it. *John admitted that he let the dog out* presupposes that the dog was supposed to be in, and asserts that John pled guilty to letting it out. Presuppositions are like background conditions that must be true for a sentence to have meaning. Often, when a hearer was not previously aware of presupposed information, he infers it when he hears a sentence. Hearing that Gloria has stopped getting drunk, a person might infer that she used to drink to excess, even if he met her only recently. A hearer who did not know where the dog was supposed to be might infer from *John admitted that he let the dog out* that it belonged in.

An interesting characteristic of presuppositions is that they do not change when a sentence is negated. *Gloria has stopped getting drunk every night* and *Gloria has not stopped getting drunk every night* both presuppose Gloria's bibulousness. *John admitted he let the dog out* and *John did not admit he let the dog out* both presuppose that the dog was not supposed to go out. It is the presuppositional character of the sentence that allows this sort of evil: *Have you stopped beating your wife?* To answer directly, a person can only deny the assertion (about stopping); he cannot deny the presupposition (about beating). And because the question is meaningless if the presupposition is false, a listener must assume that it is true in order to comprehend the sentence—even if only for an instant. Lawyers sometimes exploit this fact. When a witness is asked *Do you admit to seeing the letter?*, hearers must presuppose for a moment that it was bad to see the letter. Otherwise, the sentence is meaningless. The witness may flounder around and say *Of course I saw it. So what?* But the natural comprehension strategies of the hearer may already have awarded the lawyer his point.

Hornby (1974) demonstrated experimentally that people tend to take presuppositional information as true. He presented pictures (e.g., a boy petting a cat) so briefly that people could not see all the details. He then asked people to judge the truth of statements about the pictures. Sometimes the statements were accurate; *It is a cat the boy is petting.* Sometimes they were inaccurate in assertion, sometimes in presupposition.

(13) It is the girl who is petting the cat.
(14) It is the boy who is petting the dog.

Sentence (13) presupposes that a cat is being petted, and asserts that a girl is doing the petting. The presupposition is consistent with a picture of a boy petting a cat; but the assertion is at odds with it. The reverse is true of Sentence (14). The presupposition that the dog is being petted is not consistent with the picture, but the assertion that a boy is doing the petting is. Because the picture was presented so quickly that people would have a hard time seeing all the details, it was possible for Hornby to see whether mismatches were detected better if the presupposition was wrong or if the assertion was wrong. He found that people were more likely to make errors when the mismatch was in the presupposition. People were more likely to detect the mismatch in Sentence (13) than in Sentence (14). Hornby's outcome suggests that a normal comprehension strategy is to evaluate assertions, but to take presuppositions as true.

You can see how this comprehension strategy might be exploited to persuade people of things they might not otherwise believe. The lawyer who asks *Do you admit to seeing the letter?* may prevent the conscious evaluation of the wrongness of seeing the letter, and may thus slip one over on witness, judge, and jury. Overly obvious efforts of this sort are called leading questions.

Some excellent research on leading questions has been done by Loftus, whom you may have seen on television, advertising Anacin. Although her commercials were impeccably honest, her interest in the persuasive use of presuppositions may have stemmed from her advertising experience. Loftus' studies show that careful question wording may affect, not only the answers to questions, but also people's memory of the events they are being questioned about. In one study (Loftus & Zanni, 1975) students viewed a short film showing a multiple-car accident. Immediately afterward, they filled out a questionnaire that included such questions as *Did you see a broken headlight?* For half the subjects the question was worded *Did you see the broken headlight?* When the definite article *the* is used, the question is about the viewer's powers of observation. It asks, *There was a broken headlight. Did you happen to see it?* The indefinite article *a* does not presuppose the existence of a broken headlight. Questions with *the* more often elicited reports that the witness had seen the broken headlight than questions with *a*. This was true regardless of whether the object had actually appeared in the film.

In another study (Loftus & Palmer, 1974), subjects again viewed a film of an automobile accident and were asked about the speed of the cars at the time of the accident. Some subjects were asked *About how fast were the cars going when they smashed into each other?* Others were asked *About how fast were the cars going when they hit each other?* *Smashed* elicited higher estimates of speed than *hit,* and what is more, the wording of this question affected people's later memory of the events in the film. When they were questioned again a week later (without seeing the film again), viewers were asked a number of questions, including whether or not they had seen any broken glass. Those who had previously been asked the *smashed* question were more likely to report having seen broken glass than those who had received the *hit* question, even though there was actually no broken glass in the film. People apparently take information from questions and use it to supplement their memory. When the experimenter asks *How fast were the cars going when they smashed into each other?*, it is presupposed that the cars smashed each other, and this presupposition in turn suggests that they were going quite fast. People apparently incorporated the presupposed information into their memory of the accident, both in their immediate estimates of speed and their delayed recollection about the presence of glass.

In yet another experiment of the same general type, Loftus (1975) showed students a 3-minute videotape taken from the film *Diary of a Student Revolution.* The sequence showed eight demonstrators disrupting a class and then leaving the room after a noisy confrontation. After the videotape, subjects were given questionnaires, in which one question was critical. Half the students were asked *Was the leader of the four demonstrators who entered the classroom a male?* The rest were asked *Was the leader of the twelve demonstrators who entered the classroom a male?* A week later, the students were asked a number of additional questions, including *How many demonstrators did you see entering the classroom?* Students who had previously been asked the *twelve* question estimated more demonstrators than those who were previously asked the *four* question. Interestingly, very few of the subjects responded with the actual number twelve or four. It seemed that they averaged their memory of the film (which showed eight demonstrators) and the number presupposed in the question.

Acceptance of presuppositions is a form of inference. People normally know and believe presupposed information; but when they do not, they may acquire it when they hear it.

3. Nonliteral Comprehension

Sometimes the contribution of the listener entirely transcends the literal content of a message. When the literal message is oblique, distorted, or badly phrased, people may nevertheless extract the intended message. It is as though the literal message served only to direct the hearer to the intended message, rather than to embody the message itself. Clinical psychologists sometimes rely on people's extraction of hidden communications (usually about power relationships) from words that appear to be about something else (Watzlawick, Beavin, & Jackson, 1967). For example, when a therapist asks a husband and wife how they happened to meet, there is a power message conveyed by who speaks first. If the husband speaks first and his phrasing suggests that he "looked her over" and picked her out, he is communicating a power relationship—namely, that he controlled their meeting and courtship; she simply waited around to be looked over and picked out. The therapist would not be surprised if the wife in this example evidenced understanding of the husband's nonliteral message.

Cognitive psychology has only recently attended to the nonliteral comprehension of linguistic inputs, and our studies have not concerned the affective level as the clinical approach does. The research conducted by cognitive psychologists concerns two general issues: the interpretation of distorted sentences and indirectly conveyed requests. The latter are quite common in verbal interchanges. The sentence

(15) It's stuffy in here.

is sometimes a request to open a door or window. The analytic process in correctly interpreting Sentence (15) is likely to be the same one that might make a wife feel put down when her husband says,

(16) Oh, she was one of the girls in my office, and I thought she was kind of cute.

For both (15) and (16), the listener may extract a message that is not part of the literal statement.

A study by Fillenbaum (1974) shows how thoroughly people may disregard a message in favor of plausible interpretation. He asked people to paraphrase sentences. His instructions were emphatic that the paraphrase should preserve the meaning of the originals, not improve them. He included "perverse" sentences that would only make sense in highly unusual contexts. For example, one item was *Don't print that or I won't sue you,* which is a perverse threat because usually one threatens to sue, not to refrain from suing. In spite of Fillenbaum's strong instructions not to improve the sentences, over half of the perverse items were normalized—for example, to *I'll sue you if you print that.* Next, Fillenbaum showed people the original sentences and their own paraphrases, asking whether they meant the same thing. Less than half of the normalizations were detected, and people seemed flustered when confronted with the fact that their paraphrase had changed the meaning. Many indicated that their paraphrase was "what the speaker actually meant." Fillenbaum concluded that people more readily assume that a perverse sentence is a badly phrased statement about a normal world than that it is a well-phrased statement about a peculiar world. This suggests that it is normal to be only partly dependent on linguistic input, and to use it along with one's own knowledge to reach a plausible interpretation.

Clark and Lucy (1975) supported this interpretation in an experiment on conversationally conveyed requests. They showed people statements such as *Please color the circle blue* and *Shouldn't you color the circle blue?*, along with pictures of a blue or a pink circle. Subjects were told to regard the statement as a request, and to indicate by a *true* or *false* response whether the request had been followed. For both the preceding examples, then, subjects should have said *true* if a blue circle appeared, and *false* if a pink circle appeared. People's responses of *true* and *false* indicated that they responded to the request in its intended form. This conclusion is based on the fact that people can generally say *false* faster to a *negative* stimulus, but they can say *true* faster to an *affirmative* stimulus. Some of the requests in Clark and Lucy's study were superficially negative, but had affirmative conveyed meanings:

(17) Why not color the circle blue?

For example, Sentence (17) is actually an affirmative request to color the circle blue, despite the negative word *not.* If people respond to the literal meaning of this sentence, they should be faster to say *false* to a pink circle than *true* to a blue one. But they responded *true* more quickly, indicating that their response was based on the affirmative nature of the conveyed request.

However, Clark and Lucy found some evidence in the reaction times that people did at some point compute the literal meaning. *Unless* is an "inherent negative"; although not conventionally negative, such words yield latencies similar to ordinary negatives in comprehension tasks (Clark & Clark, 1977). Negation, like interrogation, is a surface structure characteristic that usually yields slower processing times than affirmation and declaration. In the Clark and Lucy experiment, negative and interrogative surface structures, such as Sentences (18) and (19), resulted in slower response times:

(18) I'll be very happy unless you color the circle blue.
(19) Can you make the circle blue?

than their affirmative and declarative counterparts

(20) I'll be very happy if you color the circle blue.
(21) Please make the circle blue.

Clark and Lucy proposed that people first compute the literal meaning, then test it against the context to see whether it is plausible. If it is not, they use rules of conversation to compute the conveyed or intended meaning. Thus, a person hearing *Would you mind opening the window?* first computes the literal meaning, and realizes that it is an implausible question; the speaker knows that the hearer would not mind. He then applies conversational rules to deduce the intended meaning: *Please open the window.*

This study marked a turning point in Clark's interests. While his previous models (Clark, 1974; Clark & Chase, 1972) were appropriate for the comparison of sentences and pictures, the earlier experiments required nothing but literal comprehension. Conversation requires attention to intended meanings, too. Along with Haviland, Clark set out to build a model to explain conversational practices. The result is a comprehension theory that attempts to integrate experimental data on inference, presupposition, and nonliteral comprehension.

V. A MODEL OF CONVERSATIONAL COMPREHENSION

Clark's model (Clark, 1976, 1978; Clark & Haviland, 1977; Haviland & Clark, 1974) considers comprehension to be the adding of new information to information already known. For example, upon hearing the sentence

(22) It was Margaret who phoned last night.

the listener's job is to access his previous knowledge that someone phoned and add the novel information that it was Margaret. Clark calls the material that should already be known Given information (someone called), and the novel component of the message New information (it was Margaret). A presupposition is a linguistic device to convey Given information. The relationship between presupposition and Given information is a little like that between shoes and feet: They are not identical, but in the well-dressed person, one contains the other. Likewise, in the well-formed sentence, presuppositions contain Given information and assertions contain New information.

Such linguistic devices help the hearer separate what he is supposed to know already from what he is not expected to know. He can then locate information he has already stored that corresponds to the Givens, and add to or modify them as directed by the New information. In Sentence (22), the hearer who is aware that someone called last night must locate the entity in memory corresponding to *the one who phoned last night*. Let us give this entity, which is called the Antecedent, the arbitrary label X_{56}. Therefore,

X_{56} = *the one who phoned last night.*

The hearer of Sentence (22) should seek entity X_{56}, because the construction of the sentence informs him that the speaker expects it to be in his memory. He can then add the new information,

X_{56} = Margaret,

and he has comprehended.

We have spoken of three closely related concepts, whose similarities and differences we should clarify. First, there is the presuppositional component of a sentence, indicated by certain syntactic constructions. Second, there is Given information, which corresponds to what a speaker thinks his hearer already knows. A competent speaker will put the Given information into the presuppositional part of his sentences, which will help the hearer in seeking (within his own memory) the intended Antecedent. The Antecedent corresponds to the entity that in fact *is* in the hearer's memory.

An interesting feature of Clark's view of comprehension is that a speaker must do some "mind reading" and a listener must expect the speaker to be good at "reading his mind." The speaker must assess the mental world of the listener so as to say neither more nor less than necessary to direct the search for intended Antecedents, while adding manageable parcels of information. The hearer, for his part, must follow a comprehension strategy that assumes that: (1) the Given information is contained in linguistic presuppositions; (2) there will be in his memory an entity corresponding to the Given information; and (3) if the speaker is telling him too much or too little, then the message must be nonliteral. Comprehension will proceed smoothly as long as speaker and hearer do their parts; but if the speaker does not follow the rules, the hearer's strategy fails and communication breaks down. It is as if the speaker and hearer are parties to a contract: The speaker contracts to follow certain rules of conversation, and the hearer contracts to use a comprehension strategy that depends on those rules being followed. In fact, Clark and Haviland (1977) have proposed exactly this metaphor, suggesting that listeners' strategies depend on adherence to the Given–New Contract.

At the heart of the Contract is the need for speakers to direct hearers to the intended Antecedent. The Antecedent information is, to the best of the speaker's knowledge, available to the listener. The listener may consider that the hearer has the Antecedent available for several reasons. It may be general knowledge, as in Sentence (23):

(23) *Airport security measures* have greatly reduced the incidence of skyjackings.

We believe that the italicized portion of Sentence (23) will direct a normally informed reader to an Antecedent in his memory. Of course, we could be wrong. If so, the reader must do some additional processing, as a result of which comprehension will be relatively slow. The speaker may assume that the hearer has the Antecedent available because it has been supplied by linguistic context, as in (24):

(24) I have two sons. *My sons* are both avid sports fans.

In this case, *my sons* is not general knowledge, but the speaker of the sentence pair can assume that the hearer has the Antecedent corresponding to *my sons* in memory because the sons were just mentioned. Previous linguistic context, or previous interactions between speaker and hearer, may give the speaker reason to expect particular Antecedents to be in the hearer's memory. If you have visited my home, met my two sons, and interacted extensively with my family, I can say *My sons are both avid sports fans* with the reasonable expectation that you should have an Antecedent corresponding to my two sons. Nonlinguistic context can also provide a speaker with the expectation of available Antecedents on his listener's part. For example, the speaker of Sentence (25) makes the assumption that a hearer can identify the Antecedents for *it* and *one:*

(25) I didn't like *it* as much as the *one* we saw last week.

The assumption is reasonable if the sentence is uttered by a girl to her steady companion as they leave a movie, and the couple had seen another movie the previous week. She can assume that he has Antecedents corresponding to the movie they just saw and to the one they had seen the previous week without having to mention them.

In most speech, the speaker introspects unconsciously for his hearer. However, the accuracy with which he is able to guess at his hearer's preexisting knowledge determines his effectiveness at getting his message across. A speaker who underestimates his listener's knowledge will say things the hearer knows. The hearer will feel bored, patronized, or both. A speaker who overestimates his hearers' knowledge will talk over their heads, leaving them confused and uninformed.

Table 11.4 illustrates Clark and Haviland's model further. It gives examples of speaker beliefs, hearer knowledge, well-formed sentences to provide the hearer with directions to an Antecedent and new information to add to the Antecedent, and the outcome of hearer processing. Notice that sentences like the last one in the table are easy to understand, even by someone who does not know that the speaker owned a Porsche. But the model requires that there be Antecedent information for comprehension to occur. If the listener does not have the Antecedent in memory, how does he understand? He infers the Antecedent. Relying on the Given–New Contract, the hearer first tries to locate the Antecedent in memory. If he cannot find it there, he tries to construct it by inference. Such inferences are important, for they have empirical consequences.

A hearer using the Given–New Strategy will sometimes find that the speaker has directed him to an Antecedent he does not have. For example, Sentence (26) makes reference to an Antecedent that is probably not in your memory:

(26) *The student who flunked his test* has dropped the course.

However, you have available a capacity to overcome this problem. You can construct an Antecedent, using reasoning such as, "If the student who flunked his test dropped the course, there must be a student who flunked his test." This is inference, for you have inferred the existence of the student from a sentence that was not literally about his existence, but about his dropping a course. It is a small inference, to be sure, and probably done without conscious awareness; but it is an inference nevertheless. Clark (1977) calls this kind of inference *implicature*. It is implicature by addition. *Bridging* is another kind of implicature. These sentences will probably require you to construct a bridge:

(27) Alex went to a party last night. He's going to get drunk again tonight.

The word "again" signals that it is Given that Alex got drunk before. You will attempt to locate an Antecedent corresponding to the Given information— namely, "the previous occasion on which Alex got drunk." Nothing in your knowledge of Alex, or in the surrounding linguistic context, could supply you with this Antecedent. But you will probably not be stumped; you will most likely resort to bridging. By noting that Alex went to a party last night, and that people often drink at parties, you can draw the plausible inference that Alex got drunk last night, thereby constructing the intended Antecedent.

TABLE 11.4

Examples of Given Information, New Information, Suitable Constructions, and Hearer Processing According to Smoothly Operating Given–New Contract

Given Information (What the Speaker Believes the Hearer Already Knows)	New Information (What the Speaker Wants to Add for the Hearer)	Sentence	Antecedent[a] Located (What the Hearer Actually Has in Memory)	Outcome of Sentence Processing
Someone kissed Oscar.	Olivia did it.	It was Olivia who kissed Oscar.	X_{32} = the person who kissed Oscar.	X_{32} = Olivia.
Olivia kissed someone.	Oscar was the one.	It was Oscar that Olivia kissed.	X_{98} = the person Olivia kissed.	X_{98} = Oscar.
There exists a particular garbage truck.	It hit my Porsche.	The garbage truck hit my Porsche.	X_{185} = the particular garbage truck.	X_{185} hit the speaker's Porsche.
Speaker owns a Porsche.	A garbage truck hit it.	My Porsche was hit by a garbage truck.	X_{210} = the speaker's Porsche.	Garbage truck hit X_{210}.

[a]The numbers of the Antecedents are arbitrary. They are intended to show that some specific parcel of information in the memory, which corresponds to the Given information, is accessed. The Antecedents could be, for example, particular nodes in a network structure like that of Collins, Loftus, and Quillian (1975) or Rumelhart, Lindsay, and Norman (1972).

Clark (1977) notes that various bridges can be built for any sentences lacking an existing Antecedent in memory. For (27), we assumed the bridge that Alex got drunk at last night's party. But you could have inferred that Alex got drunk at last night's party because he always gets drunk at parties, and this is because he always meets women at parties, and all women speak in high voices, and high voices invariably make him think of his mother, and every time he thinks of his mother he gets angry, and whenever he gets angry he gets drunk. This bridge would have constructed the intended Antecedent as well as the shorter one. Clark assumes that people usually construct the shortest bridge sufficient to provide an Antecedent.

Restructuring is a third device available to hearers under the Given–New Strategy. This is necessary when speakers violate the Given–New contract by putting Given information in the assertion and New information in the presupposition. Here is an example:

(28) Agnes saw somebody. It was Agnes who saw Maxine.

This sequence seems wrong to most people. The cleft object construction of the second sentence implies the Given information *someone saw Maxine.* The New information should be that it was Agnes. A hearer of the second sentence, assuming the contract is being followed, will search for an Antecedent corresponding to *the person who saw Maxine,* and will fail to find one. All he should have is *the person that Agnes saw.* But by interchanging the Given and New information in the second sentence—that is, restructuring, the hearer can get around the problem.

To summarize the Given–New Strategy, then, the steps are as follows:

1. Isolate the Given and New information in the current sentence.
2. Locate in memory the intended Antecedent identified by the Given information. If none is directly available, try to construct one by bridging, addition, or restructuring.
3. Integrate the New information into the memory structure by attaching it to the Antecedent found or constructed in Step 2.

The preceding discussion of the Given–New Strategy covers the way Clark's theory characterizes the listener's role; but speakers must also follow the rules. The rules are implicit in the contract. First, the speaker should be appropriate: He should use syntactic constructions that facilitate the hearer's separation of Given and New information, thereby facilitating the search for an Antecedent. He should be relevant: The techniques of addition, bridging, and restructuring will not work unless the hearer can count on the present context for cues to the inferences he is intended to make. As an example, suppose a person says, *I was talking to your brother the other day.* Then he changes the subject and thinks of the used-car dealer who sold him a lemon. Violating the requirement of relevance, he gives no signal of the changed subject but says, *I think I'll go back and kill the lousy creep.* His hearer, assuming that the requirement of relevance is being followed, constructs the plausible bridge *the lousy creep* is *your brother.* This does supply an Antecedent for *the lousy creep,* but not the intended one. The hearer could be forgiven if he moved to protect his brother! A third requirement is uniqueness: Only one Antecedent should be designated by the Given information. The following sentence repeatedly violates the requirement of uniqueness, for it is impossible to determine the referents of all the pronouns:

(29) The lawyer told a colleague that he thought a client of his more critical of himself than any of his rivals.

We have all known people who talk this way, particularly when excited. A fourth requirement is computability. The hearer must not be asked to do too much bridging. This requirement is frequently violated by authors of statistics textbooks, who follow lists of formulas with the offhand remark, *Obviously therefore ...*, drawing a very unobvious conclusion. Oftentimes, the conclusion relies on ancillary assumptions that are automatic to the writer and unheard of by the reader. Parents often violate the requirement of computability when speaking to their young children. A mother says, *Don't get your hands dirty. I'm about to set the table.* Computing the bridges to relate these two sentences requires the child to know that mother sets the table right before serving food, that mother does not want the child to eat with dirty hands, that hand-washing after the food is served will delay eating, that delay will cause the food to get cold, that mother does not want to begin dinner until the child is seated, and that mother and father like their food hot. This is well within the capacity of the average 10-year-old, but such things are often said to far younger children. To keep from violating the requirement of computability, a speaker must estimate well his listener's skill in bridging.

Bridging, addition, and restructuring should take time, allowing a test of the Given–New model. Haviland and Clark (1974) tested this prediction by asking people to press a button as soon as they understood the second of two sentences. Their sentence pairs were of the following types:

(30) Horace got some beer out of the trunk. The beer was warm.
(31) Horace was especially fond of beer. The beer was warm.

Notice that the first sentence in (30) postulates a particular batch of beer, which provides a direct Antecedent for *the beer* in the second sentence. The first sentence in (31) does not posit any particular beer; so this pair requires bridging or addition, which should take time. Haviland and Clark found that pairs like (31) did take longer than pairs like (30), providing support for the idea that people must construct an Antecedent by means of extra processing if it is not directly supplied.

What happens when the hearer computes an Antecedent, adds the New information to it, and finds the result implausible? According to the theory, the hearer should make a nonliteral interpretation of the sentence. Sometimes, this may be exactly what is intended, as in the request phrased as a question, *Would you mind opening a window?* Sometimes, however, the hearer computes inferences the speaker did not intend. Clark calls these inferences *unauthorized*. A classic unauthorized inference was made by the press when Nixon said at a news conference, *I am not a crook.* Nixon intended to assure everybody that he was honest, but the effect was quite the opposite. The statement *I am not a crook* is only meaningful when someone believes you are crooked; recall Wason's (1965) results on the contexts of plausible denial. The press computed the bridge, "Hmmm. He thinks people believe he is a crook," and they took Nixon's statement as a public admission that he was on the defensive. This admission signaled a change in his public posture. Most of us stopped our bridging there; but the Washington press corps made many further inferences, all of them unauthorized, for Nixon did not intend them to be made.

Here is another example of unauthorized inference:

> Ian has just arrived home after a late night at work, and his wife Maggie calls out, "Is that you, honey?" Now Maggie meant for Ian to take this as a mere question of concern, one to be answered by "Yes" or some such response. But Ian infers something more. He recalls that whenever she has called out like this in the past, she has been worried all evening, watched television for consolation, and been cranky all the next day. He therefore infers that she worried and watched television that night and will be cranky the next day. Maggie didn't mean to convey this by what she said, and so Ian has drawn unauthorized inferences [Clark, 1978, p. 27].

Just as the speaker must know the listener in order to construct sentences that pinpoint Antecedent information, the hearer must know the speaker. Whenever the intended Antecedent is not explicitly provided, the hearer must construct it by inference. In doing so, he will rely on everything he knows about the speaker, for he calculates what the speaker intended. If he cannot calculate, he must guess. When the speaker does not pinpoint Antecedents well, he loses control over the hearer's processing and risks the drawing of unauthorized inferences.

Sometimes there are intentional violations of the terms of the contract, as when people speak ironically or sarcastically, or writers introduce new characters as if they were old friends. To communicate effectively, such violations must carry signals that they are intended. If suitable signals (facial expression, tone of voice, or the like) do not accompany the violations, the hearer will continue to use the Given–New Strategy, and he will extract the wrong meaning from what he hears.

Clark's theory is quite new, and it will be a while before it has been well tested. Nevertheless, it does seem to integrate much of the literature summarized in this chapter. For example, it encompasses the data on constructive synthesis; the constructive parts are the products of addition and bridging. It accounts for nonliteral comprehension (Clark & Lucy, 1975) and the force of presuppositions. Because presuppositions are treated as Given information, the natural strategy is to locate or construct the Antecedent mentioned in a presupposition rather than to evaluate its truth (Hornby, 1974). When Given information cannot be located, it is constructed by addition; this feature of Clark's theory accounts for the findings of Loftus (1975), Loftus and Palmer (1974), and Loftus and Zanni (1975). Even though Clark's theory is too new to have generated a great deal of experimentation, it has consequences that might be tested, and it is consistent with the available data. It does justice to people's ability to transcend the literal content of linguistic messages and to divine what speakers have in mind. This ability must be handled by any adequate theory, for it probably pervades the vast majority of comprehension activities.

Discourse Processing and Global Models of Comprehension

ABSTRACT

I. *Introduction*

The psycholinguistic approach to comprehension, covered in the preceding chapter, takes sentences as its units of analysis. The global models of comprehension are concerned with larger units, and they strive to give a completely sufficient account of people's comprehension activities.

II. *Discourse Processing*

Research and theory on discourse comprehension stands midway in scope between psycholinguists' work and the work of the global modelers.
  A. *Content of Passages* Psychological research on story comprehension was begun by Bartlett (1932) but was abandoned during the years when behaviorism and linguistics held predominant sway over psychologists. Bartlett's and later research showed that people's previously stored knowledge supplies themes around which they organize new inputs, even those that are vague or metaphorical.
  B. *Structure of Passages* Several scholars consider that there may be a kind of "grammar" of stories, which can be represented by rewrite rules or tree diagrams. Efforts to predict the importance and memorability of various elements in the story from such structures have been successful.

III. *Comprehensive Theories in General*

In 1973, the first comprehensive model appeared (Anderson & Bower, 1973). It was called HAM and marked a change in some of the conventional components of the information-processing paradigm. Within 4 years, several more of these large-scale theories appeared, and HAM was revised. These models are more rational and less empirical than is customary for cognitive psychologists. The detail in which they are specified and the rapid rate at which they change has made them less than universally popular. However, the extraordinary scholarship that characterizes them makes it impossible to ignore them.

450

A. *Why Global Theory?—Some Shared Motives*
  1. *Limitations of Smaller Models* Global theorists reject as problem-limited the small-scale models resulting from experiments on one task such as sentence–picture verification. They intend their models to be adequate to a large range of human comprehension capacities.
  2. *Theories, Models, or Experiments in Conceptualization?* The global models are not theories in the conventional sense. They seem, instead, to be efforts to stretch the information-processing paradigm to make it answer timeless questions of meaning that have preoccupied thinkers for centuries.
  3. *Influence of Artificial Intelligence* The global models trace their ancestry to Quillian (1968) and continue to draw on developments in the discipline of artificial intelligence. The relationship works both ways, as AI draws on psychological accounts too.
B. *Agreed-Upon Features of the Comprehension System* All the global modelers have adopted a similar strategy: Define the range of human memory and then develop a system that can represent this range. Then develop interfaces between the environment and the memory system. The modelers agree on what human capacities are important. All are content-dependent. All borrow from artificial intelligence. All agree that the comprehension system has at least these four components: an interface parser, a representational structure, control systems, and output synthesizing mechanisms.
C. *Some Differences in Approach* The models differ in starting point and amount of attention devoted to the four components. Some have completely ignored one or another component, while the same component may be the very heart of an alternative model. Some are implemented as computer simulations; others are not.

IV. *Some Particulars of Four Theories*
  A. *HAM (Anderson & Bower, 1973)*
  B. *ACT (J. Anderson, 1976)*
  C. *LNR (Norman & Rumelhart, 1975)*
  D. *Kintsch's (1974) Theory*

V. *Where the Theories Stand on Some Major Issues*
  A. *The Formal Representation of World Knowledge* Each system contains a theoretical representation of the human representational system. The main characteristics of the system that must be accommodated are its size, its efficiency, and its inferential ability.
    1. *Obvious Requirements for Representational Systems* The necessary feature of the sufficiency, efficiency, and inferential aspects of the system are described.
    2. *Network Notation* Several of the systems utilize network notation in characterizing the representational part of their theories.
    3. *Propositional Representation*
      a. *Why propositional representation?* Some of the arguments for the universal choice of propositional representation are presented.
      b. *Formal properties of propositional representation* Illustrations of propositional notation are provided.
      c. *Summary*
  B. *The Declarative–Procedural Distinction* Anderson (1976) has incorporated this distinction in ACT for reasons described here.

C. *The Meaning of Words*
 1. *What We Know About Word Meaning*   Abstract conceptual entities
    constitute the meaning of words. Meaning cannot be reduced to reference.
    Some word meaning is tied to human perceptual and motor capacities.
    Some word meanings can be expressed in terms of more "primitive"
    concepts.
 2. *Semantic Decomposition*   Some theorists prefer to develop a small set of
    semantic primitives that capture word meanings. Their propositions
    are relatively complex. Others prefer to use concepts at the level of
    complexity of words in the propositions; for their theories, the
    representational system carries a relatively heavy burden of expressing
    meanings. Both positions have attractive and problematic features.
D. *The Interface Problem*   The models have not as yet given much attention to
   the interface between the environment and the memory.

VI. *Summary of Comprehensive Theories*

I. INTRODUCTION

Psycholinguistic research on comprehension takes individual sentences as its
units of analysis. As we saw in the last chapter, this focus has revealed
interesting things about people's comprehension strategies. But people
comprehend much larger units than isolated sentences. They grasp
paragraphs, chapters, stories, books, and situations. A growing body of
research and theory is now focusing directly on the comprehension of such
larger units of discourse. This chapter discusses that work, and particularly
the approach of global modelers to comprehension. We begin with some
experiments on discourse processing, which provide the only bridge for the
enormous gap between studies of sentence memory and comprehension and
the larger task set for themselves by the global modelers. Discourse
processing originated in experimental psychology alone. The comprehensive
theories represent influences from both psychology and artificial intelligence.

II. DISCOURSE PROCESSING

A. Content of Passages

Sir Frederick Bartlett (1932) deserves credit for beginning the enterprise with
his now famous studies on memory for stories, of which this is one:

The War of the Ghosts

One night two young men from Egulac went down to the river to hunt seals, and
while they were there it became foggy and calm. Then they heard war-cries, and

they thought: "Maybe this is a war-party." They escaped to the shore, and hid behind a log. Now canoes came up, and they heard the noise of paddles, and saw one canoe coming up to them. There were five men in the canoe, and they said:

"What do you think? We wish to take you along. We are going up the river to make war on the people."

One of the young men said: "I have no arrows."

"Arrows are in the canoe," they said.

"I will not go along. I might be killed. My relatives do not know where I have gone. But you," he said, turning to the other, "may go with them."

So one of the young men went, but the other returned home.

And the warriors went on up the river to a town on the other side of Kalama. The people came down to the water, and they began to fight, and many were killed. But presently, the young man heard one of the warriors say: "Quick, let us go home: that Indian has been hit." Now he thought: "Oh, they are ghosts." He did not feel sick, but they said he had been shot.

So the canoes went back to Egulac, and the young man went ashore to his house, and made a fire. And he told everybody and said: "Behold I accompanied the ghosts, and we went to fight. Many of our fellows were killed, and many of those who attacked us were killed. They said I was hit, and I did not feel sick."

He told it all, and then he became quiet. When the sun rose he fell down. Something black came out of his mouth. His face became contorted. The people jumped up and cried.

He was dead.

This story is a Kwakiutl Indian folktale. It must have seemed very odd to Bartlett's British subjects, who knew little about North American Indians' customs and beliefs. When asked to recall the story, Britons changed it so that it conformed more to their culture, making it more sensible and coherent to them. As time passed between reading and recalling the story, more and more details were omitted or changed. Bartlett invoked the idea of a *schema* (pluralized *schemata*) to explain these effects. He claimed that schemata "form models of themselves." They are a mental framework into which new facts and ideas are incorporated. Bartlett believed that schemata modify new inputs so as to make them coherent and meaningful, thereby influencing both initial understanding and later recall.

The concept of schemata was too loosely defined and mentalistic to receive much attention during the neobehaviorist period, and it was largely ignored during the ensuing 30 years. During the 1960s, a trickle of studies on prose comprehension picked up the thread of Bartlett's work, but by then the focus was on single sentences because of the influence of linguistics on psychology. When psycholinguistics began to drift away from linguistics proper, research on discourse comprehension was resumed.

Pompi and Lachman (1967) did one of the earliest American studies to be influenced by Bartlett's work. Their subjects read stories lacking words that were high associates of the story's theme. For example, one story concerned a surgical operation:

> Chief Resident Jones adjusted his face mask while anxiously surveying a pale figure secured to the long gleaming table before him. One swift stroke of his small sharp instrument and a thin red line appeared. Then an eager young assistant carefully extended the opening as another aide pushed aside glistening surface fat so that vital parts were laid bare. Everyone present stared in horror at ugly growth too large for removal. He now knew it was pointless to continue.

After reading the passage, subjects were asked to identify which words on a list had appeared in the story. Words that normally would appear in an account of surgery, such as *doctor, nurse, scalpel,* and *operation,* were included in the test list, though they were not in the story. Nevertheless, people "recalled" that such words had been in the story. Pompi and Lachman concluded that people extract a story's theme and then compare this theme to the test words to decide whether they were in the story. It seems hard to believe that such an intuitively reasonable idea had to be proved by experiment, but the preoccupation of neobehavioristic psychologists with overt stimuli made it necessary. To a neobehaviorist, a subject's recognition behavior is a response, and therefore it must follow some identifiable stimulus. The stimulus in the Pompi and Lachman study could only come from inside the subject's head, where his knowledge of surgical procedures was stored. The experiment was thus a challenge to the associationist and neobehaviorist way of looking at higher mental processes. In today's terms, subjects invoked their schema of surgical operations to judge the likelihood that particular words were used in the story.

The theme a person attributes to a passage will depend on his own experience and knowledge. The closer the correspondence between the theme selected by the reader and the one intended by the writer, the more the person's theme will facilitate his recall of the passage. This point was demonstrated by Dooling and Lachman (1971). Their subjects attempted to recall a highly metaphorical passage. Half the subjects were given a title, and half were not. Here is one passage:

> With hocked gems financing him, our hero bravely defied all scornful laughter that tried to prevent his scheme. Your eyes deceive, he had said. An egg, not a table, correctly typifies this unexplored planet. Now three sturdy sisters sought proof. Forging along sometimes through calm vastness, yet more often over turbulent peaks and valleys, days became weeks. As many doubters spread fearful rumors about the edge, at last, from nowhere, welcome winged creatures appeared signifying momentous success.

People who read this story with no title recalled it poorly. Those who were given the title "Christopher Columbus Discovering America" recalled it fairly well. You will appreciate the difference if you read the passage again. The theme gave meaning to such expressions as *three sturdy sisters* and *the edge*.

A study by Bransford and Johnson (1972) made the same point using vague rather than metaphorical prose. They also showed that a picture could provide a theme, even if it depicted unusual events. They arranged the elements of a picture two ways, as shown in Fig. 12.1. One of the arrangements (A) provided a theme to relate the elements of the following story, whereas the other (B) did not:

If the balloons popped, the sound wouldn't be able to carry since everything would be too far away from the correct floor. A closed window would also prevent the sound from carrying, since most buildings tend to be well insulated. Since the whole operation depends on a steady flow of electricity, a break in the middle of the wire would also cause problems. Of course, the fellow could shout, but the human voice is not loud enough to carry that far. An additional problem is that a string could break on the instrument. Then there could be no accompaniment to the message. It is clear that the best situation would involve less distance. Then there would be fewer potential problems. With face to face contact, the least number of things could go wrong [pp. 392–393].

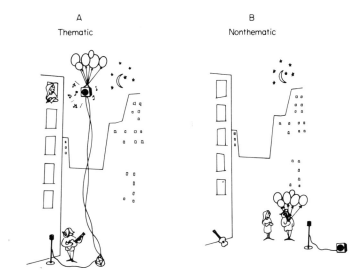

A
Thematic

B
Nonthematic

FIG. 12.1. Thematic and nonthematic pictures used by Bransford and Johnson (1972).

People who saw the thematic picture recalled more of the story than those who saw the nonthematic picture.

B. Structure of Passages

People have expectations about how texts should be structured. If a text does not conform to a recognizable structure, it will seem choppy, chaotic, and unorganized. If it conforms to a familiar structure, it will flow smoothly and logically.

There have been several efforts to devise formal accounts of passage organization (Restle, 1975; Rumelhart, 1975; Thorndyke, 1975). Thorndyke's approach has been to use rewrite rules, rather like Chomsky's (see Fig. 10.5). Thorndyke's rules for the organization of one kind of passage are shown in Table 12.1. An implication of using rewrite rules to describe story structure is that the story elements are hierarchical. As you may remember from our discussion of Chomsky (see Fig. 10.6, p. 374), rewrite rules and tree diagrams provide the same kind of information about structure, making it possible for Thorndyke (1975) to construct tree diagrams from the rewrite rules for a passage. Story elements that are at a high level in the tree are those that give meaning to many other events in the story. Those that are relatively incidental would be at a low level in the tree. In the child's story "The Wizard of Oz," for example, a superordinate element is the fact that Dorothy is lost and trying to get back to Kansas. It explains many of the events in the story. In contrast, the

TABLE 12.1
Grammar Rules for Simple Stories[a]

Rule Number		
(1)	Story	Setting + Theme + Plot + Resolution
(2)	Setting	Characters + Location + Time
(3)	Theme	(Event) + Goal
(4)	Plot	Episode
(5)	Episode	Subgoal + Attempts + Outcome
(6)	Attempt	Event episode
(7)	Outcome	Event state
(8)	Resolution	Event state
(9)	Subgoal goal	Desired state
(10)	Characters location time	Stative

[a]After Thorndyke (1975).

subordinate fact that the Wicked Witch produced a rainstorm is relatively incidental to the story; it figures only in one subplot concerning the Tin Woodsman.

If, as Thorndyke's system suggests, the elements in a story are hierarchically ordered, some elements should be judged more important, salient, or central than others. In fact, Thorndyke (1975) showed that ratings of elements' importance are predicted by the rewrite rules for stories. You might also expect that central and important elements should be remembered best, and they are (deVilliers, 1974; Kintsch & Keenan, 1973; Thorndyke, 1975).

Literature and the arts would be pretty dull if authors and playwrights stuck slavishly to one kind of organization, however informative. One way diversity and creativity are expressed is by varying the order in which setting, theme, plot, and resolution are presented (Restle, 1974). For example, flashbacks vary the order of events. Some plays present their resolution first, and then flash back to the events leading up to it. Other plays have no plot at all, but are character studies. But authors cannot use such violations of familiar structures haphazardly. The writer who deviates from expectation must provide signals so that his listeners can follow the story as he intends. It will not serve his purpose if the audience treats his resolution as if it were a setting; it will only cause confusion. He must provide cues that he is not adhering to the expected order of elements, so that his audience may assign elements to their appropriate categories. In fact, taking liberties with structure may be a luxury that only the literate can afford. People told stories long before they wrote, and their stories filled important cultural functions. Because story tellers must rely on their memories, it may be necessary for a few simple structures to accommodate many different tales. Folk historians recognize similar structure in thousands of tales and fables from all parts of the world. Writing and filming, of course, allow storage of diverse and elaborate structures.

Research on the understanding of discourse is a growing field. There is general agreement that narratives are understood by reference to previous knowledge. The knowledge may be about the narrative's content, or about the components of a well-formed story and when each component is usually presented.

Discourse comprehension has been central to the work of several of the comprehensive modelers, to whom we now turn. In principle, none is interested in the comprehension of single isolated sentences as an end in itself. All consider that sentences are understood in relation to other material, nonlinguistic and linguistic alike. Although they account for such factors in different ways, all comprehensive modelers strive to give roles in their theories to linguistic and situational context, previous knowledge, and inferential processes. The comprehensive models are a new and significant development in the information-processing paradigm. The methods of their makers are unorthodox. They rely less on experimental data than is conventional, and more on rational methods. The recent emergence of these large theories may signal further evolution of the information-processing paradigm, or it may mark the beginning of another revolution.

III. COMPREHENSIVE THEORIES IN GENERAL

Neobehaviorists built large-scale theories, the last of which was published as a book in 1956 (Spence, 1956). It took 17 years before experimental psychologists (Anderson & Bower, 1973) published another book-length theory, called HAM. HAM stands for Human Associative Memory, which sounds as if it might be a theory of forgetting based on associationism. But Anderson and Bower's model was actually in the intellectual tradition of Newell and Simon (1972). It was the first of a genre that is a major new force in cognitive psychology. HAM was an extraordinarily sophisticated effort to construct a theory of how knowledge is stored and then retrieved in the course of understanding new linguistic input. The major concern of the theory was permanent memory and its contents. It also focused squarely on language, including how knowledge about it is stored and how linguistic input is matched against stored knowledge. Most of Anderson and Bower's analyses and exposition of their theory concerned single sentences and their knowledge content, but later models have somewhat remedied that.

Prior to HAM, information-processing psychologists had largely confined their theorizing to particular problems, such as iconic storage, memory scanning, ambiguity resolution, and brief memory for letter triplets. When cognitive psychologists rejected neobehaviorism, they seemed also to reject the goal of large-scale theory. HAM was a rejection of that rejection. Without apology, Anderson and Bower set out to model the processes that underlie people's performance in all the tasks that cognitive psychology's smaller models deal with.

HAM was not received with universal adulation. Some of Anderson and Bower's information-processing colleagues might even have dismissed it were it not for the great scholarship and technical quality of the product. HAM could not be ignored. Its authors had mastered and reconciled technical achievements in the propositional logic, computer simulation, and probability theory. Moreover, they had mastered theoretical accomplishments in several disciplines, including linguistics, artificial intelligence, and psychology. At least six experts reviewed HAM, and all applauded its scholarship.

It was only a year later when the next book-length model appeared. Kintsch's (1974) *The Representation of Meaning in Memory* described his theory of propositional knowledge, which was designed to explain the understanding of paragraphs and longer discourses. Superficially, Kintsch's model was entirely different from HAM, but its long-range goals were the same, and the problems with which Kintsch wrestled were similar to those confronted by Anderson and Bower.

In 1975, there appeared two more book-length comprehension theories. Both were influenced by studies of artificial intelligence, and both involved extensions of earlier, shorter papers. Norman and Rumelhart, who are two productive cognitive psychologists, designed their model (1975) for computer implementation. They followed the custom in artificial intelligence of supplying human names for intelligent programs: they took the initials, LNR, of the authors of the original, short version of the model (Rumelhart, Lindsay & Norman, 1972) and pronounced them ELINOR. Schank (1975) also published a revision of his earlier Conceptual Dependency Theory, abbreviated CDT (Schank, 1972). Schank is a computer scientist who makes strong psychological claims for his theory. He believes that global models must correspond with how people understand language and make inferences, and he has constructed his theory accordingly. The same year, Frederiksen (1975) reported a model designed to describe the logical and semantic content of text. He explicitly rejected the single sentence as his primary unit of analysis in favor of accounting for comprehension of extended discourse. Barely 3 years after HAM's appearance, Anderson updated it and published a 500-page revision called ACT (Anderson, 1976). At about the same time, Miller and Johnson-Laird (1976) reported yet another book-length theory of meaning, which attempts to relate perception, language, and knowledge.

Within 4 short years, seven comprehensive models of knowledge were published, and this after 17 years of no large-scale theorizing. Most of these models have already been revised, at least once. The reaction of most cognitive psychologists can best be described as ambivalent. Many are committed to the idea that theory should be sufficient to human processing capacities, and if these models strive for anything, it is sufficiency. All address central questions about people: How do they know what they know? How do they understand what they are told? How do they think and reason so as to create new knowledge from old? The dedication of the global modelers to sufficiency is seen as a virtue, but they sometimes seem to be marching to a different drummer than scholars in psychology's strong empirical tradition. Creative thinking about what would constitute an adequate comprehension theory is as important to most of them as doing experiments to devise one. Anderson (1976) for example, has argued convincingly for the value of "rational experiments," in which the data are everyday facts of life and logical proofs rather than systematic observations from the laboratory. These strategies are an unanticipated, and sometimes unappealing, development for some strict laboratory scientists.

When the authors of global models do report experimental data, it is not always easy to tell how well the outcomes support central premises of their models—often because it is not apparent what *are* the central premises. Each model is very elaborate and complex, with many details; it can be difficult to know which details are critical and which are not. Moreover, each model uses idiosyncratic notational conventions and a unique set of assumptions, and it is difficult to master even one of them completely, let alone several. Because theoretical thinking can often move faster than laboratory data collection, the models have tended to change at an alarming rate. These factors have given the global models a rather problematical status in cognitive psychology. Although most practitioners know the models exist, acknowledge their potential importance, and recognize the high level of scholarship they involve, relatively few are conversant with their details. Even fewer have attempted to conduct experiments that are responsive to the models.

Some cognitive psychologists are deliberately ignoring the comprehensive models except, perhaps, for an occasional sour remark. Others are standing at the sidelines applauding the intent and purposes, but waiting for the models to stabilize somewhat before taking any of them seriously. A small number are designing experiments suggested by the models, working to supply the data that mandates the next revision. All of these psychologists probably agree that global models are here to stay, and that more are on the way. It is exciting to see new possibilities for addressing problems that have preoccupied leading intellectuals throughout history.

Here is our dilemma as authors of a scientific text. The global models are part of the information-processing paradigm as surely as are short-term memory, psycholinguistics, and attention. But their details have been changing rapidly so that much of what we might write about them could be incorrect before it was printed. What is more, the models are not easily compared, because they have different emphases and are variously explicit on different points. At present there is no disciplined basis for choice among them, at least according to Anderson's (1976) conclusion; therefore, we cannot even concentrate on the most promising. Accordingly, we will cover those shared features of the models that we think will endure. These turn out not to be the particulars of any of them, but instead their goals and motivations, and the problems they seek to resolve. We present no more detail of any model than is needed to illustrate how it approaches these issues. Having spoken of their shared goals and motivations, we describe the models' different approaches to these questions: How is knowledge of the world represented in people's memories? How are word meanings represented in people's linguistic knowledge? How does the perception of language or visual scenes contact information in memory?

A. Why Global Theory?—Some Shared Motives

1. Limitations of Smaller Models

While global theorists differ on many details, they unanimously reject task-limited theory. None of them values theories of particular experimental tasks, however elegant those theories might be. They are unimpressed by the proliferation of task-specific models that do not relate coherently to one another. They view theoretical and experimental analyses of isolated cognitive subsystems as a scientific failure. Their approach amounts to a new paradigmatic convention, according to which the whole language processing and comprehension system should be studied all at once. This convention runs counter to the analytic commitment of virtually all scientific paradigms, which is stiff competition.

While the global models come from the same tradition as the semantic memory models presented earlier, the global theorists tend to reject the semantic memory models because they are all based on some version of the sentence-verification task. People do more with language than verify sentences. They tell jokes and are amused, they inform and are informed, they ask and answer questions, they write poetry, play word games, and so on indefinitely. When faced with particular tasks, people probably supplement their general comprehension strategies with task-specific strategies, which they use at no other time. From the global theorists' vantage, the problem with a model based on data from a specific task is that one does not know how much of it is about people's general capabilities and how much is about task-specific strategies. Global theorists want to know about the capabilities people bring to all tasks requiring language. It remains to be seen whether such pessimism about ever being able to add up smaller models to make a comprehensive theory is warranted. It is clear, however, that any experiment requires particular procedures, so that global modelers will somehow have to find a way around people's use of task-specific strategies.

2. Theories, Models, or Experiments in Conceptualization?

We have used the terms theory and model interchangeably to describe the ideas of global thinkers, and we continue to do so. But all of the global formulations are more than either models or theories in the conventional sense. They are also rational tests of the limits of the information-processing paradigm. As we said in the first chapter, paradigms provide a framework of assumptions, a set of concepts, a language, and a central analogy within which testable hypotheses can be formulated. The scholars whose work we cover in this chapter are launching a nontrivial effort to see whether the assumptions, concepts, language, and analogies of the information-processing paradigm are good conceptual tools for dealing with age-old questions about people's mental capacities. You can think of efforts as "experiments in conceptualization."

In a sense, experiments in conceptualization reverse the usual direction of influence between paradigm and research. Normally, it is the paradigm that suggests researchable problems. Most of the experiments described in this book were done because the paradigm suggested they were important and feasible. Iconic and echoic storage, choice reaction time, and much of the memory literature are examples of problems suggested by the paradigm. The issues addressed by the global models are not the province of any particular paradigm; they are timeless questions about the human mind. Armed with a new view of the mind as a general-purpose symbol-manipulating system, the global modelers are re-asking these ancient questions. The test of the paradigm will be whether it provides researchable hypotheses about those questions, and whether the research moves us closer to the answers. Few of the global modelers may think of themselves as testing the limits of their paradigm, but this will be an outcome of their collective effort, and it seems to us to be implicit in their shared goals.

3. Influence of Artificial Intelligence

Psychology has drawn considerably on the ideas of workers in artificial intelligence, and this is especially true of the global theorists. Like the global theorists, workers in artificial intelligence have been vitally interested in language comprehension. Because information-processing psychologists have accepted the idea that a computer program is an acceptable formalism for expressing theory, they have readily viewed artificial intelligence programs designed to understand language as psychological theories about people's use of language. As a result, developments in artificial intelligence are of special interest to psychologists who theorize about language, especially because some of these developments have indeed been very impressive. For example, Winograd (1972) built a computer program that follows natural-language instructions to move blocks about. His computer program's world is restricted; it knows nothing of shoes, ships, sealing wax, cabbages, or kings. But it does know about the shapes, colors, and balancing properties of cones, cylinders, and rectangles; and it knows about the spatial relationships among these objects. It can thus view objects as arranged in Panel A of Fig. 12.2 and change them to the arrangement of Panel B in response to the command, *Put the red block on top of the black one.* To make room for the red one, it has to move the green one away; but it understands

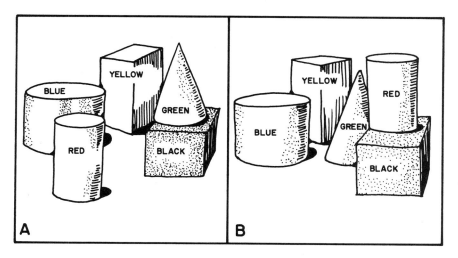

FIG. 12.2. Objects before (A) and after (B) rearrangement by Winograd's (1972) computer simulation.

and can do so. Winograd's program also refuses to follow a command to place a block on the point of a cone. Building this bit of intelligent language-understanding into a computer program took a formidable intellectual effort on Winograd's part. Many of the techniques he developed have been adopted and emulated.

Several of the global theories incorporate ideas developed for artificial intelligence programs. One of these ideas is to use active procedures rather than static storage to represent semantic knowledge (see Winograd, 1975). That is, word meanings are represented as separate programs, rather than as contents of memory locations (facts) to be accessed by a main program. When a word is input and the main program must comprehend it, the separate word program can be called on to determine whether the word is being employed in a correct semantic–syntactic sense. Both ACT and ELINOR have incorporated this idea, which may be part of the way around the problem that words have different meanings in different contexts. Another contribution of artificial intelligence is a program for grammatical analysis of sentences, called Augmented Transition Networks (Woods, 1970, 1973). It divides sentences into syntactic constituents, but not by principles stemming from transformational grammar. Many global theorists find this program attractive, because it works. Whether it works like people remains to be seen.

The flow of ideas is not all from artificial intelligence to psychology. Artificial intelligence theorists are responsive to the psychological literature as well. Schank (1976), whose work spans both disciplines, has argued that automata will understand language only if they are made to work as people do. Because psychological theorists are a long way from explaining people's use of language, and because computer scientists are a long way from making computers use language as flexibly as people, each has something to learn from the other.

B. Agreed-Upon Features of the Comprehension System

Most of the global theorists use the same approach to their "experiments in conceptualization." They try to define the type and range of information in permanent memory. They then develop a system that might encode and represent everything a person could know. The goal is to make that system compatible with the types of human knowledge and adequate to its range. Once they have a representational system, the theorists develop interface systems to provide interaction between the memory representations and the environment. The goal is to account for people's ability to access memory contents relevant to particular linguistic and perceptual inputs and to account for the enormous range of human response capabilities.

Quillian's Teachable Language Comprehender is the intellectual ancestor of all the global theories, and all borrow ideas and implementation techniques from each other and from the discipline of artificial intelligence. Most of them employ a network structure and graph-theoretic concepts resembling those of TLC. They use the concepts of *nodes* and *links* much as Quillian did. All are content-dependent: They are designed to process people's everyday knowledge and comprehension, not just lists of words and sentences. This contrasts sharply with older theories based on classic associationism, which is content-independent: Associationism invoked the idea of S–R connections to explain all learning, without respect to the meanings of the connected elements or the types of links between them. All of the global theories try to specify the mechanisms and processes that underlie comprehension. These include segmentation devices that break down and/or build up input information into recognizable units corresponding to some part of the internally stored data base—what we earlier called *input synthesis.*

None of the global theories was induced from data of the sort presented in this chapter or the previous one. While the outcomes of some studies imposed some constraint on some theories, the theorists' pretheoretical conceptions, intuitions, and rational considerations played a much larger role in shaping their models, as is appropriate. Insights and rational analysis are not verification methods, but they are good starting points for experiments in conceptualization.

The global modelers agree that a mature theory of comprehension will have at least four components. It will have an interface parser that takes language strings or visual experiences and converts them from physical signals to representations compatible with the structure of memory. In other words, the interface parser is responsible for input synthesis, which may consist of many small recodings. The second component is the representational structure. It is a system of world and language knowledge, such as those discussed in the chapter on semantic memory. Third, there are control systems that operate on memory, guide and determine processing, and determine the extent and character of memory searches, inferential processes, and the like. The fourth component is metaphorically the mirror image to the first; it consists of output synthesizing mechanisms that convert information from the ideational form of the representational system into speech, writing, or other behavior.

While all of the global theorists agree that these four components need to be included in any comprehensive theory of comprehension, only Winograd (1972) has yet dealt with all four. The others have given heaviest attention to the representational structure. The interface parser has been conceptualized extensively by some. Control systems are important in some theories and ignored in others. Very few have treated output synthesizing mechanisms. There are also other differences among the models.

C. Some Differences in Approach

All of the theories describe the interaction between synthesized inputs and the permanent memory structures, but not all include mechanisms for the modification of memory by new input. In HAM, permanent memory was used to understand new inputs, but it was not itself modified by them. LNR did include mechanisms for the modification of permanent memory. HAM also emphasized fact retrieval, the storing of individual sentences, and their subsequent location in memory. It said little about inferential processes. Schank's CDT (Schank, 1972, 1975; Schank & Abelson, 1977) focused primarily on the role of inference and had less to say about fact retrieval. Kintsch (1974) and Frederiksen (1975) both sought to develop text grammars, or formal summaries of the contents of paragraphs, stories, and other extended narratives. It cannot be said that the others fail to handle texts. Rather, they have been developed for other purposes, and it is not clear how difficult it ultimately will be to make them handle text.

Parts of several theories (i.e., HAM, ACT, LNR, CDT) are implemented in computer programs. Kintsch and Frederiksen have not so implemented theirs. Those that have been so implemented can be tested to see what their knowledge-representation systems can do with specific language inputs, by examining the output of the programs. Some experimental tests have been made of some of the models, but not of all. One of Anderson's motives for replacing HAM with ACT was HAM's failure to properly predict experimental data in sentence memory experiments (e.g., King & Anderson, 1976). Kintsch's experiments usually have not involved isolated sentence learning, but instead people's memory and inference making in extended discourse (Kintsch, 1974). LNR, in contrast, has been motivated less by experimental results than by rational considerations concerning the adequacy of its assumptions and strategies for dealing with knowledge representation. Schank does no experiments at all.

IV. SOME PARTICULARS OF FOUR THEORIES

Here is a brief summary of the characteristics of four global models to serve as background for the rest of our discussion. These thumbnail sketches mention the major focus of each model and the kind of experimental task favored by its author or authors.

A. HAM (Anderson & Bower, 1973)

HAM posits a long-term memory that is *strategy-free*. In other words, the memory is separate from control processes that operate on it. It stores or locates information by a fixed set of rules, whatever the occasion for such storage or location. HAM further assumes that memory structures are not changed by comprehension processes, although additions may be made. These assumptions are implausible for many human performances, and Anderson and Bower knew this. However, they were not trying to construct a system that would immediately simulate everything a person could do from birth to death. In fact, HAM's major task was to model the performance of young adults learning lists of sentences. HAM's assumptions may be satisfactory for this situation, although they may not encompass other situations, such as comprehension.

Knowledge in HAM's memory is represented with abstract propositions. You have already encountered similar propositions in the work of Clark (Clark & Chase, 1972) and Carpenter and Just (1975). Although these psychologists used propositions to represent the information contained in sentences, they work equally well for the information contained in memory. As you also already know from Collins and Loftus' (1975) Spreading Activation Theory, the configuration of propositions in a hypothetical memory can be described in graph network notation. Anderson and Bower used a version of such notation to represent HAM's knowledge. In the propositions of HAM's memory, concepts form the nodes, and grammatical or logical relations such as *time* and *predicate* form the links. The system has no mechanism for inference. It is limited to parsing and storing input sentences and subsequently retrieving the stored information. Its strongest suit, then, is modeling the outcome of sentence-memory experiments.

The theory contained in HAM is partly implemented in a computer simulation that answers certain kinds of questions. Suppose HAM was told:

(1) The spectator disrobed the singer at the concert.

The program would convert this sentence into the graph structure shown in Fig. 12.3, and check to see whether the same information was already in memory. If not, the program would store it. The numbers and letters in the figure are arbitrary; we have used 52 to designate the proposition expressed in Sentence (1). Node 53 is a *context* linked to the proposition. The context consists of a *location,* 55, and a *time,* 56. These are particular instances of *Concert* and *Past.* The more general knowledge of concerts is node J, which is linked to other information about concerts and designated by its natural-language name CONCERT. The figure is thus an explicit theoretical claim about what people extract from a sentence such as (1). The claim is that people derive from sentences abstract propositional structures, such as Fig. 12.3, and that they identify the proposition as a set of specific relationships among particular instances of general concepts having natural-language names.

HAM contains a subset of processing rules called MATCH, which controls the storage and location of information. MATCH determines whether the information in the tree is already in memory, and it also controls the location of information to answer *yes* or *no* questions like *Did the spectator disrobe the singer?* and *Was the spectator at the concert?*

HAM suggested a number of experiments on sentence recognition and recall, and it accommodated many of the results. It also handled the results of earlier studies on rote learning, interference, fact retrieval, memory scanning, effects of imagery instructions, and other data. However, there were some experiments on sentence memory that did not turn out according to HAM's predictions and this, along with rational and pragmatic considerations, led Anderson to revise HAM. He named the new version ACT.

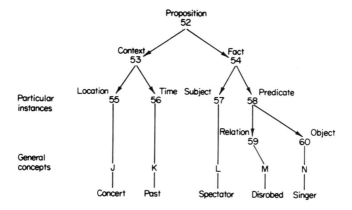

FIG. 12.3. HAM's propositional representation of the sentence "The spectator disrobed the singer at the concert."

B. ACT (J. Anderson, 1976)

The structure of ACT's memory is different from HAM's. In HAM, all stored knowledge was represented by a propositional graph structure. In ACT, only factual or declarative knowledge such as that in Sentence (1) is so represented. Procedural knowledge (knowing how to do things) is represented with *production systems.* Production systems are a special kind of program that specify conditional actions. The "conditions" are the values of variables or patterns of variables, and the actions may include modification of the conditions—leading in turn to another action. At present, production systems are the only "effective procedures" we know of that might describe the control processes of an information-processing system.

ACT's production systems take the place of HAM's MATCH component, because they locate and compare information. But MATCH conducted serial memory searches, whereas the production system searches in parallel. The search, along with many other capabilities of the model, works on the principle of spreading activation utilized by Collins–Loftus–Quillian. The production systems also allow ACT to draw inferences, which HAM could not.

ACT uses a different network notation from HAM. Sentence (1) would be represented by ACT as shown in Fig. 12.4. It is represented as three propositions. ACT's notation allows the encoding of complex sentences that were too awkward in HAM's notation.

ACT's postulates are extremely technical, and would require too extensive an explication to present here. They are based in part on the outcomes of sentence memory experiments (e.g., Anderson, 1976; King & Anderson, 1976).

C. LNR (Norman & Rumelhart, 1975)

LNR's memory representation is contained in what the authors call an *active procedural network,* which means that the memory does not distinguish declarative or factual knowledge from procedural knowledge, as ACT does. A single network accommodates word meanings, facts, task information and strategies, inferences, and other manipulations of words and facts. The LNR memory is represented in a graph network notation, into which sentences are converted. LNR would represent Sentence (1) as shown in Fig. 12.5. The figure reveals a significant aspect of the theory: Verbs are broken into primitive action components. A verb such as *disrobe* is said to consist of elemental ideas, such as *cause* (a body) to *change state* from *covered* to *uncovered* (by clothing). Various "primitive" components of verbs have been specified, along with rewrite rules to combine them into more complex

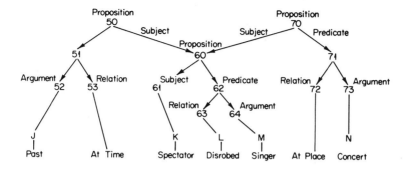

FIG. 12.4. ACT's propositional representation of the sentence "The spectator disrobed the singer at the concert."

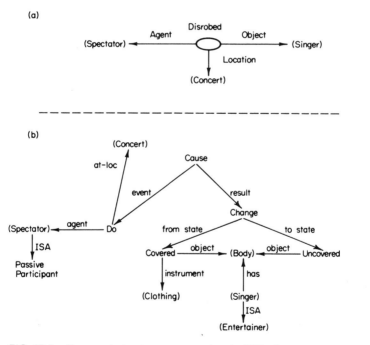

FIG. 12.5. Two graph structure representations by LNR of the sentence "The spectator disrobed the singer at the concert."

concepts. We have more to say about the use of semantic primitives, which is a controversial issue among the global modelers and in cognitive psychological research. The upper structure in Fig. 12.5 represents a relatively superficial kind of comprehension, according to LNR. A deeper kind of comprehension is achieved when the primitives are extracted, as in the lower structure of the figure.

LNR, like ACT, has been implemented as a computer simulation, having three components. The first is the memory network, already described. Second, there is an interface parser that takes sentence-like utterances as inputs and converts them into network structures compatible with the memory network. This parser uses an augmented transition network system (Woods, 1970, 1973), a device from computational linguistics that is growing increasingly popular among global modelers. Third, an interpreter controls the examination, modification, and incrementing of the node structure of the memory network. Interestingly, a portion of the network itself controls the interpreter. This reflexive feature of the LNR model seems intuitively satisfying. The human cognitive system also must contain the procedural information by which it is itself used, modified, and expanded.

D. Kintsch's (1974) Theory

Unlike the theories so far described, Kintsch's does not represent permanent memory with network notation. His theory does not explain the understanding of single sentences, nor the way a person relates the content of a single sentence to permanent knowledge. The purpose of Kintsch's system is to convert extended discourse into lists of propositions. The propositions are a way of representing the knowledge contained in a discourse. Kintsch's propositional format is modeled after systems of mathematical logic. Because these systems are expressly designed for deductive inference, their use gives Kintsch's model powerful inferential capability.

Kintsch uses a set of tentative and intuitive rules to capture the meanings of natural-language prose in propositional format. The rules require that the propositions be ordered and that the relationships among different propositions be represented. For example, if a story contains the sentence *John is stupid* and later the sentence *John flunked history,* the system must explain how the comprehender takes these to be about the same *John* and how the probable causal relationships between the two sentences are represented.

Kintsch does not decompose semantically complex words into primitives. He argues that people treat complex words as unitary concepts. In his system, word meanings are represented by *meaning postulates.* These postulates supply the same kind of information as semantic primitives. The difference is that the meaning postulates are available if the comprehender wishes to scrutinize them and draw inferences from them, but they are not necessarily accessed in the course of comprehending prose and discourse. In Kintsch's system, Sentence (1) would be represented as follows:

1. (DISROBE, SPECTATOR, SINGER)
2. (TIME: PAST, 1)
3. (LOCATION: AT, 1, CONCERT)

The "1s" in these propositional notations reflects the understanding that the time and location information pertain to the time and location of the events described in Proposition 1.

The theory was developed to guide research on comprehension and memory for prose and the inferences people make from the propositional content of prose. Kintsch (1974, 1977) reports numerous relevant experiments.

V. WHERE THE THEORIES STAND ON SOME MAJOR ISSUES

Three major issues with which all the models must cope are the representation problem, the status of procedural knowledge, and the issue of word meaning.

A. The Formal Representation of World Knowledge

All the theorists are concerned with comprehension; so all must include in their theories some account of the knowledge that underlies comprehension —how it is organized, stored, and retrieved. This account is the "representational system" in their theories. It is important to distinguish between the *human* representational system and *theoretical* representational systems. The goal of all the theorists is to construct a theoretical representational system that does justice to the human representational system. Most agree on the aspects of the human representational system that, at the very least, must be accommodated by an adequate theoretical representational system. Certainly it has vast content, it must be efficient, and it obviously supports inference making. No experiments are necessary to decide that these capacities exist in people. Hence, there has been some shift from empirical to rational considerations in the work of the global modelers. It is enough of a task (nowhere near finished) to conceive a theoretical representational system that is adequate to the most manifest human capacities. If a proposed representational system cannot account for such obvious abilities, it does not matter whether it can account for nonobvious ones such as might be revealed in carefully done experiments. Just now, therefore, laboratory studies play a less central role in evaluating the theoretical adequacy of the models than is traditional in psychological normal science. It would be different if we had several theories that accounted for the most conspicuous human abilities and were trying to choose among them. Then, extensive experimentation would be needed to see how well the different theories handled subtleties.

1. Obvious Requirements
for Representational Systems

A theoretical representational system must be sufficient. There is no point to constructing a theoretical representation that cannot incorporate the kinds of information people use. The telephone switchboard model of simple associations between words, for example, could never be extended to accommodate the richness of people's knowledge. Such a model could not hope to be a sufficient representation of the interrelations between concepts in memory.

A theoretical representation must allow efficient search and retrieval. People can retrieve any of a large number of facts quickly. Remember, it was estimated, for example, that an educated person has from 70,000 to 120,000 words in his productive vocabulary; yet while speaking, he locates about two concepts per second and puts them together for vocal expression. This is a strikingly rapid search through an enormous stored array. The theories with computer implementation (HAM, ACT, LNR, and CDT) all use *content-addressable storage*. Content-addressable means that when a concept or idea is needed, some element in the stimulus requiring it contains its "address," or the necessary information for locating it.

To illustrate content-addressable storage, imagine the ways you might organize a library full of books. One way is to put books on the same general subject near each other, alphabetized by content. Thus, a book about aardvarks would be first in the zoology section, and one on abortion would be the first in the section on surgery. This would be a content-addressable store. A person might find a book about any subject by simply going to the content. An eccentric librarian might use some other device, such as organizing the books by the number of words they contain. Anyone who wanted a book 493,212 words long could easily find one by going to the long-book shelves. This is a length-addressable, not a content-addressable system. Imagine using it to find all of the books about sex, or motorcycle repair, or any other content!

Alternatives to content-addressability as an indexing system in psychological models might be addressability by frequency, codability, or age of acquisition. Age-of-acquisition storage would allow easy retrieval only if something in the stimulus identified the age at which the concept was learned. Although Carroll and White (1972) and Lachman, Shaffer, and Hennrikus

(1974) proposed this as a storage mode for words in a person's vocabulary, no one has proposed it for the concepts in the person's repertoire of knowledge. In fact, it is widely assumed that human memory is content-addressable (Bower, 1975; Frijda, 1972), because people go quickly from idea to idea on the basis of the content of the various ideas. It is possible, however, that the indexing of human memory is far more complicated than direct content-addressability, and current theories are rather unspecific about the form and nature of the codes that provide the information for locating a concept. Are they the sensory features of a stimulus, or more complex perceptual constructions, or even an abstract ideational component relatively free of sensory data? This is one of the issues that the theories must tackle. A believable theory must provide evidence that it can reproduce a memory search similar to that of the human mind.

A theoretical representational system must allow for rapid inference. Language processing is largely the drawing of inferences from input strings, as we have already seen. If knowing X and Y makes possible inference Z, then something about the way X and Y are stored and related to each other must contain the implicit information that Z is also true, or probably true. The representational system must specify relationships among elements so that plausible inferences are easily made and implausible ones are not. A theoretical representational system should also allow ready conversion of simple ideas into complex ones and provide for such abilities as classification and similarity detection, to name a few. Finally, it should foster accretion: People's knowledge grows by the addition of external information and by generating new information. Various theorists have suggested other representational requirements (e.g., Bower, 1975), but these are enough for the present state of theory. The list inevitably will grow.

2. Network Notation

Anderson (1976) has noted that all of the comprehensive theories use propositions to represent knowledge. Although they use several types of notation to describe their propositional systems, the most popular are networks, which can be drawn in two dimensions. Figure 9.1 (p. 309) is an example of a network structure. The reasons network notation is so popular are its convenience, readability, and nice mathematical properties.

Networks consist of linked nodes. The nodes are indifferent to what they represent. A theorist can use them to stand for anything from individual concepts to whole scenarios. A node can be postulated for unitary concepts such as *fish, John,* and *Mary,* for more complex concepts such as *John and Mary's fishing trip,* and for whole configurations of concepts such as *the events that occurred on John and Mary's last fishing trip.* Nodes can even stand for whole programs that operate on the network itself. This flexibility makes them convenient. A network's links can be labeled to designate various relationships between nodes; they can be assigned strength values and can be given directionality. This adds to the flexibility of network notation, giving the theorist considerable latitude in his model building and considerable room to revise his model as data suggest. He can change the substance of his theory by changing the type of node admitted, the scope of information contained in single nodes, the kinds of relations designated by links, the choice of strength values, and so on.

Network representations are also quite readable. They can illustrate the tracing of paths through the represented knowledge structure. These paths are very important, for they constitute the mechanism by which the models understand, remember, and infer. In theory, such paths are the mental routes traversed by a person locating information, matching information, or making inferences from input information. It would be possible to communicate the paths to a reader by giving him/ her a print-out of the simulation program; but presented this way the essentials would be hard to grasp. Network representation makes it possible to show any given path in a way that can be easily apprehended by a reader. It is less easy to recover paths from other notational systems.

The third advantage of network notation is that it can be manipulated mathematically with the formalism called *finite labeled graph theory*. This provides the theorist with a set of derivational tools to discover the logical implications of his theory. Unfortunately, this formalism has rarely been used. It is so far only a potential advantage of network representation.

3. Propositional Representation

a. Why Propositional Representation? All of the global theories represent permanently stored information with propositions. Propositional representation takes some getting used to. Many ideas that can be presented clearly and concisely in plain English are tortuously complex, intricate, and difficult to read when translated into propositional representation (see, for example, Table 12.2). Why, then, do all global theories use propositions to represent meanings? The reasons are partly rational, partly accident, and partly value judgments.

Some of the reasons are data-based. Data on memory for text shows that people are likelier to recall the gist of prose, or essential ideas, than the exact wordings (Bransford, Barclay & Franks, 1972; Pompi & Lachman, 1967; Sachs, 1967). This suggested to Anderson and Bower (1973) that people retain the abstract "essence" of what they hear. Propositions can capture the essence of a statement. Also, they can mediate rapid inference making.

Empirical considerations also contributed to Kintsch's (1974) use of propositional representation of text, defined as a set of sequentially

TABLE 12.2
Comprehension and Recall of Text as a
Function of Content Variables[a]

	The *Joseph* Paragraph: Long, Few Different Arguments
1	(BECOME, JOSEPH, RULER)
2	(ISA, JOSEPH, SLAVE)
3	(LOC: IN, 2, EGYPT)
4	(RISE, SLAVE, CLASS)
5	(HIGHER, CLASS)
6	(DIFFICULT, 4)
7	(CONJUNCTION, 2, 6)
8	(CONCESSION, 7, 10)
9	(BRIGHT, JOSEPH)
10	(CAUSALITY, 9, 1)
11	(LOC: IN, 1, EGYPT)
12	(GREAT, RULER)
13	(HAVE, JOSEPH, BROTHER)
14	(SEVERAL, BROTHER)
15	(WICKED, BROTHER)
16	(PLAIN, BROTHER, 17)
17	(KILL, BROTHER, JOSEPH)
18	(TIME: PAST, 17)
19	(COME, BROTHER, EGYPT)
20	(GET, BROTHER, BREAD)
21	(FINALITY, 19, 20)
22	(FIND, BROTHER, 1)
23	(LOC: IN, 22, EGYPT)

Arguments: JOSEPH, RULER, SLAVE, EGYPT, CLASS, BROTHER, BREAD (7).

Text: Although Joseph was a slave in Egypt and it was difficult to rise from the class of slaves to a higher one, Joseph was so bright that he became a ruler in Egypt. Joseph's wicked brothers, who had once planned to kill him, came to Egypt in order to beg for bread. There they found that Joseph had become a great ruler (66 words).

Note: CONJUNCTION, CONCESSION, and FINALITY are abstract word concepts, realized in the text as *and, although,* and *in order to,* respectively.

[a]From Kintsch, Kozminsky, Streby, McKoon, and Keenan (1975), *Journal of Verbal Learning and Verbal Behavior.*

connected sentences of natural language. Psychologists tried to study text understanding during the demise of neobehaviorism, but the effort failed for lack of a suitable meaning unit. There was no suitable way to quantify recall for text. Various quantifiable units were tried, such as number of words recalled, but these did not do justice to people's paraphrases. Other more intuitively attractive units of meaning, such as "idea units," proved unreliable and difficult to apply consistently. Kintsch (1974, 1976) judged that the meaning of a text can be effectively captured by lists of propositions and that their recall can be scored for its match with propositional units. Table 12.2 shows a sample of text (bottom) and the way propositions represent it (top).

Besides the empirical data on people's memory for gist, rational considerations suggest the use of propositional representation. For example, the rational argument against representing the contents of memory as natural language sentences is that the same ideas can be expressed in many sentences. There are far too many paraphrases of any utterance to permanently store all possible versions of each in a finite storage system. A related argument relies on the fact that people recognize various parts of utterances as references to the same given or antecedent information (Clark & Haviland, 1978; Haviland & Clark, 1974). If the antecedent occurred only once, various subsequent utterances have to be referred back to a single previously stored event. This seems possible only if there are canonical or rule-governed forms for encoding meanings so that every new stimulus can be transformed into a form for comparison to experience coded in the past. If various versions of an utterance (called *tokens*) are stored in an identical canonical form (called a *type*), then there must be a system for translating types into tokens and vice versa. Propositional representation has been adopted because it seems to capture type–token relationships, thereby providing an explicit view of what input and output synthesis systems have to do.

The arguments for a propositional representation are not limited to language processing. They can be extended to perception as well. When you look at something, you end up knowing what it is. You do not merely see; you also understand. Although there may be many processing steps between light hitting the eyeball and knowing, the knowing seems more easily described as a system of propositions than any other way (Pylyshyn, 1973). We presented this argument earlier in connection with dual encoding of episodic memories and synthesized codes.

Despite the foregoing considerations, the issue of how best to represent meaning is far from resolved. It is a metatheoretical problem with which theorists will wrestle for many years. It may be their most important metatheoretical problem. Given the centrality of representation to theories in the information-processing paradigm, the representational system must support inference, retrieval, problem solving, and most other cognitive processes as well. If the representational system selected is off the mark, the theories will fail to accommodate the data from all these areas of research.

b. *Formal Properties of Propositional Representation.*   A proposition is neither a sentence nor a string of words. It is a meaning, or ideational unit. Propositions can be expressed as sentences, but they are assumed to have a nonlinguistic form in the mind. The same proposition can be expressed in many different ways in a given language, and in different languages as well.

A proposition contains symbols representing one or more concepts. The symbols may be words or not. In addition, propositions may also contain logical operators that relate the concepts in various ways, such as *if . . . then, all x's are y's,* and so on. The propositions used in the global models are *n-tuples* of concepts. One concept serves as a predicator and the others as arguments with specific semantic roles (Kintsch, 1974). An *n*-tuple is a group of *n* things; in the proposition, it is a construction of *n* concepts. In most of the examples used by the global theorists, the concepts are expressible as words; so usually a word is used in the propositional representation of concepts. Typically, *n* ranges from two to about a dozen. The predicator is a concept that designates the relationship among the other (*n*-1) concepts in the proposition. The other concepts are called arguments. Consider the proposition expressed in the sentence *Horses like hay.* Three easily named concepts are involved: HORSES, LIKE, and HAY. Which one is the predicator? It is the one that defines the relationship between the other two. The predicator in this proposition is LIKE. It specifies the relationship between the arguments HORSES and HAY. The proposition is written

LIKE (HORSES, HAY)

It might seem to you that the predicator should be HORSES, which defines the relationship between LIKE and HAY as a thing that horses do. If the predicator were HORSES, the proposition would be written

HORSES (LIKE, HAY)

This proposition is legitimate in some theories, but it corresponds more closely to what people mean when they say *What likes hay is horses* than when they say *Horses like hay.* Most global theorists concern themselves with rather typical declarative sentences, in which the verb is usually the predicator.

The *n*-tuples used by LNR (Norman & Rumelhart, 1975) closely resemble those used by Kintsch. HAM (Anderson & Bower, 1973) and ACT (Anderson, 1976) use another propositional structure consisting of pairs of relationships embedded within other pairs, forming a tree structure with binary branches. The number of elements in their *n*-tuples is thus always divisible by two. The reason for the family resemblances among the models in the appearance of their propositions is that all draw on mathematical logic. Mathematical logic was developed to deal with that subset of human ideas that is quantifiable or logically coherent. When theorists in psychology and artificial intelligence began representing meaning in propositional form, they borrowed the formalisms and notation of propositional logic and predicate calculus. These systems contain rules for constructing formuli. Those formuli whose truth or falsehood can be determined are called propositions. It is important to note that propositions so defined cannot represent all statements people make. They are not designed to accommodate expressions that are vague, ambiguous, nonliteral, metaphorical, or fanciful. They cannot include the full range of implications, even of literal statements; recall our *firecracker* sentence at the beginning of the chapter on semantic memory. It would take a forbidding proposition indeed to represent all the world knowledge underlying comprehension of this sentence.

Thus, psychologists have borrowed representational systems that are not completely sufficient, and they are working to extend them. Different theorists approach this extension in different ways, but all seek to put natural-language utterances into a form resembling the propositions upon which predicate calculus can operate. The reason is to allow objective construction of proofs and derivations, and straightforward evaluation of the truth value of propositions. Once a natural-language statement is couched in the proper form, the powerful formalisms of propositional logic and predicate calculus can be used for these purposes.

The big stumbling block in the strategy of using propositional representation is the difficulty of translating natural language utterances into forms comparable to those required by propositional logic. The precise and objective rules specified by the formal logical systems for creating propositions cannot be used, because they exclude those ideas of people that do not fit precisely into the system's logical structure. The global theorists have all adopted a strategy that requires that they figure out how to represent any human idea in the notation of propositional logic. They are all doing this, because they do apply propositional notation to natural-language sentences, but their rules for accomplishing the job are intuitive and informal. Kintsch has acknowledged his informality (van Dijk & Kintsch, 1977), but he is not alone. None of the global modelers have precisely specified their rules for converting utterances into propositional notation. Until they do, it is difficult for vast armies of normal-science experimenters to put their theories to the test of the laboratory.

In first-order predicate calculus, there are predicators and arguments. Several of the global theorists treat verbs and prepositions as predicators and nouns as arguments. Using this method, the ideas expressed in the natural-language sentence

(2) Mary exploded a firecracker in Sue's house.

can be represented as axioms in the predicate calculus as follows:

IN (MARY, HOUSE)
POSSESSES (SUE, HOUSE)
EXPLODED (MARY, FIRECRACKER)

This is similar to the representational format used in computer simulations for inference making and question answering (see Newell & Simon, 1972; Raphael, 1976), and this example reveals the principal disadvantage of predicate calculus: It fails to capture the many nuances and inferences that would be available to the ordinarily intelligent adult hearer of Sentence (2). In the case of the expression *to explode a firecracker,* some of these were mentioned in connection with our earlier sentence about firecrackers. People know that this expression contains the meaning that "something is done to a firecracker to ignite it and cause it to cease to exist as an entity, by changing its state to yield new entities, with a loud noise during the change of state and possible physical harm to persons close to the location where the change of state occurs...." Most people also would have some notion of the social acceptability of the described event, what probably ensued, as well as some theories of Mary's personality, probable age range, and so on. To identify all the propositions implicit in the sentence and to construct them in predicate calculus representation would be so heroic an undertaking that some consider it impossible (Anderson, 1976).

Anderson (1976) has identified a further problem: Predicate calculus provides many ways to represent each assertion. This is a problem because a primary motive for adopting propositional notation in the first place was the need to convert many sentences with the same meaning into one and only one proposition. Propositional representation was supposed to accommodate the need for a consistent type–token relationship. A single *type,* or meaning, was to be extracted from different utterances, or *tokens.* Comprehension could then be viewed as the storing of a token in working memory until its unique type was located or constructed in permanent memory. This way of looking at comprehension is problematic, however, if there is not a unique propositional form for each meaning. To handle this problem, Anderson has adopted the position that there is only weak invariance under paraphrase. That is, he allows ACT to accept as identical somewhat different encoded and stored propositions. He has relaxed the requirement that there be one and only one propositional representation for every paraphrase of the same idea.

The propositional representations of many of the global theorists have also incorporated conventions from case grammar (Fillmore, 1968, 1971). In Fillmore's system, which we presented in Chapter 10, a verb serves as the relational operator for a set of arguments, including the ideas of actor, agent, recipient, source, time, place, and so on. Fillmore called these arguments *cases.* Sentence (2) about Mary and the firecracker might be represented in a case format by

EXPLODE(MARY, FIRECRACKER, INSTRUMENT NOT
SPECIFIED, PAST, INTERIOR SUE'S HOUSE,...)

The case approach can be used to cast a wide net and capture large schools of meaning elements, but the list of cases is arbitrary and changes from verb to verb, with no principled restriction on its size.

Propositions in LNR are based on case grammar, which has also played a significant role in the development of Kintsch's (1974, pp. 23ff.) propositional representation. However, Kintsch's set of cases is very different from Fillmore's.

c. Summary.   All the comprehensive theories represent the meanings of utterances and other surface forms with an abstract unit of knowledge called a proposition, which is a configuration of concepts and their interrelations. The proposition is a meaning atom intended to represent surface relationships in their most reduced but coherent form. The propositional unit is abstract because the knowledge it represents is not tied to any input modality, language, situation, or other aspect of concept acquisition. Propositional representation was borrowed from the logical formalisms of propositional logic and predicate calculus, but it is has been necessary to extend these formalisms to cover ideas they were not designed to represent. The global theorists have used several ways to represent the rich variety of meanings expressed in natural language with the notation of propositional logic, but none has provided precise rules for forming propositions. Aspects of the logical formalisms—some logical operators for example—were dropped; and ideas from case grammar were added by some of the theorists. LNR incorporates the propositions into a network representation by identifying predicators with links and arguments with nodes. HAM and ACT include both as nodes. Something like this network implementation of propositions seems essential to allow for such cognitive operations as locating, altering, or adding to memory.

It was the great inferential power of propositional logic that made it attractive as a source of formalism and notation. It seemed to do justice to the inferential capacities of human language comprehenders. Its major disadvantage is that it does not do justice to the content of human thought, being originally designed to deal only with a small part of people's ideation. There are things in heaven, on earth, and in the minds of humans that can so far be expressed consistently only in natural language. Ultimately, all features of human conception and of natural-language semantics must be expressible in the representation of a global theory. Otherwise the theory is a failure. Theories of propositional storage are too new to have worked out precise procedures or rules for assigning meaning representations to sentences or other stimuli. Utlimately, however, there must be a rule-governed way of going from surface features to underlying propositions. The theorist must discover or invent a finite and workable set of mechanisms or programs that assigns some appropriate propositional representation to each of the utterances that people can process. Then, and only then, will experiments play a major role in answering the question, Is this the way that meaning is represented in the mind?

It is too soon to conclude that it will be impossible to devise a sufficient propositional representation. Current systems may be improved, or some entirely different method of representation may be necessary.

B. The Declarative–Procedural Distinction

The memory structure of some contemporary theories contains two kinds of knowledge: declarative and procedural. The former is propositional and consists of facts about language and the world. Procedural knowledge is about how to do things. Procedural knowledge is analogous to computer programs, while factual knowledge is analogous to data. The idea that knowledge can be represented as processes is a recent development, and it is causing a minor revolution in certain areas of computer science (Raphael, 1976). The conception of procedural knowledge has its most detailed development in Winograd's block-moving model (1972) and in the production systems of Newell and Simon (1972) and Newell (1973). In Winograd's model, all things are defined by procedures to prove some new, unknown thing is an X. Anderson (1976) uses Newell and Simon's production systems in ACT, which is the most fully developed global theory. ACT's world knowledge is divided about equally between a propositional network and its production systems. Thus, its memory contains both data and control processes, and the control processes (production systems) examine, test, modify, and extend the contents of the propositional network. LNR also includes both procedures and data in its representation scheme, but it does not formally distinguish them (Norman & Rumelhart, 1975).

Anderson used production systems in his theory primarily to make its language processing more like that of humans, but he also had intuitive reasons. The idea of production systems presupposes the declarative–procedural distinction. This distinction is essential if we are to take seriously the strong intuition that a person can communicate most of his declarative knowledge but little of his procedural knowledge. For example, one of this book's authors (JL) was once an inveterate roller skater. She stopped skating in her mid-teens. About 20 years later she tried again to skate, and was quite successful. This surprised her. She had not known whether she would be able to do it, and she could not describe how she did it. It just "came back." In contrast is the knowledge she has of the places she has lived. Twenty years after leaving California she could also name and describe most of its major cities, but this did not surprise her, and she can tell you how she does it. ACT's procedural knowledge component captures the idea of automatic pathway activation underlying behaviors that we do without conscious awareness or intention (Shiffrin & Schneider, 1977). The production systems that represent ACT's procedural knowledge actually do have an automatic quality, although this is difficult to convey to a reader without a technical explanation of how they work. The utilization of ACT's propositional network seems to correspond better with the strategic direction of conscious cognitive behavior (Posner & Snyder, 1975). Of course, strategy-controlled behavior can initiate procedural knowledge.

C. The Meaning of Words

As far as the representation of meaning is concerned, we have spoken only about the use of propositions to capture the ideas in sentences. The meanings of words need to be represented too. Most global theorists believe that words are part of a linguistic system, while the concepts they stand for are part of a separate knowledge system. The surface properties of the word—the way it is pronounced or spelled—interest them very little; that is a problem for the future. Presently, they are concerned with how to represent the conceptual entities to which words direct people. From the information-processing view, these conceptual entities are words' meanings.

1. What We Know About Word Meaning

Words' meanings are abstract, and somehow the surface features of words lead to their meanings. Words have syntactic properties, phonological properties, and meanings. All must be interrelated; moreover, word meanings must bear some relationship to world knowledge, but there is disagreement on how to represent this relationship in a model. Likewise, there is no agreement about the psychological and linguistic properties of the abstract entities that constitute word meaning.

Controversy over word meaning antedates the global models. It has sometimes been held that word meaning can be reduced to *reference,* or naming. Reference is the notion that words "mean" what they stand for. On this view, the meaning of *John Smith* is the person, John Smith; analogously, the meaning of *pig* is the class of physical objects that are referred to by the word *pig*. Learning a word's meaning, according to the referential theory, is learning an association between a word and its referents—the things it names. This view has been questioned ever since the nineteenth century (Frege, 1892). Most contemporary psycholinguists agree that word meaning is not reducible to reference, although reference may be part of the meaning of some words.

The first objection to meaning as reference is that many words have no conceivable referent. Abstract words such as *justice*, for example, simply do not refer to physical objects and events. Such concrete referents as might be proposed—a blindfolded lady carrying scales to stand for *justice*—are peripheral or superfluous to what the word means to most people. The second objection is that there is more to meaning than reference, even in the case of concrete nouns. If this were not so, then the sentence *Polaris is the North Star* would mean nothing more than *Polaris is Polaris,* because *Polaris* and *North Star* refer to the same object. Clearly, though, there is more information in the former sentence than the latter. Third, some of the meaning of at least some words is tied to human perceptual and motor capabilities. There are no physical characteristics of *chair* that define all chairs, except a shape that accommodates sitting. Queen Anne chairs have hardly any physical characteristic in common with beanbag chairs, not to mention barrels, orange crates, and other objects that can serve as a chair, and may rightly be called *chair* while doing so. Somehow, the meaning of the word *chair* must reflect what people do to sit. There are many other objections to reference as a complete theory of word meaning. An excellent discussion can be found in Fodor, Bever, and Garrett (1974).

2. Semantic Decomposition

Most theorists accept the idea that the meaning of some words can be expressed in terms of primitive concepts. For example, the meaning of *sell* seems to involve the ideas of *exchange for money*. Dictionaries usually define words by this means. However, dictionaries do not reduce word meanings as far as possible. For example, *exchange for money* involves two transfers of possessions: money from the buyer to the seller and some object from the seller to the buyer. This transaction is permanent rather than temporary, as in *rent* or *borrow*. Some implication of relative desirability exists—namely, that the seller desires the money more than the object and that the buyer desires the object more than his money. Everyone who knows the meaning of *sell* knows these things; and the potential exists for interminable decomposition. This is where the theorists disagree. While most would accept *exchange for money* as *a proper characterization of the meaning of sell,* not all care to decompose it further.

What are the implications of a theorist's position on semantic decomposition? First, the extent to which a theorist decomposes the concepts named by words determines the number and generality of elements in his theory's permanent memory representation. A theorist who does no decomposition will have to postulate at least as many permanent-memory concepts as there are words in his language. A theorist who views words as labels for combinations of more primitive concepts should be able to get by with fewer stored elements. Some theorists would like to construct a relatively small and manageable set of semantic primitives from which all complex concepts in memory can be built up, and some consider it possible. Others believe that the search for semantic primitives is misguided and quixotic.

One of the earliest semantic theories by psycholinguists (Katz & Fodor, 1963) tried to characterize word meanings in terms of atomic, hierarchically organized semantic components such as animateness, humanness, maleness, and the like. Perhaps its most notable achievement was to expose the difficulties of decomposition. A given word's meaning may have many aspects, and as we have already seen, context determines which aspects of meaning are salient in a given utterance. Consider the following sentences:

(3) He is a politician, but he was appointed to office.
(4) He is a politician, but he is honest.
(5) He is a politician, but he is very dumb.
(6) He is a politician, but he is very smart.

Sentence (3) highlights the meaning of *politician* as one who is elected to office. Other meanings of *politician* may or may not be activated by (3). Sentence (4) highlights the meaning of *politician* that concerns questionable honesty; so *politician* must contain that meaning too. In fact, any meaning that can be accessed as a component of *politician* by people when they hear the word should be available to the theoretical memory as a part of the meaning of the concept labeled by that word. The number of relevant dimensions of *politician* is quite large, but that is not the big problem. The serious problem is a logical one, illustrated by Sentences (5) and (6). Sentence (5) points up the meaning of *politician* as one who is expected to be smart, while Sentence (6) points up the meaning of *politician* who is expected to be dumb. Can *expected to be smart* and *expected to be dumb* both be stored with *politician*? It seems not, which raises the question of principles to guide the selection of meaning components.

One tack is to store only those aspects that are always part of a word's meaning. But you will recall from our example of *eating* with tramps, lords, and ladies in Chapter 11 that it can be difficult to identify any common element of meaning in all possible uses of a word. Here is an example studied by R. C. Anderson, Pichert, Goetz, Schallert, Stevens, and Trollip (1976).

(8) The container held the cola.
(9) The container held the door.
(10) The brick held the door.
(11) The policeman held the suspect.
(12) The policeman held the traffic.
(13) The speaker held their attention.

Each of these sentences may involve a single aspect of *held*'s meaning, but any such commonality is extraordinarily difficult to characterize. R. C. Anderson et al. were led to the conclusion that there is no such thing as a defining feature, if a defining feature is a common characteristic of meaning present in every use of a word. This position contrasts with that of Smith, Shoben, and Rips (1974), who distinguished defining from characteristic features. R. C. Anderson and associates argue that there are no defining features for words, only characteristic ones. It remains to be seen whether they have made too large a leap from the fact that word meanings change with context to the claim that there is no core meaning at all.

How have the global theorists reacted to the notion of semantic primitives? J. Anderson (1976) has rejected it. He argues that decomposition into primitives is nothing more than a translation from one arbitrary symbol structure, natural language, to another. He does not believe that theoretical elegance or simplicity is thereby gained, nor that any set of semantic primitives is more manageable than the set of words. While he has rejected primitives, he has put nothing in their place to represent word meaning. ACT works with words themselves, matching them to previously stored words on the basis of their surface properties.

Schank (1972, 1975) takes a different route. He tries to break all verbs into action components, such as CAUSE, TRANSFER, and the like. He calls them ACTs, but they should not be confused with Anderson's (1976) model. Schank now uses 11 primitive actions and a larger set of primitive states to build up the meanings of words. Norman and Rumelhart (1975) also use semantic primitives. They have assumed decomposition into a small set of states, state changes, and causal relations. Kintsch (1974) uses yet another strategy. He has borrowed a tool called *meaning postulates* from linguistics, trying to relate meanings to the way the word's concept functions in his propositional representation. He acknowledges that people can decompose complex semantic concepts into more primitive underlying components, but he argues that they do not always do so. From his perspective, the psychologists' problem is to specify the circumstances under which decomposition normally occurs, and the amount of decomposition that actually does occur. So far, no experimental data exist to recommend any particular decomposition level. This leaves the problem of how word meanings are to be represented in psychological models empirically unconstrained. Various approaches recommend themselves to the theorists on the basis of feasibility, logical consistency, computer programmability, and the like. All the global modelers have addressed the matter of representing word meanings, but none has solved it. It is a problem they must continue to face.

D. The Interface Problem

Anderson and Bower (1973) recognized that models such as HAM must have interfaces: They must have an input parser and an output synthesizer. The input parser is needed to convert sentences to a form compatible with permanent memory, where concepts, ideas, and beliefs are stored. In short, the parser would do input synthesis. The output interface would recode from the format of permanent memory to that of language or other behavior.

It is easy to summarize what the global modelers have done to solve the interface problem—with the exception of Winograd (1972), nothing. This is one of the reasons we suggested that their work not be evaluated as conceptually mature theory, but as experiments in conceptualization. Although they are imaginative, formal, and significant, they are still insufficiently complete to be judged as full-fledged theories.

VI.   SUMMARY OF COMPREHENSIVE THEORIES

The global models signal a change from problem-limited theory to comprehensive models. How comprehensive are they? At present, they are more comprehensive in intent than in fact. Each still models a fairly restricted set of experimental tasks. For example, experimental tests of ACT are still largely sentence-memory studies. Kintsch's model has been tested primarily in experiments on prose recall. The authors of LNR report relatively few experiments, but are concentrating on eliciting realistic question-answering from the model.

Nevertheless, it is clear that the objectives of the modelers are justly called "comprehensive." They clearly wish their models to extend to such wide-ranging human capabilities as language acquisition and comprehension, conversation, learning, reading, reconstructing past events, and perhaps all the topics covered in this book.

The models are very new and are probably best viewed as experiments in conceptualization rather than theories or even models. Whether they forecast a major change in paradigmatic commitments is uncertain.

There are major problems with which all global models must deal. The first is how to represent the knowledge in permanent memory. Most of the proposed solutions have come from efforts of computer scientists who specialize in artificial intelligence. Some of the global modelers have adopted network representation, and all have adopted the proposition as the unit of representation. Their notion of propositions comes from systems of mathematical logic. But propositional logic and predicate calculus defined propositions too narrowly to handle all the ideas people are capable of. In extending propositions to cover more, the objectivity of their mathematical formation rules has been lost. The global modelers have so far been unable to formulate a precise description of how they translate the ideas expressed in natural language into propositions, though they continue to do such translations. Objectifying this process is an important task for the future.

Representation of word meanings is also a problem. The flexibility of word meanings makes it difficult to decide which nuances should be directly stored with a concept and which should be indirectly accessible. Some theorists have sought semantic primitives, which are a few meaning elements from which more complex concepts are built. Others have rejected this approach and offer logical arguments against it. Each approach has its costs. A theorist who opts for semantic primitives will have a relatively small and efficient system for representing word meanings, but his propositions will have to carry the weight of combining the primitives into word concepts as well as combining the word concepts into larger utterances. As a consequence, the propositions may be unwieldy. On the other hand, a theorist who keeps the entries in his model's propositions at about the level of natural-language words will have a heavier burden to bear in designing his model's permanent memory, for the nuances of meaning and all the interrelationships among concepts will have to be available there.

The global modelers recognize the need to solve the interface problem, but few have yet tried.

Their colleagues have mixed feelings about the global modelers. On the one hand, most information-processing psychologists concede that they are asking the right questions. On the other hand, there is some objection to the movement away from traditional experimentation on the part of some modelers. The global modelers are similar to linguists in their willingness to use rational argument, and they are similar to artificial intelligence specialists in their willingness to be pragmatic for the purpose of implementing parts of their models on computers. To at least some information-processing psychologists, and perhaps to many, these are character flaws.

It is our expectation that these influences will balance each other. The global modelers, we anticipate, will prosper and multiply. They will keep important questions about cognition in sharp focus. They will act as a counterforce to any tendency for cognitive psychology to degenerate into trivial, puzzle-solving experiments. On the other hand, those who treasure the experimental tradition will constrain the more stratospheric flights of the modelers' fancy. Unless they provide evidence that their models can be subjected to laboratory test, the modelers will be ignored by many of the most important cognitive psychologists. The silent treatment is deadly for scientists. We welcome the global models, and wish them well. We also look to the experimentally oriented to keep them scientifically respectable.

13 Pattern Recognition

James F. Juola[1]

ABSTRACT

I. *Information Processing and Pattern Recognition*
Meaningful interaction with the world requires pattern recognition, which is illustrated by the fact that reading, understanding speech, and distinguishing the familiar from the unfamiliar all require the recognition of patterns. Pattern recognition is not a simple matter of matching sensory input with memories, because the neural signals arising from stimulation undergo many changes on their way from the senses to the brain, and the existence of illusions shows that these changes are determined by internal factors. How people recognize patterns was one of the first questions that information-processing psychologists tried to answer. It remains one of the few questions about cognition for which a consideration of neurophysiology is pertinent.

II. *Some Sensory Physiology*
The study of sensory physiology has produced data and theory about how external information enters the cognitive system, and psychological theories of perception, memory, and language must be consistent with these biological data and theories. To show how and the extent to which knowledge of sensory physiology constrains theories of pattern recognition, selected aspects of auditory and visual physiology are described.
  A. *Aspects of the Visual System* The retina, which lines the rear of the eye, contains two sorts of light receptors: rods and cones. These receptors synapse with bipolar cells that synapse in turn with ganglion cells, whose axons combine to form each eye's optic nerve, which carries electrical impulses from the receptors in each eye to its corresponding visual cortex in the brain.

---

[1] I wish to thank the authors of this book for the many additions and revisions that they made to improve the quality and readability of this chapter.

Cells represent information only in their firing rate—that is, only with the rate at which they transmit electrical impulses. Each cell has a characteristic firing rate that remains the same as long as the cell is unstimulated. When stimulated, a cell's baseline (unstimulated) firing rate changes. By placing tiny electrodes in a cell, it is possible to measure its firing rate and to see what sorts of external stimulation change it. Sensory physiologists have used this technique to determine how various parts of the visual system represent different patterns of light presented to various parts of the eye. They have discovered that cells which synapse to a receptor (rod or cone) in the eye increase their firing rate when light strikes the receptor. Moreover, cells adjacent to the one whose rate is increased show a reciprocal decrease in their firing rate. This decrease as a consequence of an increase in a neighboring neuron's firing rate is called *lateral inhibition*, and it serves to enhance the perception of edges and other discontinuities in the visual field. Also, lateral inhibition helps explain various illusions.

There are fewer receptor cells in the eye than there are ganglion cells in the optic nerve, which suggests that each nerve cell conveys information from a number of receptor cells. This has been verified by monitoring the firing of cells in the optic nerve. The group of receptor cells that synapses to a ganglion nerve cell is called that cell's *receptive field*. Different receptive fields respond to different sorts of visual stimulation, including edges, angles, spots, movement, etc. Cells in the visual cortex also have receptive fields that are specialized for various sorts of visual events.

From the information-processing point of view, there are several important generalizations to be drawn from knowledge of the neurophysiology of vision. The relationships between receptors, nerve cells, and cells in the visual cortex show that information is transformed several times on its way from the eye to the brain, which is entirely consistent with the paradigm's pretheoretical beliefs. Also, different neural units respond to different features of the environment, and as information moves from the eye to the brain, its representation becomes at once more specific and more organized like templates of environmental objects.

B. *Aspects of the Auditory System*   While the neurophysiolgy of the auditory system has been studied less than that of the visual system, what is known suggests strongly that the same general principles apply to both systems.

C. *Neurosensory Constraints on Theories of Pattern Recognition*   Study of sensory physiology has shown that the cortical representation of auditory and visual stimuli are recoded abstractions, but it has said very little about the character of these abstractions; far more is known about peripheral than about central neurophysiology. Therefore, neurosensory data constrain psychological theories of stimulus encoding far more tightly than they constrain theories about abstract central representation and decision making. Pattern-recognition theories deal mainly with comparisons among abstract, central representations. Consequently, pattern-recognition theory is constrained only loosely by neurophysiological data.

III. *Theories of Pattern Recognition*
To recognize a pattern in the here and now as being equivalent to one from the past, people must compare the here and now to their memory of the past. The comparison must be made centrally, and to work, the compared representations must have similar forms. Pattern-recognition theories differ primarily in the forms they attribute to the representations that are compared. Some theories view

the compared representations as lists of features. Other theories view the representations as templates. As far as knowledge of neurophysiology is concerned, either sort of theory could be correct.

A. *Feature-Comparison Models*   The computer simulation called *Pandemonium* is used to illustrate feature-comparison models of visual pattern recognition. Psychologists have concluded that such models are not as active as people's pattern-recognition procession must be. For example, there are no mechanisms in models like Pandemonium to account for the facts that people make allowances for perceptual context and that their expectations influence their recognition of patterns. Also, pattern-recognition theories have not yet incorporated featural information about orientation and symmetry, but people do use such information.

B. *Template Matching and Structural Models*   Template-matching theories postulate a memory structure of idealized images that are compared with incoming images of whole objects or large parts of objects. Most cognitive psychologists have abandoned such models because they seem to require an unbelievably large memory store, which should cause people to process pattern information very slowly. Though the abandonment of template-matching models is quite complete, it is based more on psychologists' knowledge of computers (which slow down as their memory becomes larger) than on data from people.

IV. *Speech Perception Research*

The idea that pattern recognition requires comparison of incoming perceptual codes with memory codes flows directly from the computer analogy. Despite the fact that both feature-comparison and template-matching models are viewed as inadequate, psychologists have continued to search for the units of the perceptual and memory codes whose existence is suggested by the computer analogy. The search has produced two sorts of research. One sort focuses on events near the peripheral (receptor) end of the processing chain that is presumed to underlie perception, and this research is said to concern data-driven processes. The second sort focuses on processes near the central (cortical) end of the processing chain, and this research is said to concern conceptually driven processes.

A. *Data-Driven Processes*   Information-processing psychologists concerned with the data-driven aspects of speech recognition have drawn their hypotheses about perceptual units from phonetic and acoustic analysis of speech and from anatomical analyses of the mechanisms of speech. Various experiments have asked whether the perceptual units of speech are distinctive features (isolated with anatomical and acoustic analyses), phonemes (from phonetic analysis), vowels, consonants, and syllables (from acoustic and phonetic analyses) or larger units. Taken together, these experiments suggest that the smallest probable perceptual unit for speech is the syllable. Whether there are larger perceptual units for speech is uncertain, though some investigators believe not.

B. *Conceptually Driven Processes*   Research on conceptually driven processes has concentrated on showing that factors such as a person's knowledge of language, his expectations, and his reactions to situational context influence his perception of speech. Theoretical acknowledgment that all of these things are so has been made by advancing analysis-by-synthesis models, according to which perceptual analysis is guided by conceptual factors.

C. *Relating Data-Driven to Conceptually Driven Research*   So far, it has been impossible to test the information-processing view that the units of information in memory are the same as incoming perceptual units. Research on the data-driven aspects of speech recognition has clarified some aspects of perceptual units, but as yet there are no methods for comparably clarifying the units of memory. There is thus a disjunction between knowledge of data-driven and conceptually driven aspects of speech perception, and this disjunction gives models of pattern recognition more the status of metaphors than theories. Nevertheless, the models continue to guide new research into speech recognition, which should lead to new conceptions of pattern recognition, even if methods are not found for examining the nature of memory units.

V. *Visual Perception and Reading Research*
Most theories of visual pattern recognition are based on analyses of the information extracted from single fixations of the eye, without regard for the possibility that some sorts of pattern recognition may require several fixations to allow the extraction of visual change that occurs over time.

A. *Data-Driven Processes* Just as research on data-driven aspects of speech perception has been concerned with whether the syllable is the main perceptual unit, research on the data-driven aspects of visual perception during reading has been concerned with whether the word is the basic unit. While there is no question that people can treat letters or smaller visual elements as perceptual units, there is question as to whether letters are the first or most basic unit used during reading. Various experiments to answer the question have yielded no definitive result. The data do suggest that people adopt different strategies for different perceptual tasks, and that the unit upon which they depend varies with their strategy, which is like saying that conceptually driven processes are important in visual perception as well as in auditory perception.

B. *Conceptually Driven Processes* The main way that investigators have shown the effects of conceptual processes on visual perception is by varying the visual context preceding or accompanying a pattern to be perceived. Context does influence recognition, evidently by bringing different conceptual information to bear during stimulus analysis.

VI. *Theoretical Overview*
There are several points of agreement between models of auditory and visual pattern recognition. Both presume that features are extracted from stimuli before the stimuli are categorized, that categorization requires a comparison or perceptual and memory codes, and that conceptually driven processes influence pattern recognition. Neither auditory nor visual models have adequately specified their basic units of perception, and neither has documented the processes it postulates during comparison of perceptual and memory units.

I. INFORMATION PROCESSING AND PATTERN RECOGNITION

Adults, children, and animals recognize common objects in their environment. You undoubtedly would recognize a picture of the Statue of Liberty; very young children recognize their parents' faces; and dogs can recognize such things as their food dishes. Objects are only one type of the many kinds of patterns present in environmental stimulation that people recognize. For example, to understand speech we must recognize the auditory patterns that correspond to meaningful words. Reading similarly involves recognition of the arbitrary visual patterns used to represent letters of the alphabet. These examples illustrate that pattern recognition is essential to almost all our waking activities. In fact, every living thing must recognize patterns when it interacts meaningfully with its world.

Pattern recognition research is an important part of cognitive psychology, as well as of such other disciplines, as neurobiology, computer science, and communications engineering. All of these disciplines are concerned with systems (man, animal, or machine) that convert complex inputs (such as patterns of lights and sounds) into recognizable and meaningful words, objects, or events. From the information-processing point of view, how people recognize patterns is one of the more interesting and researchable aspects of the larger question of how they perceive and interact with their environment. Yet the study of pattern recognition was not always thought to be important for understanding perception and cognition.

Nineteenth- and early twentieth-century experimental psychologists took their task to be the discovery of the elements of sensation and the explanation of how the laws of association combined these elements into larger complexes or patterns. In the view of the earliest experimental psychologists, the elements of sensation existed entirely in the stimulus, and the function of the peripheral nervous system was to decompose complex physical stimuli into their simpler elements. The function of the brain was to combine the elemental sensations into perceptions. Peripheral decomposition and central combination were thought to occur passively, in accordance with the laws of association. By this view, the first research goal was to identify the elements into which complex stimuli are decomposed. Early in this century, psychologists did many experiments in which a trained observer introspectively analyzed and described sensations arising from various stimuli, but little progress resulted. Introspective methods were unreliable; even highly trained observers produced different introspective reports. Furthermore, the existence of visual illusions (e.g., the moon looking larger near the horizon than high in the sky) suggested that the nervous system is not so passive as the associationists supposed. Research has shown that perception is not always veridical (true to the world), so that some transformation of the input must take place between stimulation and perception. This idea was advocated energetically by Gestalt psychologists (e.g., Wertheimer, 1923), who argued that unique organizing principles of the nervous system influence the way external stimulation is turned into conscious perception.

Kolers (1968) marshaled physiological evidence to bolster the conclusion suggested by visual illusions that perception cannot be a passive transmission of impulses from physically defined stimuli. For example, even though the retinal image is an imperfect record of the stimulation entering the eye, it yields sharp vision. Also, there are more receptors in the eyes than fibers in the optic nerve, which precludes a one-to-one relationship between them. Kolers concluded that transforming operations occur at each of several "stations" in the visual system; the outputs of these stations are different from their inputs.

Conceiving vision in this way—and, by analogy, audition as well—contemporary psychologists have applied information-processing language and concepts to perception. According to the information-processing view, the eyes and ears are input devices or energy transducers. A transducer changes energy of one form (e.g., light) into another (e.g., the electrochemical energy of the nervous system). Inputs are recoded by means of operations performed on them in several processing stages in the visual system. In other words, sensory information is transformed in accordance with the structures and processes of the perceptual system. Because new stimulation is recognized, some of the recoded information must be compared and matched with information in memory. Discovering how recoded stimuli are compared to memories will not only increase our understanding of people, but also pave the way for many technical advances. For example, computer scientists have long tried with only limited success to make computers read handwriting and interpret ordinary speech. There is reason to believe that machines will be made to do these things only after adequate theories of human pattern recognition processes have been constructed.

Given the physiological evidence that perception involves successive transformations of input information, information-processing models have been readily applied to pattern recognition problems. Indeed, language understanding and character recognition have been two of the most enthusiastically researched but continuously perplexing problems for psychologists and computer scientists alike. Neisser's (1967) textbook, *Cognitive Psychology*, is now viewed as a classic, and was one of the earliest comprehensive treatments of the information-processing approach. Neisser based many of his examples on pattern recognition problems, and the influence of his approach spread information-processing methods and models to a wide range of applications in psychology. Hence, we have earlier discussed many topics such as long-term memory and language comprehension, where the stage-model approach is not as specific in its description of the cognitive processes involved as it often is in pattern recognition theories.

Pattern recognition continues to be important because it is one of the few topics in cognitive psychology that make unequivocal and scientifically meaningful contact with neuropsychological data. Theories of how animals recognize objects can be tested against data obtained at different steps in the sensory nervous system.

Neuropsychology has diverse intellectual antecedents, a special language and a system of concepts, an accepted data base, analogies, and a domain of agreed-upon problems that are different from those of cognitive psychology. Besides experimental psychology, neuropsychology has intellectual antecedents in anatomy, physiology, chemistry, and biophysics. Its fundamental subject matter is brain mechanisms that mediate both overt and covert behavior. Neuropsychology has no single most important analogy, but has employed a variety of metaphors from machines to molecular dynamics in its research on local and general brain mechanisms. Among the many research techniques it has developed over the years are neurosurgical methods, procedures for recording the electrical activity of large groups of nerve cells, electrophysiological recording from single nerve cells, and various ways of correlating behavior with neural events. Some of these methods cannot be applied to normal human subjects. For example, electrophysiological recording from single brain cells is not possible without penetrating the skull, which is a dangerous practice for people as well as laboratory animals. Animal experimentation is necessarily far more common in neuropsychology than it is in cognitive psychology. For example, we later discuss research on the optic nerve of *limulus*, the horseshoe crab. This animal is particularly well suited to the use of single-cell recording techniques for studying visual pattern perception because it has a large and accessible optic nerve. Inferences from such animal data to humans are made by neuropsychologists, even though they realize that it is not always safe to assume that physiological evidence from one animal provides conclusive data about another. There are cases in which direct measurements (involving surgery or other drastic procedures) on animals are supported by indirect evidence from humans, and in such cases it is safe to assume that the two organisms function similarly.

II. SOME SENSORY PHYSIOLOGY

Thought and action have two origins: autonomous events internal to the nervous system, and external sources of information that stimulate peripheral receptors. Data and principles from the study of sensory physiology and brain function concern how external information enters the cognitive system. Such data and principles provide boundary conditions for theories about higher cognitive processes. Any theory of perception, memory, or language comprehension must be partly about what happens to information received by the sense organs. If the theory is inconsistent with what we know of sensory physiology, it can only fail. Research programs initiated to test it will be a waste of both human and financial resources. Therefore, data from sensory physiology can provide constraints on theories of higher mental processes, even though such theories cannot be derived from physiological data alone. For this reason, we briefly review some physiology of the visual and auditory systems.

A. Aspects of the Visual System

Recently developed recording techniques allow reserchers to measure electrical activity in the visual and auditory pathways to animal brains. Tiny sensing devices (called electrodes) are placed in individual cell bodies or in fibers (called axons) that lead from one cell body to another or to other fibers. The electrodes are used to measure the neural activity that various stimuli produce at different points along sensory pathways. This makes it possible to infer how the eye and the ear encode stimuli and what kinds of changes occur in these sensory codings on their way to the brain. These neural messages are the basis of the brain's representation of the environment. Theories of human pattern recognition must also begin with a stimulus representation, and it should be consistent with knowledge of the neural codings that occur as information moves from the senses to the brain.

Hartline was one of the first neuroscientists to use single-cell recording techniques to obtain information about the visual pathway. He and his colleagues (Hartline & Ratliff, 1957, 1958; Hartline, Wagner, & Ratliff, 1956; Ratliff & Hartline, 1959) implanted tiny electrodes in single axon fibers of nerve cells in the eye of limulus. Though not light-sensitive themselves, the implanted cells synapsed to (came in close enough contact to intercommunicate with) light-sensitive cells of the limulus eye. Recordings taken through the electrodes indicated that the cells in the limulus eye, like most nerve cells, send a nearly steady rate of electrical impulses along their axons as long as they remain unstimulated. This unstimulated or baseline firing rate is relatively constant for each neuron but ranges between neurons from nearly zero to a few hundred spikes (impulses) per second.

Because all neural impulses or spikes are alike, their rate is the *only* source of information reaching the brain along sensory pathways. Any change (increase or decrease) from the baseline rate is a potential source of sensory information for the brain. Changes in the pattern of light projected to the eye alter the baseline firing rate of visual neurons. Hartline and his colleagues found that a small spot of light projected directly onto a light-sensing cell in the eye increased the firing rate of nerve cells with which it synapsed. More importantly, the light spot decreased the rate of firing by cells adjacent to the area being stimulated by light. The capacity of an excited nerve to reduce the activity of its neighbors is called lateral inhibition. Hartline and his colleagues were able to observe lateral inhibition directly, and they showed that the amount of inhibition that any cell exerts on its neighbors is directly related to its own level of excitation (Hartline & Ratliff, 1957).

Lateral inhibition is a general principle of exceptional importance. Among other things it enhances the perception of edges in the visual field. It also operates in sensory modalities other than vision (e.g., the skin pressure sense, Somjen, 1972; Uttal, 1973), and it explains many otherwise puzzling perceptual phenomena. As an example of a perceptual phenomenon explainable by lateral inhibition, consider the illusion known as "Mach bands" (named after its discoverer, Ernst Mach, a German physicist; see Ratliff, 1965). The illusion is shown in Fig. 13.1.

Each of the vertical bars is a uniform shade of gray; yet each bar appears lighter near its edge with a darker neighbor and darker near its edge with a lighter neighbor. The illusory lightening and darkening arise from lateral inhibition among the many visual nerve cells stimulated by looking at the vertical bars. Cells stimulated by the center of a bar receive equal light energy

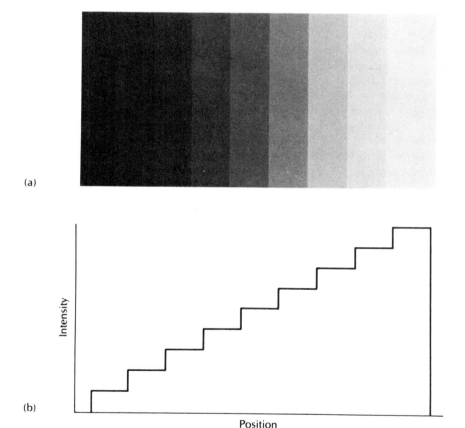

(a)

(b)

Position

FIG. 13.1. Mach bands. In the upper part of the figure, a series of vertical gray stripes is shown. Even though each stripe is of uniform brightness, each appears to be lighter near a darker neighbor and darker near a lighter neighbor. This illusion is due to differences in the relative amounts of lateral inhibition that visual nerve cells receive if they are located in a uniformly illuminated area of the retinal projection or if they are located near an edge.

and are excited to the same level. Moreover, the lateral inhibition among equally excited cells is the same, yielding identical firing rates and consequently identical perception from cells stimulated by the center of any bar. But neighboring cells stimulated by different bars receive different light input. Cells stimulated by a lighter bar fire at a more rapid rate, which is the neural basis for perceiving the bar as lighter. Furthermore, because a cell in the lighter region more strongly inhibits its neighbor in the darker region, the activity of the cell in the dark will be even less than if all of its neighbors were also stimulated by the darker bar. As a result, cells near the edge of a darker bar will fire less rapidly than those in the middle of a darker bar, making the edge of the dark bar seem even darker. Conversely, cells at the edge of a brighter bar are only inhibited strongly by neighboring cells that are also in the light, and they receive less inhibition from their neighbors in the darker region. A cell on the brighter side of an edge receives less total inhibition than one in the middle of a bright field, and its net firing rate is therefore greater, making it seem brighter. In sum, lateral inhibition causes cells that lie on opposite sides of an edge to have the greatest discrepancies in their rates of firing, thus enhancing the perception of edges, but also producing illusory bands of apparently lighter and darker regions near edges.

Figure 13.2 illustrates some of what is known about the eyes of higher animals and their neural characteristics. Light enters the eyeball through the cornea and the lens, which projects a focused image of the viewed scene onto the retina (see Fig. 13.2). The retina covers most of the inside surface of the eyeball, and it contains light-sensitive cells called rods and cones. The cones are packed most densely into the rear central part of the retina, called the fovea. When we look directly at an object, its image is focused by the lens onto the fovea. Because of the density of cones in the fovea, we can see the object more clearly than if we looked less directly at it, thereby focusing the object on the periphery of the eye. Peripheral vision is also handled by cones, but they are packed far less densely outside the fovea. Instead of densely packed cones, there are large numbers of rods in the periphery. Rods respond to dim light and are among the most sensitive light detectors in nature (Hecht, Schlaer, & Pirenne, 1942; see also Cornsweet, 1970).

In the mammalian retina (see Fig. 13.2), rods and cones synapse with bipolar cells, which in turn synapse with retinal ganglion cells. The ganglion cells send out long axonal projections that combine to form the optic nerve, which relays information from each eye to visual centers in the brain. Humans have about 100 times as many receptor cells as ganglion cells; so recording the activity of any particular ganglion cell may capture the combined outputs of many light-sensitive receptors. The receptor cells that activate a particular ganglion cell determine its receptive field. The number of cells in a ganglion's receptive field varies from perhaps one or two in the fovea to several hundred in the periphery.

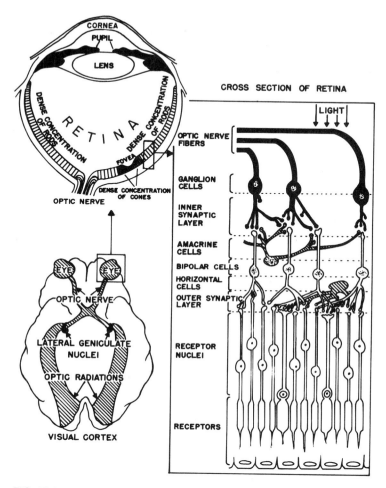

CROSS SECTION OF RETINA

LIGHT

OPTIC NERVE FIBERS

GANGLION CELLS

INNER SYNAPTIC LAYER

AMACRINE CELLS

BIPOLAR CELLS

HORIZONTAL CELLS

OUTER SYNAPTIC LAYER

RECEPTOR NUCLEI

RECEPTORS

CORNEA
PUPIL
LENS
R E T I N A
DENSE CONCENTRATION OF RODS
DENSE CONCENTRATION OF RODS
FOVEA
DENSE CONCENTRATION OF CONES
OPTIC NERVE

EYE
EYE
OPTIC NERVE
LATERAL GENICULATE NUCLEI
OPTIC RADIATIONS
VISUAL CORTEX

FIG. 13.2. A detailed drawing of a section of the retina taken from a human eye. Notice that light entering the eye through the pupil is focused by the lens onto the inside lining of the eyeball, and it must pass through several layers of cells before it reaches the light-sensitive receptors. The receptor cells eventually send their messages to the retinal ganglion cells, whose axons combine to form the optic nerve. The optic nerve leads from the eyes to a partial crossing point before the lateral geniculate nuclei. Here new fibers carry the messages to the back part of the brain, called the visual cortex. Because of the partial crossing, the left visual cortex receives information only about the right half of the visual field and vice versa, although we are not aware of any split in the visual field.

The responses of single retinal cells to various light stimuli have been studied by many investigators, including Lettvin, Maturana, McCulloch, and Pitts (1959). Lettvin et al. studied the responses of single cells in the optic nerve of the frog. As in Hartline's work with limulus, recordings were not taken from light-sensitive cells located in the eye, but rather from cells in the nerve that transmits messages from the eye to the brain. That is, Lettvin et al. recorded from retinal ganglion cells. Bodies of these ganglion cells are located in the retina, and their axons combine to form the optic nerve (see Fig. 13.2). Lettvin et al. inserted an electrode into the optic nerve until pulses recorded from it indicated that the electrode had penetrated a nerve cell. Various stimuli were then put into the frog's line of sight in order to discover what maximally excited each cell. Different cells responded most to different stimuli. Four cell types were found—those that responded maximally to (1) stationary edges, (2) moving edges, (3) dimming, and (4) small moving spots—all of which seem to be important to frogs. For example, cells that respond most to small moving spots should help detect flying insects, which is what frogs eat. The cells responded not only to specific types of stimuli but also to specific locations in the field of view, and hence to corresponding areas on the retina of the eye. Each ganglion cell seemed to monitor the activity of a group of receptor cells in a different part of the retina. This area of sensitivity is called the receptive field of a cell.

Kuffler (1952, 1953) studied the organization of receptive fields in the retinas of cats, and sensory psychologists feel comfortable generalizing most of his observations to humans. Kuffler's findings concern the organization of receptive fields of individual ganglion cells. Using small spots of light as stimuli, he found circular regions of the retina, portions of which respond with increased firing rates (called excitation) of the ganglion cells and portions of which respond with decreased rates (inhibition). Most cells showed excitatory and inhibitory regions in a center–surround relationship. In other words, if a light spot fell at the center of a circular "on-center, off-surround" field, the ganglion cell would begin firing at a higher rate shortly after the onset of the spot. On the other hand, if the light spot fell outside the central area and on the surrounding "off" area, there was a decrease in firing rate while the light was on and a burst of activity when it was turned off. An approximately equal number of ganglion cells showed the opposite relationship in their receptive fields—that is, off-centers and on-surrounds. Thus, the simple lateral inhibition found in the eye of limulus has an analogue in the organization of the receptive fields of mammals, whose center–surround regions work in comparable antagonistic ways.

Figure 13.3 shows how center–surround antagonism might account for such perceptual phenomena as edge enhancement and Mach bands. The top portion of the figure shows where on the retina a light bar is focused. The middle portion shows that each receptor cell operates at a hypothetical rate of

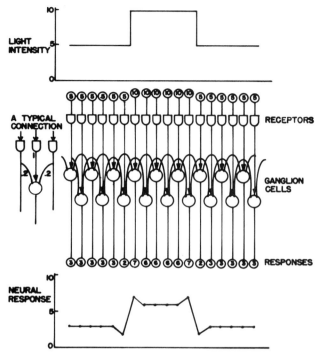

FIG. 13.3. A schematic representation of how on-center, off-surround ganglion cells could combine their activities to emphasize light discontinuities at an edge. A light bar shown in the top of the figure excites all receptor cells by an arbitrary 10 units of activity, whereas the background results in only 5 units of activity. The ganglion cells preserve the level of excitation exactly for the receptors in the center of their fields, whereas they are inhibited by the two neighboring receptors by an amount equal to 0.2 times the receptor's activity. The algebraic sums of excitations and inhibitions produce the numerical response rates shown at the bottom of the figure. Thus the antagonistic center–surround organization of retinal ganglion cells serves to enhance the perception of edges. The same phenomenon could be demonstrated by using off-center, on-surround cells in the figure or a combination of both types of cells, as in a living retina.

10 spikes per second where the bar hits the retina and five spikes per second where it does not. Receptor cells communicate with the ganglion cells by means of excitatory (arrows) and inhibitory (dots) synapses. The connections in Fig. 13.3 represent on-center, off-surround receptive fields.

All excitatory connections are shown as if they preserve the activity rate of the receptor cells in the ganglia so that the ganglia would fire at the rate of either 5 or 10 spikes per second without inhibition. The inhibitory connections from each ganglion cell to its immediate neighbors are assumed to reduce the activity of the neighbors by .2 times the amount of the central cell's activity. Thus, a cell in the light region (bar present) reduces its neighbors' activity by .2 × 10 = 2 spikes per second, and a cell in the dark region (bar absent) reduces its neighbors' activity by .2 × 5 = 1 spike per second. Because each cell receives one excitatory connection and two inhibitory connections, the algebraic sum of the inputs determines the final firing rate, which is shown at the bottom of the figure. Notice that the difference in firing rate is greatest at the boundaries of the light bar—greater in fact than the light gradients in the real world (top part of figure). The figure is a gross oversimplification of the neural circuits in the mammalian retina, but it shows how lateral inhibition might enhance perceptual contrasts between light sources of different energies. The antagonistic relations of regions of receptive fields can enhance the boundaries between objects or between an object and its background, making them more noticeable than they would be if the eye produced a more exact reproduction of the physical stimulus. Even at the simple level of the receptive field, information is transformed by processing mechanisms such as lateral inhibition, which is one reason so many researchers embrace the information-processing approach to cognition.

Lateral inhibition is not the only mechanism that accentuates visual discontinuities in the environment. Retinal ganglion cells with center-surround antagonism are of two types: sustained and transient (e.g., Wright & Ikeda, 1974). Sustained cells have receptive fields concentrated near the fovea, and they transmit information about a stimulus as long as it is projected onto a receptive field. Transient cells have larger receptive fields located more often in the periphery, and they change their rate of firing for only a short period after the stimulus in the receptive field changes. It is as though transient cells are specialized for detecting changes or motion in the environment, while sustained cells are used to inspect an interesting stimulus once it is detected.

Transient cells are particularly important for edge and discontinuity detection. Our eyes are in two types of constant motion. There is a gross type, which you can see by watching anyone read or look about. Everyone's eyes jump from point to point about four times each second. Each point is fixated for about 200 msec, and the movement time between fixations averages about 50 msec, with the result that our view of the world is composed of brief "snapshots." During each snapshot or fixation, there is a finer sort of movement that is not observable without special instruments. By magnifying the image of the eye and observing slow-motion films of its activity, it can be seen that the eye is constantly jerked and pulled short distances by rapid involuntary contractions of the eye muscles. These movements constantly change the location on the retina of images projected through the eye's lens during fixation. Any transient cell that is located near an edge (light discontinuity) on the retinal image will thus continually fire as the fine eye movements bring the edge back and forth across its receptive field. Transient cells located in areas of uniform illumination will fire briefly at the start of each new fixation, and will revert to their baseline rates during fixation. Edges are thus signaled to the brain by the continuous neural activity resulting from eye movements, as well as by environmental signals. In fact, eliminating the effects of fine eye movements by stabilizing the image on the retina makes edges invisible (Neisser, 1967). This is so because most retinal cells are transient rather than sustained. Eliminating the effects of fine eye movements causes the transient cells to return to their normal rate of firing, which produces functional blindness.

So far we have spoken of mechanisms located in or near the eye, but much is also known about more central processes of the visual system. The optic nerve sends information from the retina through a pair of relay stations located below the center of the brain. From these stations, which are synapses of the lateral geniculate nuclei, neural pathways lead to the visual cortex located in the extreme rear of the brain's two hemispheres (see Fig. 13.2). Single-cell recording techniques similar to those used to study cells synapsing directly in the retina have been used to study mechanisms of cells in the visual cortex of cats and monkeys (Hubel & Wiesel, 1962, 1963, 1965, 1968).

Hubel and Wiesel identified three types of cortical cells: simple, complex, and hypercomplex. All three types have elongated or rectangular fields rather than the circular, center–surround fields of retinal ganglion cells, and most cells of each type are driven binocularly: They respond to inputs from either eye. Many of the brain cells are stimulated most by movement, and many are further specialized, responding mainly to movement in a particular direction.

The simple cortical cells (isolated by Hubel and Wiesel) have larger receptive fields than those of ganglion cells in the retina, and they are excited most by edges, dark bars, or slits of light. Different simple cells favor different orientations of their preferred stimuli. Of those stimulated by edges, some respond most to verticals, others to horizontals, and yet others to various angles between vertical and horizontal. The precise interconnections between retinal ganglion and cortical cells are unknown, but some reasonable hypotheses follow from what is known. It seems likely that each simple cortical cell receives inputs from several ganglion cells that are arranged linearly on the retina. For example, a single cortical cell could receive outputs from a string of off-center, on-surround ganglion cells arranged so that they are all stimulated by a dark bar of specific orientation and width against a light background. Other cortical cells could be connected to groups of ganglion cells arranged so as to respond as a group only when stimulated by other specific patterns of light.

Complex cortical cells are similar to simple cells except for having larger receptive fields. Thus, a given complex cell will respond maximally to a light stripe 45° off horizontal, located anywhere in a large segment of the visual field, whereas an analogous simple cell will respond only if the stripe is in a specific small area. Simple cells detect lines and edges in specific locations, whereas complex cells detect lines and edges without reporting their locations as accurately.

Hypercomplex cells respond to more specific types of stimuli than either simple or complex cells. They respond maximally to edges, corners, curves, and angles of particular sizes. Stimuli, such as edges, that excite a given simple or complex cell regardless of their length may be too short or too long to excite a hypercomplex cell, which will respond maximally only to an edge of specific length.

Single-cell recording techniques have shown much about how light patterns are represented at various points on the path from the eye to the brain. From the information-processing point of view, one important generalization from these findings is that different neural units respond to different features of the environment. Another important generalization is that as information moves from the eye to the brain, the features to which cells respond become at once more specific and more organized like templates or idealized models of environmental objects. Within the information-processing approach, pattern recognition requires the matching of incoming information with information stored in permanent memory. The available neurosensory data on the visual system suggest that sensory information might be represented in the same form as the information in memory to which it must be compared; neurosensory data suggest that memory must be organized around lists of distinctive features or around templates that represent objects or parts of objects. We see subsequently that pattern recognition theories emphasize one or the other of these two representational modes. Some are feature-matching theories and others are template-matching theories.

B. Aspects of the Auditory System

More is known about the neural aspects of recoding in the visual modality than in any other sensory channel. Of the remaining senses, most is known about audition.

The inputs to the ears are pressure changes (compressions and rarefactions of air), which are usually represented as waves that differ in frequency and amplitude. These pressure changes or sound waves vibrate the tympanic membrane (eardrum), which moves three small bones (ossicles), which in turn transmit the vibrations of the eardrum to a small membrane called the oval window of the cochlea. The cochlea is coiled like a snail's shell and is filled with fluid. The fluid surrounds several membranes, including the basilar membrane, which contains about 23,000 tiny hair cells. These hair cells are the transducer cells for hearing. Each cell sprouts several hairs, called cilia. The cilia are moved by sound-induced waves in the cochlear fluid and the internal membranes. Each hair cell synapses with bipolar cells, which eventually communicate with cells in the auditory cortex of the brain. There is an auditory cortex in each lobe of the brain (above and quite near the inner ear structures) and their dominant neural pathways are primarily contra-lateral. That is, the left ear communicates mainly with the right auditory cortex and vice versa.

Which of the 23,000 hair cells are stimulated most by a pressure wave depends on the wave's frequency. Those cells located on the part of the basilar membrane closest to the oval window are excited most by high-frequency waves, whereas low-frequency waves have their greatest effect on cells near the other end of the basilar membrane. This fact underlies the place theory of pitch perception, according to which people's subjective impression of pitch depends on the location (place) of the hair cells that are most intensely excited by a pressure wave.

Single-cell recordings from animals indicate that each neuron in the auditory nerve has a "tuning curve"; each responds maximally to a particular sound frequency. The tuning curve represents the relative displacement (by incoming sounds) of the basilar membrane, preserving in different neurons information as to the frequency of auditory inputs. A further index of frequency is the firing rate of auditory nerve cells. For low frequencies, each stimulated cell fires once per cycle of the sound wave; thus, a wave of 200 cycles per second produces 200 spikes per second in cells communicating with the maximally displaced region of the basilar membrane. Higher frequencies that exceed the maximum possible neural firing rates produce volleys in groups of cells, which are linked in their rate of firing to some fraction of the cycles per second of the high-frequency wave. For example, two cells might operate to code the exact frequency of a tone by alternately firing on odd- or even-numbered cycles of the pressure wave it represents. These facts about firing rate are the basis of the volley theory of pitch perception, which supplements the place theory.

Intensity, or perceived loudness, is apparently coded in the range or spread of stimulated hair cells. Low-intensity sounds stimulate only those nerve cells in the region of the basilar membrane appropriate to the sound's frequency. As intensity increases, a wider range of cells is stimulated, with those appropriate to the sound's frequency responding at the highest rate. For extremely intense sound, a broad range of cells is excited, and many of them fire at their maximum rates. Thus, apparent loudness is probably coded by the number of cells tuned to different frequencies.

Central mechanisms of the auditory system have been studied by monitoring single cells in the auditory cortex of such animals as cats and monkeys (Whitfield & Evans, 1965; see also Lindsay & Norman, 1977; Uttal,

1973). About 60% of the cells in the auditory system respond to pure tones. The remainder fire in response to more complex sounds. As in the visual system, some cells respond only to stimulus onset, others to stimulus offset, and still others signal both onset and offset. Some cells in the auditory cortex show narrow tuning curves, whereas others seem to respond to a broad range of frequencies. Some cells act as frequency sweep detectors, responding only to increases or decreases in frequency. These cells do not change their rates of firing for either stimulus onset or offset. About 40% of the cells in the auditory cortex apparently respond only to idiosyncratic sounds, such as clicks or bursts of noise.

The neurosensory characteristics of the auditory system have not been studied as extensively as those of the visual system, but what is known suggests that auditory information is coded by assembling the responses of cells tuned to specific frequencies of pressure waves, to the onsets and offsets of auditory inputs, to changes in frequency, and to particular complex sounds such as clicks and noise bursts. Pattern recognition theorists often argue by analogy from the visual system to the auditory system, because of some evident similarities between the two and because the visual system is better understood.

C. Neurosensory Constraints on Theories of Pattern Recognition

Data concerning sensory and brain mechanisms for coding environmental stimulation necessarily constrain theories of human pattern recognition, but the constraints apply primarily to stimulus coding. The neurosensory data provide fewer constraints on ideas about central recoding mechanisms, which are at least as crucial to pattern recognition theory as is stimulus coding. A minimum of 10 anatomical layers of cell organization and vascular networks have been identified in the retina of the eye (Polyak, 1957). Incoming light strikes the top layers first, but these are not light sensitive. Before light reaches its sensors (rods and cones), it must pass through optic fibers and ganglion cells, layers of inner synaptic structures, amacrine cells, bipolar cells, horizontal cells, outer synaptic structures, receptor nuclei, and various vascular tubes (see Fig. 13.2). The image picked up by the receptor layer is nothing like the crisp perceptions we experience. The mystery of how we perceive clearly and accurately is heightened by the fact that the topological arrangment of light on the retina is imperfectly retained during transmission to the visual cortex. It follows from all of this that cortical representations of visual stimuli are *recoded abstractions* (Kolers, 1968), and it is these with which cognitive theory deals. Cognitive theories have concerned the recoded abstractions that are particularized in conscious experience, decision making, and behavior, and these theories are relatively loosely constrained by the data of neuropsychology.

III. THEORIES OF PATTERN RECOGNITION

The problem for cognitive theories of pattern recognition is to explain how people determine that a present perceptual experience is equivalent to a previous one. The crude answer must be that they compare their present experience to some stored record of their past experiences. To recognize a pattern in the here and now as equivalent to one from the past, people must compare the here and now to their memory of the past. Without memory, the past is gone and cannot be compared to anything. Moreover, for the here and now to be compared to memory, the two must have similar form. That form cannot be a literal copy of the past, because literal copies of experience do not find their way into memory. As we have seen from the foregoing consideration of neuropsychology, every stimulus is transformed on its way to the brain, which is where memories are stored. Such transformations have counterparts in computer science, from which some pattern recognition theorists draw their theoretical analogy. The numerical inputs to computers are transformed into various electrical codes on their way to the machine's storage devices and central processor. Moreover, the present-to-past comparison that must be the heart of the recognition process has counterparts in computers, and these counterparts serve as a major source of guidance to pattern recognition theorists.

To determine whether a present input is the same as one from the past, a computer transforms the input to a form like that of its stored record of the past. It places this transformed input into its central processor. It then moves records of its past input from its memory to its central processor, and compares the new input to these memories. When one of the memories matches the transformed input, the processor has "recognized" that input. Depending on its architechture and how it is programmed, any particular computer will accomplish the transformation, transfer, and comparison processes in different ways. We need illustrate only one such way in order to clarify feature-comparison theories of pattern recognition and to show how directly such theories draw on the computer analogy.

A. Feature-Comparison Models

Pandemonium is a computer program designed to recognize visual patterns (Selfridge, 1959; Selfridge & Neisser, 1960; see also Lindsay & Norman, 1977; Rumelhart, 1977). The various stages in how it does this may be viewed as analogous to possible stages in humans' processing, but it is imperative to remember that people do not do anything precisely as computers do, no matter how compelling the effectiveness or elegance of a computer program makes it appear that the computer's way must be the only way. We remind you of this because in the pattern recognition literature, more than perhaps in any other, theorists alternate between talking *as if* people operate as computers and asserting that they *do* operate as computers. *As if*s can guide research and clarify thinking about how people function; but *do*s obscure the boundaries between hypotheses about how people might function and paradigmatic beliefs about how they must function.

Pandemonium first accepts input, which is analogous to the formation of an image on a human's retina. Suppose the input is an A. After accepting the A, Pandemonium extracts its features, which is analogous to the activation of neurons in the visual cortex. From this point on in the processing chain, we do not have the faintest idea what mental or neural processes the functions of Pandemonium might be analogous to; so speaking of what people might do that is like Pandemonium is purely hypothetical. All we know for sure is what Pandemonium does. It has in its memory a list of features that can be used to describe letters of the alphabet. Thus, the feature *cross bar* is characteristic of the letters, A, E, F, and H. The feature *oblique right* is characteristic of A, K, M, N, V, W, X, and Z. *Oblique left* is a feature of A, M, V, W, X, and Y. Notice that these features are at least roughly like ones to which cells in the visual cortex of animals are known to respond. Pandemonium's memory structure contains concepts that consist of lists of features. Each concept has a feature list that contains the concept's perceptual characteristics: cross bar, oblique left, and so on. The model works by marking a tally in a register corresponding to each concept in memory whose list contains a feature extracted from the present perceptual event. Thus, as features are extracted from our hypothetical input, A, every concept in memory receives a tally mark for every feature it shares with A. The name of the concept that has the most tallies when feature extraction is complete is assigned to the input event; Pandemonium recognizes the input as an instance of the category receiving the largest number of tallies. When the feature set in memory is designed so that its various combinations distinguish exclusively among all possible inputs, a system such as Pandemonium will make no recognition errors, unless some source of noise is introduced to interfere with feature extraction. Speaking as if Pandemonium were a person, "noise" might amount to insufficient illumination to allow the formation of a clear retinal image.

The processes used by Pandemonium can be spoken of in quasi-neurological terms, making it sound more like an account of human pattern recognition. Thus, Pandemonium's tally marking can be spoken of as *activation* or *excitation* of a cortically represented concept's features that are extracted from visually registered stimuli. In fact, all contemporary theories of human pattern recognition that incorporate the idea of feature comparison are translations of mechanisms that can be programmed into computers. Such theories are among the best examples of the computer analogy at work in cognitive psychology.

Only two criticisms need to be leveled at feature-comparison models to establish the need for their revision. First, they are too passive. People's perceptions are influenced by their expectations and the contexts in which stimuli appear, but most feature comparison models make no allowance for such factors and contain no mechanisms that can account for expectancy and contextual effects. Second, patterns that have identical features (as they are defined in pattern recognition models) may nevertheless be discriminably different to people. That is, two objects that share the same features may be discriminated by inversion or by their degree of symmetry. People use their knowledge of how features are properly combined to form patterns and of how features relate to one another in patterns, but feature comparison models of the Pandemonium type do not.

B. Template Matching and Structural Models

Template-matching theories postulate a memory structure containing idealized images that are compared with incoming images of whole objects or large parts of objects. Such models have sometimes been criticized as inadequate because they require a huge number of templates to be stored in memory (at least as many as there are categories of objects), which would seem to require enormous storage capacity and consequently unreasonably long comparison times to locate the template corresponding to any particular incoming image. Moreover, template matching might not work if the stimulus input differed slightly from an idealized template of it. The latter problem might be solved by employing approximate criteria of matching between incoming events and memory templates, but this might result in inaccurate recognition of perceptually similar objects and events. The degree of perceptual variance that can be tolerated from an ideal model and still square with people's perceptual accuracy is difficult to specify. There has been no satisfactory estimate of how large people's memory arrays are; so it is difficult to judge how many templates they might be able to store. There is also no satisfactory estimate of how rapidly people make template comparisons, so that the effects of large memory arrays on their perceptual speed cannot be judged precisely. Despite such vagaries, template-matching theories have been largely abandoned as unlikely to account for much of human pattern recognition behavior. The best explanation for their abandonment seems to be that theorists have been influenced by their knowledge of computers (e.g., computers can slow down drastically when memory becomes exceedingly large and many memory registers must be checked against the current input). Also, matches are generally detected by computers only when the memory information and current input are exactly alike, and any noise is likely to result in errors. To account for human performance, more flexibility in using information is required in the theory.

Structural models of pattern recognition are similar to template-matching models in that they postulate memory structures composed of holistic descriptions of stimuli, but these descriptions are not images. Rather, they specify stimulus features and the relations among them as bases for recognizing things like objects and three-dimensional scenes (Reed, 1973). Some of the criticisms that apply to template-matching models also apply to structural models, but structural models do provide a possible way of compensating for the degradation of stimulation that occurs during sensory registration. Structural models are also theoretically more efficient than template models because they allow a single set of rules for determining relations among features to apply to a wide variety of objects and scenes. Neisser (1976) has suggested that stimulus descriptions in memory, which he calls schemas, are not compared directly to incoming representations of environmental events. Rather, the (hypothetical) descriptions or schemas only direct what we look and listen for. Neisser suggests that schemas are organizational plans of what to look for and how to interpret what is found in the environment. Recall, however, from the discussion in Chaper 12 that the nature of schemas and their mode of operation is entirely conjectural. Suggesting that holistic descriptions are schemas that operate as plans has not yet achieved theoretical precision; and Neisser's argument notwithstanding, most researchers have assumed that pattern recognition involves the comparison of some perceptual units (features or images) with some memory units of the same form.

IV.   SPEECH PERCEPTION RESEARCH

The idea that perceptual and memory units are compared prior to recognition flows directly from the computer analogy. Even though the models suggested by that analogy are not regarded as sufficient to account for human pattern perception, the analogy has motivated the search for units that might be employed by people when they recognize patterns. If, as suggested by the computer analogy, pattern recognition requires the internal comparison of sensory and memory representations, then it makes good sense to try to discover the nature of those representations. The goal of much pattern recognition research has been to find the units with which incoming data are represented and the units of memory representations to which they are compared.

   The information-processing view suggests that the comprehension of speech requires a chain of cognitive operations to link the sensory transduction of the speech signal (patterns of pressure changes) to conceptual processes that give meaning to the signal. Recognizing speech patterns is a part of this presumed processing chain, and investigations of speech pattern recognition can be divided roughly into those that focus on events near the input or sensory end and those that focus on events near the conceptual end of the chain. Viewing input as data, this division of studies follows the data-driven versus conceptually driven distinction drawn by Norman and Bobrow (1975) and described in Chapter 6.

A. Data-Driven Processes

Because the data-driven end of the processing chain begins with speech itself, information-processing psychologists have drawn their hypotheses about perceptual units from phonetic and acoustic analyses of speech and from anatomical analyses of the mechanisms of speech. These analyses give rise to many hypotheses about what the units of speech perception might be, and most of the research designed to choose among these hypotheses can be organized around the question of whether the unit is smaller or larger than the syllable. Syllables are combinations of vowels and consonants; so one research question has been whether vowels and consonants, rather than syllables, are the units of speech perception. You will recall from the psycholinguistics chapter that linguists have devised a system of units, called phonemes, which are smaller than syllables and which might serve as the perceptual units people rely on when they analyze incoming speech. And, in principle, larger units such as words might be the perceptual units of speech.

Every person's voice is unique, which is to say that the sound wave patterns each of us creates when speaking are different from those produced by everyone else. It follows that to understand each other, we must pay attention to only part of the sound waves created by speaking. Linguists have developed various phonetic systems to characterize that part of the speech signal to which we attend when we listen to one another's language. The unit of these systems is called a phoneme. A phoneme is a perceptual pattern that distinguishes one sound from another, and words are made up of strings of phonemes. Thus, the word *bill* is composed of three phonemes, /b/ /i/ /l/, and it differs by one phoneme from the word *pill*, /p/ /i/ /l/. But notice that phonemes may or may not correspond to single letters; spoken English has about 45 phonemes, but there are only 26 letters in the English alphabet. Phonemes are units of spoken language, not written language. Just as words are formed from combinations of sound units called phonemes, phonemes are formed by combinations of units called distinctive features. Distinctive features are defined in terms of the vocal operations required to produce them, and they are either present or absent. Thus, the nasality feature refers to the presence or absence of sound created by the passage of air through the nose. When producing a nasal sound, people lower their soft palate so that some air escapes through the nose, but when making a non-nasal (oral) sound, they keep their soft palate raised and all escaping air passes through the mouth. By combining such features as nasality with others, such as the positions of the tongue and lips, we produce different sounds, whose perceptual classes are the phonemes of a language.

It has recently become possible to record the intensity, frequency, and timing of the sounds people create when they speak. Graphic displays of such recordings typically represent frequency on the vertical axis and time on the horizontal axis. Intensity is shown by the darkness of the marking on the record. The darker the mark, the more intense the frequency it corresponds to on the vertical axis. Figure 13.4 shows a graphic display of a speech segment. The graph is called a sound spectrogram. The dark bands or stripe-like segments of the spectrogram are called formants, and they result from the concentration of the most intense sound in different frequency ranges. Notice that formants are most clearly defined for vowels. (The sounds represented in the spectrogram are written below the horizontal axis.) Formants are believed to be the most important cues for vowel perception, and they result from the resonance of air through the vocal tract during the articulation of vowels. But the absolute frequencies of the formants cannot be used to identify a vowel, because the frequency range of each formant varies from speaker to speaker. That is one of the things that makes each person's voice unique. It is apparently the relative differences in frequencies of the formants that define particular vowels (Wilder, 1975).

All vowels are voiced. Voicing corresponds to vibration of the vocal chords during a speech sound. Only some consonants are voiced. Voiced consonants (e.g., /b/ and /d/) share some features with vowels, but unvoiced ones (e.g., /p/ and /t/) do not. Voiced consonants thus show formants in speech spectrograms and can be differentiated from unvoiced consonants by the relative time of onset of different formants. Other consonants are cued by bursts of high frequency noise or yet other acoustic characteristics. The exact nature of the features of consonants and vowels is less important here than the fact that, having isolated such features with spectrographic techniques, we can synthesize speech sounds. That is, electronic devices have been used to simulate the features of spectrograms, and the result has been speech-like sounds. By electronically manipulating the characteristics of such synthetic speech and then asking people to judge the sounds they hear, we can devise experiments to secure data about whether vowels and consonants might serve as the perceptual units of speech. Liberman, Cooper, Shankweiler, and Studdert-Kennedy (1967) synthesized formants for the vowels /i/ and /u/ and combined them with the appropriate initial format transitions to produce clearly recognizable "di" and "du" sounds. The beginning, presumably consonant part of the syllable, when played by itself, was heard as a nonspeech sound, similar to a chirp or whistle. Successively adding segments of the initial part of the total pattern never resulted in hearing /d/ alone; rather, the perception changed abruptly from a nonspeech sound to the full recognition of the "di" or "du" syllable. These data say that the consonant /d/

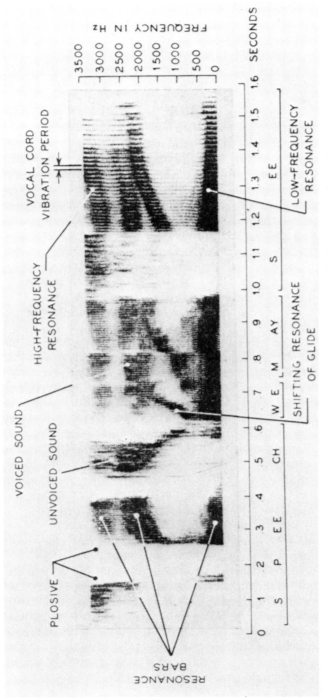

FIG. 13.4. Example of a speech spectrogram. The recording is of a human speaker saying "Speech we may see," as indicated along the bottom of the record. The horizontal axis is time, and the vertical axis is the frequency of the sounds emitted. The sounds themselves are represented by the dark tracings, with the darkest tracings corresponding to the most intense sounds. Notice that the distinct bands of sounds, called formants, are most clearly evident for vowels and for voiced consonants, such as /m/. Formants are produced by vibrations of the vocal cords and their resulting resonant frequencies amplified by the vocal tract.

513

cannot be perceived unless it is attached to a vowel, which is some evidence against the idea that some perceptual units for speech are smaller than syllables. Other experiments using synthetic stimuli provide further evidence that the syllable is the smallest probable unit of speech perception.

If syllables are the basic units of speech perception, then efforts to perceive smaller units should fail. Liberman, Harris, Kinney, and Lane (1961) tested people's abilities to perceive units smaller than the syllables "do" and "to." They constructed a large number of synthetic syllables that differed mainly with respect to features that might have influenced consonant (d or t) perception. That is, the onset time of the formant representing voicing was systematically varied from an early onset, appropriate for "do," to a late onset, appropriate for "to." When people listened to them, they identified half of the syllables as "do" and half as "to." In other words, half the stimuli fell into one phonemic category and half fell into another, according to judgments made about each syllable in isolation. Next, Liberman et al. played sequences of three of these syllables to people. The first two were always equally different from each other on the physically specified dimension of formant onset time, but sometimes both were previously judged to sound like "do," sometimes both were judged to sound like "to," and sometimes one had been judged to be from each syllable category. The third syllable was always identical with one of the first two, and the listener's job was to say which of the first two syllables matched the third. This procedure is called an ABX discrimination task. In the experiment by Liberman et al., the letters stand for syllables ("do" or "to"); the listener's task was to say whether syllable X was the same as A or B. People did this very accurately when A and B were syllables from different categories ("do" and "to"), but they did it very inaccurately when A and B came from the same category, even though the differences between the physical stimuli were always the same. That is, the categorization judgments made by the first group of subjects predicted the ABX discriminations of the second group. This sort of predictive relationship is generally taken as evidence of categorical perception, which means that people do not discriminate within perceptual categories, but they do discriminate between them. In the present context, the existence of categorical perception for consonant–vowel syllables is evidence that people do not discriminate among units smaller than syllables.

Research with natural speech has also suggested that units smaller than the syllable are not perceptible. Savin and Bever (1970) and Warren (1971) had people listen for prespecified target phonemes and syllables in lists of syllables or in normal spoken sentences. Syllables were detected more rapidly than consonant phonemes alone, and Warren reported that the presence of certain consonants was often missed entirely by his subjects.

In summary, research on speech perception suggests that there are no perceptual units smaller than syllables. Whether there are larger perceptual units is uncertain. Massaro (1975) has argued that there are not, on the grounds that syllables are generally about 250 msec long. He has severely criticized the evidence on precategorical acoustic storage (reviewed in Chapter 7) and has concluded that it does not show that auditory information can be maintained in the sensory register for longer than 250 msec. According to Massaro, syllables are recognized serially from the sensory store and held in categorical form in a short-term working memory until they can be integrated into larger perceptual units, either words or phrases. In other words, Massaro believes that memory models such as Atkinson and Shiffrin's can be generalized to explain the data-driven aspects of speech perception.

B. Conceptually Driven Processes

So far, we have concentrated on the more-or-less passive, data-driven aspects of speech perception. However, most theorists believe that conceptually driven processes are equally important, in that speech perception and speech production both rely on knowledge of language and its properties. They believe that people make active use of their phonological, syntactic, and semantic knowledge when they perceive speech as well as when they speak. Thus, phonological knowledge can be used to break up the essentially continuous and noisy stream of speech sounds into recognizable units. Recognizing the units of speech might also be aided by anticipating coarticulation effects—that is, the effects that pronouncing one phoneme or syllable has on the pronunciation of ones following it. Knowledge of syntax and semantics can be used to identify words and phrases and to interpret their meanings given the constraints of the context.

Just how linguistic knowledge might function in speech perception is suggested by *analysis-by-synthesis* models. For example, a model of speech perception by Stevens (1972; Stevens & Halle, 1967) presumes that several sources of information combine in our analysis of incoming speech sounds. The primary source is speech itself, or its analysis by auditory feature detectors into phonemes or syllables. According to Stevens, categorized sounds (phonemes or syllables) are held for a few seconds in short-term memory. This much of the Stevens' model is very similar to Atkinson and Shiffrin's, but in Stevens' account sources of information enter the perceptual system that do not enter Atkinson and Shiffrin's model. These other sources include the results of preceding analyses, which provide linguistic and situational context for the current input. From such contexts, expectations are said to be generated about the form of the stimulus, and these expectations contribute to the synthesis of the perceived speech sound. If the expectations are appropriate for the incoming sensory information, the perceptual process continues to generate new expectations and syntheses. However, if the expectations begin to yield mismatches with sensory signals, more attention is directed to the current auditory input and new expectations are derived. As a result, part of the incoming message might be lost or misunderstood until the correct track is picked up.

Analysis-by-synthesis models have gained a good deal of acceptance among speech perception theorists, and similar models have been applied to processes operating in visual perception and reading. The various models differ in how they involve expectations generated from linguistic knowledge. In some models, expectations take the form of subvocalizations that precisely match incoming signals. In other models, expectations are merely vague schemas involving, perhaps, anticipated phrase structures and meaningful components of the speech input. But the models agree that synthetic or constructive operations facilitate perception by using several sources of information to narrow down the set of possible categorizations for the sensory input. With fewer alternatives to choose from, decisions based on the noisy speech signal generated by humans are bound to be more accurate. It should be noted, however, that relatively little research has been done to establish the importance of conceptually driven processes like those postulated in the various models of speech perception. Experimental work has concentrated either on data-driven aspects of speech perception or on how context affects comprehension. The reasons are paradigmatically determined. The speech signal is the most obvious determinant of speech perception, and highly sophisticated analytic technologies (e.g., sound spectrography) and computerized synthetic technology have evolved to study it. The availability of these techniques, in turn, has dictated the questions that many researchers ask. At the same time, context effects were introduced into cognitive psychology by linguistically and mnemonically oriented investigators, who have continued to use dependent measures that say little or nothing about perception. The study of contextual effects upon perception has therefore fallen largely between the paradigmatic cracks created in the discipline by its scientific ancestry.

The small amount of pertinent research that has been done suggests that analysis-by-synthesis models may explain such phenomena as being able to follow a conversation while listening attentively only part of the time, or reading through a novel rapidly while not attending to every word. It is as though we are able to fill in the missing parts of the message through our knowledge of language and our ideas about what the speaker/writer intends to say. For example, Warren (1970) replaced the phoneme /s/ in normal English sentences with a noise burst or other nonspeech sound. Subjects did not report anything unusual about the altered sentences. Apparently, context provided by the sentences allowed the subjects to synthesize the correct phoneme when it was missing from the sensory input. Cole (1973) similarly showed that people are much less likely to notice that a syllable is mispronounced when it is embedded in a sentence than when presented alone. Against a noisy background, words are also much more likely to be identified correctly if they occur in a sentence than if they are presented in isolation (Miller, Heise, & Lichten, 1951; Miller & Isard, 1963).

All of these results would be difficult to explain if one did not accept the idea that context facilitates perception. Presumably, this facilitation is due to contextually based expectations about what the missing or degraded stimulus is. If expectations are exact enough, no information need be registered for a stimulus to be "identified" correctly. Even in the absence of precise expectations, however, any elimination of alternatives makes the categorization task in perception easier, quicker, and more likely to be correct—all of which favors analysis-by-synthesis processes.

C. Relating Data-Driven to Conceptually Driven Research

According to the information-processing view, the units of information in memory must have the same features as perceptual units; otherwise the two could not be compared. No research has tested this view because no one has devised a way to study memory units. It has been possible to study the size and nature of perceptual units, as described under the rubric of data-driven aspects of perception, but it remains impossible to relate these findings to the nature of memory units, because we have no direct knowledge of them.

Research on conceptually driven aspects of pattern perception serves to make the point that the process of unitizing sensory information is far more complex than it would seem if cognitive psychologists studied only the data-driven aspects of the pattern recognition problem. The main way this point has been made is by showing experimentally that context can facilitate perception. The information-processing interpretation of this fact is that context triggers internal processes that draw on stored knowledge, and that stored knowledge guides the processing that shows itself in experiments on context. Conceptually driven research has not looked directly at processing mechanisms, but rather has concentrated on demonstrations that internal knowledge influences perception. The theoretical statements made by pattern recognition researchers are more metaphors than they are precise specifications of internal processes. The various analysis-by-synthesis views reflect the commitments of information-processing psychologists at least as much as they reflect the results of conceptually driven research.

V. VISUAL PERCEPTION AND READING RESEARCH

The units of auditory perception are necessarily spread over time. The units must be long enough to allow the extraction of frequency information from the speech signal, and spectrographic analyses show that the speech cues for vowels are relational. Extracting relational properties presumably takes time in itself. Moreover, spectrographic analyses have shown that the cues for at least some consonants are time-based changes in relational aspects of the speech signal. It is not so clear that the units of visual perception must have a temporal aspect. Instead, visual information seems more clearly spread across space than across time. At least, this is the implicit assumption of research on the units of visual perception. Most pattern recognition theories of human vision are based on analyses of information abstracted from a single eye fixation; the temporal distribution of visual events has been minimized experimentally. Stimuli used in most studies of human pattern recognition have been brief (10–200 msec) exposures of light patterns designed to produce a high-quality visual image that persists for some time after the stimulus. Such stimuli are assumed to mimic what is seen in a normal eye fixation.

A. Data-Driven Processes

We confine our consideration of data-driven visual processes in pattern recognition to research with linguistic stimuli—that is, to reading research. Research on the data-driven aspects of speech perception has revolved around the question of whether the syllable is the basic perceptual unit. In reading research, there is an analogous question—namely, whether the word is the basic perceptual unit. While there is no question that people can treat letters or smaller visual events as perceptual units, there is the question of whether letters are the first or most basic unit used during reading. To answer this question, psychologists have studied how rapidly words and letters are identified. If words are identified as rapidly as letters, then one information-processing inference is that people must not first recognize letters and then combine them into words. This inference is based squarely on the assumption that cognitive processes require time for their execution.

Huey (1908/1968) reviewed the available evidence that familiar words are identified as quickly as single letters. The studies that he considered demonstrated that the threshold for identification (i.e., the briefest exposure time that would reliably result in stimulus identification) was about the same for common words as for single letters. Also, Huey reported that words are sometimes identified under conditions that preclude identifying their component letters—for example, when words are viewed from a distance greater than that required for clear visibility of single letters. Contemporary research has also indicated that single letters and common words are about equally perceptible. Thus, the data seem to argue that words are the basic perceptual units during reading, but there is considerable theoretical dispute on this matter. Some theorists argue that equally rapid identification time for words and letters does not resolve the matter. There are data to indicate that people sometimes process letters before recognizing the word they spell, and some theorists have claimed that this is always necessary for word recognition. Because people know a good deal about how letters combine to make words, not all letters in a word need to be analyzed before the word is identified. If some letters can be identified more quickly than others and if a word can be inferred before all of its letters are identified, then letters might be identified no more quickly, on average, than words. Thus, the debate continues. Do readers use letters as their basic perceptual units, filling in with inferences letters not identified from their visual features (Massaro, 1975), or do they directly recognize words or even phrases from featural information about them (Henderson, 1977; Juola, Schadler, Chabot, McCaughey, & Wait, in press; Smith & Spoehr, 1974)?

One reason for the debate is the inadequacy of much of the data that might resolve the issue. Many early word perception experiments took this form: (1) a brief display of a string of letters; (2) the subject reporting everything he can about the display. For example, Miller, Bruner, and Postman (1954) presented eight-letter strings that varied in their degree of approximation to English words. In this experiment, YRULPZOC was a zero-order string (no relation to English orthography), and VERNALIT was a fourth-order string (i.e., all successive groups of four letters actually occur in English words). The dependent measure was the number of letters correctly reported after the exposure. As the strings more closely approximated English words, more letters were identified correctly. Similar results have been reported by Gibson, Pick, Osser, and Hammond (1962) for regularly spelled pseudowords such as GLURCK versus irregular nonwords composed of the same letters such as CKURGL.

Whole-report studies, such as those by Miller et al. and Gibson et al., are insufficiently analytic to resolve the perceptual unit question. We cannot judge from them whether the advantages for orthographically regular strings lie in perceptual processes or in other cognitive operations between the stimulus and response. It may well be that regular letter strings are perceived more clearly than irregular strings when they are briefly presented. It is just as likely, however, that the regular strings (words and pseudowords) are maintained in short-term memory more easily (perhaps by being chunked into pronounceable syllables) and that guesses during response output are more likely to be correct for regular than for irregular strings. It seems reasonable that guessing strategies should be influenced by spelling habits. In sum, there are several processing stages that might be influenced by orthographic regularity, and the whole-report task does not say which. Some recent studies have been designed to eliminate confoundings of perceptual factors with short-term memory and response processes. They follow the general logic of Sperling's research that was described in Chapter 7.

The first evidence for a clearly perceptual advantage of words over nonword letter strings was obtained by Reicher (1969). He presented four-letter words, such as WORD, and anagrams, such as OWRD, for about 60 msec, followed by a masking field to limit stimulus processing (see Chapter 7 for details of such experiments). The masking field was accompanied by response alternatives located above and below the position where one of the alternatives had occurred in the stimulus. In such an example, the letters D and K might appear above and below the fourth-letter position, and the subjects' task would be to indicate which had occurred. As the example suggests, the alternatives were chosen so that both would have made a word if they had been included in the display on word trials, whereas neither would have made a word on nonword trials. This procedure minimized short-term memory contributions to performance, and it eliminated the chance for guessing strategies to bias the results. Reicher's results were clear: Subjects were much more accurate in picking the alternative letter from common words than from nonword letter strings. Several subsequent studies have also found that letters are recognized more accurately in regular pseudoword contexts than when presented in irregularly spelled nonwords (Aderman & Smith, 1971; Baron & Thurston, 1973).

One interpretation of experimentation of the sort done by Reicher is that some letters are identified before words they make up, and then the perceiver uses his knowledge of spelling rules to infer any unknown letter that falls in the tested position. One difficulty with this interpretation is that recent experiments with Reicher's procedure have found a perceptual advantage for words over orthographically regular pseudowords (Juola, Leavitt, & Choe, 1974; Manelis, 1974). Orthographically regular pseudowords use the same spelling rules as real English words, and knowledge of these rules is presumably drawn on to infer the masked letters. It seems to follow that inferences should be the same for words and orthographically regular pseudowords, but because the data indicate that they are processed differently there might be some additional information present in common words that facilitates their perception. Words must have an advantage because they can be recognized as wholes. A more likely possibility is that there is no single basic perceptual unit, but what one sees in a display depends on what is expected.

Some experimental procedures result in no perceptual differences between words, pseudowords, and irregular nonwords, and they look very much like the procedure used by Reicher. The difference appears to be that they allow different processing strategies, which implies that words exist as units in memory that are sometimes used and sometimes not used when attempting to recognize incoming sensory information. Perhaps people must expect that attempts to recognize higher-order units such as words will help perception before they will use those units to guide perception. Thus, Aderman and Smith (1971) demonstrated that letters could be recognized more accurately in regular letter strings only when people expected to see the regular strings rather than irregular ones. Similarly, Juola, Choe, and Leavitt (1974) found that when people looked repeatedly for the same pair of letter alternatives in a block of display strings, the advantage of words over nonwords disappeared. Practice with a specific pair of items evidently promoted a strategy based on the featural difference between the target letters in the sensory input. This featural difference could presumably be detected before either letters or words were recognized.

There are often several strategies available to participants in perceptual experiments, which suggests that there is no single basic perceptual unit. Rather, there may be different units, depending on the nature of the task set for people and on the strategy required of them. The effect of strategies on visual perception, like the effects of context on auditory perception, shows that pattern recognition theories cannot restrict themselves to the data-driven aspects of perception. We turn now to a brief consideration of the effects of context upon visual perception, after which we examine pattern recognition theory in view of what we have said about both visual and auditory perception.

B. Conceptually Driven Processes

Several investigations have shown that the context in which an object is viewed can have large effects on what it is seen as, and even on whether it is successfully perceived at all. For example, in an experiment by Palmer (1975), people viewed a drawing of a scene, such as a kitchen counter, and then a briefly presented drawing of a common object. The original scene was appropriate to the object on some trials (a loaf of bread followed the kitchen scene) and inappropriate on others (a mailbox followed the kitchen scene). Objects were correctly identified about twice as often when the preceding context was appropriate. Without any preceding context, performance was less accurate than that for an object following an appropriate scene and more accurate than that following an inappropriate scene. Presumably, a context activates information in memory, which influences perceptual synthesis when an object is presented. When the context is appropriate, the synthesis proceeds more successfully, improving the perceptibility of the object.

It has also been shown that the context in which an object is embedded affects its perception. Biederman (1972; Biederman, Glass, & Stacy, 1973) showed that people find a target object in a scene much more rapidly if the scene is a normal one than if its components are arranged unnaturally. The target object was the same in both natural and altered scenes, leading to the conclusion that context is used to make predictions about where objects should be located as well as what they are. Such predictions cannot be made when the structure is disrupted. Even as simple a task as detecting a line in a briefly exposed field is improved by context. If the line combines with others in the field to form a familiar object, it is more likely to be detected than if the lines are arranged randomly (Weisstein & Harris, 1974). Thus, the perception of any object can be affected by the context in which it is presented.

Presumably this is due to the use of stored information about how objects and their environments normally relate to one another. When contextual relations are as expected, they help people find desired objects.

Context also influences perception during reading. Tulving and his colleagues (Tulving & Gold, 1963; Tulving, Mandler, & Baumel, 1964) have shown that a briefly presented word is identified much more readily when preceded by a phrase or sentence than when presented alone. Also, an irrelevant or misleading phrase or sentence reduced the likelihood of correctly identifying a subsequent word, relative to a condition in which no context was provided.

VI.   THEORETICAL OVERVIEW

From the information-processing perspective, there are many similarities between auditory and visual perception, which is shown in the similarity of the models designed to account for auditory and visual pattern recognition (e.g., Massaro, 1975). Models of both types postulate first some sort of feature extraction from stimulus input, which is followed by an interpretation or categorization of the stimulus. Feature extraction is viewed as largely data driven, although it can be influenced by conscious decisions about where to seek information. Consistent with information-processing premises, categorization has been hypothesized to involve several substages, including especially a comparison between feature-based codes extracted from sensory input and codes that are stored in memory. In both auditory and visual models, the best-matching memory code is used to represent the meaning of the stimulus. Both visual and auditory models also allow the possibility that a memory code that best matches stimulus input will be overlooked because of incompatible synthesis activities. For example, when proofreading for content, an editor is likely to overlook many errors of spelling and punctuation, and vice versa. Auditory and visual models both posit the use of perceptual input to activate memory information, which is used to anticipate other perceptual events. The fact that both auditory and visual perception are influenced by context has encouraged modelers to employ analysis-by-synthesis notions, according to which conceptually driven processes importantly influence pattern recognition.

The foregoing points of agreement between theories of auditory and visual pattern recognition are substantial evidence of the power of the information-processing paradigm, but whether these agreements will be maintained in the face of continuing research is uncertain. What is certain is that important details of theory remain to be clarified.

Perhaps the most important theoretical challenge for information-processing approaches to pattern recognition is to specify the basic units of perception, and there remains substantial murkiness about what those units might be for both speech and visual perception. Research about possible units of speech perception seems more definitive than research about the units of visual perception, but even in regard to the former, the picture is fuzzy. The syllable seems to be the smallest unit possible for speech perception, but it is not at all clear that larger units are impossible. The main argument against a larger unit is based on pegging the maximum duration of the precategorical acoustical code at 250 msec. It is also true that the research tradition of students of speech perception has led to a relative neglect of contextual effects on speech perception. If more contextual research were done with smaller auditory segments, then it might appear (as it does in the visual domain) that the size of the unit employed depends on the strategic demands of the tasks used to study it.

The second most important challenge for information-processing models of pattern recognition is to specify the details of the matching procedures that are supposedly used to compare transformed sensory input with coded memories. Hardly any experimental evidence has been collected to allow selection among the various comparison processes that have been suggested in models of pattern recognition. The best that can be said is that sensory codes might be compared to information stored in memory in any of several ways. One possibility is that in order to keep memory comparisons straight, features are compared from one location or object at a time. Alternatively, several objects might be worked on simultaneously, with several categorizations being attempted at once. The serial versus parallel processing question has turned out to be as difficult to resolve for pattern recognition theorists as it has been in other branches of cognitive psychology, though it does appear that the visual system has a limited capacity to recognize several different objects simultaneously. Although several small letters projected onto the fovea can often be processed as efficiently as one, performance drops off for large numbers of letters or symbols presented peripherally (e.g., Estes, 1975b; Massaro, 1975; Shiffrin & Gardner, 1972).

To explain reading, some constructive processes such as analysis-by-synthesis seem mandatory, because reading rates are often faster than word-by-word processing would allow. When synthesis during reading draws on concepts and propositions to extract meaning from text, it is obviously far removed from the sensory code. Thus, we need to look beyond theories of pattern recognition for a complete understanding of how we use both written and oral language. The contributions of psycholinguistic theories and theories of pattern recognition to the understanding of complex behaviors such as reading will continue to be substantial. Indeed, the most elaborate, detailed, and in the long run the most practical theories of how we recognize external objects and events have been couched largely in linguistic terms.

14

Epilogue:
Critiques of the Paradigm

ABSTRACT

I. *Introduction*
Information-processing cognitive psychology has moved into a stage of normal science. Some criticisms are beginning to appear, but these may be more pertinent to normal science in general rather than only to that of information-processing psychology.

II. *Normal Science and Narrowing of Focus*
During scientific revolutions, much research concerns the focal, central issues whose importance is self-evident. As the discipline moves into normal science, much experimentation becomes responsive to a growing technical literature. It may diverge from the main issues and come to appear irrelevant, narrow, and insular.

III. *Critiques*
    A. *Noncumulative and Irrelevant Research*   Neisser (1976) has called for more ecological validity. By this he means research methods of greater sufficiency, and also a particular approach to cognition initially formulated by Gibson (1966). His negative views and proposed alternative have not been widely accepted, although the neo-Gibsonian position is a potential challenge to information-processing views. Newell (1973) considers the field to be in a fragmented state of disarray. He deplores the failure of most theorists to develop the concept of control processes. He also considers that flowcharts may sometimes be substituted for theoretical precision, and he objects to the practice of couching research questions as binary oppositions. Tulving has noted that 100 years of memory research has failed to yield a cumulative structure of knowledge.

    These critiques may reflect the inevitable consequences of maturing normal science in combination with the relative newness of the paradigm. They are not universally shared. Another pioneer of information-processing psychology (Broadbent, 1971) expresses optimism for the prospects of our experimental traditions.

B. *The Problem of Inferred Theoretical Mechanisms* Particularly with respect to global models, some complain that there is a poor fit between theory and experiment. Some despair of the possibility of uniquely specifying theoretical mechanisms and entities. Examples from the physical sciences show that this problem is not unique to psychology. What theoretical mechanisms and entities are empirically justified is, in the last analysis, a matter of consensus supported by the persuasive use of the rational and conventional components of the scientific enterprise.

I. INTRODUCTION

The scientific study of cognitive psychology has moved dramatically forward under the pretheoretical commitments of the information-processing approach. Great progress is reflected in the way our discipline has refocused its research effort toward accounting for intelligent human behavior. This refocusing required a revolution: The significant issues simply could not be addressed adequately within the framework of neobehavioristic psychology.

Now information-processing is an established paradigm, and it guides the vast bulk of psychological research in human cognition. Our revolution is complete, and the atmosphere is one of normal science.

Our book, with its paradigmatic theme, would be incomplete if we were to exclude all mention of critics of the approach. You may wonder whether the seeds of the next revolution are now being sown. Are there anomalies and insoluble problems that are causing an accumulation of discontent within the ranks? Can we identify elements to suggest what will take the place of the current paradigm?

It may be that, as committed practitioners of information-processing psychology ourselves, we are in a poor position to tell. However, it is our impression that the paradigm has as yet no insurmountable dead ends, and that its potential is by no means exhausted. No alternative view has yet been proposed that is sufficiently well specified to attract large numbers of cognitive psychologists away from the approach described in this book.

This is not to imply that no criticisms exist. They do; there are a handful of published papers that purportedly offer a critique of information-processing psychology. However, we think that many of the criticisms are pertinent to normal science in general—not uniquely appropriate to the normal science of contemporary cognitive psychology. We examine these criticisms in this final chapter, and mention one current effort to launch an alternative approach. We also offer a cautious prognosis for the information-processing paradigm and the field of cognitive science.

II. NORMAL SCIENCE AND NARROWING OF FOCUS

Some criticisms of information-processing may actually be criticisms of the normal-science tradition the paradigm has produced. We have suggested that they may be criticisms of normal science in general. Why should this be so? Because some scholars find normal science unappealing; to them, it may appear narrow, insular, and even pedestrian. They prefer the exhilarating environment of revolutionary science.

During scientific revolutions, attention is focused on foundation issues and central substantive problems that, at least for the revolutionary scientists, are the focal matters the discipline must face. These matters, self-evidently important, are confronted; approaches to them are criticized and debated under circumstances where two apparently viable alternatives are available. The immediate postrevolutionary period is characterized by optimism; there is a sense of breakthrough, and progress seems to be rapid. Much of the experimental work in the new paradigm is rather directly responsive to the focal problems identified during the revolutionary period.

Then, revolution shades into normal science. A growing research literature accumulates. Some experimentation begins to develop that is responsive to prior experimentation, with its partially accidental course of development. These lines of research may diverge more and more from the major, self-evidently important research questions that initiated them. At the same time, various lines initiated by a common focal problem may diverge more and more from each other, tending to insularity. The longer normal science endures, the more likely it is that some research programs will be narrowly focused and the more experimentation will tend toward inwardly directed puzzle solving. Cognitive psychology, in the information-processing tradition, has not escaped this general principle. Thus, much of the criticism that has been made may reflect the inevitable consequences of maturing normal science.

Even so, it is worthwhile to examine the criticisms with an eye to potential resolution of the difficulties. It is also interesting to reflect on the possibility that some particular specification of an existing malaise is the opening shot in a new paradigm clash.

III. CRITIQUES

A. Noncumulative and Irrelevant Research

Neisser's (1967) book was a landmark event in the cognitive revolution. Today, he believes that cognitive psychology is distorting human nature by a slavish commitment to standard laboratory procedures and standard ways of conceptualizing consciousness and attention (Neisser, 1976). He calls for research and analyses that are "ecologically valid."

By ecological validity, Neisser means two things. One meaning is related to what we have called sufficiency; Neisser considers that too many of our experimental tasks have no counterpart outside the laboratory, nor will they tell us anything worth knowing about extralaboratory cognitive functioning. However, Neisser's call for ecologically valid research is more than a demand for sufficiency—it calls for sufficiency within a particular conceptual scheme. That scheme, which is the second aspect of ecological validity, is a version of Gibson's (1966) theme of the perceptual cycle: the time-extended environment–organism interaction that determines perceived information. This view is attracting some interest (Shaw & Bransford, 1977; Turvey & Shaw, 1978). It places great weight on the evolutionary history of a perceiving species, emphasizing the fact that organisms have evolved in interaction with a relatively stable environment. That environment impinges on organisms with its characteristic patterns of light, spaces, textures, and so on. How an organism organizes its percepts of these patterns depends on what it can do about them. For example, a small animal that can organize light patterns into a percept of "a small hole, suitable for hiding" is at a genetic advantage. Small holes will be perceived, and the animal will take advantage of the hiding places they afford. It may then live to reproduce another day, and transmit its ability to perceive small holes to its offspring. An elephant, in contrast, gains little by the ability to organize percepts of small holes—it cannot hide in them nor does it prey on other animals that can. The percept of a small hole must thus be characterized differently for an elephant than for, let us say, a rabbit.

This position, called the neo-Gibsonian view, is attracting some prominent and talented adherents. It is difficult to dispute the emphasis on evolutionary-environmental determinants of cognitive organization, though it is apparently true that information-processing psychologists have insufficiently exploited this potential source of theoretical constraint. More controversial is the claim of some neo-Gibsonians that cognitive psychology can do without the concept of representation (Shaw & Bransford, 1977). If this position can be defended, neo-Gibsonianism will truly strike at the heart of information-processing psychology, because representation is centrally implicated in every topic we have covered. However, the proponents of this view have still only partially developed their alternative position. It remains to be seen whether it will be further developed and formalized. If all these conditions are met, will it command the allegiance of many psychologists?

Neisser's views, and his advocacy of a neo-Gibsonian approach, have not been widely accepted (Posner & McLean, 1977; Weimer, 1977). In fact, the information-processing paradigm may have a trump card against such competing approaches as Gibson's. As you recall, the general-purpose symbol-manipulating system is equivalent in power to a Turing machine; and a Turing machine can simulate any effective procedure that has yet been devised. Armed with this kind of power, the overall concept of the human being as a general-purpose symbol manipulator will be able to subsume any account of human behavior that can be specified and formalized in precise terms. It is as though the information-processing approach, in its technical expression at least, can virtually swallow competing positions by simulating them! Of course, this does not mean that all the ancillary facets of the paradigm—the language, concepts, methods, and so on—are impervious to change. These components are subject to revision. Should this happen, it will occur because the collective judgment of cognitive psychologists is that some other approach works better. It is hard to see how another approach will damage the technical formulation of Newell and Simon, however, Change is likelier in the looser, analogical deployment of the computer metaphor.

Neisser's critique does not appear symptomatic of a general malaise. The more commonly perceived difficulty with the information-processing paradigm has been published only occasionally, though it is often discussed informally. It concerns the fragmented and noncumulative nature of contemporary research (cf. Newell, 1973; Tulving, in press). Newell, for example, asks what would happen if you take all the work some of our most creative and sophisticated researchers have done since the start of their careers, and project the same to their retirement. He seems to conclude that psychology will still be in the same fragmented disarray that he describes now. Moreover, he projects the beginning of new, similarly fragmented sequences of experiments by others at that future point in time. We take this to be a correct prognosis. Unlike Newell, we see the general situation that he describes as an unavoidable consequence of normal science. We also would contend that there is a genuine cumulative advance of knowledge; it results not from this particular characteristic of normal science but despite it.

Newell also describes some specific characteristics of the contemporary scene that are partly responsible for our difficulties but that are correctable. First, he deplores the failure of most theorists to develop the notion of control processes. Atkinson and Shiffrin (1969) were typical in that they labeled a box in their flowchart "control process" and then failed to give it any specific formal properties. The research done focused on other aspects of the system. But Newell views the control processes as centrally important in accounting for behavior. An individual's control processes, in conjunction with his goals, determine what information he will process and what he will do in a given situation. The omission of the control structure in theoretical formulations allows an indefinitely large set of alternative behaviors for a given task, and nonspecifiable or unprincipled changes of behavior from task to task. The detailed specification of human control systems should sharply curb the tendency for unrelated and unintegrated sequences of experiments, at least from the laboratories of any given scientist.

A related problem diagnosed by Newell is the licentious use of flowchart representation. As we proposed earlier in the book, flowcharting is an excellent format for communicating one's theoretical infrastructure. However, it is not a substitute for a detailed and formal specification of mechanisms. The articulation of detailed theoretical mechanisms for subsystems designated by boxes is a slow and difficult business. It will take time—successful theoretical specification of underlying mechanisms may span several research careers. Sometimes, the best that can be done is to provide a fertile soil for future growth. Nevertheless, it would be better to begin with some formal specification than to conceal ignorance with another arrow or box in the flow diagram.

Newell also decries the fact that much contemporary research is cast in the form of binary opposites—for example, single codes versus multiple codes, features versus templates, and so on. Because research outcomes are cast in terms of their support for or contradiction of one of the binary opposites, numerous details of processing and various aspects of the task domain remain suppressed. The consequence is that it is impossible to compare current research outcomes with previous ones. Are they commensurate or contradictory? Is knowledge cumulating? The problem is that generally there is no way to tell! This is a problem confronting all of psychology, not just the information-processing tradition.

Tulving (in press) approaches the problem from a different perspective, but he comes to a similar conclusion. The single most important characteristic of an advancing discipline, according to Tulving, is that the results of previous research are deeply embedded in "a cumulatively developing structure of knowledge." The result should be a relatively permanent structure for contemporary knowledge. Tulving concludes that this state of affairs has *not* been achieved after 100 years of the study of memory. His diagnosis is that the technology of doing experiments and collecting data has far outstripped and overwhelmed conceptual developments. This is probably true in part. But the foundation work has been done in characterizing the human capacity for memory and other things in the context of a general-purpose information-processing system. The formal rationale for this view was developed over two decades ago by Newell and Simon and reported fully in 1972. The technical doctrine of humankind as a symbol manipulating system has enormous power and potential, and it is only recently that it has been explored in areas of cognition outside of problem solving. It will take as much imagination to properly implement this formal doctrine as was required for its original formulation. Likewise, great technical skill and originality will be needed to superimpose it on the field represented by the various chapters of this book. These advances, if they occur, will lend psychology the kind of stable structure Tulving desires; but they will not happen overnight.

The view of the degenerative character of research in the normal science of cognitive psychology is not universally shared. Broadbent (1958), who authored a seminal monograph during the beginnings of the information-processing revolution, recently concluded (Broadbent, 1971) that the empirical approach in cognitive psychology is enormously rich by virtue of the fact that it encourages a steady, continuing revision and modification of its ideas. One of Broadbent's current views, however, sharply contrasts with the view presented in this book. He finds any idea of a perfect or persistent vision of human nature—what we have called the paradigm's pretheoretical thema—a dangerous illusion (Broadbent, 1971, p. 476). He believes that such visions adulterate the appeal to observation, whereas we have argued that they guide this appeal. Perhaps our arguments and perspective will persuade him.

B. The Problem of Inferred Theoretical Mechanisms

Reviewers of global cognitive theories, such as Kintsch's model (Schank, 1976) and LNR (Chi, 1976), have asserted that there is little or no relationship between data and theory. This criticism is worth discussing in detail, for it is likely to be said of any cognitive theory that is broad enough to account for any substantial amount of cognitive behavior. Any nonsimplistic theoretical account of virtually any cognitive behavior will contain a veritable zoo of inferred hypothetical structures and processes. These will be expressed in one or another formalism, whose logico-mathematical forms may be viewed as reflecting mental structures and mechanisms. "Relation of theory to experiment" is basically a matter of how to test these inferred entities experimentally, an issue that must eventually confront all psychologists for whom theories of general cognitive processes are important. This surely includes the vast majority of scholars cited in this book, whether empirically or theoretically oriented. The problem has lain dormant since the demise of general neobehaviorist theory in the 1960s. The appearance of several comprehensive theories and the promise of more brings the issue once again to center stage. How are the hypothetical microprocesses of such multicomponent theories related to observable behavior? What kind of experiment constitutes a satisfactory empirical test?

The prudent theorist is usually obscure on these points, because he usually does not know what ontological claims to make for his inferred mechanisms, nor what would constitute empirical corroboration. This problem is neither new nor unique to psychology. Competent scholars still disagree on how to evaluate hypothetical mechanisms and inferred structures by means of observable events, even in fully developed natural sciences. Recently, debate has been reopened on these issues in cognitive psychology. Townsend (1972, 1974), for example, has carefully analyzed research and logical issues in the determination of specific sets of inferred mechanisms. He examined four sets of polar-opposite processing issues: independent versus dependent processing, self-terminating versus exhaustive search, limited versus unlimited capacity, and serial versus parallel processing. Townsend's careful analyses demonstrated the considerable difficulty of experimentally supporting one of the pairs of inferred processing mechanisms. The study of serial and parallel processing, in particular, has been prone to illogical conclusions and experimental indeterminacy. Anderson (1976, pp. 6ff.) has extended Townsend's analysis and concluded that the unique identification of many internal processes and structures is impossible. We would like to place the issue of inferred entities in a broader perspective, because it arises in any science that deals with complex systems.

The atom of contemporary quantum theory and the molecule of turn-of-the-century physical chemistry have been reified to strong ontological claims about the subvisible microscopic structure of material things. At the end of the nineteenth century, the ontological status of atoms and molecules was no more secure than that of our self-terminating serial searches, links, nodes, or propositions. In fact, such hypothetical particles stood at the center of a long and bitter controversy that had forced the scientific giants of the middle and late nineteenth century into warring camps. It is informative to consider the evidentiary basis on which the controversy was resolved, and the way cleared for the reification of atoms and molecules. Early in this century Einstein (1905) developed a theory explaining the phenomenon of Brownian motion, a theory that was subsequently supported by the experiments of Perrin (1910). The theory entailed a concrete mechanical conception of individual molecular agitation, and is said to have re-established the reality of molecules and atoms as material particles (Polanyi, 1964). Two aspects of this event in physical science are important from our viewpoint. First, during half a century of debate on the molecular hypothesis, it was never clear what kind of evidence would ultimately support an ontological claim for molecules and atoms. Brownian motion was not new; the phenomenon had long been known (Brown, 1866). But no one knew that it would figure in the resolution of the debate over the reality of subvisible particles. Nothing directly aimed at that issue finally resolved it. Einstein's theory and the subsequent experiments were undertaken to explain Brownian motion. The theory *assumed* the existence of subvisible particles, and its success as a theory swept its assumptions in with it. A second important point about the Einsteinian resolution of the molecular hypothesis is that the theory, and the experiments that supported it, were not decisive in and of themselves. The end of the controversy reflected a collective heuristic judgment that, in the context of the cumulative data and theory of almost 50 years, Einstein's work supported an ontological claim.

In psychology, we are in no better position than the physical scientists of the last century to know in advance what kind of experimental evidence will ultimately appear decisive in supporting (or rejecting) ontological claims for our theoretical entities. We are therefore unable to make definitive statements about how well the hypothetical mechanisms of limited or general cognitive theories relate to experimentation. Cognitive theories and the hypothetical processes they propose, like their counterparts in other fields, will not be confirmed or disconfirmed directly by experiment. A collective heuristic judgment by information-processing psychologists will eventually consign them to prosperity or oblivion. Some may survive; most will certainly fail. Experimental outcomes will weigh in the judgments, but so will formal adequacy, sufficiency, plausibility, and other values—with different practitioners assigning different weights to the various factors. Theory choice is not a totally canonical process; accounts that describe it as such are reconstructions or idealizations of what actually happens. This is not to say that the process is frivolous, random, or unscientific. It is only to say that a preponderance of evidence of an antecedently unspecifiable sort is responsible for the conclusions of a science, although the conclusions of individual scientists will vary and may be reached somewhat differently. Weizenbaum (1977) has recently gone as far as to conclude that all scientific claims, even those based directly on mathematics and formal logic, are fundamentally acts of persuasion. This conclusion may sit badly with some of our colleagues; however, it is consistent with some well-thought-out views of the scientific enterprise. We cannot but agree with the conclusion. It is our final hope that our treatment of the information-processing paradigm has been persuasive.

References

Aderman, D., & Smith, E. E. Expectancy as a determinant of functional units in perceptual recognition. *Cognitive Psychology*, 1971, *2*, 117–129.

Anderson, J. R. FRAN: A simulation model of free recall. In G. H. Bower (Ed.), *The psychology of learning and motivation.* Vol. 5. New York: Academic Press, 1972.

Anderson, J. R. *Language, memory, and thought.* Hillsdale, N.J.: Lawrence Erlbaum Associates, 1976.

Anderson, J. R. Arguments concerning representations for mental imagery. *Psychological Review*, 1978, *85*, 249–277.

Anderson, J. R., & Bower, G. H. *Human associative memory.* Washington, D.C.: Winston, 1973.

Anderson, J. R., & Reder, L. M. Elaborative processing of prose material. In L. S. Cermak & F. I. M. Craik (Eds.), *Levels of processing and human memory.* Hillsdale, N.J.: Lawrence Erlbaum Associates, 1978.

Anderson, J., & Whitten, L. Oddsmaker makes Humphrey 7–6 favorite over Ford. *Record-Courier* (Kent-Ravenna, Ohio), November 24, 1975, p. 9.

Anderson, R. C., & Ortony, A. On putting apples into bottles—A problem of polysemy. *Cognitive Psychology*, 1975, *7*, 167–180.

Anderson, R. C., Pichert, J. W., Goetz, E. T., Schallert, D. L., Stevens, K. V., & Trollip, S. R. Instantiation of general terms. *Journal of Verbal Learning and Verbal Behavior*, 1976, *15*, 667–679.

Angell, J. R. The province of functional psychology. *Psychological Review*, 1907, *14*, 61–91.

Atkinson, R. C., & Crothers, E. J. A comparison of paired-associate learning models having different learning and retention axioms. *Journal of Mathematical Psychology*, 1964, *1*, 285–315.

Atkinson, R. C., Herrmann, D. J., & Wescourt, K. T. Search processes in recognition memory. In R. L. Solso (Ed.), *Theories in cognitive psychology: The Loyola Symposium.* Potomac, Md.: Lawrence Erlbaum Associates, 1974.

Atkinson, R. C., & Juola, J. F. Factors influencing speed and accuracy of word recognition. In S. Kornblum (Ed.), *Attention and performance IV.* New York: Academic Press, 1973.

Atkinson, R. C., & Juola, J. F. Search and decision processes in recognition memory. In D. H. Krantz, R. C. Atkinson, R. D. Luce, and P. Suppes (Eds.), *Contemporary developments in mathematical psychology*. San Francisco: Freeman, 1974.

Atkinson, R. C., & Shiffrin, R. M. Human memory: A proposed system and its control processes. In K. W. Spence & J. T. Spence (Eds.), *Advances in the psychology of learning and motivation research and theory*. Vol. 2. New York: Academic Press, 1968.

Averbach, I., & Coriell, A. S. Short-term memory in vision. *Bell System Technical Journal*, 1961, *40*, 309–328.

Axelrod, S., & Guzy, L. T. Underestimation of dichotic click rates: Results using methods of absolute estimation and constant stimuli. *Psychonomic Science*, 1968, *12*, 133–134.

Ayer, A. J. (Ed.). *Logical positivism*. New York: Free press, 1959.

Baddeley, A. D. *The psychology of memory*. New York: Basic Books, 1976.

Baddeley, A. D., & Ecob, J. R. Reaction time and short term memory—Implications of repetition effects for the high speed exhaustive scan hypothesis. *Quarterly Journal of Experimental Psychology*, 1973, *25*, 229–240.

Baddeley, A. D., Grant, S., Wight, E., & Thompson, N. Imagery and visual working memory. In P. M. Rabbitt & S. Dornic (Eds.), *Attention and performance* (Vol. 5). New York: Academic Press, 1975.

Baddeley, A. D., & Hitch, G. Working memory. In G. Bower (Ed.), *Recent advances in learning and motivation* (Vol. 8). New York: Academic Press, 1974.

Baggett, P. Memory for explicit and implicit information in picture stories. *Journal of Verbal Learning and Verbal Behavior*, 1975, *14*, 538–548.

Baker, L., & Santa, J. L. Semantic integration and context. *Memory & Cognition*, 1977, *5*, 151–154.

Bamber, D. Reaction time and error rates for "same"–"different" judgments of multidimensional stimuli. *Perception and Psychophysics*, 1969, *6*, 169–174.

Barclay, J. R. The role of comprehension in remembering sentences. *Cognitive Psychology*, 1973, *4*, 229–254.

Barclay, J. R., Bransford, J. D., Franks, J. J., McCarrell, N. S., & Nitsch, K. Comprehension and semantic flexibility. *Journal of Verbal Learning and Verbal Behavior*, 1974, *13*, 471–481.

Baron, J., & Thurston, I. An analysis of the word-superiority effect. *Cognitive Psychology*, 1973, *4*, 207–228.

Bartlett, F. C. *Remembering: An experimental and social study*. Cambridge: Cambridge University Press, 1932.

Battig, W. F., & Montague, W. E. Category norms for verbal items in 56 categories: A replication and extension of the Connecticut category norms. *Journal of Experimental Psychology Monograph*, 1969, *80*, 1–46.

Begg, I., & Paivio, A. U. Concreteness and imagery in sentence meaning. *Journal of Verbal Learning and Verbal Behavior*, 1969, *8*, 821–827.

Bever, T. G., Fodor, J. A., & Garrett, M. A formal limitation of associationism. In T. R. Dixon & D. L. Horton (Eds.), *Verbal behavior and general behavior theory*. Englewood Cliffs, N.J.: Prentice-Hall, 1968.

Bever, T. G., Fodor, J. A., & Weksel, W. On the acquisition of syntax. *Psychological Review*, 1965, *72*(6), 467–482. (a)

Bever, T. G., Fodor, J. A., & Weksel, W. Is linguistics empirical? *Psychological Review*, 1965, *72*(6), 493–500. (b)

Bever, T. G., Lackner, J. R., & Kirk, R. The underlying structures of sentences are the primary units of immediate speech processing. *Perception and Psychophysics*, 1969, *5*, 225–234.

Biederman, I., Glass, A. L., & Stacy, E. W. Searching for objects in real-world scenes. *Journal of Experimental Psychology*, 1973, *97*, 22–27.

Biederman, I., & Stacy, E. Stimulus probability and stimulus set size in memory scanning. *Journal of Experimental Psychology*, 1974, *102*, 1100–1107.

Bjork, R. A. Theoretical implications of directed forgetting. In A. W. Melton & E. Martin (Eds.), *Coding processes in human memory*. Washington, D.C.: Winston, 1972.

Bloomfield, L. *Language*. New York: Henry Holt, 1933.

Blumenthal, A. Observations with self-embedded sentences. *Psychonomic Science*, 1966, *6*, 453–454.

Blumenthal, A. L. Prompted recall of sentences. *Journal of Verbal Learning and Verbal Behavior*, 1967, *6*, 203–206.

Blumenthal, A. L., & Boakes, R. Prompted recall of sentences: A further study. *Journal of Verbal Learning and Verbal Behavior*, 1967, *6*, 674–676.

Bobrow, D. G., & Collins, A. (Eds.). *Representation and understanding studies in cognitive science*. New York: Academic Press, 1975.

Bobrow, S. A., & Bower, G. H. Comprehension and recall of sentences. *Journal of Experimental Psychology*, 1969, *80*, 455–461.

Boring, E. G. *History of experimental psychology*. New York: Appleton-Century-Crofts, 1950.

Boring, E. G. *A history of experimental psychology* (2nd ed.). New York: Appleton-Century-Crofts, 1957.

Bousfield, W. A. The occurrence of clustering in the recall of randomly arranged associates. *Journal of General Psychology*, 1953, *49*, 229–240.

Bower, G. H. Stimulus-sampling theory of encoding variability. In A. W. Melton & E. Martin (Eds.), *Coding processes in human memory*. Washington, D.C.: Winston & Sons, 1972.

Bower, G. H. Cognitive psychology: An introduction. In W. K. Estes (Ed.), *Handbook of learning and cognitive processes*. Hillsdale, N.J.: Lawrence Erlbaum Associates, 1975.

Bower, G. H., & Reitman, J. S. Mnemonic elaboration in multilist learning. *Journal of Verbal Learning and Verbal Behavior*, 1972, *11*, 478–485.

Braine, M. D. S. On learning the grammatical order of words. *Psychological Review*, 1963, *70*(4), 323–348.

Braine, M. D. S. On the basis of phrase structure. *Psychological Review*, 1965, *72*(6), 483–492.

Bransford, J. D., Barclay, J. R., & Franks, J. J. Sentence memory: A constructive versus interpretive approach. *Cognitive Psychology*, 1972, *3*, 193–209.

Bransford, J. D., & Franks, J. J. The abstraction of linguistic ideas. *Cognitive Psychology*, 1971, *2*, 331–350.

Bransford, J. D., Franks, J. J., Morris, C. D., & Stein, B. S. An analysis of memory theories from the perspective of problems of learning. In L. S. Cermak & F. I. M. Craik (Eds.), *Levels of processing and human memory*. Hillsdale, N.J.: Lawrence Erlbaum Associates, 1978.

Bransford, J. D., & Johnson, M. K. Contextual prerequisites for understanding: Some investigations of comprehension and recall. *Journal of Verbal Learning and Verbal Behavior*, 1972, *11*, 717–726.

Brewer, W. F., & Harris, R. J. Memory for deictic elements in sentences. *Journal of Verbal Learning and Verbal Behavior*, 1974, *13*, 321–327.

Broadbent, D. E. The role of auditory localization in attention and memory span. *Journal of Experimental Psychology*, 1954, *47*, 191–196.

Broadbent, D. E. *Perception and Communication*. London: Pergamon Press, 1958.

Broadbent, D. E. *Decision and stress*. New York: Academic Press, 1971.

Brooks, L. R. The suppression of visualization in reading. *Quarterly Journal of Experimental Psychology*, 1967, *19*, 289–299.

Brooks, L. R. Spatial and verbal components in the act of recall. *Canadian Journal of Psychology*, 1968, *22*, 349–368.

Brown, J. A. Some tests of the decay theory of immediate memory. *Quarterly Journal of Experimental Psychology*, 1958, *10*, 12–21.

Brown, R. A brief account of microscopic observations. In J. J. Bennett (Ed.), *The miscellaneous botanical works* (Vol. 1). London: Robert Hardwicke, 1866.

Brown, R., Cazden, C. B., & Bellugi, U. The child's grammar from I to III. In J. P. Hill (Ed.), *Minnesota symposia on child psychology* (Vol. 2). Minneapolis: University of Minnesota Press, 1969.

Brown, R., & Lenneberg, E. H. A study in language and cognition. *Journal of Abnormal and Social Psychology*, 1954, *49*, 454–462.

Brown, R., & McNeill, D. The "tip of the tongue" phenomenon. *Journal of Verbal Learning and Verbal Behavior*, 1966, *5*, 325–337.

Bugelski, B. R. Presentation time, total time, and mediation in paired–associate learning. *Journal of Experimental Psychology*, 1962, *63*, 409–412.

Bugelski, B. R. Images as mediators in one-trial paired–associate learning. II: Self-timing in successive lists. *Journal of Experimental Psychology*, 1968, *77*, 328–334.

Burrows, D., & Murdock, B. B. Effects of extended practice on high speed scanning. *Journal of Experimental Psychology*, 1969, *82*, 231–237.

Butterfield, G. B., & Butterfield, E. C. Lexical codability and age. *Journal of Verbal Learning and Verbal Behavior*, 1977, *16*, 113–118.

Carpenter, P. A., & Just, M. A. Sentence comprehension: A psycholinguistic processing model of verification. *Psychological Review*, 1975, *82*, 45–73.

Carpenter, P. A., & Just, M. A. Models of sentence verification and linguistic comprehension. *Psychological Review*, 1976, *83*, 318–322.

Carr, H. A. *Psychology: A study of mental activity*. New York: Longmans, Green, 1925.

Carroll, J., & Payne, J. (Eds.). *Cognition and social behavior*. Hillsdale, N.J.: Lawrence Erlbaum Associates, 1976.

Carroll, J. B., & White, M. N. Word frequency and age of acquisition as determiners of picture-naming latency. *Quarterly Journal of Experimental Psychology*, 1973, *25*, 85–95.

Cermak, L. S., & Craik, F. I. M. (Eds.). *Levels of processing and human memory*. Hillsdale, N.J.: Lawrence Erlbaum Associates, 1978.

Charness, N. Memory for chess positions: Resistance to interference. *Journal of Experimental Psychology: Human Learning and Memory*, 1976, *2*, 641–653.

Chase, W. G. (Ed.). *Visual information processing*. New York: Academic Press, 1973.

Chase, W. G., & Clark, H. H. Mental operations in the comparison of sentences and pictures. In L. W. Gregg (Ed.), *Cognition in learning and memory*. New York: Wiley, 1972.

Cherry, E. C. Some experiments on the recognition of speech, with one and with two ears. *Journal of the Acoustical Society of America*, 1953, *25*, 975–979.

Cherry, E. C. *On human communication* (2nd ed.). Cambridge: MIT Press, 1966.

Chi, M. T. H. The representation of knowledge (Review of *Explorations in cognition* by D. A. Norman, D. E. Rumelhart, and the LNR Research Group). *Contemporary Psychology*, 1976, *21*, 784–785.

Chomsky, N. *Syntactic structures*. The Hague: Mouton, 1957.

Chomsky, N. A review of Skinner's *Verbal Behavior*. *Language*, 1959, *35*, 26–58.

Chomsky, N. *Aspects of the theory of syntax*. Cambridge: MIT Press, 1965.

Church, A. An unsolvable problem of elementary number theory. *American Journal of Mathematics*, 1936, *58*, 345–363.

Clark, H. H. Linguistic processes in deductive reasoning. *Psychological Review*, 1969, *76*, 387–404.

Clark, H. H. On the evidence concerning J. Huttenlocher and E. T. Higgens' theory of reasoning: A second reply. *Psychological Review*, 1972, *79*, 428–432.

Clark, H. H. The language-as-fixed-effect fallacy: A critique of language statistics in psychological research. *Journal of Verbal Learning and Verbal Behavior*, 1973, *12*, 335–359.

Clark, H. H. Semantics and comprehension. In T. A. Sebeok (Ed.), *Current trends in linguistics. Volume 12: Linguistics and adjacent arts and sciences*. The Hague: Mouton, 1974.

Clark, H. H. Inferences in comprehension. In D. LaBerge & S. J. Samuels (Eds.), *Perception and comprehension*. Hillsdale, N.J.: Lawrence Erlbaum Associates, 1976.

Clark, H. H. *Bridging*. Stanford University Working Paper, 1977.

Clark, H. H. Inferring what is meant. In a forthcoming book edited by W. J. M. Levelt & G. B. F. d'Arcais, 1978.

Clark, H. H., & Chase, W. G. On the process of comparing sentences against pictures. *Cognitive Psychology*, 1972, *3*, 472–517.

Clark, H. H., & Clark, E. V. *Psychology and language: An introduction to psycholinguistics*. New York: Harcourt Brace Jovanovich, 1977.

Clark, H. H., & Haviland, S. E. Comprehension and the given–new contract. In R. O. Freedle (Ed.), *Discourse, production, and comprehension*. Norwood, N.J.: Ablex Publishing, 1977.

Clark, H. H., & Lucy, P. Understanding what is meant from what is said: A study in conversationally conveyed requests. *Journal of Verbal Learning and Verbal Behavior*, 1975, *14*, 56–72.

Clifton, C., Jr., Kurcz, I., & Jenkins, J. J. Grammatical relations as determinants of sentence similarity. *Journal of Verbal Learning and Verbal Behavior*, 1965, *4*, 112–117.

Cofer, C. N. On some factors in the organizational charateristics of free recall. *American Psychologist*, 1965, *20*, 261–272.

Cofer, C. N., Chmielewski, D. L., & Brockway, J. P. Constructive processes and the structure of human memory. In C. N. Cofer (Ed.), *The structure of human memory*. San Francisco: Freeman, 1976.

Cole, R. A. Listening for mispronounciations: A measure of what we hear during speech. *Perception and Psychophysics*, 1973, *13*, 153–156.

Coleman, E. B. Approximations to English: Some comments on the method. *American Journal of Psychology*, 1963, *76*, 239–247.

Collins, A. M., & Loftus, E. F. A spreading activation theory of semantic processing. *Psychological Review*, 1975, *82*, 407–428.

Collins, A. M., & Quillian, M. R. Retrieval time from semantic memory. *Journal of Verbal Learning and Verbal Behavior*, 1969, *8*, 240–247.

Collins, A. M., & Quillian, M. R. Experiments on semantic memory and language comprehension. In L. W. Gregg (Ed.), *Cognition in learning and memory*. New York: Wiley, 1972.

Conrad, C. Cognitive economy in semantic memory. *Journal of Experimental Psychology*, 1972, *92*, 149–154.

Conrad, R. Acoustic confusions in immediate memory. *British Journal of Psychology*, 1964, *55*, 75–84.

Cooper, L. A. Mental rotation of random two-dimensional shapes. *Cognitive Psychology*, 1975, *7*, 20–43.

Cooper, L. A., & Shepard, R. N. Chronometric studies of the rotation of mental images. In W. G. Chase (Ed.), *Visual information processing*. New York: Academic Press, 1973.

Cornsweet, T. N. *Visual perception*. New York: Academic Press, 1970.

Corteen, R. S., & Wood, B. Autonomic responses to shock-associated words in an unattended channel. *Journal of Experimental Psychology*, 1972, *94*, 308–313.

Craik, F. I. M. The fate of primary items in free recall. *Journal of Verbal Learning and Verbal Behavior*, 1970, *9*, 143–148.

Craik, F. I. M., & Jacoby, L. L. A process view of short-term retention. In F. Restle, R. M. Shiffrin, N. J. Castellan, H. R. Lindman, and D. B. Pisoni (Eds.), *Cognitive theory* (Vol. 1). Hillsdale, N.J.: Lawrence Erlbaum Associates, 1975.

Craik, F. I. M., & Lockhart, R. S. Levels of processing: A framework for memory research. *Journal of Verbal Learning and Verbal Behavior*, 1972, *11*, 671–684.

Craik, F. I. M., & Tulving, E. Depth of processing and the retention of words in episodic memory. *Journal of Experimental Psychology: General*, 1975, *104*, 268–294.

Dallett, K. M. Implicit mediators in paired–associate learning. *Journal of Verbal Learning and Verbal Behavior,* 1964, *3,* 91–94.

D'Amato, M. R. *Experimental psychology: Methodology, psychophysics, and learning.* New York: McGraw-Hill, 1970.

Danks, J. H., & Schwenk, M. A. Prenominal adjective order and communication context. *Journal of Verbal Learning and Verbal Behavior,* 1972, *11,* 183–187.

Danks, J. H., & Schwenk, M. A. Comprehension of prenominal adjective orders. *Memory & Cognition,* 1974, *2, 1A,* 34–38.

Danks, J. H., & Sorce, P. A. Imagery and deep structure in the prompted recall of passive sentences. *Journal of Verbal Learning and Verbal Behavior,* 1973, *12,* 114–117.

Darwin, C. J., Turvey, M. T., & Crowder, R. G. An auditory analogue of the Sperling partial report procedure. *Cognitive Psychology,* 1972, *3,* 255–267.

Davies, D., & Isard, S. D. Utterances as programs. In D. Michie (Ed.), *Machine Intelligence 7.* Edinburgh: Edinburgh University Press, 1972.

Deese, J. Serial organization in the recall of disconnected items. *Psychology Reports,* 1957, *3,* 577–582.

Deese, J. *The structure of associations in language and thought.* Baltimore: Johns Hopkins Press, 1965.

Deininger, R. L. Human factors engineering studies of the design and use of push-button telephone sets. *Bell System Technical Journal,* 1960, *39,* 995–1012.

Deutsch, J. A., & Deutsch, D. Attention: Some theoretical considerations. *Psychological Review,* 1963, *70,* 80–90.

deVilliers, P. A. Imagery and theme in recall of connected discourse. *Journal of Experimental Psychology,* 1974, *103,* 263–268.

Dewar, K. M., Cuddy, L. L., & Mewhort, D. J. K. Recogniton memory for single tones with and without context. *Journal of Experimental Psychology: Human Learning and Memory,* 1977, *3,* 60–67.

Donders, F. C. Over de snelheid van psychische processen. Onderzoekingen gedaan in het Psyiologish Laboratorium der Utrechtsche Hoogeschool: 1868–1869. Tweede Reeks, II, 92–120. Translated by W. G. Koster in W. G. Koster (Ed.), Attention and Performance II. *Acta Psychologica,* 1969, *30,* 412–431.

Dooling, D. J., & Lachman, R. Effects of comprehension on retention of prose. *Journal of Experimental Psychology,* 1971, *88,* 216–222.

Dresher, E., & Hornstein, N. On some supposed contributions of artificial intelligence to the scientific study of language. *Cognition,* 1976, *4,* 321–398.

Dumas, J. Scanning memory for multidimensional stimuli with extended practice. *Perception and Psychophysics,* 1972, *11,* 209–212.

Ebbinghaus, H. *Uber das Gedachtnis,* 1885. [Reprinted as *Memory* (H. A. Ruger & C. E. Busenius, trans.). New York: Teachers College, 1913.]

Efron, R. The relationship between the duration of a stimulus and the duration of a perception. *Neuropsychologia,* 1970, *8,* 37–55. (a)

Efron, R. The minimum duration of a perception. *Neuropsychologia,* 1970, *8,* 57–63. (b)

Efron, R. Effect of stimulus duration on perceptual onset and offset latencies. *Perception & Psychophysics,* 1970, *8,* 231–234. (c)

Egeth, H. Parallel versus serial processes in multidimensional stimulus discrimination. *Perception and Psychophysics,* 1966, *1,* 245–252.

Egeth, H., Jonides, J., & Wall, S. Parallel processing of multielement displays. *Cognitive Psychology,* 1972, *3,* 674–698.

Einstein, A. Ueber die von der molikular-kinetischen Theorie der Wärme geforderte Bewegung von in ruhenden Flüssigkeiten suspendierten Teilchen. *Annalen der Physik*, 1905, *17*, 549–560. [Translation in Einstein *Investigations on the theory of the Brownian motion* (A. D. Cooper, trans.). With notes by R. Fürth. London: Methuen, 1926.]

Ekstrand, B., & Underwood, B. J. Paced versus unpaced recall in free learning. *Journal of Verbal Learning and Verbal Behavior*, 1963, *2*, 288–290.

Ellis, J. A. Transfer failure and proactive interference in short-term memory. *Journal of Experimental Psychology: Human Learning and Memory*, 1977, *3*, 211–221.

Epstein, W. The influence of syntactical structure on learning. *American Journal of Psychology*, 1961, *74*, 80–85.

Eriksen, C. W. Temporal luminance summation effects in backward and forward masking. *Perception and Psychophysics*, 1966, *1*, 87–92.

Estes, W. K. The statistical approach to learning theory. In S. Koch (Ed.), *Psychology: A study of a science* (Vol. 2). New York: McGraw-Hill, 1959.

Estes, W. K. Some targets for mathematical psychology. *Journal of Mathematical Psychology*, 1975, *12*, 263–282. (a)

Estes, W. K. Memory, perception, and decision in letter identification. In R. L. Solso (Ed.), *Information processing and cognition: The Loyola Symposium*. Hillsdale, N.J.: Lawrence Erlbaum Associates, 1975. (b)

Estes, W., Koch, S., MacCorquodale, K., Meehl, P., Mueller, C., Schoenfield, W., & Verplanck, W. (Eds.). *Modern learning theory*. New York: Appleton-Century-Crofts, 1954.

Fiksel, J. R., & Bower, G. H. Question-answering by a semantic network of parallel automata. *Journal of Mathematical Psychology*, 1976, *13*, 1–45.

Fillenbaum, S. Pragmatic normalization: Further results for some conjunctive and disjunctive sentences. *Journal of Experimental Psychology*, 1974, *102*, 574–578.

Fillenbaum, S., & Rapoport, A. Verbs of judging, judged: A case study. *Journal of Verbal Learning and Verbal Behavior*, 1974, *13*, 54–62.

Fillmore, C. J. The case for case. In E. Bach and R. T. Harms (Eds.), *Universals in linguistic theory*. New York: Holt, Rinehart & Winston, 1968.

Fillmore, C. J. Some problems for case grammar. In R. J. O'Brien (Ed.), Linguistics: Developments of the sixties—Viewpoints for the seventies. *Monograph series on languages and linguistics*, 1971, *24*, 35–56.

Fitts, P. M. Cognitive aspects of information processing: III. Set for speed versus accuracy. *Journal of Experimental Psychology*, 1966, *71*, 849–857.

Fitts, P. M., & Seeger, C. M. S–R compatibility: Spatial characteristics of stimulus and response codes. *Journal of Experimental Psychology*, 1953, *46*, 199–210.

Fitts, P. M., & Switzer, G. Cognitive aspects of information processing: The familiarity of S–R sets and subsets. *Journal of Experimental Psychology*, 1962, *63*, 321–329.

Fodor, J. A. Could meaning be an r_m? *Journal of Verbal Learning and Verbal Behavior*, 1965, *4*, 73–81. [Also in R. C. Oldfield & J. C. Marshal (Eds.), *Language: Selected readings*. Baltimore: Penguin Books, 1968.]

Fodor, J. A., & Bever, T. G. The psychological reality of linguistic segments. *Journal of Verbal Learning and Verbal Behavior*, 1965, *4*, 414–420.

Fodor, J. A., Bever, T. G., & Garrett, M. F. *The psychology of language*. New York: McGraw-Hill, 1974.

Franks, J. J., & Bransford, J. D. The acquisition of abstract ideas. *Journal of Verbal Learning and Verbal Behavior*, 1972, *11*, 311–315.

Frederiksen, C. H. Representing logical and semantic structure of knowledge acquired from discourse. *Cognitive Psychology*, 1975, *7*, 371–458.

Frege, G. On sense and reference. *Zeitschrift für philosophie und philosophische kritik.* 1892, *100,* 25–50.

Frijda, N. H. Simulation of human long-term memory. *Psychological Bulletin,* 1972, *77,* 1–31.

Gardner, H. The naming of objects and symbols by children and aphasic patients. *Journal of Psycholinguistic Research,* 1974, *3,* 133–149.

Gardner, R. A., & Gardner, B. T. Teaching sign language to a chimpanzee. *Science,* 1969, *165,* 664–672.

Gardner, R. A., & Gardner, B. T. Two-way communication with an infant chimpanzee. In A. M. Schrier & F. Stollnitz (Eds.), *Behavior of nonhuman primates* (Vol. 4). New York: Academic Press, 1971.

Gardner, R. A., & Gardner, B. T. Early signs of language in child and chimpanzee. *Science,* 1975, *187,* 752–754.

Garner, W. R. *Uncertainty and structure as psychological concepts.* New York: Wiley, 1962.

Garner, W. R. The stimulus in information processing. *American Psychologist,* 1970, *25,* 350–358.

Garner, W. R. Information integration and form of encoding. In A. W. Melton & E. Martin (Eds.), *Coding processes in human memory.* Washington, D.C.: Winston, 1972.

Garner, W. R. *The processing of information and structure.* Potomac, Md.: Lawrence Erlbaum Associates, 1974.

Garner, W. R., & Clement, D. E. Goodness of pattern and pattern uncertainty. *Journal of Verbal Learning and Verbal Behavior,* 1963, *2,* 446–452.

Garner, W. R., & Felfoldy, G. Integrality and separability of stimulus dimensions in information processing. *Cognitive Psychology,* 1970, *1,* 225–241.

Garner, W. R., Hake, H. W., & Eriksen, C. W. Operationism and the concept of perception. *Psychological Review,* 1956, *63,* 149–159.

Garrett, M. F., Bever, T. G., & Fodor, J. A. The active use of grammar in speech perception. *Perception and Psychophysics,* 1966, *1,* 30–32.

Gibson, E. J. A systematic application of the concepts of generalization and differentiation to verbal learning. *Psychological Review,* 1940, *47,* 196–229.

Gibson, E. J., Pick, A., Osser, H., & Hammond, M. The role of grapheme–phoneme correspondence in the perception of words. *American Journal of Psychology,* 1962, *75,* 554–570.

Gibson, J. J. *The senses considered as perceptual systems.* Boston: Houghton-Mifflin, 1966.

Glanzer, M. Storage mechanisms in recall. In G. H. Bower & J. T. Spence (Eds.), *The psychology of learning and motivation.* Vol. 5. New York: Academic Press, 1972.

Glanzer, M., & Clark, W. H. Accuracy of perceptual recall: An analysis of organization. *Journal of Verbal Learning and Verbal Behavior,* 1962, *1,* 289–299.

Glanzer, M., & Clark, W. H. The verbal loop hypothesis: Binary numbers. *Journal of Verbal Learning and Verbal Behavior,* 1963, *2,* 301–309.

Glanzer, M., & Cunitz, A. R. Two storage mechanisms in free recall. *Journal of Verbal Learning and Verbal Behavior,* 1966, *5,* 351–360.

Glass, A. L., & Holyoak, K. J. Alternative conceptions of semantic memory. *Cognition,* 1975, *3,* 313–339.

Glucksberg, S., & Cowen, G. N. Memory for nonattended auditory material. *Cognitive Psychology,* 1970, *1,* 149–156.

Glucksberg, S., Trabasso, T., & Wald, J. Linguistic structures and mental operations. *Cognitive Psychology,* 1973, *5,* 338–370.

Gödel, K. Über formal unentscheidbare Sätze der *Principia Mathematica* und verwandter Systeme. *Monatschefte der Mathematik und Physik,* 1931, *38,* 173–198. [Translated in: Davis, M. (Ed.). *The undecidable: Basic papers on undecidable propositions, unsolvable problems and computable functions.* Hewlitt, N.Y.: Raven Press, 1956.]

Goldman-Eisler, F. *Psycholinguistics: Experiments in spontaneous speech.* New York: Academic Press, 1968.

Gough, P. B. Grammatical transformations and speed of understanding. *Journal of Verbal Learning and Verbal Behavior,* 1965, *4,* 107–111.

Gough, P. B. The verification of sentences: The effects of delay of evidence and sentence length. *Journal of Verbal Learning and Verbal Behavior,* 1966, *5,* 492–496.

Gray, J. A., & Wedderburn, A. A. I. Grouping strategies with simultaneous stimuli. *Quarterly Journal of Experimental Psychology,* 1960, *12,* 180–184.

Green, D. W. The effects of task on the representation of sentences. *Journal of Verbal Learning and Verbal Behavior,* 1975, *14,* 275–283.

Griffith, D. The attentional demands of mnemonic control processes. *Memory and Cognition,* 1976, *4,* 103–108.

Haber, R. N. *Information-processing approaches to visual perception.* New York: Holt, Rinehart & Winston, 1969.

Haber, R. N., & Standing, L. G. Direct measures of short-term visual storage. *Quarterly Journal of Experimental Psychology,* 1969, *21,* 43–54.

Hanson, N. R. *Patterns of discovery.* Cambridge, Mass.: Harvard University Press, 1958.

Harris, R. J. Memory and comprehension of implications and inferences of complex sentences. *Journal of Verbal Learning and Verbal Behavior,* 1974, *13,* 626–637.

Harris, R. J., & Brewer, W. F. Deixis in memory for verb tense. *Journal of Verbal Learning and Verbal Behavior,* 1973, *12,* 590–597.

Hartline, H. K., & Ratliff, F. Inhibitory interaction of receptor units in the eye of *Limulus. Journal of General Physiology,* 1957, *40,* 357–376.

Hartline, H. K., & Ratliff, F. Spatial summation of inhibitory influence in the eye of the *Limulus,* and the mutual interaction of receptor units. *Journal of General Physiology,* 1958, *41,* 1049–1066.

Hartline, H., Wagner, H., & Ratliff, F. Inhibition in the eye *Limulus. Journal of General Physiology,* 1956, *39,* 651–673.

Haviland, S. E., & Clark, H. H. What's new? Acquiring new information as a process in comprehension. *Journal of Verbal Learning and Verbal Behavior,* 1974, *13,* 512–521.

Hayes, C. *The ape in our house.* New York: Harper & Row, 1951.

Hays, D. G. *Introduction to computational linguistics.* New York: American Elsevier, 1967.

Hebb, D. O. *The organization of behavior.* New York: Wiley, 1949.

Hecht, S., Schlaer, A., & Pirenne, M. H. Energy quanta and vision. *Journal of General Physiology,* 1942, *25,* 819–840.

Henderson, L. Word recognition. In N. S. Sutherland (Ed.), *Tutorial essays in psychology.* Hillsdale, N.J.: Lawrence Erlbaum Associates, 1977.

Hendrick, C. (Ed.). *Perspectives on social psychology.* Hillsdale, N.J.: Lawrence Erlbaum Associates, 1977.

Hick, W. E. On the rate of gain of information. *Quarterly Journal of Experimental Psychology,* 1952, *4,* 11–26.

Holding, D. H. Guessing behavior and the Sperling store. *Quarterly Journal of Experimental Psychology,* 1970, *22,* 248–256.

Holmes, V. M., & Langford, J. Comprehension and recall of abstract and concrete sentences. *Journal of Verbal Learning and Verbal Behavior,* 1976, *5,* 559–566.

Holton, G. *Thematic origins of scientific thought: Kepler to Einstein.* Cambridge: Harvard University Press, 1973.

Holton, G. On the role of themata in scientific thought. *Science,* 1975, *188,* 328–334.

Holyoak, K. J., & Glass, A. L. The role of contradictions and counterexamples in the rejection of false sentences. *Journal of Verbal Learning and Verbal Behavior,* 1975, *14,* 215–239.

Hornby, P. A. Surface structure and presupposition. *Journal of Verbal Learning and Verbal Behavior,* 1974, *13,* 530–538.

Hubel, D. H., & Wiesel, T. N. Receptive fields, binocular interaction and functional architecture in the cat's visual cortex. *Journal of Physiology* (London), 1962, *160,* 106–154.

Hubel, D. H., & Wiesel, T. N. Shape and arangement of columns in cat's striate cortex. *Journal of Physiology* (London), 1963, *165*, 559–568.

Hubel, D. H., & Wiesel, T. N. Receptive fields and functional architecture in two non-striate visual areas (18 & 19) of the cat. *Journal of Neurophysiology*, 1965, *28*, 229–289.

Hubel, D. H., & Wiesel, T. N. Receptive fields and functional architecture of monkey striate cortex. *Journal of Physiology* (London), 1968, *195*, 215–243.

Huey, E. B. *The psychology and pedagogy of reading*. Cambridge, Mass.: MIT Press, 1968.

Hull, C. L. *Principles of behavior*. New York: D. Appleton-Century, 1943.

Hyman, R. Stimulus information as a determinant of reaction time. *Journal of Experimental Psychology*, 1953, *45*, 188–196.

Jacoby, L. L., & Craik, F. I. M. Effects of elaboration of processing at encoding and retrieval: trace distinctiveness and recovery of initial context. In L. S. Cermak & F. I. M. Craik (Eds.), *Levels of processing and human memory*. Hillsdale, N.J.: Lawrence Erlbaum Associates, 1978.

Jakobson, R., Fant, G., & Halle, M. *Preliminaries to speech analysis: The distinctive features and their correlates*. Cambridge, Mass.: MIT Press, 1963.

Jakobson, R., & Halle, M. *Fundamentals of language*. The Hague: Mouton, 1956.

James, W. *The principles of psychology*. New York: Holt, 1890. [Reprinted by Dover, New York, 1950.]

Jenkins, J. J. *Recognition memory for picture sequences*. Colloquium presented at the University of Houston, 1977.

Jennings, J. R. Wood, C. C., & Lawrence, B. E. Alcohol and speed/accuracy trade-off. *Perception and Psychophysics*, 1976, *9*, 85–91.

Johnson, M. K., Bransford, J. D., Nyberg, S. E., & Cleary, J. J. Comprehension factors in interpreting memory for abstract and concrete sentences. *Journal of Verbal Learning and Verbal Behavior*, 1972, *11*, 451–454.

Johnson, M. K., Bransford, J. D., & Solomon, S. K. Memory for tacit implications of sentences. *Journal of Experimental Psychology*, 1973, *98*, 203–205.

Johnson, M. K., Doll, T. J., Bransford, J. D., & Lapinski, R. H. Context effects in sentence memory. *Journal of Experimental Psychology*, 1974, *103*, 358–360.

Johnson, N. The psychological reality of phrase-structure rules. *Journal of Verbal Learning and Verbal Behavior*, 1965, *4*, 469–475.

Johnson, W. A., Greenberg, S. N., Fisher, R. P., & Martin, D. W. Divided attention: A vehicle for monitoring memory processes. *Journal of Experimental Psychology*, 1970, *83*, 164–171.

Johnson-Laird, P. N. Procedural semantics. *Cognition*, 1977, *5*, 189–214.

Jorgensen, C. C., & Kintsch, W. The role of imagery in the evaluation of sentences. *Cognitive Psychology*, 1973, *4*, 110–116.

Jung, J. *Verbal learning*. Toronto: Holt, Rinehart & Winston, 1968.

Juola, J. F. Repetition and laterality effects on recognition memory for words and pictures. *Memory & Cognition*, 1973, *1*, 183–192.

Juola, J. F., & Atkinson, R. C. Memory scanning for words vs. categories. *Journal of Verbal Learning and Verbal Behavior*, 1971, *10*, 522–527.

Juola, J. F., Choe, C. S., & Leavitt, D. D. *A reanalysis of the word superiority effect*. Paper presented at the Psychonomic Society meeting, Boston, 1974.

Juola, J. F., Fischler, I., Wood, C. T. & Atkinson, R. C. Recognition time for information stored in long-term memory. *Perception and Psychophysics*, 1971, *10*, 8–14.

Juola, J. F., Leavitt, D. D., & Choe, C. S. Letter identification in word, nonword, and single-letter displays. *Bulletin of the Psychonomic Society*, 1974, *4*, 278–280.

Juola, J. F., Schadler, M., Chabot, R., McCaughey, M., & Wait, J. What do children learn when they learn to read? In L. Resnick & P. Weaver (Eds.), *Theory and practice of beginning reading* (Vol. 2). Hillsdale, N.J.: Lawrence Erlbaum Associates, in press.

Kahneman, D. Remarks on attention control. *Acta Psychologica*. In A. F. Sanders (Ed.), *Attention and performance III*, 1970, 118–131.

Kahneman, D. *Attention and effort*. Englewood Cliffs, N.J.: Prentice-Hall, 1973.

Katz, J. J., & Fodor, J. A. The structure of a semantic theory. *Language*, 1963, *39*, 170–210.

Keele, S. W. *Attention and human performance*. Pacific Palisades, Calif.: Goodyear, 1973.

Kellogg, W. N., & Kellogg, L. A. *The ape and the child*. New York: McGraw-Hill, 1933.

Kessel, F. S. The philosophy of science as proclaimed and science as practiced. *American Psychologist*, 1969, *24*, 999–1005.

King, D. R. W., & Anderson, J. R. Long-term memory search: An intersecting activation process. *Journal of Verbal Learning and Verbal Behavior*, 1976, *15*, 587–605.

Kintsch, W. *The representation of meaning in memory*. Hillsdale, N.J.: Lawrence Erlbaum Associates, 1974.

Kintsch, W. Memory for prose. In C. N. Cofer (Ed.), *The structure of human memory*. San Francisco: Freeman, 1976.

Kintsch, W. On comprehending stories. In M. A. Just & P. A. Carpenter (Eds.), *Cognitive processes in comprehension*. Hillsdale, N.J.: Lawrence Erlbaum Associates, 1977.

Kintsch, W., & Keenan, J. Reading rate and retention as a function of the number of propositions in the base structure of sentences. *Cognitive Psychology*, 1973, *5*, 257–274.

Kintsch, W., Kozminsky, E., Streby, W. J., McKoon, G., & Keenan, J. M. Comprehension and recall of text as a function of content variables. *Journal of Verbal Learning and Verbal Behavior*, 1975, *14*, 196–214.

Klahr, D., & Wallace, J. C. *Cognitive development: An information-processing view*. Hillsdale, N.J.: Lawrence Erlbaum Associates, 1976.

Klee, H., & Eysenck, M. W. Comprehension of abstract and concrete sentences. *Journal of Verbal Learning and Verbal Behavior*, 1973, *12*, 522–529.

Koch, S. (Ed.). *Psychology: A study of a science*. New York: McGraw-Hill, 1959.

Kochen, M., MacKay, D. M., Maron, M. E., Scriven, M., & Uhr, L. *Computers and comprehension*. Rand Corporation Memorandum RM-4065-PR, April 1964.

Kolers, P. A. Some psychological aspects of pattern recognition. In P. A. Kolers & M. Eden (Eds.), *Recognizing patterns*, Cambridge, Mass.: MIT Press, 1968.

Kolers, P. A. A pattern analyzing basis of recognition. In L. S. Cermak & F. I. M. Craik (Eds.), *Levels of processing and human memory*. Hillsdale, N.J.: Lawrence Erlbaum Associates, 1978.

Kosslyn, S. M., & Pomerantz, J. R. Imagery, propositions, and the form of internal representations. *Cognitive Psychology*, 1977, *9*, 52–76.

Kroll, N. E. A. Short-term memory and the nature of interference from concurrent shadowing. *Quarterly Journal of Experimental Psychology*, 1972, *24*, 414–419.

Kroll, N. E. A. Visual short-term memory. In J. A. Deutsch (Ed.), *Short-term memory*. New York: Academic Press, 1975.

Kroll, N. E. A., & Kellicutt, M. H. Short-term recall as a function of covert rehearsal and of intervening task. *Journal of Verbal Learning and Verbal Behavior*, 1972, *11*, 196–204.

Kroll, N. E. A., Parks, T., Parkinson, S. R., Bieber, S. L., & Johnson, A. L. Short-term memory while shadowing: Recall of visually and of aurally presented letters. *Journal of Experimental Psychology*, 1970, *85*, 220–224.

Kucera, H., & Francis, W. N. *Computational analysis of present-day American English*. Providence, R.I.: Brown University Press, 1967.

Kuffler, S. W. Neurons in the retina: Organization, inhibition, and excitation problems. *Cold Spring Harbor Symposium on Quantitative Biology*, 1952, *17*, 281–292.

Kuffler, S. W. Discharge patterns and functional organization of mammalian retina. *Journal of Neurophysiology*, 1953, *16*, 37–68.

Kuhn, T. S. *The structure of scientific revolutions*. Chicago: University of Chicago Press, 1962.

Kuhn, T. S. *The structure of scientific revolutions* (2nd ed.). Chicago: University of Chicago Press, 1970. (a)

Kuhn, T. S. Logic of discovery or psychology of research? In I. Lakatos & A. Musgrave (Eds.), *Criticism and the growth of knowledge.* London: Cambridge University Press, 1970. (b)

Kuhn, T. S. Reflections on my critics. In I. Lakatos & A. Musgrave (Eds.), *Criticism and the growth of knowledge.* London: Cambridge University Press, 1970. (c)

Kuhn, T. S. Second thoughts on paradigms. In F. Suppe (Ed.), *The structure of scientific theories.* Urbana: University of Illinois Press, 1974.

Lachman, R. Uncertainty effects on time to access the internal lexicon. *Journal of Experimental Psychology,* 1973, *99,* 199–208.

Lachman, R., Shaffer, J. P., & Hennrikus, D. Language and cognition: Effects of stimulus codability, name-word frequency, and age of acquisition on lexical reaction time. *Journal of Verbal Learning and Verbal Behavior,* 1974, *13,* 613–625.

Lakatos, I. Falsification and the methodology of science research programs. In I. Lakatos & A. Musgrave (Eds.), *Criticism and the growth of knowledge.* London: Cambridge University Press, 1970.

Lakoff, G. Presupposition and relative well-formedness. In D. D. Steinberg & L. A. Jakobovits (Eds.), *Semantics.* Cambridge: Cambridge University Press, 1971.

Lakoff, R. Some reasons why there isn't any some–any rule. *Language,* 1969, *45,* 608–615.

Landauer, T. K., & Freedman, J. L. Information retrieval from long-term memory: Category size and recognition time. *Journal of Verbal Learning and Verbal Behavior,* 1968, *7,* 291–295.

Landauer, T. K., & Meyer, D. E. Category size and semantic memory retrieval. *Journal of Verbal Learning and Verbal Behavior,* 1972, *11,* 539–549.

Lantz, D., & Stefflre, V. Language and cognition revisited. *Journal of Abnormal and Social Psychology,* 1964, *69,* 472–481.

Layton, P., & Simpson, A. J. Surface and deep structure in sentence comprehension. *Journal of Verbal Learning and Verbal Behavior,* 1975, *14,* 658–664.

Lenneberg, E. H. *Biological foundations of language.* New York: Wiley, 1967.

Leonard, J. A. Partial advance information in a choice reaction task. *British Journal of Psychology,* 1958, *49,* 89–96.

Lesgold, A. M. Pronominalization: A device for unifying sentences in memory. *Journal of Verbal Learning and Verbal Behavior,* 1972, *11,* 316–323.

Lettvin, J. Y., Maturana, H. R., McCulloch, W. S., & Pitts, W. H. What the frog's eye tells the frog's brain. *Proceedings of the IRE,* 1959, *47(11),* 1940–1951.

Levy, B. A. Role of articulation in auditory and visual short-term memory. *Journal of Verbal Learning and Verbal Behavior,* 1971, *10,* 123–132.

Lewis, J. L. Semantic processing of unattended messages using dichotic listening. *Journal of Experimental Psychology,* 1970, *85,* 225–229.

Liberman, A. M., Cooper, F. S., Shankweiler, D. P., & Studdert-Kennedy, M. Perception of the speech code. *Psychological Review,* 1967, *74,* 431–461.

Liberman, A. M., Harris, K. S., Kinney, J. A., & Lane, H. L. The discrimination of relative onset time of the components of certain speech and nonspeech patterns. *Journal of Experimental Psychology,* 1961, *61,* 379–388.

Lieberman, P. *On the origins of language.* New York: Macmillan, 1975.

Lieberman, P., Crelin, E. S., & Klatt, D. H. Phonetic ability and related anatomy of the newborn, adult human, Neanderthal man and the chimpanzee. *American Anthropology,* 1972, *74,* 287–307.

Lindsay, P. H., & Norman, D. A. *Human information processing: An introduction to psychology.* New York: Academic Press, 1972.

Lindsay, P. H., & Norman, D. A. *Human information processing.* New York: Academic Press, 1977.

Loftus, E. F. Leading questions and the eyewitness report. *Cognitive Psychology,* 1975, *7,* 560–572.

Loftus, E. F. Organization and retrieval of attribute and name information. In S. Ehrlich and E. Tulving (Eds.), *La Memoire Semantique.* Paris: Bulletin de Psychologie, 1976.

Loftus, E. F. How to catch a zebra in semantic memory. In R. Shaw & J. Bransford (Eds.), *Perceiving, acting and knowing.* Hillsdale, N.J.: Lawrence Erlbaum Associates, 1977.

Loftus, E. F., & Palmer, J. C. Reconstruction of automobile destruction: An example of the interaction between language and memory. *Journal of Verbal Learning and Verbal Behavior,* 1974, *13,* 585–589.

Loftus, E. F., & Zanni, G. Eyewitness testimony: The influence of the wording of a question. *Bulletin of the Psychonomic Society,* 1975, *5,* 86–88.

MacCorquodale, K. On Chomsky's review of Skinner's *Verbal Behavior. Journal of the Experimental Analysis of Behavior,* 1970, *13,* 83–99.

Mahoney, M. J. *Cognition and behavior modification.* Cambridge, Mass.: Ballinger, 1974.

Malmberg, B. *Structural linguistics and human communication* (2nd ed.). Heidelberg: Springer, 1963.

Mandler, G. Organization in memory. In K. W. Spence & J. T. Spence (Eds.), *Psychology of learning and motivation* (Vol. 1). New York: Academic Press, 1967.

Mandler, G. Consciousness: Respectable, useful, and probably necessary. In R. L. Solso (Ed.), *Information processing and cognition: The Loyola Symposium.* Hillsdale, N.J.: Lawrence Erlbaum Associates, 1975.

Manelis, L. The effect of meaningfulness in tachistoscopic word perception. *Perception and Psychophysics,* 1974, *16,* 182–192.

Marks, L. E. Some structural and sequential factors in the processing of sentences. *Journal of Verbal Learning and Verbal Behavior,* 1967, *6,* 707–713.

Marks, L. E., & Miller, G. A. The role of semantic and syntactic constraints in the memorization of English sentences. *Journal of Verbal Learning and Verbal Behavior,* 1964, *3,* 1–5.

Mascall, E. L. *Christian theology and natural science.* New York: Longmans, Green, 1956.

Massaro, D. W. Preperceptual auditory images. *Journal of Experimental Psychology,* 1970, *85,* 411–417.

Massaro, D. W. Preperceptual images, processing time, and perceptual units in auditory perception. *Psychological Review,* 1972, *79,* 124–145.

Massaro, D. W. *Experimental psychology and information processing.* Chicago: Rand McNally, 1975.

Masterman, M. The nature of a paradigm. In I. Lakatos & A. Musgrave (Eds.), *Criticism and the growth of knowledge.* Cambridge: Cambridge University Press, 1970.

McCrary, J. W., Jr., & Hunter, W. S. Serial position curves in verbal learning. *Science,* 1953, *117,* 131–134.

McGeoch, J. A. *The psychology of human learning: An introduction.* New York: Van Rees Press, 1942.

McMahon, L. E. *Grammatical analysis as part of understanding a sentence.* Unpublished doctoral dissertation, Harvard University, 1963.

McNeill, D. *The acquisition of language.* New York: Harper & Row, 1970.

Mehler, J., & Carey, P. Role of surface and base structure in the perception of sentences. *Journal of Verbal Learning and Verbal Behavior,* 1967, *6,* 335–338.

Meier, N. *Deutsche Sprachstatistik* (Vols. 1 and 2). Hildesheim: G. Olms, 1964.

Melton, A. W., & Martin, E. *Coding processes in human memory.* Washington, D.C.: Winston & Sons, 1972.

Merkel, J. Die zeitlichen Verhältnisse der Willensthätigkeit. *Philosophische Studien,* 1885, *2,* 73–127.

Meyer, D. E. On the representation and retrieval of stored semantic information. *Cognitive Psychology*, 1970, *1*, 242–300.

Meyer, D. E. Verifying affirmative and negative propositions: Effects of negation on memory retrieval. In S. Kornblum (Ed.), *Attention and Performance IV*. New York: Academic Press, 1973.

Meyer, D. E., & Ellis, G. B. Parallel processes in word recognition. Paper presented at the meeting of the Psychonomic Society, San Antonio, November 1970.

Meyer, D. E., & Schvaneveldt, R. W. Meaning, memory structure, and mental processes. In C. N. Cofer (Ed.), *The structure of human memory*. San Francisco: Freeman, 1976.

Milgram, N. A. Microgenetic analysis of word associations in schizophrenic and brain damaged patients. *Journal of Abnormal and Social Psychology*, 1961, *62*, 364–366.

Miller, G. A. What is information measurement? *American Psychologist*, 1953, *8*, 3–11.

Miller, G. A. The magical number seven, plus or minus two: Some limits on our capacity for processing information. *Psychological Review*, 1956, *63*, 81–97.

Miller, G. A. Some psychological studies of grammar. *American Psychologist*, 1962, *17*, 748–762.

Miller, G. A. Toward a third metaphor for psycholinguistics. In W. B. Weimer & D. S. Palermo (Eds.), *Cognition and the symbolic processes*. Hillsdale, N.J.: Lawrence Erlbaum Associates, 1974.

Miller, G. A., Bruner, J. S., & Postman, L. Familiarity of letter sequences and tachistoscopic identification. *Journal of Genetic Psychology*, 1954, *50*, 129–139.

Miller, G. A., Galanter, E., & Pribram, K. H. *Plans and the structure of behavior*. New York: Henry Holt & Co., Inc., 1960.

Miller, G. A., Heise, G. A., & Lichten, W. The intelligibility of speech as a function of the text of the test materials. *Journal of Experimental Psychology*, 1951, *41*, 329–335.

Miller, G., & Isard, S. Some perceptual consequences of linguistic rules. *Journal of Verbal Learning and Verbal Behavior*, 1963, *2*, 217–228.

Miller, G. A., & Johnson-Laird, P. N. *Language and perception*. Cambridge, Mass.: Harvard University Press, 1976.

Miller, G. A., & Selfridge, J. A. Verbal context and the recall of meaningful material. *American Journal of Psychology*, 1950, *63*, 176–185.

Milne, E. A. *Modern cosmology and the christian idea of god*. Oxford: Oxford University Press, 1952.

Milner, B. The memory defect in bilateral hippocampal lesions. *Psychiatric Research Reports*, 1959, *11*, 43–52.

Milner, B. Neuropsychological evidence for differing memory processes. Abstract for the symposium on short-term and long-term memory. *Proceedings of the 18th International Congress of Psychology, Moscow*, 1966.

Milner, B. Amnesia following operation on the temporal lobes. In C. W. M. Whitty & O. L. Zangwill (Eds.), *Amnesia*. London: Butterworths, 1967.

Minsky, M. L. *Computation: Finite and infinite machines*. Englewood Cliffs, N.J.: Prentice-Hall, 1967.

Minsky, M. L. A framework for representing knowledge. In P. Winston (Ed.), *The psychology of computer vision*. New York: McGraw-Hill, 1975.

Mistler-Lachman, J. Levels of comprehension in processing of normal and ambiguous sentences. *Journal of Verbal Learning and Verbal Behavior*, 1972, *11*, 614–623.

Mistler-Lachman, J. Levels of comprehension and sentence memory. *Journal of Verbal Learning and Verbal Behavior*, 1974, *13*, 98–106.

Moeser, S. D. Memory for meaning and wording in concrete and abstract sentences. *Journal of Verbal Learning and Verbal Behavior*, 1974, *13*, 682–697.

Moray, N. Attention in dichotic listening: Affective cues and the influence of instructions. *Quarterly Journal of Experimental Psychology*, 1959, *11*, 56–60.

Moray, N. *Listening and attention.* Baltimore: Penguin, 1969.

Moray, N. *Attention: Selective processes in vision and hearing.* New York: Academic Press, 1970.

Moray, N., Bates, A., & Barnett, T. Experiments on the four-eared man. *Journal of Acoustical Society of America,* 1965, *38,* 196–201.

Morris, C. D., Bransford, J. D., & Franks, J. J. Levels of processing versus transfer appropriate processing. *Journal of Verbal Learning and Verbal Behavior,* 1977, *16,* 519–534.

Mowbray, G. H., & Rhoades, M. V. On the reduction of choice reaction times with practice. *Quarterly Journal of Experimental Psychology,* 1959, *11,* 16–23.

Mowrer, O. H. The psychologist looks at language. *American Psychologist,* 1954, *9,* 600–694.

Murdock, B. B. The immediate retention of unrelated words. *Journal of Experimental Psychology,* 1960, *60,* 222–234.

Murdock, B. B., Jr. The retention of individual items. *Journal of Experimental Psychology,* 1961, *62,* 618–625.

Murdock, B. B., Jr. Four channel effects in short-term memory. *Psychonomic Science,* 1971, *24,* 197–198.

Naus, M. J., Glucksberg, S., & Ornstein, P. A. Taxonomic word categories and memory search. *Cognitive Psychology,* 1972, *3,* 643–654.

Neisser, U. Decision-time without reaction time: Experiments in visual scanning. *American Journal of Psychology,* 1963, *76,* 376–385.

Neisser, U. Visual search. *Scientific American,* 1964, *210,* 94–102.

Neisser, U. *Cognitive psychology.* New York: Appleton-Century-Crofts, 1967.

Neisser, U. *Selective reading. A method for the study of visual attention.* Nineteenth International Congress of Psychology, London, 1969.

Neisser, U. *Cognition and reality.* San Francisco: Freeman, 1976.

Neisser, U., & Becklen, R. Selective looking: Attending to visually specified events. *Cognitive Psychology,* 1975, *7,* 480–494.

Nelson, D. L. Remembering pictures and words: Significance and appearance. In L. S. Cermak & F. I. M. Craik (Eds.), *Levels of processing and human memory.* Hillsdale, N.J.: Lawrence Erlbaum Associates, 1978.

Newell, A. You can't play 20 questions with nature and win: Projective comments on the papers of this symposium. In W. G. Chase (Ed.), *Visual information processing.* New York: Academic Press, 1973.

Newell, A., Shaw, J. C., & Simon, H. A. Elements of a theory of human problem solving. *Psychological Review,* 1958, *65,* 151–166.

Newell, A., & Simon, H. A. The simulation of human thought. In *Current trends in psychological theory.* Pittsburgh: University of Pittsburgh Press, 1961.

Newell, A., & Simon, H. *Human problem solving.* Englewood Cliffs, N. J.: Prentice-Hall, 1972.

Newell, A., & Simon, H. A. Computer science as empirical inquiry: Symbols and search. *Communications of the ACM,* 1976, *19,* 113–126.

Nickerson, R. S. Binary classification reaction time: A review of some studies of human information processing capabilities. *Psychonomics Monograph Supplement,* 1972, *4*(Whole No. 65), 275–318.

Norman, D. A. Toward a theory of memory and attention. *Psychological Review,* 1968, *75,* 522–536.

Norman, D. A. *Models of human memory.* New York: Academic Press, 1970.

Norman, D. A. Memory, knowledge, and the answering of questions. In R. L. Solso (Ed.), *Contemporary issues in cognitive psychology: The Loyola Symposium.* Washington, D. C.: Winston, 1973.

Norman, D. A., & Bobrow, D. G. On data limited and resource limited processes. *Cognitive Psychology,* 1975, *7,* 44–64.

Norman, D. A., & Bobrow, D. G. On the role of active memory processes in perception and cognition. In C. Cofer (Ed.), *The structure of human memory*. San Francisco: Freeman, 1976.

Norman, D. A., & Rumelhart, D. E. A system for perception and memory. In D. A. Norman (Ed.), *Models of human memory*. New York: Academic Press, 1970.

Norman, D. A., Rumelhart, D. E., & the LNR Research Group. *Explorations in cognition*. San Francisco: Freeman, 1975.

Oldfield, R. C. Individual vocabulary and semantic currency. *British Journal of Social and Clinical Psychology*, 1963, *2*, 122–130.

Oldfield, R. C. Things, words and the brain. *Quarterly Journal of Experimental Psychology*, 1966, *18*, 340–353.

Oldfield, R. C., & Wingfield, A. The time it takes to name an object. *Nature*, 1964, *202*, 1031–1032.

Oldfield, R. C., & Wingfield, A. Response latencies in naming objects. *Quarterly Journal of Experimental Psychology*, 1965, *17*, 273–281.

Olson, D. R., & Filby, N. On the comprehension of active and passive sentences. *Cognitive Psychology*, 1972, *3*, 361–381.

Osgood, C. E. *Method and theory in experimental psychology*. New York: Oxford University Press, 1953.

Ostry, D., Moray, N., & Marks, G. Attention, practice, and semantic targets. *Journal of Experimental Psychology: Human Perception and Performance*, 1976, *2*, 326–336.

Pachella, R. G. The interpretation of reaction time in information processing research. In B. Kantowitz (Ed.), *Human information processing: Tutorials in performance and cognition*. Hillsdale, N.J.: Lawrence Erlbaum Associates, 1974.

Paivio, A. Mental imagery in associative learning and memory. *Psychological Review*, 1969, *76*, 241–263.

Paivio, A. *Imagery and verbal processes*. New York: Holt, Rinehart & Winston, 1971.

Paivio, A., & Csapo, K. Concrete-image and verbal memory codes. *Journal of Experimental Psychology*, 1969, *80*, 279–285.

Palmer, S. E. Visual perception and world knowledge. In D. A. Norman, D. E. Rumelhart, & the LNR Research Group (Eds.), *Explorations in cognition*. San Francisco: Freeman, 1975.

Palmer, S. E. Fundamental aspects of cognitive representation. In E. Rosch & B. B. Lloyd (Eds.), *Cognition and categorization*. Hillsdale, N. J.: Lawrence Erlbaum Associates, 1978.

Parker, E. S., Birnbaum, I. M., & Noble, E. P. Alcohol and memory: Storage and state dependency. *Journal of Verbal Learning and Verbal Behavior*, 1976, *15*, 691–702.

Parkinson, S. R. Short-term memory while shadowing: Multiple-item recall of visually and of aurally presented letters. *Journal of Experimental Psychology*, 1972, *92*, 256–265.

Parkinson, S. R., Parks, T. E., & Kroll, N. E. A. Visual and auditory short-term memory: Effects of phonemically similar auditory shadow material during the retention interval. *Journal of Experimental Psychology*, 1971, *87*, 274–280.

Patterson, F. G. The gestures of a gorilla: Language acquisition in another pongid. *Brain and Language*, 1978, *5*, 72–97.

Pavlov, I. P. *Conditioned reflexes*. London: Oxford University Press, 1927.

Perrin, M. *Brownian movement and molecular reality*. London: Taylor and Francis, 1910.

Peirce, J. R. *Symbols, signals, and noise: The nature and process of communication*. New York: Harper & Row, 1961.

Peterson, L. R. Verbal learning and memory. *Annual Review of Psycyhology*, 1977, *28*, 393–415.

Peterson, L. R., & Johnson, S. T. Some effects of minimizing articulation on short-term retention. *Journal of Verbal Learning and Verbal Behavior*, 1971, *10*, 346–354.

Peterson, L. R., & Peterson, M. J. Short-term retention of individual verbal items. *Journal of Experimental Psychology*, 1959, *58*, 193–198.

Pew, R. W. The speed accuracy operating characteristic. *ACTA Psychologica,* 1969, *30,* 16–26.

Phillips, W. A. & Baddeley, A. D. Reaction time and short-term visual memory. *Psychonomic Science,* 1971, *22,* 73–74.

Polanyi, M. *Personal knowledge: Towards a post-critical philosophy.* Chicago: University of Chicago Press, 1962.

Pollack, I. Speed of classification of words into superordinate categories. *Journal of Verbal Learning and Verbal Behavior,* 1963, *2,* 159–165.

Pollatsek, A., & Battencourt, H. O. The spaced-practice effect in the distractor paradigm is related to proactive interference but not to short-term store. *Journal of Experimental Psychology: Human Learning and Memory,* 1976, *2,* 128–141.

Polyak, S. L. *The vertebrate visual system.* Chicago: University of Chicago Press, 1957.

Pompi, K. F., & Lachman, R. Surrogate processes in the short-term retention of connected discourse. *Journal of Experimental Psychology,* 1967, *75,* 143–150.

Popper, K. R. *The logic of scientific discovery.* New York: Basic Books, 1959.

Popper, K. R. Normal science and its dangers. In I. Lakatos & A. Musgrave (Eds.), *Criticism and the growth of knowledge.* London: Cambridge University Press, 1970.

Posner, M. I. Abstraction and the process of recognition. In G. H. Bower & J. T. Spence (Eds.), *The psychology of learning and motivation: Advances in research and theory* (Vol. 3). New York: McGraw-Hill, 1969.

Posner, M. I. Coordination of internal codes. In W. G. Chase (Ed.), *Visual information processing.* New York: Academic Press, 1973.

Posner, M. I., & Boies, S. J. Components of attention. *Psychological Review,* 1971, *78,* 391–408.

Posner, M. I., & Klein, R. M. On the functions of consciousness. In S. Kornblum (Ed.), *Attention and performance IV.* New York: Academic Press, 1973.

Posner, M. I., Klein, R. M., Summers, J., & Buggie, S. On the selection of signals. *Memory and Cognition,* 1973, *1,* 2–12.

Posner, M. I., & McLean, J. P. Cognition: Forwards or backwards? *Contemporary Psychology,* 1977, *7,* 481–482.

Posner, M. I., & Rogers, M. G. K. Chronometric Analysis of Abstraction and Recognition. In W. K. Estes (Ed.), *Handbook of learning and cognitive processes* (Vol. 6). Hillsdale, N. J.: Lawrence Erlbaum Associates, 1978.

Posner, M. I., & Snyder, C. R. R. Attention and cognitive control. In R. L. Solso (Ed.), *Information processing and cognition: The Loyola Symposium.* Potomac, Md.: Lawrence Erlbaum Associates, 1974.

Post, E. L. Finite combinatory processes—Formulation I. *Journal of Symbolic Logic,* 1936, *1,* 103–105.

Postman, L. The present status of interference theory. In C. N. Cofer (Ed.), *Verbal learning and verbal behavior.* New York: McGraw-Hill, 1961.

Postman, L. Verbal learning and memory. *Annual Review of Psychology,* 1975, *26,* 291–335.

Premack, D. A. A functional analysis of language. *Journal of Experimental Analysis of Behavior,* 1970, *14,* 107–125.

Premack, D. A. Language in chimpanzee? *Science,* 1971, *172,* 808–822.

Pribram, K. H. *Why a neuropsychologist must know the literature in memory, perception and cognition as well as physiological psychology.* (To be published by Lawrence Erlbaum Associates.)

Pylyshyn, Z. W. What the mind's eye tells the mind's brain: A critique of mental imagery. *Psychological Bulletin,* 1973, *80,* 1–24.

Quillian, M. R. Semantic memory. In M. Minsky (Ed.), *Semantic information processing.* Cambridge, Mass.: MIT Press, 1968.

Quillian, M. R. The teachable language comprehender: A stimulation program and theory of language. *Communications of the ACM,* 1969, *12,* 459–476.

Radtke, R. C., & Grove, E. K. Proactive inhibition in short-term memory: Availability or accessibility? *Journal of Experimental Psychology: Human Learning and Memory*, 1977, *3*, 78–91.

Raphael, B. *The thinking computer: Mind inside matter.* San Francisco: Freeman, 1976.

Ratliff, F. *Mach bands.* San Francisco: Holden Day, 1965.

Ratliff, F., & Hartline, H. K. The responses of *Limulus* optic nerve fibers to patterns of illumination on the receptor mosaic. *Journal of General Physiology*, 1959, *42*, 1241–1255.

Reed, S. K. *Psychological processes in pattern recognition.* New York: Academic Press, 1973.

Reicher, G. M. Perceptual recognition as a function of meaningfulness of stimulus material. *Journal of Experimental Psychology*, 1969, *81*, 274–280.

Reitman, J. S. Mechanisms of forgetting in short-term memory. *Cognitive Psychology*, 1971, *2*, 185–195.

Reitman, J. S. Without surreptitious rehearsal: Information and short-term memory decays. *Journal of Verbal Learning and Verbal Behavior*, 1974, *13*, 365–377.

Restle, F. Critique of pure memory. In R. L. Solso (Ed.), *Theories in cognitive psychology: The Loyola Symposium.* Potomac, Md.: Lawrence Erlbaum Associates, 1974.

Restle, F. Answering questions from cognitive structures. In F. Restle, R. M. Shiffrin, N. J. Castellan, H. R. Lindman, & D. B. Pisoni (Eds.), *Cognitive theory* (Vol. 1). Hillsdale, N.J.: Lawrence Erlbaum Associates, 1975.

Rips, L. J. Quantification and semantic memory. *Cognitive Psychology*, 1975, *7*, 307–340.

Rips, L. J., Shoben, E. J., & Smith, E. E. Semantic distance and the verification of semantic relations. *Journal of Verbal Learning and Verbal Behavior*, 1973, *12*, 1–20.

Rosch, E. On the internal structure of perceptual and semantic categories. In T. M. Moore (Ed.), *Cognitive development and the acquisition of language.* New York: Academic Press, 1973.

Rosch, E. Cognitive representations of semantic categories. *Journal of Experimental Psychology: General*, 1975, *104*(3), 192–233.

Rosch, E., & Mervis, C. B. Family resemblances: Studies in the internal structure of categories. *Cognitive Psychology*, 1975, *7*, 573–605.

Rosch, E., Mervis, C. B., Gray, W., Johnson, D., & Boyes-Braem, P. Basic objects in natural categories. *Cognitive Psychology*, 1976, *8*, 382–439.

Rothstein, L. D. *Recognition reaction time: Searching for search.* Unpublished doctoral dissertation, Kent State University, 1973.

Rothstein, L. D., & Morin, R. E. *The effects of size of stimulus ensemble and the method of set size manipulation on recognition reaction time.* Paper presented at the meeting of the Midwestern Psychological Association, Cleveland, May 1972.

Rumelhart, D. E. Notes on a schema for stories. In D. G. Bobrow & A. M. Collins (Eds.), *Representations and understanding: Studies in cognitive science.* New York: Academic Press, 1975.

Rumelhart, D. E. *An introduction to human information processing.* New York: Wiley, 1977.

Rumelhart, D. E., Lindsay, P. H., & Norman, D. A. A process model for long-term memory. In E. Tulving & W. Donaldson (Eds.), *Organization of memory.* New York: Academic Press, 1972.

Sachs, J. S. Recognition memory for syntactic and semantic aspects of connected discourse. *Perception and Psychophysics*, 1967, *2*, 437–442.

Salzberg, P. M. On the generality of encoding specificity. *Journal of Experimental Psychology: Human Learning and Memory*, 1976, *2*, 586–596.

Salzberg, P. M., Parks, T. E., Kroll, N. E. A., & Parkinson, S. R. Retroactive effects of phonemic similarity on short-term recall of visual and auditory stimuli. *Journal of Experimental Psychology*, 1971, *91*, 43–46.

Savin, H. B., & Bever, T. G. The nonperceptual reality of the phoneme. *Journal of Verbal Learning and Verbal Behavior*, 1970, *9*, 295–302.

Savin, H. B., & Perchonock, E. Grammatical structure and the immediate recall of English sentences. *Journal of Verbal Learning and Verbal Behavior*, 1965, *4*, 348–353.

Schaeffer, B., & Wallace, R. Semantic similarity and the comparison of word meanings. *Journal of Experimental Psychology*, 1969, *82*, 343–346.

Schaeffer, B., & Wallace, R. The comparison of word meanings. *Journal of Experimental Psychology*, 1970, *86*, 144–152.

Schallert, D. L. Improving memory for prose: The relationship between depth of processing and context. *Journal of Verbal Learning and Verbal Behavior*, 1976, *15*, 621–632.

Schank, R. C. Conceptual dependency: A theory of natural language understanding. *Cognitive Psychology*, 1972, *3*, 552–631.

Schank, R. C. *Conceptual information processing.* New York: American Elsevier, 1975.

Schank, R. C. The role of memory in language processing. In C. N. Cofer (Ed.), *The structure of human memory.* San Francisco: Freeman, 1976.

Schank, R., & Abelson, R. *Scripts, plans, goals and understanding.* Hillsdale, N. J.: Lawrence Erlbaum Associates, 1977.

Scheffler, I. Vision and revolution: A postscript on Kuhn. *Philosophy of Science*, 1972, *39*, 366–374.

Schendel, J. D. Analysis of the rehearsal processes in the release from proactive interference. *Journal of Experimental Psychology: Human Learning and Memory*, 1976, *2*, 76–82.

Schneider, W., & Shiffrin, R. M. Controlled and automatic human information processing: I. Detection, search, and attention. *Psychological Review:* 1977, *84*, 1–66.

Schweller, D. G., Brewer, W. F., & Dahl, D. Memory for illocutionary forces and perlocutionary effects of utterances. *Journal of Verbal Learning and Verbal Behavior*, 1976, *15*, 325–337.

Segal, E. M., & Lachman, R. Complex behavior or higher mental process: Is there a paradigm shift? *American Psychologist*, 1972, *27*, 46–55.

Segal, S. J., & Fusella, V. Influence of imaged pictures and sounds on detection of visual and auditory signals. *Journal of Experimental Psychology*, 1970, *83*, 458–464.

Selfridge, O. G. Pandemonium: A paradigm for learning. In *Symposium on the mechanization of thought processes.* London: HM Stationery Office, 1959.

Selfridge, O. G., & Neisser, U. Pattern recognition by machine. *Scientific American*, 1960, *203*, 60–68.

Seymour, P. H. K. Judgments of verticality and response availability. *Bulletin of the Psychonomic Society*, 1973, *1*, 196–198.

Shafto, M. The space for case. *Journal of Verbal Learning and Verbal Behavior*, 1973, *12*, 551–562.

Shallice, T. Dual functions of consciousness. *Psychological Review*, 1972, *79*, 383–393.

Shallice, T., & Warrington, E. K. Independent functioning of verbal memory stores: A neuropsychological study. *Quarterly Journal of Experimental Psychology*, 1970, *22*, 261–273.

Shannon, C. E. A mathematical theory of communication. *Bell System Technical Journal*, 1948, *27*, 379–423, 623–656.

Shapere, D. Critique of the paradigm concept. *Science*, 1971, *172*, 706–709.

Shapere, D. Scientific theories and their domains. In F. Suppe (Ed.), *The structure of scientific theories* (2nd ed.). Urbana: University of Illinois Press, 1977.

Shaw, R., & Bransford, J. Approaches to the problem of knowledge. In R. Shaw & J. Bransford (Eds.), *Perceiving, acting, and knowing.* Hillsdale, N.J.: Lawrence Erlbaum Associates, 1977.

Shepard, R. N. Recognition memory for words, sentences, and pictures. *Journal of Verbal Learning and Verbal Behavior*, 1967, *6*, 156–163.

Shepard, R. N., & Metzler, J. Mental rotation of three-dimensional objects. *Science*, 1971, *171*, 701–703.

Shiffrin, R. M. Information persistence in short-term memory. *Journal of Experimental Psychology*, 1973, *100*, 39–49.

Shiffrin, R. M. The locus and role of attention in memory systems. In P. M. A. Rabbit & S. Dornic (Eds.), *Attention and performance V.* New York: Academic Press, 1975.

Shiffrin, R. M. Introduction to "Human memory: A proposed system and its control processes." In G. H. Bower (Ed.), *The psychology of learning and motivation* (Vol. 11). New York: Academic Press, 1978.

Shiffrin, R. M., & Atkinson, R. C. Storage and retrieval processes in long-term memory. *Psychological Review,* 1969, *76,* 179–193.

Shiffrin, R. M., & Gardner, G. T. Visual processing capacity and attentional control. *Journal of Experimental Psychology,* 1972, *93,* 73–82.

Shiffrin, R. M., & Grantham, D. W. Can attention be allocated to sensory modalities? *Perception and Psychophysics,* 1974, *15,* 460–474.

Shiffrin, R. M., KcKay, D. P., & Shaffer, W. O. Attending to forty-nine spatial positions at once. *Journal of Experimental Psychology: Human Perception and Performance,* 1976, *2,* 14–22.

Shiffrin, R. M., & Schneider, W. Controlled and automatic human information processing: II. Perceptual learning, automatic attending, and a general theory. *Psychological Review,* 1977, *84,* 127–190.

Shoben, E. J., Rips, L. J., & Smith, E. E. *Issues in semantic memory: A response to Glass and Holyoak* (Tech. Rep. No. 101). Urbana, Ill.: Center for the Study of Reading, University of Illinois, 1978 (in press).

Shulman, H. G. Encoding and retention of semantic and phonemic information in short-term memory. *Journal of Verbal Learning and Verbal Behavior,* 1970, *9,* 499–508.

Shulman, H. G. Semantic confusion errors in short-term memory. *Journal of Verbal Learning and Verbal Behavior,* 1972, *11,* 221–227.

Simon, H. A. *Information processing theory of human problem solving* (C.I.P. Working Paper No. 324). Carnegie-Mellon University, May 28, 1976.

Simon, H. A., & Feigenbaum, E. A. An information-processing theory of some effects of similarity, familiarization, and meaningfulness in verbal learning. *Journal of Verbal Learning and Verbal Behavior,* 1964, *3,* 385–396.

Simon, H. A., & Newell, A. Information processing in computer and man. *American Scientist,* 1964, *53,* 281–300.

Skinner, B. F. *Verbal behavior.* New York: Appleton-Century-Crofts, 1957.

Slobin, D. I. Grammatical transformations in childhood and adulthood. *Journal of Verbal Learning and Verbal Behavior,* 1966, *5,* 219–227.

Smith, E. E. Effects of familiarity on stimulus recognition and categorization. *Journal of Experimental Psychology,* 1967, *74,* 324–332.

Smith, E. E. Choice reaction time: An analysis of the major theoretical positions. *Psychological Bulletin,* 1968, *69,* 77–110.

Smith, E. E. Theories of semantic memory. In W. K. Estes (Ed.), *Handbook of learning and cognitive processes* (Vol. 5). Hillsdale, N.J.: Lawrence Erlbaum Associates, 1978.

Smith, E. E., Shoben, E. J., & Rips, L. J. Structure and process in semantic memory: A featural model for semantic decision. *Psychological Review,* 1974, *81,* 214–241.

Smith, E. E., & Spoehr, D. T. The perception of printed English: A theoretical perspective. In B. H. Kantowitz (Ed.), *Human information processing: Tutorials in performance and cognition.* Hillsdale, N.J.: Lawrence Erlbaum Associates, 1974.

Smith, M. C., & Schiller, P. H. Forward and backward masking: A comparison. *Canadian Journal of Psychology,* 1966, *20,* 191–197.

Somjen, G. *Sensory coding in the mammalian nervous system.* New York: Plenum Press, 1972.

Spelke, E., Hirst, W., & Neisser, U. Skills of divided attention. *Cognition,* 1976, *4,* 215–230.

Spence, K. W. *Behavior theory and conditioning.* New Haven, Conn.: Yale University Press, 1956.

Spencer, T. J. Some effects of different masking stimuli on iconic storage. *Journal of Experimental Psychology,* 1969, *81,* 132–140.

Spencer, T. J., & Shuntich, R. Evidence for an interruption theory of backward masking. *Journal of Experimental Psychology*, 1970, *85*, 198–203.

Sperling, G. The information available in brief visual presentations. *Psychological Monographs*, 1960, *74*(Whole No. 11).

Spyropoulos, T., & Ceraso, J. Categorized and uncategorized attributes as recall cues: The phenomenon of limited access. *Cognitive Psychology*, 1977, *9*, 384–402.

Staats, A. W., & Staats, C. K. *Complex human behavior*. New York: Holt, Rinehart & Winston, 1963.

Standing, L. Learning 10,000 pictures. *Quarterly Journal of Experimental Psychology*, 1973, *25*, 207–222.

Stanners, R. F., Headley, D. B., & Clark, W. R. The pupillary response to sentences: Influences of listening set and deep structure. *Journal of Verbal Learning and Verbal Behavior*, 1972, *11*, 257–263.

Stegmuller, W. *The structure and dynamics of theories*. New York: Springer-Verlag, 1976.

Stein, B. The effects of cue-target uniqueness on cued recall performance. *Memory and Cognition*, 1977, *5*, 319–322.

Sternberg, S. *Retrieval from recent memory: Some reaction time experiments and a search theory*. Paper presented at the meeting of the Psychonomic Society, Bryn Mawr, August 1963.

Sternberg, S. High-speed scanning in human memory. *Science*, 1966, *153*, 652–654.

Sternberg, S. Two operations in character recognition: Some evidence from reaction-time measurements. *Perception and Psychophysics*, 1967, *2*, 45–53.

Sternberg, S. The discovery of processing stages: Extensions of Donders' method. *Acta Psychologica*, 1969, *30*, 276–315. (a)

Sternberg, S. Memory-scanning: Mental processes revealed by reaction-time experiments. *American Scientist*, 1969, *57*, 421–457. (b)

Sternberg, S. *Decomposing mental processes with reaction-time data*. Invited address, Midwestern Psychological Association, Detroit, May 1971.

Sternberg, S. Memory scanning: New findings and current controversies. *Quarterly Journal of Experimental Psychology*, 1975, *27*, 1–32.

Stevens, K. N. Segments, features, and analysis by synthesis. In J. F. Kavanagh & I. G. Mattingly (Eds.), *Language by ear and by eye: The relationship between speech and reading*. Cambridge, Mass.: MIT Press, 1972.

Stevens, K. N., & Halle, M. Remarks on analysis by synthesis and distinctive features. In W. Wathen-Dunn (Ed.), *Models for perception of speech and visual form*. Cambridge, Mass.: MIT Press, 1967.

Stevens, S. S. Psychology and the science of science. *Psychological Bulletin*, 1939, *36*, 221–262.

Stolz, W. A study of the ability to decode grammatically novel sentences. *Journal of Verbal Learning and Verbal Behavior*, 1967, *6*, 867–873.

Suppe, F. *The structure of scientific theories* (2nd ed.). Urbana: University of Illinois Press, 1977.

Tanenhaus, M. K., Carroll, J. M., & Bever, T. G. Sentence-picture verification models as theories of sentence comprehension: A critique of Carpenter and Just. *Psychological Review*, 1976, *83*, 310–317.

Taylor, D. A. Stage analysis of reaction time. *Psychological Bulletin*, 1976, *83*, 161–191.

Teichner, W. H., & Krebs, M. J. Laws of visual choice reaction time. *Psychological Review*, 1974, *81*, 75–98.

Theios, J. Reaction-time measurements in the study of memory processes: Theory and data. In G. H. Bower (Ed.), *The psychology of learning and motivation* (Vol. 7). New York: Academic Press, 1973.

Theios, J., Smith, P. G., Haviland, S. E., Traupmann, J., & Moy, M. C. Memory scanning as a serial self-terminating process. *Journal of Experimental Psychology*, 1973, *97*, 323–336.

Thomson, D. M., & Tulving, E. Associative encoding and retrieval: Weak and strong cues. *Journal of Experimental Psychology*, 1970, *86*, 255–262.

Thorndike, E. L., & Lorge, I. *The teacher's work book of 30,000 words.* New York: Teachers College of Columbia University, 1944.

Thorndyke, P. W. Conceptual complexity and imagery in comprehension and memory. *Journal of Verbal Learning and Verbal Behavior*, 1975, *14*, 359–369.

Toulmin, S. *Human understanding* (Vol. 1). Princeton, N.J.: Princeton University Press, 1972.

Townsend, J. T. Some results on the identifiability of parallel and serial processes. *British Journal of Mathematical and Statistical Psychology*, 1972, *25*, 168–199.

Townsend, J. T. Issues and models concerning the processing of a finite number of inputs. In B. H. Kantowitz (Ed.), *Human information processing: Tutorials in performance and cognition.* Hillsdale, N.J.: Lawrence Erlbaum Associates, 1974.

Treisman, A. M. Contextual cues in selective listening. *Quarterly Journal of Experimental Psychology*, 1960, *12*, 242–248.

Treisman, A. M. Selective attention in man. *British Medical Bulletin*, 1964, *20*, 12–16. (a)

Treisman, A. M. Monitoring and storage of irrelevant messages in selective attention. *Journal of Verbal Learning and Verbal Behavior*, 1964, *3*, 449–459. (b)

Treisman, A. M. Strategies and models of selective attention. *Psychological Review*, 1969, *76*, 282–292.

Treisman, A. M., & Davies, A. Divided attention to ear and eye. In S. Kornblum (Ed.), *Attention and performance IV.* New York: Academic Press, 1973.

Treisman, A., Squire, R., & Green, J. Semantic processing in dichotic listening: A replication. *Memory and Cognition*, 1974, *2*, 641–646.

Tulving, E. Subjective organization in free recall of "unrelated" words. *Psychological Review*, 1962, *69*, 344–354.

Tulving, E. Intratrial and intertrial retention: Notes towards a theory of free recall verbal learning. *Psychology Review*, 1964, *71*, 219–237.

Tulving, E. Theoretical issues in free recall. In T. R. Dixon & D. L. Horton (Eds.), *Verbal behavior and general behavior theory.* Englewood Cliffs, N.J.: Prentice-Hall, 1968.

Tulving, E. Episodic and semantic memory. In E. Tulving & W. Donaldson (Eds.), *Organization of memory.* New York: Academic Press, 1972.

Tulving, E. *Memory research: What kind of progress?* Paper presented at the memory conference in Uppsala, Sweden, June 1977. [To be published in: Nilsson, L.-G. (Ed.). *Perspectives on memory research: Essays in honor of Uppsala University's 500th anniversary.* Hillsdale, N.J.:Lawrence Erlbaum Associates, 1979.]

Tulving, E. Relation between encoding specificity and levels of processing. In L. S. Cermak & F. I. M. Craik (Eds.), *Levels of processing and human memory.* Hillsdale, N.J.: Lawrence Erlbaum Associates, 1978.

Tulving, E., & Gold, C. Stimulus information and contextual information as determinants of tachistoscopic recognition of words. *Journal of Experimental Psychology*, 1963, *66*, 319–327.

Tulving, E., Mandler, G., & Baumel, R. Interaction of two sources of information in tachistoscopic word recognition. *Canadian Journal of Psychology*, 1964, *18*, 62–71.

Tulving, E., & Osler, S. Effectiveness of retrieval cues in memory for words. *Journal of Experimental Psychology*, 1968, *77*, 593–601.

Turing, A. M. On computable numbers, with an application to the Entscheidungsproblem. *Proceedings of the London Mathematics Society* (Series 2), 1936, *42*, 230–265.

Turvey, M. T., & Shaw, R. E. Memory (or, knowing) as a matter of specification not representation: Notes toward a different class of machines. In L. S. Cermak & F. I. M. Craik (Eds.), *Levels of processing and human memory.* Hillsdale, N.J.: Lawrence Erlbaum Associates, 1978.

Tversky, A. Features of similarity. *Psychological Review*, 1977, *84*, 327–352.

Underwood, B. J., & Schulz, R. W. *Meaningfulness and verbal learning*. Philadelphia: Lippincott, 1960.

Underwood, G. Moray vs. the rest: The effects of extended practice on shadowing. *Quarterly Journal of Experimental Psychology*, 1974, *26*, 368–373.

Uttal, W. R. *The psychobiology of sensory coding*. New York: Harper & Row, 1973.

van Dijk, T. A., & Kintsch, W. Cognitive psychology and discourse. In W. Dressler (Ed.), *Text linguistics*. Berlin: deGruyeter, 1977.

Volkova, V. D. On certain characteristics of the formation of conditioned reflexes to speech stimuli in children. *Fiziol. Zh. SSSR*, 1953, *39*, 540–548. Cited in G. Razran, The observable unconscious and the inferable conscious in current Soviet psychophysiology: Interoceptive conditioning, semantic conditioning, and the orienting reflex. *Psychological Review*, 1961, *63*(2), 81–147.

von Frisch, K. Dialects in the language of the bees. *Scientific American*, 1962, *207*, 79–87.

von Frisch, K. Honeybees: Do they use direction and distance information provided by their dancers? *Science*, 1967, *158*, 1072–1076.

von Neumann, J. *The computer and the brain*. New Haven: Yale University Press, 1958.

Von Wright, J. M., Anderson, K., & Stenman, U. Generalization of conditioned GSR's in dichotic listening. In P. M. A. Rabbitt & S. Dornic (Eds.), *Attention and performance V*. New York: Academic Press, 1975.

Wanner, E. *On remembering, forgetting, and understanding sentences*. The Hague: Mouton, 1974.

Warren, R. E., & Warren, N. T. Dual semantic encoding of homographs and homophones embedded in context. *Memory & Cognition*, 1976, *4*, 586–592.

Warren, R. M. Perceptual restoration of missing speech sounds. *Science*, 1970, *167*, 392–393.

Warren, R. M. Identification times for phonemic components of graded complexity and for spelling of speech. *Perception & Psychophysics*, 1971, *9*(4), 345–349.

Wason, P. C. The contexts of plausible denial. *Journal of Verbal Learning and Verbal Behavior*, 1965, *4*, 7–11.

Watkins, M. J., Ho, E., & Tulving, E. Context effects in recognition memory for faces. *Journal of Verbal Learning and Verbal Behavior*, 1976, *15*, 505–517.

Watson, J. B. *Behaviorism* (rev. ed.). New York: Norton, 1930.

Watzlawick, P., Beavin, J. H., & Jackson, D. D. *Pragmatics of human communication*. New York: Norton, 1967.

Waugh, N. C. Free versus serial recall. *Journal of Experimental Psychology*, 1961, *62*, 496–502.

Waugh, N. C., & Norman, D. A. Primary memory. *Psychological Review*, 1965, *72*, 89–104.

Waugh, N. C., & Norman, D. A. The measure of interference in primary memory. *Journal of Verbal Learning and Verbal Behavior*, 1968, *7*, 617–626.

Weimer, W. B. Overview of a cognitive conspiracy: Reflections on the volume. In W. B. Weimer & D. S. Palermo (Eds.), *Cognition and the symbolic processes*. Potomac, Md.: Lawrence Erlbaum Associates, 1974.

Weimer, W. B. Cognition: Forwards or backwards? *Contemporary Psychology*, 1977, *7*, 483–484.

Weimer, W. B., & Palermo, D. S. Paradigms and normal science in psychology. *Science Studies*, 1973, *3*, 211–244.

Weimer, W. B., & Palermo, D. S. (Eds.). *Cognition and the symbolic processes*. Potomac, Md.: Lawrence Erlbaum Associates, 1974.

Weingartner, H., Adefris, W., Eich, J., E. & Murphy, D. L. Encoding-imagery specificity in alcohol state-dependent learning. *Journal of Experimental Psychology: Human Learning and Memory*, 1976, *2*, 83–87.

Weisstein, N., & Harris, C. S. Visual detection of line segments: An object-superiority effect. *Science*, 1974, *186*, 752–755.

Weizenbaum, J. *Computer power and human reason: From judgment to calculation.* San Francisco: Freeman, 1976.

Welford, A. T. *Fundamentals of skill.* London: Methuen, 1968.

Welford, A. T. *Skilled performance: Perceptual and motor skills.* Glenview, Ill.: Scott, Foresman, 1976.

Wertheimer, M. Untersuchungen zur Lehre von der Gestalt. II. *Psychologische Forschung,* 1923, *4,* 301–305.

Whitehead, A. N., & Russell, B. A. W. *Principia mathematica* (Vols. 1–3). Cambridge: 1910–1913; 2nd ed., 1925–1927.

Whitfield, I. C., & Evans, E. F. Responses of auditory cortical neurons to stimuli of changing frequency. *Journal of Neurophysiology,* 1965, *28,* 655–672.

Wickelgren, W. A. Speed–accuracy tradeoff and information processing dynamics. *Acta Psychologica,* 1977, *41,* 67–85.

Wickens, D. D. Encoding categories of words: An empirical approach to meaning. *Psychological Review,* 1970, *77,* 1–15.

Wickens, D. D., Moody, M., & Shearer, P. W. Lack of memory for nonattended items in dichotic listening. *Journal of Experimental Psychology: Human Learning and Memory,* 1976, *2,* 712–719.

Wilder, L. Articulation and acoustic characteristics of speech sounds. In D. W. Massaro (Ed.), *Understanding language: An information-processing analysis of speech perception, reading and psycholinguistics.* New York: Academic Press, 1975.

Wilkins, A. J. Conjoint frequency, category size, and categorization time. *Journal of Verbal Learning and Verbal Behavior,* 1971, *10,* 382–385.

Winograd, E., & Rivers-Bulkeley, N. T. Effects of changing context on remembering faces. *Journal of Experimental Psychology: Human Learning and Memory,* 1977, *3,* 397–405.

Winograd, T. Understanding natural language. *Cognitive Psychology,* 1972, *3,* 1–191.

Winograd, T. Frame representations and the declarative-procedural controversy. In D. Bobrow & A. Collins (Ed.), *Representations and understanding.* New York: Academic Press, 1975.

Wiseman, S., & Tulving, E. Encoding specificity: Relation between recall superiority and recognition failure. *Journal of Experimental Psychology: Human Learning and Memory,* 1976, *2,* 349–361.

Woods, W. Transition network grammars for natural language analysis. *Communications of the ACM,* 1970, *13,* 591–606.

Woods, W. An experimental parsing system for transition network grammars. In R. Rustin (Ed.), *Natural language processing.* New York: Algorithmics Press, 1973.

Woodworth, R. S. *Experimental Psychology.* New York: Henry Holt, 1938.

Wright, P. Some observations on how people answer questions about sentences. *Journal of Verbal Learning and Verbal Behavior,* 1972, *11,* 188–195.

Wright, M. J., & Ikeda, H. Processing of spatial and temporal information in the visual system. In F. O. Schmitt, F. G. Worden, & G. Adelman (Eds.), *The neurosciences: Third study program.* Cambridge, Mass.: MIT Press, 1974.

Wundt, W. Zur Kritik tachistosckopischer Versuche. *Philosophische Studien,* 1899, *15,* 287–317.

Zelniker, T. Perceptual attenuation of an irrelevant auditory verbal input as measured by an involuntary verbal response in a selective attention task. *Journal of Experimental Psychology,* 1971, *87,* 52–56.

Zipf, G. K. *Human behavior and the principle of least effort.* Cambridge, Mass.: Addison-Wesley, 1949.

Author Index

Italicized page numbers denote pages with complete bibliographic information.

A

Abelson, R., 465, *551*
Adefris, W., 283, *555*
Aderman, D., 520, *533*
Anderson, J. R., 54, 106, 120, 137, 138, 180, 271, 279, 285, 421, 427, 450, 451, 458, 459, 460, 465, 466, 468, 473, 474, 477, 479, 481, 485, 486, 531, *533, 543*
Anderson, K., 196, *555*
Anderson, R. C., 282, 431, 432, 433, 485, *533*
Angell, J. R., 47, *533*
Atkinson, R. C., 126, 132, 157, 171, 172, 173, 174, 210, 214, 217, 219, 220, 262, 263, 268, 272, 287, 288, 289, 290, 291, 330, 335, 528, *533, 534, 542, 552*
Averbach, I., 211, 212, 230, 232, 233, 240, 267, *534*
Axelrod, S., 192, *534*
Ayer, A. J., 40, *534*

B

Baddeley, A. D., 157, 171, 172, 267, 272, 285, *534, 549*
Baggett, P., 435, *534*
Baker, L., 281, 282, *534*
Bamber, D., 179, *534*
Barclay, J. R., 429, 432, 433, 434, 474, *534, 535*
Barnett, T., 237, *547*
Baron, J., 520, *534*
Barlett, F. C., 118, 407, 450, 452, *534*
Bates, A., 237, *547*
Battencourt, H. O., 273, *549*
Battig, W. F., 315, 317, 325, *534*
Baumel, R., 522, *554*
Beavin, J. H., 439, *555*
Becklen, R., 198, 199, *547*
Begg, I., 406, 423, *534*
Bellugi, U., 346, 359, *536*
Bever, T. G., 38, 82, 348, 384, 392, 421, 483, 514, *534, 539, 540, 550, 553*
Bieber, S. L., 266, 267, 285, *543*
Biederman, I., 157, 521, *534, 535*
Birnbaum, I. M., 283, *548*
Bjork, R. A., 213, 248, *535*
Bloomfield, L., 78, *535*
Blumenthal, A. L., 391, 392, 393, *535*
Boakes, R., 392, 393, *535*
Bobrow, D. G., 109, 197, 205, 208, 270, 271, 511, *535, 547, 548*
Bobrow, S. A., 282, *535*

557

Subject Index

Theoretical formalisms *(contd.)*
propositional logic, 478–479
rewrite rules, 373–375
Theory, 104–110
black-box, 107
choice of, 264–265
comprehensive, 458–460
evolution of, 290
experiments in conceptualization, 461–462
inferred mechanisms in, 530–532
levels of abstraction in, 108–109
neurosensory constraints on, 506
parsimony in, 314
rejection of, 261–262
structural, 107, 313–315, 324–326
tripartite structure, 262
Thinking, 102, 207–208
Three term series problems, 416–417
Tip-of-the-tongue, 325, 326, 343
Total time hypothesis, 276
Transformational grammar, 83, 85, 375–381
psychological reality of transformations, 384–389
rules in, 85
Turing machines, 95, 96, 112, 527–528
Typicality, 307, 315, 316, 320–322, 325, 331

U

Uncertainty, *see also* Information
and codability, 339–340
illustrated, 73

Uncertainty *(contd.)*
and information, 136–138
of stimulus set, 73
Understanding, *see* Comprehension
Universal machine, *see* Turing machine

V

Verbal learning, 44, 46–56, 264, 270
and Atkinson–Shiffrin model, 262–263
clustering, 53
decay vs. interference, 54, 268
paired-associate, 49–50, 51
serial, 49
S–R associations in, 50–51
subjective organization in, 52–54
Visual analogue storage, 249–251, 283–286, 335, 426

W

Word(s), *see also* Lexicon
age of acquisition, 341–343, 472–473
codability, 338–344
frequencies, 336–342, 360–361
as labels for concepts, 325
meaning, 431–434, 482–486
perception, 518–521
production, 335–344
and reference, 482–483
segmentation of, 414